Criminal Justice

An Introduction

Fifth Edition

Freda Adler
Rutgers University

Gerhard O. W. Mueller
Rutgers University

William S. Laufer
University of Pennsylvania

 **Higher Education**

Boston   Burr Ridge, IL   Dubuque, IA   New York   San Francisco   St. Louis
Bangkok   Bogotá   Caracas   Kuala Lumpur   Lisbon   London   Madrid   Mexico City
Milan   Montreal   New Delhi   Santiago   Seoul   Singapore   Sydney   Taipei   Toronto

Dedication

To David S., Daniel A., Julia A., Noah A., Zoë A., Hannah M., Nicolai A., John J., Lauren E., Stephen W., and Anna L.

The McGraw-Hill Companies

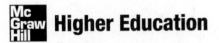 **Higher Education**

Published by McGraw-Hill, an imprint of The McGraw-Hill Companies, Inc., 1221 Avenue of the Americas, New York, NY 10020. Copyright © 2009, 2006, 2003, 2000, 1996. All rights reserved. No part of this publication may be reproduced or distributed in any form or by any means, or stored in a database or retrieval system, without the prior written consent of The McGraw-Hill Companies, Inc., including, but not limited to, in any network or other electronic storage or transmission, or broadcast for distance learning.

This book is printed on acid-free paper.

1 2 3 4 5 6 7 8 9 0 QPD/QPD 0 9 8

ISBN: 978-0-07-337995-1
MHID: 0-07-337995-6

Editor in Chief: *Mike Ryan*
Publisher: *Frank Mortimer*
Sponsoring Editor: *Katie Stevens*
Marketing Manager: *Leslie Oberhuber*
Developmental Editor: *Phil Butcher*
Project Editor: *Regina Ernst*
Manuscript Editor: *Leslie Anne Weber*
Text Designer: *Kay Fulton*
Cover Designer: *Allister Fein*
Photo Research: *Poyee Oster*
Production Supervisor: *Louis Swaim*
Composition: *10/12 Times Roman by Aptara, Inc.*
Printing: *PMS 7455, 45# New Era Matte Plus, Quebecor Dubuque*

Cover: (c) Royalty-Free/CORBIS
Credits: The credits section for this book begins on page C1 and is considered an extension of the copyright page.

Library of Congress Cataloging-in-Publication Data

Adler, Freda.
    Criminal justice : an introduction / Freda Adler, Gerhard O. Mueller, William Laufer.—5th ed.
      p. cm.
    Includes index.
    ISBN-13: 978-0-07-337995-1 (alk. paper)
    ISBN-10: 0-07-337995-6 (alk. paper)
    1. Criminal justice, Administration of—United States. I. Mueller, Gerhard O. W. II. Laufer, William S. III. Title.
  HV9950.A353 2009
  364.973—dc22

2008014420

The Internet addresses listed in the text were accurate at the time of publication. The inclusion of a Web site does not indicate an endorsement by the authors or McGraw-Hill, and McGraw-Hill does not guarantee the accuracy of the information presented at these sites.

www.mhhe.com

About the Authors

Freda Adler is Emeritus Distinguished Professor of Criminal Justice at Rutgers University, School of Criminal Justice. She received her BA in sociology, her MA in criminology, and her PhD in sociology from the University of Pennsylvania. Dr. Adler began her career in criminal justice as an evaluator of drug and alcohol treatment programs for federal and state governments. Teaching since 1968, her subjects include criminal justice, criminology, comparative criminal justice systems, statistics, and research methods. She has served as criminal justice advisor to the United Nations, as well as to federal, state, and foreign governments. Dr. Adler's published works include eleven books as author or coauthor, nine books as editor or coeditor, and over eighty journal articles. She has served on the editorial boards of the *Journal of Criminal Justice, Criminology,* and the *Journal of Research on Crime and Delinquency.* Dr. Adler is editorial consultant to the *Journal of Criminal Law and Criminology,* and is coeditor of *Advances in Criminological Theory.* She also has served as president of the American Society of Criminology (1994–1995).

Gerhard O. W. Mueller is the late Distinguished Professor of Criminal Justice at Rutgers University, School of Criminal Justice. After earning his JD degree from the University of Chicago, he went on to receive a master of laws degree from Columbia University. He was awarded the degree of DrJur (hc) by the University of Uppsala, Sweden. His career in criminal justice began in 1945, when he served as a chief petty officer in the British Military Government Water Police, where he commanded a Coast Guard cutter. His teaching in criminal justice, begun in 1953, was partially interrupted between 1974 and 1982 when, as Chief of the United Nations Crime Prevention and Criminal Justice Branch, he was responsible for all of the United Nations' programs dealing with problems of crime and justice worldwide. He continues his service to the United Nations as chair ad interim of the Board of the International Scientific and Professional Advisory Council of the United Nations Crime Prevention and Criminal Justice Programme. Professor Mueller has been a member of the faculties of law at the University of Washington, West Virginia University, New York University, and the National Judicial College, with visiting appointments and lectureships at universities and institutes in the Americas, western and eastern Europe, Africa, Asia, and Australia. He is the author of some 50 authored or edited books and 270 scholarly articles.

William S. Laufer is Professor of Legal Studies and Business Ethics, Sociology, and Criminology at the Wharton School of the University of Pennsylvania, and chairperson, Department of Criminology, School of Arts and Sciences. Dr. Laufer received his BA in social and behavioral sciences at the Johns Hopkins University, his JD at Northeastern University School of Law, and his PhD at Rutgers University, School of Criminal Justice. Dr. Laufer's research has appeared in law reviews and a wide range of criminal justice, legal, and psychology journals, such as the *Journal of Research in Crime and Delinquency, American Journal of Criminal Law, Law and Human Behavior, Journal of Personality and Social Psychology,* and *Business Ethics Quarterly.* His most recent book is *Corporate Bodies and Guilty Minds.* Dr. Laufer is coeditor of the *Handbook of Psychology and Law; Personality, Moral Development and Criminal Behavior;* and *Crime, Values and Religion.* He is series coeditor of *Advances in Criminological Theory,* with Freda Adler.

Brief Contents

Contents

The Police 133

The Courts 231

PART 4 Corrections 335

**Challenges for the
Twenty-First Century 419**

List of Boxes

In Their Own Words

21st Century Challenge

Crime Scene

Preface

Criminal justice is always a subject of intense debate, but never more so than today. As the focus of the country seems fixed on armed conflicts in Iraq and Afghanistan, and the attacks of September 11, 2001, serve as the historical milestone of our new century, a host of challenges facing the field of criminal justice are just beginning to set in. The boundaries of our field have been extended, from strategies for policing our borders and developing the structure of homeland security, to reconceiving the idea of corporate deviance, and punishing corporate criminals. Yet even with a significant shift in law enforcement priorities, many of the old challenges are still with us. This includes the plight of victims in the criminal justice system, and matters of juvenile justice. Certainly, the field of criminal justice reflects times that are exciting and, at the same time, disturbing and tragic.

Our goal with *Criminal Justice* remains the same: to discuss these problems and challenges, their origins, and their possible solutions in a clear, practical, straightforward fashion that brings the material to life for students. We invite teachers and students alike to join us in traveling along the path of criminal justice, rediscovering old controversies, exploring its new domains, and mapping out its immediate future.

The Fifth Edition

In the four preceding editions of this textbook, we prepared students in criminal justice to understand the contemporary problems with which criminal justice is concerned and to anticipate the challenges that society would have to face in the beginning of this new century.

- With the advent of international terrorism on our soil, we have entered into a new century with new challenges. Foremost among these challenges is the need to conceive of criminal justice in the United States as a system that affects, and is affected by, events around the world.
- Because of the forward-looking orientation of previous editions of *Criminal Justice*, and our desire not to sensationalize acts of terrorism, we chose not to depart from the book's established structure and approach. We have, however, researched, refined, and updated every chapter in the text—not only to maintain the book's scholarly integrity, but also to ensure its relevance.
- In addition to updating every chapter's statistical information, we have significantly expanded coverage on terrorism and corporate crime.
- Also, we have increased our coverage of the criminal law, asking students to grapple with the most significant cases in the substantive law. Of course, *Criminal Justice: An Introduction, 5/e,* remains as objective, as critical, and as encompassing as its earlier editions.

Organization

The text contains fifteen chapters, arranged in five parts.

- Part 1 introduces students to the universe of crime and justice, with chapters focusing on the origins, evolution, and global nature of the science and profession of criminal justice (Chapter 1), the types of crime (Chapter 2), the measurement and explanation of criminal behavior (Chapter 3), and a discussion of the legal definitions of crime and the component parts that make up the criminal justice system (Chapter 4).

- Part 2 reviews the law enforcement response to the problem of crime. Chapters 5 and 6 examine the history and organization of policing, police functions, and the culture of policing. Chapter 7 considers the rule of law in law enforcement.

- Part 3 discusses the origin and role of the courts, lawyers and judges, prosecution and adjudication, and sentencing.

- Part 4 covers the correctional system, from its history to community-based alternatives to institutional corrections.

- The text concludes in Part 5 with a discussion of two persistent challenges to criminal justice: juvenile crime and victims of crime.

Pedagogical Aids

Working together, the authors and the editors have developed a format for the text that supports the goal of a readable, practical, and attractive text. Chapter outlines, margin notes and key terms, chapter review sections, and a comprehensive glossary all help students master the material.

- To address the emergence of international terrorism as a domestic problem of criminal justice, we have raised the issue of terrorism in different parts of the text. Students are asked to consider how terrorism as a crime changes the criminal justice system.

- Two dramatic four-pages photo essays have been added, bringing the tragic events of September 11 into focus and considering the effects of a long series of corporate scandals. Accompanying text for the first photo essay raises questions about the readiness of our criminal justice system to mount an effective response to terrorist acts. What should be done to protect against the inevitability of future attacks? How should federal and local law enforcement coordinate efforts? The text for the second photo essay asks students to grapple with the ways in which corporations are regulated by state and federal authorities. How should we mount an effective response to corporations that violate environmental, antitrust, tax, and fraud laws? How should we punish offending corporations?

- Our box program continues along the same themes as in previous editions, though a number of boxes have been replaced in light of the fifth edition's emphasis on the challenges of policing terrorism. Most chapters have one or more boxes—21st Century Challenge, In Their Own Words, and Crime Scene.

  - *21st Century Challenge* inserts focus on recent changes to the criminal justice system and give students a window into the forces that will have the most significant influence on tomorrow's system. The release of the 9/11 Commission Report; cyberpolicing—law enforcement and information systems; overcrowding of prisons; and the consequences of Megan's Law are just a few of the issues explored in these boxes.

  - *In Their Own Words* boxes provide compelling first-person accounts by practitioners in the field, enabling students to experience a typical day in the life of a professional. Examples include an account by an inner-city police captain who tells why, in 25 years on the force, he never had to draw his gun; a medical examiner, who takes readers through a typical day of reconstructing crimes at the scene of death; and a warden, who describes the difficult challenges he faces in running a county jail.

  - *Crime Scene* boxes, an immensely popular feature among students, bring current issues to life. Topics such as road rage, Court TV, prison violence, and stalking are included. Many of the Crime Scene boxes are new to this edition; others have been updated.

  - Finally, each chapter closes with Thinking Critically about Criminal Justice questions and Internet Connection exercises to guide students in their further exploration of key issues raised in the chapter.

Supplements Package

For the Student

- *By the Book* Website—weekly terrorism updates to keep students current, and invaluable vocabulary flashcards and pretests to help them study for exams.

For the Instructor

- Instructor's Manual/Testbank—chapter outlines, key terms, overviews, lecture notes, discussion questions, a complete testbank, and more.
- Computerized Testbank—easy-to-use computerized testing program for both Windows and Macintosh computers.
- PowerPoint Slides—complete, chapter-by-chapter slideshows featuring text, tables, and illustrations.

Acknowledgments

At Rutgers University, Phyllis Schultze, the librarian of the National Council on Crime and Delinquency, Criminal Justice Collection, has been most helpful in patiently tracking and tracing sources. At the University of Pennsylvania, Crystalyn Calderon assisted in revising and editing the text. We are especially grateful to those faculty who reviewed this and prior editions of *Criminal Justice,* including: Katherine A. Cameron, *Pittsburgh State University;* Lisa Decker, *Indiana State University;* John Doherty, *Marist College;* Malcolm Holmes, *University of Wyoming;* Matrice Hurrah, *Southwest Tennessee Community College;* Emmanuel Onyeozili, *University of Maryland–Eastern Shore;* Lee Ross, *University of Wisconsin–Parkside;* Clayton Steenberg, *Arkansas State University at Mountain Home;* Jose Texidor, *Pennsylvania State University;* and Oliver M. Thompson, *Riverside Community College.*

We again owe a special debt of gratitude to the team at McGraw-Hill: To publisher Phil Butcher, senior sponsoring editor Carolyn Henderson Meier, developmental editor Craig Leonard, and copyeditor Sharon O'Donnell, proofreader Dorothy Hoffman, project manager Jean R. Starr, designer Gino Cieslik, and production supervisor Jason Huls for efficiently and expertly turning manuscript into bound book; and to Natalia Peschiera for another outstanding photo program.

It takes many intelligent, dedicated, motivated, and well-educated men and women to run the criminal justice system in a world where all local problems have international connections, and in the face of ever-changing political demands. We hope that this book will be an important part of the introductory curriculum for the next generation of criminal justice practitioners and policymakers.

Freda Adler
Gerhard O.W. Mueller
William S. Laufer

The Universe of Crime and Justice

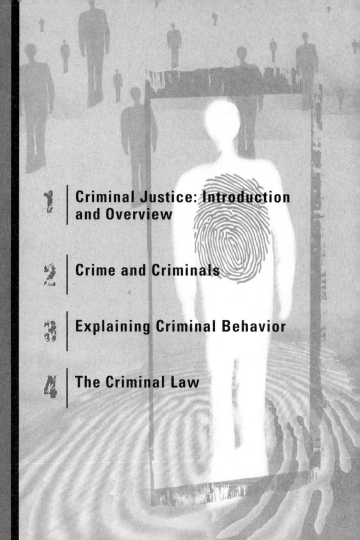

1 | Criminal Justice: Introduction and Overview

2 | Crime and Criminals

3 | Explaining Criminal Behavior

4 | The Criminal Law

• PART 1 of this book is the gateway to the universe of criminal justice, a universe that is vast, dramatic, fascinating, challenging, disturbing, frustrating, and at times tragic. It is a universe that reflects the highest degree of professionalism, discipline, and commitment, as well as the lowest forms of depravity, violence, and lost human potential. The chapters in Part 1 set the stage for Parts 2, 3, and 4, which focus on the individual segments of the criminal justice system: the police (Part 2), the courts (Part 3), and corrections (Part 4). Part 5 takes a forward look into challenges of the twenty-first century.

• CHAPTER 1 previews the book as a whole. After describing the origin and evolution of the science and profession of criminal justice, it reviews the stages of the criminal justice system. This is followed by a brief overview of challenges of juvenile justice and globalization. Chapter 2 looks at the amount and types of crimes, including transnational and corporate crimes, and discusses the characteristics of those who are arrested. Chapter 3 provides an overview of criminological theory, including biological, psychological, and sociological explanations. The law that underlies our criminal justice system and the criminal justice system itself are the focus of Chapter 4. When a crime appears to have been committed and authorities such as police or prosecutors have been notified, a legal apparatus is set in motion. This apparatus is the criminal justice system. The system is described as a whole, with all of its component parts, paths, processes, and outcomes.

CHAPTER 1

Criminal Justice:
Introduction and Overview

—Two armored car guards murdered
—Jail for "wolf pack" teen
—Suspicious powder brings hazmat unit to school
—Corruption panel probes governor
—Predator online rape
—Thieves steal copper pipes from vacant buildings
—Ex-street couple pleads guilty to insider trading

• You cannot hide from it. There is no way of escaping it. Read about it online or in a newspaper. Watch the evening news. Listen to the radio. Criminal justice is a continuing drama with real-life players, set in small towns and large cities, disintegrating ghettos and affluent suburbs, bedrooms, and boardrooms. The actors in the drama are young and old, victims and perpetrators, strangers and loved ones. They were born here or abroad. They bleed, feel physical or emotional pain, and often die. Others live a life filled with the pain of losing a child, a parent, or a sibling; the loss of innocence; the shame of neglect or the guilt of having neglected. Many do no more than survive in a cell or a yard surrounded by razor wire and concrete walls. Some wait decades before they are put to death.

• And there are those who make their careers by tediously and often heroically policing the streets; objectively and dispassionately judging the innocent and guilty; and bravely or fearfully controlling the incarcerated. Unfortunately, there are also those who enforce our laws unfairly and with bias and who discriminate consciously or unconsciously in assessing guilt in sentencing those adjudged guilty and brutally disciplining the condemned.

• The human drama of criminal justice touches every one of us, whether we are an unfortunate victim, a chronic offender, a frightened inner-city dweller, or a rookie correctional officer.

Criminal Justice: The Origins of a Young Discipline

As we know, policy and legislation in matters of criminal justice are often the result of the publicity given to emotion-charged media reports. Such reports are more likely to promote political careers than evidenced-based crime control. While references are made to the human drama that crime creates every day, this book is about understanding the drama in terms of the social and behavioral science of criminal justice.

Criminal justice is a young but increasingly sophisticated and demanding discipline that seeks to answer difficult questions about crime and justice. Research in criminal justice is intended to reform policy, legislation, and the practice of crime control.

Before there was a special field called criminal justice, most legislation and policy rested on a foundation of hunches, folk wisdom, political expediency, media pressure, and emotion, which collectively has been called the "moral consensus" of the community. Today we live in an era when all of this is changing, with increasing speed. Attorneys general, legislative committees, chiefs of police, and others have begun to listen to experts on criminal justice, and more and more governmental initiatives are based on criminal justice research findings and evaluations. The field of criminal justice is increasingly influenced by an emerging evidenced-based movement in the social sciences. This movement calls for systematic reviews of criminal justice policies and programs that look for solid empirical support for what works, what doesn't work, and what looks promising.

This development is not merely of national relevance. With globalization, advances in communications and commerce, transportation, and information technology have turned separate nations and regions into a global village in which every society is affected by every other society. Independence has been replaced by interdependence, and that has had an enormous impact on crime and the effectiveness of the criminal justice response.

There are, as yet, far too few criminal justice specialists to undertake the studies needed for the creation of effective and humane crime control measures. Nevertheless, the discipline is growing and is critically important. A generation ago there were no students majoring in criminal justice. Today there are several hundred thousand! Of course, not all of these majors are seeking or advancing their careers in the field. Many students take these courses because they cover such a wide range of issues that are of concern to all those who are fascinated by crime, or are committed to the idea of justice. Courses on criminal justice are both interesting, compelling, and important.

criminal justice
The sum total of society's activities to defend itself against the actions it defines as criminal.

So, let us begin this book with a definition of the concept of criminal justice. **Criminal justice** is the sum total of society's activities to defend itself against the actions it defines as criminal. These activities reflect a broad range of social, legal, economic, political, and moral interests. Today in the United States, criminal justice functions as a system, run by professionals and increasingly assessed, evaluated, and advanced by social scientists. To be successful and effective, the criminal justice system must be perceived as having authority by the community that it serves. The perception of authority and its legitimacy require confidence in the criminal justice system. The police, courts, and correctional agencies strive for the public's confidence (see Table 1.1).

Creating a Criminal Justice System

For centuries, everywhere in the world, criminal justice was a fragmented, chaotic process or event. Law enforcers would round up suspects for offenses, real or imagined, in violation of laws enacted for the supposed good of all the people but without any basis in the real needs of the society. Judges would adjudicate as many or as few defendants as their time, or the capacity of their courtrooms, would permit. Those convicted would then be turned over to administrators of the penal system. Sometimes these administrators would have little to do; at other times they would be swamped with convicts and would literally have to farm them out (to prison farms) or sell them as slaves on prison galleys.

TABLE 1.1
Reported Confidence in the
Criminal Justice System by
Demographic Characteristics,
United States, 2005

Question: "I am going to read you a list of institutions in American society. Please tell me how much confidence you, yourself, have in each one—a great deal, quite a lot, some, or very little: the criminal justice system?"

	Great Deal/ Quite a Lot	Some	Very Little	None[a]
National	26%	45%	26%	2%
Sex				
Male	29	40	28	2
Female	28	50	24	2
Race				
White	25	48	24	2
Nonwhite	29	33	32	4
Black	24	35	40	0
Age				
18 to 29 years	34	36	26	4
30 to 49 years	29	46	24	1
50 to 64 years	19	50	28	1
50 years and older	20	48	28	2
65 years and older	21	45	29	2
Education				
College postgraduate	33	50	17	(b)
College graduate	34	49	15	1
Some college	23	48	26	3
High school graduate or less	24	38	33	2
Income				
$100,000 and over	32	49	19	(b)
$75,000 to $99,999	24	58	19	1
$50,000 to $74,999	23	49	24	4
$30,000 to $49,999	91	43	26	(b)
$20,000 to $29,999	20	38	39	2
Under $20,000	15	41	37	6
Community				
Urban area	25	44	27	3
Suburban area	29	44	24	2
Rural area	22	49	27	1
Region				
East	31	42	22	4
Midwest	21	49	27	2
South	29	42	26	2
West	23	49	27	1
Politics				
Republican	31	49	17	2
Democrat	28	44	26	1
Independent	10	43	35	3

NOTE: The "don't know/refused" category has been omitted; therefore percents may not sum to 100.
[a]Response volunteered.
[b]Less than 0.5%.
SOURCE: Table constructed by *Sourcebook* staff from data provided by The Gallup Organization, Inc. Reprinted by permission. Adapted from the *Sourcebook of Criminal Justice Statistics 2005*, Table 2.11.

FEDERAL CRACK COCAINE SENTENCING*

Overview

After two decades of contentious debate regarding the federal sentencing disparities between crack cocaine and powder cocaine, new momentum to reform current policy has emerged. In 2007, the United States Sentencing Commission (Commission) issued recommendations that call on Congress to address the lengthy sentences for low-level crack offenses. Congress has responded with at least two bipartisan crack sentencing reform bills and a new Senate bill that would equalize penalties for crack and powder cocaine offenses without increasing mandatory sentences. Over the last year, newspapers from Alabama to California have published commentary highlighting the bias associated with federal crack penalties and the federal government's concentrated prosecution of street-level dealers of crack, instead of drug kingpins and importers. This briefing paper provides background on the cocaine sentencing debate, explores the racial impact of the crack sentencing disparity, clarifies the misperceptions regarding crack addiction, and offers recommendations for eliminating unfairness in crack cocaine sentencing.

Origins of Federal Cocaine Sentencing Policy

Crack cocaine became prevalent in the 1980s and received extensive media attention, due in part to its exponential growth in the drug market. The popularity of crack cocaine was associated with its cheap price, which for the first time made cocaine available to a wider economic class. Crack is made by taking powder cocaine and cooking it with baking soda and water until it forms a hard rocky substance. These "rocks" are then broken into pieces and sold in small quantities.

Public concern about crack cocaine addiction and its accompanying violent drug market spread quickly. Newscasters used words like "crisis" and "epidemic"—later shown to be exaggerated—to describe the impact of crack. The drug was considered a social menace more dangerous than powder cocaine in its physiological and psychotropic effects. The political hysteria that ensued led Congress to pass the Anti-Drug Abuse Act of 1986. The law's mandatory penalties for crack cocaine offenses were the harshest ever

adopted for low level drug offenses and established drastically different penalty structures for crack and powder, under the belief that crack cocaine was more dangerous than powder cocaine and posed a greater threat. The result is that defendants convicted with just 5 grams of crack cocaine, the weight of less than two sugar packets and a quantity that yields about 10 to 50 doses, are subject to a five-year mandatory minimum sentence. The same five-year penalty is triggered for the sale of powder cocaine only when an offense involves 500 grams, 100 times the minimum quantity for crack, which yields between 2,500 and 5,000 doses.[1] Similarly, while the sale of 5,000 grams of powder, which can yield up to 50,000 doses, subjects defendants to a 10-year sentence, the same mandatory sentence is triggered by selling only 50 grams of crack, which produces about 100 to 500 doses.

The mandatory sentencing structure which continues today results in average sentences for crack cocaine offenses that are three years longer than for offenses involving powder cocaine. As seen in Figure 1.1, crack cocaine sentences for quantities less than 25 grams are far more severe than for powder cocaine offenses, 65 months compared to 14 months. Sentences for crack cocaine are also nearly two years longer than for methamphetamine and four years longer than for heroin. Crack is the only drug that carries a mandatory prison sentences for a first-time possession offense. A person convicted in federal court of simple possession of 5 grams of crack is subject to a mandatory five-year prison term while a per-

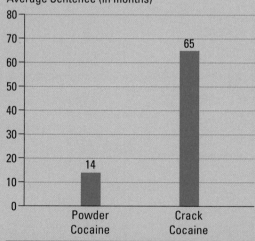

Average Sentence (in months)

FIGURE 1.1 Cocaine Sentences for Quantities Less Than 25 Grams

SOURCE: U.S. Department of Justice, *Federal Cocaine Offenses: An Analysis of Crack and Powder Penalties*, March 17, 2002.

*This paper was adapted from an earlier report by The Sentencing Project entitled *Race and Class Penalties in Crack Cocaine Sentencing*.

Drug	Median Drug Weight	Applicable Mandatory Minimum
Crack cocaine	52 grams	10 years
Powder cocaine	340 grams	none

TABLE 1.2 Median Street Level Dealer Drug Quantities and Mandatory Minimums

son convicted of possessing 5 grams of powder will probably receive a probation sentence. In fact, the maximum sentence for simple possession of any other drug, be it powder cocaine or heroin, is one year in prison.

Drug Quantities and Crack Cocaine Penalties

The federal sentencing laws Congress passed in the 1980s were intended to impose tough sentences on high-level drug market operators, such as manufacturers or heads of organizations distributing large quantities of narcotics, and serious traffickers with a substantial drug-trade business.[2] However, the weights attached to the sentences failed to capture the different roles within the crack trade. As research from the Commission has shown, the 5 grams of crack set by Congress as the trigger for a five-year mandatory sentence is not a quantity associated with mid-level, much less serious, traffickers.[3] The median drug quantity for a crack cocaine street level dealer charged in federal court (comprising two-thirds of federal crack defendants) in 2000 was 52 grams, enough to trigger a 10-year mandatory sentence. For powder cocaine, the median quantity for a street level

dealer was 340 grams, not enough even to trigger the five-year sentence. (See Table 1.2.)

These skewed calculations resulted in two serious consequences. First, they have led to extremely severe prison terms for low-level crack offenses, with represent more than 60 percent of federal crack defendants (see Figure 1.2). Second, with mandatory minimum sentences focusing solely on quantities, defendants with different levels of culpability are often lumped together. The unfortunate reality, according to the Commission, is that crack cocaine penalties "apply most often to offenders who perform low-level trafficking functions, wield little decision-making authority, and have limited responsibility."[4]

Racial Impact of Crack Sentencing

Government data demonstrate that drug use rates are similar among all racial and ethnic groups. For crack cocaine, two-thirds of users in the United States are white or Hispanic.[5] Furthermore, research on drug market patterns demonstrates that drug users generally purchase drugs from sellers of the same racial or ethnic background.[6] Despite these facts, people of color are

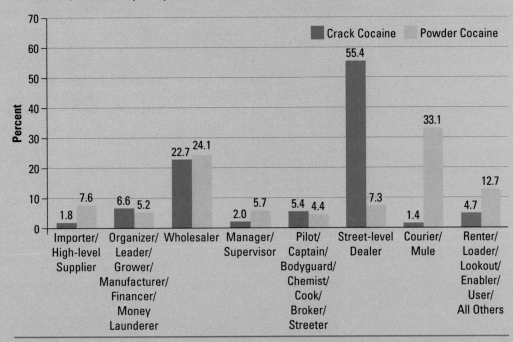

FIGURE 1.2 Defendant Function in Crack/Powder Cocaine Cases
SOURCE: U.S. Sentencing Commission, 2005 Drug Sample.

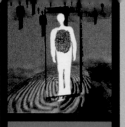

disproportionately subject to the penalties for both types of cocaine. Indeed, 81.8 percent of crack cocaine defendants in 2006 were African American (see Figure 1.3).[7]

African American drug defendants have a 20 percent greater chance of being sentenced to prison than white drug defendants.[8] Between 1994 and 2003, the average time served by African Americans for drug offenses increased by 62 percent, compared to an increase of 17 percent for white drug offenders.[9] Moreover, African Americans now serve virtually as much time in prison for a drug offense (58.7 months) as whites do for a violent offense (61.7 months).[10] As a result, the Commission reported in 2004 that "[r]evising the crack cocaine thresholds would better reduce the [sentencing] gap than any other single policy change, and it would dramatically improve the fairness of the federal sentencing system."[11] Moreover, these inequalities have substantial consequences for the way in which the African American community views the criminal justice system. According to the Commission's report to Congress, even "[p]erceived improper racial disparity fosters disrespect for and lack of confidence in the criminal justice system."[12]

Legislation that seeks to reduce the sentencing disparity between crack and powder by lowering the powder weight necessary to trigger a mandatory minimum, as has been proposed in some bills, would still have the effect of incarcerating large numbers of people of color in prison. According to data from the Commission, though the proportion of black defendants in powder cases is lower than for crack cases, the majority of powder defendants are Hispanic (see Figure 1.3). Therefore, decreasing the amount of powder required to trigger a mandatory sentence would not eliminate the racial and ethnic disparity in federal drug sentencing.

Crack Myths

Initially, the violence associated with the crack market fostered a perception that crack use instigated violent behavior in the individual user. In its May 2002 recommendations to Congress, the Commission stated that the crack penalties were based on beliefs about the drug's association with violence which had been shown to be inaccurate. In fact, the 2007 report notes a decline in associated violence, such as bodily injury or threats, for both crack and powder cocaine charges.[13] The Commission concluded that the violence associated with crack is primarily related to the drug trade and not to the effects of the drug itself, and that both powder and crack cocaine cause distribution-related violence, as do all drug markets. From an analysis of federally prosecuted cocaine cases, the Commission reported that, for 2005, a substantial majority of both powder cocaine offenses (73 percent) and crack cocaine offenses (57.3 percent) did not involve a weapon.[14] Indeed, the frequency with which weapons are "accessible, possessed, or used by the offender" is extremely low, 0.8 percent of powder cases and 2.9 percent of crack cases.[15]

Crack cocaine was also initially viewed as a menace that was ravaging not only inner-city adults but also babies. The notion of the "crack baby" became common and was associated mostly with African American infants who experienced the effects of withdrawal from crack. Over time, the medical field determined the effects of crack on a fetus had been overstated.[16] Deborah Frank, a professor of Pediatrics at Boston University, describes the "crack baby" as "a grotesque media stereotype [and] not a scientific diagnosis."[17] She found that in pregnant crack users the drug's impact on the fetus is similar to the negative effects of tobacco or alcohol use, poor prenatal care, or poor nutrition.

Crack Cocaine

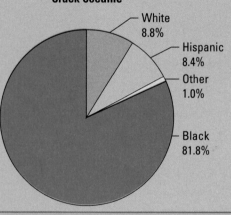

- White 8.8%
- Hispanic 8.4%
- Other 1.0%
- Black 81.8%

Powder Cocaine

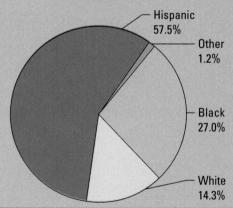

- Hispanic 57.5%
- Other 1.2%
- Black 27.0%
- White 14.3%

FIGURE 1.3 Race/Ethnicity of Cocaine Defendants
SOURCE: U.S. Sentencing Commission 2006 Datafile, USSCFY06.

Over time, numerous studies have shown that the physiological and psychotropic effects of crack and powder are the same, and the drugs are now widely acknowledged as pharmacologically identical. For example, a 1996 study published in the *Journal of the American Medical Association* finds analogous effects on the body for both crack and powder cocaine.[18] Similarly, Charles Schuster, former director of the National Institute on Drug Abuse and professor of Psychiatry and Behavioral Sciences, found that once cocaine is absorbed into the bloodstream and reaches the brain its effects on brain chemistry are identical regardless of whether it is crack or powder.[19]

Sentencing Commission Calls for Reform

In 1984 Congress created the Commission to develop federal sentencing guidelines that would, among other goals, reduce unwarranted sentencing disparity. In 1994, as part of the Omnibus Violent Crime Control and Law Enforcement Act, the Commission was directed to study the differing penalties for powder and crack. After a year-long study the Commission recommended to Congress a revision of the crack/powder 100:1 quantity disparity, finding it to be unjustified by the small differences between the two forms of cocaine. The Commission advised equalizing the quantity ratio that would trigger the mandatory sentences. The Commission also recommended that the federal sentencing guidelines consider factors other than drug quantity to determine sentence lengths. Congress rejected the recommendations, which marked the first time it did so in the Commission's history.

Two years later, in April 1997, the Commission once more recommended that the quantity disparity between crack and powder cocaine be reduced, this time providing Congress a range of 2:1 to 15:1 to choose from. The new recommendation was based on both raising the quantity of crack and lowering the quantity of powder required to trigger a mandatory minimum sentence. Congress, however, again did not act on the recommendation.

In 2002 there was a new movement to reconsider crack cocaine policies. The Commission's *Report to Congress,* which again called for reducing sentencing disparities, documented the conclusions of an extensive body of research, as well as testimony presented at three public hearings by medical and scientific professionals, federal and local law enforcement officials, criminal justice practitioners, academics, and civil rights organizations. Moreover, the Drug Sentencing Reform Act was introduced by Senator Jeff

Sessions (R-AL)—a modest proposal to reform crack cocaine sentencing policy. The legislation never passed but set an important precedent of Republican support for reducing unfairness in crack cocaine sentencing.

The bipartisan support for crack cocaine sentencing reform reemerged in 2006, and the Commission renewed its commitment to resolving the sentencing controversy. In July 2006, Senator Sessions again introduced his legislation to reduce the inequality in cocaine sentencing. The proposal would raise the crack trigger amount for the five-year mandatory minimum to 20 grams from 5 grams, but lower the trigger threshold for powder cocaine to 400 grams from 500 grams.

In November 2006, the Commission held another public hearing to assess whether the differences in punishment for crack and powder cocaine offenses were justified in light of any recent developments. The Commission heard testimony from the Department of Justice, law enforcement, medical and drug treatment professionals, academics, and advocacy organizations. At the hearing, commissioners expressed concern that the current crack cocaine law was ineffective at targeting the upper echelon of drug distributors. According to United States Attorney R. Alexander Acosta's testimony, the highest level cocaine trafficking takes place almost exclusively in the powder form. This was affirmed by Joseph Rannazzisi of the Drug Enforcement Administration, who noted that crack cocaine sellers are at the lowest end of the powder cocaine distribution chain. Acosta testified that the administration's top priority for drug policy enforcement was targeting the highest level leaders in the drug market, but Vice Chair Judge Ruben Castillo pointed out that only 7 percent of federal cocaine cases involve high-level traffickers.

In May 2007, the Commission released a new report detailing findings from the hearing and recommended modification to the 100:1 quantity ratio. The Commission called on Congress to raise the crack cocaine quantities that trigger the five-year and ten-year mandatory minimum sentences in order to focus penalties on serious and major traffickers and to repeal the simple possession mandatory minimum. Additionally, the commission cautioned against any reduction in the quantity trigger for the powder cocaine mandatory minimum, "as there is no evidence to justify such an increase in quantity-based penalties for powder cocaine offenses."[20] Congress has responded with three bills introduced in the Senate's 110th session. In addition to Senator Session's proposal first introduced in 2001, Senators Orrin Hatch

(R-UT) and Joseph Biden (D-DE) each introduced bills that either reduce or eliminate the sentencing disparity between crack and powder cocaine. While Hatch's bill, like Sessions's, calls for a 20:1 ratio, he achieved this end by raising the five-year mandatory minimum quantity trigger for crack cocaine to 25 grams and leaving the powder cocaine level untouched at 500 grams. Biden advocates raising the crack cocaine quantity triggers to those of powder cocaine, thereby eliminating the disparity. Both bills eliminate the simple possession mandatory minimum.

Conclusion

The impact of the crack cocaine sentencing provisions has been troubling on two counts. First, a significant racial disparity in prosecutions and confinement has ensued. Along with disproportionate law enforcement practices that target blacks, the crack sentencing policies have resulted in more than 80 percent of crack cocaine defendants being African American despite the fact that a majority of crack cocaine users in the United States are white or Hispanic.

Second, a serious misdirection of federal resources has developed. The crack law fails as an effective drug strategy by inappropriately targeting low-level offenders. While the federal courts are intended to focus on high-level drug operations, more than 60 percent of federal crack cocaine defendants have only low-level involvement in drug activity, such as street-level dealers, couriers, or lookouts. This pursuit of low-level offenders diverts resources away from the most troublesome contributors to the illegal drug market, drug kingpins and importers. As noted by the Commission in its report to Congress in 1997, "federal cocaine policy inappropriately targets limited federal resources by placing the quantity triggers for the five-year mandatory minimum penalty for crack cocaine too low."[21]

The misinformation and hysteria that clouded the public debate on crack cocaine have done a disservice to developing responsible sentencing policy, while exacerbating the tragic racial disparities that plague our prison system. Two decades later, a new consciousness about the impact of the war on drugs, the costs of incarceration to urban communities, and the effectiveness of drug treatment has emerged. Restoring fairness to the cocaine sentencing structure requires Congress to equalize the

Despite various reform efforts in policing, in court administration, and especially in corrections, there was no systematic reform effort in the United States until 1929, when former Attorney General George W. Wickersham was instructed to conduct a nationwide study of prevailing conditions in the administration of justice. The findings of his commission (1929–1931), known as the Wickersham Report, were devastating: There was little justice in the criminal justice system; there was not even a system; most of those running the various agencies were untrained. Scholarship in the field was nonexistent.[1] But the Great Depression of the 1930s and the subsequent war years made it impossible to improve criminal justice. Only in the 1960s, a decade of civil disturbances on a wide spectrum of social issues, did the movement for reform again gain momentum. In part this was due to the realization by an increasing number of Americans that many of the rights and opportunities that the Constitution provided on paper were in fact not granted equally or made accessible to all citizens. It was clear, for example, that people of color continued to be oppressed and disenfranchised, and that women were not afforded the same rights and privileges as men. Citizens charged with crimes were denied the due process guarantees that the Constitution provided. The U.S. Supreme Court, under the leadership of Chief Justice Earl Warren, squarely addressed these problems and in case after case ruled that constitutional guarantees must be honored.[2]

In *Gideon v. Wainwright* (1963), for example, the Supreme Court mandated that every criminal defendant—in whatever court—is entitled to the assistance of counsel (legal advice).[3] In a series of related decisions, culminating in *Miranda v. Arizona* (1966),[4] the Court placed the burden on the police to warn arrestees and those in custody of their Fifth Amendment right to remain silent and their Sixth Amendment right to have counsel appointed. The cost of not advising arrestees of their rights includes having the defendant's statements excluded from evidence at trial, including any and all evidence obtained as a result of those statements. *Miranda* was a rude awakening for law enforcement agencies all across the country. Overzealous and inadequately trained officers found it difficult to cope with the demands the Supreme Court imposed. Improved recruitment procedures training, standards of integrity, and professionalism were needed.

penalties for crack and powder offenses without increasing the current mandatory sentences. Harsh mandatory drug penalties have not protected communities or reduced drug addiction. Now is the time for new ideas about sentencing. An important first step to address the need for reform begins with correcting the inequity in crack cocaine penalties.

SOURCES

1. United States Sentencing Commission [USSC], *Report to Congress: Cocaine and Federal Sentencing Policy* (May 2007), p. 73.
2. Testimony of Commisioner John R. Steer before the Subcommittee on Criminal Justice, Drug Policy and Human Resources, May 11, 2000.
3. USSC, *Report to Congress: Cocaine and Federal Sentencing Policy,* May 2002 p. 45, Figure 10.
4. Ibid, p. 100.
5. Substance Abuse and Mental Health Services Administration, *Results from the 2005 National Survey on Drug Use and Health:* Detailed Table J (Washington, DC: September 2006), Table 1.43a.
6. Dorothy Lockwood, Anne E. Pottieger, and James A. Inciardi, "Crack Use, Crime by Crack Users, and Ethnicity," in Darnell F. Hawkins, ed., *Ethnicity, Race and Crime.* New York: State University of New York Press, 1995, p. 21.
7. USSC, *Report to Congress: Cocaine and Federal Sentencing Policy,* May 2007, p. 15.
8. USSC, *Fifteen Years of Guidelines Sentencing* (November 2004), p. 122.
9. Bureau of Justice Statistics [BJS], *Compendium of Federal Justice Statistics, 1994* (Washington, DC: March 1998), Table 6.11, p. 85; and BJS, *Compendium of Federal Justice Statistics, 2003* (Washington, DC: October 2004), Table 7.16, p. 112.
10. *Compendium of Federal Statistics, 2003* (October 2005), Table 7.16, p. 112.
11. USSC, *Fifteen Years of Guidelines Sentencing* (November 2004), p. 132.
12. USSC, *Report to Congress: Cocaine and Federal Sentencing Policy,* May 2002, p. 103.
13. USSC, *Report to Congress: Cocaine and Federal Sentencing Policy,* May 2007, p. 36.
14. Ibid., p. 32.
15. Ibid., p. 33.
16. Ibid., p. 68.
17. Testimony of Deborah A. Frank, M.D., before the United States Sentencing Commission, February 21, 2002.
18. Dorothy K. Hatsukami and Marian W. Fischman, "Crack Cocaine and Cocaine Hydrochloride: Are the Differences Myth or Reality?" *Journal of the American Medical Association,* November 20, 1996.
19. Testimony of Charles Schuster before the Subcommittee on Crime and Drugs of the Senate Judiciary Committee, May 22, 2002.
20. USSC, *Report to Congress: Cocaine and Federal Sentencing Policy,* May 2007, p. 8.
21. USSC, *Special Report to Congress: Cocaine and Federal Sentencing Policy,* April 1997, p. 7.
22. Available at http://www.sentencingproject.org/Admin/Documents/publications/dp_cracksentencing.pdf.

The Supreme Court also touched the field of corrections by granting prisoners rights they had not had before, thereby creating new responsibilities for correctional administrators and staff. These developments led to the need for intensive training of corrections officers.

Congress began to realize that the Supreme Court's demands required a new type of professional, well selected and highly trained, to run the criminal justice enterprise, which needed to become an integrated system of criminal justice with component parts. The police, courts, and correctional agencies had to operate in a coordinated fashion.

President Lyndon B. Johnson realized this objective in establishing the President's Commission on Law Enforcement and Administration of Justice (1967),[5] and urged congressional passage of the Omnibus Crime Control and Safe Streets Act (1968),[6] which established the federal Law Enforcement Assistance Administration (LEAA). The report of the President's Commission clearly defined the tasks of criminal justice and in so doing identified criminal justice as an approach, a governmental aim, and—indeed—a science, leaving it to the LEAA to implement a national strategy.

The President's Commission, with Nicholas DeBelleville Katzenbach as chair, a former attorney general, included some of the foremost scholars in law and justice who produced voluminous reports on the workings of criminal justice, often probing what works and what does not and making sound recommendations.[7] The field and "system" of criminal justice was born.

Criminal Justice as a System

The term "criminal justice system" is so familiar that you have probably never questioned whether or not there is in fact a "system." The components of a system are meant to form a unified whole. The steps and processes of a system are meant to be interdependent, and its agencies and actors are supposed to serve a common purpose. Are these truly the characteristics of the criminal justice system? Do the police, courts, and corrections operate in this way? Are their actions interactive, interdependent, and unified?

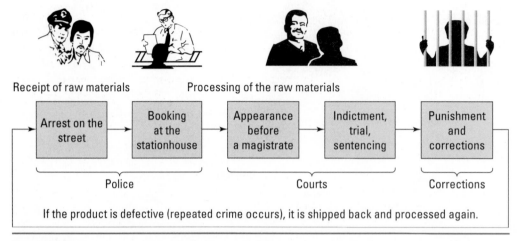

Receipt of raw materials   Processing of the raw materials

| Arrest on the street | → | Booking at the stationhouse | → | Appearance before a magistrate | → | Indictment, trial, sentencing | → | Punishment and corrections |

Police   Courts   Corrections

If the product is defective (repeated crime occurs), it is shipped back and processed again.

FIGURE 1.4   The Production Process Model

These questions have challenged criminal justice specialists for years. Some see the criminal justice system as a production process—a process where "raw materials" are screened and refined (Figure 1.4). The raw materials of the criminal justice process are the criminal suspects. Specialists from three segments of the system are actively involved in processing this raw material: police, courts, and corrections. As the raw material moves along in the production line, it changes in character. A suspect becomes an accused, an accused becomes a defendant, a defendant becomes a convicted offender, and a convicted offender becomes a probationer or inmate. Finally, in almost every case, an inmate becomes an ex-convict.

But the criminal justice "production process" differs, for example, from a typical cell phone manufacturing plant in a number of important respects. First, cell phones are assembled in a series of interconnected production lines and supervisors oversee the entire manufacturing process. Unfortunately, the criminal justice process lacks the same oversight and coordination. In the field of criminal justice, there is no equivalent to a board of directors or a top management team that is responsible for ensuring product quality throughout the system.

Second, the raw material in criminal justice is human, typically reluctant to participate, and experiencing feelings of helplessness or loss of control and perhaps even anger. Because this is not the processing of the component parts that compose a cell phone, criminal justice agencies must use forms of social control (coercive processes, including physical detention) to ensure that the processing of human beings will be efficient, orderly, and ultimately just and effective.

Third, the criminal justice system must maintain legitimacy in the community. Law enforcement officers, judges, and correction officials must have credibility and standing in the community. The criminal justice process is open to public inspection, criticism, and reform. The vast majority of manufacturing facilities are closed to public scrutiny. Consumers must wait until the latest cell phone is displayed in a retail store or marketed online.

Fourth, the "dropout" rate in the criminal justice system is much higher than in the manufacturing process. There are many diversion points along the line; very few of the original "raw materials" reach the end. Cell phone manufacturers would go out of business with so many products diverted from the production line!

The process begins: an officer interviewing witnesses at the scene of a crime.

The production line analogy has prompted some researchers to propose innovative models. Samuel Walker argues that the straight-line production analogy fails to consider that criminal cases receive differential treatment, both in the press and in the criminal justice system. He depicts criminal justice processes in the shape of a wedding cake (see Figure 1.5). At the top are the celebrated cases that receive disproportionate press coverage and public scrutiny. As we move down the layers of the cake, the seriousness of the crimes decreases, as do the penalties. At the lowest layer, misdemeanors, there is much less concern for procedural rights.

The wedding cake model is not an alternative explanation of the system. Rather, it shows that we are dealing with perhaps three distinct processes: The most refined and ideal one is found at the top of the cake (dispositions of highly visible cases); the least refined and most hurried one lies at the bottom (misdemeanor dispositions).

As you think about the production line and wedding cake models, consider one last problem: Cell phone components at different stages of assembly ride on an automated conveyor belt and are bar coded and quality inspected. Criminals, however, do not ride through an automated criminal justice system, guided by the artificial intelligence of the latest robotics. Rather, human beings make decisions at every stage of the criminal justice process—decisions that affect the fate of another human being. In short, the criminal justice system is a human system.

FIGURE 1.5
The Wedding Cake Model
SOURCE: Adapted from Samuel Walker, *Sense and Nonsense About Crime* (Belmont, CA: Wadsworth, 1985).

Models of the Criminal Justice System

The Goals

The prevention of crime is often discussed as one of the ends or goals of the criminal justice system. When a law enforcement officer separates quarreling lovers, when a probation officer guides a client away from a bar, when a judge orders the arrest of a drug dealer, each acts to prevent crime. It is easy to conclude, then, that the criminal justice system is dedicated to preventing crime. But critics will immediately counter with statistics proving that the system does a poor job of this, and that it even fosters crime in a variety of ways: by criminalizing conduct in the first place, by raising the statistics, by labeling individuals as "criminals" (thus creating criminal careers), by making inmates unfit for life in a free society, and so on. This is not the place to argue how well the system works. Nor is it the place to point to other options for the prevention of crime, like better secondary schools, equal access to economic opportunities, and a loving caretaker. Here we simply note that crime prevention is a recognized, although sometimes disputed, goal or end of the criminal justice system.

The other major goal or end is said to be justice itself. That sounds a bit like the chicken and the egg—the goal of criminal justice is justice. Yet this is what proponents argue: The criminal justice system can do no more than deliver criminal justice. The end product must be fair and deserved, and at each stage of the process justice must also be applied and delivered. (See "Federal Crack Cocaine Sentencing," 21st Century Challenge.)

The Means

Herbert Packer, in *The Limits of the Criminal Sanction*,[8] has made an important contribution to identifying the methods by which criminal justice seeks to achieve its goals. He presents two approaches for the criminal justice process: the due process model and the crime control model. The due process model requires strict adherence to the Constitution. The focus is on the accused and on his or her rights. The focus is also on providing some balance to the power and authority of the state. Quite simply, due process protections under the Constitution force the state to fulfill its burden of proving its case against the accused. The crime control model focuses on the efficiency and effectiveness of the process. The criminal process exists to investigate crimes, screen suspects, detain dangerous defendants, and secure convictions of guilty parties. This should be done with speed and finality. Each agency at every stage of the process assumes the responsibility for dealing efficiently with the criminal case.

Packer describes the due process model as an obstacle course. Each stage creates barriers to the successful prosecution of an accused, whereas the crime control model resembles an assembly line. Efficiency, productivity, and reliability are its hallmarks, with constitutional rights taking second place to the desirability of processing offenders quickly and successfully.

This identification of two different approaches explains many of the differences in policymakers' views. The two models are the practical and theoretical extremes of how the process can be conducted. They neither explain the goals at the end of the criminal justice system nor pinpoint the operational ideal, which is to operate a criminal justice system under the rule of law.

Wayne R. LaFave and Jerold H. Israel identify eight goals for the ideal criminal justice system:[9]

1. **Establishing an adversarial system of adjudication.** Neutral decision makers must make decisions in a forum where opponents can present interpretations of facts and law in a light most favorable to their case.
2. **Establishing an accusatorial system of prosecution.** In such a system the state bears the burden of proving the guilt of the accused.
3. **Minimizing erroneous convictions.** Protecting an accused from erroneous conviction is an important goal of the process.
4. **Minimizing the burdens of accusation and litigation.** The process must reduce the likelihood that innocent people will be accused of crimes.
5. **Providing lay participation.** The criminal justice process must not be left entirely to government officials. Lay participation can ensure objectivity and independence.
6. **Respecting the dignity of the individual.** The criminal process must ensure respect for privacy and autonomy, as well as freedom from physical and emotional abuse.
7. **Maintaining the appearance of fairness.** Ensuring fairness in the process is not enough. There must also be an appearance of justice and fairness to the participants and the public.
8. **Achieving equality in the application of the process.** Ensuring the just treatment of an accused is not enough. The criminal justice process must also ensure that like cases are treated alike.

Stages of the Criminal Justice Process

In 1967 the President's Commission on Law Enforcement and the Administration of Justice characterized the criminal justice system as an orderly process comprising five interrelated phases with four paths.[10] Every criminal case may potentially flow through all the phases, though most do not. In the first phase, called entry into the system, citizens play an important role by bringing criminal events to the attention of the police. The police investigate the case and identify a suspect. The judiciary issues search and arrest warrants.

The second phase, prosecution and pretrial services, is dominated by prosecutors, who prepare the charges; grand juries, who indict defendants; and judges, who conduct a series of hearings, including the initial appearance of an arrested person at court and a preliminary hearing.

The third phase, adjudication, begins with an arraignment, at which the officially accused person pleads to (answers) the formal charges (indictment or information) against him or her, and ends with a judgment of guilty or not guilty. This phase is conducted by a judge, with or without a jury. The prosecutor, representing the state and people, and the defense lawyer play the most active roles.

The fourth phase consists of sentencing and sanctions. In most cases, in most states, jurors do not participate in sentencing. The judge imposes the sentence, usually after hearing a presentence investigation (PSI) report prepared by a probation officer. Prosecutors, defense lawyers, and defendants have their say, and in many states victims do as well.

The fifth and final phase, corrections, is in the hands of the executive branch of government. Its Department of Corrections executes the sentence imposed by the court. Even though courts defer to correction officials in matters of inmate care, custody, and control, courts require them to comply with the law.

The revised flowchart first devised by the President's Commission shows four different paths through the system (Figure 1.6). The first path is for major crimes, or felonies (the top layers of Walker's wedding cake); the second is for minor crimes, or misdemeanors (the bottom layer of the cake). The paths differ. Misdemeanors normally require no grand jury indictment and no trial by jury, and the sanctions imposed are jail sentences of one year or less or fines, rather than imprisonment (meaning confinement in a prison for more than a year). A third path is for petty offenses, with summary proceedings resulting in minor sanctions, usually fines. A fourth path is for juveniles. It resembles the paths for adults in many respects, except that the proceedings are less formal and rarely include juries.

As the flowchart indicates, the traditional paths through the criminal justice system do not end at a single exit; they lead to many exits. An accused person's path through the system is not fixed or predestined. The direction that path takes, and its end, depend on the actions of several decision makers, including the accused. Let's see how this works.

Entry into the System

Decisions by Victims

The mere fact that a crime has taken place does not, in and of itself, activate the criminal justice system. A series of decisions—some complex, others simple—must be made to activate the machinery. For a criminal act to be *known to the police,* initiating the process, the act must first be *perceived* by an individual (the car is not in the garage where I left it). The act must then be *defined* or *classified* as one that places it within the jurisdiction of the criminal justice system (a theft has taken place), and it must be *reported* to the police. Once the police are notified, they classify it and often *redefine* what may have taken place (a youngster has taken the car without parental permission) before *recording* the act as a *crime known to the police* (Figure 1.7).

Victims of criminal acts have been called the "most influential" of all the decision makers, or the "principal gatekeepers" of the entire criminal justice process.[11] For many offenses, except for the victim's report of the crime to the police, the system would never become involved. Early studies of the role of victim reporting reveal that approximately 95 percent of all crimes known to the police come from victim initiatives.[12]

But surveys also reveal that victims often do not report offenses to the police (Table 1.3). Some researchers attribute this failure to the victims' concern for their present and future safety.[13] Others have found that feelings of self-blame and loss of personal control may inhibit reporting. One recent study has suggested that much of the nonreporting of minor criminal victimization may be accounted for by efforts on the part of the victim to engage in self-help—that is, by ignoring it, talking it out, engaging in interpersonal violence, or receiving insurance proceeds.[14] The literature on victim reporting is certainly clear on one issue—reasons for reporting or not reporting vary according to the crime committed. Consider why victims of rape may fail to report. Recent victimization surveys reveal that 35 percent of victims consider it a "private/personal matter," 18 percent are of the opinion that nothing can be done because they cannot prove they have been victimized, and 16 percent fear reprisals.[15]

Decisions by the Police

Once information about a possible crime has come to the attention of the police, a decision has to be made whether to investigate the case. The police cannot possibly investigate every complaint. Because of heavy caseloads in large municipalities, for example, police emphasize the investigation of major crimes. Petty larcenies are rarely investigated because of the sheer bulk of the cases and the shortage of police detectives.

What is the sequence of events in the criminal justice system?

Entry into the system   **Prosecution and pretrial services**   **Adjudication**

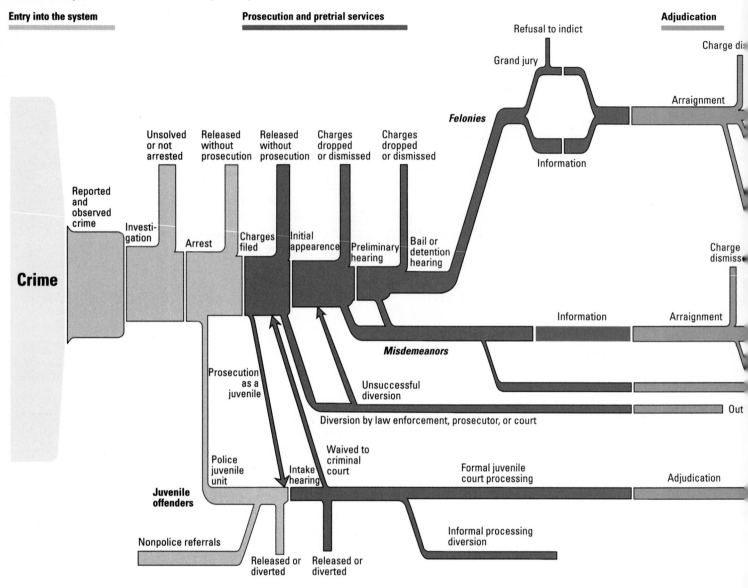

FIGURE 1.6   The Criminal Justice Process

SOURCE: Adapted from the President's Commission on Law Enforcement and Administration of Justice, *The Challenge of Crime in a Free Society* (Washington, DC: U.S. Government Printing Office, 1967), pp. 8–9; in U.S. Department of Justice, Bureau of Justice Statistics, *Report to the Nation on Crime and Justice*, 2nd ed. (Washington, DC: U.S. Government Printing Office, 1998).

Other factors are also on the minds of police when they decide to make an arrest or to seek an arrest warrant, or to drop an investigation entirely. They consider, for example, public ambivalence about the significance of a given criminal law, the probability that a witness will or will not cooperate, and whether an arrest is too harsh a response to a particular act. The police may choose from a series of alternatives to arrest ranging from outright release to release with a citation to release of a youngster into the custody of parents or guardians.[16] It is worth considering that (1) not all those known to have committed a crime are arrested; (2) after arrest a "desk officer" may change the charge or go so far as to reject the arrest; and (3) investigating officers may, at any point in their investigation, consider the arrest too weak and therefore reject it.

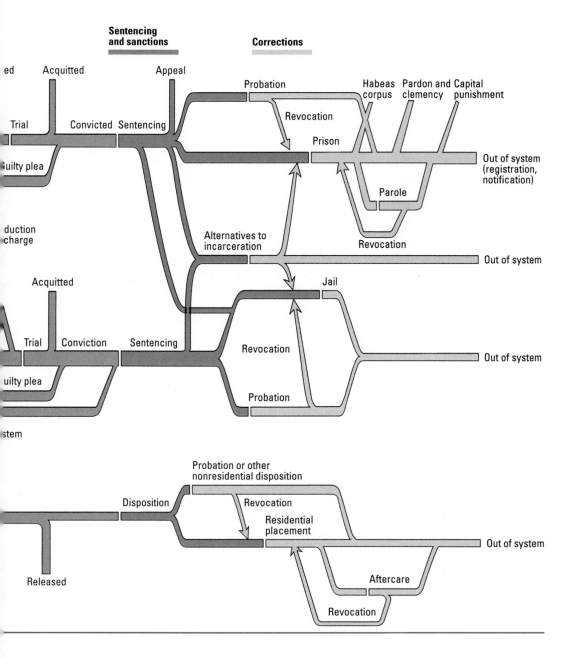

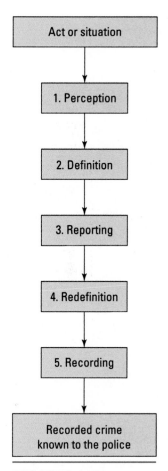

FIGURE 1.7

The Process of Bringing Crime to the Attention of Police

SOURCE: R. F. Sparks, H. G. Genn, and D. J. Dodd, *Surveying Victims: A Study of the Measurement of Criminal Victimization, Perceptions of Crime, and Attitudes to Criminal Justice* (Chichester, England: Wiley, 1977), p. 6.

Legal Standards

What legal criteria determine when and whether a suspect can be brought into the criminal justice system? When may the system do something to or about a suspect? As we will see in later chapters, the Constitution, as interpreted by the Supreme Court, provides some of these criteria.

The Constitution states that no one may be "seized" (taken into the criminal justice process) except on a warrant issued on the basis of probable cause of having committed a crime. For almost two centuries, the **probable cause** requirement was deemed to establish the point at which potential guilt is clear enough to take a person into custody. Ideally this determination is made by a judge or magistrate on the basis of the testimony of witnesses (including the police), delivered under oath, that a given suspect has committed a given crime. In practice, the probable cause decision is frequently made by a law enforcement officer at the scene of the crime. The Supreme Court has ruled that the police have probable cause to take a suspect into custody when "the facts and circumstances within their knowledge and of which

probable cause
Set of facts that would lead a reasonable person to believe that an accused person committed the offense in question; the minimum evidence requirement for an arrest, according to the Fourth Amendment.

TABLE 1.3
Estimated Percent Distribution of Reasons for Not Reporting Personal and Property Victimizations to Police By Type of Crime, United States, 2004[a].

Reasons for Not Reporting to Police	Total[b]
Number of reasons for not reporting victimizations[d]	3,126,410
Total	100%
Reported to another official	13.9
Private or personal matter	19.2
Object recovered; offender unsuccessful	20.3
Not important enough	6.7
Insurance would not cover	0.1[e]
Not aware crime occurred until later	0.5[e]
Unable to recover property: no ID number	0.5[e]
Lack of proof	2.5
Police would not want to be bothered	4.8
Police inefficient, ineffective, or biased	3.0
Fear of reprisal	4.6
Too inconvenient or time consuming	4.1
Other reasons	19.9

[a]Detail may not add to total because of rounding.
[b]Includes crimes of violence and purse snatching/pocket picking not listed separately.[c]
[c]Includes rape and sexual assault not listed separately.
[d]Some respondents may have cited more than one reason for not reporting victimizations to the police
[e]Estimate is based on about 10 or fewer sample cases.
SOURCE: U.S. Department of Justice, Bureau of Justice Statistics, *Criminal Victimization in the United States, 2004 Statistical Tables*, NCJ 200561, Table 102 [Online],http://www.ojp.usdoj.gov/bjs/pub/pdf/cvus02.pdf (Aug. 7, 2006). Table adapted by *Sourcebook* staff.

they [have] reasonable trustworthy information [are] sufficient to warrant a prudent man in believing that the [suspect] had committed or was committing an offence."[17]

This definition relies on vague terms such as "reasonable trustworthy information" and "prudent man." Nevertheless, arrests made without probable cause or without a warrant that has been issued on sworn testimony before a judge and based on a determination of probable cause are considered unreasonable seizures of the person and in violation of the Fourth Amendment. Evidence taken in the course of an illegal arrest may be ruled inadmissible and barred from use at a trial.

The practice of finding inadmissible evidence that is illegally obtained is called the **exclusionary rule.** This is a judicially created rule of law designed to deter the police from engaging in illegal practices and to keep the courts from condoning such conduct. The Supreme Court ruled in 1969, in *Mapp v. Ohio,* that all state courts in the country must apply the exclusionary rule as a matter of constitutional law.[18] The ruling has been hailed by civil libertarians, who view it as a necessary safeguard against police misconduct, and strongly attacked by conservatives, who argue that now an arbitrary measure "handcuffs" the police.

These two positions illustrate the fundamental issues present in a Fourth Amendment analysis—that is, the need for effective law enforcement versus the need to protect individual rights and liberties. Conservatives call for unhampered law enforcement and liberals ask for the protection of rights. Research, as we will see in later chapters, suggests that law enforcement has not been seriously hindered by the exclusionary rule.

Recent Supreme Court decisions have strengthened police powers. Faced with mounting public concern over street crime in the 1960s, the Supreme Court was under pressure to legitimize prudent police action for the purpose of preventing a specific crime about to be committed, even when an officer had no probable cause to make an arrest. In 1968, the Supreme Court acknowledged the propriety of police intervention when evidence against a suspect falls short of probable cause. If a police officer has **reasonable suspicion** that a person might be engaged in the commission of a crime, the officer is authorized to stop

exclusionary rule
Rule prohibiting use of illegally obtained evidence in a court of law.

reasonable suspicion
Suspicion (short of probable cause) that a person has been or may be engaged in the commission of a crime.

the person, ask questions, and frisk him or her to make sure that the suspect is not armed and dangerous.[19]

The Right to Counsel

Assume that a police officer or a magistrate has made the decision to arrest a suspect, and a suspect has in fact been arrested. What happens now?

Immediately after the arrest, when the person is in custody, the arresting officer has the duty to recite the *Miranda* **warning,** which explains the rights of an arrestee. The *Miranda* warning derives from one of the Supreme Court's most important rulings, which laid down the standards of procedural fairness mandated by the Fourth, Fifth, and Sixth Amendments to the Constitution.[20] If the warning is not given, a judge may exclude from evidence presented at trial any incriminating statement the arrestee may have made, as well as any evidence that resulted from it.[21] Once the suspect has been taken into custody, the processing of the event and the offender begins with booking, the taking of fingerprints and mug shots (identifying photographs), the filling out of forms, and detention in a holding pen.

In the case of *Gideon v. Wainwright* (1963), the Supreme Court laid down the rule that every person charged with a crime that may lead to incarceration has the right to an attorney and that the state must pay for that service if the defendant cannot afford to do so.[22] This case, which involved an indigent Florida defendant, established the universal right to free defense counsel for the poor. It has been implemented nationwide by the provision of assigned counsel, public defenders, contract counsel, or legal aid attorney. As we will see in later chapters, however, these defense lawyers, under tremendous caseload pressures, often suggest plea bargains.[23] So their decisions, too, have a considerable impact on the direction and outcome of the process.

Miranda warning
Warning that explains the rights of an arrestee, and that police recite at the time of the arrest or prior to interrogation.

Prosecution and Pretrial Services

During the prosecution and pretrial services phase, prosecutors and judges make the decisions. Far fewer persons go through this phase than enter the system. Many arrested persons have already been diverted out of the system by this stage; others will be diverted at this stage, when charges are dropped or cases dismissed. Charges may be dropped for many reasons. Perhaps the evidence is not strong enough to support probable cause. Perhaps the arrested person is a juvenile who should be dealt with by the juvenile justice system or a mentally disturbed person who requires hospitalization. Perhaps the judge believes that justice is best served by compassion.

The Judicial Decision to Release

An arrested person must promptly be taken before a magistrate, a judge at the lowest level of the judicial hierarchy, who makes a determination that probable cause exists. The magistrate will use a standard of probable cause that is a bit tougher than that of the police officers. For one thing, the magistrate has more time to view the evidence, to reflect, and then to decide than the police officer had at the scene of the crime. The magistrate must also repeat the *Miranda* warning and then decide whether to release the defendant on bail or on percentage bail (the defendant deposits with the court only a certain percentage of the bail that has been set); to release on recognizance or ROR (no bail is required on condition that the defendant appears for trial and remains law-abiding in the meantime); to release the defendant into someone's custody; or to detain the defendant in jail pending further proceedings.

In making the decision to release, judges or magistrates are strongly influenced by prosecutors' views as to whether a given defendant is a safe risk for release. In most states, release criteria have been enacted into law. Historically, however, the only criterion for release on bail has been whether the defendant can be relied on to be present for the next court appearance. In practice, judges tend to rely on such factors as the gravity of the charge and the probability that the defendant may commit a crime or harass victims if released.[24]

THOMAS J. NESTEL, III, PHILADELPHIA POLICE DEPARTMENT

Introduction

On the fateful day when Islamic extremists flew passenger airliners into the World Trade Center, I was the commanding officer of Philadelphia's 25th District. As the events unfolded in New York City, Washington, D.C., and Shanksville, Pennsylvania, my only sources of information regarding the attacks were cable news networks. When my six-year-old daughter called begging that I come home where I would be safe, I assured her that my area of command had no potential targets for attack. At that point, I remembered that one of my neighborhoods was largely populated by Arab Americans, and they would need protection from any misguided retaliation. The next 12 hours were spent identifying critical infrastructure locations and providing the necessary security to protect them. What did law enforcement learn from the tragedy of 9/11? Has policing changed in America?

Pre-9/11/2001

Police officers have always been the masters of re-actionary response. No other profession can quickly and effectively react to emergency situations. When innocent people face a threat to their safety, law enforcement professionals make up the line of defense that confronts and neutralizes the danger. Police officers routinely move from one treatening event to another. Time spent conducting disaster drill, and pre-event planning did not exist before 9/11/2001.

Prior to the attacks, information gathered by police officers stayed in that department's cone of secrecy and was not shared with any outside organization. Historically, the topic of information sharing has been strongly discouraged. The causes of poor intelligence sharing can be attrib-

uted to liability resulting from the unintended release of confidential information, competitive nature of information gathering, and mistrust of anyone outside of the work group.

The Philadelphia Police Department staffed myriad units tasked with gathering intelligence, but little occurred on the municipal level to analyze the data or to provide worthwhile information to assist field commanders in deployment and prevention efforts. The police department did not have any analysts on its staff so raw information tended to receive only a cursory review. Pre-9/11 intelligence products for field operations in Philadelphia were few and far apart and always came from federal and state entities.

The normal response to major incidents in a municipality had been limited to police and fire departments. The two groups of first responders have specific functions and, prior to 9/11, operated without much coordination. The law enforcement profession tended to operate independently of other service and public safety agencies. Although the police and fire departments in Philadelphia have a tremendous relationship and mutual respect, they definitely work in separate pipelines at the scene of an incident. Radio communication served as another issue that fostered independence. The various communication channels were not compatible, and any messages transmitted to and from the field elements were done by messenger.

The National Commission on Terrorist Attacks upon the United States published its report in 2002 and began an evolution. The Commission pointed out several shortcomings in the response to terrorist attacks by the nation's intelligence community and law enforcement. The factors noted in the report definitely apply to the Philadelphia Police Department. Until the attacks, we lacked a level of planning that would assist in the seamless response of multiple departments and mass evacuations. We did not conduct drills that challenged the capabilities of public safety in the city. The department failed to focus on developing intelligence to aid field commands. Perhaps, most important, we did not possess the financial support to purchase equipment to train and plan for terrorism incidents.

Post-9/11/2001

So, has the Philadelphia Police Department adapted to the new threat facing America? In some ways, improvements have launched the department into the future, while other attempts seem to be baby steps in the walk toward protecting the city. Some of the outstanding efforts involve the purchase of equipment and the delivery of training. A classified number of police officers now possess duffel bags filled with equipment that would be used in the event of an incident that causes mass casualties. Protective and tactical gear that would enable a well-protected police response anywhere in the region now exists in Philadelphia. Prior to 9/11/2001, a response of such magnitude would have taken hours and perhaps days.

The training modules for hundreds of Philadelphia police officers now serve as a model for emergency response throughout the country. Training builds confidence and enables officers to react in a manner that will assist in mitigating an incident. These programs have even stretched across county borders and created a unified response that did not exist prior to 9/11/2001. The point where the progress halts lies in the drills that are conducted to test large-scale response. A police commander active in these drills refers to them as "Kabuki Theater." He regularly attempts to draw attention to the fact that each drill is scheduled and resources are staged, thus enabling a glowing success. He asserts that each response element knows its part in the play before it is presented for display. In order to successfully evaluate an emergency response, the incident must actually be an emergency response, not a pre-planned show.

Much has been said about the need for communications interoperability. Each organization in the emergency management realm has a separate radio channel. Those channels are secure and do not allow other agencies to gain access. An example would be if police and emergency medical personnel respond to a shooting incident, and the police observe a sniper in a position to threaten the safety of first responders. The police cannot immediately contact the EMS elements to warn them of the impending danger. A relay of the information would have to occur, and this wasted time could negatively affect the safety of the responders. Post-9/11, Philadelphia has established a mutual emergency channel to allow first responders to communicate directly with each other. Although this is a step in the right direction, the reality is that mutual emergency channel radio communications at the scene of an emergency could not handle all of the traffic initiated by the first responders. Monitoring the emergency channel would actually require an additional person to listen and relay transmissions to the main communications channel of police, fire, or other responders. The time saved between the newly created interoperable method and the former relay method is marginal.

The biggest failure leading up to the attacks of 9/11/2001 resides in the lack of information sharing. The multitude of intelligence gathering agencies did not talk to each other. They were unable to share because of institutional regulations and a simple unwillingness to provide hard-earned information to other people. Sometimes, the information sharing problem did not even rise to the agency-to-agency issue. Often, information did not flow within the department that gathered the raw data.

In the Philadelphia Police Department, four intelligence gathering units competed for information—Narcotics Intelligence, School Violence Intelligence, Organized Crime Unit, and the Street Gang Unit. These units did not share information. After the World Trade Center attacks, the intelligence gathering function within the Philadelphia Police Department was reevaluated. The logical answer was to combine the police department's information gathering elements and engage this robust group of investigators in developing worthwhile intelligence for field commanders. Unfortunately, the newly created Homeland Security Unit remains independent of the combined intelligence element. The other shortcoming that continues to exist in Philadelphia is the lack of buying from field commanders. Intelligence products disseminated to patrol districts and special enforcement units are not used in deployment and tactical strategies. At this point, despite vigorous information gathering and data analysis, the commanders responsible for the safety of Philadelphians place little or no value on that product.

The federal government has supplemented crime fighting efforts in cities and states for decades. Municipalities struggle to handle the growing calls for service while addressing blossoming crime problems. Without the resources and funding provided by federal entities, the cities and states could not possibly afford the costs that are accumulated by unexpected problems. After the attacks, the federal funding that had been the crutch for local and state crime fighting efforts shifted to terrorism prevention, response, and recovery. The grip that police had on criminals before 9/11/2001 has loosened because of the intense interest in preventing terrorist attacks on American soil.

The close scrutiny on the processes that should have alerted those responsible for protecting the country guided law enforcement to intelligence-led policing. Instead of being reactionary, policy are now expected to pay attention to the precursors of crime. Contacts with community sources, social network analysis, group affiliations, and other such connections can assist investigators in identifying potential criminal offenders. Once identified, the information is channeled to field operatives for surveillance and action. By operating in this fashion, law enforcement has shifted from reactionary to preventive mode. Only time will tell if this post-9/11 strategy can become a meaningful method of reducing crime and terrorism in America.

NIGHT COURT—GATEWAY TO THE CRIMINAL JUSTICE SYSTEM

What do film director Quentin Tarantino, a children's services supervisor, actor Daniel Baldwin, the chef at famed New York restaurant Le Chantilly, an air-quality inspector, ex-football player Mark Gastineau, and the mother of an eleven-year-old girl who sold sex to junkies have in common? All were arraigned recently in Manhattan Criminal Court on charges ranging from endangering the welfare of a child (the children's services supervisor) to grand larceny (the flamboyant celebrity chef). Federal law requires that all those arrested in New York City must appear before a Manhattan Criminal Court judge within 24 hours to be "arraigned."

Manhattan Criminal Court is the gateway to one of the most elaborate criminal justice systems in the world—a system that processes tens of thousands of defendants each year with resources that have been called no more than scarce and courtroom conditions that often approach squalor. The court is like a dingy convenience store, open 24 hours a day, 365 days a year, serving the poor and rich alike with consistently slow and often mediocre service.

All those arrested in Manhattan are promptly arraigned; some are then released due to insufficient evidence to support the crime charged; others are placed on bail or released on their own recognizance; and, finally, the poor, the disaffiliated, and those charged with the most serious of all crimes are sent to Rikers Island (a jail/detention facility) to await their next court appearance.

In recent years, the two arraignment parts of Manhattan Criminal Court have become a favorite place to take a date, as well as a popular vacation destination for German, Dutch, and Spanish tourists who grow tired of the Statue of Liberty, Central Park, the Empire State Building, or visiting the site where the "Twin Towers" used to be. Surprising as it may be, the court is listed in Frommer's *Guide to New York* as a free attraction worth seeing. Busloads of foreign tourists arrive on Friday and Saturday evenings for a sneak peek at this unique style of American justice, a style made popular by the hit NBC sitcom *Night Court*. This is no coincidence. The night sessions of Manhattan Criminal Court bear the same name. Veteran court clerks take pride in the fact that NBC based this highly rated show on its arraignment parts.

Wide-eyed tourists to Night Court sit among prostitutes, drug dealers, witnesses, relatives, and victims. Some stare at the poor that line the pews of the courtroom. A few visitors doze off in a deep sleep, while many watch the arraignment judge dispense justice, case after case, in intervals that rarely exceed five minutes. Bailiffs, clerks, legal aid lawyers, assistant district attorneys, defendants, and victims move around the

The District of Columbia and a few other jurisdictions permit "preventive detention" when there is a high probability that the defendant may commit a crime if released. Despite the difficulty of predicting human behavior, the Supreme Court has ruled that it is constitutional to deny bail to a person who is considered dangerous.[25]

What Do You Think?

If you were asked to provide advice to the American Civil Liberties Union (ACLU) following the events on 9/11, what would you say about the need for national security given their concerns over government repression?

National Security, American Civil Liberties Union Freedom Network

"History teaches that grave threats to liberty often come in times of urgency, when constitutional rights seem too extravagant to endure."
—Justice Thurgood Marshall, *Skinner v. Railway Labor Executives' Assn.* (1989)

Throughout this country's history, the shibboleth of "national security" has often been used as a pretext for massive violations of individual rights. In the name of national security, President Jefferson countenanced internment camps for political dissidents; President Wilson authorized the round-up and deportation of thousands of foreign-born suspected "radicals" during the Palmer Raids; and President Franklin Roosevelt interned 120,000 Japanese Americans. The Cold War era brought loyalty oaths, blacklisting, and travel restrictions; the Vietnam War era saw the government's

(continued)

bench in a furious pace. With acoustics that inhibit sound, even the most experienced of lawyers find it difficult if not impossible to follow the proceedings if seated in the back of the courtroom.

In the turmoil of these two courtrooms, tourists, young couples out for a romantic evening, members of the press, and veteran court watchers are offered only two guarantees. First, those with even the slightest sensitivity will leave surprised if not shocked by the sheer number of criminal cases in a city that today appears as safe as it was thirty years ago. By the end of any one eight-hour session in Night Court, as many as 200 defendants will either go back on the streets of New York City or take the long bus ride to Rikers Island with new dates for a hearing or trial.

Second, even the most hardened New Yorkers will walk away from Night Court with the feeling that "there but for the grace of God go I." This gateway to New York City's court and correctional system is nothing less than a frightening example of an overburdened and outdated criminal justice production line. Overworked and underpaid judges pass judgment on pimps, drug heads, arsonists, and wife beaters without expression or emotion. Beleaguered legal aid lawyers are often introduced to their indigent clients several minutes before beginning their efforts at zealous representation in open court. The better judgment of assistant district attorneys is frequently held hostage to a historically overcrowded correctional system that, due to court order, can afford to warehouse only the most serious of offenders.

Foreign visitors armed with travel guides to this fine city will always seek titillating evening entertainment. To some, this real-life crime drama is better than a prime-time network sitcom. Fortunately, many see Night Court for what it really is.

Questions for Discussion

1. How different is the gateway to the criminal justice system in your hometown or city?

2. Do you believe that prosecutors in New York generally consider the problems of its overcrowded court and correctional systems in deciding how aggressively to pursue a criminal case?

attempt to censor the "Pentagon Papers." None of these measures were actually necessary to preserve national security; all of them violated civil liberties.

Today, although many of these abuses are behind us, "national security" is still invoked to justify government repression. The most recent example is the counterterrorism legislation introduced into Congress after the April 19, 1995, bombing in Oklahoma City. This terrible tragedy was thereby compounded by repressive—and ineffective—legislation.

SOURCE: Text adapted from American Civil Liberties Union, *Issue Summary: National Security,* http:www.aclu.org/issues/security/isns.html (June 4, 2002).

The Preliminary Hearing

The next step in the process in many states is the **preliminary hearing,** a preview of the trial that takes place in court before a judge. At this hearing, the prosecution must produce enough evidence to convince the judge that the case should proceed to trial or to the grand jury. In many jurisdictions the preliminary hearing is officially considered another probable cause hearing, but what emerges is more than probable cause. In this proceeding, conducted with some of the rights given the accused at trials—such as the cross-examination of witnesses and the introduction of evidence under stringent rules—enough evidence must be produced to *bind the defendant over* to the grand jury; in other words, to constitute reasonable inference of guilt or reasonable grounds to believe the defendant is guilty. In the preliminary hearing, in which the defense need not present any evidence, the defendant (and the defense attorney) have the advantage of finding out how the prosecution is developing

preliminary hearing
Preview of a trial held in court before a judge, in which the prosecution must produce sufficient evidence for the case to proceed to trial.

grand jury
Panel of sixteen to twenty-three citizens who screen the prosecution's evidence, in secret hearings, to decide whether someone should be formally charged with a crime.

prima facie case
Case in which there is evidence that would warrant the conviction of the defendant unless otherwise contradicted; a case that meets evidentiary requirements for grand jury indictment.

indictment
Accusation against a criminal defendant rendered by a grand jury on the basis of evidence constituting a *prima facie* case.

information
Accusation against a criminal defendant prepared by a prosecuting attorney.

its case. The defense attorney's decision—whether to enter a plea or to engage in plea negotiations—depends very much on what happens during the preliminary hearing.

The Decision to Charge and to Indict

No matter what the result of the preliminary hearing, the decision to charge the defendant with a crime rests with the prosecutor. Even in states where a grand jury must determine whether a defendant is to be indicted for a felony, it is the prosecutor who decides in the first place whether to place a case before the grand jury. The prosecutor also decides what evidence to present to the grand jury and how to present it.

The **grand jury** is one of the oldest institutions of the Anglo-American criminal justice system. It has been abolished in the United Kingdom, but in most American states it has been retained for serious (felony) cases to screen the prosecution's evidence, in secret hearings, and decide whether the defendant should be formally charged with a crime.

Federal grand juries are composed of sixteen to twenty-three citizens, and an indictment in the federal criminal process requires the concurrence of at least twelve grand jurors.[26] State rules are similar. The indictment must rest on evidence indicating a *prima facie* case against the defendant. A *prima facie case* exists when there seems to be sufficient evidence to convict the defendant. The case may still be defeated by evidence at trial that raises reasonable doubt or constitutes a legal excuse. Since that is a strong requirement, most indicted defendants are inclined to make a plea bargain at this point. And most of those convicted of a felony go to prison. In 1998, state courts convicted over 928,000 adults of a felony. Sixty-eight percent were sentenced to some form of incarceration (jail or prison).[27]

As soon as the grand jury has indicted, or the prosecutor has made a decision to charge the defendant and has informed defense counsel accordingly, the stage is set for plea bargaining. This process is part of the Anglo-American system, under which a trial always proceeds in accordance with the prosecution's charge and the defendant's response to it: a plea of not guilty.

Plea Bargaining

Every criminal defendant exercises some power over the way his or her case is to be conducted. A defendant who pleads guilty admits all the facts alleged in the accusation, whether it is an **indictment** or an **information,** and all the legal implications of those facts. He or she admits to being guilty as charged, and no trial is needed. A defendant who pleads not guilty denies all the facts and their legal implications and forces the government (the prosecutor) to prove guilt in a criminal trial.

The idea arose centuries ago that both prosecution and defense could benefit if both sides were to agree on a plea that would save the government the expense of a trial and the defendant the risk of severe punishment if he or she were found guilty. By the mid-twentieth century it had become common practice in the United States for prosecutors and defense attorneys to discuss the charges against criminal defendants and to agree on a reduced or modified plea that would spare the state the cost of a trial and guarantee the defendant a sentence more lenient than the original charge warranted.

At first such plea negotiations were quite secret and officially denied. In fact, when accepting a plea, the judge would always inquire whether the plea was freely made, and the defendant would always answer yes, when in fact the plea represented a bargain reached by the defendant and the prosecutor together.

In a highly publicized case, Scott Peterson stood trial for the murder of his wife and unborn child, was convicted, and sentenced to death in 2005.

The practice of plea bargaining is widespread today. Nevertheless, the process of plea bargaining invites injustices. Defendants who are legally not guilty, for example, may feel inclined to accept a plea bargain in the face of strong evidence. Other defendants may plead guilty to a lesser charge even though the evidence was obtained in violation of constitutional guarantees. In some cases, by "overcharging" (charging murder instead of manslaughter, for example), a prosecutor may coerce a defendant into pleading guilty to the lower charge, in effect forcing him or her to relinquish the right to a jury trial. Of course, if no plea bargain is agreed upon, the case will be set for trial.

Adjudication and Sentencing

Defendants may choose to be tried by a judge (a bench trial) or by a jury (consisting usually of twelve citizens, but as few as six in some states for lesser offenses).[28] In a jury trial the judge rules on matters of law, instructs the jurors about relevant legal questions and definitions, and tells them how to apply the law to the facts of the case.

A defendant may prefer a jury trial or a bench trial for any number of reasons. When a defense is based largely on the application and interpretation of technical legal propositions, a judge is likely to be the preferable choice. If the defense appeals more to sympathy and emotion, a jury is likely to be the better choice.

If a defendant has not been diverted out of the system, has pleaded guilty, or, after a plea of not guilty, has been tried and convicted, the next step in the process is the imposition of a sentence. In some states, with respect to some crimes, the statute leaves the sentencing judge no choice: A mandatory sentence is imposed by law. But in most states judges still have some choice. The judge must decide whether to place the defendant on probation and, if so, on what type of probation; whether to impose a sentence of incarceration and for what length of time; whether to impose a minimum or maximum term (or both) or to leave the sentence open-ended (indeterminate) within statutory limits; whether to impose a fine and how much; whether to order compensation for the victims; whether to impose court costs; and so on.

In making sentencing decisions, judges consider the offenders' personal characteristics, their past, their problems, and their needs. The principal guidance and advice come from probation departments. These are part of the court system, and they operate under the court's supervision. To help the court find the most appropriate sentencing decision, the probation department supplies the judge with a presentence investigation report on every convicted offender.

To avoid bias, which could result in different sentences for more or less similar offenses and offenders, policymakers and researchers have developed **sentencing guidelines.** These guidelines assign specific values to the important sentencing criteria—principally, the seriousness of the offense and, possibly, the existence of a prior record and other factors. Such guidelines, used in both state and federal trial courts, are meant to assist judges in selecting the length and type of punishment warranted by the crime.

sentencing guidelines System for the judicial determination of a relatively firm sentence based on specific aggravating or mitigating circumstances.

Corrections

The correctional sector of the criminal justice system is composed of institutions with different objectives, degrees of security, and treatment programs. In making its placement decision, the correctional staff takes into consideration such factors as security requirements, the availability of treatment and rehabilitation programs, and organizational needs. All inmates are placed into categories for the purposes of placement. In some institutions, given overcrowded conditions, placement is a function of availability.[29] In others, factors such as offense severity and psychopathology are considered.

Let us look now at what sentencing options are available to the court and what correctional implications the court's judgment may have.

Community Decisions

If the offense is not serious and the offender is a good candidate for reform, the judge may decide on a *community* sentence. The judge may place the convicted offender on **probation,** the release of a prison-bound offender into the community, usually with specified conditions (e.g., that the convict must not commit another offense, must not leave the county without permission, must make payments to the victim, or must attend meetings of Alcoholics Anonymous, and so on).

More recently, states have experimented with a variety of additional options, called **alternative sanctions.** These options include placement in restitution programs, intensive supervision programs (ISPs), shock incarceration, and regimented discipline programs (RDPs), which are also called boot camps.

Institutional Decisions

Suppose the court has decided a defendant's crime is too serious to allow for a sentence to be served in the community. In that case, an institutional sentence will be imposed. But while the judge may express his or her preferences, it is now entirely up to the executive department of government, the Department of Corrections, to decide on the placement of the convicted offender.

These decisions may be very difficult and have far-reaching consequences, yet they are often made with little information beyond that contained in the presentence report. Classifications of security level or status, for example, may have to be made primarily on the basis of the offense of which the person stands convicted. Predicting the success of educational programs, vocational training, or any other treatment program is also difficult. It is often easier to place inmates in the jobs that keep an institution running. For example, inmates may do clerical and classification work, or they may work in the library, the infirmary, the laundry, or the kitchen. But even these placement decisions require considering other factors, especially safety. A host of objective classification measures have been devised that offer some hope for increasing the predictive validity of inmate classification.

Release and Parole Decisions

One of the most important decisions in the entire criminal justice process is when to release an inmate from an institution. There are two types of release from the correctional system. One is release at the expiration of a sentence. Correctional administrators have little choice in this case, although the expiration point depends to some degree on administrative decisions. In the course of disciplinary proceedings, for example, correctional administrators must decide whether an inmate will lose "good-time" benefits because of violations of the institution's rules. Good-time benefits, which have the effect of reducing prison sentence lengths, are given to inmates for institutional behavior that conforms to rules and regulations. An inmate who violates the rules loses the benefit of the early release that comes with good behavior. Today, release decisions are further complicated by policy decisions made at higher governmental levels or by judges, who frequently order prisoners released to make space for new ones in an effort to relieve prison overcrowding.

The second way an inmate may be released is through **parole.** In its original and ideal form, parole was a benefit bestowed on a prisoner for good behavior in prison and a promise of good conduct after discharge. Success on parole was to be achieved with the aid of a parole officer. As parole officers' caseloads increased in the 1960s, however, that ideal faded, until today parole is simply an early release from prison, based on the decision of a parole board. Parole boards make these decisions with very little information. Conduct within the institution, however, has been demonstrated to relate to behavior outside. Some progress has been made in the development of devices to predict success on parole.[30] Nevertheless, the decision remains difficult. The federal system and a growing number of states have abolished parole, and others are using it with steadily declining frequency. (Several special forms of parole, such as intensive supervision parole with and without electronic monitoring, are discussed in subsequent chapters.)

probation
Alternative to imprisonment, allowing a person found guilty of an offense to stay in the community, under conditions and with supervision.

alternative sanctions
Punishments or other dispositions imposed instead of the principal sanctions currently in use, such as imprisonment or probation.

parole
Supervised conditional release of a convicted prisoner before expiration of the sentence of imprisonment.

Diversion

Throughout the criminal justice process, the number of persons within the system steadily decreases. This decrease is usually reported as the **attrition,** or **mortality rate.**

As we have seen, there are three reasons for the enormous amount of diversion from the system at various stages. First, decision makers may, for a variety of reasons, deem a case inappropriate for further processing. If they did not do this, the system would become clogged, dispositions would be unreasonably delayed, and the flow would stop. Moreover, this exercise of discretion keeps an already punitive system from becoming overly punitive. Prosecutorial discretion and type of offense charged are often related. Second, in many situations decision makers have no choice but to dismiss a case. At each stage of the process the authorities must meet a legal standard of proof. When that standard is not met, the case leaves the criminal justice process. These standards become progressively stricter as the case (and the person) proceeds through the various stages. And third, many cases are simply lost, for example, by failure of the accused to appear on a selected court date.

Now that we have discussed the criminal justice process for adult offenders, we shall describe the processes designed for juveniles and for violators of international law.

attrition (mortality) rate
Rate at which the numbers decrease in the course of the criminal process because persons are diverted out of the system.

The Challenge of Juvenile Justice

Approaches to Juvenile Delinquency

How are we to react to children who commit acts that we call criminal when committed by adults?

The American public and its politicians are confused as to what to do about juvenile delinquency, and especially juvenile violence: Should we get tough, or ever tougher, or should we seek to nurture and guard the nation's youngest, to socialize them to become productive citizens?

CAMERA_01

18:21:35 02/01/2004

Video camera records the abduction of eleven-year-old Carlie Brucia in Sarasota, Florida. Carlie was found dead five days later.

There is a historical reason for this confusion. Two thousand years ago, the Romans developed conflicting approaches, and we have used both ever since. One of these approaches is punitive: Children above age seven are potentially subject to criminal liability if their actions show that they were aware of the wrongfulness of their action.

The greatest of English legal scholars, Sir William Blackstone (1723–1780), suggested in his 1758 lectures that if a child of tender years had killed another, evidence that he hid the body might be sufficient to prove he understood the wrongfulness of his action.[31] By age seven, children are socialized enough to attend school. But children below age fourteen may still not be held accountable for their actions if they lack the maturity to realize the wrongfulness of their conduct.

The other ancient root is that of concern for children. It was expressed by the legal concept of *parens patriae* (parent of the country) which to the Romans meant that the emperor, and in medieval times the monarch, could exercise *patria potestas* (parental power) *in loco parentis* (in the place of a parent deemed unable or unworthy) over children in trouble or in danger of becoming wayward. The power of the monarch was eventually transferred to the state, as represented by the juvenile court judge. We find its traces in the concepts used today in juvenile court proceedings.

In re Gault: A Landmark Case

There has been a see-saw battle between these two approaches—the punitive and the caring—ever since. The caring approach gained the upper hand in 1899, when the first American juvenile court was established in Chicago. This approach found adherents all over the world. The switch back to the punitive approach occurred in the 1960s when, faced with rising juvenile crime rates, there was a swing toward a get-tough approach. The spark that fueled the switch was the case of Gerry Gault.

> Gerald Francis Gault, then aged fifteen, was accused of having made obscene phone calls. (He never admitted the charge, nor was it ever proven.) The sheriff—a police officer—arrested Gault. The same officer, now acting as a jailer, kept him in custody. The same officer, now acting as a prosecutor, presented charges against Gault in juvenile court. Gault's family was never properly notified. There was no witness against him, yet the juvenile court ordered him to be confined in a juvenile correctional facility for six years. (An adult could have been punished for this offense, if proven, by a fine of $5 to $50 and a two-month jail term.)

Everything seemed to have gone wrong in the Gault case. A single official had acted as police officer, social worker, prosecutor, and jailer. Having been refused the constitutional right to be confronted by a witness, to receive counsel, to be given notice of the charges, and to be protected against self-incrimination, and having been committed to a multiyear detention sentence (in lieu of perhaps a warning or a fine), the conclusion was inescapable that a young man was being confined for a crime that was never proven, properly or otherwise.

When the case finally reached the U.S. Supreme Court, the Court decided that juveniles in juvenile court must be accorded the same constitutional rights available to adults charged with crime. These rights include:

- The right to receive adequate and timely notice of the charges.
- The right to counsel.
- The right to be confronted by and to examine witnesses.
- The privilege against self-incrimination.[32]

The Supreme Court's decision sent mixed signals. Juvenile court judges were worried that this might mean the end of the benevolent/paternalistic approach to dealing with delinquents. For the politicians, the *Gault* decision raised another issue: If we are to give juvenile offenders the same rights and privileges as adult offenders, why don't we hold them to the same responsibilities and duties? Thus began the effort to adjust juvenile court proceedings to the standards of adult criminal proceedings, and the parallel effort to subject more and more juveniles to adult criminal processes.

Treating Juveniles as Adults

The first step was an initiative by the Institute of Judicial Administration at New York University and the American Bar Association calling for juvenile proceedings to be based on the seriousness of the offense committed.[33]

The states responded with four strategies:[34]

1. Lowering the age at which juveniles are subject to adult criminal liability to as low as ten years
2. Reducing the upper age at which juveniles are subject to original juvenile court jurisdiction to as low as fifteen years of age
3. Excluding certain serious offenses from the jurisdiction of juvenile courts altogether
4. Investing prosecutors with the power to **direct file** juveniles for trial in adult criminal courts (mostly for serious offenses)

direct file
Prosecutors' power to try juveniles directly in adult criminal courts.

In many states, prosecutors are empowered to bring charges against juveniles directly in criminal court, bypassing the juvenile justice system altogether. The net effect has been an erosion of juvenile court jurisdiction and the transfer of more and more juvenile offenders into the already overburdened adult criminal justice system. How far down on the age ladder should we go? Not so long ago, in Chicago, two young boys, seven and eight years old, stood charged with having murdered an eleven-year-old girl by striking her with a rock, suffocating her with her underwear, molesting her, and then dragging her body into nearby underbrush. They then stole her bicycle.[35] At their arraignments they occupied themselves with drawing crayon pictures of houses and hearts, oblivious to their situation, their attorneys and prosecutors, the court, the trial, life and death. As it turned out, the two little boys are probably innocent of the crimes for which they had been arraigned. Their "confessions" had been the result of suggestive police interrogation, and their innocence was corroborated by semen stains on the victim's underwear, which could not possibly have come from a seven- or eight-year-old.[36] Subsequent investigation indicated that the two boys may well have thrown stones at their little victim, but that it was a sex deviant who committed a sexual crime on the body of the little girl.[37]

The magnitude of juvenile delinquency and crime is demonstrated by the following statistics: In 2004, law enforcement agencies made over 1.26 million arrests of persons under age eighteen, but only 289,131 of these were for index crimes. (For a discussion of index crimes see Chapter 2.)[38] So the vast majority of those arrested continue to travel the road of juvenile justice, albeit a road paved with due process guarantees.[39]

careers

Changing the Juvenile Justice Process

The steps in the juvenile process (Figure 1.8) are comparable to those of criminal proceedings, though there are some differences in terminology and function:

- While in criminal cases the process normally starts with an arrest, juveniles are actually "taken into custody."
- Booking procedures for juveniles are called "intakes."
- In criminal proceedings, charges are filed to start the process. Juvenile proceedings start with a petition.
- Adults charged with a crime may be bailed or jailed; juveniles are normally released into the custody of their parents before an adjudicatory hearing.
- Adults charged with a crime face a trial; juveniles face an adjudicatory hearing.
- Adults may be found guilty of crimes charged; juveniles may be determined to be delinquent.

There are many divergent calls to change the processes by which juveniles charged with crime are dealt with. Some want the juvenile court to be replaced by either a family court or the placement of all juvenile offenders under adult criminal court jurisdiction. Initiatives to abolish the juvenile court system do not hold much promise. Adult criminal courts are notoriously inept at dealing with juvenile offenders, especially the very young.

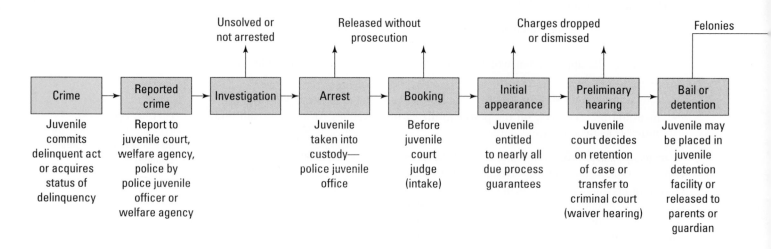

FIGURE 1.8   The Juvenile Justice Process

SOURCE: From Freda Adler, Gerhard O. W. Mueller, and William S. Laufer, *Criminal Justice: An Introduction* (New York: McGraw-Hill, 1996), pp. 482–483.

The statistical evidence indicates that juvenile violent crime peaked in 1993 and has been declining ever since. While the arrest rates for other offenses with which juveniles are charged have shown divergent patterns, the overall juvenile share of violent crime has been decreasing since 1994—more than seven years in a row (Figure 1.9). And there is no evidence that system changes had anything to do with it. But even if they had, many experts believe there is something wrong with the systems we have developed for dealing with juvenile offenders. Children are not simply young adults, and the transformation of an infant into an adult is a complicated process. The challenge for the future, as far as juvenile justice is concerned, is to take this transformational process into account, adjust our procedures accordingly, and develop separate yet integrated approaches for preventing juvenile delinquency on the one hand, and dealing with juvenile offenders on the other.[40] This calls for an open-minded approach that must rely on research in psychology and child development. In all probability, a new approach will emerge, with the following ingredients:

• not to prematurely interrupt childhood;

• not to throw children into the adult world of criminal justice;

• not to subject children to punishment in the adult sense of this term; but rather,

• to protect and promote childhood;

• to discourage detrimental (adult) values from intruding on childhood;

• to respond to youthful deviance in a graduated manner that respects crucial developmental differences as a child matures from infancy, to prepubescence, to pubescence, to young adulthood, to maturity.

The Challenge of Globalization

On December 21, 1988, Pan Am flight 103, en route from Frankfurt, Germany, to New York, filled with Americans on their way home to celebrate the holidays, exploded in mid-air. The debris fell on Lockerbie, Scotland. There were 270 casualties in passengers, crew,

ADJUDICATIONS   SENTENCING
                                 AND SANCTIONS

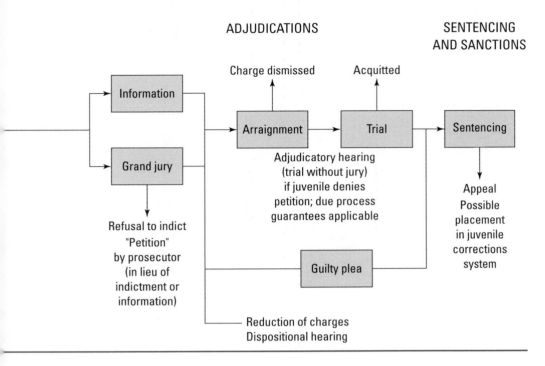

and people on the ground. From the outset it was clear that this was no accident. But it took investigators three years to assemble evidence sufficient to satisfy an American grand jury that a crime, or crimes, had been committed.

The dimensions of this case were broad and the details complex: An American airliner, en route from Frankfurt, Germany, explodes over a Scottish (United Kingdom) town. Of those killed, 189 were Americans and the others had a multitude of nationalities, including of course British (those on the ground). Since the impact of the crime was in Scotland, the Scottish police force was the principal agency for investigation. U.S. federal law enforcement agencies joined their Scottish colleagues. But American officers cannot just descend on Scotland. They have no "jurisdiction," no power or authority, there. Such cooperation requires agreement, either preexisting or specially achieved.

The joint Scottish–U.S. investigation quickly spread all over the world. Leads to Iranian-backed Syrian terrorist groups led nowhere. But searches on the ground in Lockerbie revealed fragments of a bomb timer. Photographs obtained in Senegal (Africa) led investigators to intact bomb timers in Togo (Africa). These, it turned out, had been manufactured in Switzerland. Some of them had been sold to Libyans. Further investigation established that the bomb (and its timer) had been placed in a shirt (the fragments of which were found at Lockerbie) that had been purchased in Malta (Mediterranean island nation) by the station agent of the Libyan airlines.

An indictment for murder and conspiracy (193 counts) was issued on Friday, November 15, 1991, against three Libyans—after investigators had conducted 14,000 interviews and extended their investigation to fifty countries (about 25 percent of the world's countries).

The Libyan government was requested to surrender those indicted to the United States for trial. Despite backing of the American request by the United Nations Security Council, the Libyan government refused and was placed on an embargo: Libya became a political and economic outlaw. Under this pressure Libya finally agreed to surrender the indictees for trial by a special international tribunal, composed of Scottish judges, sitting in The Hague, Netherlands. The trial resulted in a conviction, with sentence to be served in international custody, in the Netherlands. Finally, in 2003, Libya "sort of" acknowledged its act of terrorism and offered millions of dollars to each of the victimized families. Subsequently, in 2004, in a surprise move, Libya's leader Col. Muammar Qaddafi renounced its past policies, vowed to terminate its program of weapons of mass destruction, and agreed to end all terrorism. In 2004, the Libyan leader paid a visit to the European

The juvenile Violent Crime Index arrest rate in 2004 was lower than in any year since at least 1980 and half the peak rate in 1994

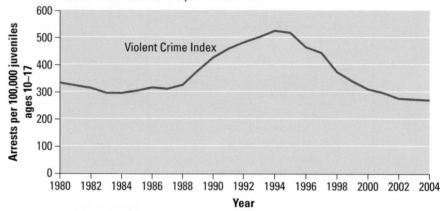

- In 2004, there were 269 arrests for Violent Crime Index offenses for every 100,000 youth between 10 and 17 years of age. If each of these arrests involved a different juvenile (which is unlikely), then about 1 in every 370 persons ages 10–17 was arrested for a Violent Crime Index offense in 2004, or about one-third of 1% of all juveniles ages 10–17 living in the U.S. (Because some juveniles likely were arrested more than once, the actual percentage is probably lower.)

  Data source: Analysis of arrest data from the FBI and population data from the U.S. Census Bureau and the National Center for Health Statistics. *[See data source note on p. 12 for detail.]*

After years of relative stability, the juvenile Property Crime Index arrest rate began a decline in the mid-1990s that continued through 2004

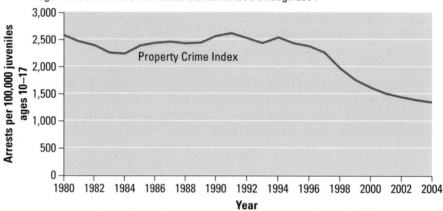

- The juvenile arrest rate for Property Crime Index offenses in 2004 was about half the 1980 level—down 48% over the period. The large declines over the last decade in the two arrest indexes the FBI uses to monitor juvenile crime indicate a substantial reduction in the law-violating behavior of America's youth.

  Data source: Analysis of arrest data from the FBI and population data from the U.S. Census Bureau and the National Center for Health Statistics. *[See data source note on p. 12 for detail.]*

FIGURE 1.9   Juvenile Arrest Rates for Violent Crimes and Property Crimes

Source: Howard N Synder, "Juvenile Arrests 2004," December 2006, OJJDP available http://www.ncjrs.gov/pdffiles1/ojjdp/214563.pdf.

Union, where he was welcomed back into the fold of "civilized" nations. The U.N. ended its embargo, and the United States allowed business to resume relations with Lybia, and visitors to enter that country. So, does international criminal justice work?

Globalization

Indeed, one of the greatest challenges to criminal justice in the twenty-first century is posed by globalization. What is globalization? Look at it this way: When people lived primarily in villages (some of us still do) daily life centered on the village—food growing, handicrafts, trade, social life, and, indeed, policing. When villages grew into towns and into large metropolitan areas, these new large settlements defined most aspects of life—including the task of keeping the peace. States and nations then combined many smaller communities, and they became the boundaries of social life, economic life, and law enforcement and criminal justice. Development did not stop there: Over the last several decades, we have witnessed the expansion of commerce, the arts and entertainment, travel and communications, and disease control and crime control to the entire globe. With the click of the mouse you can communicate with people in Peru and Poland, India and Italy, or anyplace in the world. What once was a ten-month journey from San Francisco to Tokyo now takes ten hours by jetliner or less than ten seconds in cyberspace.

Globalization has seemed to come out of nowhere. No one person, or group of persons, has designed or directs it, and there is no director general of the Internet. Yet all nations and their citizens have become globally interdependent. Export and import figures demonstrate how globalization has taken place. In 1950 the United States exported $10 billion worth of goods and services; in 2000 it exported over $1 trillion worth of goods and services. By 2010 exports will reach well over $2 trillion. The world has become a single huge marketplace.

Globalization has brought many advantages. Satellite TV lets us witness events thousands of miles away. Commerce now functions in a global market in which our manufacturers compete against—or make alliances with—their counterparts all over the world. The car you drive may be a Chrysler product, yet Chrysler is owned by the Daimler-Benz (Mercedes) company of Germany. And your American car may have from 30 percent to 60 percent of its parts made elsewhere in the world. The car may have been built in Japan or Korea in the first place. Currency traders transfer $1.3 trillion daily in any of the world's currencies.

Yet globalization also has its negative aspects. Diseases that once were local can now become global epidemics, as the HIV virus has demonstrated. The global linkage of economies also means that when Asia suffers an economic slump (as it did in 1998), companies in the United States will also suffer the consequences (e.g., the Boeing Company of Seattle was forced to lay off 48,000 workers). Jetliners that carry legitimate travelers can, with equal ease, carry terrorists from anywhere to everywhere. Electronic transfers convey not only the proceeds of legitimate business transactions, but also those derived from the drug trade, bribery, and corruption. The Internet can be used equally by legitimate communicators and by scoundrels and con artists or industrial spies.

The negative aspects of globalization are posing incredible challenges to criminal justice systems. Local law enforcement could deal easily with the crime problems of the village. But the crime problems of the global village are far beyond the capacity of even national justice systems. And there are many costs to policing across borders. Consider how countries differ with respect to fundamental protections and safeguards against surveillance by law enforcement. (See Figure 1.10.) This is but one example of the complexity of international or transnational law enforcement.

Transnational Crimes

Since the mid-1970s it has become clear that much of local crime is affected by forces abroad and beyond our local control. The gun with which a local robbery is committed may have come from Italy or China; the heroin or cocaine being traded likely comes from places such as the Golden Triangle and the Golden Crescent in Asia, or the Andean mountains of South America.

In addition to the types of local crime being affected by activities abroad, there is a category of criminal activity that by its nature transcends national boundaries. The crimes in this category are called **transnational crimes.**[41] Transnational criminality, it is important to note, is not a legal term. Rather, it is a criminological concept, used to describe broad groupings of criminal activities, each of which may contain a variety of different crimes, centering on a common theme. By now, eighteen distinct groups of transnational crimes have been recognized:

transnational crimes
Criminal activities extending into, and violating the laws of, several countries.

1. Money laundering
2. Illicit drug trafficking
3. Corruption and bribery of public officials, party officials, and elected representatives as defined in national legislation

Map of Surveillance Societies Around the World

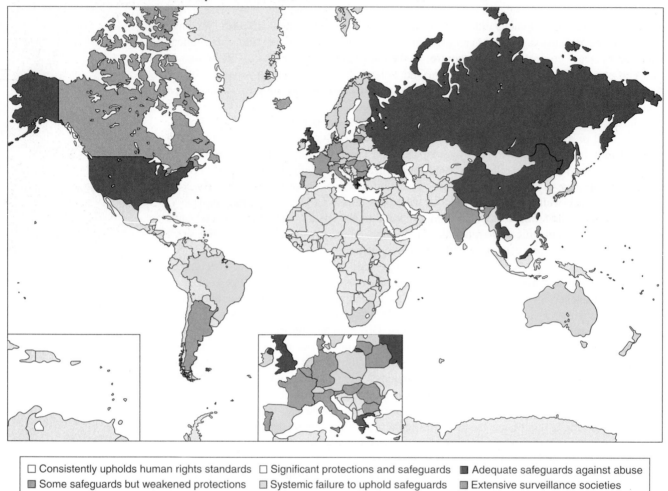

☐ Consistently upholds human rights standards ☐ Significant protections and safeguards ■ Adequate safeguards against abuse
■ Some safeguards but weakened protections ☐ Systemic failure to uphold safeguards ■ Extensive surveillance societies
■ Endemic surveillance societies

FIGURE 1.10   Leading Surveillance Societies in the EU and the World

Source: Available at http://www.privacyinternational.org/article.shtml?cmd[347]=x-347-545269&als[theme]=P... 10/4/2007

4. Infiltration of legal business
5. Fraudulent bankruptcy
6. Insurance fraud
7. Computer crime
8. Theft of intellectual property
9. Illicit traffic in arms
10. Terrorist activities
11. Aircraft hijacking
12. Sea piracy
13. Land hijacking
14. Trafficking in persons
15. Trade in human body parts
16. Theft of art and cultural objects
17. Environmental crime
18. Other offenses committed by organized criminal groups[42]

Since transnational crime is not a legal concept, national agencies do not collect statistics. Moreover, it would be difficult to assess statistics for transnational crime, since it affects so many different countries simultaneously. Our knowledge about its extent often comes from industry sources, for example from the insurance industry (insurance fraud), the Software Publishers Association (theft of intellectual property), or private maritime industry groups (sea piracy). Nearly all transnational crime is also organized crime, committed by global alliances of criminals.[43] (We shall continue this discussion in Chapter 2.)

How can local or even national law enforcement agencies deal with this massive, intricate web of transnational crime? The answers are by no means identical for all forms of transnational crime. For example, it may be possible for U.S. law enforcement officers to curb the transport of stolen motor vehicles by tighter customs inspections at seaports and border crossings. (At present an estimated 300,000 stolen automobiles are exported from the United States to Latin America and Africa annually.) But while the United States may succeed in controlling this criminal activity by conventional means, the same does not hold true for Europe. There the flow of stolen motor vehicles goes from western to eastern Europe, and there are few border controls.

Carlos Rohm, who operated an Argentinian bank called Banco General de Negocios (BGN), was arrested in late January 2002. Rohm was charged with illegally moving clients' funds from Argentina to Uruguay, contributing to Argentina's economic collapse.

Conventional law enforcement measures have proved relatively ineffective in stemming the flow of illicit drugs around the world. Even a diversified approach aimed at curbing consumption at home, limiting production overseas, and providing for interception in between, has had only modest success. Many countries have made bilateral or multilateral arrangements to assist each other in controlling the production and export and import of narcotic drugs. Drug Enforcement Administration agents have been posted at American embassies overseas to cooperate with their local counterparts. FBI agents have liaison offices around the world. Most countries have ratified various United Nations narcotics control conventions. But still the drugs flow from country to country in vast amounts.

As for terrorist activities, while some terrorists operate locally or nationally (the abortion clinic bombers, the self-styled militias, or the so-called Unabomber in the United States), much terrorist activity is transnational. There may not be a global command structure, yet regional organizations have cooperated to act interregionally. The problem threatens global security.

Most of the transnational terrorist organizations have been identified, and transnational terrorist acts have been chronicled for some time. Global, regional, and intergovernmental initiatives to deal with terrorism are in place. These include **extradition** treaties with other governments, providing for the transfer of all indicted persons to the requesting country; the stationing of law enforcement officers overseas; the exchange of information and evidence; and other forms of cooperation, including the network of the International Criminal Police Organization (Interpol). But there are limits to extradition. By their own law, some countries will not extradite if:

careers

extradition
Process of ancient origin by which an alleged offender is transferred from one sovereign country to another for trial.

- The offense charged is political in nature.
- The requested person is a national of the requested country.
- The requesting country has capital punishment.
- There is no standing extradition agreement.

Some countries (notably the United States) have resorted to unilateral measures to resolve transnational crime problems, especially terrorism. U.S. agents have repeatedly kidnapped wanted criminals abroad and conducted military strikes against suspected terrorist sites overseas. But such actions are in violation of international law and the law of the country where the activities are carried out.

ENTRY INTO THE SYSTEM   PROSECUTION AND SERVICES

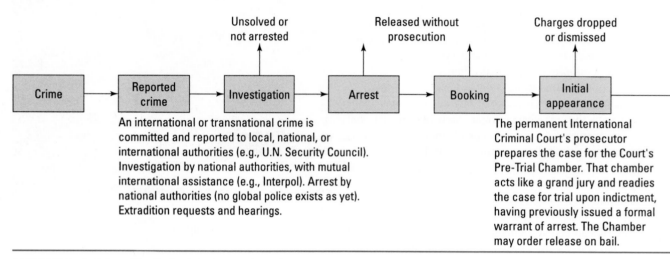

FIGURE 1.11   The Path of the International Criminal Justice System

Note: The proceedings before the ad hoc international criminal courts are similar to those before the ICC, but somewhat simple. The prosecutor also fulfills the grand jury function in both the International Criminal Tribunal for the former Yugoslavia and the International Criminal Tribunal for Rwanda. Other so-called international criminal courts vary widely as to their procedures, and have so their procedures, and have far less international participation (e.g., the tribunal for Campuches and that for Sierra Leone).

Source: Adapted from the President's Commission on Law Enforcement and Administration of Justice, *The Challenge of Crime in a Free Society,* 1967 [pp. 8–9], in U.S. Department of Justice, Bureau of Justice Statistics, *Report to the Nation on Crime and Justice,* 2nd ed. (Washington, DC: U.S. Government Printing Office, 1988), pp. 56–57. Revised pursuant to the Rome Statute for an International Criminal Court (ICC), 1998.

international crimes
Crimes, established largely by conventions, violative of international law including but not limited to crimes against the peace and security of humankind.

convention
International agreement by which many nations commit themselves to common, legally binding obligations.

treaty
An agreement, usually among two sovereign states, binding them to abide by common standards and to enforce them.

jurisdiction
Power of a sovereign state to make and enforce its own laws. Also, the power granted to a court to adjudicate matters in dispute within its competence and territory.

To help resolve the problems, a number of transnational crime categories have been elevated to the level of international crimes, thus providing access to measures and sanctions specifically applicable to international crimes.

International Crimes

International crimes are crimes legally defined by international **conventions** and **treaties.** Apart from defining such crimes, these international agreements also provide for the exercise of **jurisdiction;** in other words, they specify which country has the right or duty to try international offenders, who has the right or duty to surrender them to whom for trial, and what measures of cooperation must be extended among nations that sign such agreements. By now there are twenty-five categories of international crimes:

1. **Aggression**
2. **Genocide**
3. Crimes against humanity
4. War crimes
5. Crimes against the United Nations and associated personnel
6. Unlawful possession and/or use of weapons
7. Theft of nuclear materials
8. Mercenarism
9. Apartheid
10. Slavery
11. Torture

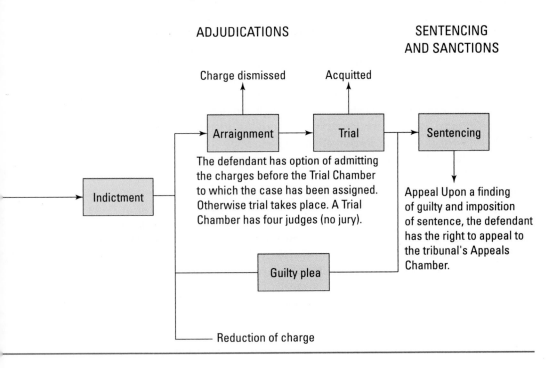

ADJUDICATIONS

SENTENCING
AND SANCTIONS

Charge dismissed

Acquitted

Arraignment → Trial → Sentencing

Indictment

The defendant has option of admitting the charges before the Trial Chamber to which the case has been assigned. Otherwise trial takes place. A Trial Chamber has four judges (no jury).

Appeal Upon a finding of guilty and imposition of sentence, the defendant has the right to appeal to the tribunal's Appeals Chamber.

Guilty plea

Reduction of charge

12. Unlawful human experimentation
13. Piracy
14. Aircraft hijacking
15. Unlawful acts against maritime navigation
16. Unlawful acts against internationally protected persons
17. Taking of civilian hostages
18. Unlawful use of the mail
19. Unlawful traffic in drugs
20. Destruction/theft of national treasures
21. Unlawful acts against the environment
22. International traffic in obscene materials
23. Falsification and counterfeiting
24. Unlawful interference with international submarine cables
25. Bribery of foreign public officials[44]

Some of these crimes are ancient. Piracy, for example, has been an international crime for about 2,500 years, although it is now defined in a modern treaty, the Law of the Sea Treaty.[45] Some international crimes are a century old (counterfeiting, cutting of submarine cables); some were created (from customary law precedents) for the trial of the war criminals at Nuremberg (1945–1946); still others have been created under the auspices of the United Nations in more recent years.

Ideally, the **International Criminal Court** (Figure 1.11) should have the power to try all persons charged with any international crime. Yet, for the most part, nations have retained the power to try those international criminals they have apprehended. However, the example of the trial of the major Nazi war criminals at Nuremberg in 1945–1946 demonstrated that an international criminal court, composed of judges and prosecutors from many countries, and with defendants from yet another country, can work, and can provide justice.

Over the last few years, the United Nations has established two temporary international criminal courts for trials involving war crimes committed in the 1990s in the former Yugoslavia (which includes Kosovo province, where massive ethnic cleansing was reported in 1999) and in Rwanda. The crimes in question involve genocide (destroying a national,

aggression
Use of armed force by a state against the sovereignty or territory of another state, inconsistent with the Charter of the United Nations; an international crime.

genocide
International crime defined by convention (1948) and consisting of specific acts of violence committed with intent to destroy, in whole or in part, a national, ethnic, racial, cultural, or religious group.

international criminal court
Established by the United Nations, ad hoc (temporary) criminal courts created to try defendants accused of crimes under international law. A permanent International Criminal Court was agreed upon in 1998.

ethnic, racial or religious group, in whole or in part), **crimes against humanity** (including systematic or mass violations of human rights), aggression, and war crimes.

Pessimists predicted that these courts would fail, because those indicted could not be apprehended. The opposite was the case with respect to Rwanda, however, where thousands were detained pending trial on charges of genocide committed against the Tutsi minority. As of Fall 2007, more than 161 defendants have been indicted and asked to appear before the International Criminal Tribunal for the former Yugoslavia, a court established in 1993 following significant violations of international humanitarian law committed in the territory of the former Yugoslavia. The most notable defendant is former Serbian and Yugoslavian President Slobodan Milosevic.

The international community of scholars in international criminal law has long advocated the creation of a permanent international criminal court. After many decades of pressure, the governments of most countries have decided to establish such a permanent international criminal court. The Statute on the International Criminal Court was passed in Rome on July 17, 1998. The court has its seat in The Hague, the Netherlands, with judges drawn from countries that sign the agreement. The judges have been selected based on equitable representation of gender, legal systems, and cultural areas. The statute grants this permanent international criminal court jurisdiction over the major international crimes, including genocide, crimes against humanity, and war crimes.

The governments of some 104 countries signed the statute. Those that have not signed include China, Iraq, Libya, Qatar, and Israel. The United States, which feared that U.S. military personnel engaged in international peacekeeping operations as well as government personnel and contractors might be subjected to the international court's jurisdiction, signed in 2000.

The world has taken a mighty step forward on the route to protecting itself against criminals who threaten the peace and security of all people. On the basis of experience with the temporary international tribunals for the former Yugoslavia and Rwanda, it is expected that this new world level of jurisdiction for exceptionally grave crimes will be successful. By now the vast majority of the world's governments have ratified the statute.

Looking Ahead: A Preview of This Book

This chapter has surveyed criminal justice as a discipline, a science, a profession, a career, a challenge, and a means of dealing with the crime problems that face the United States as well as the world in the twenty-first century.

Chapter 2 provides the student with fundamental information on crime and offenders: the rates of crime, the types of crime, and the characteristics of offenders.

Chapter 3 explains why some people commit crime.

Chapter 4 provides an introduction to the law by which we define people as criminals and the procedures by which we do so.

While the four chapters in Part 1 impart basic, fundamental knowledge, in Part 2 we enter into an examination of the work of the component parts of the criminal justice system. Thus, we shall examine the history and organization of the police (the largest employer in criminal justice). We then turn to an analysis of police functions, which have undergone rapid developments in the past decade.

"The police" can be understood only if we closely examine the professional culture in which police officers function. Above all, law enforcement activities are subject to the rule of law, as laid down by legislators and constantly interpreted and reinterpreted by the courts, especially the United States Supreme Court. As we shall see, the courts, too, function within, and thus reflect, the moral consensus and standards of the community. It should come as no surprise, therefore, that in some eras the courts favor individual rights (the due process or civil libertarian ideals), while at other times they favor crime control. Actually, we shall question whether these two different approaches should be in conflict with one another (Chapter 8), especially in this new millennium.

In Part 3 we shall discuss the work and role of the courts in our system. In Chapter 9 we review the history of the courts and the traditions that have had an impact on their role both today and in the future. More specifically, in Chapters 10 and 11, we describe the functions of lawyers and judges in prosecuting, defending, and adjudicating criminal cases. We shall detect many deficiencies and shortcomings that surely will require improvement in this new century, yet there are also promising developments.

Part 3 concludes with a discussion of the complex problems of sentencing those convicted of crime—including the sentence of capital punishment (Chapter 12). No issue in criminal justice has experienced as many dramatic changes during the past quarter century as that of sentencing, and in all likelihood judicial sentencing will undergo additional dramatic changes in the twenty-first century. But which way should we move?

The chapter on sentencing also serves as a bridge to Part 4 of the book, on corrections, for the simple reason that corrections must deal with all those sentenced by the judiciary. Once again, we shall introduce the subject by looking at the historical background of our current practices (Chapter 14). This is followed by a detailed analysis of institutional corrections, including prisons and jails and their vast populations (Chapter 14). Were it not for the expansion of noninstitutional alternatives (community corrections), our incarcerated population would be far larger than it is. This topic is our focus in Chapter 15. While community corrections started in the nineteenth century (probation and parole), new approaches of community corrections have been developed only over the last quarter century. Their use will predictably expand in the twenty-first century.

Throughout the book we have asked ourselves several questions: What have we done wrong in the past? What must we do better in the future? In short, what are the challenges of our discipline? We have identified problems and suggested remedies to be forged.

1. How should the criminal justice system handle crimes committed by children? The past record is dismal!

2. How can better services be provided for the victims of crime? After some promising starts, we seem to have reached a stalemate. Does the answer lie in *restorative justice,* by which offenders are sentenced to repair the damage, the harm, they have caused?

3. The biggest question of all is how do we cope with crime that is no longer just local but has become global, just as everything else has become global: the economy, financial services, electronic communication and information, mass transport, and entertainment? How can we do so if all of our past training of criminal justice officials has emphasized local—or national—levels?

We believe that with this book we are taking you on an exciting voyage, full of puzzles, full of surprises, full of hope, full of potential, yet often reflecting human tragedy. By the end of studying *Criminal Justice: An Introduction,* you will understand criminal justice as a human system, striving to be a humane system.

Review

In this introductory chapter we have demonstrated that, for all too long, crime control decisions have been based on guesses and emotions. They were frequently based on outrage created by the media and exploited by politicians in election agendas. We then related the history of the various reform efforts. Ultimately driven by the U.S. Supreme Court's imposition of high standards for law enforcement, the legislative and executive branches of government, in the 1960s, started programs, including LEAA and LEEP, which promoted education and research in criminal justice, led to the recognition that criminal justice is, or should function as, a system, and encouraged the development of a new discipline: criminal justice. This discipline has evolved into a profession and a science, drawing on the experiences and research methods of many other social and behavioral sciences.

We concluded this chapter with a discussion of two major challenges facing the criminal justice system in

M. CHERIF BASSIOUNI, PROFESSOR OF LAW, DEPAUL UNIVERSITY; CHAIR, U.N. SECURITY COUNCIL COMMISSION TO INVESTIGATE VIOLATIONS OF INTERNATIONAL HUMANITARIAN LAW IN THE FORMER YUGOSLAVIA, 1992–1994

In 1992 the Security Council appointed a special commission to investigate the international crimes resulting from the conflict in the former Yugoslavia.

The conflict was essentially between Serbia and Croatia, and between Serbia and Bosnia.

There was also conflict between Bosnian Catholics and Muslims.

From its inception, the U.N. commission encountered difficulties because the war was still going on and not all the parties to the conflict were willing to allow the investigation to proceed. These problems were compounded by political, bureaucratic, and financial difficulties. Curious as it may seem, though the Security Council provided a broad investigatory mandate, it did not provide funds to conduct the necessary fieldwork.

To overcome the lack of funds and resources, I established a centralized database operation at DePaul University in Chicago, staffed mostly with volunteer lawyers and law students, whose number totaled 165 over a two-year period. In addition, we relied on over 200 personnel assigned to us by the governments of Canada, the Netherlands, and Norway, as well as volunteers from fourteen countries. These people worked as fact finders, investigators, and legal and forensic analysts. Funding for this and other work came from a few governments and private foundations.

The commission identified six different parties to the conflict, each with a separate army, plus a total of twenty-nine paramilitary groups working alongside these armies, but largely out of control. Many of these paramilitary groups operated as criminal gangs, killing, raping, destroying and stealing property, and looting. The demarcation lines between military, paramilitary, police, and

---

the twenty-first century. First there is the challenge of juvenile justice. We have yet to resolve the conflict between a caring and a punitive approach, both of which are deeply rooted in history. Over the last decade, juvenile justice has become more punitive—at least as far as legislation is concerned. This increased punitiveness appears to be motivated by political and emotional considerations. Scientific evidence does not support it. We concluded the chapter with the increasing problems posed by globalization, which currently affects all aspects of life, including crime. Local criminal justice systems and officials are ill-equipped to deal with criminal activi-

ties reaching around the globe. We are witnessing the emergence of global approaches to dealing with globalized crime problems.

Thinking Critically about Criminal Justice

1. Who played the greatest role in creating our new discipline, profession, and science of criminal justice: The courts? Congress? The administration? The universities? Explain your answer.

> "Some two million persons became refugees, most of them as a result of the 'ethnic cleansing policy.'"

civilian combatants were fluid and changing. The country was riddled with strongholds and checkpoints that impeded our passage, and roads were frequently impassable, especially in winter.

We also encountered other difficulties. For example, we tried to exhume a mass grave near the city of Vukovar in Croatia. The grave, in a remote farmhouse, contained 204 bodies of Croatian prisoners of war. The area was within firing range of the Serb militia forces who had committed this crime and they were a constant threat. The location was also far from any facility that could accommodate forensic analysis. Then, too, this work was done in late fall by assigned military personnel and civilian volunteers who were living in tents, cooking their food in the field, and heating water on stoves to wash off the muck.

As a result of the conflict, some 2 million persons became refugees, most of them because of the "ethnic cleansing" policy conducted mostly by the Serbs. It was accompanied by the commission of crimes that fall in the category of genocide, crimes against humanity, and war crimes. Similar crimes, though in much lesser numbers, were also committed against the Serbs.

The commission established that some 500,000 persons were imprisoned for different periods in over 800 places of detention, and among them some 50,000 persons were tortured and an estimated 20,000 women raped. One hundred fifty-one mass graves were identified, containing

between 5 and 3,000 bodies each. Over 3,000 towns and villages were destroyed, as were a significantly large number of Muslim mosques. Catholic churches and Jewish synagogues were also destroyed, as well as some Serbian Orthodox churches. Most of the victims were Bosnian Muslims. The second largest number of victims were Catholic Croatians, followed by a lesser number of Orthodox Serbs.

The commission conducted 35 field investigations, including the largest rape investigation in history, which resulted in identifying 573 rape victims, interviewing 223 such victims, and collecting information on close to 1,500 cases. The work was done under my direction by thirty-three women volunteers—prosecutors, psychiatrists, psychologists, and linguists.

The commission produced the most significant record on war crimes, crimes against humanity, and genocide ever compiled. The report, published by the Security Council, was approximately 3,500 pages long, backed by over 65,000 documents, over 300 hours of videotapes, and a database which had some unique data about the crimes committed and the nature of the conflict.

No one today can imagine it, and few even know or remember the difficulties and hardships, and the horrors we heard about and witnessed. All the work was done in a climate of political skepticism and cynicism. At times we could not figure out what was worse, the objective difficulties we faced or the political forces that sought to paralyze us. But our determination kept us going until we succeeded.

[As a result of the commission's successful investigation and recording of evidence, in 1993 the U.N. Security Council established the International Criminal Tribunal for the former Yugoslavia.]

2. Why was criminal justice not regarded as a "system" in the past and why is it now regarded as such?

3. Do you think that every college student should study criminal justice, even if he or she is not interested in a criminal justice career? Why?

4. Should capital punishment be imposed on persons as young as eleven years who are charged with homicide? List the arguments for and against this proposition.

5. It has been argued that the United States does not need the International Criminal Court, nor any convention against transnational crime, as it is strong enough to protect its own interest. Argue for and against this proposition.

Internet Connection

Note: *While all of the URLs listed were current as of the printing of this book, these sites often change. Please check our website (http://www. mhhe.com/socscience/crimjustice/adlercj) for updates.*

What initiatives have the FBI engaged in to counter international terrorism? See: **http://www.fbi.gov/publish/terror/terroris.pdf.**

Violence on the part of juvenile street gangs continues to be a significant problem. What countermeasures have been taken by federal law enforcement? See: **http://www. fbi.gov/archives/congress/gang/gang.htm.**

The United States Department of State has long been active in fighting transnational crime. What kinds of initiatives are currently embraced? For a discussion of a range of initiatives from alien smuggling to the training of Bosnian Police, see: **http://www.ncjrs.org/intloicj.htm.**

In recent years the tactic of mass rape during war has come to light. Read about victims of rape during war in the context of history and reflect on why this tactic is still used to victimize women and children. See: **http://condor_de-paul.edu/-rrotenbe/aeer/aeer13_1/Olujic.html.**

What kinds of employment opportunities in the field of juvenile justice exist in the private sector versus the state and federal government? See the juvenile justice job bank: **http://www.fsu.edu/~crimdo/jjclearinghouse/jjboard. html.**

Notes

1. See Gerhard O. W. Mueller, *Crime, Law and the Scholars* (London: Heinemann; Seattle: University of Washington Press, 1969), pp. 95–104.

2. Aptly described in Charles H. Whitebread and Christopher Slobogin, *Criminal Procedure,* 3rd ed. (Mineola, NY: The Foundation Press, 1993), pp. 1–9.

3. *Gideon v. Wainwright,* 372 U.S. 335 (1963).

4. *Miranda v. Arizona,* 384 U.S. 436 (1966).

5. The President's Commission on Law Enforcement and Administration of Justice, *The Challenge of Crime in a Free Society* (Washington, DC: U.S. Government Printing Office, 1967).

6. Publ. L. No. 90-351, 82 Stat. 212 (1968); 18 U.S.C. Secs. 2510–2521.

7. The task force reports covered the following subjects: the police, courts, corrections, juvenile delinquency and youth crime, organized crime, science and technology, assessment of crime, narcotics and drugs, and drunkenness. In addition there were research studies and related consultant papers.

8. Herbert Packer, *The Limits of the Criminal Sanction* (Stanford, CA: Stanford University Press, 1968).

9. Wayne R. LaFave and Jerold H. Israel, *Criminal Procedure,* 1992 ed. (St. Paul, MN: West Publishing., 1991).

10. President's Commission, *The Challenge of Crime.*

11. Michael R. Gottfredson and Don M. Gottfredson, *Decision Making in Criminal Justice,* 2nd ed. (NY: Plenum Press, 1988), pp. 21–22.

12. Ibid., p. 22.

13. Robert F. Kidd and Ellen F. Chayet, "Why Do Victims Fail to Report? The Psychology of Crime Victimization," *Journal of Social Issues* 40 (1984), pp. 39–50.

14. Leslie W. Kennedy, "Going It Alone: Unreported Crime and Individual Self-Help," *Journal of Criminal Justice* 16 (1988), pp. 403–412.

15. Ibid., Chapter 2.

16. Ibid., Chapter 3.

17. *Beck v. Ohio,* 379 U.S. 89 (1964).

18. *Mapp v. Ohio,* 367 U.S. 643 (1961).

19. *Terry v. Ohio,* 392 U.S. 1 (1968).

20. *Miranda v. Arizona,* 384 U.S. 436 (1966). *Miranda* warnings are not always recited at the time of arrest and may, depending on the jurisdiction, be recited when the suspect is booked or prior to any custodial interrogation.

21. But there is an exception to this rule: When public safety is at risk, the warning may be postponed. See *New York v. Quarles,* 467 U.S. 649 (1984).

22. *Gideon v. Wainwright,* 372 U.S. 335 (1963), as amplified by, among others, *Argersinger v. Hamlin,* 407 U.S. 25 (1972), and *Strickland v. Washington,* 466 U.S. 668 (1984) (counsel must be competent). See also Anthony Lewis, *Gideon's Trumpet* (NY: Random House, 1974).

23. Robert Hermann, Eric Single, and John Boston, *Counsel for the Poor* (Lexington, MA: Lexington Books, 1977), especially page 153.

24. Gottfredson and Gottfredson, *Decision Making in Criminal Justice,* Chapter 4.

25. *United States v. Salerno,* 481 U.S. 739 (1987).

26. Federal Rules of Criminal Procedure, Rule 6.

27. Matthew R. Durose, David J. Levin, and Patrick A. Langan, *Felony Sentences in State Courts, 1998* (Washington, DC: United States Department of Justice, Bureau of Justice Statistics, 2001), p. l.

28. Held constitutional in *Williams v. Florida,* 399 U.S. 25 (1972).

29. Hans Toch, with contributions by John Gibbs, John Seymour, and Daniel Lockwood, *Living in Prison* (NY: Free Press, 1977).

30. Michael R. Gottfredson and K. Adams, "Prison Behavior and Release Performance: Empirical Reality and Public Policy," *Law and Policy Quarterly* 4 (1982), pp. 373–391. Also see Allen J. Beck and Bernard E. Shipley, *Recidivism of Young Parolees: Special Report,* U.S. Department of Justice, Bureau of Justice Statistics (Washington, DC: U.S. Government Printing Office, 1987).

31. Blackstone, *Commentaries,* IV: 23–24, first published 1765.

32. *In re Gault,* 387 U.S. 1 (1967). Subsequent decisions added that juvenile charges must be proven by evidence beyond a reasonable doubt and other rights. See Christopher P. Manfredi, *The Supreme Court and Juvenile Justice* (Lawrence: The University of Kansas Press, 1998).

33. Institute of Judicial Administration—American Bar Association, *Juvenile Justice Standards: A Summary and Analysis,* 2nd ed., ed. Barbara Dansiger Flicker (Cambridge, MA: Ballinger, 1982).

34. Jeffrey A. Butts and Adele V. Harrell, *Delinquents or Criminals: Policy Options for Young Offenders* (Washington, DC: The Urban Institute, 1998), pp. 5, 6.

35. Pam Belluck, "Chicago Boys, 7 and 8, Charged in the Brutal Killing of a Girl, 11," *The New York Times,* August 10, 1998, pp. 1, 14.

36. Julie Grace, "The Things Kids Say," *Time,* September 14, 1998, p. 50; "Chicago Police Are Reviewing Juvenile Policy," *The New York Times,* September 9, 1998, p. 26.

37. John McCormick and Peter Annin, "Who Killed Ryan Harris?" *Newsweek,* October 5, 1998, pp. 42–43.

38. Howard H. Snyder, *Juvenile Arrests 1996* (Washington, DC, U.S. Department of Justice, OJJDP, November 1997).

39. Carol J. DeFrances and Kevin J. Strom, *Juveniles Prosecuted in State Criminal Courts* (Washington, DC: U. S. Department of Justice, OJP, BJS, March 1997).

40. Coordinating Council on Juvenile Justice and Delinquency Prevention, *Combating Violence and Delinquency: The National Juvenile Justice Action Plan* (Washington, DC: U.S. Government Printing Office, 1996); Kevin Wright and Karen Wright, *Family Life, Delinquency and Crime: A Policymaker's Guide: Research Summary* (Washington, DC: Office of Juvenile Justice and Delinquency Prevention, 1994); Butts and Harrell, *Delinquents or Criminals. United Nations Standard Minimum Rules for the Administration of Juvenile Justice (The Beijing Rules)* (NY: United Nations), in *Compendium of United Nations Standards and Norms in Crime Prevention and Criminal Justice, 1992,* pp. 169–179; *United Nations Guidelines for the Prevention of Juvenile Delinquency (The Riyadh Guidelines)* (NY: United Nations), in *Compendium of United Nations Standards and Norms in Crime Prevention and Criminal Justice, 1992,* pp. 180–191.

41. The term "transnational crimes" was coined by G. O. W. Mueller, then chief of the United Nations Crime Prevention and Criminal Justice Branch. See Department of Economic and Social Affairs, *Fifth United Nations Congress on the Prevention of Crime and the Treatment of Offenders, Report Prepared by the Secretariat* (NY: United Nations, 1976, A/CONF./56/10, Sales No. E.76.IV.2); see also *Organized Crime—A Compilation of U.N. Documents, 1975–1998,* ed. M. Cherif Bassiouni and Eduardo Vetere (Ardsley, NY: Transnational Publishers, 1998).

42. As it turns out, "catch-all" group 18 currently consists mainly of a lively trade in stolen motor vehicles, from West to East and North to South. (Note: The categories have been rearranged. See A.CONF.169/15/Add. 1, 4 April 1995.)

43. See G. O. W. Mueller, "Transnational Crime: Definitions and Concepts," and G. O. W. Mueller, "Responding to the Challenges of Transnational Crime: Where Do We Go from Here?" in *Transnational Crime,* ed. Phil Williams (Milan, Italy: ISPAC, 1999).

44. M. Cherif Bassiouni, *International Criminal Law Conventions and Their Penal Provisions* (Irvington-on-Hudson, NY: Transnational Publishers, 1997), pp. 20–21.

45. United Nations Convention on the Law of the Sea (Montego Bay Convention) 516 UNTS 205 (entered into force November 16, 1994), which adopted the definition of the Convention on the High Seas, of April 27, 1958, 450 UNTS 82, 13 UST 2312, Article 15.

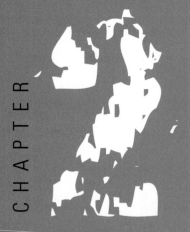

CHAPTER

2

Crime and Criminals

The phone number Americans call when they need police protection from a criminal attack or similar emergency is 911. In a very real sense, then, 911 starts the process of criminal justice and its inquiry about perpetrators and victims, causes and motivations, offenses and defenses. Therefore, 911 is a good symbol with which to start a course—or a book—dedicated to criminal justice. In 2001, 911 took on yet another meaning, not only to the worldwide public, in general, but to criminologists, in particular.

It was in the morning hours of September 11, 2001, that four airliners were diverted in flight, by perpetrators who had subdued or killed the crews. Two of the jets crashed into the New York World Trade Center. The third plane smashed into the Pentagon, in Washington, DC. The fourth plane, apparently headed toward Washington, DC, crashed into a field in Pennsylvania, as a result of passengers trying to overpower the hijackers.

The World Trade Center collapsed within the hour; the Pentagon was in flames; all passengers and crews of the airplanes died in fiery crashes. The death toll was nearly three thousand. It was the worst criminally caused catastrophe in American history. To this day the events of September 11, 2001, are coded as painful and traumatic images in the minds of many Americans.

• As any exposure to the media will tell you, there is a competition for attention among those who deem terrorism to be the most significant national problem, and those pointing to the occupation of Iraq, the failure to develop comprehensive health care coverage in the United States, and uncertainty over our economy and erratic markets. No one would disagree, though, that investor lack of confidence in the financial markets over the past five years came from anything other than corporate scandals and abuses. Corporate giants like Enron, WorldCom, Adelphia, Tyco, and many others, are now bankrupt or continue to seriously suffer financially because management deceived shareholders, business partners, the government, and the public. Billions of dollars were embezzled, stolen, illegally transferred, and withheld from tax authorities.

• It is the oceans, covering nearly three quarters of the world's surface, that make life on earth possible. Yet the oceans are being threatened by many types of criminality, of which the most deadly is pollution. In earlier editions of this book we discussed the case of the supertanker *Exxon Valdez,* which negligently had ruptured its hull in Alaska waters, spilling eleven million gallons of crude oil. This caused the greatest environmental disaster North America had ever known. At the time we expressed our hope that this criminally caused disaster would lead to greater efforts to prevent recurrences. But no. Oil spill disasters that should have been prevented have occurred with increasing regularity, off the coasts of China, South Africa, the Galapagos Islands, the United States, American Samoa, Denmark, Thailand, Brazil, Finland, Germany, the Netherlands, and Vietnam, among others. This criminality, destroying the environment, is called "ecocide."

The collapse of Tower One of the World Trade Center.

Today's focus of the media on a given crime problem is no indication of the extent of tasks for the criminal justice system. In the 1960s the emphasis was on juvenile delinquency; in the 1970s attention turned to street crime in general and drugs, in particular, which led in the 1980s to a focus on prison overcrowding, on the one hand, and target hardening, on the other. Then, in the 1990s and well into the first decade of the twenty-first century, more attention was being paid to foreign influences on our crime rates, in the wake of globalization. Terrorism dictated the market for ideas, competing for attention with computer, white-collar, and corporate criminality. Regardless of the media focus, one thing is certain: The challenges to our criminal justice system continue to grow.

Transnational Crime

Transnational crimes are activities extending into, and violating the laws of, several countries (see Chapter 1).

Terrorism

In the federal and state penal codes there are a number of crimes referring to terrorism. The federal penal code has listed several new crimes regarding terrorism, including "acts of terrorism transcending national boundaries," "use of certain weapons of mass destruction," and "financial transactions" to finance terrorism. Several states have adopted similar legislation, much of which is based on global United Nations conventions. Few of these laws define terrorism as such. Most incorporate crimes that terrorists are likely to commit in furtherance of their objective, such as murder, arson, kidnapping, and so on. The U.S. Department of State has defined "terrorism" as the "premeditated, politically motivated violence perpetrated against noncombatant targets by sub-national groups or clandestine agents, usually intended to influence an audience"[1] (Table 2.1). Most definitions imply the use of violence or other significant forms of criminality to achieve the perpetrators'

Foreign Terrorist Organization (FTO)
Abu Nidal Organization (ANO)
Abu Sayyaf Group (ASG)
Al-Aqsa Martyrs Brigade
Ansar al-Sunna (AS)
Armed Islamic Group (GIA)
Asbat al-Ansar
Aum Shinrikyo (Aum)
Basque Fatherland and Liberty (ETA)
Communist Party of Philippines/New People's Army (CPP/NPA)
Continuity Irish Republican Army (CIRA)
Gama'a al-Islamiyya (IG)
HAMAS
Harakat ul-Mujahedin (HUM)
Hizballah
Islamic Jihad Union (IJU)
Islamic Movement of Uzbekistan (IMU)
Jaish-e-Mohammed (JEM)
Jemaah Islamiya Organization (JI)
Al-Jihad (AJ)
Kahane Chai (Kach)
Kongra-Gel (KGK/PKK)
Lashkar e-Tayyiba (LT)
Lashkar i Jhangvi (LJ)
Liberation Tigers of Tamil Eelam (LTTE)
Libyan Islamic Fighting Group (LIFG)
Moroccan Islamic Combatant Group (GICM)
Mujahedin-e Khalq Organization (MEK)
National Liberation Army (ELN)
Palestine Liberation Front (PLF)
Palestinian Islamic Jihad (PIJ)
Popular Front for the Liberation of Palestine (PFLP)
Popular Front for the Liberation of Palestine-General Command (PFLP-GC)
Al-Qaida (AQ)
Al-Qaida in Iraq (AQI)
Al-Qaida in the Islamic Maghreb (AQIM) [Formerly Salafist Group for Call and Combat (GSPC)]
Real IRA (RIRA)
Revolutionary Armed Forces of Colombia (FARC)
Revolutionary Nuclei (RN)
Revolutionary Organization 17 November
Revolutionary People's Liberation Party/Front (DHKP/C)
Shining Path (SL)
United Self-Defense Forces of Colombia (AUC)

(continued)

SOURCE: Office of the Coordinator for Counterterrorism, Terrorist Organizations, April 30, 2007, available at www.state.gov/s/ct/rls/crt/2006/82738.htm.

TABLE 2.1 U.S. Department of State's Designated Foreign Terrorist Organization List

Terrorist Exclusion List Designees (alphabetical listing)

- Afghan Support Committee (a.k.a. Ahya ul Turas; a.k.a. Jamiat Ayat-ur-Rhas al Islamia; a.k.a. Jamiat Ihya ul Turath al Islamia; a.k.a. Lajnat el Masa Eidatul Afghania)
- Al Taqwa Trade, Property and Industry Company Ltd. (a.k.a. Al Taqwa Trade, Property and Industry; a.k.a. Al Taqwa Trade, Property and Industry Establishment; a.k.a. Himmat Establishment; a.k.a. Waldenberg, AG)
- Al-Hamati Sweets Bakeries
- Al-Ittihad al-Islami (AIAI)
- Al-Manar
- Al-Ma'unah
- Al-Nur Honey Center
- Al-Rashid Trust
- Al-Shifa Honey Press for Industry and Commerce
- Al-Wafa al-Igatha al-Islamia (a.k.a. Wafa Humanitarian Organization; a.k.a. Al Wafa; a.k.a. Al Wafa Organization)
- Alex Boncayao Brigade (ABB)
- Anarchist Faction for Overthrow
- Army for the Liberation of Rwanda (ALIR) (a.k.a. Interahamwe, Former Armed Forces (EX-FAR))
- Asbat al-Ansar
- Babbar Khalsa International
- Bank Al Taqwa Ltd. (a.k.a. Al Taqwa Bank; a.k.a. Bank Al Taqwa)
- Black Star
- Communist Party of Nepal (Maoist) (a.k.a. CPN(M); a.k.a. the United Revolutionary People's Council; a.k.a. the People's Liberation Army of Nepal)
- Continuity Irish Republican Army (CIRA) (a.k.a. Continuity Army Council)
- Darkazanli Company
- Dhamat Houmet Daawa Salafia (a.k.a. Group Protectors of Salafist Preaching; a.k.a. Houmat Ed Daawa Es Salifiya; a.k.a. Katibat El Ahoual; a.k.a. Protectors of the Salafist Predication; a.k.a. El-Ahoual Battalion; a.k.a. Katibat El Ahouel; a.k.a. Houmate Ed-Daawa Es-Salafia; a.k.a. the Horror Squadron; a.k.a. Djamaat Houmat Eddawa Essalafia; a.k.a. Djamaatt Houmat Ed Daawa Es Salafiya; a.k.a. Salafist Call Protectors; a.k.a. Djamaat Houmat Ed Daawa Es Salafiya; a.k.a. Houmate el Da'awaa es-Salafiyya; a.k.a. Protectors of the Salafist Call; a.k.a. Houmat ed-Daaoua es-Salafia; a.k.a. Group of Supporters of the Salafiste Trend; a.k.a. Group of Supporters of the Salafist Trend)
- Eastern Turkistan Islamic Movement (a.k.a. Eastern Turkistan Islamic Party; a.k.a. ETIM; a.k.a. ETIP)
- First of October Antifascist Resistance Group (GRAPO) (a.k.a. Grupo de Resistencia Anti-Fascista Premero De Octubre)
- Harakat ul Jihad i Islami (HUJI)
- International Sikh Youth Federation
- Islamic Army of Aden
- Islamic Renewal and Reform Organization
- Jamiat al-Ta'awun al-Islamiyya
- Jamiat ul-Mujahideen (JUM)
- Japanese Red Army (JRA)
- Jaysh-e-Mohammed
- Jayshullah
- Jerusalem Warriors
- Lashkar-e-Tayyiba (LET) (a.k.a. Army of the Righteous)
- Libyan Islamic Fighting Group
- Loyalist Volunteer Force (LVF)
- Makhtab al-Khidmat
- Moroccan Islamic Combatant Group (a.k.a. GICM; a.k.a. Groupe Islamique Combattant Marocain)
- Nada Management Organization (a.k.a. Al Taqwa Management Organization SA)
- New People's Army (NPA)
- Orange Volunteers (OV)
- People Against Gangsterism and Drugs (PAGAD)
- Red Brigades-Combatant Communist Party (BR-PCC)
- Red Hand Defenders (RHD)
- Revival of Islamic Heritage Society (Pakistan and Afghanistan offices—Kuwait office not designated) (a.k.a. Jamia Ihya ul Turath; a.k.a. Jamiat Ihia Al-Turath Al-Islamiya; a.k.a. Revival of Islamic Society Heritage on the African Continent)
- Revolutionary Proletarian Nucleus
- Revolutionary United Front (RUF)
- Salafist Group for Call and Combat (GSPC)
- The Allied Democratic Forces (ADF)
- The Islamic International Brigade (a.k.a. International Battalion; a.k.a. Islamic Peacekeeping International Brigade; a.k.a. Peacekeeping Battalion; a.k.a. The International Brigade; a.k.a. The Islamic Peacekeeping Army; a.k.a. The Islamic Peacekeeping Brigade)
- The Lord's Resistance Army (LRA)
- The Pentagon Gang
- The Riyadus-Salikhin Reconnaissance and Sabotage Battalion of Chechen Martyrs (a.k.a. Riyadus-Salikhin Reconnaissance and Sabotage Battalion; a.k.a. Riyadh-as-Saliheen; a.k.a. the Sabotage and Military Surveillance Group of the Riyadh al-Salihin Martyrs; a.k.a. Riyadus-Salikhin Reconnaissance and Sabotage Battalion of Shahids (Martyrs))
- The Special Purpose Islamic Regiment (a.k.a. the Islamic Special Purpose Regiment; a.k.a. the al-Jihad-Fisi-Sabililah Special Islamic Regiment; a.k.a. Islamic Regiment of Special Meaning)
- Tunisian Combat Group (a.k.a. GCT; a.k.a. Groupe Combattant Tunisien; a.k.a. Jama'a Combattante Tunisien; a.k.a. JCT; a.k.a. Tunisian Combatant Group)
- Turkish Hizballah
- Ulster Defense Association (a.k.a. Ulster Freedom Fighters)
- Ummah Tameer E-Nau (UTN) (a.k.a. Foundation for Construction; a.k.a. Nation Building; a.k.a. Reconstruction Foundation; a.k.a. Reconstruction of the Islamic Community; a.k.a. Reconstruction of the Muslim Ummah; a.k.a. Ummah Tameer I-Nau; a.k.a. Ummah Tameer E-Nau; a.k.a. Ummah Tameer-I-Pau)
- Youssef M. Nada & Co. Gesellschaft M.B.H.

SOURCE: Office of Counterterrorism, United States, December 29, 2004, available at http://www.state.gov/s/ct/rls/fs/2004/32678.htm.

TABLE 2.1 (Continued)

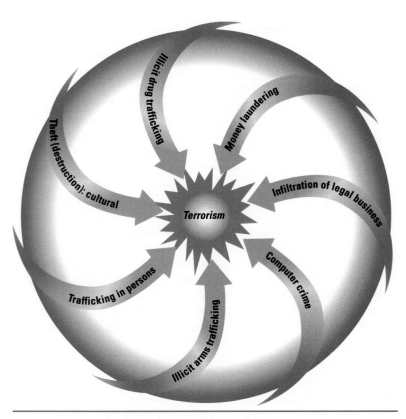

FIGURE 2.1 Wheel of Terrorism

purpose. We are proposing our own definition of **terrorism:** The use or threat of violence directed at people or governments to punish them for a past action or to bring about a change of policy that is to the terrorist's liking. This concept incorporates many forms of criminal conduct and is therefore of prime significance to criminologists.

There is a second and equally important reason to study terrorism: It is at the hub of many forms of criminality that feed or are fed by terrorism. This can best be demonstrated by a wheel, the hub of which is terrorism. The seven spokes of the wheel are the seven forms of transnational criminality that are directly relevant to terrorism, either because they support it or because they are a consequence or by-product of it. Let us examine these seven categories. (See Figure 2.1)

Illicit Drug Trafficking

Terrorists need money for their operations. The drug trade provides easy access to large funds. The Taliban have financed their terrorist activities from the vast opium production of Afghanistan. Terrorists in Colombia derive their funds from the coca trade of Latin America. That holds true for just about every other terrorist group around the world. Globally, there is about $500 billion in "dirty" drug money available for financing illegal activities, including terrorism. United Kingdom Prime Minister Tony Blair, in a speech at a party conference on February 10, 2001, bluntly declared: "the arms the Taliban are buying today are paid for with the lives of young British people buying their drugs on British streets. That is another part of their regime we should seek to destroy."[2] While the "war on drugs" had received widespread attention in the media and on the part of government officials and criminologists, the "war against terrorism" has virtually replaced the prior emphasis. This is particularly disturbing when it is becoming ever more clear that the drug trade nurtures terrorism and fosters the growth of international criminal organizations.[3]

terrorism
The use or threat of violence directed at people or governments to punish them for past action or to bring about a change of policy that is to the terrorist's liking.

Money laundering allows crime to pay by permitting criminals to hide and legitimize proceeds derived from illegal activities. According to one recent estimate, worldwide money laundering activity amounts to roughly $1 trillion a year.

Source: U.S. State Department, "The Fight against Money Laundering," *Economic Perspectives* 6(2), May 2001. http://usinfo.state.gov/journals/ites/0501/ijee/ijee0501.htm.

Money Laundering

"Dirty" (illegally obtained) money cannot be spent freely. While there is evidence that terrorist weapons have been obtained by direct exchange for drugs, or for "dirty" money, most expenditures by terrorists are for goods or services obtained on the free market, which demands clean cash. Hence, much of the dirty money must be laundered in a vast criminal enterprise called "money laundering." Of course, it is not just drug money that requires laundering. All illegally obtained funds, for example, bribery, black market activities, corruption, extortion, and embezzlement, require laundering. Thus, money laundering is an activity aimed at making illegally obtained and, therefore, untaxed funds appear legitimate. Usually this is done by depositing such funds in numbered but unnamed (secret) accounts in banks of a number of countries where that is still possible. From there the funds are rapidly transferred elsewhere, and yet again, until it becomes impossible to trace them to the criminal activity that created them.[4] Despite increased international cooperation to curb money laundering, it appears that terrorism has benefited greatly from this criminal activity. Law enforcement is trying to keep pace. By mid-year 2006, 473 cases were investigated resulting in 161 indictments and 95 convictions—all within a 12-month period.

Infiltration of Legal Business

Dirty money, once laundered, can be used freely, for example, to buy or establish a legitimate business. By way of example, police in Hamburg, Germany, discovered that the innocent-looking import-export firms Tatari Design and Tatex Trading G.m.b.H. were not so innocent at all. They had been established as fronts for Al Qaeda operatives to smuggle money, agents, and supplies.[5] Of course, it is just as likely that laundered funds, rather than directly financing terrorist enterprises, will be invested in businesses controlled by organized crime, like trash hauling, construction, seafood, or investment banking.[6]

Computer Crime

Cyberspace is there for everyone to use—or to abuse, and these abuses are increasingly being discovered and, indeed, legislated as crime. Above all there is the abuse of cyberspace for money laundering, ultimately to support terrorist groups.[7] Beyond that, there is the potential of cyberattacks on the national security of the United States. The security community generally expects terrorists to launch major strikes through computer networks in the immediate future.[8] Al Qaeda is deemed to possess the capacity for these major cyberattacks.[9]

Internet cafes, like this one in Istanbul, Turkey, can be found in most cities of the world. Without them, transnational crime would be difficult to conduct

Illicit Arms Trafficking

The wars of the past have provided terrorists of the past—and the present—with surplus and remnant arms and munitions to fight for their causes. The market in small arms is vast and mostly clandestine. The novelty, however, is the market for weapons of mass destruction: nuclear, bacteriological, and chemical. There is considerable evidence that nuclear materials have been diverted from now-defunct former Soviet installations. It is feared that rogue states that have traditionally supported terrorism are seeking these materials for the creation of weapons of mass destruction.

Traffic in Persons

Smuggling would-be illegal migrants from less-desirable homelands to more promising lands of opportunity has become a significant criminal enterprise, involving millions of human beings, billions in funds paid to smugglers, and the loss of a great number of innocent lives. Many of the countries of destination fear the growth of immigrant communities that might be a terrorist haven, like the refugee camps of Palestine. Even greater is the fear that terrorist organizations deliberately infiltrate their members into immi-

Sailors of a Spanish naval vessel—part of an international armada—boarding an unflagged ship, the *Sosan*, 600 miles off the coast of East Africa, after the caption refused to identify the vessel. Initially, the North Korean master of the vessel claimed she was carrying cement. The Spanish search revealed fifteen missiles and other sophisticated weaponry.

grant populations. To their dismay, for example, Italian law enforcement authorities have learned that among the waves of illegal immigrants washing ashore in Sicily, there are increasing numbers of persons linked to terrorist organizations.[10] There are also masses of illegal aliens who have moved from Iran, Iraq, and Turkey—across the Aegean Sea—into Northern Africa where they become vulnerable recruits for terrorist activities.

Destruction of Cultural Property

Lenin's terrorists became infamous for their effort to destroy the evidence of a culture past: Christian churches were destroyed. Hitler's terrorists burned down the synagogues of Germany and every other cultural symbol, especially literature, art, and music deemed inconsistent with the new "culture" they wanted to impose. The Taliban took delight in firing artillery shells into two ancient statues of Buddha, the largest in the world—reducing them to rubble. And when the 911 terrorists destroyed the World Trade Center, they eradicated not only a symbol of American trade leadership but also a beautiful, unique structure of American architecture. Terrorists, especially those with millennial goals, or of religious or political extremism, seek to destroy past cultures and to impose their own vision of culture.

We have completed our examination of the hub and the seven spokes of our criminological wheel. These represent terrorism and seven other forms of criminality that support or are the product of terrorism. These eight forms of criminality are part of a group of eighteen which the United Nations has defined as "transnational criminality." Not crimes by themselves, but rather a mixture of other crimes, they all have in common that they transcend national boundaries, affecting several nations, and therefore are hard to deal with by just one nation.

While few would contest the importance of these forms of criminality, and the link to terrorist activity, criminologists are still exploring their incidence and the extent of their connection. Recent evidence, for example, disputes estimates of human trafficking of women and children in the United States.[11] Critics of the drug-terrorist connection also ask those who boast about narco-terrorism to provide supportive data that the link is that significant.[12] Deriving accurate estimates of the strength of these spokes on the wheel of terrorism remains an unmet challenge.

Types of Crime

Now that you are acquainted with crimes that transcend our borders, let us turn to those crimes that are the major focus of our criminal justice system. All crimes may be placed into four broad categories: violent crime, property and economic crimes, organized crime, and crimes against public morality.

TABLE 2.2
Where Does Your State Rank According to Rates of Violent Crime (per 100,000 population)?

Area	Rate per 100,000	Area	Rate per 100,000
District of Columbia[5]	1,508.4	New Jersey	351.6
South Carolina[2]	765.5	Ohio[2]	350.3
Tennessee[2]	760.2	Washington	345.9
Nevada	741.6	Indiana	314.8
Florida	712.0	Minnesota[4]	312.0
Louisiana	697.8	Mississippi	298.6
Alaska	688.0	Wisconsin[2]	284.0
Delaware	681.6	Iowa[2]	283.5
Maryland	678.6	Virginia[2]	282.2
New Mexico[2]	643.2	Nebraska[2]	281.8
Michigan[2]	562.4	Hawaii	281.2
Arkansas[2]	551.6	Connecticut[2]	280.8
Missouri	545.6	Oregon	280.3
Illinois[2,3,4]	541.6	West Virginia[2]	279.7
California	532.5	Kentucky	263.0
Texas	516.3	Montana	253.7
Arizona	501.4	Idaho	247.2
Oklahoma	497.4	Wyoming	239.6
North Carolina	475.6	Rhode Island[2]	227.5
Georgia	471.0	Utah	224.4
Massachusetts[2]	447.0	South Dakota[2]	171.4
Pennsylvania	439.4	New Hampshire[2]	138.7
New York	434.9	Vermont[2]	136.6
Alabama	425.2	North Dakota[2]	127.9
Kansas[2]	425.0	Maine	115.5
Colorado	391.6		

[1]Populations are U.S. Census Bureau provisional estimates as of July 1, 2006, and July 1, 2005.
[2]The 2005 crime figures have been adjusted.
[3]Limited data for 2005 and 2006 were available for Illinois.
[4]The data collection methodology for the offense of forcible rape used by the Illinois (with the exception of Rockford, Illinois) and the Minnesota state (2006 data only) Uniform Crime Reporting (UCR) Programs do not comply with national UCR Program guidelines. Consequently, their figures for forcible rape were estimated for inclusion in this table.
[5]Includes offenses reported by the Zoological Police and the Metro Transit Police.
*Less than one-tenth of 1 percent.
NOTE: Although arson data are included in the trend and clearance tables, sufficient data are not available.
SOURCE: Adapted from Sourcebook of Criminal Justice Statistics (available at: www.albuy.edu/sourcebook/pdf/f452006.pdf).

Violent Crime

The taking of life is the most serious harm one human being can inflict on another (see Table 2.2). Consequently, we begin this section on violent crime with criminal homicide. Serious attacks that do not result in death include assaults of various types, among them sexual assault (rape) and the forceful taking of property from another person (robbery).

Homicide

On November 11, 2000, Judy Chandler had been arguing with her boyfriend, Arthur Lee Gales, Jr. Gales beat Chandler with a hammer and left her on the side of the road near their Omaha apartment where police found her incoherent and bleeding from massive head wounds. Upon investigation, authorities found her children's bodies, thirteen-year-old LaTara

TABLE 2.3
Criminal Homicides

Murder	
First degree:[1]	Premeditated, deliberate, malicious,[2] intentional killing of another human being.
Second degree:	Malicious, intentional[3] killing of another human being.
Felony murder	Causing the death of another human being while committing a felony dangerous to life.[4]
Manslaughter	
Voluntary:	Intentional killing of another human being in the heat of passion.
Involuntary:	Reckless[5] killing of another human being.
Negligent homicide	Negligent[6] killing of another human being.

[1]In some states, first degree is restricted to, for example, killing a law enforcement officer.
[2]Technically referred to as "malice aforethought."
[3]Or with total disregard of human life.
[4]Felonies dangerous to life include: burglary, robbery, arson, kidnapping, escape, and sexual assault.
[5]Serious, conscious risk-taking.
[6]Less serious and usually unconscious risk-taking.

Chandler and seven-year-old Tramar. LaTara had been raped and strangled in an attack that lasted four minutes. Tramar was drowned and strangled to death. Gales was found guilty of two counts of first-degree murder and one count of attempted second-degree murder. Nearly a year after the crimes were committed, on November 5, 2001, Gales was sentenced to die in the electric chair for the murders of two children. "Now I can go on with my life," Judy Chandler said. "Now my children can rest."[13]

Homicide is the killing of one human being by another. Unjustified, unexcused killings are **criminal homicides** (Table 2.3). They are subdivided into three categories: murder, manslaughter, and negligent homicide (a lesser form of involuntary manslaughter). A premeditated and deliberate, intentional and malicious killing is **murder in the first degree.** Without premeditation and deliberation, it is **murder in the second degree.** In some states the charge of murder in the first degree has been reserved for the killing of a law enforcement officer or a corrections officer, and for the killing of any person by a prisoner serving a life sentence. Additionally, when death is caused during the commission of a felony considered dangerous to life, the law considers it murder on the part of all participants. This is called **felony murder.**

Voluntary manslaughter is a killing committed intentionally but without malice, as in the heat of passion or in response to strong provocation without an opportunity to cool off. A crime is called an **involuntary manslaughter** when a person causes the death of another unintentionally but recklessly by consciously disregarding a substantial and unjustifiable risk that endangers the other person's life. For example, on October 1, 1998, an ambulance driver was arrested in Brooklyn after speeding through a red light and crashing into a car, killing three little sisters, ages seven, five, and three. State laws allow emergency vehicle drivers to go through stop signs and red lights but only after slowing down to check traffic conditions. In some jurisdictions there exists a lesser form of involuntary manslaughter called *negligent homicide,* a killing usually in conjunction with automobile or industrial accidents.

Extent. The murder rate for 2006 was 5.7 per 100,000, with a total of 17,034 murders. Juveniles under eighteen committed 710 of them. The murder rate has decreased steadily since 1993, with a 33.9 percent decrease. Three quarters of victims were male, with firearms used in approximately seven out of ten murders.[14]

Mass and Serial Murder. On April 7, 2004, suspected mass murderer Marcus Wesson, 57, was charged with 33 felony counts—including rape and sexual assault of a minor—in addition to nine counts of **mass murder.** Investigators believe the victims, ranging in age

homicide
The killing of one person by another.

criminal homicide
Unjustified, unexcused killing of another human being.

murder in the first degree
Killing done with premeditation and deliberation or, by statute, in the presence of other aggravating circumstances.

murder in the second degree
Killing done with intent to cause death but without premeditation and deliberation.

felony murder
Criminal liability for murder for one who participates in a felony that is dangerous to life and causes the death of another.

voluntary manslaughter
Intentionally but without malice causing the death of another person, as in the heat of passion.

involuntary manslaughter
Unintentionally but recklessly causing the death of another by consciously taking a grave risk.

mass murder
The murder of multiple victims, in one act or transaction, by one perpetrator or a group of perpetrators.

from 1 to 25, were all his children. Police stated that Wesson engaged in polygamy and incest, fathering the victims with six women, including two of his daughters and three of his nieces. All of the bodies were found in the bedroom of his Fresno home.[15]

Who can forget the Unabomber, Ted Kaczynski, who committed another type of murder that is particularly unnerving to the community: **serial murder,** the killing of several victims over time.[16] Most serial murderers, unlike Kaczynski, see their victims face to face. Aileen Carol Wuornos, a Florida prostitute considered to be the country's first female serial killer, was sentenced to death. In February 1999, Charles Chitat Ng was found guilty of eleven murders. Ng, along with Leonard Lake (who killed himself in police custody) is believed to have killed over twenty people in the mid- to late-1980s, and was thought to have used many of them as sex slaves before killing them. Ng had escaped to Canada but was found after an arrest for attempting to steal clothing from a department store.[17]

serial murder
Killing of several victims over a period of time.

Yolanda Manuel, mother of seven-year-old sexual assault and murder victim Sherrice Iverson, speaks at a rally on the U.C. Berkeley campus, 1998. The rally was staged to protest the presence, on the Berkeley campus, of sophomore David Cash, who watched and did nothing as friend Jeremy Strohmeyer dragged Sherrice into a Las Vegas casino bathroom stall where he killed her.

For more than 30 years a serial killer who called himself BTK ("Bind, Torture, Kill") defied capture. The BTK killer would break into a home, wait for the occupant to return, and viciously kill his victim. Women in Wichita, Kansas, were justifiably scared until suddenly the murders stopped. After more than a decade lapse, law enforcement surmised that the killer moved, was arrested elsewhere for another crime, or had died.

In March 2004, a letter was sent to a local newspaper with the author taking responsibility for the murder of Vicki Wegerle in September 1986. The letter contained photographs of the victim's body that only the killer could have taken, along with a copy of Wegerle's driver's license.

Less than a year later, on February 25, 2005, Dennis L. Rader, 60, of Park City was arrested after a number of other letters were sent by the apparent killer. Rader confessed to being Wichita's BTK serial killer and pleaded guilty to 10 murders dating back to 1974. He will serve 10 consecutive life sentences with no chance of parole.

Mass and serial murderers are particularly difficult for law enforcement personnel to track down because they have no apparent motive for committing their crimes.

Gang Murder.   In Chicago, a ten-year-old boy riding his bike near his home was trapped in a gang crossfire and killed. Just a few days before, a three-year-old boy sitting on his mother's lap was partially blinded when he was caught in the midst of a gang fight.[18] In Atlanta, a gang member was charged with murder in the death of two infants after throwing a Molotov cocktail into the home of their eighteen-year-old mother, who had argued with a friend of the gang.[19] In Los Angeles, a small girl handed out flyers saying, "Let's have a no-killing weekend for Easter."[20]

Since the 1950s the nature of gang violence has changed dramatically. Gun violence began in the 1980s when gang members started selling crack and cocaine. It is estimated that one gang alone, the Eight Tray Gangster Crips, has distributed hundreds of kilos of the drug worth over $10 million on the streets of Los Angeles and five other cities, as far east as Birmingham, Alabama, and Atlanta. The FBI reports that this network is only one of perhaps a hundred more operating nationwide.[21] Illicit firearm markets that supply the guns for resolving gang conflicts have spread across the country. About 80 percent of guns taken from youths are handguns, and over half of these are semiautomatic weapons. Serial numbers have been removed.[22] Between 50 and 70 percent of gang members own or have access to guns. Use of these guns, rather than knives and clubs, turns violent events into life-and-death situations; gangs battle gangs in a kind of street guerrilla warfare. Drive-by shootings, in particular, have become a favored method of operation. A "drive-by" involves members of one gang driving onto a rival gang's turf to shoot at someone, followed by a high-speed escape. Some drive-bys are for "fun," some are for defending gang honor, some for initiation rites, and others to get rid of competition in the drug field. In Brooklyn, New York, all three brothers in one family fell victim to street violence. Homicides by gangs of offenders differ from homicides by single offenders with respect to the age of the offenders (gang killers are five years younger on average), their ethnicity (they're more likely to be members of the same ethnic group), and the victim–offender relationship (gang killers are twice as likely not to know their victims).[23]

Assault

An **assault** is an attack on another person with apparent ability to inflict injury and at least the intent to frighten. Modern statutes usually recognize *two types of assault:* a **simple assault** is one that inflicts little or no physical harm; a *felonious* or **aggravated assault** is one in which the perpetrator inflicts serious harm on the victim or uses a deadly weapon. The National Crime Victimization Survey estimates that 4,357,190 assaults were committed in 2005.[24] These figures grossly underestimate the real number of assaults because many persons prefer to keep such incidents private—especially if the assault has occurred within the household or family. In 1994, for instance, Hedda Nussbaum brought a $3.6 million suit against Joel Steinberg for the permanent disfigurement she suffered as a result of eight years of beatings. The assaults came to light when, on November 1, 1987, Steinberg, a disbarred lawyer, beat to death their illegally adopted daughter, Lisa. As the criminal justice system pays increasing attention to family-related violence (spouse and child abuse), more persons are reporting such offenses to the police.

assault
Unlawful offer or attempt with force or violence to hurt another.

simple assault
Attack that inflicts little or no physical harm on the victim.

aggravated assault
Attack on a person in which the assailant inflicts serious harm or uses a deadly weapon.

Rape and Sexual Assault

According to the Uniform Crime Reports, 92,455 forcible rapes (31 per 100,000 population) were reported in 2006. This is the lowest rate of forcible rape in 20 years.[25] The extent of the problem is largely unknown. The UCR do not include most rapes of wives by husbands or rapes among acquaintances because they are not reported to the police. Unlike rapes committed by persons who know the victim, rapes by strangers often receive widespread coverage in the news media. A prime example is the 1997 case of Lawrence Singleton, who sexually molested and murdered the mother of three children ages three to eleven. After his arrest, the sixty-nine-year-old male confessed to the crime, all the while proclaiming that he had been framed in a much earlier case. In 1978, he bound and raped a fifteen-year-old Las Vegas, Nevada, girl. After the attack he axed off her arms and left her in a large concrete pipe to die. Somehow, she survived. Singleton served 8 1/3 years for that crime.

The common law defined rape as an act of forced intercourse by a man of a woman, not his wife. While most laws in our penal codes have retained their original form, the law on forcible rape has changed drastically in many states. This change includes the name of the crime (sexual assault), its definition, the rules of evidence and procedure, and society's reaction to it. Recent legislation in several states has removed some of the difficulties women had previously encountered in rape prosecutions. In some states they are no longer required to reveal prior sexual activity, the requirement of corroborative evidence has been reduced or eliminated, and a wife may now charge her husband with rape.

Robbery

Robbery is the taking of property from a victim by force and violence or by the threat of violence. Approximately 447,403 robberies were reported to the police in 2006.[26] Over time, armed robbery has taken many forms. In transportation we have witnessed a progression from stagecoach holdups, to train robberies, to armed carjackings, which in some U.S. cities have reached epidemic proportions. In Los Angeles during a recent reporting period, more than 4,000 vehicles were stolen by assailants who threatened victims with handguns, knives, machetes, simulated guns, and even a broken bottle.[27] It is estimated that there are 34,000 attempted or successful carjackings each year.[28] In a particularly notorious case,

robbery
The taking of the property of another out of his or her presence by means of force and violence or the threat thereof.

Pamela Basu was dragged to her death trying to rescue her 20-month-old daughter who had become tangled in her seat belt. The carjackers threw her infant daughter out of the car into the roadway. Another carjacking victim, Laura Christ, was forced from her car and shot in the heart in March 1995.

Property Crimes

Traditional property crimes include larceny (theft), obtaining property by fraud, burglary, and arson, which not only deprives the owner of property but also can endanger lives. Larceny is the property crime committed most frequently.

Larceny.   The crime of **larceny** is:

larceny
Trespassory taking and carrying away of personal property belonging to another with the intent to deprive the owner of the property permanently.

- a "trespassory" (any absence of permission or authority for the taking)
- taking and
- carrying away of
- personal property
- belonging to another
- with the intent to deprive the owner of the property
- permanently (a condition no longer required in many states).

The UCR reported 6,607,013 thefts in 2006, or a rate of 2,207 thefts per 100,000 persons. Most thefts do not include personal contact (e.g., pocket-picking and purse-snatching). **Shoplifting,** the stealing of goods from retail merchants, makes up about 13 percent of all larcenies. While shoplifting may appear to be a rather insignificant crime, the cost to the public is high. Each thief may steal goods with an average value of only $200, but together these thefts add up to over $10 billion a year, a cost that is ultimately passed on to consumers through increases in the price of various products.[29]

shoplifting
Stealing of goods from stores or markets.

Nearly 1.2 million motor vehicles, mostly passenger cars, were stolen in 2006,[30] with an overall loss to owners of more than $8 billion. Recently, young car thieves have used stolen vehicles for racing, for "showing off" among their friends, or for the "kick" of destroying them. Older, professional thieves steal designated cars on consignment for resale in an altered condition (with identifying numbers changed) or for sale to "chop shops," which strip the cars for resale of their parts.

Fraud

fraud
Acquisition of the property of another through deception.

Fraud is the acquisition of the property of another person through deception. Deception includes false pretenses, confidence games, check forgery, and illegal credit and cash transactions. Two rapidly growing types of fraud involve auto and health insurance claims. The amount and types of fraud have changed through the years with technological developments. Just as the introduction of checks for the payment of goods and services opened up opportunities for thieves to gain illegitimate financial advantage, so did the introduction of "plastic money." Major credit card companies report billions of dollars in losses from fraud annually. Stolen, lost, or expired credit cards are now modified with computers and encoding devices so that they appear to be valid. Totally counterfeit credit cards are also fabricated with the help of laser copiers or other duplicating machines. More recently, credit card account numbers are being stolen from the Internet, where credit purchases are now possible. In 2000, the FBI and the White-Collar Crime Center created a national reporting mechanism to track fraud on the Internet by establishing the Internet Fraud Complaint Center (IFCC) (Figure 2.2).

High-Tech Crimes

In addition to credit card fraud carried out on the Internet, the rise of computers and other high-technology equipment has paved the way for other new types of crime as well. These crimes present yet another set of challenges for potential victims, law enforcement personnel, and criminal justice professionals. What exactly *is* high-technology crime? It is generally

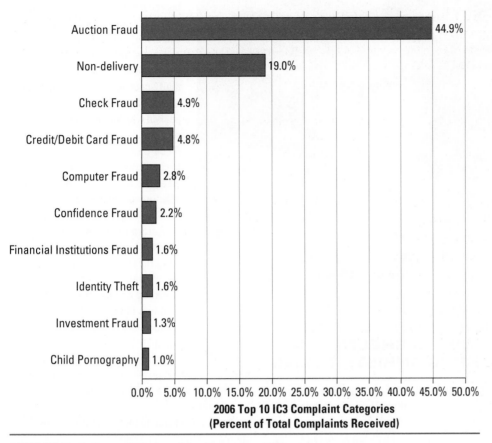

FIGURE 2.2 IFCC Complaint Categories, 2006

SOURCE: Table adapted from *IFCC 2002 Internet Fraud Report,* National White Collar Crime Center and the Federal Bureau of Investigation, 2006, p. 6.

agreed that **high-tech crime** involves an attempt to pursue illegal activities through the use of sophisticated electronic devices—computers, cellular telephones, and other digital communications—that are in common use today. The financial loss associated with computer crimes alone is staggering. Consider the loss to a small sample (269) of corporations surveyed about cyber crime.[31] Consider, as well, the effect of a single virus. In January 2004, the "MyDoom" worm became the fastest spreading virus to date. One out of every twelve e-mail messages, at a certain point in time, had the virus. The National White Collar Crime Center estimates that this worm alone caused $38.5 billion worth of damages worldwide.

New types of crime include "cyberspying" into competitors' computer systems to gather proprietary information, the distribution of illegal or illegally obtained images such as child pornography, and video piracy. For example, it is not unusual for a major motion picture to open in movie theaters—and for bootleggers' videotape versions to appear on the streets the same day.

high-tech crime
The pursuit of illegal activities through the use of advanced electronic media.

Burglary

The common-law definition of **burglary** is:

- the breaking
- and entering
- of the dwelling house
- of another person
- at night
- with the intention to commit a felony or larceny inside.

burglary
According to common law, the nighttime breaking and entering of the dwelling house of another, with the intention to commit a crime or larceny therein; a felony.

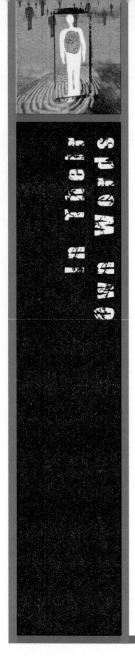

HÉLICA GONZÁLEZ, CARE MANAGER, THE WOMEN'S SHELTER, INC., CORPUS CHRISTI, TEXAS

There are currently 36 individuals at this residence: 14 women and 21 children. The perimeter doors and windows are constantly locked. Cameras at each doorway and intercoms are all working. The locks are not to keep the individuals inside but to keep individuals out—those who wish to harm those who seek safety with us. There are no signs outside of the building to suggest what we do or who we are. Those who know of us are women and children who are victims of domestic violence.

The time is 4:00 P.M. on a Saturday afternoon and I have just been buzzed into the shelter to begin my eight-hour shift. I walk into the hotline office; a phone with 24 lines awaits the calls that will notify us of the abuse which occurs throughout the 12 counties we serve. Throughout the office are folders and books, packed with information and resources for the clients that we serve. A board sits above the desk. I scan it to check who has remained this week and how much space is available for women who will seek safety from us tonight.

Before I can even begin to look over the logbook, where everything that happens is recorded, the woman who came in last weekend comes into the office with two of her children to speak to me. Her body looks like that of a boxer rather than a woman of 26: she has a broken nose, scars all over her body, mostly on her face, and her mouth is permanently scarred from the several busted lips she has not been able to have stitched.

As I sit and listen to her reasons why she should go back (she has no home, no job, and no education), all I can do is reassure her of her ability to make it with our help. After about two hours of active listening, she has assured me that she will not go back as she is tired of the abuse and the fear of her children watching her abuser kill her in front of them.

Statutes have added buildings other than dwellings to the definition and no longer limit the offense to nighttime attacks. There were close to 2.2 million burglaries reported to the police in 2006. Although these crimes still account for almost 19.1 percent of all index offenses, the burglary rate was the lowest in more than twenty years.

Criminal justice experts believe that the decline in burglaries may be due to greater awareness on the part of homeowners of the risks of leaving doors and windows open or newspapers on a doorstep. Greater use of burglar alarms, street lights, and other devices that limit opportunities for burglars to commit crimes may also have contributed to the decline.

Arson

arson
The malicious burning of the dwelling house of another, or the burning of other structures or even personal property.

The common law defines **arson** as the malicious burning of or setting fire to the dwelling of another person. Modern statutes have increased its scope to include other structures, personal property such as automobiles, and fires set by property owners themselves in an effort to collect insurance money. While arson is a fairly infrequent offense, it can cause a great deal of damage. The seriousness of this crime was underscored by the inferno created by arsonists in the Du Pont Plaza Hotel in San Juan in 1987. Ninety-seven people died.

The traditional property crimes just discussed are typically committed by a lone perpetrator with a single target—a house, an automobile, or merchandise.

At about 9:30 P.M. we have already had about seven calls for help, some of the women just needing a friend, others needing shelter. At about 9:40 P.M. a female calls looking for shelter. She has been running from her abuser for the past three hours; she has been able to get to a pay phone where he can't see her; a man at a convenience store is hiding her behind the counter. I call the police department and they agree to pick her up and bring her to the shelter. Thirty minutes later she is at the front door, soaked, with her three children (ages four, two, and three weeks), the youngest in a carrier with a trash bag covering him so he would not get wet.

Once in the shelter, we tend to her and the children. They have only the clothes on their backs and none of them have shoes. We go to our donation room and find clothing for all of them. As the other case manager on shift tends to the children, I concentrate on her intake paperwork. She begins by telling me that her abuser has been hitting her since yesterday afternoon and it has just gotten worse over the course of the night. She has several bruises all over her body, as he has kicked and punched her repeatedly. Her right lip is cut open and her left eye is swollen shut. She is refusing medical treatment because she fears he will be at the hospital. She asks me to show her the locks on the doors and windows, because "If he wants me, he will get me."

At about 11:16 P.M. the women come out of their rooms; the children have been put to bed and they come together in the dining area to talk. They sit and talk of their abuse. One woman who had come in about one month ago shows off her new checking account. She has been working for the past 12 years, but had never seen one penny of her money because her abuser controlled all of her finances.

At about 11:46 P.M., the woman who came in to talk to me earlier shows up at the door of the office with her children and her belongings. She wants to go home, she feels that this time he will change and that everything will be all right. As she tells me how everything will be different this time, she cries, and the fear shows in her eyes. As we speak, I go over a personal safety plan with her and assure her that we are here to help again if she needs us. She states that she doesn't think it will happen again, and I am sure that in her heart she really wishes this were true. As she leaves, the women in the dining room give her support and the woman with her first checking account hands her a check, "just in case."

I offer her advice as she leaves and remind her to "Get out before it is too late."

It is 12:22 A.M.. and my shift at the shelter has ended.

White-Collar Crime

David Duncan, a fired Arthur Andersen LLP partner, took the witness stand a week into the criminal trial of Andersen in May 2002, and admitted that he intentionally obstructed justice when he asked his employees to shred documents relating to the Enron Corporation. "Yes, I obstructed justice. I instructed people on the [Enron audit] team to follow the document retention policy, which I knew would result in the destruction of documents." Duncan's statements all but sealed the fate of the Arthur Andersen partnership—one of the largest and most highly respected accounting firms in the world. Andersen (as a partnership) was convicted of obstruction of justice nearly a month later and is now in bankruptcy—one more casualty in the latest round of corporate scandals.

Add Tyco International CEO Kozlowski to this list of scandals for possible tax evasion. Next, add CEO Rigas of Adelphia for securities fraud charges. We cannot help but mention Enron for securities, insider trading, and perjury charges against senior management and fraud charges against the company. Daily, the list of casualties appears never ending, with recent allegations of insider trading and securities fraud in Global Crossing; and high-profile civil investigations of WorldCom, Qwest, Martha Stewart, Dynegy, CMS Energy, El Paso Corporation, Halliburton, and Williams Companies.

Martha Stewart, an icon of good homemaking, is accused of selling thousands of shares of ImClone Systems, Inc., stock just prior to the company's announcement that it failed to receive Food and Drug Administration approval for an anticancer drug. Was this insider trading? Did she trade on material, non-public information?

Defining White-Collar Crime. From 2001 to 2005 there was a near daily barrage of media reports on the latest corporate scandal— from allegations against Martha Stewart to ex-General Electric's CEO Jack Welch. For a long while, it was only natural to think that we were in the midst of an unprecedented wave of white-collar and corporate crime. On reflection, there is no empirical evidence that there was much of a change.

Not surprisingly, politicians seized the opportunity to call for corporate reforms in light of almost daily accusations of illegalities. With little reflection, President Bush signed the Sarbanes-Oxley Act of 2002 to quell public concerns over the legitimacy and integrity of the markets. This act adopts tough provisions to deter and punish corporate and accounting fraud and corruption.

According to a press release from the White House, the act "ensures justice for wrongdoers, and protects the interests of workers and shareholders. This bill improves the quality and transparency of financial reporting, independent audits, and accounting services for public companies."

To its credit, the Sarbanes-Oxley Act of 2002 does the following:

- Creates a public company accounting oversight board to enforce professional standards, ethics, and competence for the accounting profession
- Acts to strengthen the independence of firms that audit public companies
- Increases corporate responsibility and the usefulness of corporate financial disclosure
- Increases penalties for corporate wrongdoing
- Protects the objectivity and independence of securities analysts
- Increases Securities and Exchange Commission resources

Perhaps most noteworthy, CEOs and chief financial officers must personally vouch for the truth and fairness of their company's disclosures.

For those who think that the problem of white-collar and corporate crime is young, consider that in ancient Greece public officials reportedly violated the law by purchasing land slated for government acquisition. Much of what we today define as white-collar crime, however, is the result of laws passed within the last century. For example, the Sherman Antitrust Act, passed by Congress in 1890, authorized the criminal prosecution of corporations engaged in monopolistic practices. Federal laws regulating the issuance and sale of stocks and other securities were passed in 1933 and 1934. In 1940 Edwin H. Sutherland provided criminologists with the first scholarly account of white-collar crime. He defined it as crime "committed by a person of respectability and high social status in the course of his occupation.[32]

The conviction of Arthur Andersen, LLP, demonstrates that Sutherland's definition is not entirely satisfactory: White-collar crime can be committed by a corporation as well as by an individual. As Gilbert Geis has noted, Sutherland's work is limited by his own definition. He has a "striking inability to differentiate between the corporations themselves and their executive management personnel."[33] Other criminologists have suggested that the term "white-collar crime" not be used at all; we should speak instead of "corporate crime" and "occupational crime."[34] Generally, however, **white-collar crime** is defined as a violation of the law committed by a person or group of persons in the course of an otherwise respected and legitimate occupation or business enterprise.[35]

white-collar crime
A violation of the law committed by a person or group of persons in the course of an otherwise respected and legitimate occupation or business enterprise.

Just as white-collar and corporate offenses include a heterogeneous mix of corporate and individual crimes, from fraud, deception, and corruption (as in the S&L case) to pollution of the environment, victims of white-collar crime range from the savvy investor to the unsuspecting consumer. No one person or group is immune.[36] The Vatican lost millions of dollars in a fraudulent stock scheme; fraudulent charities have swindled fortunes from unsuspecting investors; and many banks have been forced into bankruptcy by losses due to deception and fraud. Perhaps as important, public perceptions of the legitimacy of financial institutions and markets have been undermined, at least in part, by allegations of corporate abuses.

Types of White-Collar Crimes. White-collar crimes are as difficult to detect as they are easy to commit.[37] The detection mechanisms on which police and government traditionally rely seem singularly inadequate for this vast new body of crimes. Moreover, though people have learned through the ages to be wary of strangers on the street, they have not yet learned to protect themselves against vast enterprises. Much more scientific study has to be undertaken on the causes, extent, and characteristics of white-collar crimes before we can develop workable prevention strategies.[38]

Eight categories of white-collar offenses committed by individuals can be identified:

* Securities-related crimes
* Bankruptcy fraud
* Fraud against the government
* Consumer fraud
* Insurance fraud
* Tax fraud
* Bribery, corruption, and political fraud
* Insider-related fraud[39]

Let us briefly examine each type of crime.

Securities-Related Crimes. State and federal securities laws seek to regulate both the registration and issuance of a security and the employment practices of personnel in the securities industries. After the stock market crash on October 26, 1929, the federal government enacted a series of regulatory laws, including the Securities Act of 1933 and the Securities Exchange Act of 1934, aimed at prohibiting manipulation and deceptive practices. The 1934 act provided for the establishment of the Securities and Exchange Commission (SEC), an organization with broad regulatory and enforcement powers. The SEC is empowered to initiate civil suits and administrative actions and to refer criminal cases to the U.S. Department of Justice.

Crime in the securities field remains common. The problem of securities fraud was made more apparent in recent years with some notable cases. The significance of the problem, however, is highlighted by the sheer size of the equities market.

Four kinds of offenses are prevalent: churning, trading on insider information, stock manipulation, and boiler-room operations.

Churning is the practice of trading a client's shares of stock frequently in order to generate large commissions. A broker earns a commission on every trade, so whether or not the stock traded increases or decreases in value, the broker makes money. Churning is difficult to prove, because brokers typically are allowed some discretion. Therefore, unless the client has given the broker specific instructions in writing, a claim of churning often amounts to no more than the client's word against the broker's.

Insider trading is the use of material, nonpublic, financial information to obtain an unfair advantage in trading securities.[40] A person who has access to confidential corporate information may make significant profits by buying or selling stock on the strength of that information. The prototype case of insider trading was against Dennis Levine. Levine, a 34-year-old managing director of the securities firm formerly known as Drexel Burnham Lambert, used insider information to purchase stock for himself and others in such corporations as International Telephone and Telegraph, Sperry Corporation, Coastal Corporation, American National Resources, and McGraw Edison. After the SEC found out, Levine implicated other Wall Street executives—including Ivan Boesky, who had made millions of dollars in illegal profits.

Stock manipulation is common in the "pink sheets" over-the-counter market, in which some stocks are traded at very low prices, but it is by no means limited to such stocks. Brokers who have a stake in a particular security may make misleading or even false statements to clients to give the impression that the price of the stock is about to rise and thus to create an artificial demand for it.

Fact Update

2006: 108,823 arrests for forgery/counterfeiting. 280,693 arrests for fraud. 20,012 arrests for embezzlement (50 percent women). In federal courts, 1,172 convicted of forgery/counterfeiting (73.2 percent got some prison, 9 month median), 6,958 for fraud (68.8 percent got some prison, 10 month median), 584 embezzlement (51.7 percent got some prison, 6 month median), 912 money laundering (80.4 percent got prison, 22.5 month median), 622 racketeering/extortion (93 percent got some prison, 60 month median).

SOURCE: "White Collar Crime Statistics," September 2007, National White Collar Crime Center.

Securities and Commodities Fraud.

Estimates $40 billion lost to securities fraud each year ($6 billion from market manipulation). 1,655 cases pending in FY 2006, 203 indictments, 164 convictions. $1.9 billion in Restitutions, $20.6 million in Recoveries, $80.7 million in Fines, and $62.7 million in Seizures.

SOURCE: "Financial Crimes report to the Public Fiscal Year 2006," FBI Financial Crimes Section, Criminal Investigative Division. Available at: http://www.fbi.gov/filelink.html?file=publications/financial/fcs_report2006/publicrpt06.pdf.

churning
Practice of trading a client's shares of stock frequently to generate large commissions.

insider trading
Use of material, nonpublic financial information about securities to obtain unfair advantage.

stock manipulation
Brokers who have a stake in a particular security make misleading or false statements to clients to give the impression that the price of the stock is about to rise, creating an artificial demand for it.

boiler rooms
Operations run by stock manipulators who, through deception and misleading sales techniques, seduce unsuspecting and uninformed individuals into buying stocks in obscure and often poorly financed corporations.

bankruptcy fraud
Scam designed to take advantage of loopholes in the bankruptcy laws.

Fired Arthur Andersen auditor David Duncan, appearing on Capitol Hill Thursday, January 24, 2002, before a House Energy subcommittee hearing on the destruction of Enron-related documents. Duncan cited his Fifth Amendment rights, declining to testify to Congress about anything he knows or anything he did in the destruction of Enron documents.

Boiler rooms are operations run by stock manipulators who, through deception and misleading sales techniques, seduce unsuspecting and uninformed individuals into buying stocks in obscure and often poorly financed corporations. Significant federal and state legislation has been passed (Penny Stock Reform Act of 1990) to curtail these operations, but the manipulation continues. The problem is particularly significant in Florida where the state has warned the public.

Bankruptcy Fraud.   The filing of a bankruptcy petition results in proceedings in which the property and financial obligations of an insolvent person or corporation are disposed of. Bankruptcy proceedings are governed by laws enacted to protect insolvent debtors. Unscrupulous persons have devised numerous means to commit **bankruptcy fraud**—any scam designed to take advantage of loopholes in the bankruptcy laws. The most common are the "similar-name" scam, the "old-company" scam, the "new-company" technique, and the "successful-business" scam.

The similar-name scam involves the creation of a corporation that has a name similar to that of an established firm. The objective is to create the impression that this new company is actually the older one. If the trick is successful, the swindlers place large orders with established suppliers and quickly resell any merchandise they receive, often to fences. At the same time the swindlers remove all money and assets of the corporation and either file for bankruptcy or wait until creditors sue. Then they leave the jurisdiction or adeptly erase their tracks.

The old-company scam involves employees of an already established firm who, motivated by a desire for quick profits, bilk the company of its money and assets and file for bankruptcy. Such a scam is typically used when the company is losing money or has lost its hold on a market.

The new-company scam is much like the similar-name scam: A new corporation is formed, credit is obtained, and orders are placed. Once merchandise is received, it is converted into cash with the assistance of a fence. By the time the company is forced into bankruptcy, the architects of this scheme have liquidated the corporation's assets.

The successful-business scam involves a profitable corporation that is well positioned in a market but experiences a change in ownership. After the new owners have bilked the corporation of all its money and assets, the firm is forced into bankruptcy.

The Federal Bureau of Investigation estimates that 10 percent of all bankruptcy filings involve fraud. On average, in recent years, this suggests that approximately 250 fraudulent bankruptcies were filed every day. Two-thirds of these cases involve some form of hidden assets.

The FBI launched a series of joint undercover investigations with multiple field offices, for example, Remington Raider and Total Disclosure. Operation Total Disclosure alone resulted in the arrest of 110 bankruptcy fraud subjects.

Fraud against the Government.   Governments at all levels are victims of a vast amount of fraud, which includes collusion in bidding, payoffs and kickbacks to government officials, expenditures by a government official that exceed the budget, the filing of false claims, the hiring of friends or associates formerly employed by the government, and offers of inducements to government officials.

Consider, for example, the fall of Wedtech—a military contractor with annual sales in excess of $100 million. At one time the Wedtech Corporation was hailed as the first major employer of blacks and Hispanics in New York City's blighted South Bronx. Before its fall from grace, Wedtech was a high flier on the New York Stock Exchange. What fueled the company? As a minority-controlled business, it won defense contracts without the need to bid. But in early 1986 Wedtech lost its status as a minority business, and by the end of that year the company was in ruins.

Fiscal Year	Criminal Indictments[a]	Criminal Convictions[a]	Military Article 15*	Criminal Judgment Amount	Civil Settlement Amount	Administrative Amount	Investigative Recoveries and Seizures
2001	177	137	6	$38.6	$103.5	$4.9	$0.6
2002	200	109	14	$919.6	$528.4	$2.4	$4.8
2003	176	121	10	$40.7	$492.4	$19.9	$3.8
2004	86	113	7	$28.0	$61.8	$40.2	$0.7
2005	79	85	2	$27.1	$269.6	$23.7	$0.0
Total	718	565	39	$448.1	$1,449.6	$90.4	$9.9

[a]Conditions sometimes occur in the year or years following indictments and therefore may be less than or exceed the number of indictments. In addition, some indictments do not result in convictions.

*For minor fraud committed by military personnel, punishment is usually labeled by the commanding officer. Such non-judical punishment is referred to as an Article 15 procedure.

SOURCE: GAO-06-838R, "Contract Management: DOD Vulnerabilities to Contracting Fraud, Waste, and Abuse," July 7, 2006.

TABLE 2.4 DOD Procurement Fraud Case Results for Fiscal Years 2001–2005 (dollar amounts in millions)

Wedtech officials had used fraudulent accounting methods, issued false financial reports, and counted profits before they were received. Caught in the cross fire of charges was member of Congress Mario Biaggi, who was later convicted of soliciting bribes in order to obtain special government support for Wedtech. Other company and government officials either pleaded guilty or were convicted.[41]

Is the Wedtech scandal an isolated case? Clearly not. From 2001 through 2005, the Department of Defense reported that 718 defense contractors were indicted and thousands of individuals and firms have been banned from receiving federal contracts.[42] (See Table 2.4.)

An important step to curb government contract fraud was taken with the passage of the Major Fraud Act (1988), creating a separate offense of government contract fraud in excess of $1 million. What kinds of activities does this act cover? Federal prosecutors seek indictments against contractors who engage in deceptive pricing or overcharging by submitting inaccurate cost and pricing data; mischarging by billing the government for improper or nonallowable charges; collusion in bidding (a conspiracy between presumed competitors to inflate bids); product substitution or the delivery of inferior, nonconforming, or untested goods; or the use of bribes, gratuities, conflicts of interest, and a whole range of other techniques designed to influence procurement officials.

Clearly there is more to government-related fraud than the manipulation of contractors and consultants.[43] The Inspector General's Office in the Department of Health and Human Services reported that an estimated $20 billion may be lost annually to fraud in the Medicare program alone.[44]

Consumer Fraud. **Consumer fraud** is the act of causing a consumer to surrender money through deceit or a misrepresentation of a material fact. These offenses range from home repair fraud to mail order fraud (see Figure 2.3). Consumer frauds often appear as confidence games and may take some of the following forms:

consumer fraud
The act of causing a consumer to surrender money through deceit or a misrepresentation of a material fact.

- *Home-improvement fraud.* Consumers have been defrauded through the promise of low-cost home renovation. The home owners give sizable down payments to the contractors, who have no plans to complete the job. In fact, contractors often leave the jurisdiction or declare bankruptcy.

- *Deceptive advertising.* Consumers are often lured into a store by an announcement that a product is priced low for a limited period of time. Once in the store, the customer is told that the product is sold out, and he or she is offered a substitute, typically of inferior quality or at a much higher price. Such schemes are known as "bait-and-switch advertising."

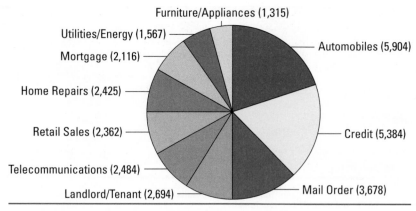

FIGURE 2.3   The Range of Consumer Fraud Complaints, 2001

- *Telemarketing fraud.* You are no doubt familiar with the old adage "If a deal sounds too good to be true, it probably is!" Each day, countless phone calls are made to homes around the United States with a very familiar opening script: "Congratulations! You are a grand prize winner." "Please donate money to. fund or. charity." Telemarketers lure consumers by making attractive offers (e.g., vacations, prizes, discounts on household items) that are nothing more than scams. Once you pay, your name is often added to a "sucker list" that may be sold to other scam telemarketers.

  Of course, not all telemarketing is fraudulent. The New York State Attorney General, for example, estimates that approximately 10 percent of over 140,000 New York businesses using telemarketing to sell their products are frauds.

- *Land fraud.* Consumers are easy prey for land fraud swindlers. Here the pitch is that a certain piece of vacation or retirement property is a worthy investment, many improvements to the property will be made, and many facilities will be made available in the area. Consumers often make purchases of worthless or overvalued land.

- *Business opportunity fraud.* The objective of business opportunity fraud is to persuade a consumer to invest money in a business concern through misrepresentation of its actual worth. Work-at-home frauds are common: Victims are told they can make big money by addressing envelopes at home or performing some other simple task. Consumers lose large sums of money investing in such ventures.

Insurance Fraud.   There are many varieties of insurance fraud: Policyholders defraud insurers, insurers defraud the public, management defrauds the public, and third parties defraud insurers. Policyholder fraud is most often accomplished by the filing of false claims for life, fire, marine, or casualty insurance. Sometimes an employee of the insurance company is part of the fraud and assists in the preparation of the claim. The fraud may be simple—a false death claim—or it may become complex when multiple policies are involved.

A different type of insurance fraud is committed when a small group of people create a "shell" insurance firm without true assets. Policies are sold with no intent to pay legitimate claims. In fact, when large claims are presented to shell insurance companies, the firms disband, leaving a trail of policyholder victims. In yet another form of insurance fraud, middle-and upper-level managers of an insurance company loot the firm's assets by removing funds and debiting them as payments of claims to legitimate or bogus policyholders.[45]

Criminologists Paul Tracy and James Fox conducted a field experiment to find out how many auto-body repair shops in Massachusetts inflate repair estimates to insurance companies, and by how much. These researchers rented two Buick Skylarks with moderate damage, a Volvo 740 GLE with superficial damage, and a Ford Tempo with substantial damage. They then obtained 191 repair estimates, some with a clear understanding that the car was insured, others with the understanding that there was no insurance coverage. The results were unequivocal: Repair estimates for insured vehicles were significantly higher than those for noncovered cars. This finding is highly suggestive of fraud.[46]

Coalition Against Insurance Fraud (CAIF) estimates that the cost of fraud in the industry is as high as $80 billion each year. This cost is passed on to consumers in the form of higher premiums. In fact, the National Insurance Crime Bureau (NICB) calculates that insurance fraud raises the yearly cost of premiums by $300 for the average household. During 2006, 233 cases investigated by the FBI resulted in 53 indictments and 54 convictions, $30 million in Restitutions and $3 million in Seizures.

Tax Fraud. The Internal Revenue Code makes willful failure to file a tax return a misdemeanor. An attempt to evade or defeat a tax, nonpayment of a tax, or willful filing of a fraudulent tax return is a felony. What must the government prove? In order to sustain a conviction, the government must present evidence of income tax due and owing, willful avoidance of payment, and an affirmative act toward tax evasion.[47] How are tax frauds accomplished? Consider the following techniques:

- *Keeping two sets of books.* A person may keep one set of books reflecting actual profits and losses and another set for the purpose of misleading the Internal Revenue Service.
- *Shifting funds.* In order to avoid detection, tax evaders often shift funds continually from account to account, from bank to bank.
- (*Faking forms.* Tax evaders often use faked invoices, create fictitious expenses, conceal assets, and destroy books and records.

The IRS lacks the resources to investigate all suspicious tax forms. When the difficulty of distinguishing between careless mistakes and willful evasion is taken into account, the taxes that go uncollected each year are estimated to exceed $100 billion.[48]

Bribery, Corruption, and Political Fraud. Judges who fix traffic tickets in exchange for political favors, municipal employees who speculate with city funds, businesspeople who bribe local politicians to obtain favorable treatment—all are part of the corruption in our municipal, state, and federal governments. The objectives of such offenses vary including favors, special privileges, services, and business. The actors include officers of corporations as well as of government; indeed, they may belong to the police or the courts.

Bribery and other forms of corruption are ingrained in the political machinery of local and state governments. Examples abound: Mayors of large cities attempt to obtain favors through bribes; manufacturers pay off political figures for favors; municipal officials demand kickbacks from contractors.[49] In response to the seriousness of political corruption and bribery, Congress established two crimes: It is now a felony to accept a bribe or to provide a bribe.[50] Of course, political bribery and other forms of corruption do not stop at the nation's borders. Kickbacks to foreign officials are common practice and countries develop reputations for facilitating corruption and tolerating corruption. (See Table 2.5.)[51] Business sectors develop reputations for corruption as well.

Corruption also can be found in private industry. One firm pays another to induce it to use a product or service; a firm pays its own board of directors or officers to dispense special favors; two or more firms, presumably competitors, secretly agree to charge the same prices for their products or services.

Insider-Related Fraud. Insider-related fraud involves the use and misuse of one's position for pecuniary gain or privilege. This category of offenses includes embezzlement, employee-related thefts, and sale of confidential information.

Embezzlement is the conversion (misappropriation) of property or money with which one is entrusted or for which one has a fiduciary responsibility. Yearly losses attributable to embezzlement are estimated at over $1 billion.[52]

Employee-related thefts of company property are responsible for a significant share of industry losses. Estimates place such losses between $4 billion and $13 billion each year. Criminologists John Clark and Richard Hollinger have estimated that the 35 percent rate of employee pilferage in some corporations results primarily from vocational dissatisfaction and a perception of exploitation.[53] And not only goods and services are taken; time and money are at risk as well. Phony payrolls, fictitious overtime charges, false claims for business-related travel, and the like, are common.

Finally, in a free marketplace where a premium is placed on competition, corporations must guard against the *sale of confidential information* and trade secrets. The best insurance policy is employee loyalty. Where there is no loyalty, or where loyalty is compromised, abuse of confidential information is possible. The purchase of confidential information from employees willing to commit industrial espionage is estimated to be a multimillion-dollar business.[54]

embezzlement
The conversion (misappropriation) of property or money with which one is entrusted or for which one has a fiduciary responsibility.

Rank	Country/ Territory	Number of Respondents	Average Score (Scale 0–10)	Standard Deviation	Margin of Error (at 95% confidence)
1	Switzerland	1744	7.81	2.65	0.12
2	Sweden	1451	7.62	2.66	0.14
3	Australia	1447	7.59	2.62	0.14
4	Austria	1560	7.50	2.60	0.13
5	Canada	1870	7.46	2.70	0.12
6	UK	3442	7.39	2.67	0.09
7	Germany	3873	7.34	2.74	0.09
8	Netherlands	1821	7.28	2.69	0.12
9	Belgium	1329	7.22	2.70	0.15
	US	5401	7.22	2.77	0.07
11	Japan	3279	7.10	2.87	0.10
12	Singapore	1297	6.78	3.04	0.17
13	Spain	2111	6.63	2.73	0.12
14	UAE	1928	6.62	3.09	0.14
15	France	3085	6.50	3.00	0.11
16	Portugal	973	6.47	2.79	0.18
17	Mexico	1765	6.45	3.17	0.15
18	Hong Kong	1556	6.01	3.13	0.16
	Israel	1482	6.01	3.14	0.16
20	Italy	2525	5.94	2.99	0.12
21	South Korea	1930	5.83	2.93	0.13
22	Saudi Arabia	1302	5.75	3.17	0.17
23	Brazil	1317	5.65	3.02	0.16
24	South Africa	1488	5.61	3.11	0.16
25	Malaysia	1319	5.59	3.07	0.17
26	Taiwan	1731	5.41	3.08	0.15
27	Turkey	1755	5.23	3.14	0.15
28	Russia	2203	5.16	3.34	0.14
29	China	3448	4.94	3.29	0.11
30	India	2145	4.62	3.28	0.14

The margin of error at 95 percent confidence is provided to demonstrate the precision of the results. The confidence level indicates that there is a 95 percent probability that the true value of the results lies within the range given by the margin of error above and below each score.

SOURCE: Transparency International Bribe Payers Index 2006.

TABLE 2.5   The Full Results of the BPI 2006

Corporate Crime

The idea of white-collar crime is straightforward. Employees in a business step over the line by pocketing corporate funds. Tax avoiders become tax evaders. Home owners file fraudulent insurance claims. The crimes of white-collar criminals make fascinating television and movie scripts, from complex insider trading scandals to smoke-filled, boiler-room stock frauds. There are, however, other kinds of crimes that take place in the course of a respected and legitimate business enterprise. For the balance of this chapter, we will consider crimes by one or more employees of a corporation that are attributed to the organization itself—corporate crimes. The concept of **corporate crime,** which may be defined as a criminal act committed by one or more employees of a corporation that is subsequently

corporate crime
Criminal act committed by one or more employees of a corporation that is subsequently attributed to the organization itself.

attributed to the organization itself, may be familiar if you have heard or read about the fall of Arthur Andersen and other companies that were convicted—as corporations—of a host of criminal law violations. In fact, the concept of a "corporate" crime is more than a century old.

Frequency and Problems of Definition. There is no central repository for data on the number of cases of corporate crime either in state or federal courts. The best source of data, the United States Sentencing Commission, is less than ideal. The commission compiles information on cases of corporations that have been convicted of a federal crime.

On average, between 200 and 350 corporations are convicted each year in federal courts for offenses ranging from tax law violations to environmental crimes. The vast majority of these companies are small- to medium-size privately held corporations. In fact, over the past decade a large majority of all corporations convicted had fewer than 100 employees. Fewer than 5 percent of all convicted corporations had more than 500 employees.

One problem with corporate crime is defining it. In 1989 the supertanker *Exxon Valdez* ran aground in Prince William Sound, Alaska, spilling 250,000 barrels of oil. The spill became North America's largest ecological disaster. Prosecutors were interested in determining the liability of the captain, his officers, and his crew. But there were additional and far-reaching questions. Was the Exxon Corporation liable? If so, was this a corporate crime? The same problem presented itself with the filing of criminal charges against Arthur Andersen. Should the firm bear the brunt of the crimes of its employees?

Governmental Control of Corporations. Corporate misconduct is covered by a broad range of federal and state statutes, including the federal conspiracy laws; the Racketeer Influenced and Corrupt Organizations (RICO) Act; federal securities laws; mail-fraud statutes; the Federal Corrupt Practices Act; the Federal Election Campaign Act; legislation on lobbying, bribery, and corruption; the Internal Revenue Code (especially regarding major tax crimes, slush funds, and improper payments); the Bank Secrecy Act; and federal provisions on obstruction of justice, perjury, and false statements.

The underlying theory is that if the brain of the artificial person (usually the board of directors of the corporation) authorizes or condones the act in question, the body (the corporation) must suffer criminal penalty. That seems fair enough, except for the fact that if the corporation gets punished—usually by a substantial fine—the penalty falls on the shareholders, most of whom had no say in the corporate decision. And the financial loss resulting from the fine may be passed on to the consumer. The counterargument, of course, is that shareholders often benefit from the illegal actions of the corporation. Thus, in fairness, they should suffer some detriment or loss when and if the corporation is apprehended and convicted.

Reliance on Civil Penalties. Beginning in the nineteenth century, corporations were suspected of wielding monopolistic power to the detriment of consumers. The theory behind monopoly is simple: If you buy out all your competitors or drive them out of business, then you are the only one from whom people can buy the product you sell. So you can set the price, and you set it very high, for your profit and to the detriment of the consumers. The Sugar Trust was one such monopoly. A few powerful businesspeople eliminated all competitors and then drove the price of sugar up, to the detriment of the public. Theodore Roosevelt fought and broke up the Sugar Trust.

In 1890 Congress passed the **Sherman Antitrust Act,** which effectively limited the exercise of monopolies.[55] The act prohibited any contract, conspiracy, or combination of business interests in restraint of foreign or interstate trade. This legislation was followed by the Clayton Antitrust Act (1914), which further curbed the ability of corporations to enrich their shareholders at the expense of the public, by prohibiting such acts as price-fixing.[56] But the remedies this act provided consisted largely of splitting up monopolistic enterprises or imposing damages, sometimes triple damages, for the harm caused. In a strict sense, this was not a use of the criminal law to govern corporate misconduct.

Sherman Antitrust Act
Congress passed this law in 1890 to prohibit any contract, conspiracy, or combination of business interests in restraint of foreign or interstate trade.

Criminal Liability.   A movement away from exclusive reliance on civil remedies was apparent in the 1960s, when it was discovered that corporate mismanagement or negligence on the part of officers or employees could inflict vast harm on identifiable groups of victims. Negligent management at a nuclear power plant can result in the release of radiation and injury to thousands or millions of people. The marketing of an unsafe drug can cause crippling deformities in tens of thousands of bodies.[57] Violation of environmental standards can cause injury and suffering to generations of people who will be exposed to unsafe drinking water, harmful air, or eroded soil. The manufacture of hazardous products can result in multiple deaths.[58]

The problem of corporate criminal liability since the 1960s, then, goes far beyond an individual death or injury. Ultimately, it concerns the health and even the survival of humankind. Nor is the problem confined to the United States. It is a global problem. It thus becomes necessary to look at the variety of activities attributable to corporations which in recent years have been recognized as particularly harmful to society.

When it comes to proving corporate criminal liability, prosecutors face formidable problems: Day-to-day corporate activity has a low level of visibility. Regulatory agencies that monitor corporate conduct have different and uncoordinated recording systems. Offending corporations operate in a multitude of jurisdictions, some of which regard a given activity as criminal, while others do not. Frequently, the facts of a case are not adjudicated at a trial; the parties may simply agree on a settlement approved by the court. Those corporations that are convicted tend to be first offenders without effective compliance programs.

Investigating Corporate Crime.   We know very little about the extent of economic criminality in the United States. There is no national database for the assessment of corporate criminality, and corporations are unlikely to release information about their own wrongdoing. The situation is worse in other countries, especially in the developing countries of Africa south of the Sahara, where few national crime statistics are kept and where corporations are least subject to governmental control. Yet the evidence in regard to corporate crime is gradually coming in.[59]

As we noted earlier, the first American criminologist who was alert to the potential for harm in corporate conduct was Edwin Sutherland, who described the criminal behavior of 70 of the 200 largest production corporations in his 1946 book *White Collar Crime.*[60] An even more ambitious study was completed by Marshall B. Clinard and Peter C. Yeager, who investigated corporations within the jurisdiction of 25 federal agencies during 1975 and 1976. Of 477 major American corporations whose conduct was regulated by these agencies, 60 percent had violated the law. Of the 300 violating corporations, 38 (or 13 percent) accounted for 52 percent of all violations charged in 1975 and 1976, an average of 23.5 violations per firm.[61] Large corporations were found to be the chief violators, and a few particular industries (pharmaceutical, automotive) were the most likely to violate the law.

According to Clinard and Yeager, what makes it so difficult to curb corporate crime is the enormous political power corporations wield in the shaping and administration of the laws that govern their conduct. This is particularly the case in regard to multinational corporations that wish to operate in developing countries. The promise of jobs and development by a giant corporation is a temptation too great for the governments of many such countries to resist. They would rather have employment opportunities that pollute air and water than unemployment in a clean environment. Government officials in some Third World countries can be bribed to create or maintain a legal climate favorable to the business interests of the corporation, even though it may be detrimental to the people of the host country.

The work of Sutherland, Clinard, Yeager, and other traditional scholars, as well as that of a group of radical criminologists,[62] hearings on white-collar and corporate crime held by the Subcommittee on Crime of the House Judiciary Committee, under the leadership of Congress member John Conyers, Jr. in 1978; the consumer protection movement, spearheaded by Ralph Nader; and investigative reporting by the press have all contributed to public awareness of large corporations' power to inflict harm on large population groups.

In 1975 James Q. Wilson still considered such crime to be insignificant,[63] but more recent studies show that the public considers corporate criminality at least as serious as, if not more serious than, street crime. Marvin Wolfgang and his associates found in a national survey that Americans regard illegal retail price-fixing (the artificial setting of prices at a high level, without regard for the demand for the product) as a more serious crime than robbery committed with a lead pipe.[64] Within the sphere of corporate criminality perhaps no other group of offenses has had so great an impact on public consciousness as crimes against the environment. Enforcement of major environmental statutes has been weak in the past. There is some evidence that this is changing.

The Future of White-Collar and Corporate Crime. Some of the most respected names on Wall Street are under investigation or indictment. Others have been criminally convicted and are bankrupt—desperately reinventing themselves or out of business entirely. From WorldCom to Merrill Lynch, the very companies that made billions for investors in the 1990s are both perpetrators and victims of fraud, mismanagement, and conflicts of interest. And repercussions from the scandals continue even if it is no longer "headline" news. Recently, ten Wall Street firms were forced to pay $1.4 billion to resolve charges that each firm issued biased research reports and hyped stocks. The firms represent the cream of the crop on the "Street"—Credit Suisse First Boston, Citigroup/Salomon Smith Barney, Bear Stearns, J. P. Morgan Chase, Lehman Brothers, UBS Warburg, Merrill Lynch, Morgan Stanley, Piper Jaffray, and Goldman Sachs.

The icon of this wave of corporate scandals is a company that now lays in ruin, bankrupt. Some of its property is still up for auction. If you are ever on eBay, you can buy a copy of the company's ethics code put up for sale by former employees looking to make a couple of dollars and prove the point that what companies say they are doing and what they actually do are often two very different things. In 2000 this company had worldwide assets of more than $65 billion and revenue of $101 billion. If you have guessed that this company was the pride of Houston, Texas, you are right! As of 2000, *Fortune* magazine called it "The Most Innovative Company in America." That year, the same magazine ranked it twenty-second of the "100 Best Companies to Work for in America."

One cannot imagine working for a more ethical and socially minded company. In its 2000 *Corporate Responsibility Annual Report,* the chair and CEO of this company, Kenneth Lay, articulated four of its guiding principles:

Respect: We will work to foster mutual respect with communities and stakeholders who are affected by our operations; we will treat others as we would like to be treated ourselves.

Integrity: We will examine the impacts, positive and negative, of our business on the environment and on society, and will integrate human health, social, and environmental considerations into our internal management and value system.

Communication: We will strive to foster understanding and support with our stakeholders and communities, as well as measure and communicate our performance.

Excellence: We will continue to improve our performance and will encourage our business partners and suppliers to adhere to the same standards.

The name of this company, in case you have not yet guessed it, is Enron Corporation. Enron was created in 1985 following a merger of Houston Natural Gas and InterNorth, a natural gas company with headquarters in Omaha, Nebraska. Both companies were in the business of transporting and selling natural gas and their merger created a network of more than 37,000 miles of gas pipeline. Soon after the merger, however, deregulation of the nation's energy markets, including the natural gas market, posed a significant challenge for Enron's business model. With the help of the large and prestigious consulting firm of McKinsey &

Co., Enron diversified, going into the business of creating its own natural gas market, that is, buying and selling gas through contracts while controlling costs and prices.

Jeff Skilling, the young McKinsey consultant who brought the idea of Enron creating its own energy market, was hired as chair and CEO of Enron Finance Corporation, later becoming president and chief operating officer of Enron. And the rest is history, a very sad page of business history. The history of Enron is marked by a single employee corporate whistle-blower Sherron Watkins, who sent a one-page anonymous letter to Ken Lay (then chief executive officer) immediately after Jeff Skilling resigned, unexpectedly. Portions of it read:

> Has Enron become a risky place to work? For those of us who didn't get rich over the last few years, can we afford to stay? . . . The spotlight will be on us, the market just can't accept that Skilling is leaving his dream job. I think that the valuation issues can be fixed and reported with other good will writedowns to occur in 2002. How do we fix the Raptor and Condor deals? They unwind in 2002 and 2003, we will have to pony up Enron stock and that won't go unnoticed.
>
> To the layman on the street, it will look like we recognized funds flow of $800 million from merchant asset sales in 1999 by selling to a vehicle (Condor) that we capitalized with a promise of Enron stock in later years. Is that really funds flow or is it cash from equity issuance?
>
> We have recognized over $550 million of fair value gains on stocks via our swaps with Raptor. Much of that stock has declined significantly—Avici by 98 percent from $178 million, to $5 million; the New Power Company by 80 percent from $40 a share, to $6 a share. The value in the swaps won't be there for Raptor, so once again Enron will issue stock to offset these losses. Raptor is an LJM entity. It sure looks to the layman on the street that we are hiding losses in a related company and will compensate that company with Enron stock in the future.
>
> I am incredibly nervous that we will implode in a wave of accounting scandals. My eight years of Enron work history will be worth nothing on my résumé, the business world will consider the past successes as nothing but an elaborate accounting hoax. Skilling is resigning now for "personal reasons" but I would think he wasn't having fun, looked down the road and knew this stuff was unfixable and would rather abandon ship now than resign in shame in two years.

You need not understand the accounting alchemy that Enron used to defraud investors, for example, special purpose entities like Raptor or Condor and "related party transactions and disclosures." Many accountants still find these technicalities difficult to explain. Suffice it to say, Enron was built on an accounting house of cards. When that house tumbled down, a host of victims emerged, from the thousands of loyal and hardworking Enron employees to countless investors whose pensions and retirement plans dramatically lost value. Once nearly a $90 per share stock, Enron stock certificates trade on eBay as collectors' items. The accounting firm that offered advice and counsel to Enron, Arthur Andersen, LLP, was indicted and convicted of obstruction of justice for shredding thousands of documents relating to Enron audits. They, too, suffered corporate death. Tens of thousands of Andersen employees sought employment elsewhere as the accounting world watched in horror. It was common to refer to Andersen as one of the top five accounting firms. Now there are four.

Most important, Enron and the fall of Arthur Andersen sent a strong signal that Wall Street has a problem with corporate governance, that is, the way in which a corporation is managed and overseen. Principles of corporate governance require that both senior management and the board of directors participate in the affairs of the company. But they do so differently. Senior managers run the day-to-day operations of the company. The board of directors has the special function of providing an independent oversight of senior managers—an independent check on managers. This is accomplished through audit committees, finance committees, and compensation committees that tirelessly review the health of the company. In recent years, boards were called upon to see that systems of internal controls are implemented and monitored.

What happened to the systems of control and governance structures of Enron? Why did they fail? Answers are difficult to find, particularly because Enron followed many of the "best practices" of corporate governance, including an independent board of directors of competent outsiders. Enron had all of the trappings of an ethical, Fortune 500 company with a bright future. Until answers to the many questions of Enron emerge, it is only fair to ask: How significant is the problem of corporate misgovernance in the United States? To this the only answer is that the future of Wall Street and its perceived legitimacy hang in the balance.

Organized Crime

Organized crime got its start in the United States early in this century when immigrants from the region of Sicily in Italy replicated their traditional family structure in organizing criminal activity.[65] A traditional Sicilian family has been described as an extended family, or clan. This family (*famiglia*) is hierarchically organized and administered by the head of the family (the Capo *di famiglia*) to whom all members owe obedience and loyalty. Upon migration to the United States, members of Sicilian families soon found that the social environment was hostile. They could not find a legitimate means to achieve the wealth they sought. Some found themselves involved in a system of politics in which patronage and protection were dispensed by corrupt politicians and petty hoodlums from earlier immigrant groups—among them the German, Irish, and Jewish. The Sicilian family structure helped its members to survive in this hostile environment. It also created the organizational basis that permitted them to respond to the opportunity created when, on January 16, 1920, the Eighteenth Amendment to the Constitution outlawed the manufacture, sale, and transportation of alcoholic beverages. During the years of Prohibition in the 1920s, Al Capone, Lucky Luciano, Frank Costello, and many other Sicilians became well-known mobsters. Sicilian families (frequently referred to as the Mafia) were so successful in controlling bootlegging, gambling, loansharking, prostitution, labor racketeering, drug trafficking, and other illegal enterprises that they were able to take over many legitimate businesses. In recent years other organized crime groups—Latin Americans, Jamaicans, Israelis, Japanese, Russians, Chinese—have gained major influence.

Starting in the 1930s and continuing to the present, major investigations have established the magnitude of organized crime in the United States. Specific legislation has been designed to control it. Many cases have been successfully prosecuted under the Racketeer Influenced and Corrupt Organizations (RICO) Act. *Racketeering* refers to the extortion of money or other advantages by threats of violence, by blackmail, or by unlawful interference with business or employment. RICO attacks racketeering activities by prohibiting the investment of funds derived from racketeering in any business that is engaged in interstate commerce. In addition, witnesses from within organized crime have been more willing to testify since, under the **Federal Witness Protection Program,** enacted as part of the Organized Crime Control Act of 1970, they are assured of a new identity, thereby protecting them against revenge. Currently over 14,000 persons are in this program.

The activities of the Mafia appear to have shifted from the once extremely violent bootlegging and street crime operations to a far more sophisticated level of criminal activity.[66] Modern organized crime has assumed international dimensions.[67] It extends not only to international drug traffic, but also to such legitimate enterprises as real estate and trade in securities, as well as to many other lucrative business enterprises. This transition has been accomplished both by extortion and by entry with laundered money derived from illegitimate activity. It is tempting to wonder whether we may be witnessing the same kind of metamorphosis that occurred a century ago, when the robber barons became legitimate business tycoons and, ultimately, philanthropists.

The New Ethnic Diversity in Organized Crime.   Organized crime is not necessarily synonymous with the Mafia. Other groups also operate in the United States. Foremost among them are the Colombian crime families, whose brutality is unrivaled by any other organized-crime group, and Bolivian, Peruvian, and Jamaican crime families, which since

Federal Witness Protection Program
Program under the Organized Crime Control Act of 1970 to protect witnesses who testify in court by relocating them and assigning them new identities.

EMERGING ETHNIC ORGANIZED-CRIME GROUPS

Over a decade ago a dramatic event on our own shoreline opened our eyes to a highly dangerous method of getting illegal immigrants into the United States.

The *Golden Venture* had run aground, or was run aground, on one of New York City's beaches during a storm in June 1993. Waves pounded the old rust bucket. Hundreds of Chinese passengers jumped overboard into the cold waters of the Atlantic, seeking safety ashore. Six drowned. A few made their escape into the anonymity of the big city. Most were rounded up by law enforcement officers.

The ship was one of many operated by Chinese organized-crime groups to ferry illegal would-be immigrants into the United States. This particular vessel—like much of the smuggling network—was controlled by twenty-seven-year-old Guo Liang Qi, who had become crime boss by executing his competitors and lieutenants. Guo is now in custody in Hong Kong, and two of his brothers have been killed by rivals in Teaneck, New Jersey. Their business—undoubtedly now carried on by others—is as ruthless as it is profitable: Each illegal immigrant brings the crime group a minimum of $30,000. A part of this sum has to be paid prior to their departure; the rest is paid upon their arrival in the United States. And if there is no payment, the immigrant is enslaved—often in chains—in some dungeon in Chinatown, where he or she has to work off the debt washing dishes or working in a massage parlor. Many are tortured or killed. The Chinese slave trade is now a multibillion-dollar enterprise.

People smuggling is not the only illegal business run by Chinese organized-crime groups. According to criminologist Ko-lin Chin, an expert in this area:

> Chinese crime groups are now considered by U.S. law enforcement authorities as the second most serious organized crime problem in America, right behind the Italian Mafia. In America, Chinese crime groups such as the triads, tongs, street gangs, heroin trafficking organizations, and human smuggling groups or snakeheads are active in a variety of crimes such as extortion, illegal gambling, prostitution, kidnapping, credit card fraud, money laundering, heroin trafficking, and alien smuggling. They are also involved in legitimate businesses. These legitimate businesses not only facilitate and conceal their criminal operations but also enable them to establish themselves as businessmen rather than "criminals."[1]

> "And if there is no payment, the immigrant is enslaved—often in chains—in some dungeon in Chinatown."

Other ethnic groups have their own criminal organizations. The end of the Cold War and the collapse of the Soviet Union have opened new windows of opportunity for Russian entrepreneurs—legal and illegal.[2] A thriving Russian colony in Brighton Beach, New York, is the seat of Russian gangs as ruthless as those of any other ethnic origin. Working between Moscow and New York, they smuggle anything worth smuggling, including nuclear material, gold, and Russian army surplus—often passing it off as a high-grade Japanese product. Russian organized crime has a hold on the

the 1970s have organized the production, transportation, and distribution within the United States of cocaine and marijuana.

Another form of organized crime, initiated by disillusioned veterans of the Korean War and reinforced by veterans of Vietnam, appears in the outlaw motorcycle gangs. Among them are the Hell's Angels, the Pagans, the Outlaws, the Sons of Silence, and the Bandidos. All are organized along military lines; all are devoted to violence; all are involved in the production and distribution of narcotics and other drugs. Many members are also involved in other criminal activities, including extortion and prostitution, trafficking in stolen motorcycles and parts, and dealing in automatic weapons and explosives.

Among other organized groups engaged in various criminal activities are Chinese gangs (see Figure 2.4), the so-called Israeli Mafia, the recently emerging Russian–Jewish Mafia, Jamaican posses, and the "Tattooed Men" of Japan's Yakuza, whose Yamaguchi-Gumi family alone has over 56,000 members, or nearly twenty times the number of fully initiated Italian organized-crime members in all the crews of all the families in the United States. All these groups have demonstrated potential for great social disruption.[68]

sale of bootlegged gasoline, distributed throughout the United States. Members use extortion and murder to strengthen their operations. Some of the gang leaders are experienced criminals with long histories of economic offenses in Russia. Russians call them "thieves-in-law."

Some law enforcement authorities and some in the media describe Russian criminals operating in the United States as being structured like La Cosa Nostra, even tracing their roots back to the Solntsevskaya gang, the largest gang in the former Soviet Union. Another view is that Russian organized crime has not yet developed a complex organizational structure and that the persons involved in the various enterprises are not rigidly controlled. Instead, they create partnerships for various illicit activities. There is little loyalty based on shared ethnicity.[3]

Gangs made up of immigrant Albanians and former Yugoslavians have been committing burglaries along the East Coast since the early 1990s. Their targets are retail shops, banks, and automated teller machines. They specialize in supermarket safes because these stores generally have a great deal of cash on hand. Their techniques are highly sophisticated, rather than run-of-the-mill break and enter. The burglars rarely carry guns; every detail is carefully planned (oxygen tanks may be brought for their safe-cracking torches); and they are equipped with an arsenal of tools, gloves, and walkie-talkies. Often they cut phone lines to set off alarms, wait until the police come and go, and then strike.

Korean, Cambodian, and Laotian gangs have sprung up in the middle of the country. Other groups hail from the Pacific Islands. The Tongan Crips gangsters and Sons of Samoa, demonstrating their macho values, have spread fear in once quiet, pastoral Utah. The Vietnamese have established a reputation as "housebreakers"; they burglarize the homes of other, wealthier Vietnamese immigrants. And then there are the deadly Jamaican posses, specializing in the drug and weapons trade.

No longer does the Italian Mafia enjoy a monopoly on organized crime in America, and no longer is organized crime a national phenomenon. Ethnic organized groups exist side-by-side; many operate nationally or in international networks. They reflect America's ethnic composition, indeed that of the world. It was hard enough to infiltrate the Italian Mafia. Law enforcement is not quite ready to tackle the new problem created by such a vast array of ethnically divergent gangs operating at the same time.

Questions for Discussion

1. Dealing with gangs may require infiltrating them. What if there are no young police officers from the gangs' ethnic groups? What else can be done?

2. Global migration is changing rapidly, due to a flurry of regional political–economic developments. Countries like the United States are likely destinations for migrants, some of whom are imported by organized criminal groups. What should criminal justice agencies do to anticipate or prevent the potential impact on crime and the criminal justice system of these new immigrants?

SOURCES

1. Personal communication from Ko-lin Chin, author of *Smuggled Chinese Immigrants in America* (Philadelphia: Temple University Press, forthcoming); and *Chinatown Gangs: Extortion, Enterprise and Ethnicity* (New York: Oxford University Press, 1996).

2. Dennis Kenney and James O. Finckenauer, *Organized Crime in America* (Belmont, CA: Wadsworth, 1995).

3. James O. Finckenauer and Elin J. Waring, *Russian Mafia in America: Crime, Immigration, and Culture* (Boston: Northeastern University Press, 1998).

Crimes against Public Morality: Drugs, Alcohol, and Vice

The category of "crimes against public morality" includes a variety of criminal activities that were once known as "victimless" crimes. Perhaps that is because it was assumed that people who engage in them choose to do so. They include drug use, alcohol abuse, and prostitution and other sex acts between consenting adults. Often no one complains to the police about being victimized by such consensual activities. But contemporary forms of these activities may entail massive victimizations. That is especially true of a broad range of drug-related crimes.

Drug-Related Crime. In Queens, New York, there is no need to leave your home to buy drugs. You just call your local drug delivery service, say you're "hungry," and a pager-carrying delivery person quickly arrives with cocaine or marijuana—just like a pizza delivery service. If you aren't happy with the batch, you get a discount on the next one.[69] In Miami's Coconut Grove, you don't have to get out of your car to buy a $15 "cap" (capsule) of "boy" (heroin) from the local vendors. Even though their illegal drug marketplace is well known to law enforcement, it remains open.[70]

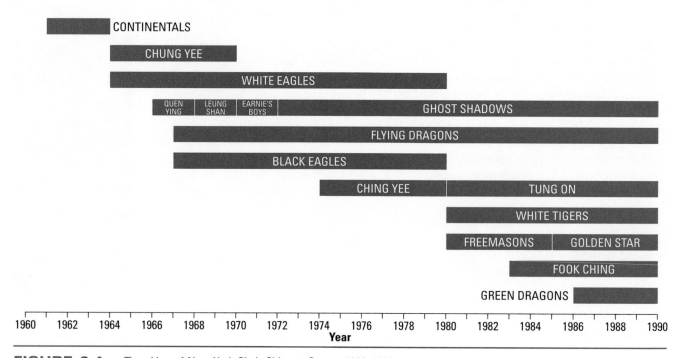

FIGURE 2.4   Time Line of New York City's Chinese Gangs: 1960–1990

SOURCE: Ko-lin Chin, *Chinese Subculture and Criminality* (New York: Greenwood Press, 1990), p. 76.

On a college campus in the Midwest, a crowd sits in the basement of a fraternity house drinking beer and smoking pot through the night. At a beachfront house in California three young professional couples get together for a barbecue. After dinner, they sit down at a card table in the family room. On a mirror, someone lines up a white powdery substance into rows about 1/8-inch wide and an inch long. Through rolled-up paper they breathe the powder into their nostrils and await the "rush" of cocaine.

The "drug problem" in the United States is not a single problem but a broad range of problems that involves all social classes and in one way or another touches most people's lives. Moreover, it is a global problem involving vast international networks. There are growers, smugglers (who import drugs from foreign countries), wholesalers, and dealers (who sell drugs on the streets); there are corrupt criminal justice officials, abusers who endanger people's lives through negligence (pilots, bus drivers), addict mothers, and even unborn addict babies. Many of the crimes discussed in this chapter are drug related.

A national household survey found that in 2006 an estimated 112 million Americans (46 percent of the population) reported illicit drug use at least once in their lifetime.[71] In the 1980s cocaine constituted the country's major drug problem. The popularity of cocaine waned by the 1990s. The same is not true for crack (a derivative of cocaine), however, which spread to the inner-city population. Crack is cheaper than powdered cocaine, fast-acting, and powerful. Though individual doses are inexpensive, once a person is hooked on crack, a daily supply can run between $100 and $250. The use of heroin is less pervasive, but it is once again becoming popular on the streets. Marijuana continues to be the substance (other than alcohol) most frequently abused in the United States. The national household survey had shown a decline in its use between 1978 and 1991 among high school seniors. The most recent data demonstrate that marijuana use is still declining. (See Figure 2.5.)[72]

Use of illicit drugs is most prevalent among those who are between the ages of eighteen and thirty-four, but a substantial number of children twelve and younger have tried cocaine, marijuana, and other drugs. The most common drugs abused in America, in order of the numbers of people who use them, are: marijuana, cocaine, hallucinogens, stimulants, inhalants, tranquilizers, crack, and heroin.

Lifetime Drug Use, High School Seniors*

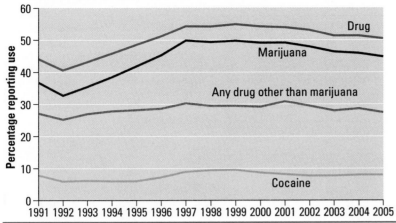

FIGURE 2.5   Lifetime Drug Use by High School Seniors, by Drug Type: 1991 to 2005

*2005 National Survey on Drug Use and Health (http://www.ojp.usdoj. gov/bjs/dcf/du.htm) reports that 112 million Americans age 12 and older (46 percent population) have used an illicit drug in their lifetime; 14 percent within past year, 8 percent within past month. Marijuana was the most common drug, followed by cocaine.

SOURCE: The National Institute on Drug Abuse, *Monitoring the Future Study* (Washington, DC: U.S. Department of Justice, 2005), p. 10.

Drugs and Crime.   Until recently, information about drugs and crime comes from a nationwide program called Arrestee Drug Abuse Monitoring (ADAM). In 1999, the ADAM program collected data about drug use among 30,000 adult males arrested at thirty-four sites and 10,000 adult females arrested at thirty-two sites. Drug abuse was monitored through drug urinalysis and self-report information. The investigation shows that at each site a majority of its adult male arrestees tested positive for at least one drug. The same was true of adult female arrestees in twenty-two of thirty-two sites where they were studied. The crack/cocaine epidemic is easing in many ADAM cities, but the problem is only just beginning in others. Opiate use remained low compared to cocaine and marijuana in the sample. However, more than 75 percent of arrestees who tested positive for opiates also tested positive for other drugs.[73] These data remained consistent through 2003 (Table 2.6).

Alcohol and Crime.   Alcohol abuse is another major social problem. In the United States, the average annual consumption of alcoholic beverages by each person fourteen years of age and over is equivalent to 591 cans of beer, 115 bottles of wine, and 35 fifths of liquor; this is more than the average individual consumption of milk and coffee.[74] Alcohol continues to grow in popularity among teenagers and young adults. On campuses across the nation, "binge drinking," defined as frequently guzzling five or more drinks at a time, has become a popular pastime in collegiate culture. Some of the alcohol-related problems that affect the criminal justice system are violent crime, drunken driving, negligence at the workplace, and public intoxication.

National surveys of inmates in prisons and jails show that approximately 30 percent of the offenders incarcerated for violent crimes (particularly assaults) admitted the use of alcohol and/or drugs immediately before the crimes.[75] Results from ADAM support this finding. (See Table 2.7.) Among inmates convicted of homicide, assault, rape, and robbery, 34 to 45 percent described themselves as heavy drinkers.[76] The role of alcohol in violent family disputes has been increasingly recognized.

Each year there are nearly one and a half million arrests for driving under the influence of alcohol, and over a million persons are injured in alcohol-related crashes.[77] When Cari Lightner, age thirteen, was killed in May 1980 by a drunken driver (who had been arrested a few days before on a DUI charge, "driving while under the influence"), her mother Candy

Primary City	% of Arrestees Testing Positive for:						
	Any of 5 Drugs*	Multiple Drugs (Any of 5)	Any of 9 Drugs**	Multiple Drugs (Any of 9)	Any of 9 Drugs or Alcohol**	Multiple 9 Drugs or Alcohol**	Interviews with Completed Urine Tests (%)
Albany, NY	72.3	19.9	74.7	22.3	78.2	29.3	67.7
Albuquerque, NM	66.6	25.2	70.3	30.1	74.6	35.6	95.3
Anchorage, AK	66.3	18.0	66.6	22.5	70.7	28.5	90.1
Atlanta, GA	72.4	22.8	73.5	24.1	77.2	27.7	93.4
Birmingham, AL	66.1	19.8	67.5	22.6	72.1	29.1	87.8
Boston, MA	80.3	16.8	82.7	18.4	84.3	20.8	85.6
Charlotte, NC	65.9	17.4	66.8	20.7	69.5	23.7	86.8
Chicago, IL	86.0	38.1	86.0	40.3	86.2	41.9	91.6
Cleveland, OH	74.5	25.0	74.9	27.3	77.8	31.7	93.6
Dallas, TX	62.3	21.7	63.8	24.4	67.1	27.5	95.7
Denver, CO	66.4	23.3	72.6	27.2	75.0	31.3	95.7
Des Moines, IA	68.7	22.1	71.3	24.8	76.2	31.0	92.0
Honolulu, HI	62.9	21.4	64.7	23.6	72.6	27.6	84.7
Houston, TX	61.7	16.1	61.9	23.8	62.9	24.4	96.6
Indianapolis, IN	64.6	22.4	66.4	27.2	70.8	30.8	97.8
Las Vegas, NV	65.3	22.4	70.0	26.3	75.7	30.1	96.7
Los Angeles, CA	68.6	26.3	68.9	26.9	71.7	29.2	80.9
Miami, FL	63.2	26.9	64.7	28.5	68.6	29.5	95.9
Minneapolis, MN	64.7	19.3	66.1	21.7	71.6	25.5	92.2
New Orleans, LA	78.4	29.4	79.6	32.3	82.4	36.8	98.7
New York, NY	69.7	22.2	72.7	26.7	73.9	28.2	95.2
Oklahoma City, OK	70.9	25.3	73.5	31.9	77.5	34.7	98.4
Omaha, NE	71.0	24.9	72.9	27.6	78.2	33.0	88.4
Philadelphia, PA	67.0	28.2	68.8	32.9	71.2	35.1	91.8
Phoenix, AZ	74.1	27.8	76.8	31.5	80.8	36.2	95.0
Portland, OR	71.5	29.8	72.7	31.5	75.9	34.2	94.6
Rio Arriba, NM	77.2	34.6	80.7	46.0	87.4	51.8	90.8
Sacramento, CA	78.9	32.2	81.1	36.6	83.8	39.9	98.1
Salt Lake City, UT	56.2	21.1	60.0	22.3	62.9	25.1	95.7
San Antonio, TX	59.6	23.4	65.2	28.8	68.0	32.3	96.6
San Diego, CA	66.8	23.9	71.2	27.4	73.4	28.6	96.4
San Jose, CA	62.8	25.2	63.7	27.0	66.5	29.3	90.8
Seattle, WA	67.3	25.3	69.4	28.8	73.1	32.4	92.2
Spokane, WA	69.5	25.1	70.4	29.0	74.7	30.8	94.8
Tampa, FL	60.1	19.5	62.1	22.5	67.7	26.4	86.6
Tucson, AZ	73.3	31.3	76.4	33.4	80.1	38.6	89.3
Tulsa, OK	69.8	23.6	71.9	29.9	80.0	34.0	98.1
Washington, D.C.	65.6	17.7	65.8	21.1	70.9	26.6	81.8
Woodbury, IA	41.6	10.3	41.6	11.1	52.2	12.8	93.4
Median	67.0	23.4	70.3	27.2	73.9	30.1	93.4

*The 5 drugs are cocaine, marijuana, mathamphistamina, opiates, and phencyclidine (PCP).

**The 9 drugs are barbiturates, benzodiazepines, cocaine, marijuana, methadone, methamphetamine, opiates phencyclidine (PCP), and propoxyphene.

SOURCE: Zhiwei Zhang, ADAM, Drug and Alcohol Use and Related Matters Among Arrestees.

TABLE 2.6   Urine Test Results on Any or Multiple Drug or Alcohol Use among Adult Male Arrestees 2003

Primary City	Arrestees Testing Positive for Alcohol (%)	Binge Drinking, Past 30 Days[a]	Heavy Drinking, Past 30 Days[b]	At Risk for Alcohol Dependence[c] (%)
Albany, NY	14.5	54.4	32.4	33.9
Albuquerque, NM	14.0	61.1	35.0	37.2
Anchorage, AK	12.1	68.3	33.0	38.2
Atlanta, GA	9.2	41.2	26.6	28.6
Birmingham, AL	12.6	44.0	23.1	23.3
Boston, MA	4.7	54.8	30.1	35.5
Charlotte, NC	7.5	38.9	21.9	21.0
Chicago, IL	2.3	37.0	20.9	20.2
Cleveland, OH	9.1	48.6	32.9	27.9
Dallas, TX	8.1	41.1	21.4	21.3
Denver, CO	8.4	54.1	29.6	28.6
Des Moines, IA	11.8	46.6	24.6	24.5
Honolulu, HI	13.7	47.6	28.7	27.8
Houston, TX	1.8	47.9	27.6	22.6
Indianapolis, IN	10.0	50.2	29.9	36.1
Las Vegas, NV	11.2	48.3	25.7	30.3
Los Angeles, CA	6.6	42.4	20.0	24.3
Miami, FL	5.0	45.1	21.0	22.6
Minneapolis, MN	11.5	51.5	24.6	30.9
New Orleans, LA	9.5	47.0	34.9	20.9
New York, NY	2.8	35.0	23.5	20.0
Oklahoma City, OK	8.4	51.1	29.1	33.1
Omaha, NE	13.0	45.2	23.2	24.9
Philladelphia, PA	4.9	37.4	21.7	23.4
Phoenix, AZ	10.8	45.6	25.5	26.0
Portland, OR	7.0	42.0	24.1	32.3
Rio Arriba, NM	20.2	65.7	32.9	46.2
Sacramento, CA	9.6	47.7	28.3	31.0
Salt Lake City, UT	6.7	48.1	26.1	27.1
San Antonio, TX	7.7	57.5	31.1	28.8
San Diego, CA	4.5	54.6	29.4	33.7
San Jose, CA	6.0	47.7	23.2	30.0
Seattle, WA	9.6	47.5	25.6	28.3
Spokane, WA	6.8	52.6	25.9	35.2
Tempa, FL	11.2	53.1	29.0	30.6
Tucson, AZ	11.0	54.3	30.4	32.8
Tulsa, OK	13.5	56.0	33.7	36.6
Washington, D.C.	12.1	25.6	12.7	15.0
Woodbury, IA	13.1	48.7	22.9	23.1
Median	9.5	47.9	26.1	28.6

[a]Binge drinking is defined in the National Household Survey on Drug Abuse as consumption of five or more drinks on at least one occasion in a month.

[b]Heavy drinking is defined in the National Household Survey on Drug Abuse as consumption of five or more drinks on the same occasion on five or more days in a month.

[c]Dependences, an ideication of need for treatment, is measured by a clinically based dependency screen regarding alcohol use experience during the prior year.

NOTE: Questions were asked of arrestees who reported consuming alcohol.

TABLE 2.7 Alcohol Use and Risk for Dependence among Adult Male Arrestees 2003

took action almost immediately to push for new legislation that would mandate stiffer penalties for drunk driving. By the end of that year, Mrs. Lightner had organized the Governor's Task Force on Drinking and Driving in California. Her advocacy group, Mothers Against Drunk Driving (MADD), was soon in the national spotlight. Remove Intoxicated Drivers (RID) and Students Against Drunk Driving (SADD) have joined the campaign.

Sex-Related Offenses.   The last group of offenses to be mentioned are those existing under statutes that seek to regulate sexual morality, or at least to document society's views on sexual morality. These range from the prohibition of sexual activity other than consensual spousal intercourse (thus covering "adultery," "fornication" or "lewd cohabitation," and "sodomy"; "prostitution" offenses; and others) to the sale and distribution of obscene or indecent material.

Such legislation has had no discernible effect on human behavior, and law enforcement agencies have always dreaded the task of enforcing it. Officers often find such enforcement efforts to be futile, demeaning, and corrupting. Legislative statements of morality often lack popular support and consensus. However, in recent years women active in a number of important organizations have tried to shape public attitudes on such matters as prostitution (more specifically the exploitation of prostitution), sexual harassment, and pornography.

Counting Crime

In this section we examine the major sources of information that are used most frequently to estimate the extent of crime in the United States. We then discuss the amount of crime and who is arrested for committing it.

Sources of Information

Estimates of the extent and nature of crime in the United States come primarily from two sources: the Federal Bureau of Investigation's Uniform Crime Reports, based on information compiled by the police; and the National Crime Victimization Survey, which measures crime based on reports by victims.

Uniform Crime Reports.   When your local paper reports that the number of robberies has doubled or that every thirty minutes (2006) a murder takes place, where do the reporters get their numbers? More likely than not, they have relied on information "known to the police," which the FBI compiles into the Uniform Crime Reports (UCR), published annually. Each month approximately 16,000 city, county, and state law enforcement agencies, covering 97 percent of the total population, voluntarily send information on twenty-nine types of offenses brought to their attention, whether or not an arrest has been made.

index crimes
The eight major crimes included in Part I of the UCR: criminal homicide, forcible rape, robbery, aggravated assault, burglary, larceny-theft, motor vehicle theft, and arson.

The UCR separate offenses into two major groups: Part I and Part II. Part I offenses include eight crimes divided into crimes against the person (criminal homicide, forcible rape, robbery, aggravated assault) and crimes against property (burglary, larceny-theft, motor vehicle theft, and arson). Because these **index crimes** are serious, they tend to be reported to the police more reliably than others, and they are used collectively as a *crime index,* or indicator, of changes in crime rates over time. Except for traffic violations, all twenty-one other offenses are Part II crimes. They include fraud, embezzlement, weapons offenses, vandalism, and simple assaults. Since crime definitions differ from state to state, the UCR use a rather broad set of descriptions; while they may not be legally correct in any one state, these descriptions encompass most criminal events in each category. Moreover, there are some crimes that are not included in any of the UCR categories, for example, stalking and hate crime.

In addition to the number and rates of reported crimes, the UCR include the number of crimes where an arrest has been made ("cleared by arrest"), information about the circumstances of crimes (such as time, place, and geographic region), descriptions of offenders (age, gender, and race), and the distribution of law enforcement personnel. Despite the fact that the UCR are among the main sources of crime statistics, the reports have their limitations. The statistics present the amount of crime known to law enforcement agencies, but they do not reveal how many crimes have actually been committed. Another serious limitation is the

Crime Clock 2006	
Every 22.2 Seconds	**One Violent Crime**
Every 30.9 minutes	One murder
Every 5.7 minutes	One forcible rape
Every 1.2 minutes	One robbery
Every 36.6 seconds	One aggravated assault
Every 3.2 Seconds	**One Property Crime**
Every 14.4 seconds	One burglary
Every 4.8 seconds	One larceny-theft
Every 26.4 seconds	One motor vehicle theft

FIGURE 2.6 Crime Clock, 2006

Uniform Crime Reports—2007
(Washington, D.C.: United
States Printing Office, 2007, p. 5).

fact that when several crimes are committed in one event, only the most serious offense is included in the UCR; the others go unreported. At the same time, when certain other crimes are committed, each individual act is counted as a separate offense. If a person robs a group of six people, for example, the UCR list one robbery. But if a person assaults six people, the UCR list six assaults. UCR data are further obscured by the fact that they do not differentiate between completed and attempted acts.

Improving the Uniform Crime Reports. In 1986 the International Association of Chiefs of Police, the National Sheriffs' Association, and the state-level UCR programs joined forces with the FBI to deal with the limitations of the UCR. A new reporting system was developed, called the National Incident-Based Reporting System (NIBRS; for an example of NIBRS data, see Table 2.8). Reporting by local law enforcement agencies to the NIBRS is voluntary and coexists with the UCR. Each offense is considered an "incident" and information is recorded about the offender, victim, property, and so forth. The NIBRS is a computerized system. Local agencies transmit by computer their crime data directly to state- and federal-level agencies, reducing the need for standardized reporting forms. The implementation of NIBRS depends on the resources and abilities of law enforcement agencies. Thus far, nineteen states contribute data in the NIBRS format; other states are testing the system or are in various planning stages.

The NIBRS is a major attempt to improve the collection of crime data. But it deals only with crimes that come to the attention of the police. What about those crimes that remain unreported? For this "dark figure of crime" we rely on victimization data.

Victimization Surveys. Victimization surveys measure crime by interviewing individuals about their experiences. The best-known national study, compiled annually by the Bureau of the Census in cooperation with the Bureau of Justice Statistics, is called the National Crime Victimization Survey (NCVS). The NCVS estimates the total number of offenses committed by asking individuals from a large national sample about their experiences as victims during a given time period.

NCVS Information. The NCVS includes victimization by rape, robbery, assault, theft, burglary, and motor vehicle theft. Nationwide, NCVS data give us variations in crime rates by region, season, time of day, and specific places, among others. The survey gathers information about crimes (where and when they occur, use of weapons, number of offenders); offenders (perceived age, gender, race); and the victims themselves. Interviewers also try to identify the reasons why people do not report crimes to the police. The reasons victims give include, among others: a belief that the offense is too minor; a determination that the police will do nothing about it; a dislike of the red tape surrounding the reporting process; and fear of reprisal. In other cases, people simply do not want to "get involved."

Bias Motivation	Incidents	Offenses	Victims[1]	Known Offenders[2]
Total	**7,163**	**8,380**	**8,804**	**6,804**
Single-Bias Incidents	**7,160**	**8,373**	**8,795**	**6,800**
Race:	**3,919**	**4,691**	**4,895**	**3,913**
Anti-White	828	935	975	963
Anti-Black	2,630	3,200	3,322	2,581
Anti-American Indian/Alaskan Native	79	95	97	73
Anti-Asian/Pacific Islander	199	231	240	163
Anti-Multiple Races, Group	183	230	261	133
Religion:	**1,227**	**1,314**	**1,405**	**580**
Anti-Jewish	848	900	977	364
Anti-Catholic	58	61	61	22
Anti-Protestant	57	58	58	32
Anti-Islamic	128	146	151	89
Anti-Other Religion	93	102	106	54
Anti-Multiple Religions, Group	39	42	47	18
Anti-Atheism/Agnosticism/etc.	4	5	5	1
Sexual Orientation:	**1,017**	**1,171**	**1,213**	**1,138**
Anti-Male Homosexual	621	713	743	715
Anti-Female Homosexual	155	180	186	146
Anti-Homosexual	195	228	233	237
Anti-Heterosexual	21	23	23	18
Anti-Bisexual	25	27	28	22
Ethnicity/National Origin:	**944**	**1,144**	**1,228**	**1,115**
Anti-Hispanic	522	660	722	691
Anti-Other Ethnicity/National Origin	422	484	506	424
Disability:	**53**	**53**	**54**	**54**
Anti-Physical	21	21	21	21
Anti-Mental	32	32	33	33
Multiple-Bias Incidents[3]	**3**	**7**	**9**	**4**

[1]The term *victim* may refer to a person, business, institution, or society as a whole.

[2]The term *known offender* does not imply that the identity of the suspect is known, but only that an attribute of the suspect has been identified, which distinguishes him/her from an unknown offender.

[3]In a *multiple-bias incident* two conditions must be met: (1) more than one offense type must occur in the incident and (2) at least two offense types must be motivated by different biases.

SOURCE: Uniform Crime Reports, 2006 (Washington, D.C.: United States Printing Office, 2007) (available at: www.FBI.gov/UCR/H62006).

TABLE 2.8   Incidents, Offenses, Victims, and Known Offenders by Bias Motivation, 2005

Comparison: UCR and NCVS. Figure 2.7 shows that the number of crimes reported to the police and the number of crimes reported in the victimization survey are far apart. According to the NCVS data for 2002, there were 23.0 million victimizations. But the UCR shows that only 11.8 million index crimes (excluding arson) were reported to the police, underscoring the extent to which many crimes go unreported.

The Amount of Crime

Both scholarly journals and the news media typically discuss the amount of crime, or whether crime is going up or down, in terms of rates. Crime rates are computed in the following way:

Crime rate = Number of reported crimes / Total population × 100,000

National Crime Victimization Survey
(Number of Offenses)

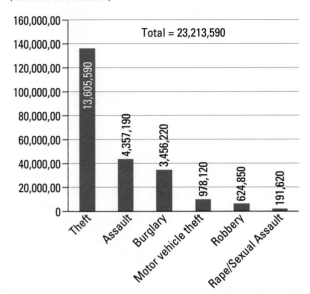

Total = 23,213,590

Uniform Crime Reports
(Number of Offenses)

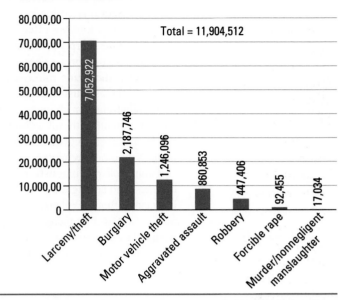

Total = 11,904,512

FIGURE 2.7 National Crime Victimization Survey (Number of Offenses); Uniform Crime Reports (Number of Offenses)

SOURCES: *National Crime Victimization Survey, Criminal Victimization, 2000.* Adapted from U.S. Department of Justice, Bureau of Justice Statistics, NCJ 187007 (Washington, DC: U.S. Government Printing Office, June 2001), p. 3, http://www.ojp.usdoj.gov/bjs/.

Uniform Crime Reports: Index of Crime, 1999. Adapted from U.S. Department of Justice, Federal Bureau of Investigation, *Crime in the United States, 1999* (Washington, DC: U.S. Government Printing Office, 2000), http://www.fbi.gov.

If we say, for example, that the robbery rate is 257, we mean that there were 257 robberies for every 100,000 persons in the population under consideration (e.g., all persons over eighteen years of age; the total U.S. population). Calculating crime in terms of rates enables us to show whether changes in the population have resulted in changes in the amount of crime or whether the actual prevalence of crime has changed.

The UCR show that the U.S. crime rate increased slowly between 1930 and 1960 and then began to rise much more quickly. This trend continued until 1980, when the rate was 5,950 per 100,000 (Figure 2.8). From that peak the rate dropped steadily until 1984, when there were 5,031.3 crimes per 100,000. After that year the rate rose again until 1991, and then began a steady drop, decreasing to the present rate of 4,118.[78] Moreover, the NCVS property and violent crime rates for 2002 are the lowest recorded since the survey began in 1973 (see most recent data, Table 2.9).[79]

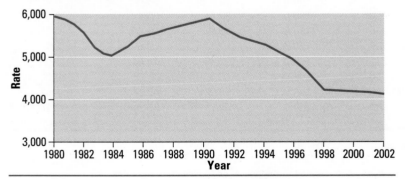

FIGURE 2.8 Uniform Crime Reports, per 100,000 Population, 1980–1999

SOURCE: *Uniform Crime Reports: Index of Crime, 1999.* Adapted from U.S. Department of Justice, Federal Bureau of Investigation, *Crime in the United States, 1999* (Washington, DC: U.S. Government Printing Office, 2000), http://www.fbi.gov.

Several reasons have been presented for the changes in the crime rate over time. One important factor in the decline from 1980 to 1984 was the age distribution of the population. Given the fact that young people tend to have the highest crime rate, age distribution of the population has a major effect on the number of crimes committed. After World War II, the birth rate rose sharply in what is known as the "baby boom." As the baby-boom generation reached its crime-prone years in the 1960s, the crime rate rose; as the baby-boom generation grew older, the crime rate became more stable and in the early 1980s began to decline.

While the age distribution and other factors such as reporting practices have been offered as explanations for changes in the crime rate, there are no definitive answers. We are not able to explain with any certainty why the rate falls and rises. The rise from 1984 to 1990 has been linked to drug-related crime against persons and property; the number of children of baby boomers reaching their crime-prone years; and the economic recession.

Crime fell precipitously in the 1990s in all parts of the country, across all categories of offenses, and among all demographic populations. Few people anticipated this decline of crime, but many offered explanations. Innovative policing was the most popular reason offered to the media, followed by increased incarceration, changes in drug markets, an aging population, gun control laws, a strong economy, and larger police forces.[80] One academic has credited lower levels of lead in the blood due to a reduction in lead-based paints and leaded gasoline.[81]

Sector and Type of Crime	Number of Victimizations	Percent of Victimizations			
		Total	Yes/a	No	Not known and not Available
All Crimes	**23,440,720%**	**100.0%**	**41.3%**	**57.4%**	**1.3%**
Personal crimes	**5,400,790**	**100.0%**	**46.9%**	**51.3%**	**1.8%**
Crimes of violence	5,173,720	100.0	47.4	50.7	1.8
Completed violence	1,658,660	100.0	61.5	37.4	1.1*
Attempted/threatened violence	3,515,060	100.0	40.8	57.0	2.1
Rape/Sexual assault	191,670	100.0	38.3	61.7	0.0*
Rape/Attempted rape	130,140	100.0	42.1	57.9	0.0*
Rape	69,370	100.0	45.2*	54.8	0.0*
Attempted rape/b	60,770	100.0	38.7*	61.3	0.0*
Sexual assault/c	61,530	100.0	30.2*	69.8	0.0*
Robbery	624,850	100.0	52.4	46.9	0.7*
Completed/property taken	415,320	100.0	60.5	38.5	1.0*
With Injury	142,830	100.0	73.8	26.2	0.0*
Without injury	272,490	100.0	53.6	44.9	1.5*
Attempted to take property	209,530	100.0	36.4	63.6	0.0*
With injury	64,450	100.0	39.6*	60.4	0.0*
Without injury	145,090	100.0	35.0	65.0	0.0*
Assault	4,357,190	100.0	47.1	50.8	2.1
Aggravated	1,052,260	100.0	62.4	36.6	1.0*
With injury	330,730	100.0	76.2	23.8	0.0*
Threatened with weapon	721,530	100.0	56.0	42.5	1.5*
Simple	3,304,930	100.0	42.3	55.3	2.4

NOTE: Detail may not add to total shown because of rounding.

*Estimate is based on about 10 or fewer sample cases.

a/Figures in this column represent the rates at which viclimizations were reported to the police, or "police reporting rates,"

b/Includes verbal threats of rape.

c/Includes threats.

SOURCE: Shunnan M. Catalano, Criminal Victimization, 2005 (Washington D.C.: Bureau of Justice Statistics, 2006) P.3.

TABLE 2.9   Personal and Property Crimes, 2005: Percent Distribution of Victimizations, by Type of Crime and Whether or Not Reported to the Police

Intrigued by this phenomenon, Steven Levitt, an economist at the University of Chicago, tested these popular theories. His economic models and survey of others' work concluded that six commonly cited factors likely had little impact on the crime rate: the strong economy, changing demographics, better policing strategies, gun control, less restrictions on carrying a concealed weapon, and increased use of the death penalty. He argued that four factors account for almost all of the decline: an increase in the number of police officers, an increase in the prison population, the receding crack epidemic, and the legalization of abortion after *Roe v. Wade* in 1973.[82]

Arrests

Behind each crime is a criminal, or several criminals. These criminals can be grouped into categories (age, gender, race, class, and others), and it is these categories that criminal justice agencies and researchers find useful. In 2006 there were 14.4 million arrests for all crimes except traffic violations.

Age. Six armed men who have been called the "over-the-hill gang" were arrested trying to rob an elegant bridge and backgammon club in midtown New York City. The robbery began at 10:25 P.M. when the men, wearing rubber gloves and ski masks and armed with two revolvers, a shotgun, and a rifle, forced the customers and employees to lie down in a back room while

Sector and Type of Crime	Number of Victimizations	Reported to the Police			Not known and not Available
		Total	Yes/a	No	
With minor injury	795,240	100.0	59.0	39.2	1.8*
Without injury	2,509,690	100.0	37.0	60.4	2.6
Purse snatching/Pocket picking	227,070	100.0	35.2	63.6	1.2*
Completed purse snatching	43,550	100.0	51.2*	48.8*	0.0*
Attempted purse snatching	3,260*	100.0*	0.0*	100.0*	0.0*
Pocket picking	180,260	100.0	32.0	66.5	1.5*
Property crimes	**18,039,930**	**100.0%**	**39.6%**	**59.3%**	**1.1%**
Household burglary	3,456,220	100.0	56.3	42.6	1.1
Completed	2,900,460	100.0	57.1	41.9	0.9*
Forcible entry	1,068,430	100.0	74.7	24.7	0.5*
Unlawful entry without force	1,832,030	100.0	46.9	52.0	1.2*
Attempted forcible entry	555,760	100.0	51.7	46.2	2.1*
Motor vehicle theft	978,120	100.0	83.2	15.9	0.8*
Completed	774,650	100.0	92.4	7.1	0.4*
Attempted	203,470	100.0	48.2	49.4	2.3*
Theft	13,605,590	100.0	32.3	66.6	1.1
Completed	13,116,270	100.0	32.0	66.9	1.1
Less than $50	4,079,120	100.0	18.6	80.5	0.9*
$50–$249	4,656,120	100.0	27.6	71.5	0.9
$250 or more	3,231,440	100.0	52.7	46.2	1.1*
Amount not available	1,149,590	100.0	39.0	58.3	2.7*
Attempted	489,320	100.0	38.6	59.5	1.8*

Year	Population[1]	Violent Crime	Violent Crime Rate	Murder and Nonnegligent Manslaughter	Murder and Nonnegligent Manslaughter Rate	Forcible Rape	Forcible Rape Rate
1987	242,288,918	1,483,999	612.5	20,096	8.3	91,111	37.6
1988	244,498,982	1,566,221	640.6	20,675	8.5	92,486	37.8
1989	246,819,230	1,646,037	666.9	21,500	8.7	94,504	38.3
1990	249,464,396	1,820,127	729.6	23,438	9.4	102,555	41.1
1991	252,153,092	1,911,767	758.2	24,703	9.8	106,593	42.3
1992	255,029,699	1,932,274	757.7	23,760	9.3	109,062	42.8
1993	257,782,608	1,926,017	747.1	24,526	9.5	106,014	41.1
1994	260,327,021	1,857,670	713.6	23,326	9.0	102,216	39.3
1995	262,803,276	1,798,792	684.5	21,606	8.2	97,470	37.1
1996	265,228,572	1,688,540	636.6	19,645	7.4	96,252	36.3
1997	267,783,607	1,636,096	611.0	18,208	6.8	96,153	35.9
1998	270,248,003	1,533,887	567.6	16,974	6.3	93,144	34.5
1999	272,690,813	1,426,044	523.0	15,522	5.7	89,411	32.8
2000	281,421,906	1,425,486	506.5	15,586	5.5	90,178	32.0
2001[2]	285,317,559	1,439,480	504.5	16,037	5.6	90,863	31.8
2002	287,973,924	1,423,677	494.4	16,229	5.6	95,235	33.1
2003	290,788,976	1,383,676	475.8	16,528	5.7	93,883	32.3
2004	293,656,842	1,360,088	463.2	16,148	5.5	95,089	32.4
2005[3]	296,507,061	1,390,745	469.0	16,740	5.6	94,347	31.8
2006	299,398,484	1,417,745	473.5	17,034	5.7	92,455	30.9

TABLE 2.10   Crime in the United States Percent By Volume and Rate per 100,000 Inhabitants, 1987–2006

[1]Populations are U.S. Census Bureau provisional estimates as of July 1 for each year except 1990 and 2000, which are decennial census counts.
[2]The murder and nonnegligent homicides that occurred as a result of the events of September 11, 2001, are not included in this table.
[3]The 2005 crime figures have been adjusted.
NOTE: Although arson data are included in the trend and clearance tables, sufficient data are not available to estimate totals for this offense.

Years	Violent Crime	Violent Crime Rate	Murder and Nonnegligent Manslaughter	Murder and Nonnegligent Manslaughter Rate	Forcible Rape	Forcible Rape Rate
2006/2005	+1.9	+1.0	+1.8	+0.8	−2.0	−3.0
2006/2002	−0.4	−4.2	+5.0	+1.0	−2.9	−6.6
2006/1997	−13.3	−22.5	−6.4	−16.3	−3.8	−14.0

TABLE 2.11   Crime in the United States Percent Change in Volume and Rate per 100,000 Inhabitants for 2 Years, 5 Years, and 10 Years

they loaded a nylon bag with wallets, players' money, and the club's cash box. A club worker slipped out a side door to alert police, who arrived within minutes. They surprised and disarmed one member of the gang, a forty-eight-year-old, whom they found clutching a .22-caliber revolver. They took a .38-caliber revolver from another gang member, forty-one years old.

During the scuffle with the officers, one suspect tried to escape, fell, and broke his nose. The officers then found and arrested a forty-year-old man standing in the hallway with a 12-gauge Winchester shotgun. Meanwhile, the other gang members abandoned their gloves and masks and lay down among the people they had robbed. One of the suspects, age seventy-two, who wore a back brace, complained of chest and back pain as police locked handcuffs on him. He was immediately hospitalized.[83]

Robbery	Robbery Rate	Aggravated Assault	Aggravated Assault Rate	Property Crime	Property Crime Rate	Burglary	Burglary Rate
517,704	213.7	855,088	352.9	12,024,709	4,963.0	3,236,184	1,335
542,968	222.1	910,092	372.2	12,356,865	5,054.0	3,218,077	1,316
578,326	234.3	951,707	385.6	12,605,412	5,107.1	3,168,170	1,283
639,271	256.3	1,054,863	422.9	12,655,486	5,073.1	3,073,909	1,232
687,732	272.7	1,092,739	433.4	12,961,116	5,140.2	3,157,150	1,252
672,478	263.7	1,126,974	441.9	12,505,917	4,903.7	2,979,884	1,168
659,870	256.0	1,135,607	440.5	12,218,777	4,740.0	2,834,808	1,099
618,949	237.8	1,113,179	427.6	12,131,873	4,660.2	2,712,774	1,042
580,509	220.9	1,099,207	418.3	12,063,935	4,590.5	2,593,784	987
535,594	201.9	1,037,049	391.0	11,805,323	4,451.0	2,506,400	945
498,534	186.2	1,023,201	382.1	11,558,475	4,316.3	2,460,526	918
447,186	165.5	976,583	361.4	10,951,827	4,052.5	2,332,735	863
409,371	150.1	911,740	334.3	10,208,334	3,743.6	2,100,739	770
408,016	145.0	911,706	324.0	10,182,584	3,618.3	2,050,992	728
423,557	148.5	909,023	318.6	10,437,189	3,658.1	2,116,531	741
420,806	146.1	891,407	309.5	10,455,277	3,630.6	2,151,252	747
414,235	142.5	859,030	295.4	10,442,862	3,591.2	2,154,834	741
401,470	136.7	847,381	288.6	10,319,386	3,514.1	2,144,446	730
417,438	140.8	862,220	290.8	10,174,754	3,431.5	2,155,448	726
447,403	149.4	860,853	287.5	9,983,568	3,334.5	2,183,746	729

Robbery	Robbery Rate	Aggravated Assault	Aggravated Assault Rate	Property Crime	Property Crime Rate	Burglary	Burglary Rate
+7.2	+6.1	−0.2	−1.1	−1.9	−2.8	+1.3	+0.3
+6.3	+2.3	−3.4	−7.1	−4.5	−8.2	+1.5	−2.4
−10.3	−19.7	−15.9	−24.8	−13.6	−22.7	−11.2	−20.6

In another case, 94-year-old "career criminal" Wesley (Pop) Honeywood, from Jacksonville, Florida, was sentenced to seven years after he pointed an unloaded gun at another man who warned him not to eat grapes growing in the man's yard. Mr. Honeywood was given the option of going to a nursing home instead of prison, but he resisted, saying, "If I go to jail, I may be out in a couple of years. If I go to a nursing home, I may be there the rest of my life."[84]

These cases are extraordinary for at least two reasons. First, in any given year approximately half of all arrests are of individuals under the age of twenty-five; and second, gang membership is ordinarily confined to the young. Though persons under eighteen years of age comprise about 8 percent of the population, they account for almost one-third of the arrests for index crimes. Arrest rates decline after age thirty and taper off to about 2 percent or less from age fifty on[85] (See Figure 2.9).

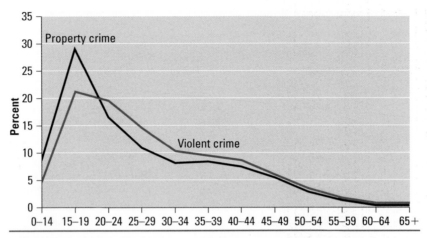

FIGURE 2.9   Share of Index Crime Arrests across Age Groups

Increasing attention is being paid to the effects of social class on the response of the criminal justice system.

Gender.   Most crimes are committed by males. But while 11 percent of the total number of people arrested in 1960 were women, this figure rose to 24 percent in 2005.[86] According to the UCR for 2005, for example, female arrestees accounted for 17 percent of violent crime arrests, and 32 percent of property crime arrests.[87]

Gang membership has been primarily limited to young, inner-city males. Twenty-three cities nationwide had known street gangs in 1961. In 2004, the National Youth Gang Center survey estimated approximately 24,000 active gangs and 760,000 gang members.[88] Gangs such as the Logan Heights Calle Treinte and the Syndo Mob (both Hispanic) that have come into existence in newly emerging gang cities are more disorganized and informal than those that exist in established gang cities like Chicago.[89] Among them are the "wannabes" and the "gonnabes," younger boys waiting to go through initiation rites that sometimes demand a drive-by murder. Two of the most violent gangs are the Crips and the Bloods. Crips wear blue; Bloods wear red. Their rivalry often results in gun battles with automatic assault weapons. Recently, females have increased their participation in gangs. In San Francisco, for example, an all-female group, the Potrero Hill Posse, was formed when the young women realized that their gang-affiliated boyfriends were not distributing the profits of their crack sales fairly.[90]

Social Class.   Relating social class to crime is more difficult than relating age or gender to crime. Some researchers claim any association found between class and crime could be related to bias on the part of the police, who may be more likely to arrest a lower-class suspect than a middle-class suspect.[91] While there are debates on the social class of persons who commit crime, there is no debate about the social class of prisoners.

The probability that a person such as Dan Rostenkowski, former chair of the federal House of Representatives Ways and Means Committee who served 451 days for mail fraud, will in fact get a prison sentence is extremely low. Rostenkowski does not fit the profile of the hundreds of inmates in our nation's jails and prisons. He is educated. Only 28 percent of prison inmates have completed high school.[92] His income was that of a high-ranking politician. The average yearly income of jail inmates who work is $5,600. He had a white-collar job. Eighty-five percent of prison inmates are blue-collar workers. He committed a white-collar offense. Only 18 percent of those convicted of such offenses go to prison for more than one year, whereas 39 percent of the violent offenders do.[93]

Race.   Information on race and crime shows that while blacks make up approximately 13 percent of the population, they account for 28 percent of all arrests.[94] African Americans account for 39 percent of all arrests for violent crime. Fifty percent of black urban males are arrested for an index crime at least once during their lives, compared with 14 percent of white males. Moreover, the leading cause of death among young African-American men is murder.[95]

Criminal justice specialists need to look carefully at these numbers because they raise a number of important questions about how the criminal justice system operates. Are blacks stopped, interrogated, and taken into custody as suspects more often than whites? Is there a disproportionate amount of police surveillance in black neighborhoods? Do blacks receive different treatment in the courts? In prisons? And, if blacks commit a disproportionately higher number of offenses than whites, why is this the case?

Review

Initially, our discussion centered on the increasing forms and dimensions of crimes that transcend our borders, particularly those that support terrorism. These transnational crimes are activities that extend into, and violate, the laws of several countries.

We learn about the amount of crime that exists from two major sources: the Uniform Crime Reports and victimization surveys. Recently there has been a sharp drop in crime rates. Of the total number of index crimes, violent crimes make up only about 12 percent. Murder, assault, rape, and robbery all share the common characteristic of violence. The traditional property crimes are larceny, obtaining property by frauds of various sorts, burglary, and arson.

The spread of computers and other high-technology equipment has paved the way for new types of crime such as the distribution of child pornography and video piracy. Some property-oriented crimes deprive people of their property through business operations of legitimate enterprises. Individual or corporate white-collar offenses include securities-related crimes and various types of fraud. There are also property-oriented offenses that deprive people of their property through the use of illegitimate business practices. Some illegal activities—drug, alcohol, and sex-related—once were commonly called victimless crime. But contemporary forms of such activities entail massive victimization.

Thinking Critically about Criminal Justice

1. You are asked to be a member of a national committee that will devise a plan to help local criminal justice agencies to deal with transnational crime. What ideas would you present?
2. Which type of crimes does the public fear more—white collar and corporate *or* street crime?
3. What experiences have you had as a crime victim? How many of these victimizations did you report to the police? If you did not report the crime, then why?

Internet Connection

Note: *While all of the URLs listed were current as of the printing of this book, these sites often change. Please check our website (http://www.mhhe.com/socscience/crimjustice/adlercj/) for updates.*

Did you know that criminal justice specialists consider age to be one of the most powerful predictors of criminality? This is not surprising given the early onset of criminality. Examine the distribution of the population arrested by age group as found in *The Sourcebook of Criminal Justice Statistics* (**http://www.albany.edu/sourcebook/**). What can you conclude about the rise and fall of criminality in different age groups? When do crime rates decrease? Can you explain this decrease?

As you make your way through *Criminal Justice: An Introduction,* it is helpful to refer to *The Sourcebook* for up-to-date statistics on crime, criminals, courts, and corrections. Each year *The Sourcebook* is reprinted at: **http://www.albany.edu/sourcebook/.**

Notes

1. *Patterns of Global Terrorism 1999* (Washington, DC: U.S. State Department, April 2000).

2. Transform Drug Policy Foundation, http://www.transform-drugs.org.uk/drug&terrorism.htm.

3. Robert Spear and Philip Shenou, "Customs Switches Priority from Drugs to Terrorism," *New York Times,* October 10, 2001, http://www.crimelynx.com/custswitch.html; Jerry Seper, "Mexicans, Russian Mob New Partners in Crime," *Washington Times,* September 14, 2002, http://www.rusnet.nl/info/cis-today/archive/01-05/28wnl.shtm.

4. Secret bank account transfers are not the only method of laundering money. Other methods are Market Peso Exchange, cash smuggling, gold transfers, and many others.

5. Steven Erlanger, "Hamburg Police Raid 2 Import-Export Firms," http://www.nytimes.com/2002/09/11/international/11GERM.html; "3 Former Executives Indicted in Fraud," *New York Times,* September 6, 2002, Sec. C, p. 4.; Leif Pagrotsky and Joseph Stiglitz, "Blocking the Terrorists' Funds: The Global Financial System Provides Hiding Places for Dirty Money," *Financial Times,* December 7, 2001; Daniel Williams, "Swiss Probe Illustrates Difficulties in Tracking Al Qaeda's Cash," *Washington Post,* November 12, 2001.

6. P. K. Semler, "Rich Linked to Money Laundering," *Washington Times,* June 21, 2002, http://www.washtimes.com/world/20020621-417508.htm. The reference to the American fugitive financier, Mark Rich, who defrauded clients of millions of dollars, found safe haven (and business opportunities), in Zug, Switzerland, and was ultimately pardoned by President Clinton.

7. R. Mark Bortner, "Cyberlaundering; Anonymous Digital Cash and Money Laundering," http://www.law.miami.edu/~fro@mkin/seminar/papers/bortner.htm (1996).

8. Jim Wolf, "Cyber Attack Fears Stir Security Offices," http://story.news.yahoo.com/news?tmplstory2@cidncid-564@e-11@u-lnm/2002.

9. Barton Gellman, "Cyber-Attacks by Al Qaeda Feared," http://www.crime-research.org/eng/library/Barton.htm (2002).

10. For example, Associated Press, International News, "Italian Police Arrest 15 Alleged Islamic Extremists," September 16, 2002, http://famulus.msnbc.com/FamulusIntl/ap09-12-150217.asp?reg=Europe.

11. Government Accounts often, Human Trafficking: Better Data, Strategy, and Reporting Needed to Enhance U.S. Antitrafficking Efforts Abroad, (Washington, DC.: GAO, 2006).

12. Id.

13. Associated Press, "Man Sentenced to Death for Killing Two Children Sits in Silence," *The Arizona Daily Wildcat,* November 7, 2001. http://wildcat.arizona.edu/papers/95/57/05.html (June 1, 2002).

14. U.S. Department of Justice, Federal Bureau of Investigation, *Crime in the United States* 1975; 1980; 1993; 1997; 1999 (Washington, DC: U.S. Government Printing Office, 1976, 1981, 1994, 1998, 2000), pp. 13, 41, 49, 58, 67, hereafter cited as *Uniform Crime Reports.*

15. FresnoBee.com, http://www.fresnobee.com/special/ 2004/massacre/story/8407716p-9238181c.html.

16. Jack Levin and James Alan Fox, *Mass Murder: America's Growing Menace* (New York: Plenum Press, 1985).

17. Bill Wallace, "Family of Missing Man Finds Peace in Ruling," *The San Francisco Chronicle,* March 12, 2001, p. A20.

18. Don Terry, "A Fight for Peace on Chicago's Streets," *The New York Times,* April 4, 1994, p. A8.

19. Fox Butterfield, "Police Find Pattern of Arson by Gangs," *The New York Times,* October 29, 1994, p. 7.

20. Yusef Jah and Sister Shah' Keyah, *Uprising: Crips and Bloods Tell the Story of American Youth in the Crossfire* (New York: Scribner's, 1995).

21. John Bonfante, "Entrepreneurs of Crack," *Time,* February 27, 1995, p. 22.

22. David M. Kennedy, *Juvenile Gun Violence and Gun Markets in Boston* (National Institute of Justice, March 1997).

23. Cheryl L. Maxson, Margaret A. Gordon, and Malcolm W. Klein, "Differences between Gang and Nongang Homicides," *Criminology* 23 (1985), pp. 209–222.

24. *Criminal Victimization,* 2005, p. 1.

25. *Uniform Crime Reports,* 2006, p. 25.

26. Ibid., p. 18.

27. Tod W. Burke and Charles E. O'Rear, "Armed Carjackings: A Violent Problem in Need of a Solution," *Police Chief* 60 (1993), pp. 18–24.

28. John L. Mitchell, "Suspect Arraigned in Carjacking Death," *Los Angeles Times,* April 16, 1996, p. B1.

29. Gail A. Caputo, *What's in the Bay?: A Shoplifting Treatment and Education Program* (Lanham, MD: American Correctional Association), 2003.

30. *Uniform Crime Reports,* Federal Bureau of Investigation (Washington, DC: U.S. Government Printing Office, 2003), p. 45.

31. Computer Security Institute and the Federal Bureau of Investigation, *Computer Crime and Security Survey* (Washington, DC: CSI, 2004), p. 10.

32. Edwin H. Sutherland, "White Collar Criminality," *American Sociological Review* 5, (1940), pp. 1–20.

33. Gilbert Geis, *On White Collar Crime* (Lexington, MA: Lexington Books, 1982), p. 9.

34. Marshall B. Clinard and Richard Quinney, *Criminal Behavior Systems,* 2nd ed. (New York: Holt, Rinehart & Winston, 1982); Marshall B. Clinard, *Corporate Corruption: The Abuse of Power* (Westport, CT: Praeger, 1990); Gilbert Geis and Paul Jesilow, eds., "White-Collar Crime," *Annals of the American Academy of Political and Social Science* 525 (1993), pp. 8–169; David Weisburd, Stanton Wheeler, and Elin Waring, *Crimes of the Middle Classes: White-Collar Offenders in the Federal Courts* (New Haven, CT: Yale University Press, 1991); John Braithwaite, "Poverty, Power, White-Collar Crime and the Paradoxes of Criminological Theory," *Australian and New Zealand Journal of Criminology* 24 (1991), pp. 40–48; Frank Pearce and Laureen Snider, eds., "Crimes of the Powerful," *Journal of Human Justice* 3 (1992), pp. 1–124; Hazel Croall, *White Collar Crime: Criminal Justice and Criminology* (Buckingham, England: Open University Press, 1991); Stephen J. Rackmill, "Understanding and Sanctioning the White Collar Offender," *Federal Probation* 56 (1992), pp. 26–33; Brent Fisse, Michael Bersten, and Peter Grabosky, "White Collar and Corporate Crime," *University of New South Wales Law Journal* 13 (1990), pp. 1–171; Susan P. Shapiro, "Collaring the Crime Not the Criminal: Reconsidering the Concept of White-Collar Crime," *American Sociological Review* 55 (1990), pp. 346–365; Kip Schlegel and David Weisburd, eds., *White-Collar Crime Reconsidered* (Boston: Northeastern University Press, 1992); David Weisburd, Stanton Wheeler, Elin Waring, et al., *Crimes of the Middle Classes: White-Collar Offenders in the Federal Courts* (New Haven, CT: Yale University Press, 1991); David Weisburd, Ellen F. Chayet, and Elin J. Waring, "White-Collar Crime and Criminal Careers: Some Preliminary Findings," *Crime and Delinquency* 36 (1990), pp. 342–355; David Weisburd, Elin Waring, and Stanton Wheeler, "Class, Status, and the Punishment of White-Collar Criminals," *Law and Social Inquiry* 15 (1990), pp. 223–243; Lisa Maher and Elin J. Waring, "Beyond Simple Differences: White Collar Crime, Gender and Workforce Position," *Phoebe* 2 (1990), pp. 44–54; John Hagan and Fiona Kay, "Gender and Delinquency in White-Collar Families: A Power-Control Perspective," *Crime and Delinquency* 36 (1990), pp. 391–407.

35. See James W. Coleman, *The Criminal Elite: The Sociological White-Collar Crime,* 2nd ed. (New York: St. Martin's Press, 1989); and Michael L. Benson and Elizabeth Moore, "Are White-Collar and Common Offenders the Same? An Empirical and Theoretical Critique of a Recently Proposed General Theory of Crime," *Journal of Research in Crime and Delinquency* 29 (1992), pp. 251–272. See also Lori A. Elis and Sally S. Simpson, "Informal Sanction Threats

and Corporate Crime: Additive versus Multiplicative Models," *Journal of Research in Crime and Delinquency* 32 (1995), pp. 399–424. For a view of white-collar offending in which the risks and rewards are considered by potential offenders, see David Weisburd, Elin Waring, and Ellen Chayet, "Specific Deterrence in a Sample of Offenders Convicted of White-Collar Crimes," *Criminology* 33 (1995), pp. 587–605.

36. Not only are governments at all levels victimized by corporate crimes, governments of all nations are also victimized; see Karlhans Liebl, "Developing Trends in Economic Crime in the Federal Republic of Germany," *Police Studies* 8 (1985), pp. 149–162. See also Jurg Gerber and Susan L. Weeks, "Women as Victims of Corporate Crime: A Call for Research on a Neglected Topic," *Deviant Behavior* 13 (1992), pp. 325–347; Elizabeth Moore and Michael Mills, "The Neglected Victims and Unexamined Costs of White-Collar Crime," *Crime and Delinquency* 36 (1990), pp. 408–418.

37. For an outline of a general theory of crime causation applicable to both street crime and white-collar crime, see Travis Hirschi and Michael Gottfredson, "Causes of White-Collar Crime," *Criminology* 25 (1987), pp. 949–974; James W. Coleman, "Toward an Integrated Theory of White Collar Crime," *American Journal of Sociology* 93 (1987), pp. 406–439; and James R. Lasley, "Toward a Control Theory of White Collar Offending," *Journal of Quantitative Criminology* 4 (1988), pp. 347–362.

38. Donald R. Cressey, "The Poverty of Theory in Corporate Crime Research," in *Advances in Criminological Theory,* vol. 1, ed. William Laufer and Freda Adler (New Brunswick, NJ: Transaction, 1989); for a response, see John Braithwaite and Brent Fisse, "On the Plausibility of Corporate Crime Theory," in *Advances in Criminological Theory,* vol. 2, ed. William Laufer and Freda Adler (New Brunswick, NJ: Transaction, 1990). See also Travis Hirschi and Michael Gottfredson, "The Significance of White-Collar Crime for a General Theory of Crime," *Criminology* 27 (1989), pp. 359–371; and Darrell Steffensmeier, "On the Causes of 'White Collar' Crime: An Assessment of Hirschi and Gottfredson's Claims," *Criminology* 27 (1989), pp. 345–358.

39. Bequai, *White Collar Crime.* Bequai also includes antitrust and environmental offenses, which are corporate crimes, discussed in the next section.

40. Kenneth Polk and William Weston, "Insider Trading as an Aspect of White Collar Crime," *Australian and New Zealand Journal of Criminology* 23 (1990), pp. 24–38. In a report before Congress, insider trading scandals were said to have cost the securities industry nearly half a billion dollars in the early 1970s; see U.S. Congress House Select Committee on Crime, *Conversion of Worthless Securities into Cash* (Washington, DC: U.S. Government Printing Office, 1973). For a review of the insider trading that persists on Wall Street, see Gene G. Marcial, *Secrets of the Street: The Dark Side of Making Money* (New York: McGraw-Hill, 1995); Martin Mayer, *Nightmare on Wall Street: Salomon Brothers and the Corruption of the Marketplace* (New

York: Simon & Schuster, 1993); Nancy Reichman, "Insider Trading," in *Beyond the Law: Crime in Complex Organizations,* ed. Michael Tonry and Albert J. Reiss, Jr. (Chicago: University of Chicago Press, 1993).

41. For a more extensive review of the Wedtech debacle, see Mark S. Hamm, "From Wedtech and Iran-Contra to the Riots at Oakdale and Atlanta: On the Ethics and Public Performance of Edwin Meese III," *Journal of Crime and Justice* 14 (1991), pp. 123–147; Marilyn W. Thompson, *Feeding the Beast: How Wedtech Became the Most Corrupt Little Company in America* (New York: Charles Scribner's Sons, 1990); William Power, "New York Rep. Biaggi and Six Others Indicted as Wedtech Scandal Greatly Expands," *The Wall Street Journal,* June 4, 1987, p. 9.

42. See http://www.fas.org/man/gao/gao9621.htm.

43. For a discussion of the many ways in which a person may be defrauded, see Phil Berger and Craig Jacob, *Twisted Genius: Confessions of a $10 Million Scam Man* (New York: Four Walls Eight Windows, 1995). For an Australian perspective of fraud, see M. Kapardis and A. Kapardis, "Co-regulation of Fraud Detection and Reporting by Auditors in Australia: Criminology's Lessons for Non-compliance," *Australian and New Zealand Journal of Criminology* 28 (1995), pp. 193–212.

44. Bequai, *White Collar Crime,* pp. 70–71.

45. For a European perspective on insurance fraud, with a particular focus on the enforcement activities in France and Belgium, see Andre Lemaitre, Rolf Lemaitre, Rolf Arnold, and Roger Litton, "Insurance and Crime," *European Journal on Criminal Policy* 3 (1995), pp. 7–92. For a description of insurance fraud prevalent in the American insurance industry, see Kenneth D. Myers, *False Security: Greed & Deception in America's Multibillion-Dollar Insurance Industry* (Amherst, NY: Prometheus Books, 1995); Andrew Tobias, *The Invisible Banker* (New York: Washington Square Press, 1982).

46. Paul E. Tracy and James A. Fox, "A Field Experiment on Insurance Fraud in Auto Body Repair," *Criminology* 27 (1989), pp. 589–603.

47. Kathleen F. Brickey, *Corporate Criminal Liability,* 2 vols. (Wilmette, IL: Callaghan, 1984). See also Thomas Gabor, *Everybody Does It! Crime by the Public* (Toronto: University of Toronto Press, 1994). For a uniquely British perspective, see Doreen McBarnet, "Whiter Than White Collar Crime: Tax, Fraud, Insurance and the Management of Stigma," *British Journal of Sociology* 42 (1991), pp. 323–344.

48. Alan Murray, "IRS Is Losing Battle against Tax Evaders Despite Its New Gain," *The Wall Street Journal,* April 10, 1984, p. 1.

49. Ralph Salerno and John S. Tompkins, "Protecting Organized Crime," in *Theft of the City,* ed. John A. Gardiner and David Olson (Bloomington: Indiana University Press, 1984); Edwin Sutherland, *The Professional Thief* (Chicago: University of Chicago Press, 1937).

50. 18 U.S.C. Secs. 166(b) and (c).

51. Bequai, *White Collar Crime,* p. 45.

52. Ibid., p. 87. See Virginia Department of Social Services, *Report of the Financial Exploitation of Older Adults and Disabled Younger Adults in the Commonwealth* (Richmond, VA: Senate Document no. 37, 1994). For steps to take to avoid being a victim of embezzlement, see Russell B. Bintliff, *Complete Manual of White Collar Crime Detection and Prevention* (Englewood Cliffs, NJ: Prentice Hall, 1993). For a historic account of embezzlement in the United Kingdom from 1845 to 1929, see George Robb, *White Collar Crime in Modern England: Financial Fraud and Business Morality, 1845–1929* (Cambridge, England: Cambridge University Press, 1992).

53. John Clark and Richard Hollinger, *Theft by Employees in Work Organization* (Washington, DC: U.S. Government Printing Office, 1983).

54. Bequai, *White Collar Crime,* p. 89.

55. Sherman Antitrust Act, Act of July 2, 1890, c. 647, 26 Stat. 209, 15 U.S.C. Secs. 1–7 (1976).

56. Clayton Antitrust Act, Act of October 15, 1914, c. 322, 38 Stat. 730, 15 U.S.C. Secs. 12–27 (1976); Robinson-Patman Act, Act of June 19, 1936, c. 592, Sec. 1, 49 Stat. 1526, 15 U.S.C. Sec. 13(a) (1973). See also Brickey, *Corporate Criminal Liability.*

57. Phillip Knightly, Harold Evans, Elaine Potter, and Marjorie Wallace, *Suffer the Children: The Story of Thalidomide* (New York: Viking Press, 1979).

58. The Ford Pinto case is fully described in Cullen et al., *Corporate Crime under Attack.* For more information on crimes against consumer safety, see Raymond J. Michalowski, *Order, Law, and Crime* (New York: Random House, 1985), pp. 334–340. For a description of corporate greed in its most vile form, see James S. Kunen, *Reckless Disregard: Corporate Greed, Government Indifference, and the Kentucky School Bus Crash* (New York: Simon & Schuster, 1994).

59. For an examination of corporate criminality in the United States and the response of the criminal justice system of America, see Spencer and Sims, *Corporate Misconduct.* See also Russell Mokhiber, *Corporate Crime and Violence: Big Business Power and the Abuse of the Public Trust* (San Francisco: Sierra Club, 1988); Susan P. Shapiro, *Wayward Capitalists: Target of the Securities and Exchange Commission* (New Haven, CT: Yale University Press, 1984); M. David Ermann and Richard J. Lundman, *Corporate and Governmental Deviance: Problems of Organizational Behavior in Contemporary Society,* 2nd ed. (New York: Oxford University Press, 1982); Cullen et al., *Corporate Crime under Attack;* Knightly et al., *Suffer the Children;* and W. Byron Groves and Graeme Newman, *Punishment and Privilege* (New York: Harrow & Heston, 1986).

60. See Edwin Sutherland, *White Collar Crime* (1946). Sutherland had earlier published articles on the topic, including "White Collar Criminality," *American Sociological Review* 5 (1940), pp. 1–12, and "Is White Collar Crime 'Crime'?" *American Sociological Review* 10 (1945), pp. 132–139.

61. See Gary E. Reed and Peter Cleary Yeager, "Organizational Offending and Neoclassical Criminology: Challenging the Reach of a General Theory of Crime," *Criminology* 34 (1996), pp. 357–382; Clinard and Yeager, *Corporate Crime,* p. 116. See also Peter C. Yeager, "Analysing Corporate Offences: Progress and Prospects," *Research in Corporate Social Performance and Policy* 8 (1986), pp. 93–120. For similar findings in Canada, see Colin H. Goff and Charles E. Reasons, *Corporate Crime in Canada* (Scarborough, Ontario: Prentice Hall, 1978).

62. Richard Quinney, *Critique of Legal Order: Crime Control in Capitalist Society* (Boston: Little, Brown, 1974); Richard Quinney, *Class, State, and Crime: On the Theory and Practice of Criminal Justice* (New York: David McKay, 1977); Ian Taylor, Paul Walton, and Jock Young, *The New Criminology: For a Social Theory of Deviance* (London: Routledge & Kegan Paul, 1973); William Chambliss and Robert Seidman, *Law, Order, and Power,* 2nd ed. (Reading, MA: Addison-Wesley, 1982).

63. James Q. Wilson, *Thinking about Crime* (New York: Basic Books, 1975). For a competing school of thought, see Gilbert Geis, "Criminal Penalties for Corporate Criminals," *Criminal Law Bulletin* 8 (1972), pp. 377–392; Chamber of Commerce of the United States, *White Collar Crime* (Washington, DC: U.S. Government Printing Office, 1974); John Collins Coffee, Jr., "Beyond the Shut-Eyed Sentry: Toward a Theoretical View of Corporate Misconduct and an Effective Legal Response," *Virginia Law Review* 63 (1977), pp. 1099–1278; Gilbert Geis and Robert F. Meier, *White-Collar Crime: Offenses in Business, Politics, and the Professions* (New York: Free Press, 1977); Marshall B. Clinard, *Illegal Corporate Behavior* (Washington, DC: U.S. Government Printing Office, 1979); Miriam S. Saxon, *White-Collar Crime: The Problem and the Federal Response* (Report no. 80-84 EPW, Library of Congress, Congressional Research Service, Washington, DC, April 14, 1980); Laura S. Schrager and James F. Short, Jr., "How Serious a Crime? Perceptions of Organizational and Common Crimes," in *White-Collar Crime: Theory and Research,* ed. Gilbert Geis and Ezra Stotland (Beverley Hills, CA: Sage, 1980). Contemporary works include James W. Coleman, *The Criminal Elite: The Sociology of White-Collar Crime* (New York: St. Martin's Press, 1989); Laureen Snider, "The Regulatory Dance: Understanding Reform Processes in Corporate Crime," *International Journal of the Sociology of Law* 19 (1991), pp. 209–236; Kip Schlegel and David Weisburd, *White-Collar Crime: The Parallax View* (Boston: Northeastern University Press, 1993); Michael Tonry and Albert J. Reiss, *Beyond the Law: Crime in Complex Organizations* (Chicago: University of Chicago Press, 1993); Robert Tillman and Henry Pontell, "Organizations and Fraud in the Savings and Loan Industry," *Social Forces* 73 (1995), pp. 1439–1463.

64. Patsy Klaus and Carol Kalish, *The Severity of Crime,* Bureau of Justice Statistics Bulletin NCJ-92326 (Washington, DC: U.S. Government Printing Office, 1984). See also Schrager and Short, "How Serious a Crime?" Francis Cullen, B. Link, and C. Polanzi, "The Seriousness of Crime Revisited," *Criminology* 20 (1982), pp. 83–102.

65. Howard Abadinsky, *Organized Crime,* 2nd ed. (Chicago: Nelson Hall, 1985). For a debate on the existence of a Sicilian–American crime syndicate, see Jay Albanese, *Organized Crime in America* (Cincinnati: Anderson, 1985), p. 25.

66. James Walston, "Mafia in the Eighties," *Violence, Aggression, and Terrorism* 1 (1987), pp. 13–39. For a look into organized crime's once mighty and still lingering hand on gambling in the United States, see Jay Albanese, "Casino Gambling and Organized Crime: More Than Reshuffling the Deck," in Albanese, *Contemporary Issues in Organized Crime;* Ronald A. Farrelland and Carole Case, *The Black Book and the Mob: The Untold Story of the Control of Nevada's Casinos* (Madison: University of Wisconsin Press, 1995); Nicholas Pileggi, *Casino: Love and Honor in Las Vegas* (New York: Simon & Schuster, 1995); David Johnston, *Temples of Chance: How America Inc. Bought Out Murder Inc. to Win Control of the Casino Business* (New York: Doubleday, 1992).

67. Organized-crime activities are certainly not limited to local communities. Rather, an ever-evolving organized-crime syndicate feeds off ever-increasing global opportunities; see Petrus van Duyne and Alan A. Block, "Organized Cross-Atlantic Crime: Racketeering in Fuels," *Crime, Law and Social Change* 22 (1995), pp. 127–147; Umberto Santino, "The Financial Mafia: The Illegal Accumulation of Wealth and the Financial-Industrial Complex," *Contemporary Crises* 12 (1988), pp. 203–243.

68. For a description of the damage inflicted on society by contemporary Russian organized-crime figures, see New York State Organized Crime Task Force, New York State Commission of Investigation, New Jersey State Commission of Investigation, *An Analysis of Russian-Émigré Crime in the Tri-State Region* (White Plains, NY: New York State Organized Crime Task Force, June 1996); Dennis J. Kenny and James O. Finckenauer, *Organized Crime in America* (Belmont, CA: Wadsworth, 1995).

69. Kit R. Roane, "Police Say Drug Ring Thrived by Saying 'We Deliver,'" *The New York Times,* April 23, 1998, p. B3.

70. "Miami's Grove of Crack," *Newsweek,* June 13, 1994, p. 63.

71. National Institute on Drug Abuse, 2005 *National Household Survey* (Washington, DC: U.S. Government Printing Office, 2000).

72. L. Johnston, P. O'Malley, and J. Bachman, *Monitoring the Future* (Washington, DC: National Institute on Drug Abuse, 1995).

73. *ADAM, 1999 Annual Report on Adult and Juvenile Arrestees,* National Institute of Justice Research Report (U.S. Department of Justice, 1999), pp. 1–3. http://www.ncjrs.org/pdffiles1/nij/ 181426.pdf.

74. James B. Jacobs, *Drunk Driving: An American Dilemma* (Chicago: University of Chicago Press, 1989), p. xiii.

75. *Profile of State Prison Inmates* (Washington, DC: U.S. Government Printing Office, 1989).

76. U.S. Department of Justice, *Report to the Nation,* 2nd ed., p. 50.

77. *Uniform Crime Reports, 1996,* p. 218; Lawrence A. Greenfeld, *Drunk Driving,* Bureau of Justice Statistics (Washington, DC: U.S. Government Printing Office, February 1998), p. 1.

78. U.S. Department of Justice, Federal Bureau of Investigation, *Crime in the United States,* 2002 (Washington, DC: U.S. Government Printing Office, 2003). http://www.fbi.gov/.

79. U.S. Department of Justice, Bureau of Justice Statistics, National Crime Victimization Survey, *Criminal Victimization,* 2002 (Washington, DC: U.S. Government Printing Office, December 2002), p. 1.

80. Alfred Blumstein and Joel Wallman, *The Crime Drop in America* (New York: Cambridge University Press, 2005).

81. Jessica Wolpaw Reyes, "The impact of Childhood Lead Exposure on Crime," 2002. Unpublished paper, Harvard Department of Economits.

82. See, e.g., John S. Donohue and Steven Levitt, The Impact of Crime, Quarterly Journal of Economics, 2001.

83. *New York Post,* April 20, 1989; *The New York Times,* April 20, 1989.

84. "The Week in Review," *The New York Times,* November 6, 1994, p. 24.

85. *Uniform Crime Reports,* 2002, p. 24

86. Freda Adler, *Sisters in Crime* (New York: McGraw-Hill, 1975); Meda Chesney-Lind, "Girls' Crime and Woman's Place: Toward a Feminist Model of Female Delinquency," *Crime and Delinquency* 25 (1989), pp. 5–29.

87. *Uniform Crime Reports,* 2002, p. 210.

88. Arlen Egley, *Highlights of the 1999 National Youth Gang Survey* (Washington, DC: OSSDP, 2000), p. 1

89. Scott H. Decker, Tim Bynum, and Deborah Weisel, "A Tale of Two Cities: Gangs as Organized Crime Groups," *Justice Quarterly* 15 (1998), pp. 396–425.

90. David Lauderback, Joy Hansen, and Dan Waldorf, "Sisters Are Doin' It for Themselves: A Black Female Gang in San Francisco," *Gang Journal* 1 (1992), pp. 57–72; Liqun Cao, Anthony Adams, and Vickie J. Jensen, "A Test of the Black Subculture of Violence Thesis: A Research Note," *Criminology* 35 (1997), pp. 367–379.

91. Charles R. Tittle and Robert F. Meier, "Specifying the SES/Delinquency Relationship," *Criminology* 28 (1990), pp. 271–299; Christina De Jong and Kenneth C. Jackson, "Putting Race into Context: Race, Juvenile Justice Processing, and Urbanization," *Justice Quarterly* 15 (1998), pp. 487–504.

92. The data on socioeconomic factors come from the U.S. Department of Justice, *Report to the Nation on Crime and Justice,* pp. 48–49.

93. U.S. Department of Justice, Bureau of Justice Statistics, *Annual Report, Fiscal 1986* (Washington, DC: U.S. Government Printing Office, April 1987), p. 39.

94. *Uniform Crime Reports,* 2002, p. 232.

95. James W. Balkwell, "Ethnic Inequality and the Rate of Homicide," *Social Forces* 69 (1990), pp. 53–70.

CHAPTER

3

Explaining Criminal Behavior

John A. Muhammad and his young companion Lee Malvo made the headlines of the nation's newspapers long before their names were known. They were "the snipers." They had fitted their old car so that, through a hole in the trunk, a sharpshooter's rifle could be aimed at unsuspecting persons. They killed fifteen victims and always eluded the police—until, through the tip of a truck driver, the pair were arrested. In late 2003, after trials in Virginia, John was sentenced to death and Lee to life in prison.

• Most questions about the two have been answered: Who are they? What is their relationship to each other? Who were their victims? Yet there is one lingering question: Why did they go on their killing spree? They will not tell. What do the facts tell us? Muhammad might simply have joined the global terrorist fervor. After the first few sniper killings, the pair made a $10 million ransom demand. Was that merely an afterthought when the snipers realized that they had spread enormous fear throughout the Washington, DC area? Or had that been their principal purpose? Was it their aim to terrorize the U.S. government which, after all, resides in Washington? Had Muhammad brainwashed young Lee to become a serial killer? According to Malvo, the answer to this last question is yes. In an interview with the young sniper in October 2007, Malvo said that he could not control himself; that he was under total control of Muhammad during the killings. He also admitted that they had conceived a larger plan that was never instituted, a mass-scale terrorism campaign, shooting groups of children leaving school buses along with a series of mass explosions. Even if all of these questions could be answered, there still remains the ultimate question: Why?

• People from all walks of life may come to their own conclusions: Lawyers, judges, and jurors have their own answers. But those of us who work in criminal justice cannot be satisfied with partial or unscientific answers. If we want to prevent crime, we have to determine precise reasons for a person's turning to crime in the first place.

Street gangs flourish in communities throughout the United States. Bound by strong ethnic and racial ties, criminologists have developed elaborate theories to explain their many crimes, from illegal drugs, auto theft, extortion, property crimes, and home invasion, to the trafficking in fraudulent identification papers.

This chapter opened with an account of serial killers, John A. Muhammad and Lee Malvo, and their crimes. Most people who study criminal behavior agree that no one explanation would account for their crimes. Rather, we would have to look to a combination of biological, psychological, and social causes. Biological and psychological explanations assume that criminal behavior results from physical or mental conditions that distinguish criminals from noncriminals. They tell us about individual cases, but they do not explain why crime rates vary from place to place and from one situation to another. Sociological explanations differ from biological and psychological explanations in that they look for causes of criminal behavior in the environment in which a person grows up.

Biology and Crime

Over the past several decades, scientists have followed in the tradition of some of the early pioneers in the field of criminology by trying to find meaningful associations between human biology and criminal behavior. Geneticists, for example, have argued that the predisposition to act violently or aggressively in certain situations may be inherited. In other words, while criminals are not born criminal, as some criminologists long ago might have thought, the predisposition to be violent and, thus, commit crime, may be present at birth.

To demonstrate that certain traits are inherited, geneticists have studied children born of criminals but reared from birth by noncriminal adoptive parents. They wanted to know whether the behavior of the adoptive children was more similar to that of their biological parents than to that of their adoptive parents. Their findings play an important role in the debate on heredity versus environment. Other biologists, sometimes called biocriminologists, take a different approach. Some ask whether brain damage or inadequate nutrition results in criminal behavior. In recent years, a subspecialty within biocriminology has emerged—neurocriminology. Those who study neurocriminology examine the "neuro-correlates" of criminal behavior, for example, anatomical differences in brains of criminals versus noncriminals. Others are interested in the influence of hormones, chromosomal abnormalities, and allergies. They investigate interactions between brain and behavior, and between diet and behavior.

In a highly publicized case involving the 1979 murder of San Francisco mayor George Moscone, the impact of the amount of sugar in the blood was used as a defense in the trial. The testimony showed that when Dan White, the defendant, was depressed, he departed from his normal healthy diet and indulged himself with high-sugar "junk" food, including Twinkies, CocaCola, and chocolate candy. Afterward his behavior became less and less controllable. The jury found White guilty of manslaughter, rather than murder, due to diminished capacity. His defense was promptly dubbed the "junk food defense," "Dan White's defense," or "Twinkie defense." (White served five years in prison and committed suicide after his release.)

To study the relationship between behavior and diets high in sugar, a series of studies was conducted on institutionalized offenders in the United States. Inmates were placed on a modified diet that included very little sugar. They received fruit juice in place of soda and vegetables instead of candy. The results showed a decline in disciplinary actions and a significant drop in aggressive behavior in the experimental group.[1] Other research on biochemical factors has investigated vitamin deficiencies, food allergies, and hormonal problems.

Psychology and Criminality

The psychological approach to understanding crime, like the biological, focuses on the differences between criminals and noncriminals. Psychological explanations all assume that criminal behavior results from underlying psychological problems. The case of Charles Cullen is a good example. Former nurse Cullen, forty-four, is one of the worst mass murderers in New Jersey's history. Cullen pled guilty on April 29, 2004, to intentionally killing at least thirteen patients by administering lethal injections. When the prosecutor asked what his intentions were he said: "To cause death."[2] In a recent interview, Mr. Cullen said that he had killed as many as forty patients. A better background check would have revealed that the ex-nurse had a history of attempted suicides and hospitalizations for mental illness.

When psychologists attempt to explain criminality, they consider four general approaches. First, they focus on failures in psychological development—a weak conscience, inner conflict, improper moral development, or perhaps a poor attachment of infant to mother. Second, they look at ways in which people learn to be aggressive. For example, what part do movies and TV play? The TV and movie industries provide a steady stream of violent films such as *American History X, Irreversible, Henry: Portrait of a Serial Killer, Hannibal, Seven, The Silence of the Lambs, Reservoir Dogs, Saw, The Hills Have Eyes, A History of Violence, A Clockwork Orange, Pan's Labyrinth,* and *Hostel.* Has the wealthy drug dealer, living a glamorous life, become a folk hero? Research in this area remains inconclusive.

The third way that psychologists attempt to explain criminal behavior is by studying personality characteristics. Some have found that criminals tend to be more impulsive, intolerant, and irresponsible than noncriminals. Fourth, psychologists have related a particular form of mental disorder, psychopathy, to crime.

Estimates are that between 20 and 60 percent of state correctional populations suffer from psychopathy. **Psychopathy,** or antisocial personality, is characterized by an inability to learn from experience, a lack of warmth, and no sense of guilt. Psychopaths lie and cheat without hesitation and engage in verbal as well as physical abuse without provocation. Theodore "Ted" Bundy is a classic example. Bundy, a former law student and former crime commission staff member, killed between nineteen and thirty-six young women in the northwestern states and Florida. The handsome physical fitness enthusiast often brutally sexually attacked his victims before murdering them. In prison interviews Bundy speculated on what he believed had motivated the murderer in the crime in which he was the suspect:

> "What really fascinated him was the hunt, the adventure of searching out his victim," Bundy said. "And, to a degree, possessing them physically as one would possess a potted plant, a painting or a Porsche. Owning, as it were, this individual.

> "No matter how hard he tried, this hypothetical killer could never fully extinguish his desires to rape and murder. Instead he rationalized.

psychopathy
Condition in which a person has no sense of responsibility; shows disregard for truth; is insincere; and feels no sense of shame, guilt, or humiliation.

"He would cling to the belief that there would be virtually no furor over it...," Bundy said. "I mean, there are so many people.

"It shouldn't be a problem. What's one less person on the face of the earth, anyway?"[3]

Bundy died in the Florida electric chair in 1989.

Biological and Psychological Explanations: Practical Applications

careers

modus operandi
Means and method by which a crime is committed.

An understanding of the relationship between criminal behavior and biological and psychological factors has been helpful to criminal justice agencies in a number of ways. At the police level, results of studies have been used to develop tests to identify perpetrators (for example, DNA tests). Investigators also match psychological profiles with *modus operandi,* the means and method by which a crime is committed.

At the judicial level, the court often uses psychological evaluations such as presentence investigation reports as an aid in imposing sentences. In correctional settings, a number of psychological tests are used to evaluate inmates for placement in rehabilitation programs. On a daily basis, decisions are made by prison psychologists as to where inmates should be housed (classification decisions), whether individuals are in need of psychiatric treatment, and so forth.

Sociology and Criminality

Biological and psychological explanations seek to identify the "kind of person" who becomes a criminal and to uncover the factors that caused the person to engage in criminal behavior. They may explain individual cases, but they do not explain why crime rates vary from one neighborhood to the next, from one group to the next, within large urban areas, or within groups of individuals. Why, for example, are there an estimated 130,000 gang members in Los Angeles County alone? Why do youngsters under fifteen years old join groups, usually of their own ethnicity, that account for over 30,000 violent felonies in a single year? Sociological explanations seek the reasons for differences in crime rates in the social environment.

Strain Theory

strain theory
Crime results when the same materialistic goals are held out to all members of society without giving them equal means to achieve them.

One argument relates the crime problem to our class-oriented society. Noted sociologist Robert Merton argues that our society holds out the same materialistic goals (the "American Dream") to all members without giving them equal means to achieve them.[4] Statistics clearly demonstrate wide differences in income among various classes. Table 3.1 shows that, according to the latest census data, nearly twelve[5] percent of all American families live below the poverty level, with notable differences according to race. A child born to a single, uneducated, thirteen-year-old girl living in a slum has practically no chance to move up, whereas the child of a middle-class family has a better-than-average chance of reaching a professional or business position. Yet people from all social classes share common goals. And those goals are shaped by billions of advertising dollars spent each year to spread the message that everyone can drive a sports car, take a well-deserved Caribbean vacation, and record the adventure on videotape. (See Figure 3.1.)

The fantasy is reinforced by instant lottery winners; superstar athletes like Tiger Woods, who earns millions from his athletic skills and commercial endorsements; the earnings of Wall Street traders; and rags-to-riches stories of people like Ray Kroc, a high school dropout who started the McDonald's restaurant phenomenon. The crime problem results, say some experts, when individuals become frustrated at not being able to attain these goals themselves through conventional means and turn to criminal behavior to get what they want.[6]

Year	All Persons	Percent	White	Percent	Black	Percent	Hispanic Origin[1]	Percent	Asian and Pac. Isl.	Percent
				Persons below Poverty Level, 1975–2005 (in thousands)						
1975	25,877	12.3%	17,770	9.7%	7,545	31.3%	2,991	26.9%	n.a.	n.a.
1976	24,975	11.8	16,713	9.1	7,595	31.1	2,783	24.7	n.a.	n.a.
1977	24,720	11.6	16,416	8.9	7,726	31.3	2,700	22.4	n.a.	n.a.
1978	24,497	11.4	16,259	8.7	7,625	30.6	2,607	21.6	n.a.	n.a.
1979	26,072	11.7	17,214	9.0	8,050	31.0	2,921	21.8	n.a.	n.a.
1980	29,272	13.0	19,699	10.2	8,579	32.5	3,491	25.7	n.a.	n.a.
1981	31,822	14.0	21,553	11.1	9,173	34.2	3,713	26.5	n.a.	n.a.
1982	34,398	15.0	23,517	12.0	9,697	35.6	4,301	29.9	n.a.	n.a.
1983	35,303	15.2	23,984	12.1	9,882	35.7	4,633	28.0	n.a.	n.a.
1984	33,700	14.4	22,955	11.5	9,490	33.8	4,806	28.4	n.a.	n.a.
1985	33,064	14.0	22,860	11.4	8,926	31.3	5,236	29.0	n.a.	n.a.
1986	32,370	13.6	22,183	11.0	8,983	31.1	5,117	27.3	n.a.	n.a.
1987	32,221	13.4	21,195	10.4	9,520	32.4	5,422	28.0	1,021	16.1%
1988	31,745	13.0	20,715	10.1	9,356	31.3	5,357	26.7	1,117	17.3
1989	31,528	12.8	20,785	10.0	9,525	30.7	6,086	26.2	939	14.1
1990	33,585	13.5	22,326	10.7	9,837	31.9	6,006	28.1	858	12.2
1991	35,708	14.2	23,747	11.3	10,242	32.7	6,339	28.7	996	13.8
1992	38,014	14.8	25,259	11.9	10,827	33.4	7,592	29.6	985	12.7
1993	39,265	15.1	26,226	12.2	10,877	33.1	8,126	30.6	1,134	15.3
1994	38,059	14.5	25,379	11.7	10,196	30.6	8,416	30.7	974	14.6
1995	36,425	13.8	24,423	11.2	9,872	29.3	8,574	30.3	1,411	14.6
1996	36,529	13.7	24,650	11.2	9,694	28.4	8,697	29.4	1,454	14.5
1997	35,574	13.3	24,396	11.0	9,116	26.5	8,308	27.1	1,468	14.0
1998	34,476	12.7	23,454	10.5	9,091	26.1	8,070	25.6	1,360	12.5
1999	32,258	11.8	21,922	9.8	8,360	23.6	7,439	22.8	1,163	10.7
2000	31,139	11.3	21,291	9.4	7,901	22.1	7,155	21.2	1,226	10.8
2001	32,907	11.7	22,739	9.9	8,136	22.7	7,997	21.4	1,275	10.2
2002	34,570	12.1	23,466	10.2	8,602	24.1	8,555	21.8	1,161[2]	10.1
2003	35,861	12.5	24,272	10.5	8,781	24.4	9,051	22.5	1,401	11.8
2004	36,997	12.7	25,301	10.8	9,000	24.7	9,132	21.9	1,209	9.8
2005	36,950	12.6	24,872[3]	10.6	9,168[4]	24.9	9,368	21.8	1,402	11.1
2006	36,460	12.3	24,416	10.3	9,048	24.3	9,243	20.6	1,447	10.1

n.a. = not available.

1 Persons of Hispanic origin may be of any race.

2 For years 2002 and 2003, figures refer to people who reported Asian and did not report any other race category.

3 The 2003 Current Population Survey allowed respondents to choose more than one race. White alone refers to people who reported White and did not report any other race category.

4 Black alone refers to people who reported Black and did not report any other race.

5 Asian alone refers to people who reported Asian and did not report any other race.

SOURCE: U.S. Bureau of the Census. Web: www.census.gov.

TABLE 3.1   Persons below the Poverty Level by Selected Characteristics, 2001

Cultural Deviance Theories

Other scholars do not see the crime problem in terms of individuals striving to conform to conventional goals of the middle class—namely, financial success. Rather, they argue that our society is made up of various groups called **subcultures,** each with its own conduct

subculture
A subdivision within the dominant culture that has its own norms, beliefs, and values.

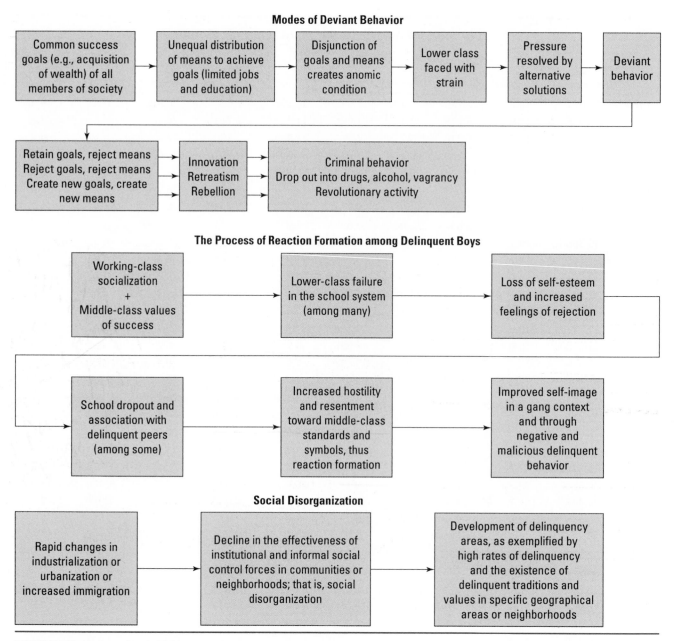

Modes of Deviant Behavior

The Process of Reaction Formation among Delinquent Boys

Social Disorganization

FIGURE 3.1   Strain Theory

SOURCE: Donald J. Shoemaker. *Theories of Delinquency: An Examination of Explanations of Delinquent Behavior,* 3rd ed. (New York: Oxford University Press, 1996), p. 107. Copyright © 1984, 1990, 1996, 2000 by Oxford University Press, Inc. Used by permission of Oxford University Press, Inc.

SOURCE: Donald J. Shoemaker. *Theories of Delinquency,* 2nd ed. (New York: Oxford University Press, 1990), p. 82. Copyright © 1984, 1990, 1996, 2000 by Oxford University Press, Inc. Used by permission of Oxford University Press, Inc.

norms (standards of right and wrong). Behavior considered normal in one group may be considered deviant by another. As a result, those who conform to the standards of cultures considered deviant may be behaving in accordance with their own norms and yet breaking the law, which is based on the norms of the dominant culture.[7]

Take, for example, motorcycle gangs. They made their appearance shortly after World War II. The Hell's Angels were the first of many gangs to be established in slum areas across the country. To become a member of the gang, initiates are subjected to grueling and revolting acts. They are conditioned to have allegiance only to the gang. Contacts with middle-class society are usually antagonistic and criminal. Motorcycle gangs finance their operations through illegal activities such as dealing drugs, running massage parlors and gambling operations, and selling stolen goods. The members' code of loyalty to one another and to their national and local groups makes the gangs extremely effective criminal organizations.

You may wonder whether the Hell's Angels are outcasts in the slum neighborhoods where they live. They are not. Many youngsters look up to them. Groups such as Hell's Angels may even meet the needs of younger boys who are looking for a way to be important in a disorganized ghetto that offers few opportunities to gain status.

According to Albert Cohen's argument, delinquent gangs emerge in economically deprived areas of larger American cities.[8] Working-class males, frustrated by their inability to compete successfully with middle-class youngsters, set up their own norms. They define "success" in ways that to them seem attainable. They turn the middle-class standards upside down, deeming behavior *right* in their gang because it is *wrong* by the standards of the middle class (for example, pleasure-seeking activities that are malicious and destructive).

Another argument is that the types of delinquent gangs that flourish depend on the types of neighborhoods in which they develop.[9] Just as means—opportunities—are unequal in the conventional world, opportunities to reach one's goals in the criminal world are also unequal. A youngster cannot simply decide to join a theft-oriented gang, or even a violence-oriented one. The types of delinquent behavior individuals engage in depend on the opportunities available in their neighborhoods—criminal (theft-oriented), conflict (violence-oriented), or retreatist ("dropout") gangs.

Some scholars argue that the general norms of behavior in inner-city slum areas are dictated by a value system that demands the use of force or violence.[10] The appearance of a weapon, a slight shove or push, or a derogatory remark may well bring about an aggressive reaction. Fists rather than words may be used to settle disputes. Knives or guns are readily available, so confrontations can quickly escalate. Violence is a pervasive part of everyday life. Child-rearing practices (hitting), gang activities (street wars), domestic quarrels, and social events (drunken brawls) are all characterized by violence.

The social disorganization of high-crime areas has been associated with poverty, rapid industrialization, increased immigration, and the growth of cities.[11] Decaying urban centers house disproportionate numbers of minority families headed by women who receive low-income assistance. In one of the most important explanations of crime causation and American criminology, Edwin Sutherland suggests that in these areas delinquent behavior is learned, transmitted from one generation to the next.[12] Not only is delinquent behavior learned, but so also are antisocial values and attitudes.

Social Disorganization

The best predictor of crime in adulthood, according to theorists, is weak social controls as a child. What are the prospects for Nathaniel Abraham, an eleven-year-old boy from Michigan, who was the youngest person ever convicted as an adult of murder. He was sentenced to a juvenile detention center until age twenty-one.

Social Control

We have been discussing why some people break the law. **Social control** explanations tell us why people do *not* break the law. It is taken for granted that drugs can tempt people; that petty fighting, petty theft, and recreational drinking may be attractive pastimes among adolescents and young adults. Why, then, do people conform in the face of so much temptation and peer pressure? The answer given by Travis Hirschi is that juveniles

social control
Deviance results when social controls are weakened or break down, so that individuals are not motivated to conform to them.

and adults conform to the law in response to certain controlling forces in their lives. They become criminals when the controlling forces are defective or absent. The forces that regulate behavior and lead to conformity, or obedience to society's rules, are the influences of family and school, religious beliefs, moral values, friends, and even beliefs about the government.[13]

Recent Explanations of Criminality

Over the past several years a number of attempts have been made to merge social control theories with other explanations of why people commit crime. These explanations are called developmental/life course theories, integrated theories, and "general theory."

Developmental/Life Course Theory. All developmental theories share one thing in common: explanations for why offending starts (onset), why it continues (continuance), why it becomes more frequent or serious (escalation), why it deescalates (deescalation), and why, inevitably, it stops (desistance). Rather than focusing exclusively on childhood, adolescence, young adulthood, or adulthood, these theories consider each developmental period in relation to the life span of an offender. In an extension of Hirschi's theory to the "life course," for example, Robert J. Sampson and John H. Laub found that family, school, and peer attachments were most strongly associated with delinquency from childhood to adolescence (through age seventeen).[14] From the transition to young adulthood through the transition to middle adulthood, attachment to work (job stability) and family (marriage) appear most strongly related to crime causation. Sampson and Laub found evidence that these positive personal and professional relationships build a "social capital" in otherwise vulnerable individuals that significantly inhibits deviance over time.

Another life course theory combines control with learning theory. Terence Thornberry argues that the potential for delinquency begins with the weakening of a person's bonds to the conventional world (parents, school, and accepted values). For this potential to be realized, there must be a social setting in which to learn delinquent values. In this setting, delinquents seek each other out and form common belief systems. There is nothing static about this kind of learning. Criminality, according to Thornberry, is a function of a dynamic social process that changes over time.[15]

The Cambridge Study of Delinquent Development reveals different explanations for the general tendency to engage in crime (long-term variables) over time, as well as the influences that prompt an individual, at any given time, to engage in crime (short-term variables). The former include impulsivity, low empathy, and belief systems favorable to law violation. The latter consider momentary opportunities and situationally induced motivating factors, such as alcohol consumption and boredom.[16]

Integrated Theory. Integrated theory combines a criminological theory, such as differential association, with a number of social controls. Researchers have integrated the social bonds of Hirschi's theory of social control with strain theories. These researchers suggest that limited or blocked opportunities and a subsequent failure to achieve cultural goals would weaken or even destroy bonds to the conventional or social order. In other words, even if someone establishes strong bonds in childhood, a series of negative experiences in school, in the community, and at home, along with blocked access to opportunity, would be likely to lead to a weakening of those social bonds. As strain weakens social bonds, the chance of delinquency increases.[17]

General Theories. In *A General Theory of Crime,* Travis Hirschi and Michael Gottfredson propose a new model of personal and social control—one designed to explain an individual's propensity to commit crime.[18] Hirschi and Gottfredson claim that their model, unlike earlier conceptualizations, explains the tendency to commit all crimes, from crimes of violence such as robbery and sexual assault to white-collar offenses such as mail fraud and federal securities violations.[19]

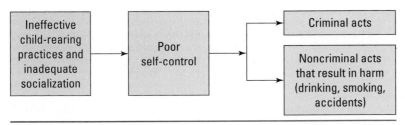

FIGURE 3.2   The Hirschi-Gottfredson Self-Control Model.
Hirschi and Gottfredson's model assumes that poor
self-control is an intervening variable that explains all
crime, as well as differences in crime rates, age,
gender, and race.

This "general theory" of propensity to commit crimes, shown in Figure 3.2, assumes that offenders have little control over their own behavior and desires. When the need for momentary pleasure and immediate gratification outweighs long-term interests, crime occurs. In short, crime is a function of poor self-control.

What leads to poor self-control? Inadequate socialization and poor child-rearing practices, coupled with poor attachment, increase the probability of impulsive and uncontrolled acts. According to Hirschi and Gottfredson individuals with low self-control also tend to be involved in noncriminal events that result in harm, such as drinking, smoking, and most types of accidents, including auto crashes, household fires, and unwanted pregnancies.

It is important to remember that all of these recent explanations of criminality share one common variable—the social bonds that are at the foundation of social control theory. The ingredients of social control theory have been used quite effectively over the last decade as building blocks for these recent developments.

Sociological Explanations: Practical Applications

As noted earlier, sociological explanations relate criminal behavior to the social environment—specifically, a lack of opportunity to attain goals and the learning of criminal values in socially disorganized neighborhoods. They also explain how social bonds promote commitment to conventional behavior in the face of frustration, poor living conditions, and other crime-oriented forces. These explanations have been the underpinning for many different types of government social programs such as Head Start. Inaugurated by President Lyndon Johnson in the 1960s, Head Start is a program for preschool children from low-income families that is intended to provide experiences that will enhance school readiness. Former President Clinton, in his 1993 State of the Union message, called Head Start a "success story," and noted that "for every dollar we invest today, we'll save $3 tomorrow."[20]

Many gang prevention and intervention strategies attempt to change the attitudes and behavior of inner city youngsters who have spent most of their lives learning unconventional street norms. The Boys and Girls Clubs of America (BGCA) Gang Prevention Through Targeted Outreach is one such program. This federally funded initiative gives juveniles at risk an alternative to gang life by recruiting them into clubs that provide structured recreation plus educational activities that focus on problem solving, decision making, school performance, and personal development. Evaluations of Targeted Outreach are very encouraging. Most of the enrolled youngsters attend once a week and one-quarter attend daily. Half of them show improved grades and better attendance at school. There are presently 157 of these programs.[21] The most comprehensive review of crime prevention programs was conducted by Lawrence W. Sherman and his colleagues. The results, in Tables 3.2 and 3.3, should force federal agencies to reevaluate their allocation of funding.

TABLE 3.2
What Works?

- **For infants:** Frequent home visits by nurses and other professionals.
- **For preschoolers:** Classes with weekly home visits by preschool teachers.
- **For delinquent and at-risk preadolescents:** Family therapy and parent training.
- **For schools:**
  —Organizational development for innovation.
  —Communication and reinforcement of clear, consistent norms.
  —Teaching of social competency skills.
  —Coaching of high-risk youth in "thinking skills."
- **For older male ex-offenders:** Vocational training.
- **For rental housing with drug dealing:** Nuisance abatement action on landlords.
- **For high-crime hot spots:** Extra police patrols.
- **For high-risk repeat offenders:**
  —Monitoring by specialized police units.
  —Incarceration.
- **For domestic abusers who are employed:** On-scene arrests.
- **For convicted offenders:** Rehabilitation programs with risk-focused treatments.
- **For drug-using offenders in prison:** Therapeutic community treatment programs.

SOURCE: Lawrence W. Sherman et al., *Preventing Crime: What Works, What Doesn't, What's Promising* (Washington, DC: NIJ, 1998), pp. 1, 7.

TABLE 3.3
What Doesn't Work

- Gun "buyback" programs.
- Community mobilization against crime in high-crime poverty areas.
- Police counseling visits to homes of couples days after domestic violence incidents.
- Counseling and peer counseling of students in schools.
- Drug Abuse Resistance Education (D.A.R.E.).
- Drug prevention classes focused on fear and other emotional appeals, including self-esteem.
- School-based leisure-time enrichment programs.
- Summer jobs or subsidized work programs for at-risk youth.
- Short-term, nonresidential training programs for at-risk youth.
- Diversion from court to job training as a condition of case dismissal.
- Neighborhood watch programs organized with police.
- Arrests of juveniles for minor offenses.
- Arrests of unemployed suspects for domestic assault.
- Increased arrests or raids on drug market locations.
- Storefront police offices.
- Police newsletters with local crime information.
- Correctional boot camps using traditional military basic training.
- "Scared Straight" programs whereby minor juvenile offenders visit adult prisons.
- Shock probation, shock parole, and split sentences adding jail time to probation or parole.
- Home detention with electronic monitoring.
- Intensive supervision on parole or probation (ISP).
- Rehabilitation programs using vague, unstructured counseling.
- Residential programs for juvenile offenders using challenging experiences in rural settings.

SOURCE: Lawrence W. Sherman et al., *Preventing Crime: What Works, What Doesn't, What's Promising* (Washington, DC: NIJ, 1998), pp. 1, 7.

Alternative Explanations for Crime

The 1960s witnessed a movement among students and professors to join advocacy groups and become activists in the social causes that rapidly were gaining popularity across the nation, such as equal rights for minorities, liberation for women, and peace. The generation of the 1960s had become disenchanted with an establishment that seemed to give only lip service to social change. The protests took many forms—demonstrations and

Ohio National Guard troops attacking student demonstrators on the Kent State campus in 1970. The killing of students shocked the nation.

rallies, sit-ins, beards and long hair, rock music and marijuana, dropping out of school, burning draft cards. Arrests of middle-class youth increased rapidly. Crime was no longer confined to the inner city. People began to ask whether arrests were being made for behavior that was not really criminal. Were the real criminals the legislators and policy-makers who pursued war in Vietnam while creating the crime of draft-card burning at home? Were the real criminals the National Guard troops who in 1970 shot and killed campus demonstrators at Kent State University? Labeling, conflict, and radical theorists provided some answers.

Labeling and conflict theorists turned away from the traditional theories that explained crime by reference to characteristics of the offender or the social environment. They set out to demonstrate that people become criminals because of what others with power, especially those in the criminal justice system, do. Unless an act is made criminal by law, no person who performs that act is a criminal. Alternative explanations of crime begin with this point. Then they ask: Who makes these laws? And why? Are all people who break these laws criminals? What part does the criminal justice system play in creating criminals?

Labeling Theory

Labeling theorists explore how and why certain acts are defined as criminal, or more broadly as deviant behavior, and others are not, and how and why certain people are defined as criminal or deviant. These theorists view criminals not as evil persons engaged in evil acts, but rather as individuals who have had a label attached to them by both the criminal justice system and the community. Viewed from this perspective, the criminal acts themselves are not particularly significant; the social reaction to them, however, is.

Labeling theory argues that society creates criminals through its criminal justice system by passing judgment on some persons as criminals, thereby permanently stigmatizing them.

labeling theory Explanation of deviance in terms of the way a person acquires a negative identity, such as "addict" or "ex-con," and is forced to suffer the consequences of outcast status.

Once it becomes known that a person has engaged in criminal or deviant acts, he or she is segregated from conventional society and is labeled a "thief," "whore," "junkie," and so forth. This process of segregation creates "outsiders" (a term used by Howard Becker), or outcasts from society, who begin to associate with others who have also been cast out.[22] As more people begin to think of these people as criminals, or deviants, and to respond to them accordingly, the labeled individuals react by continuing to engage in the behavior that society now expects of them. Gradually they begin to think of themselves as criminals or deviants.

An important question in labeling theory is: Who makes the rules that define deviant behavior, including crime? Labeling theorists answer that people in high social positions have the power to make and enforce the rules by which all members of a society must live. Certain privileged members of society therefore create the outsiders. The whole process becomes a political one, with some people making the rules that others break.

Critics of labeling theory remind us that, by and large, offenders get into the hands of the criminal justice system because they have broken the law. They question the overly active role labeling theory has assigned to the community and to criminal justice agencies, and the overly passive role it has assigned to offenders. Some suggest that punishment works as a deterrent—and therefore we need formal processing of offenders. Others argue that high rates of recidivism indicate that punishment has little to do with criminality. Moreover, those who are repeatedly arrested, convicted, and incarcerated do tend to live as outsiders in conventional communities. Labeling theorists have made a persuasive argument for more investigations in this area.

Conflict Theory

conflict theory
Model of crime in which the criminal justice system is seen as being used by the ruling class to control the lower class.

Like labeling theory, conflict theory has its roots in the questioning of values. But while labeling theorists focus on the labeling of the criminal by the system, conflict theorists question the existence of the system itself. Conflict theorists ask: If people agree on the value system, why are there so many crimes, so much threat of punishment, and so many people in prison? The answer: Laws do not exist for the good of all members of society; they represent the interests of specific groups that have the power to get them enacted.[23] Conflict theory holds that the people who have the power work to keep the powerless at a disadvantage. Powerful groups maintain their interests by making illegal any behavior that might be a threat to them. Laws thus become a means of control.

radical theory
Theory that crime is the result of a struggle for power and resources between owners of capital and workers.

Radical theory, a form of conflict theory, also argues that laws are created by the powerful to protect their own interests.[24] For radical theorists, however, there is only one dominant group, the capitalist ruling class. Radical theory demands the overthrow of capitalism, which is said to perpetuate criminality by keeping workers under the domination of capitalist oppressors. Only true socialism can reduce the crime rate. Opposition to radical theory is primarily concerned with the oversimplifications caused by an exclusive focus on capitalism. Critics also say that radical theory is more political than scientific.

Labeling and Conflict Theory: Practical Application

Labeling and conflict theorists have been instrumental in calling attention to some important questions, particularly about the way defendants are processed through the criminal justice system. Labeling theorists have carried out important scientific investigations of discrimination in the system.

Radical theorists have encouraged their more traditional colleagues to look with a critical eye at all aspects of the criminal justice system, including the response of the system to both poor and rich offenders. They challenge the system not to ignore population groups that have no share in the making of laws. Such groups include the growing number of homeless people and the increasing numbers of the population that are not working, either because they have lost their jobs or because they have not been equipped with education and working skills. (See Table 3.4.)

Perspective	Origin of Criminal Law	Causes of Criminal Behavior	Focus of Study
Traditional/consensus	Laws reflect shared values,	Psychological, biological, or sociological factors,	Psychological and biological factors (Chap. 4) unequal opportunity (Chap. 5), learning criminal behavior in disorganized neighborhoods (Chap. 5); subculture values (Chap. 6); social control (Chap .7)
Labeling	Those in power create the laws decide who will be the rule breakers.	The process that defines (or labels) certain persons as criminals.	Effects of stigmatizing by the label "criminal" sociopolitical factors behind reform legislation; origin of laws; deviant behavior (Chap. 8).
Conflict	Powerful groups use laws to support their interests.	Interests of one group do not coincide with needs of another.	Bias and discrimination in criminal justice system differential crime rates of powerful and powerless development of criminal laws by those in power, relationship between rulers and ruled (Chap. 8)
Radical (Marxist)	Laws serve interests of the ruling class.	Class struggle over distribution of resources in a capitalist system.	Relationship between crime and economics; ways in which state serves capitalist interests; solution to crime problem based on collapse of capitalism (Chap. 8)

SOURCE: Freda Adler, Gerhard O. W. Mueller, and William S. Laufer, Criminology and the Criminal Justice System (New York: McGraw-Hill, 2007), p. 190).

TABLE 3.4 Comparison of Four Criminological Perspectives

Criminal Justice In Action

Maximum-Security Schools

A rash of school shootings during the 1998–1999 academic year caused great concern across the nation. Criminologists, police, educators, lawmakers, and parents struggled to figure out why these young men and boys decided to pick up firearms and destroy the lives of their teachers and classmates. Many blamed the easy access to guns; others pointed to the social isolation these students experienced; still others looked to broader sociological explanations.

Although you would not know it, given all the media coverage surrounding these school shooting incidents, as well as experts' premonitions of doom and gloom, we are actually in the midst of a decline in violent crime in American schools. Thirty percent fewer students are carrying weapons to school than in 1991, and the number of student fights has also dropped. The number of school-related violent deaths is one-half what it was six years ago. During the 1997–1998 school year, only thirty-four students died in violent incidents in all the nation's schools. In fact, school is one of the safest places for young people, safer than the streets or even their homes. Young people are far more likely to die in alcohol-related automobile accidents (eight die per day, which represents 40 percent of all deaths of 16- to 20-year-olds), or from unintentional injury or suicide (10 and 13 percent, respectively, of deaths of those ages ten to twenty-four).[1] Even so, deaths related to school violence get much more press coverage—much of it sensationalized. As a result, parents, and the community at large, tend to panic.

Target hardening and situational crime prevention in schools are nothing new. Schools in certain parts of some cities have had metal detectors, doors with alarms, and locker searches for years. Then there are the other schools in towns few have heard of: places like Paducah, Conyers, and Littleton. The image of these suburban schools as safe havens has been shattered. Although the likelihood of a shooting

(continued)

In some inner-city schools, security measurers rival those used in prison: metal detectors, drug-sniffing dogs, frequent searches for weapons, and surveillance cameras that monitor the movement of students in and out of classrooms.

in any particular school is small, officials are not taking any chances. Interestingly, the prevention measures listed below fall squarely into Clarke and Homel's situational-crime-prevention model.

Access Control

- Intercom systems are being used at locked doors to buzz in visitors.[2]
- Students have to flash or swipe computerized identification cards to get into school buildings.
- Perimeter fences delineate school property and secure cars after hours.

Controlling Facilitators

- Students in Deltona, Florida, get an extra set of books to leave at home. The schools have banned backpacks and dismantled lockers to eliminate places to stash weapons. Other school districts are encouraging see-through lockers and backpacks.
- After the Littleton, Colorado, incident, school boards across the country banned trench coats and other oversized garments, apparently to prevent students from hiding weapons on their bodies or in their clothing.

Entry/Exit Screening

- Handheld and walk-through metal detectors keep anyone with a weapon from entering schools.

Formal Surveillance

- Uniformed police officers and private security guards, some of them armed, patrol school halls.
- Schools are installing surveillance cameras in hallways and on school buses.

Surveillance by Employees (or, in This Case, Students)

- Students are carrying small notebooks so that they can log and then report overheard threats.

Identifying Property

- Tiny microfilm is hidden inside expensive school property so that it can be identified if stolen.

On the face of it, these measures seem to make good sense. They can prevent people from bringing weapons into schools and keep unauthorized people out. They increase the ability of school officials to detect crime, identify evildoers, and prevent criminal incidents from happening. But have school officials and others gone too far? Diana Philip is the director of the American Civil Liberties Union of Texas for the northern region, which has filed several lawsuits against schools. She observes that "over the summer, we have had school boards putting together the most restrictive policies we have ever seen. A lot of them are in clear violation of the Fourth Amendment, which guarantees freedom from unreasonable searches."[3]

Chicago Tribune columnist Steve Chapman argues that schools treat students as "dangerous, incorrigible, undeserving of respect" or privacy. He asks, "What's the difference between school and prison? At school, you don't get cable TV."[4]

(continued)

SOURCES
1. *Violence in School: The Facts,* Office of the Attorney General, State of Illinois, found at http://www.ag.state.il.us/program/school/facts.htm, October 30, 1999.
2. Jacques Steinberg, "Barricading the School Door," *The New York Times,* August 22, 1999, New York section, p. 5.
3. S. C. Gwynne, "Is Anyplace Safe?" *Time,* August 23, 1999. http://www.pathfinder.com/magazine/time (accessed February 10, 2000).
4. Walter Olson, "Dial 'O' for Outrage: The Sequel—Tales from an Overlawyered America," *Reason* (November 1999), pp. 54–56.

Questions for Discussion

1. Do you think there would be as much concern over school violence if these shooting incidents had happened in urban schools? Why are people more upset when crime happens in places they perceive to be safe (such as in the suburbs)?
2. Does your high school or college campus have any security measures in place? If so, how do they fit into Clarke and Homel's sixteen techniques of situational prevention?
3. Is there a point where security measures in schools become so extreme that they can no longer be justified? Have we reached that point yet?

Situational Crime Prevention

Thus far in this chapter we have explained criminal behavior in terms of biological, psychological, and sociological factors. We also looked at alternative explanations of crime that examine the impact of lawmaking and law enforcement processes on the creation of offenders. We now turn to a new perspective that not only explains crime, but also has prevention built into it.

Environmental Criminology

Some criminologists have focused on why offenders choose to commit one offense rather than another at a given time and place. They identify conditions under which those who are prone to commit crime will in fact do so. Current research shows that both a small number of victims and a small number of places experience a large amount of all crime committed. Crimes are events. Criminals choose their targets. Certain places actually attract criminals. And there are techniques of situational prevention that make offending less likely. (See Table 3.5.)

Routine Activities and Rational Choice

Contrary to the established criminological theories that explain criminal motivation, environmental criminology begins with the assumption that some people are criminally motivated. Through mapping crimes on global, country, state, county, city, or site-specific levels, such as a particular building or plot of land, environmental criminologists can see crime patterns. They then relate these crime patterns to the number of targets; to the offender population; to the location of routine activities, such as work, school, shopping, or recreation; to security; and to traffic flow.

There are two related approaches: (1) the routine activities approach, and (2) the rational choice approach. The routine activities approach explains crime as the combination of three factors:

1. Likely and motivated offenders (for example, unemployed teenagers)
2. Suitable targets (for example, easily transportable goods)
3. An absence of capable guardians (for example, friends or neighbors)

Increasing Perceived Effort	Increasing Perceived Risks	Reducing Anticipated Rewards	Inducing Guilt or Shame
1. *Target hardening:* Slug-rejecter device Steering locks Bandit screens	5. *Entry/exit screening:* Automatic ticket gates Baggage screening Merchandise tags	9. *Target removal:* Removable car radio Women's refuges Phone card	13. *Rule setting:* Harassment codes Customs declaration Hotel registrations
2. *Access control:* Parking lot barriers Fenced yards Entry phones	6. *Formal surveillance:* Burglar alarms Speed cameras Security guards	10. *Identifying property:* Property marking Vehicle licensing Cattle branding	14. *Strengthening moral condemnation:* "Shoplifting is stealing" Roadside speedometers "Bloody idiots drink and drive"
3. *Defecting offenders:* Bus stop placement Tavern location Street closures	7. *Surveillance by employee:* Pay phone location Park attendants OCTV systems	11. *Reducing temptation:* Gender-neutral phone lists Off-street parking	15. *Controlling disinhibitors:* Drinking-age laws Ignition interlock Server intervention
4. *Controlling facilitators:* Credit card photo Caller ID Gun controls	8. *Natural surveillance:* Defensible space Street lighting Can drive ID	12. *Denying benefits:* Ink merchandise tags PIN for car radios Graffiti cleaning	16. *Facilitating compliance:* Improved library checkout Public lavatories Trash bins

SOURCE: Ronald V. Clarke and Ross Homel, "A Revised Classification of Situational Crime Prevention Techniques," In *Crime Prevention at a Crossroads*, Steven P. Lab, ed, (Cincinnati, OH: Anderson, 1997), with permission. Copyright 1997 Mathew Bender & Company, Inc., a member of the LexisNexis Group.

TABLE 3.5 Sixteen Techniques of Situational Prevention

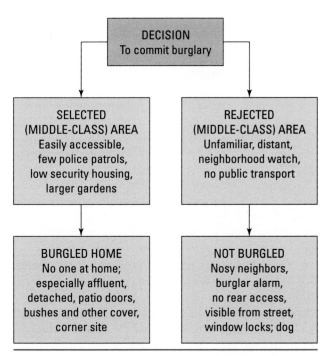

FIGURE 3.3 Event Model (*example:* burglary in a middle-class suburb).

SOURCE: Adapted from Ronald V. Clarke and Derek B. Comish, "Modeling Offenders' Decisions: A Framework for Research and Policy," In *Crime and Justice,* vol. 6, Michael Tonry and Norval Morris, eds. (Chicago: University of Chicago, 1985), p. 169. © 1985 by The University of Chicago. All rights reserved. Reprinted by permission of the University of Chicago Press.

Similarly, the rational choice approach takes into account the criminal, the motivation, and the situation. It suggests that individuals decide whether a crime is worth committing after weighing the benefits against the costs (the risk of being caught and physical danger, for example).[25]

Review

Explanations of criminal behavior focus on biological, psychological, social, and economic factors. Biological and psychological theories assume that criminal behavior results from underlying physical or mental conditions that distinguish criminals from noncriminals. These theories yield insight into individual cases, but they do not explain why crime rates vary from place to place and from one situation to another. Sociological theories seek to explain criminal behavior in terms of the social environment. Strain and cultural deviance theories focus on the social forces that cause people to engage in criminal behavior. Both theories assume that social class and criminal behavior are related. Strain theorists argue that people commit crime because they are frustrated by not being able to achieve society's goals through legitimate means. Cultural devi-

ance theorists claim that crime is learned in socially disorganized neighborhoods where criminal norms are transmitted from one generation to the next.

Those who study subcultures and the gangs that flourish within them suggest that lower-class males, frustrated by their inability to meet middle-class standards, set up their own norms by which they can find status. Often these norms are different from those of the middle class. Social control theorists explain how people remain committed to conventional behavior in the face of frustration, poor living conditions, and other criminogenic factors.

Three quite different theoretical perspectives focus on society's role in creating criminals and defining them as such. Labeling theory, conflict theory, and radical theory offer alternative explanations of crime, in the sense that they do not study individual criminal characteristics or social norms, which all the other theories associate with crime. These three theories examine the impact of the processes of lawmaking and law enforcement on the creation of offenders.

Two related approaches, routine activities and rational choice, explain why crime occurs and how it can be prevented. We consider these perspectives to be particularly practical because they suggest to the public, including the police and potential victims, ways in which crime can be prevented—both by hardening targets (better lighting, burglar alarms, etc.) and by frustrating opportunities.

Thinking Critically about Criminal Justice

1. Suppose you have been appointed a member of a team of experts that has just been given a major funding grant from the Department of Justice to reduce crime in a particular inner-city neighborhood. Based on the explanations you have learned in this chapter about why people commit crime, what recommendations would you want to include in the plan?

2. The United States has a long history of denying convicted felons the right to vote. Today there are about 4 million voting-age disenfranchised felons and exfelons. Close to 1.5 million have completed their sentence. Over one-third of the total disenfranchised population are African American males. Do you believe that given this nation's history of voting discrimination, our current disenfranchisement policy should be changed?

3. You learned in this chapter that some criminologists focus on the prevention of crimes against people, places, and valuable goods. They identify conditions under which those who are prone to commit crime will, in fact, do so. How can the police use this information?

4. Juveniles occupy a very special place in the criminal justice system. Should they be subjected to the same punishments? How about capital punishment? See www.deathpenaltyinfo.org/article php!did=205& scid=27.

Notes

1. Stephen Schoenthaler, "Diet and Crime: An Empirical Examination of the Value of Nutrition in the Control and Treatment of Incarcerated Juvenile Offenders," *International Journal of Biosocial Research* 4 (1983), pp. 25–39.

2. B. Peterson "Hospital Where 13 Were Killed Prepares to Face Lawsuits" and David Kocieniewski, "Ex-nurse pleads guilty to killing patients," *The New York Times,* April 30, 2004, pp. B1, B6.

3. Barry Bearak, "Bundy Is Electrocuted as Crowd of 500 Cheers," *Los Angeles Times,* January 25, 1989, Part 1, p. 1.

4. Robert K. Merton, "Social Structure and Anomie," *American Sociological Review* 3 (1938), pp. 672–682. See also Freda Adler and William S. Laufer, eds., *The Legacy of Anomie,* with Part I by Robert K. Merton (New Brunswick, NJ: Transaction, 1995).

5. *Statistical Abstract of the United States, 1997* (Washington, DC: U.S. Department of Commerce, Bureau of the Census, 1997), p. 465.

6. Robert Agnew, "Delinquency and the Desire for Money," *Justice Quarterly* 11 (1994), pp. 411–427.

7. Thorsten Sellin, *Culture Conflict and Crime,* Bulletin 41 (New York: Social Science Research Council, 1938).

8. Albert K. Cohen, *Delinquent Boys: The Culture of the Gang* (Glencoe, IL: Free Press, 1955). For a comprehensive examination of Chinese gangs, see Ko-lin Chin, *Chinese Subculture and Criminality* (New York: Greenwood Press, 1990).

9. Richard A. Cloward and Lloyd E. Ohlin, *Delinquency and Opportunity* (Glencoe, IL: Free Press, 1960).

10. Marvin E. Wolfgang and Franco Ferracuti, *The Subculture of Violence* (London: Tavistock, 1967).

11. Clifford R. Shaw and Henry D. McKay, *Juvenile Delinquency and Urban Areas* (Chicago: University of Chicago Press, 1969).

12. Edwin H. Sutherland, *Principles of Criminology,* 3rd ed. (Philadelphia: Lippincott, 1939).

13. Travis Hirschi, *Causes of Delinquency* (Berkeley: University of California Press, 1969).

14. Robert J. Sampson and John H. Laub, *Crime in the Making: Pathways and Turning Points through Life* (Cambridge, MA: Harvard University Press, 1993); R. J. Sampson and J. H. Laub, "Understanding Variability in Lives through Time: Contributions of Life-Course Criminology," *Studies on Crime and Crime Prevention* 4 (1995), pp. 143–158.

15. Terence P. Thornberry, A. J. Lizotte, and M. D. Krohn, "Delinquent Peers, Beliefs, and Delinquent Behavior: A Longitudinal Test of Interactional Theory," *Criminology* 32 (1994), pp. 47–83.

16. D. P. Farrington, "Explaining the Beginning, Progress, and Ending of Antisocial Behavior from Birth to Adulthood," *Advances in Criminological Theory* 3 (1992), pp. 253–286.

17. S. Menard and Delbert S. Elliott, "Delinquent Bonding, Moral Beliefs, and Illegal Behavior: A Three Wave Panel Model," *Justice Quarterly* 11 (1994), pp. 173–188.

18. Michael R. Gottfredson and Travis Hirschi, *A General Theory of Crime* (Stanford, CA: Stanford University Press, 1990); Michael Gottfredson and Travis Hirschi,

"A Propensity-Event Theory of Crime," in *Advances in Criminological Theory,* vol. 1, ed. W. Laufer and F. Adler (New Brunswick, NJ: Transaction, 1989).

19. Travis Hirschi and Michael Gottfredson, "The Significance of White-Collar Crime for a General Theory of Crime," *Criminology* 27 (1989), pp. 359–371.

20. Barbara Kantrowitz and Pat Wingert, "No Longer a Sacred Cow: Head Start Has Become a Free-Fire Zone," *Newsweek,* April 12, 1993, p. 51.

21. Terence P. Thornberry and James H. Burch, II, *Gang Members and Delinquent Behavior,* Juvenile Justice Bulletin, OJJDP (U.S. Department of Justice, June 1997).

22. Howard Becker, *Outsiders: Studies in the Sociology of Deviance* (New York: Macmillan, 1963), p. 9.

23. Austin Terrell, *Political Criminality: The Defiance of Authority* (Beverley Hills, CA: Sage, 1982).

24. Richard Quinney, *Crime and Justice in Society* (Boston: Little, Brown, 1969), pp. 26–30.

25. Ronald V. Clarke and Marcus Felson, "Introduction: Criminology, Routine Activity, and Rational Choice," in *Routine Activity and Rational Choice, Advances in Criminological Theory* 5, ed. Ronald V. Clarke and Marcus Felson (New Brunswick, NJ: Transaction, 1993), pp. 1–14.

CHAPTER

4

The Criminal Law

ALEXANDRIA, La.—A man shot five people in a downtown law office Thursday afternoon and holed up in the building, *Causation* shooting repeatedly at police with two *Punishment* victims still inside, authorities said.

Two of the victims escaped on their own and police rescued a third, but the gunman repeatedly fought off attempts to reach the others, police said.

"We've tried two or three times to enter, every time he's fired at our officers," Sgt. Clifford Gatlin said. "We have returned fire and we don't know if he's hit or not."

Police fired tear gas into the building and tried unsuccessfully to reach the shooter on his cellular telephone and the office phone, Gatlin said. A SWAT team had positioned itself behind an armored car in front of the law firm.

Gatlin would not identify the shooter.[1]

KANSAS CITY, Mo.—A woman accused of killing a pregnant woman and cutting her baby from her womb was concerned that her ex-husband was threatening to expose her faked pregnancy and get custody of her children, prosecutors said Thursday.

The night before Bobbie Jo Stinnett was killed and had her baby cut from her womb, Lisa Montgomery told her ex-husband, "I'll show you, I'll prove you wrong, I'm pregnant," federal prosecutor Matt Whitworth told jurors in opening statements.

Montgomery's attorneys, who plan an insanity defense, painted a picture of a woman who was severely troubled from repeated abuse as a teenager, and who had gone to Stinnett's house intending only to buy a puppy.[2]

• If these sound to you like plots from several episodes of a popular television series, well, you're wrong. But they could be. Deciphering the state of mind and actions of the lawful and lawless makes both fiction and nonfiction so compelling. Much of what makes both so interesting is the province of substantive criminal law—a body of law that often turns on the state of mind of the accused and the accompanying criminal act.

In this chapter, we will explore the substance of the criminal law, first by examining the seven basic principles that define all crimes. Then we describe a series of defenses, or pattern answers, created by courts and legislatures over the centuries to deal with common and frequently occurring situations.

The Criminal Law and Its Seven Basic Principles

All those who are being processed through the criminal justice system have at least one thing in common: They have been charged with a crime. And all crimes have something in common, something that distinguishes them from acts not recognized by the law as criminal. In fact, seven principles mark every crime.[3] These principles are so much a part of what we call crime that if you were to ask us for a general definition of crime, it would be an impossible task until we had put the seven principles before you. With few exceptions (which will be discussed later), it is these seven basic principles that define crime.

We start at the beginning with the one principle that is at the very source of the law—the principle of legality.

1. Legality: Is There a Law That Makes Something Criminal?

It would seem obvious that there must *be* a law before it can be applied. In terms of criminal law, there must be a criminal law before somebody can be charged with having violated it. An old maxim says: No crime without criminal law (*Nulum crimen sine lege*). Where do these laws come from? Today, for the most part, it is legislatures that make them. But this was not always the case. The common law, as our law is still called, primarily did not come to us through legislation. (In fact, the principles behind the law still are not normally contained in legislation.)

common law
Law as developed in England and later in the United States on the basis of court decisions (precedents) and as supplemented by legislation.

Reported decisions of the courts remain the hallmark of the common law: **Common law** was what the courts of England decided, and the law was always being further developed by new cases that elaborated on or extended the law of preceding cases. As far as the criminal law was concerned, however, the king's courts became increasingly reluctant to make new laws or to extend the scope of what had previously been defined as criminal. This reluctance of courts to extend the law, the preference to stick to previous decisions, is one of the hallmarks of common law. It is called the rule of *stare decisis* (to adhere to decided cases).

legality
Principle that every crime must be clearly defined by common law or legislation prior to its commission.

The principle of **legality** is firmly established in America today: Only legislatures can make laws that prohibit an act under threat of punishment. Moreover, the principle of legality also requires that the legislatures have made the law prior to the commission of the act. Human beings can be expected to act in a given manner only if there is a clear and intelligible law telling them what is expected of them and what will happen if they do not follow the law.

2. Conduct: Only the Acts of Persons Can Be Covered by Criminal Law

involuntary acts
Acts that are the product of:

- Somnambulism (sleepwalking)
- Unconsciousness
- Seizures
- Involuntary neurological responses

Modern criminal law directs itself only at human action. It is only humans, acting singly or in groups (or even as corporations), who can be alerted by the criminal law. Take a test: Look at any of the many crimes specified in the penal laws (criminal code) of your state. All prohibit *persons* from *acting* in a given manner (acts of commission). The verb *act* implies some degree of rationality or voluntariness in choosing to do or to accomplish something. A sleepwalker does not act from choice and does not act rationally. Consequently, under the criminal law the acts of a sleepwalker are considered involuntary, and the conduct of a sleepwalker cannot be deemed criminal conduct. Likewise, a convulsion or a reflex is an **involuntary act** and does not amount to action.

You Be the Judge!

Does Unconsciousness Preclude Criminal Liability?

As time passed, Ervin Mercer's strong affections for his wife Myrtle were not reciprocated. Marital difficulties were heightened when Ervin heard that his wife was having affairs with other men. Frequent separations due to Ervin's military service did not help the relationship. One day, after drinking vodka, Ervin took a gun to the house where Myrtle was staying. Myrtle threatened to call the police if he did not leave. After hearing this, Ervin "went blank in his mind," and killed Myrtle and the people she was staying with. At Ervin's trial for murder, he claimed that he was completely unconscious at the time the shooting took place.

You Be the Judge! Should a person be convicted of a crime that was committed while in a state of unconsciousness?

The court's conclusion: If Ervin was unconscious at the time of Myrtle's murder, he should not be found guilty. Absence of consciousness, if established by evidence, precludes the finding of a voluntary act and mental state—both of which are required for conviction.

State v. Mercer, 165 SE 2d 328 (N.C. 1969).

Sometimes under the law *inaction* may amount to action (acts of omission). A parent who fails to rescue a drowning child, a law enforcement officer who fails to stop a violent criminal, a firefighter who fails to put out a fire, a baby-sitter who fails to prevent an infant from strangling itself at the playground, or a person who under law must register but does not—all can be found guilty of a crime for not acting. The crime consists of inaction when there is a legal duty to act.

It follows that a person without a special legal duty to act is not obligated to come to the assistance of a person in trouble. Here law and morality differ: The biblical Good Samaritan came to the rescue even without legal obligation. This is but one of many instances where law and morality differ: Not everything immoral is illegal, and not everything illegal is immoral.

3. Harm: Protecting a Legally Recognized Value

With every criminal prohibition, the legislature seeks to protect a value, presumably one dear to all citizens. The threat to or destruction of a given value is the harm of a particular crime. Homicide legislation seeks to protect the value of human life. In the case of larceny, the harm obviously is the loss of property. In the case of treason, it is the threat to the security of the state.

Criminal Justice In Action

The Act Requirement

Ancient French court records reveal that when swarms of grasshoppers invaded the countryside and were gobbling up crops, a summons was issued to all grasshoppers to appear in court promptly on charges of devastating the harvest. In medieval Germany, goats or geese that had committed criminal mischief on a neighbor's property could be hanged as a punishment for their crimes. In 1386, a sow that had killed a child in Falaise, France, was tried, found guilty of homicide, and executed by hanging.

Punishment for Status

Today human conduct is one of the seven criteria that define a crime. Although animals have been tried, convicted, and punished for crimes in the past, we now reserve blame, responsibility, and liability for *human* action only. After all, only

(continued)

Execution of a Sow.

Fresco on a church wall in Falaise, France, depicting a 1386 execution of a sow.

human beings can act responsibly. Acting, conducting oneself, or doing something is intrinsically human. It involves the human capacity to reason, to choose among various courses of conduct. And blame can be imposed only if there was an appeal to human reason and a corresponding failure to act in accordance with the appeal.

No lawgiver can command animals to respond to reason, for they have none. Nor can a lawgiver expect mountains to move on command, or any condition of nature to change under threat of punishment. Unfortunately, we have not always recognized this truth. History records many examples of punishment for conditions of nature, status, and relationships. Under Stalin's penal code, for example, any relative of a deserter from the Red Army could be punished by ten years of exile to Siberia, simply for the family relationship—even if the person had not seen the relative in twenty years. Under Hitler's racial and martial laws, all Jews were to be executed, all gypsies, all relatives of any general officer who had surrendered. In such laws there was no appeal to reason; the punishment for being Jewish could not possibly change Jews into non-Jews.[1]

Robinson v. California

Our own law, too, from time to time has imposed punishment for a status rather than for failure to respond to an appeal to reason. Until 1964 it was possible in New York for a woman to be sent to jail for a year for being a prostitute, without regard to whether she was currently soliciting or engaging in sex for hire. She had a status: Once a prostitute, always a prostitute. This law no longer exists. But a similar law reached the Supreme Court in 1962: California had made it a misdemeanor to be a drug addict, and a drug addict, Robinson, was convicted under the statute. How could an addict have evaded the impact of this law? Drug addiction is a condition, a status. The law can say what it wants; it can make unreasoned demands; but it can no more expect people to alter their status condition than it can expect animals to abide by its commands. The Supreme Court declared the statute unconstitutional, reasoning that one may be a drug addict through no fault of one's own, for example by being born to an addict mother. To punish people for being this or that kind of person violates the Constitution's (Eighth Amendment prohibition of cruel and unusual punishment.[2] The upshot is this: Only human *action* can be prohibited under threat of punishment. Justice Fortas of the Supreme Court provided this summary:

Robinson stands upon a principle which despite its subtlety, must be simply stated and respectfully applied because it is the foundation of individual liberty and the cornerstone of the relations between a civilized state and its citizens: Criminal penalties may not be inflicted upon a person for being in a condition he is powerless to change.[3]

(continued)

The principle finally settled in *Robinson v. California* is clear: Only *human conduct* can be made criminal; every crime involves *human conduct* as a basic ingredient.

SOURCES

1. Rudolf His, *Deutsches Strafrecht bis zur karolina* (Munich: Oldenbourg, 1928), p. 18.
2. *Robinson v. California,* 370 U.S. 660 (1962).
3. Justice Fortas, dissenting in *Powell v. Texas,* 392 U.S. 514, 567 (1968).

Questions for Discussion

1. In Texas it was criminal "to be drunk in public." In *Powell v. Texas,* the U.S. Supreme Court upheld the validity of the statute. How can this be reconciled with the conduct requirement?

2. Sometimes criminal liability is based on (or increased by) a status. For example, under 8 U.S.C. Section 1726 it is unlawful, "being a postmaster," to demand unauthorized rates or gratuities. Is that reconcilable with the conduct requirement?

3. Is there a difference between the way lawyers and psychologists define conduct? Explain.

[handwritten margin note: – Void for Vagueness – Overbreadth]

The concept of harm is vital to an understanding of crime. First of all, it permits us to determine whether a crime has in fact taken place. If the legislatively prohibited harm has not been caused, then no crime has been committed. Second, harm is the evil the legislature wished to prevent, and this evil ultimately determines the punishment for committing it.

Legislators and criminal justice specialists have grouped all crimes into categories distinguished by the harm the crimes entail. Crimes against the person can be subdivided into those against life and those against physical integrity. Crimes against property include larceny, burglary, arson, and fraud. Crimes against national security include treason, and crimes against humankind include genocide.

In describing the concept, or principle, of harm as a fundamental ingredient of every crime, what is most important is this premise: A crime is not constituted, a crime is not complete, until the perpetrator has indeed brought about the harm. Murder is not complete until the victim is dead. However, if the perpetrator has tried but has not succeeded in bringing about the harm, there may still be criminal liability for an *attempt* or an *assault.* Thus, even endangerment of the legally protected interest may be a punishable harm.

Firefighters battle a blaze at the Castle Dracula, a haunted house-style ride on the Wildwood, NJ, boardwalk on January 16, 2002. Two teenagers seen running from the area were arrested and charged with arson. Did they set the fire? Evidence emerged at the trial that the two boys entered the ride when it was closed, lit torches to see where they were going, and started the fire.

Two Tests for Causation

• Factual Causation But for A's act, the result would not have occurred when and as it did. *"But for Bill's act, Harry would not have been injured in the way in which he was."*

• Proximate Causation B's injuries must have been the natural and probable consequences of A's act. B's injuries must have been foreseeable, without any intervening factors sufficient to break the causal chain that would relieve A of liability.

4. Causation: Bringing about the Harm

The law demands that a defendant's *act* must have *caused* the *harm* (*A* must have caused *B*'s injuries). If somebody else (*C*) intervened and caused the harm, the defendant (*A*) may be guilty for *trying* to cause the harm (we call this an attempt), but he cannot be blamed for the harm. In most criminal cases, attribution of the harm to the defendant's act is not a problem. Indeed, we are normally not even compelled to ask the question. When we say *A* killed *B*, we are expressing the act-causation-harm sequence in a single word. To *rape*, to *steal*, to *speed*, to *defraud*—all imply a unified concept: act, causation, and harm.

The Model Penal Code codifies the common law principle that there must be a causal link between the defendant's act and the requisite harm. In Section 2.03 it provides: "Conduct is the cause of a result when . . . it is an antecedent but for which the result in question would not have occurred." But surely there must be some limitation on how far back courts should go in the causal chain. So courts and judges have tried to shorten the causal chain by requiring that, to be a cause in the legal sense, the event in question must not be too remote; it must be "proximate." But what is proximate and what is remote? Judges tend to use the simple test: Was the result (harm) the natural and probable consequence of the act?

You Be the Judge!

When Is There Insufficient Evidence of Causation?

One night Kibbe and Krall volunteered to give Stafford a ride from one bar to another, with the intent of robbing him. On the way to the next bar, they robbed Stafford and forced him to lower his trousers and remove his boots. After robbing him, they abandoned him on a rural two-lane highway about one-quarter mile from a gas station. It was a very cold and windy night.

About half an hour later, Blake, who was driving 50 mph (10 mph over the limit), saw Stafford sitting on the road. Blake testified that he did not have time to react before impact. After the collision, Blake returned to help Stafford. Unfortunately, he was mortally injured, his trousers were around his ankles, and he had on neither his jacket nor boots. His blood alcohol level was .25 percent.

Kibbe and Krall were convicted of second-degree murder, second-degree robbery, and third-degree grand larceny without any consideration by the jury of Blake's possible contribution to Stafford's death.

You Be the Judge! Would you reverse the conviction? Should the case be retried with a consideration of the intervening actions of Blake's? When do the intervening acts of a third party break the chain of causation?

The court's conclusion: Kibbe and Krall deserved the jury's consideration of whether the intervening force of Blake was a sufficiently independent or supervening cause of Stafford's death.

Kibbe v. Henderson, 534 F2d 493 (2d Cir. 1976).

---

5. *Mens Rea* (Guilty Mind): Criminal Intent

Nothing is as well established in all legal systems as the principle that no conduct can be considered criminal unless there is a guilty mind—an intent to commit a crime or to do harm. In law this "guilty mind" is referred to by its Latin term: ***mens rea*** (evil mind). It has sometimes been said that it is the intention to do the prohibited thing that is the *mens rea:* the intention to kill (in murder), the intention to deprive the owner of property (in larceny). But that cannot be so entirely. If it were, then the soldier who kills an enemy in wartime or the executioner who carries out the death sentence would have the *mens rea* for murder. The police officer who seizes the murder weapon would have the *mens rea* for larceny.

mens rea (Latin) Guilty mind; awareness of wrongdoing. Intention to commit a criminal act, or recklessness.

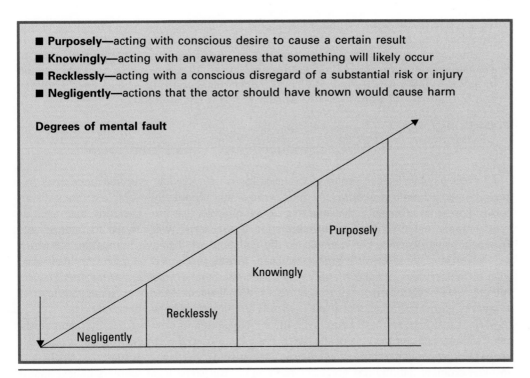

- **Purposely**—acting with conscious desire to cause a certain result
- **Knowingly**—acting with an awareness that something will likely occur
- **Recklessly**—acting with a conscious disregard of a substantial risk or injury
- **Negligently**—actions that the actor should have known would cause harm

Degrees of mental fault

Purposely

Knowingly

Recklessly

Negligently

FIGURE 4.1   Criminal Intent (*mens rea*)

Mens rea, then, is more than just intent; it is intent coupled with the knowledge or awareness that one has no right to do the act.[4] This becomes apparent when we examine how defenses work: A person who takes another's raincoat from a restaurant coatrack has the intention to take the coat; but if the person believes he is taking his own coat he is not guilty of larceny because he lacks the awareness of wrongdoing. (We will return to this issue in our discussion of various defenses.)

The Model Penal Code prescribes four states of mind that reflect an offender's *mens rea:* purposeful, knowing, reckless, and negligent (see Figure 4.1). How do courts determine one's mental state? The answer is simple—inferences about what must have been on one's mind, about one's state of mind, are deciphered from a person's actions.

In one area of the law criminal liability may be imposed without any proof of *mens rea.* This is strict, or absolute, liability. Most offenses in this area are regulatory or public welfare offenses and include violations of laws governing traffic, selling food, dispensing medicine, and operating licensed businesses. In these cases, anyone who technically violates the law, even without the slightest fault on his or her part, incurs criminal liability. The grocer who sells adulterated milk without knowledge that the milk was tampered with at the farm is guilty of a regulatory offense.

You Be the Judge!

What Evidence Satisfies an Inference of Intent?

Richard Rocker and Joseph Lava were observed sunbathing in the nude on a Hawaiian beach by police. They were arrested, tried, and convicted of sunbathing at a beach in the nude under a law that prohibits indecent exposure. The beach was frequented by local residents and anglers. In their appeal of the conviction, both Rocker and Lava claimed that they never intended to "expose" themselves to others.

(continued)

You Be the Judge! Should the appeal by Rocker and Lava be denied? Can you infer their intention to expose themselves to others from the act of nude sunbathing?

The court's conclusion: The offense of indecent exposure requires the intent to expose oneself indecently. This requirement is satisfied where one exposes oneself in a place where it is likely to be seen by others. Given Rocker and Lava's actions and the number of visitors to this beach, this is a fair inference.

State v. Rocker, 475 P2d 684 (Haw. 1970).

---

mala prohibita **(Latin)**
Wrongs that are merely prohibited.

mala in se **(Latin)**
Offenses deemed inherently evil.

Simple Formula
LEGALITY +
ACT +
HARM +
CAUSATION + CRIMINAL
INTENT +
CONCURRENCE +
PROHIBITION = Crime

Lawyers have called the group of offenses for which absolute criminal liability is frequently imposed ***mala prohibita,*** meaning wrongs that are merely prohibited. They distinguish these from offenses called ***mala in se,*** or offenses that are inherently bad, such as murder, rape, and robbery. The differentiation between the two has led to interminable discussions and disputes. For example, is the violation of a banking regulation, for which the banker may get a ten-year prison sentence, merely prohibited or inherently bad? And what difference does it make whether you attach one label or another? *Mala prohibita* are not necessarily offenses that fail to require a criminal intent. Moreover, society's views as to what is particularly bad, and what is merely prohibited, change constantly.

Various justifications have been given for the imposition of criminal liability and punishment without fault on the part of the actor. For example, so the argument goes, it is harder to get a conviction if criminal intent must be proved; the penalty usually is small; and absolute criminal liability has great deterrent value. But some legal scholars believe that if the law punishes the careful and the careless, the innocent and the guilty, alike, it will frustrate those who suffer punishment without any fault on their part.[5]

6. The Concurrence Requirement

The concurrence requirement means that the criminal act must be accompanied by an equally criminal mind. Suppose a striker throws a stone at an office window and a piece of broken glass pierces the throat of an office worker, who then bleeds to death. Property damage deserves condemnation, but far less than murder. In this case, act and intent did not concur. The striker should not be found guilty of murder.

The principle of concurrence is particularly significant in some of the doctrines of the criminal law, for example, somnambulism (sleepwalking). A person who retires to rest with the deliberate purpose of rising during the night to take the life of another inmate of the same house and who does so in a state of somnambulism, clearly established, is no more guilty of murder than if he had never entertained such an unlawful purpose. There was, to be quite sure, an original evil intent and overt act of homicide, but they did not concur or coexist.[6]

The law has created a number of exceptions to the concurrence requirement—for example, in considering the impact of intoxication on criminal liability or in the application of the felony murder rule. Again, those are deviations from the general proposition that each act requires all seven basic principles to be considered a crime.

You Be the Judge!

Can Corporations Be Charged with Crimes?

In the spring of 1991, Richard Knutson, Inc. (RKI) was hired to build a sanitary sewer line for the City of Oconomowoc, Wisconsin. On May 20, 1991, while working in an area adjacent to some power lines, a work crew from RKI tried to place a section of pipe in a trench in order to remove groundwater. A member of the crew operating a piece of heavy equipment (a "backhoe") misjudged the distance to overhead power lines and made contact with the wires. In attempting to fix the problem, an RKI employee was instantly electrocuted.

(continued)

The State of Wisconsin charged RKI, Inc. with negligent vehicular homicide under state law. The backhoe is a vehicle. RKI denied the charge, claiming that this particular law applies only to human beings, not corporations.

You Be the Judge!   Should a corporation be prosecuted under a state criminal law that makes it a crime for one to cause the death of another human being by the negligent operation of a vehicle?

The court's conclusion: RKI's attempt to limit the class of perpetrators to human beings ignores several axioms. First, elementary principles of justice demand that the same criminal liability must be imposed when two relatively similar offenses are committed under similar circumstances. Second, you do not have to be a biological person—a human being—to be criminally liable. Any actor—human or corporate—that voluntarily engages in behavior with a wrongful state of mind and without excuse may be criminally liable.

State v. Richard Knutson, Inc., 196 Wis. 2d 86; 537 NW 2d 420 (1995).

7. The Punishment Requirement

The seventh and last ingredient needed to constitute a crime is punishment. An illegal harmful act coupled with criminal intent still does not constitute a crime unless the law subjects the act to a punishment. If a sign is posted in the park saying "Do not step on the grass" and you do it anyway, have you committed a criminal offense? Not unless a law subjects that particular act to punishment. Otherwise it is simply improper or inconsiderate, no more (Figure 4.2).

FIGURE 4.2   Copyright © 1962 The Saturday Evening Post, a division of the Benjamin Franklin Literary & Medical Society. Reprinted by permission.

tort
Wrong committed by one person against another, other than mere violation of a contract, which entitles the victim to compensation.

felony
Serious crime, subject to punishment of one year or more in prison, or to capital punishment.

misdemeanor
Crime less serious than a felony and subject to a maximum sentence of one year in jail or a fine.

violation
Infraction of the law for which normally only a fine can be imposed.

The punishment requirement, more than any other, also helps us differentiate between crimes (which are subject to punishment) and **torts,** civil wrongs for which the law does not prescribe punishment but merely grants the injured party the right to recover damages.

The nature and severity of the punishment also help us to differentiate among grades of crime. Most penal codes recognize three degrees of severity: **felonies** (severe crimes subject to punishments of a year or more in prison or to capital punishment); **misdemeanors** (less severe crimes, subject to a maximum of one year in jail); and **violations,** infractions of the law for which normally only fines can be imposed. Fines can also be imposed as punishments for felonies and misdemeanors.

Criminal Justice in Action

Creation of Law—Always a Rational Effort?

We often describe the penal codes of a society as the outcome of rational efforts to deal with crime and criminals. To be considered a crime, an act should meet the seven requirements discussed in the text of this chapter. Legislators are responsible for translating these requirements into laws, and they, as society's representatives, are also responsible for creating laws that safeguard their constituents.

But in our society there appears to be a universe of many more or less powerful interest groups, or lobbies, that influence legislators while they are in the process of writing new laws. Whether an act is a crime or not may depend on who lobbies hardest as much as anything else. Gambling, and the laws affecting it, is an obvious example.

Since civilization began—and maybe before—people have risked their fortunes on all kinds of chances. They still do in the stock market and in commerce generally. That kind of chance-taking is legal in most parts of the world, although it was certainly illegal in the formerly Communist countries of eastern Europe: Free enterprise was a capital offense in these societies.

In England in the early days of the common law, gambling was legal. Later statutes made "gaming," including playing billiards or tennis, illegal. In the eighteenth century, the keeping of a gaming house became a "criminal nuisance." But in the American colonies, lotteries, another form of gambling, were perfectly legal. (They were used, in fact, to fund Columbia University [then King's College], Harvard, Yale, Dartmouth, and Williams College.) But in the nineteenth century, gambling became less and less acceptable, until finally it was prohibited in almost every state.[1]

What is the situation in the United States today? All American states except Nevada prohibit gambling in general, but there are many legal exceptions. States have legalized certain forms—for example, dog racing, horse racing, or (in Connecticut, Nevada, New Jersey, and Puerto Rico) casino gambling—and state lottery programs and church-sponsored Bingo are also defined as legal gambling in many jurisdictions.

Why is gambling sometimes legal and sometimes not? The great English jurist Sir James Fitzjames Stephen wrote in 1877: "Unlawful gaming means gaming carried on in such a manner, or for such a length of time or for such stakes (regard being had to the circumstances of the players) that it is likely to be injurious to the morals of those who game."[2] It appears, then, that the harm in gambling is the threat to gamblers' morals—the idea that the gambler who wins receives an undeserved, unearned reward.

One of the problems in the question of the legality of gambling seems to have economic roots: Gambling is extremely profitable for the operators of games. The 1976 Federal Commission on Gambling reported a turnover of $75 billion per year for American gambling activities; organized crime netted an estimated $7 billion. By now the figures are certainly much higher. So it is possible that states and localities hungry for money and facing budget cuts and the end of subsidies want some of the vast sums that now are siphoned off into illegal channels. Government, in other words, wants a

(continued)

piece of the action. Antigambling laws may seek less to protect the morals of gamblers, then, than to keep organized crime out of an extremely lucrative business.

Proposed laws prohibiting or allowing certain forms of gambling may be opposed or promoted by such diverse interest groups as churches, horsebreeders, travel agents, hotels, and citizens' groups. They all bring pressure to bear on lawmakers, who then must fashion laws that balance these competing interests with the public interest. The result may be statutes that are the product not of rational debate and careful thought, but of a long process of compromise and negotiation that focuses more on social, political and economic power than on what may in fact be right or wrong for that particular time and circumstance.[3]

Sometimes the pressures on legislators may result in corruption. In West Virginia, for example, legislators accepted large bribes from lobbyists to influence legislation—essentially criminal law—that raised the amount of the take for the state's dog tracks. A South Carolina sting operation by the FBI netted a group of legislators and lobbyists who accepted money to influence a parimutuel betting bill.[4] In Arizona, seven legislators were indicted for selling their votes (to a sting operator) on a bill that would have legalized casino gambling.

Let's ask again: Why is gambling sometimes legal and sometimes illegal?

- Is it because lawmakers are concerned about the morals of gamblers?
- Is it because lawmakers are listening to those who would profit most from making gambling legal?
- Is it because some decision makers feel that organized crime can be controlled by making gambling illegal?
- Is it because sometimes gambling is profitable to governments, communities, churches, or citizens' groups?

Making criminal laws is a complex social process—and one that is not always free of corruption.

SOURCES
1. Gresham M. Sykes, *Criminology* (New York: Harcourt Brace Jovanovich, 1978), pp. 192–193.
2. Sir James Fitzjames Stephen, *A Digest of the Criminal Law* (London: Macmillan, 1877, 5th ed. 1894), p. 143.
3. M. Cherif Bassiouni, *Substantive Criminal Law* (Springfield, IL: Charles C. Thomas, 1978), pp. 355–397.
4. Thomas B. Edsall, "South Carolina Capital Girds for Sting Arrests; Vote-Buying May Hasten Power Shift," *The Washington Post,* August 12, 1990, p. A9; "S.C. Lawmakers Convicted," *The Washington Post,* March 10, 1991, p. A12.

Questions for Discussion

1. Why is the gamble taken by "day traders" on speculative stocks "legal," when other forms of wagering are prohibited?

2. Is there a parallel between the way legislatures define what is illegal and the way universities do? Could legislatures learn anything from the universities' ways of making codes of conduct for students and professors?

3. Do you think gambling should be legal throughout the United States, illegal throughout the United States, or decided on a state-by-state basis? Defend your position.

The Principles Applied: Defenses

These seven principles are rarely referred to by name in state and federal courts. Instead, courts use legal rules and propositions that they, and the legislatures, have developed over the centuries. These propositions (also called doctrines) provide the answers to frequently occurring situations like these: What is a court to do when a child or a mentally ill person is charged with a crime? What is a court to do when somebody has been forced against his or her will to do an illegal act? and so on. For these situations the law has created patterned answers. Of these, the most frequently applied are the so-called defenses to crime. There are two types of defenses, excuses and justifications. We will explain the differences between the two after we have discussed excuses.

Excuses

Infancy.   Suppose a three-year-old pushes her baby brother down the stairs, and the baby dies. Could we try the three-year-old for murder? Did the three-year-old commit the act of killing? Did she have the requisite criminal intent *(mens rea)?* In fact, a three-year-old does not even know the meaning of life and death. To prevent silly inquiries into whether an infant has committed a criminal act with the requisite criminal intent, the common law rules flatly that all children under age seven (referred to as infants) are incapable of engaging in any kind of rational act or forming the requisite criminal intent. That is the common-law defense of infancy.

Insanity.   When an adult charged with a crime pleads insanity as a defense—which happens very infrequently—he or she, in effect, asserts: "The normal rule that all adults are presumed legally capable of committing a crime does not apply in my case, because I am so severely mentally ill that I am incapable of committing crime. Thus, what looks like a crime in my case really was not a crime at all." Under common law, the so-called M'Naghten Rules (1843) made this defense concrete. Simply stated, these rules provide that a defendant is not guilty of crime if, at the time of the act, due to severe mental illness, (1) the defendant did not know the nature and quality of his or her act (in other words, did not appreciate what he was doing so that the "act requirement" was not fulfilled), or (2) the defendant did not know the wrongfulness of his or her act (in other words, could not form the requisite *mens rea*).[7]

This test was widely used in England and America, yet it was frequently misunderstood. In fact, some courts, emphasizing the second part of the test, simply inquired whether the defendant knew the difference between right and wrong. This interpretation produced many miscarriages of justice, so that courts constantly changed and reshaped their tests of insanity. Among these (usually short-lived) insanity tests were:

- The *irresistible impulse addition* to the M'Naghten test: A defendant may be acquitted if he or she was unable to control the action due to mental illness.

  - The *Durham Rule,* or *"product test"* (1954): The defendant must be acquitted if the crime was the product of mental disease or defect.

  - The *Currens Test* (1961): The defendant must be acquitted if he or she "lacked substantial capacity to conform his conduct to the requirements of the law … as a result of mental disease or defect."

In 1982 Congress settled the issue, at least as far as federal law is concerned, by providing for an acquittal by reason of insanity if "at the time of the commission of the act the defendant, as a result of severe mental disease or defect, was unable to appreciate the nature and quality or wrongfulness of his act."[8] This text is a modern version of the old M'Naghten formula. Several states have similar tests, but the majority have adopted the version codified in the American Law Institute's Model Penal Code and known as the ALI test:

A person is not responsible for criminal conduct if at the time of such conduct as a result of mental disease or defect he lacks substantial capacity either to appreciate the criminality (wrongfulness) of his conduct or to conform his conduct to the requirements of law.[9]

John W. Hinckley's acquittal by reason of insanity of the attempted assassination of President Reagan in March 1981 caused federal and state legislative changes in the insanity defense.

This test focuses on the defendant's capacity to form the necessary criminal intent by asking whether the defendant appreciated the wrongfulness of the act. It also emphasizes, as part of the *mens rea,* the defendant's volitional capacity: Could the defendant really intend to commit the wrongful act? Did he have the "substantial capacity … to conform his conduct to the requirements of law"?

Whenever a particularly notorious crime has been committed by someone who then pleads insanity, there is public clamor for revenge by toughening the insanity test. That was as true when Daniel M'Naghten attempted to assassinate Sir Robert Peel as it was when John W. Hinckley, Jr., attempted to assassinate President Ronald Reagan in 1981. The Hinckley case prompted several states to pass legislation providing for an alternative disposition, that of "guilty but mentally ill." This novel verdict is meant to cover defendants not mentally ill enough to qualify for an outright acquittal "by reason of insanity," yet not well enough to be found fully accountable and "guilty." It is therefore an in-between solution. Unhappily, the sentence that may be imposed on an in-between defendant can be the same as that received by a normal "guilty" defendant, and while some states offer special treatment for such convicts, there is no constitutional obligation that they do so.[10]

Intoxication.   American law is and always has been tough on the issue of intoxication. Most state penal codes state flatly that intoxication is no defense. Actually, that is not true. Involuntary intoxication, for example, because of prescription medication, can constitute a defense. Moreover, most courts have held that even voluntary intoxication, when severe, may render a person incapable of forming certain types of criminal intent. For example, murder in the first degree requires, among other things, premeditation and deliberation. Many courts have held that if a defendant was so grossly intoxicated that he or she could not premeditate and deliberate, he or she can at best be found guilty of murder in the second degree.

Mistake of Fact.   Let us go back to the coatrack situation. A restaurant patron goes to the coatrack to retrieve his raincoat. He verifies the manufacturer's label, takes the coat, and begins to depart. Another patron, obviously agitated, jumps up and grabs the coat-taker. "You stole my coat!" The first man is greatly embarrassed. It turns out that the coat is not his. But is he a thief?

To be a thief, as we have seen, one has to intend to deprive someone of his or her property. That is the *mens rea* requirement. In this instance the first patron is *not* a thief because, thinking the coat to be his, he had no awareness of wrongdoing. That is the essence of the defense of mistake of fact: If there is no *mens rea,* there is no crime. When an honest mistake of fact negates the *mens rea* requirement, no crime has been committed.

Mistake-of-fact problems usually are easily resolved in pretrial proceedings or at trial, but they can be troublesome to law enforcement officers. Many suspects, caught red-handed by the police, will immediately offer some excuse, often based on mistake of fact: "Gee, Officer, I thought . . . " Suppose that in the case of the mistaken raincoat the proprietor summons a police officer. What is the officer to do? Should he or she make an arrest and let the court worry about defenses? Or should he or she ascertain the facts, determine that there is probable cause a theft has been committed, but consider that there also is the defense of mistake of fact? Police officers must know enough law to make on-the-spot decisions within the discretion vested in them. If a suspect's explanation seems reasonable (there was a "reasonable mistake"), and especially if the victim agrees, the officer probably will not make an arrest. But if the facts are complex and unclear, the officer has no choice but to let the courts adjudicate the question of whether there is a reasonable mistake that nullifies the defendant's *mens rea.*

Mistake or Ignorance of Law.   Every law enforcement officer quickly learns through practical experience that the law does not recognize a mistake of law: If an officer thinks he has a right to make an arrest, but the law says otherwise, the arrest is illegal. Similarly, if a banker believes that a given money transaction is legal, but the law says it is not, the banker has committed an offense. Everybody is supposed to know and understand the law. Obviously, however, that is impossible. Even trial judges frequently do not know the law properly or misunderstand it, so that appeals courts later reverse decisions.

To legal scholars the maxim that "ignorance or mistake of law does not excuse" made sense in ancient times, when the number of crimes was limited to serious felonies that everybody understood: murder, arson, robbery, rape, burglary, and so on. But today, they argue, when there are thousands of crimes on the statute books, the rule no longer makes sense because it violates the *mens rea* principle: A person who acts in ignorance of a legal prohibition simply has no *mens rea*.

Duress. A robber approaches a bank teller with the following demand: "Your money or you're dead!" Not a fun choice, but a simple one. The teller probably reaches into the drawer and hands over the cash. Is the teller guilty of larceny or embezzlement? It is not her money. Her job as a teller does not give her the right to steal, to embezzle, or to give away funds entrusted to her.

To deal with such situations, the law has established the defense of duress:

> It is . . . [a] defense that the actor engaged in the conduct charged to constitute an offense because he was coerced to do so by the use of, or a threat to use, unlawful force against his person or the person of another, which a person of reasonable firmness in his situation would have been unable to resist.[11]

This defense applies when the actor has done something the law prohibits. The bank teller has taken money entrusted to her and given it to someone else, without authorization. All the elements of the crime of embezzlement are there. But the teller had no choice. The law recognizes that we cannot be expected to yield our lives, our limbs, the safety of our relatives, our houses, or our property when confronted by a criminal threat that forces us to violate a law. In the defense of duress it may be said that the actor acted not of his or her own free will. Thus, the element of the required voluntary action (conduct) is not there. There is, however, a general requirement that the evil that threatens the actor ("Your money or you're dead") and the evil created by the actor (handing over cash out of the till) not be out of proportion.

You Be the Judge!

What Kind of Evidence Satisfies the Defense of Necessity?

Warshow and others traveled to Vernon, Vermont, to protest at the main gate of the Vermont Yankee nuclear power plant. The plant had been shut down for repairs and refueling, and these protestors joined a rally designed to prevent workers from gaining access to the plant and placing it online.

The police and plant officials asked that Warshow and the other demonstrators leave the main gate. They refused and were charged with unlawful trespass. Warshow was convicted after the trial court ruled that the defense of necessity was not available.

Warshow wanted to raise a defense of necessity showing that operation of the Vermont Yankee nuclear plant, over time, would introduce low-level radiation and nuclear waste, and raise the definite risk of a nuclear accident.

You Be the Judge! Is the threat of long-term risks to health, safety, and public welfare a sufficient danger to constitute the defense of necessity?

The court's conclusion: The fundamental requirements of the defense of necessity require: (1) a situation of emergency arising without fault on the part of the actor concerned; (2) an emergency that is so imminent and compelling as to raise a reasonable expectation of harm, either directly to the actor or upon those he was protecting; (3) an emergency that presents no reasonable opportunity to avoid the injury without doing the criminal act; and (4) an injury impending from the emergency of sufficient seriousness to outmeasure the criminal wrong. Long-term risks and dangers of the sort that Warshow was protesting simply do not constitute the type of danger required for the defense of necessity.

State v. Warshow, 410 A2d 1000 (Vt. 1979).

Necessity.   The rule is similar for the defense of necessity. Here the threat to the actor comes from nature. It is sometimes called an "act of God," and it may be a fire, a storm, an earthquake, or a shipwreck that compels the actor to do something that otherwise would be illegal. Suppose two hikers are surprised by a snowstorm. They stumble upon an unoccupied vacation cottage. Under the rule of necessity, they may break into and enter the cottage and use its provisions to stay alive. But here, as in cases of duress, the actor must not act out of proportion to the need. The stranded hikers may seek shelter in the cottage and use necessary provisions. They cannot feast on the owner's caviar, champagne, and cigars.

The defense of necessity is not available whenever there are legal means in existence to avert the threat: A starving person should seek public welfare rather than steal for his or her survival. This is a harsh rule. The welfare office may be miles away, and its processes may take weeks. Should the hungry, homeless person choose to die rather than steal a pretzel from a vendor's cart? This limit on the defense of necessity opens up an inquiry into the overall justness of society and its laws.

Justifications

The preceding defenses all rest, basically, on a claim that either the necessary *mens rea* or the necessary voluntary act was missing so that there was no crime. These defenses are commonly called excuses. There is a second set of defenses called **justifications.** *Jus* is Latin for "law." The law itself provides a counterlaw to the prohibitory law. The prohibitory law says: You must not kill. But the counterlaw says: If you are a soldier in combat, you must kill. That is the justification.[12]

justifications
Defenses in which the law authorizes the violation of another law within limits of proportionality.

Public Duty.   Justification is nowhere applied more appropriately than in the case of public duty, namely when force has to be used by an officer of the law. The law prohibits an act such as restraining a person, but the counterlaw commands an officer of the law to restrain a person for purposes of effecting an arrest. There is a limit: The officer must use no more force than is necessary. The use of deadly force by law enforcement officers is subject to exacting restrictions. Law enforcement officers who use more force than necessary to achieve legitimate objectives are likely to be committing a criminal offense, such as assault and battery or even criminal homicide.

Few situations arouse as much public passion as the use of excessive force by law enforcement officers in the otherwise lawful execution of their duties. Obviously, when officers abuse their authority, the law must hold them accountable and charge them for the excess, whether it constitutes assault and battery, unlawful imprisonment, or a trespass.

Self-Defense, Defense of Others, and Defense of Property.   On the Saturday before Christmas in 1984, Bernhard H. Goetz entered a subway car at the IRT station at Seventh Avenue and Fourteenth Street in Manhattan. He sat down close to four young men in their late teens. One of them offered a "How are ya?" and then approached Goetz and asked for $5. At that point, Goetz pulled out a .38-caliber revolver and shot all four youths (one in the back).[13]

Few cases have ignited so much controversy. Some people saw Goetz as the avenger of the city dweller, who suffers constantly from crime and the fear of crime. Others labeled him a vigilante. Or was he simply the meek underdog, as his appearance suggested, trying to defend himself against yet another attack on the subway? He could have been any of these. Goetz was charged with attempted murder, assault, and illegal possession of a weapon. In legal terms, the case simply raised the question of the right to use force, even deadly force, in self-defense, and the extent to which the defense exists if the actor is mistaken about the actual threat that confronts him.

THOMAS KING, DETECTIVE, RETIRED, PHILADELPHIA POLICE DEPARTMENT

I worked as a detective and detective supervisor for 15 of the 20 years that I spent with the Philadelphia Police Department. In the Detective Bureau, I worked the line squad for three years, Divisional Special Investigations Unit for six years, and then was assigned to the Federal Insurance Fraud Task Force. Finally, I was asked to initiate and supervise the Firearms Trafficking Task Force working in cooperation with the Bureau of Alcohol, Tobacco and Firearms (ATF).

Gun violence in the United States has become an epidemic. From the Civil War to the present, 567,000 Americans have died in combat, but since 1920 firearms have killed over one million civilians.

With a mandate to identify, investigate, apprehend, and help prosecute those engaging in illegal gun trafficking, the first job of the Philadelphia Firearms Trafficking Task Force was to ascertain where the majority of "crime guns" originated. Crime guns are defined as firearms that are recovered by police at the scenes of violent felonies.

I had assumed that many of these guns were stolen from gun dealers, stolen from residences during burglaries, and/or trucked from southern states with relaxed gun laws. Much to my surprise, our tracking and mapping of illegal gun sources indicated that most of the guns that were recovered by police at the scenes of violent crime in Philadelphia had been initially purchased legally from federally licensed firearms dealers (FFLs) located in the Philadelphia area. Indeed, we soon discovered that Pennsylvania is a source state for illegal firearms.

We determined that a small number of FFLs accounted for a disproportionate volume of crime guns sold. Early on, the majority of these guns were purchased from so-called "kitchen table" dealers. They were FFLs who are licensed to sell guns, but usually operated from their homes. Using a combination of federal and state laws, along with local zoning statutes, the task force reduced the number of kitchen table FFLs in Philadelphia from 160 to approximately 30.

We realized that this first step would barely make a dent in the kitchen table sales statewide—each of the five counties surrounding Philadelphia County had in excess of

Other Defenses. A few other defenses normally covered in textbooks on criminal law deserve mention, though not discussion. Some of them are of limited scope; others are much broader. (See Table 4.1.) Among them are:

- The doctrine of crime commission by innocent agent, where a perpetrator abuses the ignorance or innocence of another to commit a crime.
- The doctrine of superior orders, where a subordinate follows the orders of a superior officer, thinking such orders to be legal.
- The doctrine of entrapment, where a law enforcement officer induces an originally unwilling person to violate the law.
- The doctrine of vicarious criminal liability, where a person is held liable for the criminal act of another to whom he or she stands in a certain relationship.
- The doctrine of corporate criminal liability, under which corporations bear responsibility for the acts of corporate officers or agents.
- The defense of diplomatic or legislative immunity.
- The defense of the statute of limitations, when the time for instituting proceedings has passed.

200 FFLs. However, we were better able to concentrate on legitimate storefront dealers in and around the city, who were operating legally—but who often skirted the law. Here is how: I was surprised to learn that state law allows a citizen to obtain as many handguns as he or she wishes (with a five-day Brady waiting period) and as many rifles (including semiautomatic assault rifles) with no waiting period at all. The majority of crime guns reach the streets through a "straw purchasing" scheme.

A straw purchasing scheme is where a felon—who is prohibited from purchasing or possessing a firearm—would hire someone without a criminal record to purchase guns on his or her behalf. These felons often accompany the straw purchaser to the gun store—pointing out the weapons that they want. The paperwork was filled out—purchases of 5 to 10 guns at a time were not unusual. Very often, the straw purchasers would go to several gun stores and place orders on the same day.

Most of the firearms purchased this way were cheap handguns that are subsequently sold on the street to felons for several times their purchase price. The straw purchaser would often report to the police that the guns are stolen—in their minds separating them from the felonious recipient. The person receiving the guns often obliterates the serial numbers.

The devastating effects of straw purchases is illustrated in the murder of Lauretha Vaird, the first female Philadelphia police officer ever killed on duty. On January 2, 1996, Officer Vaird responded to a radio call of a bank robbery in progress at a bank in East Philadelphia. Two handguns were recovered from the scene of the crime—a Bryco 9mm and a Lorcin .380. The 9mm was traced to a female Philadelphia resident at a gun store in nearby Upper Darby, Pennsylvania. She subsequently admitted that she purchased the gun for her boyfriend, who was later arrested and convicted for his participation in the robbery and murder.

The actual murder weapon, the .380-caliber automatic, had an obliterated serial number. The firearms examiners in Philadelphia's Firearms Identification Unit were able to raise the serial number and it was traced to a male who purchased the gun at the same Upper Darby gun store and had subsequently reported to the police that the gun was stolen. He admitted that he had actually sold the gun to the actual killer, who was convicted for the robbery and murder.

A more recent trend is an increase in purchases by those possessing a valid permit to carry a firearm. The holder of such a permit can avoid the five-day Brady waiting period and leave the gun store with as many firearms as he or she wishes to buy. Felons seek out straw purchasers who possess permits for this reason.

I enjoyed my career as a detective. I think it is the most interesting job in the police department. You get to use your experience, seek the expertise of others, and are given significant discretion in handling investigations.

In addition to these more traditional defenses, a host of new criminal defenses have emerged, covered extensively by the media and in trade books. These defenses, ranging from claims of rotten social background and addiction to junk foods, to premenstrual syndrome, have been largely dismissed by legal scholars. They fail, so the argument goes, because these "abuse" excuses mistake matters of causation (e.g., why an offender killed) with reasons or justification for criminal blame. A person is not any less blameworthy, from the perspective of the criminal law, because the criminal act that he committed was done so for reasons of high blood sugar or because he was the product of a very poor neighborhood with limited opportunities for jobs. This may explain *why* he committed the crime. It does not, however, *excuse* it.

The Arithmetic of Crime

The patterned propositions pertaining to defenses are not the only doctrines of criminal law used to assess criminal charges. There is a whole set of doctrines concerned with the arithmetic of crime. How do we deal with a situation in which only a fraction of a crime has been committed, such as an attempted but incomplete crime? How do we deal with a crime in which several persons collaborate?

Defense	Description of Defense
The Twinkie defense (hypoglycemia—too much sugar)	Because he lost his job as a San Francisco supervisor, Dan White gorged on junk food— Twinkies, Coca-Cola, candy. Depressed, he sneaked a gun into City Hall. After killing Mayor Moscone, he killed a leader of the gay community, Supervisor Milk, in 1978.
Defendants or victims with multiple personalities	Many psychiatric experts agree that the disorder exists but disagree on how common it is. If a woman with multiple personalities complains of rape, the defendant might argue that consent to sex was given by one of the personalities. A defendant with multiple personalities might argue that he or she could not control the bad personality.
Sleepwalking and other forms of automatism (unconsciousness)	Automatism is a state in which a person is capable of action but is not conscious of what he or she is doing. This defense is statutorized in some states, including California, and held to be an affirmative defense separate from the insanity defense. *Fulcher v. State,* 633 P.2d 142, 29 CrL 2556 (Wyo. 1981).
Cultural disorientation	Some immigrants to the United States bring with them cultural practices that are in conflict with our criminal codes. For example, some continue the ancient traditions of the medicinal use of opium, the practice of capturing young brides, and the ritual slaughtering of animals. In 1985 when a young Japanese mother of two children learned that her husband was having an affair with another woman, she walked into the Pacific Ocean with her children to commit suicide (*oy ako shinju*). She was saved but the children drowned.
Premenstrual syndrome (PMS) and tension	PMS, a form of emotional and physical stress, afflicts some women before their monthly periods. In certain cases, such stress is so severe that it seriously disrupts the women's lives. In 1982, a British Appeal Court held that PMS could not be used as a defense to a criminal charge but could be used in mitigation to lessen sentences.
Television intoxication	In the 1978 case of *Zamora v. State,* 361 So.2d 776 (Fla. 1978), the defendant was convicted after arguing temporary insanity from "involuntary subliminal television intoxication."
XYY chromosome defense	Everyone has chromosomes. Some have either too few or too many, causing abnormalities. Some scientists believe that the abnormality of the supermale, or XYY in males, can cause such men to exhibit antisocial or criminal conduct. The XYY syndrome is not recognized as a defense unless the requirements of the insanity test of the state are met.

SOURCE: Adapted from Thomas J. Gardner and Terry M. Anderson, *Criminal Law: Principles and Cases* (Belmont, CA: Wadsworth, 2000), pp. 100–101.

TABLE 4.1   Defenses Sometimes Attempted by Defense Lawyers

criminal attempt
Act or omission constituting a substantial step in a course of conduct planned to culminate in the commission of a crime.

Attempt.   Foremost among these doctrines of the arithmetic of crime is the one pertaining to attempted crimes. What should the law do to someone who tries to commit a crime but does not succeed? Under early common law, attempts to commit crimes were not considered crimes because the criminal act *(actus reus)* was not completed. But a person who tries to complete a crime surely has the same *mens rea* and on that basis the same culpability as one who succeeds in creating harm. Should the would-be perpetrator be treated differently just because he or she did not succeed? In 1784 in England, it was decided that an attempt to commit a felony was indeed a crime.[14] That case laid the foundation for our present conceptualization of **criminal attempt,** as contained in the Model Penal Code: "An act or omission constituting a substantial step in a course of conduct planned to culminate in the commission of a crime."[15]

accessoryship
Criminal liability of all those who aid the perpetrator of an offense.

Accessoryship.   The common law also created a sophisticated system for determining the liability of all persons involved in the commission of a crime. Here we have an arithmetical situation involving the addition of persons. **Accessoryship** refers to the criminal liability of all those who aid the perpetrator(s) of an offense.

principal
Perpetrator of a criminal act.

Today most states recognize only **principals** (all persons who commit an offense by their own conduct) and **accomplices** (all those who aid the perpetrator). That system has not solved all problems because the line between committing a crime and aiding in its commission is a fine one. Though principals and accomplices are usually considered equally at fault, in practice judges often impose lighter sentences on accomplices.

accomplice
Person who helps another to commit a crime.

Conspiracy. Conspiracy is a concept in some ways similar to accessoryship, but with a far broader reach. A **conspiracy** is an agreement among two or more persons to commit a specified crime. As soon as these parties have committed any act (even a legitimate one) in furtherance of the conspiracy, they are guilty of the crime of conspiracy. Thus, if Rob, Pim, Jill, and Nanci agree to hold up a bank teller and Pim rents a car for getaway purposes, all four are guilty of the crime of conspiracy to commit robbery. But, unlike accessoryship, in conspiracy all of the conspirators are guilty of all crimes committed by any one of them in furtherance of the conspiracy. Thus, if Pim had not rented a car but instead had taken Victor's automobile after killing him, all four would now additionally be guilty of murder and theft. If any of them then commits the planned robbery, they are all guilty of robbery as well.

The conspiracy concept has been in disrepute as a law enforcement tool throughout history. It has been called "the lazy prosecutor's tool" because it has been easier to obtain convictions for conspiracy, with its minimal elements, than for substantive crimes, which require proof of substantial activity and harm. Today prosecutors tend to throw in a conspiracy charge for good measure when two or more perpetrators are indicted, especially as a means of inducing a plea bargain. No doubt, in organized crime prosecutions there have been some successful and proper convictions, and perhaps that is conspiracy's remaining utility.

conspiracy
Agreement among two or more persons to commit a crime, making each guilty of conspiracy and all other crimes committed in furtherance of the conspiracy.

Review

Seven principles, or definitional ingredients, mark every crime. Foremost among these is the principle of legality: No crime exists without criminal law. Where does criminal law come from? Much of it comes from court decisions, known as common law. Legislatures also create criminal laws when the public demands protection against "new" crimes and in response to new situations. The other principles that mark every crime are: the conduct requirement, the harm requirement, the causation requirement, the *mens rea* requirement, the concurrence requirement, and the punishment requirement.

General principles do not decide concrete cases, though they help us greatly in understanding the criminal law. In their everyday business, criminal court judges rarely refer to principles. Instead they use patterned formulas to solve frequently recurring problems. Most notable among these are the defenses. Most of the defenses are based on the alleged absence of one of the basic principles. A mistake-of-fact defense alleges that the defendant had no criminal intent; the defense of necessity alleges that there was no voluntary act on the part of the defendant; and the justification of public duty alleges that a law demanded that a law enforcement officer do something that normally is considered illegal (for example, use force against a suspect).

The law also has formulas to deal with situations when only a part of the crime has been committed (attempt) or when crimes are committed by several persons acting jointly. The broad propositions discussed in this chapter (called the general part of the criminal law) are not arbitrary. They can be explained largely as the result of logical reasoning heavily influenced by experience, history, and political expedience. Together they are applicable to all crimes, and in that sense they are useful, necessary, and vital to the administration of the criminal law, from the street level up to the Supreme Court.

Thinking Critically about Criminal Justice

1. What are the best arguments in favor of the view that the criminal justice system is actually a "nonsystem" or anything but a system?

Internet Connection

Note: While all of the URLs listed were current as of the printing of this book, these sites often change. Please check our website (http://www.mhhe.com/socscience/crimjustice/adlercj) for updates.

Want to keep up-to-date on the latest decisions of the United States Supreme Court? The Court's docket and decisions are maintained real-time by the Oyez Project.

Considering a visit to Court to watch an oral argument? It is difficult not to find an interesting case to watch at http://www.oyez.org/oyez/frontpage.

Notes

1. Doug Simpson, "Man Shoots Five at Louisiana Law Firm," AP Press Wire, October 4, 2007.
2. Brian Charlton, "Trial Opens in Slaying of Pregnant Woman" AP Press Wire, October 4, 2007.

3. Jerome Hall, *General Principles of Criminal Law,* 2nd ed. (Indianapolis: Bobbs-Merrill, 1960); and Gerhard O. W. Mueller, "The Law of Public Wrongs—Its Concepts in the World of Reality," *Journal of Public Law* 10, no. 2 (1962), pp. 203–260.

4. Gerhard O. W. Mueller, "On Common Law *Mens Rea,*" *Minnesota Law Review* 42 (1958), pp. 1043–1104; see also Paul H. Robinson and Jane A. Grall, "Element Analysis in Defining Criminal Liability: The Model Penal Code and Beyond," *Stanford Law Review* 35 (1983), pp. 681–762.

5. Wayne R. LaFave and Austin W. Scott, Jr., *Criminal Law* (St. Paul, MN: West, 1983), p. 222.

6. Adapted from Mueller, "The Public Law of Wrongs," pp. 203–260, especially p. 242.

7. *Daniel M'Naghten's Case,* 8 Eng. Rep. 718, 722–723 (1843), 10 C.F. 200, 210–211 (1843). See also Richard Moran, *Knowing Right from Wrong: The Insanity Defense of Daniel McNaughten* (NY: Free Press; London: Collier Macmillan, 1981). Moran proved that McNaughten spelled his name *McNaughten,* though in American legal usage the spelling *M'Naghten* gained favor.

8. See 18 U.S.C. (Sec.) 17.

9. American Law Institute, Model Penal Code, Sec. 4.01.

10. Debra T. Landis, "Guilty but Mentally Ill Statutes: Validity and Construction," *American Law Reports,* 71 ALR 4th 702 (1991).

11. Generally, the defense is not available if the actor was at fault by placing himself or herself in the situation: Model Penal Code, Sec. 2.09(1).

12. There is much dispute as to where to draw the line between justifications and excuses. Volumes have been written on the subject. The fact is that our law is fuzzy in this respect. Yet much hinges on the difference. Thus, a third party may intervene to stop somebody who acts under an excuse, but he or she may not do so with respect to somebody who acts under justification. In general, see Albin Eser and George P. Fletcher, eds., *Justification and Excuse: Comparative Perspectives* (Freiburg, Germany: Max-Planck Institut, 1987), 2 vols.

13. For a legal and factual analysis of the case, see George P. Fletcher, *A Crime of Self-Defense: Bernhard Goetz and the Law on Trial* (NY: Free Press; London: Collier Macmillan 1988).

14. *Rex v. Scofield,* 1784 Cald. 402.

15. Model Penal Code, Sec. 5.01(1)(c).

PART

2

The Police

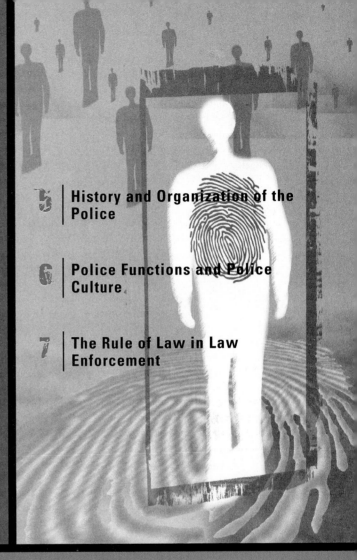

• PART 2 of this book is concerned with police and law enforcement. The police are the first criminal justice agents to take note of crime, or to be contacted by victims of crime. Their actions determine all subsequent steps of the criminal process.

• CHAPTER 5 provides an overview of the history of policing and describes the various types of law enforcement agencies, their typical structure and functioning, and their organizational responses to societal stresses and changing demands.

• CHAPTER 6 analyzes the types of activities in which police departments engage to fulfill the three functions assigned to them: the service function, the order maintenance function, and the law enforcement function. The emphasis today is on community policing, a distinct shift from the paramilitary style that prevailed until recently. The chapter also looks at police officers as human beings and as members of their own distinct subculture. Selection processes and training, peer pressure and shared dangers, common temptations, and joint griefs are described.

• The final police chapter, Chapter 7, explains the constitutional framework within which all police must conduct their activities, from arrest to arraignment. Although the Bill of Rights is two centuries old, the U.S. Supreme Court has made most of its provisions binding on the actions of state and local police only during the last forty years.

CHAPTER 5

History and Organization of the Police

Crime is everywhere. Pickpockets and purse snatchers lurk on every street. To protect their money from muggers, people carry their wallets on a leather strap around their necks. Just the other day a noted wit said: "Only a fool would go out to dinner without having made his will."[1]

The police are sparse in the neighborhoods. The city has even installed dummy police officers at intersections and school crossings. Citizens buy padlocks to protect their homes. You have never seen so many "Beware of Dog" signs! The more affluent hire private security agencies to protect their premises. It has become common practice for people to carry charms in their bags and pouches to protect them from muggers. Others simply pray to be safe from attack. At home all valuables are locked in strongboxes. Those who can afford it put their jewelry in bank safe deposit boxes. But nothing is safe from burglars, not the homes, not the banks, not even the gilding that covers public monuments. Merchants are putting chains around merchandise on display. Most shop owners have security guards. At the end of the business day they bar their doors with heavy boards and bolts. Homeowners have installed double doors for protection. More and more people take classes on self-defense techniques and carry knives not outlawed by the weapons laws. Public officials don't even ride around in public anymore without security agents in front, in back, and on the sides. Neighborhoods have formed citizens' watch groups. And everybody is upset about the lack of police presence.[2]

Does this sound like a description of the situation in your town, your neighborhood? It could well be. Actually, this is a report based on Roman documents that are 2,000 years old. Then, as now, people were looking for safety at home and on the streets, resorting to self-help, but above all looking to the police for protection.

The History of American Police

The history of policing dates back to the earliest of recorded history. American systems of policing are the product of English experiences, from the early "hue and cry" to shire reeves. In towns like Boston, Philadelphia, and Charleston, constables were appointed and watches created. Counties elected sheriffs to enforce the law. These officials, however, played a mostly reactive role, since prevailing notions of law enforcement still emphasized citizen initiative. Political entities offered rewards to the public for the apprehension of felons, and citizens could be called on to form posses in pursuit of criminals. The victim of a crime had to initiate action against the offender by going to court to swear out a warrant and by requesting the assistance of the constable in serving the warrant and making the arrest.

The problems that arose as towns grew into cities and as the social and economic order became more complex required solutions that went beyond the weak system in use throughout the early years of the nation. In the nineteenth century, and especially in the post–Civil War years, paid professional police forces were finally introduced in the United States.

The Expanding West

vigilante group
Group of private citizens taking the law into their own hands by tracking down criminals and punishing them.

The absence of effective government in many of the newly settled parts of the West created a vacuum that was often filled by private citizens taking the law into their own hands. **Vigilante groups,** which typically consisted of a few hundred people led by the town elite, would track down criminals or people creating disorder in the settlement and administer "justice" to them. At some "trials" the captured outlaws were given a chance to present a defense. Determination of guilt most often resulted in the execution of the "defendant," usually by hanging. Vigilante groups were generally well organized along military lines and had written manifestos or constitutions to which the members would subscribe.

marshal
Federal law enforcement officer of the U.S. Marshal Service; formerly, federal law enforcement officer in territories.

Law enforcement of the lawful variety also existed in the West. In federal territories, United States **marshals** were the principal law enforcement officers. Like their counterparts in the eastern constabularies, marshals were paid for the services they performed, so low-paying criminal matters tended to be neglected in favor of more lucrative civil duties.

Once an area became a state, law enforcement became the responsibility of state and local officials. In the counties, sheriffs were the chief peace officers. Cities and towns settled in the latter part of the nineteenth century created police forces like those that had by then developed in the eastern cities. The sheriffs were much like those of colonial times: important political figures drawn from the dominant power group, with duties such as tax collection, inspection of cattle brands, and the serving of civil processes, in addition to law enforcement. Even famous personalities like James "Wild Bill" Hickok and William B. "Bat" Masterson, who were known as hired guns, were willing to serve as sheriffs.

Private police were used in the West along with official and citizen forces. In the 1860s, the ambitious effort to create a transcontinental railroad provided new opportunities for crime. As trains passed through unsettled areas, they became easy targets for robbers who would "hold up" the train (the source of the term *holdup* for robbery), remove its freight or rob its passengers, and escape without fear of immediate pursuit. To provide increased protection, a number of railroad companies engaged the services of Allan Pinkerton, founder of the most famous private detective agency in America, or of hired guns like Bat Masterson and Wyatt Earp. Together with the other informal and formal law enforcement groups operating in the West, private police provided a form of "frontier justice."

The East: Urban Riots

In the growing urban centers of the East, the stress caused by social dislocation frequently erupted into riots, a phenomenon considered the most important precipitating factor in the creation of professional police forces. Riots in Boston, Philadelphia, and Louisville in the first half of the century were attributable to tensions between different immigrant groups. Racial prejudice against blacks living in northern cities and opposition to abolition also resulted in riots. There were five major race riots in Philadelphia between 1829 and 1850,

Time Frame	Event
Earliest recorded history, biblical times	Watchmen, police appointed for towns, cities in ancient Middle East
Ca. 1340 B.C.	Egypt: Nile River Police established
Ca. 1000–300 B.C.	Greece: The *polis,* which meant all municipal government activities, including police
Ca. 510 B.C.–A.D. 375	Rome: Various kinds of public and private police forces, including Praetorian Guard (like a state police) and Lictors (who protected officials)
Ca. 400–1200	England: Communal policing at various levels—tything, hundred, shire. After the Norman Conquest of 1066, centralized royal control
1285	England: Statute of Winchester sets up watch-and-ward system for towns, with citizen police, constables, justices of the peace
1300s	France: Charles V (1364–1380) establishes national police (*gens d'armes*)
17th–18th centuries	France: Louis XIV (1643–1715) establishes standing, uniformed police with "Lieutenant" of police; other European countries follow
	England: period of general lawlessness
1750–1798	England, 1750: Henry Fielding organizes official "thief-takers"; brother John Fielding creates Bow Street Runners, first salaried police in England
	England, 1798: Marine Police Establishment (Thames River Police) established
19th century	England: Sir Robert Peel establishes (London) Metropolitan Police, known as Peelers or Bobbies (1829)
	Similar police forces established all over England (1856)
17th–early 19th centuries	North America: Colonists follow English model—town watchmen, constables, sheriffs, marshals
1790	United States: Alexander Hamilton establishes first federal police force—U.S. Coast Guard (Marine Revenue Cutter Service)
19th century	United States: Politically dominated municipal police forces established (1838 Boston, 1845 New York, 1855 Milwaukee)
1890s–1920s	United States: Progressive period—International Association of Chiefs of Police founded; Leonhard Fuld publishes first police textbook; reformers Raymond Fosdick, August Vollmer
1930s–1960s	United States: Wickersham Commission documents American police as incompetent, ineffective, brutal. Reformers: professionalization (O. W. Wilson), crime fighter (J. Edgar Hoover, FBI)
1960s	United States: Crime fighter/professional police style backfires: unrest and riots. Civil libertarians call for new approach
1970s	United States: Police democratization, equal employment opportunity, community relations, better recruitment & training; search for new management models
Since 2001	United States: Expansion of police role to include "first responder" to terrorist threats; premium placed on the generation and sharing of intelligence in large municipalities. Most police departments add post-9/11 training programs, but maintain traditional police functional roles.

each requiring military intervention.[3] Some riots were economic, such as those in which depositors stormed banks during times of economic crisis. The system of constables and watchmen simply could not deal with this kind of social turmoil. Pressure mounted for finding an alternative means of maintaining order and enforcing the law.

London's newly created (1829) Metropolitan Police provided what many Americans considered the appropriate model. The "bobbies" (named for their founder, Sir Robert Peel) formed an organization that was midway between a military and a civilian force. The earliest attempt to create a replica in America was short-lived: Philadelphia in 1833 established a day police force of 24 men to supplement the night watch of 120 men, but it was disbanded two years later. In 1838, Boston appointed a force of nine police officers to deal with riots, while maintaining the night watch system already in place; the two forces were consolidated in 1854. New York City commissioned a police force in 1845. Philadelphia followed suit in 1854 and Chicago and Milwaukee in 1855.

The Problem of Political Control

From the beginning, American police forces had problems, many of which can be traced to one source: political control. The police had a vested interest in keeping in office the politicians to whom they owed their jobs. Since the police had the duty of supervising polling places, officeholders had a distinct advantage in elections. Political control was facilitated by the decentralized structure of most urban forces. This type of arrangement began in New York City, where each political ward had a separate patrol precinct. Each precinct remained under the authority of a precinct captain, who usually worked closely with the ward politicians. Police chiefs exercised little control over officers working at the precinct level. All these practices meant that the police were decidedly not a professional force.

Effective policing was hampered by other factors as well. Moral reformers wanted strict enforcement of laws dealing with prostitution, gambling, and liquor, while many working-class people and those in the liquor business opposed attempts to enforce these laws. The police were caught between the two, and enforcement became a source of chronic tension between the public and the police as well as an occasion for bribes, protection money, and corruption.

Crime detection was another area that created the image of an unprofessional force. Before the establishment of uniformed police departments, "thief-taking" had been considered a private enterprise in which a reward would be paid for the return of stolen property. Detectives continued this practice even after the formation of police departments. To recover stolen goods, detectives had to rely on contacts with criminals who could lead them to the proper sources. On occasion, this meant that criminals were hired as detectives.[4] The combination of fees paid for work and association with criminals resulted in a detective force with a lax attitude toward law enforcement.

Early Reformers: Vollmer

Reform was supported by many of the nation's early police chiefs.[5] The International Association of Chiefs of Police (IACP), founded in 1893 and given its present name in 1900, was the first professional association in law enforcement. The IACP spearheaded the movement for reform under the direction of Richard Sylvester, superintendent of the Washington, DC, police, who served as president from 1901 to 1916. Other important reformers included Leonhard Fuld, author of the first textbook on the subject of police administration; Arthur Woods, commissioner of the New York City police; and Raymond B. Fosdick, who documented American policing in a book titled *American Police Systems*.[6] The single most important reformer of this period, and the one who would prove to have the most profound influence on the development of the police, was August Vollmer.

Vollmer's career in law enforcement began with his election as town marshal of Berkeley, California, in 1905. He went on to head the Berkeley police as chief until 1932. His approach to policing emphasized professionalism among the ranks, a goal he attempted to achieve in part by selecting college students as recruits and devising a set of entrance tests.

He also established a police school to ensure proper training. Vollmer believed the primary function of the police should be crime fighting and that they should be aided in this mission by the scientific methods utilized in the crime lab he created. He was also concerned with the social dimensions of police work and established a crime prevention division as well as delinquency prevention programs.[7] Vollmer's book, *The Police and Modern Society* (1936), remained a guide for police professionals for decades.

The Wickersham Report

The early reformers made limited progress in the first decades of the twentieth century. A survey conducted in the 1920s found that only two out of three officers had finished elementary school and that only 10 percent were high school graduates. Training programs were not up to the standards proposed by Vollmer, and politicians still managed to exert some control. In 1929 the United States National Commission on Law Observance and Enforcement, under the direction of former Attorney General George W. Wickersham (and therefore commonly referred to as the Wickersham Commission), was given a mandate to investigate the criminal justice system.

Its findings painted a dismal picture of the police at that time, noting inadequacies in many areas, including recruitment, training, standards, communications, statistics, and fulfillment of the crime prevention mission. Having discovered evidence of extensive use of the **third degree**—which it labeled a "flagrant violation of the law by the officers of the law"[8]—and other forms of police brutality, the commission chose to devote an entire volume of its report to the subject of lawlessness in law enforcement.

third degree
Torturing a suspect to gain information.

The New Wave of Reform: Crime Fighters

The Wickersham report shocked the nation and provided additional impetus to reform. The most prominent leader of this new wave of reform was O. W. Wilson, a protégé of August Vollmer. Wilson was chief of police in Wichita, Kansas, from 1928 to 1935, where he fought a vigorous campaign for reform within his own department. He became a professor of police administration at the University of California and helped to create Berkeley's School of Criminology, the first of its kind in the country. From 1950 to 1960 he served as its first dean. While at Berkeley, Wilson wrote a book titled *Police Administration* (1950), which became the standard text on the subject.

The renewed reform effort focused on professionalism, with the objective of creating a well-disciplined and highly trained police force, immune to the corrupting influence of politics. Crime control was to be its primary function. The image of law enforcement officers as crime fighters was advanced especially by J. Edgar Hoover, who had been appointed director of the Federal Bureau of Investigation in 1924. The highly publicized exploits of Hoover's morally irreproachable FBI agents against the notorious criminals of the 1930s helped to foster the public's perception of police as dedicated crime fighters.

Technological advances also nurtured this image. Patrol cars were introduced just before World War I and were in widespread use by the end of the 1920s. Wilson was a strong advocate of automobile patrol, believing that the presence of distinctively marked police cars in a neighborhood would be a significant anticrime technique.[9] The advent of two-way radios in patrol cars in the late 1930s meant not only that officers could respond quickly to calls for assistance, but also that supervisors could remain in touch with those on patrol. This "quick response" ability helped to promote the idea that criminals would face an increased probability of being caught, thereby reinforcing the crime-fighting image.

The reforms that were undertaken in earnest during the 1930s had a far more profound effect than merely changing the image of the police. Departments were reorganized along functional lines. Entities such as patrol, traffic, detective, moral, and crime prevention bureaus replaced in importance the old precinct houses. Hiring guidelines raised the educational requirements for new recruits. By 1968, no large city police department would accept an applicant without a high school diploma. Psychological testing and extensive background checks were used, with the result that numerous candidates were rejected. In New York, for example, roughly five out

of six applicants were rejected during the 1950s and 1960s, while in Los Angeles and Dallas the figure went as high as nineteen out of twenty.[10] Improved training was provided to those who were appointed. Civilians began to perform some tasks within departments, freeing the police to concentrate on those duties that only well-trained professionals with special skills were able to accomplish.

The Sixties: Protests and Confrontations

By the mid-1960s, the professional model of the well-trained, highly disciplined, crime-fighting police force had taken hold across the nation. Certain features of this model, however, created tensions between the police and the public as well as within departments. In their efforts to professionalize, the police had turned themselves into a bureaucratic operation, governed by a rigid chain of command. Rank-and-file officers resented their relatively lowly status within the departments and the strict internal control exercised by commanding officers. Belief in the power of technology led to the almost exclusive use of patrol cars and the near abandonment of foot patrols. Without face-to-face contact between foot-patrol officers and the community, officers became increasingly isolated from the neighborhoods they policed.

Many departments instituted new forms of preventive patrols, known as "stop-and-search" or "stop-and-frisk," which typically would be deployed in high-crime areas. People viewed by the police as potential offenders would be rounded up on the street, frisked, and interrogated. San Francisco's Operation S, for example, stopped 20,000 people in its first year, yet only 1,000 of these people were arrested.[11] Aggressive crime-control tactics were a source of antagonism between the police and the public, especially young black males who were often the target of these patrols. As the tumultuous decade of the 1960s got under way, the professional crime-fighter model was being challenged in ways totally unanticipated by those who had struggled to bring it into existence.

The civil rights movement, opposition to the unpopular war in Vietnam, college students seeking refuge in drug use, increased television coverage of confrontations—all stressed police–community relations. At the same time, police unions became stronger and stressed the administration.[12] The fiscal crisis led to increasing "civilianization," the employment of lower-paid civilians to perform some of the functions previously performed by uniformed officers.[13] That led to intradepartmental confrontations. Aggressive policing was under attack.

In this atmosphere of rising crime rates, civil disorder, and internal pressures, several national studies evaluated the police, together with other criminal justice agencies. Among the most prominent was the President's Commission on Law Enforcement and the Administration of Justice, whose members were appointed by President Lyndon Johnson in 1965 to investigate and report on crime and the criminal justice system. The commission issued its findings in 1967 in a report titled *The Challenge of Crime in a Free Society*. The report called for many of the same reforms that had been advocated before, such as higher standards for police personnel, better training for recruits, and improved management practices. However, the report also spoke of the need for better police–community relations, recommended the hiring of minority police officers, acknowledged the need for civilian grievance procedures, and recognized the need for explicit policies to deal with issues related to the exercise of police discretion.[14]

Another significant outcome of the commission's work was the stimulus it gave to social science research in the area of the police. During its two-year investigation, the commission funded many research efforts that provided empirical information about the performance of the police. After the commission finished its work, the commitment to research was continued through the newly created Law Enforcement Assistance Administration (LEAA). LEAA-funded research provided new insight into the workings of the police. Other important sources of research sponsorship were established when the Ford Foundation created the Police Foundation in 1970, which in turn helped to found the Police Executive Research Forum (PERF).

As a result of these developments, American policing in the 1980s and 1990s differed radically from that of preceding decades. We turn now to contemporary American police forces and their structures and functions.

Post-9/11: Exploring a New Role for Police as First Responders

Following the attacks on September 11, 2001, state, municipal, and local police officers were asked to assume a very different role: intelligence gatherer. Just ask Baltimore Police Lt. David Engel, commander of the city intelligence unit (CIU), who has 36 detectives under his charge. The CIU works closely with federal agents and task forces, tracks terrorist activity, and seeks tips from informants about potential threats.

Engel's unit is part of an emerging trend that looks to local police agencies as an important source of domestic and international intelligence for any one of the 66 Joint Terrorism Task Forces of the FBI. This mission is no longer the sole province of the FBI and Central Intelligence Agency (CIA). This mission is now shared with the traditional first responders to crime on the streets.

Consider the change in police training after 9/11. In the Los Angeles Police Department, for example, officers receive an eight-hour block of training on weapons of mass destruction (WMD). "The training included information on the root of domestic and foreign Terrorism, recognition of precursor chemicals and equipment used in WMD's and response to WMD incidents. All field personnel have been issued protective equipment including nuclear, biological and chemical protective gas masks. Training has been delivered to allied agencies at the Airport and Port of Los Angeles in unified operations. This training will continue until all parts of the City are integrated."[15] Expanded training for higher-ranking officers includes coordinated counterterrorism initiatives with other first responders.

State police departments with resources have even gone further by creating bureaus of homeland security and intelligence. These larger statewide police units raise certain questions in the minds of civil rights lawyers. According to the American Civil Liberties Union, they are generally unaccountable and lack transparency. In spite of these concerns, the overriding need for real-time "street-level" intelligence—or at least the perceived need—has moved police department after police department to join in the counteroffensive against domestic and international terrorism from inside our major cities.

No municipal police department has done more, post-9/11, than the New York Police Department—from assigning officers overseas, to hiring medical staff to understand and analyze weapons of mass destruction. The department created an extensive counterterrorism bureau with more than 700 investigators, along with an intelligence bureau that boasts detectives and analysts relying on state-of-the-art technology. The department is on "war footing" by championing a proactive approach to the threat of terrorism.

Police Commissioner Raymond W. Kelly cautions, "We want to emphasize, we're not looking to supplant anything that's going on in the federal government. . . . Why are we different? Well, we've been targeted. We're sitting 10 blocks away from why we're different."[16]

Police Systems in the United States

Policing in the United States is the responsibility of a combination of federal, state, and local agencies. From its tentative beginnings a mere 150 years ago, policing has become a formidable enterprise. Nationwide, state, and local law enforcement agencies employed approximately 1,076,897 people (731,903 sworn officers) in 2004, well over half the total number of people employed in the nation's criminal justice system. The number of sworn officers was more than 10 percent greater than in 1996.[17] Furthermore, private security and citizen crime prevention programs are now a growing and important part of the system. To understand that system, it is necessary first to examine the police as a bureaucracy, and a governmental institution, and then to survey the many types of police forces in America.

Chain of Command

All but the smallest police departments in the United States are bureaucracies, marked by hierarchical structures with a clearly delineated chain of command from the top down, a division of labor among various bureaus, and a set of rules and regulations to which all officers must adhere. Police departments are not democratic organizations. They function largely along the lines of a military command structure, with military ranks and insignia. Patrol officers are responsible to their sergeants, sergeants to lieutenants, lieutenants to captains, captains to inspectors, inspectors to their chief or director.

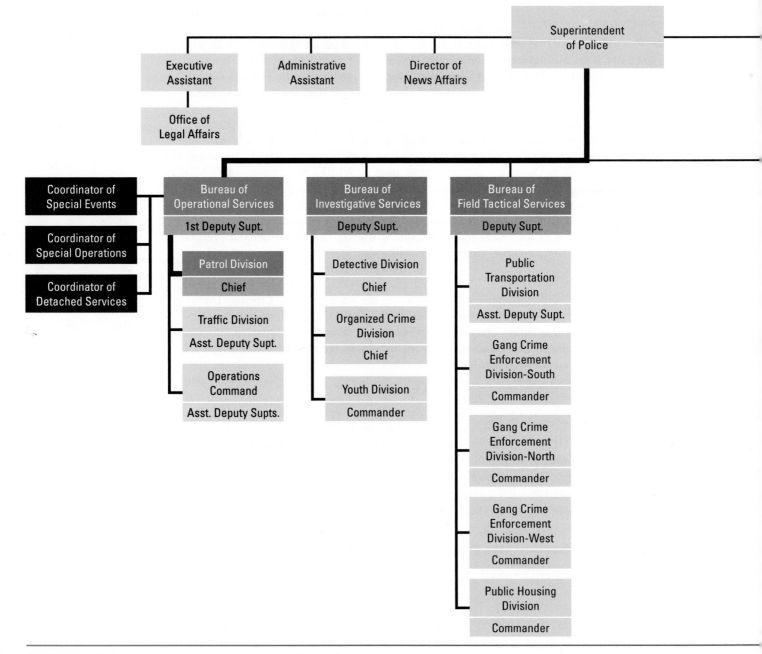

FIGURE 5.1   Organization for Command: The Chicago Police Department

SOURCE: Larry K. Gaines, Mittie D. Southerland, and John E. Angell, *Police Administration* (New York: McGraw-Hill, 1991), p. 82.

Division of Labor

Within a police department organization, the division of labor is based on needs, expertise, and experience. The division of labor is reflected in the overall responsibilities assigned to various bureaus (Figure 5.1). The **operations bureau** of a department performs the functions associated with the primary law enforcement mission of the department. These are referred to as **line functions,** and the police involved in them are called line officers. Line officers make up about 70 percent of full-time sworn local police personnel. They are the uniformed officers who are on patrol or assigned to respond to service calls. In larger forces, line activities are assigned to bureaus or divisions, which typically include patrol, traffic, detective, juvenile, and vice units. Among these the patrol division is the largest, as it delivers the bulk of crime prevention and law enforcement services.

operations bureau
Unit of a police department responsible for the functions associated with the primary law enforcement mission.

line functions
Law enforcement functions of a police department.

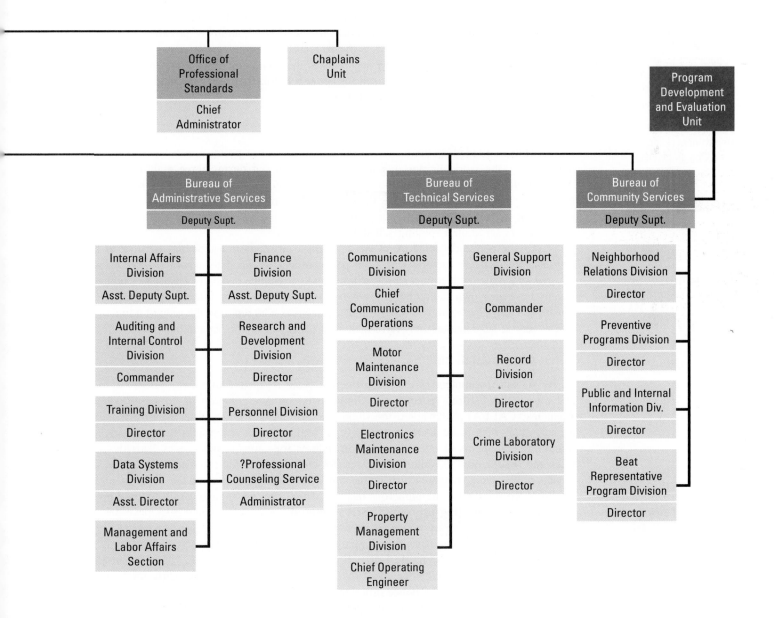

Among the line functions, those of the detective (or investigations) bureau are regarded as particularly desirable assignments. Specialized training and expertise are required for work in the various units of the detective bureaus of larger municipal departments, such as homicide, burglary, art theft (a rapidly growing problem worldwide), or the "bias" unit, the youngest specialized unit in larger departments.

The **services bureau** provides technical services to assist in the execution of line functions, such as keeping records and maintaining a crime laboratory. Services provided in the **administration bureau** include those that relate to the running of the department as an organization: personnel, finance, and research and development.

Figure 5.1 also shows a separate division called **internal affairs,** which is responsible for receiving and investigating charges against the police. Such charges may relate to violations of the criminal law or to procedural issues. Among the most frequent complaints are those of police brutality and abuse of power. The internal investigation (internal affairs) unit is typically responsible for investigating complaints filed by citizens and incidents reported by police officers themselves. It can also initiate its own investigations of possible corruption.

Another unit shown in Figure 5.1 is the Bureau of Community Services. By the 1960s a gulf separated the police and many segments of the community they were supposed to be serving; this called attention to the need for better relations between police and community. Many departments established a special division for this purpose.

The Eight-Hour Shift

Police labor is divided on the basis of time and place. Since police are on call twenty-four hours a day, the work of most departments is carried out during three eight-hour shifts. Although the most efficient way to organize officers on the basis of time may be to assign them permanently to one of these three shifts, low morale typically results because of resentment at being continuously placed on duty during an undesirable shift. Therefore, most officers serve on a rotating schedule.

To provide police coverage of all areas within a jurisdiction, a city may be divided into districts, precincts, or sectors, with each patrol officer assigned to a **beat** (a specific area covered by a police officer on a patrol) within these geographic divisions. Districts or precincts usually have their own station houses in which some officers from different specialized functional units may also be housed. For example, detectives who report to the head of a functional unit at central headquarters may have their own offices in a precinct station.

Rules and Regulations

O. W. Wilson recommended that departments create a "formal directive system" of rules and regulations.[18] More recently, the Commission on Accreditation of Law Enforcement Agencies (CALEA) underscored the importance of written policy directives by requiring agencies that wish to be accredited to have a "written directives system that includes, at a minimum, statements of agency policy, procedures for carrying out agency activities, and rules and regulations."[19] Written directives not only set forth the rules and regulations that govern police work, but they also define the policy and principles of the department and establish procedures for the numerous tasks in which officers engage. Collected and issued as a **standard operating procedure (SOP) manual,** these policies and rules have become a key tool in contemporary police management.

Although written rules have their limitations, one of their most important benefits is the role they can play in the control of discretion in the execution of duties. Many departments have in recent years issued rules about the use of deadly force that explicitly set forth the circumstances under which a police officer may shoot at a suspect. Others have adopted written policies about high-speed pursuits, spelling out the situations in which such pursuits may be undertaken and those in which a pursuit must be terminated. Other examples of such administrative rules include policies concerning mandatory arrests in cases of domestic violence and the handling of chronic alcoholics or the homeless. Some research evidence suggests that written rules restricting the use of deadly force in New York City have helped to reduce considerably the number of police shootings and injuries to both citizens and officers. There

---

services bureau
Unit of a police department that provides technical services to assist in the execution of *line functions,* such as keeping records.

administration bureau
Unit of a police department responsible for the management of the department as an organization; includes personnel, finance, and research and development.

internal affairs
Department responsible for receiving and investigating charges against the police.

beat
Territory covered by a police officer on patrol; derived from hunters, "beating" the bushes for game.

standard operating procedure (SOP) manual
Collection of departmental directives governing the performance of duties.

is also evidence that even written rules concerning matters such as hot pursuits and mandatory arrest policies in cases of domestic violence may be ignored by individual officers.[20]

The Federal System

Policing at the federal level can be dated to 1790, when Congress established a revenue marine force, subsequently called the Revenue Cutter Service and long since known as the U.S. Coast Guard, to police the nation's coasts and to enforce the revenue laws of the country. In the two centuries since then, the number of federal police forces has grown immensely. Although only 8.2 percent of all American law enforcement officers are employed in federal services, the federal role in law enforcement is an important one. The enforcement of certain laws and regulations is statutorily assigned to specific agencies. Today there are some sixty federal law enforcement agencies; here we will discuss only some of the largest.

careers

The Federal Bureau of Investigation

From a modest beginning in 1908, with only 35 agents, the FBI has become the largest federal police agency, with a staff of 27,000 people, including some 11,400 special agents in 56 field offices nationwide; about 400 resident agencies; 4 specialized field installations; and 40 foreign posts.[21] This growth is attributable to many laws passed by Congress that have widened the FBI's jurisdiction, such as the Mann Act in 1908 (prohibiting the interstate and international transportation of women for prostitution), the prohibition laws of the 1920s, and the Fugitive Felon Act of 1934. The FBI also was designated collector and disseminator of crime statistics nationwide, known as the Uniform Crime Reports (UCRs). During World War II the FBI became the guardian of national security in matters of espionage, sabotage, and violation of the neutrality laws. National security matters occupied the FBI for a long time.[22] Investigations first focused on Nazis and then switched to Communists. J. Edgar Hoover (director of the FBI from 1924 to 1972), although otherwise an outstanding professional leader, abused the national security power by investigating civil rights leaders, such as Dr. Martin Luther King, Jr. But the prestige of the FBI has been restored under subsequent directors, and today, at the end of the Cold War, the FBI is far more concerned with organized crime, street gangs, and drug groups. Overall, the bureau now has jurisdiction over some 260 federal crimes.

careers

FBI PRIORITIES

1. Protect the United States from terrorist attack.
2. Protect the United States against foreign intelligence operations and espionage.
3. Protect the United States against cyber-based attacks and high-technology crimes.
4. Combat public corruption at all levels.
5. Protect civil rights.
6. Combat transnational and national criminal organizations and enterprises.
7. Combat major white-collar crime.
8. Combat significant violent crime.
9. Support federal, state, county, municipal, and international partners.
10. Upgrade technology to successfully perform the FBI's mission.

Counterterrorism is now a top priority for the FBI, with a focus on preventing acts of terrorism before they take place. The Counterterrorism Division at FBI headquarters coordinates the work of individual field offices. An increasingly large team of intelligence analysts evaluates information gathered by the field offices. A national threat warning system is also coordinated at headquarters allowing the FBI to instantly notify local police departments.

The Counterterrorism Division focuses on both international and domestic counterterrorist efforts. At the center of this initiative is the National Joint Terrorism Task Force, located at headquarters, which includes staff from the Department of Defense, Department of Energy, Federal Emergency Management Agency, Central Intelligence Agency, Customs Service, Secret Service, and the Bureau of Citizenship and Immigration Services. The NJTTF oversees 66 local Joint Terrorism Task Force groups distributed around the United States where representatives from a host of federal agencies, state and local law enforcement organizations, and first responders coordinate counterterrorism efforts at the local level.

Questions and Criticisms

Over the years the FBI has played a highly publicized role in the investigation and capture of such criminals as Baby Face Nelson, Doc Barker, John Dillinger, Pretty Boy Floyd, Al Capone, Bonnie Parker, and Clyde Barrow. Under Hoover, the FBI acquired its sterling image as the chief investigative branch of the Department of Justice. This image was tarnished in the 1960s when it was revealed that FBI agents had been wiretapping national leaders, including Martin Luther King, Jr.; opening mail; and discrediting political radicals as "enemies of the government."

In the early 1990s the FBI's handling of a variety of cases was called into question and subjected to review. The bureau was harshly criticized for its handling of a confrontation with the Branch Davidians in Waco, Texas, in 1993. The standoff between the bureau and the Davidians came to an end on April 19 after the FBI and other federal law enforcement officers shot tear gas shells into the compound. The tragic result was that 75 Davidians, including 25 children, died in a fire that ensued. The FBI and the other federal agencies involved (such as the Bureau of Alcohol, Tobacco and Firearms [now the Bureau of Alcohol, Tobacco, Firearms and Explosives]) have learned from this tragedy and, based on advice from experts on extremist groups, have altered some of their procedures. These revised procedures have helped federal agencies respond more effectively in similar situations. For example, federal agencies peacefully resolved a 1996 standoff with a group of federal tax protestors who had barricaded themselves in an Arizona ranch.

In recent years the FBI has been criticized for its post-9/11 initiatives, including concerns over the surveillance of innocent civilians; the execution of "no-fly" terrorist watch lists; the assistance offered to local police departments with protest suppression tactics; reliance on increasingly sophisticated surveillance technologies; and the expansion of FBI powers under the USA Patriot Act, allowing the FBI to secretly obtain records and personal belongings of U.S. citizens.

A SHORT HISTORY OF THE FBI BY THE FBI

On July 26, 1908, Attorney General (AG) Charles J. Bonaparte ordered a small force of permanent investigators (organized a month earlier) to report to the Department of Justice's Chief Examiner, Stanley Finch. AG Bonaparte declared that these investigators would handle all Department of Justice (DOJ) investigative matters, except certain bank frauds. At first, little seemed to come of AG Bonaparte's reorganization.

In 1909, this investigator force was named the Bureau of Investigation (BOI). At this time, it investigated antitrust matters, land fraud, copyright violations, peonage (involuntary slavery), and twenty other matters. Over the next decade, federal criminal authority and Bureau jurisdiction were extended by laws like the 1910 "White-Slave Traffic" Act that put responsibility for interstate prostitution under the Bureau for a time and the 1919 Dyer Act that did the same for interstate auto-theft. U.S. entry into World War II in April 1917 led to further increases in the Bureau's jurisdiction. Congress and President Wilson assigned the BOI's three hundred employees responsibility for espionage, sabotage, sedition, and selective service matters.

(continued)

The 1920s brought Prohibition, the automobile, and an increase in criminal activity. Bank robbers, bootleggers, and kidnappers took advantage of jurisdictional boundaries by crossing state lines to elude capture. A criminal culture marked by violent gangsters flourished, but no federal law gave the BOI authority to tackle their crimes and other law enforcement efforts were fragmented. The Bureau addressed these matters as its jurisdiction permitted throughout the 1920s.

In 1924, Attorney General Harlan Stone appointed John Edgar Hoover as Director. Director Hoover (1924–1972) implemented a number of reforms to clean up what had become a politicized Bureau under the leadership of William J. Burns (1921–1924). Hoover reinstated merit hiring, introduced professional training of new Agents, demanded regular inspections of all Bureau operations, and required strict professionalism in the Bureau's work.

Under Hoover, the Bureau also began to emphasize service to other law enforcement agencies. The Identification Division was created in 1924 to provide U.S. police a means to identify criminals across jurisdictional boundaries. The Technical Crime Laboratory, created in 1932, provided forensic analysis and research for law enforcement, and the FBI National Academy, opened in 1935, provided standardized professional training for America's law enforcement communities.

In answer to the violent crime of the 1930s, Congress began to assign and expand new authorities to the Bureau. The kidnapping and murder of Charles Lindbergh's baby son in 1932 led to the passage of the Federal Kidnapping Act, which allowed the Bureau to investigate interstate kidnappings. The 1933 Kansas City Massacre spurred the passage of the 1934 May/June Crime Bills. These laws gave the Bureau authority to act in many new areas, to make arrests, and to carry weapons. Renamed "Federal Bureau of Investigation" in 1935, the FBI dealt with gangsters severely, earning its anonymous agents the nickname "G-Men."

As the gangster threat subsided, a threat of a different nature emerged. In 1936, President Roosevelt directed the FBI to investigate potential subversion by Nazi and Communist organizations. In 1940, he tasked the Bureau with responsibility for foreign intelligence in the western hemisphere and domestic security in the United States. In response, the Bureau created a Special Intelligence Service (SIS) Division in June 1940. The SIS sent undercover FBI Agents throughout the Western Hemisphere. These Agents successfully identified some 1,300 Axis intelligence agents (about 10 percent of whom were prosecuted). When President Truman ordered the program's end in 1947, several former SIS offices became the backbone of the FBI's foreign liaison efforts, now serving as Legal Attaché Offices. FBI efforts also thwarted many espionage, sabotage, and propaganda attempts on the home front, including Frederic Duquesne's spy ring in 1941 and George Dasch's band of saboteurs in 1942.

When Germany and Japan surrendered in 1945, concern about the threat of foreign intelligence did not end. Revelations that year from former Soviet intelligence agents like Igor Guzenko and Elizabeth Bentley, information gleaned from FBI investigations during and after the war, and decrypted/decoded Soviet cable traffic called "Venona" (available to the Bureau from 1947) convinced the FBI of the seriousness of the Soviet intelligence threat long before Senator Joseph McCarthy made his 1950 speech about communist "moles." Under the Hatch Act (1940) and Executive Orders issued in 1947 and 1951, the Bureau exercised responsibility for ensuring the loyalty of those who sought to work in the government. The FBI played a critical role in U.S. handling of the Cold War.

In the 1950s, civil rights violations and organized crime became matters of increasing concern. As in the past, lack of jurisdiction hindered the Bureau from effectively responding to these problems when they first emerged as national issues. It was under the 1964 Civil Rights Act and the 1965 Voting Rights Act that the Bureau received legislative authority to investigate many of the wrongs done to African Americans in the South and elsewhere. Under existing laws, the Bureau's efforts against organized crime also started slowly. Then, with the 1968 Omnibus Crime Control and Safe Streets Act and the 1970 Organized Crime

(continued)

Control Act, Congress gave the Bureau effective weapons with which to attack organized criminal enterprises, Title III warrants for wiretaps and the [Racketeer Influenced] and Corrupt Organizations Act (RICO).

During the 1960s, subversion remained a central focus of Bureau efforts. The counter-cultural revolution turned the Bureau's attention toward violent student movements, as criminal groups like the Weather Underground and the Black Panthers engaged in both legitimate political action and illegal crime. The Bureau responded to the threat of subversion with Counterintelligence Programs (COINTELPRO) first against the Communist Party (1956), later against other violent/subversive groups like the Black Panthers and the Ku Klux Klan (1960s). These programs resulted in the Bureau, at times, effectively stepping out of its proper role as a law enforcement agency.

During the 1970s, Bureau actions, which were publicly revealed through a strengthened Freedom of Information Act (1966, amended in 1974), resulted in congressional investigations like the Church Committee and the Pike Committee hearings in 1975. In response to criticisms emerging from these revelations, the Bureau worked with Attorney General Levi to develop guidelines for its domestic counterintelligence investigations.

In the wake of Director Hoover's death in May 1972, Director Clarence M. Kelley (1973–1977) refocused FBI investigative priorities to place less emphasis on having a high number of cases and to focus more on the quality of cases handled. Working with the Bureau and Congress in 1976, Attorney General Edward Levi issued a set of investigative guidelines to address the concerns of Bureau critics and to give the FBI the confidence of having public, legal authority behind its use of irreplaceable investigative techniques like wiretaps, informants, and undercover agents. These investigative techniques were used to great effect in cases like UNIRAC (1978), ABSCAM (1980), and GREYLORD (1984). In 1983, as concerns about terrorist acts grew, Attorney General William French Smith revised the Levi Guidelines to adjust the Bureau's ability to prevent violent radical acts.

Director William H. Webster (1977–1987) built upon Director Kelley's emphasis on investigative "quality" cases by focusing Bureau efforts on three Priority Programs: White Collar Crime, Organized Crime, and Foreign Counterintelligence. Later, Illegal Drugs (1982), Counterterrorism (1982), and Violent Crimes (1989) were also identified as priority programs. This concentration of resources brought great success against Soviet and East Bloc intelligence as more than 40 spies were arrested between 1977 and 1985. The FBI also made breakthroughs against white-collar crime in investigations like ILLWIND (1988) and LOST TRUST (1990), and in organized crime cases like BRILAB (1981) and the PIZZA CONNECTION (1985).

During the 1990s, criminal and security threats to the United States evolved as new technology and the fall of communism in the Soviet bloc changed the geopolitical world. The 1993 bombing of the World Trade Centers and the 1995 bombing of the Oklahoma City federal building highlighted the potentially catastrophic threat of both international and domestic terrorism. The FBI responded to the emerging international face of crime by aggressively building bridges between U.S. and foreign law enforcement. Under the leadership of Director Louis J. Freeh (1993–2001), the Bureau dramatically expanded its Legat Program (39 offices by fall 2000); provided professional law enforcement education to foreign nationals through the International Law Enforcement Academy (ILEA) in Budapest (opened in 1994) and other international education efforts; and created working groups and other structured liaisons with foreign law enforcement.

The Bureau also strengthened its domestic agenda. Responding to criticism of its actions in the 1993 standoffs at Waco, Texas, and Ruby Ridge, Idaho, the Bureau revamped its crisis response efforts. The FBI's commitment to law enforcement service was strengthened by the computerization of its massive fingerprint collection database, enhancements in the National Crime Information Center, and the revitalization of the FBI Laboratory. In 1997, the Bureau hired its first professional scientist to head the Lab. The Lab tightened its protocols

(continued)

for evidence control, instituted organizational changes to optimize research specialization, and earned national accreditation.

On September 4, 2001, former US Attorney Robert S. Mueller, III, (2001 to present) was sworn in as Director with a mandate to address a number of tough challenges: upgrading the Bureau's information technology infrastructure; addressing records management issues; and enhancing FBI foreign counterintelligence analysis and security in the wake of the damage done by former Special Agent and convicted spy Robert S. Hanssen.

Then within days of his starting duty, the September 11 terrorist attacks were launched against New York and Washington. Director Mueller led the FBI's massive investigative efforts in partnership with all US law enforcement, the federal government, and our allies overseas. On October 26, 2001, the President signed into law the U.S. Patriot Act, which granted new provisions to address the threat of terrorism, and Director Mueller accordingly accepted on behalf of the Bureau responsibility for protecting the American people against future terrorist attacks. On May 29, 2002, the Attorney General issued revised investigative guidelines to assist the Bureau's counterterrorism efforts.

To support the Bureau's change in mission and to meet newly articulated strategic priorities, Director Mueller called for a reengineering of FBI structure and operations that will closely focus the Bureau on prevention of terrorist attacks, on countering foreign intelligence operations against the United States, and on addressing cyber-based attacks and other high technology crimes. In addition, the Bureau remains dedicated to protecting civil rights, and to combating public corruption, organized crime, white-collar crime, and major acts of violent crime. It is also strengthening its support to federal, county, municipal, and international law enforcement partners. And it is upgrading its technological infrastructure to successfully meet each of its priorities.

At the start of the new millennium, the FBI stands dedicated to its core values and ethical standards. Commitment to these values and standards ensures that the FBI effectively carries out its mission.

SOURCE: Federal Bureau of Investigation, *Facts and Figures 2003,* http://www.fbi.gov/libref/factsfigure/shorthistory.htm.

The FBI also develops and maintains advanced forensic research capabilities, training facilities, and extensive databases of information on crime and criminals. The Laboratory Division collects and analyzes evidence for its own investigations as well as for other federal, state, and local law enforcement agencies. The division consists of thirty-five separate units organized into five sections all housed in a new facility in Quantico, Virginia, with more than 650 employees. In 1999 alone, the lab conducted more than 700,000 forensic examinations of evidence and 2.3 million latent fingerprint comparisons.[23] The Forensic Science Research and Training Center provides advanced forensic training to FBI staff and other law enforcement personnel, including a technical training course in the implementation of new DNA technology (sometimes referred to as **genetic fingerprinting**) in criminal investigations.

A genetic fingerprint, or as it is more commonly known, a DNA fingerprint, is composed of a series of DNA strands in a vertical column, representing the chromosomes from a person's mother and father. Experts study the occurrence of the combinations of these different strands in the population, and then calculate the likelihood or probability that two DNA samples have the same strands. For any particular DNA fingerprint, the likelihood of a matching fingerprint is remote. How remote depends on the number of strands examined and the number of tests performed. After five tests, the odds approach one in a million that someone else in the public will have the same DNA fingerprint.

There is strong consensus about the scientific value of DNA evidence. Few persist in questioning the evidentiary importance of DNA fingerprints. Even so, DNA evidence has its persistent critics, who are concerned about the possibility of errors. For example, errors may occur due to the mislabeling of a sample in the DNA testing laboratory or through accidents in either the collection of the bodily fluid used for the test or the analysis of the evidence.

genetic fingerprinting
Use of DNA as a technique for identifying suspects.

THE KGB—CONTROLLING INTELLIGENCE

In 1940 the NKVD, the Soviet secret police that was the forerunner of the KGB, was instructed to carry out "the supreme punishment—execution by a firing squad" of "14,700 former Polish officers, officials, landowners, policemen and gendarmes, held in camps for prisoners of war," as well as another 11,000 "members of different subversion and espionage organizations, former land- and factory owners, former Polish officers, former officials and former clergymen, arrested and held in jails in the western regions of Ukraine and Belarus."[1]

In October of 1992, Russia released secret documents detailing the Soviet massacre of 20,000 Poles in 1940. Although the bodies had been unearthed in 1943 in a mass grave in the Katyn forests west of Moscow, Soviet officials had asserted that Nazis were responsible for the deaths. In 1990, then-president of the USSR Mikhael Gorbachev admitted Soviet guilt in the Katyn massacre, but the 1992 release of secret files provided all the information that had been a mystery for fifty years.

Police forces serve to keep social order. As we pointed out at the beginning of this chapter, policing a society ensures an orderly, secure life for its members. Police forces protect the state and themselves, and not infrequently they function to protect a particular regime as well, through illegal as well as legal means. When a society undergoes some sort of upheaval, previously secret activities are exposed to view. The KGB activities that were exposed after the dissolution of the Soviet Union provide a perfect example.

Going Public: The KGB

The Soviet Union's KGB (*Komitet Gosudarstvennoy Bezpasnosti,* or Committee of State Security) was probably the most notorious of all intelligence agencies. Undoubtedly the world's largest such organization, in 1985 the KGB had 400,000 officers inside the Soviet Union, 200,000 border troops, and a vast network of informers and agents at home and abroad.

The KGB no longer exists in its old form. It lost its components in all of the newly independent republics, which formed their own intelligence services. According to Eduard Shevardnaze, chair of the Georgia State Counsel, the KGB has been replaced by the Information and Intelligence Bureau, a "totally new structure that.. . objectively informs the leadership and public opinion about home and world developments."[2] In Russia itself the new Agency for Federal Security, the "Federal Security Service" (FSB) which replaces the KGB in that republic, has been scaled down to 40,000 personnel. The head of the FSB, Nikolai Patrushev, was a senior ranking KGB official in Leningrad.

> "The KGB no longer exists in its old form."

The Katyn massacre is not the only KGB-related "mystery" that has been made public. Once the USSR collapsed, any number of top-secret files began making their way into the light. Former KGB operatives began selling their memoirs. Many former officers started lecture tours in Western countries for hard-currency honoraria. Spy satellite photographs, too, were for sale; the once "ultrasecret" spy photos were more detailed than those that any nation had made public, according to experts.[3] The old KGB headquarters were opened to Western visitors for a thirty-dollar admission charge. And new government officials in the former Soviet Union made public a variety of previously secret files.

While historians were not shocked by the information that came to light after the dissolution of the USSR, American citizens learned a great deal about the KGB in a few short months of newspaper reading. Among KGB files stamped "Top Secret" acquired in 1992 by the *Boston Globe* are those pertaining to Soviet involvement in

- the funding of Palestinian terrorists in the 1970s
- the bugging of foreign journalists
- financial support for Indian Prime Minister Indira Gandhi
- "a document from Andropov dated August 1969 offering to set up a demonstration outside

the U.S. Embassy in New Delhi . . . [by] 'not less than 20,000 Muslims' at the bargain price of 5,000 rupees—about $500 at that time"

- the funding of the decaying Polish Communist Party
- recent arms shipments to the now-fallen government of Afghanistan[4]

Some of the files indicated the extent to which the KGB violated human rights. It appears that a KGB team in 1971 unsuccessfully tried to poison the dissident novelist Alexander Solzhenitsyn, who developed severe burns after the attempt and suffered the aftereffects for three months.[5]

Standards of Conduct for Intelligence Agencies?

Attempts have been made to provide standards of conduct for all police forces, including intelligence agencies. The member states of the United Nations unanimously adopted the U.N. Code of Conduct for Law Enforcement Officials in the General Assembly of 1979. They made clear the following:

> In countries where police powers are exercised by military authorities, whether uniformed or not, or by state security forces, the definition of law enforcement officials shall be regarded as including officers of such services.[6]

In other words, the officers of intelligence services are held to the same professional standards and obligations to respect human rights as the officers of civilian police forces. As yet, there is a big gap between standards and their realization—a fact that offending countries rarely acknowledge. In 1979 two of the authors of this textbook had the extraordinary experience of being invited, under United Nations auspices, to present lectures at the KGB senior officers' academy in Moscow. The 200 bemedaled officers in the audience listened intently to the presentations—on the U.N. Code of Conduct for Law Enforcement Officials and Human Rights in Criminal Justice—and applauded politely. In concluding remarks, the KGB general in charge assured the lecturers that, of course, the lectures simply confirmed the standards by which the KGB had always been guided.

The Russian people apparently had a different view. They have toppled the statue of Dherzhinsky,

the founder of the KGB, on Moscow's Dzerzhinsky Square in front of the old KGB headquarters. Memorial, the Russian human rights organization, has erected in its place a monument dedicated to the victims of Stalin's and Dherzhinsky's secret police, the KGB.[7]

Immediately before the Victory Day parade in Red Square in 2002, a bomb exploded in a town called Dagestan. More than 30 people were killed, with 50 injured. This attack, in addition to another terrorist attack on top-ranking officials in Chechnya, resulted in calls for Nikolai Patrushev's resignation. Just like the calls for FBI Director Robert Mueller's resignation, Patrushev had been called to task for handling the most difficult and challenging problem—terrorism.[8]

Questions for Discussion

1. Is it realistic to hold the officers of intelligence services to the same standards that govern civilian police officers?

2. Should exceptions be made in (a) wiretapping, (b) arrest, (c) search and seizure, (d) the taking of human life?

3. How should the U.N.'s code of conduct be enforced, and by whom?

SOURCES
1. Celestine Bohlen, "Russian Files Show Stalin Ordered Massacre of 20,000 Poles in 1940," *The New York Times,* October 15, 1992, p. 1.
2. David Molivani, "K.G.B. Liquidated," *Soviet Press Report,* May 26, 1992.
3. William J. Broad, "Russia Is Now Selling Spy Photos from Space," *The New York Times,* October 4, 1992, p. 8.
4. Paul Quinn-Judge, "Files Show K.G.B. Ties to Terrorism," *The Boston Globe,* May 29, 1992, p. 1.
5. David Remmisck, "KGB Plot to Assassinate Solzhenitsyn Reported," *The Washington Post,* April 21, 1992, p. D1.
6. U.N. General Assembly Resolution 34/169, of December 17, 1979.
7. Nancy Adler, *Memorial* (New York: Praeger, 1993).
8. A. Gilts, *Echo of the Ongoing War,* press abstracts May 14, 2002.

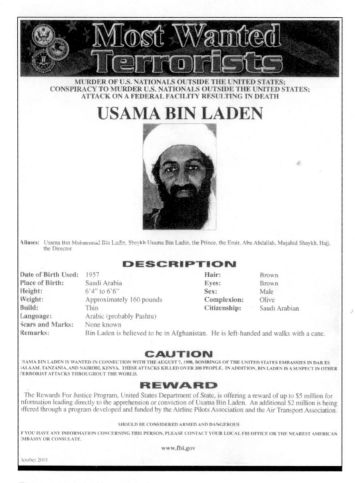

The most wanted terrorist of all time. The FBI issued this poster on Wednesday, October 10, 2001.

Despite this, DNA evidence has been introduced in hundreds of cases to convict the guilty and free the innocent. The FBI, along with 171 participating laboratories in fifty states and Puerto Rico, exchanges and compares DNA profiles in an attempt to solve violent crimes. As of November 2002, over 6,257 investigations have been aided by these exchanges, with more than 1.3 million convicted offender samples on file.[24]

Regular fingerprints are still maintained in the Identification Division that was established in 1924. Today the bureau's files contain more than 226 million fingerprint cards, representing 79 million individuals.[25] More than 96 million of these cards contain criminal history data on some 24 million people. Approximately 31,000 additional fingerprint cards arrive at the Identification Division every day. The FBI also maintains the National Crime Information Center (NCIC), a nationwide network of criminal justice information. Available to law enforcement agencies in all fifty states, the NCIC contains records on stolen property, wanted persons with outstanding arrest warrants, criminal histories on persons arrested for serious offenses, and records of certain missing persons. The NCIC serves more than 80,000 criminal justice agencies across the nation. This enables the agencies to process over 2.4 million transactions a day.[26]

In 1985, the bureau established the National Center for the Analysis of Violent Crime (NCAVC), a research and training center that provides assistance to law enforcement agencies faced with violent crimes that are unusual and/or particularly vicious or repetitive in nature, such as sexually oriented serial murders or child molestation cases involving multiple victims. The FBI also investigates police corruption. Finally, the FBI National Academy, located at Quantico, Virginia, provides training free of charge to state, local, and foreign law enforcement officials. These courses are given to more than 1,000 state and local law enforcement administrators annually.

The Drug Enforcement Administration

Established in 1973, the Drug Enforcement Administration (DEA) is the primary federal agency responsible for the enforcement of federal laws concerning the use, sale, and distribution of narcotics and other controlled substances in the United States. Of the DEA's over 9,200 staff members, half are special agents. The agency is headquartered in New York; its agents are stationed throughout the United States in twenty-one divisional offices and fourteen strike forces in major cities. Some agents are posted overseas.

In support of its investigative endeavors, the agency maintains a narcotics intelligence system that collects, analyzes, and disseminates data. (See Table 5.1.) At the international level, the DEA assists foreign governments with programs intended to reduce the availability of illicit drugs, through such measures as the eradication of crops like coca and poppies from which drugs are derived, crop substitutions, and the training of foreign officials. Other responsibilities include the investigation of drug seizures by U.S. Customs agents at border points and the regulation of the distribution of legal narcotics and drugs (see Table 5.2).

The Bureau of Alcohol, Tobacco, Firearms and Explosives

Effective January 24, 2003, the Bureau of Alcohol, Tobacco and Firearms (ATF) was transferred under the Homeland Security bill to the Department of Justice. The law enforcement functions of ATF under the Department of the Treasury were transferred to the Department

DEA Arrests (Domestic)			
Calendar Year	Number of Arrests	Calendar Year	Number of Arrests
2006	29,800	1995	25,279
2005	29,005	1994	23,135
2004	27,053	1993	21,637
2003	28,549	1992	24,541
2002	30,270	1991	23,659
2001	34,471	1990	22,770
2000	39,743	1989	25,176
1999	41,293	1988	24,853
1998	38,468	1987	22,751
1997	34,068	1986	19,884
1996	29,269	Total	568,596

SOURCE: DEA (SMARTS)
Defendant Statistical System (DSS).

DEA Drug Seizures					
Calender Year	Cocaine kgs	Heroin kgs	Marijuana kgs	Methamphetamine kgs	Hallucinogens Dosage Units
2006	69,826	805	322,438	1,711	4,606,277
2005	118,311	640	283,344	2,161	8,881,321
2004	117,854	672	265,813	1,659	2,261,706
2003	73,725	795	254,196	1,678	2,878,594
2002	63,640	710	238,024	1,353	11,661,157
2001	59,430	753	271,849	1,634	13,755,390
2000	58,674	546	331,964	1,771	29,307,427
1999	36,165	351	338,247	1,489	1,736,077
1998	34,447	370	262,180	1,203	1,075,457
1997	28,670	399	215,348	1147	1,100,912
1996	44,735	320	192,059	751	1,719,209
1995	45,326	876	219,830	876	2,768,165
1994	75,051	491	157,181	768	1,366,817
1993	55,529	616	143,055	560	2,710,063
1992	69,324	722	201,483	352	1,305,177
1991	67,016	1,174	98,592	289	1,297,394
1990	57,031	535	127,792	272	2,826,966
1989	73,587	758	286,371	896	13,125,010
1988	60,951	728	347,306	694	16,706,442
1987	49,666	512	629,839	198	6,556,891
1986	29,389	421	491,831	234.5	4,146,329

SOURCE: DEA (STRIDE).

TABLE 5.1   DEA Arrests and Drug Seizures, 1986–2006

TABLE 5.2
DEA Mission Statement

The mission of the Drug Enforcement Administration (DEA) is to enforce the controlled substances laws and regulations of the United States and bring to the criminal and civil justice system of the United States, or any other competent jurisdiction, those organizations and principal members of organizations, involved in the growing, manufacture, or distribution of controlled substances appearing in or destined for illicit traffic in the United States; and to recommend and support non-enforcement programs aimed at reducing the availability of illicit controlled substances on the domestic and international markets.

In carrying out its mission as the agency responsible for enforcing the controlled substances laws and regulations of the United States, the DEA's primary responsibilities include:

- Investigation and preparation for the prosecution of major violators of controlled substance laws operating at interstate and international levels.
- Investigation and preparation for prosecution of criminals and drug gangs who perpetrate violence in our communities and terrorize citizens through fear and intimidation.
- Management of a national drug intelligence program in cooperation with federal, state, local, and foreign officials to collect, analyze, and disseminate strategic and operational drug intelligence information.
- Seizure and forfeiture of assets derived from, traceable to, or intended to be used for illicit drug trafficking.
- Enforcement of the provisions of the Controlled Substances Act as they pertain to the manufacture, distribution, and dispensing of legally produced controlled substances.
- Coordination and cooperation with federal, state, and local law enforcement officials on mutual drug enforcement efforts and enhancement of such efforts through exploitation of potential interstate and international investigations beyond local or limited federal jurisdictions and resources.
- Coordination and cooperation with federal, state, and local agencies, and with foreign governments, in programs designed to reduce the availability of illicit abuse-type drugs on the United States market through nonenforcement methods such as crop eradication, crop substitution, and training of foreign officials.
- Responsibility, under the policy guidance of the Secretary of State and U.S. Ambassadors, for all programs associated with drug law enforcement counterparts in foreign countries.
- Liaison with the United Nations, Interpol, and other organizations on matters relating to international drug control programs.

SOURCE: Drug Enforcement Administration, *DEA Mission Statement,* http://www.dea.gov/agency/mission.htm (September 10, 2004).

of Justice. The tax and trade functions of ATF will remain in the Treasury Department with the new Alcohol and Tobacco Tax and Trade Bureau. In addition, the agency's name was changed to the Bureau of Alcohol, Tobacco, Firearms and Explosives (still referred to as the ATF) to reflect its new mission in the Department of Justice.

Careers

Although less well known than the FBI, the ATF is a federal police agency with considerable success in law enforcement, ever since Elliot Ness—one of its most famous agents—battled bootleggers and gamblers during Prohibition. Originally part of the Internal Revenue Service, the Bureau of Alcohol, Tobacco and Firearms was created to enforce the ban on alcohol that was mandated by the Volstead Act and ratified as the Eighteenth Amendment to the Constitution in 1919. ATF became an independent bureau under the Department of the Treasury in 1972.

Originally created to enforce prohibition laws banning alcohol, today's ATF is primarily concerned with firearms; its mission is to reduce the illegal use of firearms and enforce federal firearms laws. As part of this charge, ATF maintains the National Firearms Tracing Center, which completes hundreds of thousands of trace requests annually, the majority of them for other law enforcement agencies. ATF is also responsible for the issuance of federal firearms licenses and permits for the import and export of firearms. Additional duties include reducing criminal use of explosives, combating arson-for-profit schemes, and ensuring voluntary compliance with federal alcohol and tobacco taxes. A staff of more than 4,500 employees carries out the many responsibilities of this agency all across the nation.[27]

Other Federal Law Enforcement Agencies

Many other agencies within the federal government perform law enforcement functions. For example, the Internal Revenue Service, another Treasury Department agency, has agents to enforce laws relating to taxes and their collection. The Department of Justice maintains the U.S. Marshal Service, which fulfills a number of court-related and law enforcement duties. Since 1971, the service has been running the Federal Witness Protection Program, which has given protection to over 6,800 witnesses and over 14,500 family members.[28] The Supreme Court of the United States has its own police force of some 200 people. Several other agencies—such as the Federal Trade Commission (FTC), the Securities and Exchange Commission (SEC), the United States Postal Service, the Environmental Protection Agency (EPA), and the National Park Service—maintain their own law enforcement agencies to ensure compliance with the laws and regulations within their jurisdiction. There are nearly 74,500 persons employed by federal law enforcement agencies.[29]

The Department of Homeland Security

Following the September 11 terrorist attacks, the central law enforcement challenge has been one of coordination. How should a host of federal law enforcement agencies develop and share critical intelligence? How much should filter down to municipal police departments? In January 2003, Tom Ridge was sworn in as the first secretary of a new department within the United States government designed to address these and many other complex questions: the Department of Homeland Security (DHS; see Figure 5.2). Charged with coordinating the work of both intelligence and security agencies, DHS has

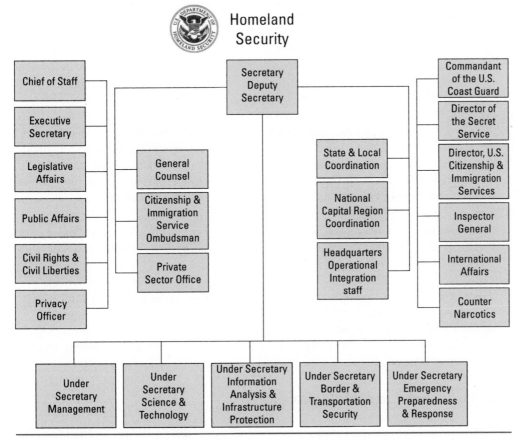

FIGURE 5.2   U.S. Department of Homeland Security Organizational Chart

SOURCE: Department of Homeland Security, http://www.dhs.gov/interweb/assetlibrary/
DHS_StratPlan_FINAL_spread.pdf.

five divisions or directorates:

I. *Border and Transportation Security (BTS).* BTS, led by Undersecretary Asa Hutchinson, is responsible for maintaining the security of our nation's borders and transportation systems. The largest of the directorates, it will become home to agencies such as the Transportation Security Administration, U.S. Customs Service, the border security functions of the Immigration and Naturalization Service, Animal & Plant Health Inspection Service, and the Federal Law Enforcement Training Center.

II. *Emergency Preparedness and Response (EPR).* This directorate ensures that our nation is prepared for, and able to recover from, terrorist attacks and natural disasters.

III. *Science and Technology (S & T).* This directorate coordinates the department's efforts in research and development, including preparing for and responding to the full range of terrorist threats involving weapons of mass destruction.

IV. *Information Analysis and Infrastructure Protection (IAIP).* IAIP merges the capability to identify and assess a broad range of intelligence information concerning threats to the homeland under one roof, issue timely warnings, and take appropriate preventive and protective action.

V. *Management.* This directorate is responsible for budget, management, and personnel issues in DHS.

Besides the five directorates of DHS, several other critical agencies have been moved into the new department or are being newly created:

• *United States Coast Guard.* The commandant of the Coast Guard reports directly to the secretary of Homeland Security. However, the USCG will also work closely with the undersecretary of Border and Transportation Security as well as maintain its existing independent identity as a military service. Upon declaration of war or when the president so directs, the Coast Guard would operate as an element of the Department of Defense, consistent with existing law.

• *United States Secret Service.* The primary mission of the Secret Service is the protection of the president and other government leaders, as well as security for designated national events. The Secret Service is also the primary agency responsible for protecting U.S. currency from counterfeiters and safeguarding Americans from credit card fraud.

• *Bureau of Citizenship and Immigration Services.* While BTS will be responsible for enforcement of our nation's immigration laws, the Bureau of Citizenship and Immigration Services will dedicate its full energies to providing efficient immigration services and easing the transition to American citizenship. The director of Citizenship and Immigration Services will report directly to the deputy secretary of Homeland Defense.

• *Office of State and Local Government Coordination.* A truly secure homeland requires close coordination among local, state, and federal governments. This office will ensure that close coordination takes place with state and local first responders, emergency services, and governments.

• *Office of Private Sector Liaison.* The Office of Private Sector Liaison will provide America's business community a direct line of communication to the Department of Homeland Security. The office will work directly with individual businesses and through trade associations and other nongovernmental organizations to foster dialogue between the private sector and DHS on the full range of issues and challenges faced by America's business sector in the post-9/11 world.

State and Local Systems

In contrast to federal law enforcement agencies, all others can be loosely referred to as the law enforcement systems of the various states, since all of them are principally enforcing state laws. However, by virtue of their territorially defined jurisdictions, and their affiliation, we must distinguish between those that operate statewide, those that operate countywide, and those that operate within the limits of cities and municipalities.

State Police

Today there are three types of state law enforcement agencies: state police, highway patrols, and state investigative agencies. While some states have several agencies, like Oklahoma, which has a separate highway patrol, a narcotics bureau, and an investigation bureau, others, like Michigan's state police, consolidate all the duties typically associated with the state police into a single agency.[30] Every state but Hawaii now has some form of state police agency.[31] Over a third of those employed by state police agencies are civilians who work in technical support positions, such as dispatching, data processing, and recordkeeping.

Belief in the principle that law enforcement should remain primarily a local responsibility has meant that the role of the state police has been somewhat circumscribed. Nevertheless, they perform several functions in addition to their highly visible role in the enforcement of highway traffic laws. A recent survey of state police agencies showed that, in addition to their enforcement activities, nearly 90 percent of them also perform accident investigations, conduct public information campaigns about traffic safety, and manage accident scenes involving hazardous materials.

All state police agencies also conduct criminal investigations and make arrests in connection with them, and in all but two states they maintain intelligence units. Nearly all of these units investigate organized crime, fraud, narcotics violations, violent crime, arson, and motor vehicle theft. Investigative services and information gathered by intelligence units are provided to local agencies without charge. Most states maintain their own forensic laboratories with capabilities in ballistics and the analysis of physical and biological evidence and fingerprints. Forensic services are also made available to local police agencies within the state.[32] A majority (78 percent) of state police agencies operate training academies, and many provide civil defense and emergency medical services.[33] Larger state police agencies, as noted earlier, have increasingly strong intelligence and counterterrorism divisions.

County Police

Law enforcement in most counties is the responsibility of a sheriff's agency, although some counties, such as those in Honolulu, Baltimore, and St. Louis, and the populous suburban counties of Nassau and Suffolk on Long Island, New York,[34] maintain police departments.

The county sheriff's position is unique among law enforcement personnel. It is an elected office in all but two states, where the sheriff is appointed.[35] The sheriff holds a considerable amount of political power; in some counties, the sheriff is the most important political figure. Most sheriff departments are responsible for regular law enforcement duties, such as patrol, criminal investigations, traffic enforcement, and accident investigations, as well as civil functions like serving civil processes and providing court security. Furthermore, 89 percent of sheriff departments maintain a jail.[36]

The most recent data on county law enforcement indicate that there are 3,328 rural and suburban county agencies employing approximately 398,610 people.[37] Nearly two-thirds (66 percent) of county law enforcement personnel are sworn officers and one-third (34 percent) are civilians.[38] The largest sheriff department is that of Los Angeles County in California, with a force of more than 8,000 full-time sworn officers (making it larger than most city police departments).[39] A sizable majority (67 percent) of sheriff departments, however, employ fewer than 25 sworn officers.[40]

Municipal Police Forces

The city's most visible government representatives are the municipal police. Citizens rely on the police for advice, service, and protection around the clock. No wonder, then, that municipal police forces are one of the largest governmental employers and consume one of the biggest slices of revenue. Local police forces account for more than three-quarters of the total employment in police agencies at all levels of government.[41]

Big-city departments account for less than 1 percent of the total number of agencies, but their employees constitute approximately 23 percent of total police employment at the local level.[42] The sheer size of some of the larger departments is intimidating. New York City has an operating expenditure of over $3.4 billion.[43] Yet fiscal management, with its constant

careers

careers

TOM HARRINGTON, ACTING SPECIAL AGENT IN CHARGE, PHILADELPHIA FBI

The Role of the FBI

Being part of the management team of any major law enforcement agency is both exciting and challenging. In today's FBI office, we are front and center in the nation's counterterrorism effort, and, at the same time, we continue to pursue the tentacles of organized crime. We are committed to addressing major fraud matters, particularly "boardroom" crime; we have developed an aggressive campaign to address violent crimes and civil rights violations in our communities; and we are guardians of the nation's secrets in our pursuit of espionage matters. The diversity of the work helps to make a career with the FBI one of the best in all of law enforcement.

As an FBI Program Manager, each day and week involve a balancing of investigative resources to address our priority investigations and ensure a safe

crises, revenue shortfalls, and budget-cutting exercises, is only one of the many challenges facing a police department. Controlling crime, controlling officers, and facing constant pressures from all segments of society make the management of large urban departments one of the most difficult governmental tasks.

The limited size of small-town departments means that they differ from their big-city counterparts in several respects. Officers who work in small departments usually work as generalists, and there is a much less formal chain of command than that found in the highly bureaucratized structure of large municipal departments. The chief of police might be found on patrol, and a detective might be making traffic stops. These departments also usually have a smaller proportion of civilian employees than those in cities.[44] City residents would probably be surprised to realize that the continuous presence and round-the-clock availability of police officers to which they are accustomed are not the norm in many departments. Agencies staffed by as few as one or two officers simply cannot provide service twenty-four hours a day, seven days a week.[45]

Special Purpose Police

Throughout the country, police agencies that are not part of the local department possess police powers within specified jurisdictional limits that may cut across political boundaries. Special police forces include transit police, public housing police, airport police, public school police, and park police. In popular conception, special police forces are often regarded as inferior to general municipal police forces. Indeed, some of them started out as guard services. By now,

environment for our employees and the communities we serve. This effort requires open communications and appropriate dissemination of information and intelligence to our law enforcement partners and the public at large. To be a successful divisional manager, you must understand the organization's mission and the strategy outlined by senior managers; convert this foundation into a vision for your office; then set your goals, plan as a team, execute the plan with open communications, and maintain a positive attitude. Our successes in the past have been achieved because of our attention to detail and the innovative, "can-do, must-do" attitude of our employees. The task can be overwhelming at times, but as a team we have had some extraordinary achievements.

Our greatest assets are our employees and the cooperation of the communities we serve. Each FBI employee must demonstrate leadership in his or her daily activities. This leadership centers on embracing a common vision and dedication to address the crime problems challenging our community. We perform our duties with the understanding that our jobs must be completed with a clear understanding of the Rule of Law. As members of the larger law enforcement community, we must earn each day the public's trust.

however, most of the special forces are as well recruited and trained as their municipal counterparts. Some have superior standards of training, given the nature of their often highly specialized duties. The New York–New Jersey Port Authority Police, for example, has reached some of the highest standards of recruitment, training, and performance.

The proliferation of police departments operating within the same jurisdiction, usually a municipality, poses a dilemma. While the need for special skills and, often, extended mobility is recognized, the problems associated with overlapping authority—and thus conflict—loom large. Cities have tried to solve this problem by creating liaisons and, especially during special events, joint commands or task forces. There is a drive to consolidate all local police forces operating within one jurisdiction. Consolidation drives are supported by those who expect higher pay scales. They are opposed by officers of special forces who enjoy their jurisdictional independence and separate status.

Private Police

Security guards, alarms, closed-circuit surveillance systems, and antitheft devices are well known in American life today. Whether at work, at home, or at leisure, Americans are now the object of surveillance or protection furnished by the private security industry more often than at any previous time. Given the extent and significance of this phenomenon, any discussion of policing in the United States would be incomplete without reference to private security forces, even though they are not part of the publicly financed system of law enforcement.

Private security today includes guard and patrol services, private investigators, alarm companies, armored car and courier services, and security consulting services for loss prevention strategies, computer security systems, and executive protection strategies. Private security forces even provide protection to entire communities, and some compare very favorably with the public police in surrounding neighborhoods in terms of crime prevention and lower levels of fear of crime.[46] The costs of private security are about $104 billion,[47] while recent expenditure figures for police protection at all levels of governmental spending amounted to only about $41 billion.[48] Over 1.5 million people work in private security.[49] Many of those employed in private security have a background in public law enforcement.

Review

In the mid-1800s, American cities created police forces that performed patrol duty in uniform. Well into the twentieth century, these forces were dependent on political patronage. Reformers sought to change this, but real professionalization (through recruitment and training) did not occur until the second half of this century.

All but the smallest police departments in the United States are bureaucracies, marked by hierarchical structures with a clearly delineated chain of command, a division of labor among a number of bureaus, and a set of rules and regulations.

The contemporary structure of American police organizations is a result of two competing forces: police professionalization within a rigid, bureaucratic, military command structure, on the one hand, and a reaction against that structure by the civil rights movement, as well as by many officers and even administrators. Today's police forces have developed strategies for more cooperative and above all more community-related management styles.

Professional police forces can be found at every level of government. Several such forces are empowered to enforce federal laws, among them the Federal Bureau of Investigation (FBI), the Drug Enforcement Administration (DEA), the Bureau of Alcohol, Tobacco, Firearms and Explosives (ATF), the Bureau of Citizenship and Immigration Services, the U.S. Secret Service, and many others. At the state level, police forces—often originating as highway patrols—were established in the first half of the twentieth century. State police forces play a vital role in policing the areas of the state outside the jurisdiction of municipal police forces, assisting the cities and counties when needed, and maintaining statewide identification systems, laboratories, and training facilities. Municipal police forces employ by far the largest number of personnel among all public police forces. They bear the brunt of law enforcement and crime prevention activities entrusted to the public police. In recent decades, however, Americans have increasingly turned to private policing, contracted for through private security firms. These private agencies employ twice as many personnel as public police agencies.

Thinking Critically about Criminal Justice

1. Many nations, such as Canada and Great Britain, have national police forces that perform many of the duties of state and county police in this country. Should the United States consider something similar? Why or why not?

2. What are the dangers to society, if any, of more and more policing responsibilities shifting to the private sector?

3. Despite repeated demands by investigatory commissions that police officers be better educated, there are some people (even within police organizations) who think more education for police is not always a good idea. Where do you stand on this issue? For example, what is an adequate level of education for a new police officer? A baccalaureate degree? An associate's degree? A high school diploma?

Internet Connection

Note: While all of the URLs listed were current as of the printing of this book, these sites often change. Please check our website (http://www. mhhe.com/socscience/crimjustice/adlercj) for updates.

The Texas Rangers are one of the oldest law enforcement organizations on the North American continent. Rangers investigate a wide range of crimes, from murder, rape, robbery, and burglary to cases of governmental corruption. What is the history of the Texas Rangers? What role did they assume in the 1800s? For an extensive history of the Rangers, see **http://www.terrytexasrangers.org.**

Notes

1. The quote is from Juvenal as quoted in William Durant, *The Story of Civilization, vol. III, Caesar and Christ* (NY: Simon & Schuster, 1935), p. 341.

2. Based on Martin A. Kelly, "Citizen Survival in Ancient Rome," *Police Studies* 11 (1988), pp. 195–201.

3. David Johnson, *American Law Enforcement: A History* (St. Louis, MO: Forum Press, 1981).

4. Roger Lane, *Policing the City: Boston, 1822–1885* (Cambridge, MA: Harvard University Press, 1967).

5. Jay Stuart Berman, *Police Administration and Progressive Reform: Theodore Roosevelt as Police Commissioner of New York* (NY: Greenwood Press, 1987).

6. Samuel Walker, *Popular Justice: A History of American Criminal Justice* (NY: Oxford University Press, 1980).

7. Nathan Douthit, "August Vollmer, Berkeley's First Chief of Police, and the Emergence of Police Professionalism," *California Historical Quarterly* 54 (Summer 1975), pp. 101–124.

8. See National Commission on Law Observance and Enforcement, *Report on Lawlessness in Law Enforcement,* no. 11 (Washington, DC: U.S. Government Printing Office, 1931), p. 5.

9. O. W. Wilson and Roy Clinton McLaren, *Police Administration,* 4th ed. (NY: McGraw-Hill, 1977).

10. Robert M. Fogelson, *Big-City Police* (Cambridge, MA: Harvard University Press, 1977).

11. Ibid.

12. George L. Kelling and Mark H. Moore, "The Evolving Strategy of Policing," *Perspectives on Policing,* no. 4

(Washington, DC: National Institute of Justice and Harvard University, November 1988).

13. U.S. Department of Justice, Federal Bureau of Investigation, *Crime in the United States, 1990* (Washington, DC: U.S. Government Printing Office, 1991); hereafter cited as *Uniform Crime Reports.*

14. President's Commission on Law Enforcement and the Administration of Justice, *The Challenge of Crime in a Free Society* (Washington, DC: U.S. Government Printing Office, 1967).

15. "Counter Terrorism and the LAPD," available at http://www.lapdonline.org/portal/generic.php?page/search.php.

16. William K. Rashbaum, "Terror Makes All the World a Beat for New York Police," *New York Times,* July 15, 2002.

17. Matthew Hickman and Brian A. Reaves, *Local Police Departments 2000* (Washington DC: U.S. Department of Justice, Bureau of Justice Statistics, 2003), p. 4.

18. Wilson and McLaren, *Police Administration,* p. 136.

19. Samuel Walker, *The Police in America: An Introduction,* 2d ed. (NY: McGraw-Hill, 1992), p. 210.

20. See, for example, James J. Fyfe, "Controlling Police Vehicle Pursuits," in *Police Practice in the '90s: Key Management Issues,* ed. James J. Fyfe (Washington, DC: International City Management Association, 1989), pp. 114–123; and Kathleen J. Ferraro, "Policing Woman Battering," *Social Problems* 36 (1989), pp. 61–74.

21. Federal Bureau of Investigation, *Frequently Asked Questions,* http://www.fbi.gov/aboutus/faqs/faqsone.html (June 1, 2002).

22. Athan G. Theoharis, "The FBI and the Politics of Surveillance, 1980–1985," *Criminal Justice Review* 15 (1990), pp. 221–230.

23. *FBI Laboratory Report 2002* (Washington, DC 2003).

24. See http://www.fbi.gov/hq/lab/labhome.htm. William S. Laufer, "The Rhetoric of Innocence," *Washington Law Review* 70 (1995), pp. 329–421.

25. Federal Bureau of Investigation, *Frequently Asked Questions,* http://www.fbi.gov/aboutus/faqs/faqsone.html (June 1, 2002).

26. Federal Bureau of Investigation, *FBI Press Room: Press Releases,* 1999 http://www.fbi.gov/pressrel/pressrel99/ncic2000.htm (June 3, 2002).

27. Bureau of Alcohol, Tobacco, and Firearms, "Fi/2000 Accountability Report," http://www.atf.treas.gov/pub/gen_pub/2000annrpt_html/structure.htm (June 1, 2002).

28. United States Marshals Service, *Witness Security,* http://www.usdoj.gov/marshals/witsec.html (June 1, 2002).

29. Reaves, *Profile of State and Local Law Enforcement Agencies, 1996,* p. 1.

30. Donald A. Torres, *Handbook of State Police, Highway Patrols, and Investigative Agencies* (Westport, CT: Greenwood Press, 1987).

31. Brian Reaves, *Profile of State and Local Law Enforcement Agencies, 1992* (Washington, DC: Department of Justice, Bureau of Justice Statistics, 1993).

32. Peter Finn and Daniel McGillis, "Public Safety at the State Level: A Survey of Major Services," *Journal of Police Science and Administration* 17 (1990), pp. 133–146.

33. Reaves, *Profile of State and Local Law Enforcement Agencies, 1992.*

34. Brian Reaves, *Police Departments in Large Cities, 1987* (Washington, DC: U.S. Department of Justice, Bureau of Justice Statistics, 1989).

35. Walker, *The Police in America,* p. 210.

36. Reaves, *Profile of State and Local Law Enforcement Agencies, 1992.*

37. *Uniform Crime Reports,* 2002, p. 328.

38. Ibid.

39. Brian Reaves and Pheny Z. Smith, *Law Enforcement Management and Administrative Statistics, 1993: Data for Individual State and Local Agencies with 100 or More Officers* (Washington, DC: Department of Justice, 1995), Table 1A, p. 1.

40. Reaves, *Profile of State and Local Law Enforcement Agencies, 1992.*

41. Sue A. Lindgren, *Justice Expenditure and Employment, 1990* (Washington, DC: U.S. Department of Justice, Bureau of Justice Statistics, 1992).

42. *Uniform Crime Reports.*

43. Reaves and Smith, *Law Enforcement Management and Administrative Statistics, 1993,* Table 7A, pp. 73–83.

44. John P. Crank, "Civilianization in Small and Medium Police Departments in Illinois, 1973–1986," *Journal of Criminal Justice* 17 (1989), pp. 167–177.

45. Victor H. Sims, *Small Town and Rural Police* (Springfield, IL: Charles C. Thomas, 1988).

46. William F. Walsh and Edwin J. Donovan, "Private Security and Community Policing: Evaluation and Comment," *Journal of Criminal Justice* 17 (1989), pp. 187–197.

47. William C. Cunningham, John J. Strauchs, and Clifford W. Van Meter, *Private Security: Patterns and Trends,* Research in Brief (Washington, DC: National Institute of Justice, August 1991).

48. Lindgren, *Justice Expenditure and Employment Extracts, 1992.*

49. Cunningham, Strauchs, and Van Meter, *Private Security.*

Police Functions and Police Culture

—The American city dweller's repertoire of methods for handling problems includes one known as "calling the cops." The practice to which the idiom refers is enormously widespread. Though it is more frequent in some segments of society than in others, there are very few people who do not or would not resort to it under suitable circumstances. A few illustrations will furnish the background for an explanation of what "calling the cops" means.

• In a tenement, officers were met by a public health nurse who took them through an abysmally deteriorated apartment inhabited by four young children in the care of an elderly woman. The babysitter resisted the nurse's earlier attempts to remove the children. The officers packed the children in the squad car and took them to Juvenile Hall, over the continuing protests of the elderly woman.

• In a middle-class neighborhood, officers found a partly disassembled car, tools, a loudly blaring radio, and five beer-drinking youths at the curb in front of a single-family home. The homeowner complained that this had been going on for several days and the men had refused to take their activities elsewhere.

The officers ordered the youths to pack up and leave. When one sassed them, they threw him into the squad car and drove him to the precinct station, from where he was released after receiving a severe tongue-lashing from the desk sergeant.

• In the apartment of a quarreling couple, officers were told by the wife, whose nose was bleeding, that the husband stole her purse containing money she earned. The officers told the man they would "take him in," whereupon he returned the purse and they left.[1]

Most encounters between the police and the public are initiated by citizens through the 911 system. This has two important consequences for the police. First, it is the citizens, not the police, who determine in large part the types of activities in which the police will become involved. Second, the police often find themselves in the reactive mode of simply responding to requests from the public.

At one time all city functions were regarded as police functions, from welfare to waste disposal, and to some extent this is still true. The police are the most visible representatives of local government: They wear distinctive uniforms, their vehicles have distinctive markings, they are usually present in the neighborhood, the station house is always open, and they are easily reached by dialing 911. It is the police whom people call when the cat ends up on top of a tall tree, the neighbor's TV is too loud, someone's car is parked across the driveway, the local teenagers are whooping it up at 3 A.M., or a tornado strikes.

The urban police we watch in endless TV series are not typical. Police work is not just cops pursuing robbers, high-speed auto chases, big drug busts, wild shoot-outs, and controlling mobs of demonstrators throwing bricks and bottles. Policing also requires tedious hours working on the Internet (see this chapter's 21st Century Challenge box). It involves handling the growing demands of drug abuse, homelessness, illegal weapons use, domestic violence, and other social problems. Moreover, much of the cop-on-the-beat work is boring and routine.

Police functions are traditionally grouped into three categories: service, order maintenance, and law enforcement. These categories are somewhat arbitrary because of the considerable overlap among them. Think of this situation: A state highway patrol car moves down the turnpike to survey the orderly flow of traffic (order maintenance). The officers spot a two-car collision, with one car ablaze. Through quick action they extricate four injured occupants, three of them children (service). They then arrest the grossly intoxicated driver of the other car (law enforcement). Moreover, the methods used to perform any of the functions may be identical.

Managing Police Functions

Community concerns necessarily shape the role of the police. For example, if the community is concerned about drug dealers or bars featuring topless dancers having moved into the neighborhood, it is likely to put the pressure on the police—and the city government in general—to "do something about it." The pressures may focus on the conduct of individual officers or community groups, or the police force in general. It is the highly decentralized structure of policing in America (every state, city, and town has its own independent police force) that allows individual departments to establish mandates based on local concerns.[2]

Management Styles

Communities across America differ from each other in many ways, including the strategies defined by their police administrators. James Q. Wilson first demonstrated the differences in styles of policing in his 1968 work, *Varieties of Police Behavior.*[3] Through close observation and analysis of police departments in eight communities (six in New York State: Albany, Amsterdam, Brighton, Nassau County, Newburgh, and Syracuse; plus Highland Park, Illinois, and Oakland, California), Wilson delineated three different styles: watchman, legalistic, and service. Each, he believed, reflected not only how police make decisions, but also the special interests of the police chief, the style of government, and expectations in the particular community.

Watchman-style departments are characterized by a concentration on the order maintenance function of policing. Police administrators allow officers to ignore minor infractions of the law, provided that order is maintained in the community. For example, someone acting in a disorderly manner may be told to "leave the area," "get out of town," or "go home"; private disputes may be settled informally; and many vice and gambling offenses may be tolerated.[4] Only when the peace has been breached and order cannot be restored are arrests made. **Legalistic-style** departments, by contrast, are those in which police work is marked by a professional orientation with an emphasis on law enforcement. Officers are expected to issue large numbers of traffic tickets, to arrest juvenile offenders, and to take action against illicit enterprises. Administrators often encourage this policing style not only because it is considered right to obey all laws, but also to protect themselves from any suspicion of corruption or criticism that they are not doing a good job.[5] The **service style** is typically true of police departments in suburban middle-class communities where residents expect and receive a high level of personal service from local government. Given the low rate of serious crimes in these communities, police officers have the time to respond to community needs. Administrators of service-style departments tend to be highly sensitive to local personalities and politics.

Alternatives to Traditional Management Styles

The civil rights movement of the 1960s may have laid the basis for reform, yet changes in policing actually occurred as a result of pressure from within the ranks. Critics viewed the traditional style as "authoritarian, hierarchical, rigid, pyramidal, paramilitary, and impersonal in its dealings with its police workers."[6] Surprisingly, many police executives agreed that traditional police bureaucracies were inflexible and rigid and often failed to adapt to rapid social change and community expectations.[7] What alternatives did the critics propose?

Community Policing

It may be difficult for students of the 1990s to visualize the American police of the 1960s. Their style of policing and their very professionalism had isolated them from the community. Minorities, who were not represented among the police, viewed them as occupation troops. A legalistic response like an arrest could ignite a whole neighborhood and lead to a riot—and still does in communities where reform programs have not been thoroughly implemented.

Only after riots leveled Watts in Los Angeles and Newark, New Jersey, did it occur to government in general, and the police in particular, that a totally new approach was needed, one that reached out and made the police part of the community. Community policing was invented, and large-scale efforts to recruit minorities into the police resulted (see Chapter 7).

Although no single definition exists, the term **community policing** is generally considered to mean programs and policies based on a commitment to a partnership between the police and the community they serve. Some have used the term *community wellness* to describe the philosophy behind this kind of policing.[8] The emphasis is on working in collaboration with residents to determine community needs and how best to address them, and to involve citizens as "coproducers of public safety."[9] But community policing requires more than just reaching out to the community. To be truly effective, there must be a restructuring of the police organization itself, to make it less hierarchical. At the very least, a "professional" police force is needed. This means, among other things, freeing police officers from partisan political control, increasing educational requirements for recruits, and paying the police more, in terms of salary and benefits. Community policing may also require a strong local tax base that can support the great expense of policing, as well as provide local accountability. At the heart of community policing is the idea of service to citizens rather than the state.[10]

watchman style
Style characteristic of police departments that concentrate on the order maintenance function.

legalistic style
Style characteristic of police departments where work is marked by a professional orientation with an emphasis on law enforcement.

service style
Style characteristic of police departments in suburban communities where residents expect and receive a high level of service from local government.

community policing
Strategy that relies on public confidence and citizen cooperation to help prevent crime and make the residents of a community feel more secure.

CYBERPOLICING—LAW ENFORCEMENT IN THE NEBULOUS WORLD OF THE INFORMATION SUPERHIGHWAY

We're familiar with the typical image of the "hacker"—a pimply-faced, gangly boy, with coke-bottle glasses, bad clothes, and no friends, who would rather play with his computer than deal with the world outside. Hackers are computer geniuses who enjoy breaking into secure computer systems and stretching the boundaries of programming, more as a means of testing their own skills than anything else. But as the domain of computers grows, as more and more naive consumers use the Internet for commerce, and as companies increasingly store sensitive data on systems that are accessible from outside, hackers have been replaced by "crackers"—those who use computers for malicious purposes.[1]

The list of deviant or illegal things people do with computers is extensive:

- A Russian cracker accessed Citicorp's computers, transferred $40 million, and withdrew $400,000.[2]

- The designer of a new razor sent out plans electronically to competitors, costing the company $1.5 million.[3]

- A twenty-two-year-old worker at a fast-food restaurant reprogrammed the drive-through computerized cash register to ring up $2.99 items as one-cent items and embezzled $3,600 before he was caught.[4]

- A former airline employee embezzled 1.4 million frequent-flier miles.[5]

- A New York state investigation known as "Operation Rip Cord" identified more than 1,500 child pornographers trading pictures of minors or soliciting child sex over the Internet.

- Hundreds of World Wide Web sites offer instruction on making car bombs, fire bombs, mail bombs, light bulb bombs, baby food jar bombs, or bombs disguised to look like telephones or burritos.[6]

- Crackers use the Internet to find credit card and calling card numbers and other personal details, then use the information for fraudulent purposes.

Cyberspace is huge. Imagine an electronic universe that doesn't really exist concretely yet spans countries and continents. Imagine that this universe has a population that is growing rapidly, and is a place where anyone can visit whenever he or she wants, totally unregulated by government, using nothing more complex than a computer and a phone line. Now imagine controlling this universe using patrol cars, Glock pistols, drug-sniffing dogs, pepper spray, and heat-sensing night vision cameras mounted on silent helicopters. The technological advances that have been so helpful in catching the traditional "bad guy" are useless when it comes to catching crackers.

Policing the information superhighway is a challenge unparalleled in law enforcement history. The police are not prepared. Fred Cotton, the training director for Search, a Sacramento-based nonprofit police training organization, estimates that there are at most 200 police investigators in the entire United States qualified to testify as expert witnesses in computer forensics.[7] But steps are being taken to increase those numbers. The Justice Department is expanding its computer training program to include joint training with industry representatives and local law enforcement.[8] The National Infrastructure Protection Center of the FBI works with a host of state and federal agencies to protect critical data sources.

At the State Police Training Center in Sea Girt, a small number of detectives from federal, state, and local law enforcement agencies are trained by the high-technology crime unit of the New Jersey State Police. They learn about the world of hackers and online stalkers, corporate spies, cell phone cloning, and cyberlaw, and about more

Among the goals of community policing are a reduction in fear of crime, the development of closer ties with the community, engagement of residents in a joint effort to prevent crime and maintain order, and an increase in the level of public satisfaction with police services. Many types of programs have been described as community policing, including increased use of foot patrol, storefront police stations, community surveys, police-sponsored youth activities, and Neighborhood Watch programs.[11]

Numerous studies have found that some aspects of community policing simply do not deliver on the promise of reducing crime. Neighborhood Watch is consistently found to be ineffective at preventing crime and may in fact increase fear of crime. Police storefronts are

mundane technical issues concerning file management and computer hardware. Seminars focus on techniques used by computer criminals to steal passwords and break into networks. Participants also learn how to examine computer files without damaging evidence.[9]

Law enforcement agencies have a hard time attracting computer talent. Assignment to special units doesn't happen immediately, so any aspiring member of a computer crime squad has to rise through the ranks in ordinary ways, typically by serving for years as a patrol officer. This can be a disincentive for potential recruits, who, if they have backgrounds in computer science, can earn much more in the private sector. Currently, even agencies with a high level of expertise, such as the New Jersey State Police high-tech crime unit, rely on experts from computer and Internet companies for assistance in evidence processing. As computers become more complex, police agencies may be forced to recruit civilians for this purpose.

Even when people with advanced computer skills do end up working for the police in one way or another, enforcing laws in cyberspace is difficult. For example, suppose one wishes to police a sex newsgroup that distributes binary pictures of child pornography. The material on this usergroup is not stored on one computer but exists in "mirror" sites in different locations around the world. Tracing one newsgroup server in Boise, and shutting down that computer (and perhaps arresting and prosecuting the computer owner), does nothing to newsgroup servers in Australia, Germany, Trinidad, Thailand, or Kenya. Former Attorney General Janet Reno has commented that "the rapid and global growth of the Internet raises a host of complex issues involving criminal law enforcement that expand beyond national boundaries."[10] Cybercrime can join the growing list of the other transnational crime categories,

"Operation Rip Cord" identified more than 1,500 child pornographers trading pictures of minors or soliciting child sex."

including drug crimes, economic crimes, organized crime, and ecological crime. With concerns over cyberterrorism, additional resources will likely be readily available.

Questions for Discussion

1. How can police agencies make themselves more appealing as career options for computer science majors?

2. Imagine what new technologies may be developed in the next ten years. What challenges will this create for law enforcement?

3. The Internet is problematic in that it spans jurisdictions. How can police at a local level address the issue of child pornography on the Internet?

SOURCES
1. "Cyberspace: The New Security Frontier," *The Lipman Report,* February 15, 1996.
2. David L. Carter and Andra J. Katz, "Computer Crime: An Emerging Challenge for Law Enforcement," *FBI Law Enforcement Bulletin* 65, no. 12 (December 1996), pp. 1–9.
3. "Cyber Sabotage: Elements of Workplace Violence in Computer Crimes," *The Lipman Report,* June 15, 1998.
4. Ibid.
5. "Cyberspace."
6. "Bombs on the Internet: New Fears about Free Speech vs. Public Safety," *CNN Interactive,* May 29, 1998, http://cnn.com/TECH/science/9805/29/t_t/bombs.on.internet./index.html (June 10, 1998).
7. Kevin Coughlin, "Hot on the Heels of Online Outlaws," *The Star-Ledger,* July 15, 1998, pp. 1, 15.
8. "U.S. Seeks World's Help to Fight Internet Crime," *CNN Interactive,* December 3, 1997, http://cnn.com/TECH/9712/03/internet.summit/index.html (June 10, 1998).
9. Coughlin, "Hot on the Heels."
10. "U.S. Seeks World's Help."

Poverty

associated with positive citizen evaluations, but they have no impact on crime. Police newsletters have no effect on the victimization rates of households that receive them. Community meetings are somewhat effective, but only if discussion centers on specific crime problems and how the police can solve them. There have been some promising findings with regard to door-to-door visits. In general, community policing works only if there is a clear focus on crime risk factors.[12]

The Violent Crime Control and Law Enforcement Act of 1994 authorized funds to promote community policing by adding 100,000 community policing officers over six years. As of 2005, the Office of Community Oriented Policing Services (COPS), which was

TABLE 6.1
How Do Police Officers
Define Their Roles: In
Terms of Traditional Policing
or Community Policing?
(A study in Indianapolis)

High Priority	Low Priority
1. Seizing drugs, guns, and other contraband.	1. Reducing citizens' fear of crime.*
2. Reactive policing—handling calls for service.	2. Reducing public disorder.*
	3. Encouraging public involvement in neighborhood improvements.
	4. Making arrests.
	5. Issuing citations.

*Goals that are associated with community policing.

SOURCE: Stephen D. Mastrofski, Roger B. Parks, Albert J. Reiss, Jr., and Robert E. Worden, *Policing Neighborhoods: A Report from Indianapolis* (National Institute of Justice, U.S. Department of Justice, July 1998).

created to oversee the community policing part of the act, had awarded grants to add more than 118,768 new police officers across the country. Tens of thousands of communities have received more than $11.3 billion in grants since its inception. The COPS program has contributed to an explosion of community policing programs across the United States; about twenty years ago, only 140 jurisdictions had some sort of community policing.[13]

Despite this rapid growth, questions about community policing remain (see Table 6.1). One of the most important is how to implement these new techniques within existing police structures.[14] Police management as well as rank-and-file officers will need to be committed to this new philosophy if programs are to work. New York City, for example, found that many police officers were resistant to the idea of community policing. The city therefore undertook a public relations campaign to sell its benefits to the department.[15]

Another question concerns the definition or the demarcation of a community. Administrative boundaries of districts and precincts may have little to do with the cultures that mark a community.[16] What may seem desirable to one group of residents may in fact have a dubious legal basis and may cause the police to unfairly represent one group's interests over those of another. Some worry that it may even encourage vigilantism.[17] In New York, one frightening example was the black community's perception that in their shared Brooklyn community the police were favoring the Hasidic residents. After the accidental death of a child in January 1992, there were confrontations, riots, and a homicide before calmer heads prevailed and a sense of community was restored.[18]

Police–Community Relations Programs

police–community relations (PCR) programs
All initiatives, whether from the police or the community, to bridge the gap between law enforcement professionals and the people they serve.

Unlike community policing, **police–community relations (PCR) programs** attempt to enhance the community's perception of the police, not to change the basic method of policing a community. The tangible results of effective PCR efforts include:

- Increased likelihood of citizen cooperation in providing information to assist in law enforcement.
- More voluntary compliance with the law.
- Improved relations with minority groups.[19]
- Community support for budget appropriations in an environment of competing demands.[20]

A recent inventory of programs in different jurisdictions showed that department-sponsored activities include "ride-along" programs in which citizens accompany the police on patrols, citizenship awards, citizen citation programs to recognize meritorious acts, liaison programs with the clergy, police headquarters' tours, and public speaking programs.[21] Various studies have shown that if the police are seen to be responsive to citizens' concerns, treat people respectfully, or even just take the time to listen to people's stories, results include lower perceived rates of serious crime, a greater willingness to obey the law, and less recidivism.[22]

Maintaining good relations with the media is a key component in shaping public opinion of police performance.[23] Many departments now employ public information specialists to deal with journalists and reporters. Some even have extensive media relations programs as part of an overall effort to achieve the goals of crime prevention and reduced fear of crime.[24]

Many students may recall visits to their schools from "Officer Friendly," a uniformed police officer who came to speak to them about safety issues. Officer Friendly is one component of police–school liaison programs intended to increase understanding of the police role. Elementary school programs commonly focus on traffic and bicycle safety and instruction about avoiding potentially dangerous circumstances. In some junior and senior high schools, police team up with teachers to provide instruction about law enforcement.[25]

Drugs and violence have altered the role police play in schools. In some inner-city areas, Officer Friendly is more likely to be engaged in frisking teenagers for weapons and is in danger of being shot by an aggressive student. Recent findings from the National Crime Victimization Survey indicate that, in one year, nearly 2 million students (9 percent of all students) had been victims of crime at school.[26] Police officers are now routinely assigned to schools for law enforcement duties, especially in high-crime, drug-infested neighborhoods in large urban centers. They have increasingly been deployed in drug education programs in the schools.

The best-known police-sponsored program is called DARE (for Drug Abuse Resistance Education). It originated in Los Angeles in 1983 and has now been adopted by a majority of the country's school districts and reaches 26 million students. Over 25,000 police officers are trained to teach DARE. The program consists of a core seventeen-lesson curriculum delivered to students in grades five or six. There are other elements of the DARE program that are less commonly used, such as police visits with younger students, and short programs for junior and senior high school students. Evaluations of the DARE core curriculum are consistent—while there is sometimes an immediate effect on students' drug use, any impact of the program is not noticeable after one year.[27] Police officers familiar with DARE have ideas about why the program is unsuccessful: "It is unrealistic to expect a child to be 'inoculated' against drugs, gangs, or violence by exposure to a forty-five to fifty-minute class, given twice weekly, when the child lives in an environment where these things are a daily occurrence," said one.[28] Another remarked more sarcastically, "When chasing a sixteen-year-old crack dealer down streets and through backyards, the thought never entered my mind that if only a policeman dressed in a dog suit had gotten to him a little earlier in grade school, this whole thing could have been avoided."[29] The chief of police in Winchester, Virginia, Gary W. Reynolds, commented that "DARE is not the solution to drug problems—but it is an integral component of many things the police and society can do to lessen the problem."[30]

Citizen Involvement

In recent years the police have encouraged citizens to take a more active role in policing their communities.[31] Some citizen crime prevention efforts merely affect personal behavior, such as locking doors, learning self-defense, marking personal property for identification, participating in police-sponsored security surveys of one's home, or buying weapons for self-protection. Other efforts take place at the community level. Neighborhood Watch programs are among the most popular, even though they are ineffective in lowering crime rates.[32] Neighbors participate by watching out for suspicious activities or people and reporting them to the police if necessary. The programs are usually organized under the sponsorship of a jurisdictionwide agency, such as the police, that works closely with residents by providing training, speakers, and liaison officers.

Civilian patrols also offer residents of a community an opportunity to participate in crime prevention. Citizens walk or drive around a neighborhood to provide added surveillance.[33] In some communities, local police departments recruit private citizens who serve as an unarmed auxiliary police force and help to patrol the streets for a few hours a week.[34]

Other patrols are organized by neighborhood residents on a local basis, with the assistance of the police.

Unlike most citizen crime prevention initiatives, the Guardian Angels, a national civilian patrol group operating in many local chapters, do not work with police. Founded in 1979 by Curtis Sliwa, this band of young people began by patrolling subway trains in New York City. They then spread out to other metropolitan areas. The concept is simple enough: A small platoon of youths, distinguishable by their red berets, make their presence felt in various places considered unsafe (such as subway trains), and through their presence deter crime or aid in apprehending offenders.[35] The National Institute of Justice has recognized the Guardian Angels as a worthy form of crime prevention but cautions that they must increase their interaction with the police, adhere to state laws and regulations, standardize their training, and meet with community leaders before setting up new patrols.

Television has provided a new means for citizens to become involved in law enforcement. *Crime Stoppers,* a program aired nationwide, typically offers rewards for information (the average reward is $77) about crimes. Interestingly, the majority of tips come from the criminals themselves or from so-called fringe players, people who associate with criminals. An estimated 641,471 arrests have been made from *Crime Stoppers* programs, with $8.2 billion worth of stolen property recovered and narcotics seized.[36] The original *Crime Stoppers* program inspired more than 1,000 organizations bearing the same name in the United States, Puerto Rico, Guam, Mexico, Canada, Great Britain, and Australia.

More recent efforts to publicize unsolved crimes or solicit public assistance in the apprehension of fugitives are the popular television series *America's Most Wanted,* which shows actual mug shots, and *Unsolved Mysteries,* in which actors recreate actual crimes. With the ability to reach millions of people across America, these shows have become powerful sources of information for law enforcement officials. After almost a decade of broadcasting, *America's Most Wanted* has resulted in the capture of over 960 fugitives. Thus, as the executive producer of *America's Most Wanted* has noted, television has organized citizens into a national Neighborhood Watch program.[37]

The Service Function

As local government's front-line response to social problems and emergencies, the police are called on to provide service to those members of the community who, by reason of personal, economic, social, or other circumstances, are in need of immediate aid.[38] They deal with people no one else will even talk to. Their duties bring them in contact with knife and gunshot wounds, drug overdoses, alcoholic delirium, and medical problems from childbirth to heart attacks to diabetic comas. They return runaway children to their parents and remove cats from trees.[39] They are the frontline troops in dealing with homeless and mentally ill people. Research conducted in a city of 400,000 found, in fact, that social service and administrative tasks accounted for 55 percent of officers' time; crime fighting accounted for 17 percent.[40] Similar analyses in other cities have likewise found that the police spend significantly more time providing service to the community and maintaining order than in fighting crime.[41]

Coping with Injury and Illness

Police are often summoned to the scene when medical emergencies occur, and sometimes they must provide first-aid services. A new health concern has arisen with the advent of the acquired immune deficiency syndrome (AIDS). The AIDS virus is transmitted through sexual contact or by contact with tainted blood. Since police often deal with people who may be infected with AIDS, such as intravenous drug users who share needles, police departments across the country are concerned about officers' exposure to the virus. Crime scene investigators who frequently have to collect samples of tissue, blood, and other body fluids are especially concerned about the risks in handling virus-carrying materials. To lessen the danger, many departments have now issued guidelines for minimizing exposure.[42] Some evidence from a recent survey of crime scene investigators and evidence technicians indicates that the guidelines work. They also help to allay officers' fear of contracting AIDS through on-the-job exposure.[43]

Coping with Mentally Ill People

In the 1960s a series of lawsuits forced the mental health community into a policy under which, in all but the most severe cases, mentally ill people are released into the community rather than kept in an institution. In the absence of psychiatric intervention, there has to be some alternative way to deal with people who sometimes engage in behavior that others find bizarre or bothersome or that actually poses a threat to themselves or others. It is typically the police who are called on to intervene in such cases. The County of Los Angeles Sheriff's Department has had a Mental Evaluation Team since 1993. It responds to calls for service from people who have attempted suicide, or who are mentally ill or developmentally disabled. The Mental Evaluation Team consists of one sergeant and five deputy sheriffs, each of whom is partnered with a Department of Mental Health technician. Most cases were stabilized at the location or resulted in placing the person in private or county hospitals. Arrest was the least common response.[44] Police are often caught in the middle of a policy dispute over which they have no control.

Order Maintenance

Several researchers have studied police work, usually by observing police on duty or by reviewing and categorizing the nature of the incidents with which police officers deal, based on the calls they receive and the incident reports they file. Specific numbers may vary, but analyses of the types of incidents reveal that the majority usually do not involve law enforcement (see Table 6.2). Many of the calls relate to what has been called order maintenance, peacekeeping, or conflict management (for example, dispersing a group of rowdy teenagers or warning an aggressive panhandler to move on).[45]

TABLE 6.2
Police Workload in Wilmington, Delaware, Unit Activity File (UAF)

Type of Activity*	Total Hours	% Hours
Free patrol	20,931	29.45
Crime-related activity	18,549	26.34
Administrative activity	8,658	12.30
Traffic-related activity	7,958	11.32
Order-maintenance activity	6,145	8.73
Unavailable for assignment	3,614	5.13
Medical-related activity	1,647	2.36
Total UAF district car time	70,396	100.00

*Type of activity:

Free patrol includes "park and walk" and "clear."

Crime-related activity includes "officer in trouble," "suspicious person/vehicle," "crime in progress," "alarm," "investigate—not in progress," "service warrant/subpoena," and "assist other police."

Administrative activity includes "meal break," "report writing," "firearms training," "police vehicle maintenance," "at headquarters," and "court-related."

Traffic-related activity includes "traffic accident investigation," "parking problems," "motor vehicle driving problems," "traffic control," and "fire emergency."

Order-maintenance activity includes "order maintenance—in progress," "animal complaint," and "noise complaint."

Unavailable for assignment includes "unavailable for assignment."

Medical-related activity includes "medical emergency" and "at local hospital."

SOURCE: Adapted from Jack R. Greene and Carl B. Klockars, "What Police Do," in *Thinking about Police,* ed. Carl B. Klockars and Stephen D. Mastrofski, 2nd ed. (New York: McGraw-Hill, 1991), pp. 273–284, 279.

Patrol: The Basic Technique

Preventive patrol, the backbone of a municipal department's activities, consists of officers driving or walking through a designated geographic area of responsibility in a varied pattern so that their presence is not predictable. Officers on patrol fulfill several important functions in addition to order maintenance: They enforce the law; provide service to the community; deter crime or catch criminals in the act; and deal with lost children, rabid dogs, trucks that lose a barrel filled with chemicals, a broken traffic light, or a big pothole.

Patrol can be fairly boring, with many hours of uncommitted or free time when an officer is not responding to a call for service or performing other identifiable activities. What do officers do with this time? According to one researcher, "the preponderance of patrol work involves not doing anything very specific, but rather taking breaks, meeting with other officers, and engaging in preventive patrolling."[46] Time is also spent on administrative duties at the police station, making court appearances, and on police-initiated activities, especially traffic law enforcement.

Types of Patrol

There are any number of modes of patrolling in addition to the most traditional and familiar—car, foot, and bicycle. Depending on the terrain to be covered, the number of police officers, and the typical problems, officers may patrol on horseback (mounted patrol); by boat or jet skis (water and harbor patrols); by air (including seaplane and helicopter patrol); or by off-road vehicle (motorcycle patrol, jeep patrol). Patrol areas may range from a few congested city blocks to miles and miles of desert or open water. In this discussion we will focus on the most-used mode, car patrol, and on some traditional modes that are being revived, like foot and bicycle patrol.

Car Patrol.   O. W. Wilson was extremely influential in persuading police throughout the country to make extensive use of the automobile for patrol. A car, he reasoned, creates a sense that the police are omnipresent in the community, provides a means of responding more rapidly to calls, and enables officers to patrol in a less predictable pattern. Today patrol is almost exclusively done in cars. A recent survey of the police in large cities showed that almost 94 percent of patrol time is taken up by motorized patrol.[47]

Theoretically it is possible to devise cost-beneficial plans for the deployment of one-officer patrol cars, at certain times, in certain areas, under certain conditions, without compromising officer safety. The issue is a highly emotional one. It takes the loss of a single life to block the continuation of one-officer patrols, as it did in New York City in the late 1970s when officer Cecil Sledge was killed while on patrol alone shortly after institution of the solo program.[48] Yet one-person cars have now become the national norm: A survey of large cities shows that 70 percent of patrol cars are staffed by one officer.

Foot Patrol. The time-honored tradition of walking the beat now accounts for only a small percentage of patrol work. Limitations of motorized patrol (for example, less contact with citizens) led to suggestions that foot patrol might have more advantages than motorized patrol. Experiments were undertaken in Newark, New Jersey, and Flint, Michigan, to evaluate the effects of foot patrol. In Newark there was no apparent effect on the amount of reported crime, but citizens seemed to be less fearful and more satisfied with police service.[49] Flint reported similar consequences with respect to fear of crime and satisfaction with police service, and in addition found decreases in reported crime.[50]

Bicycle Patrol. Before Henry Ford motorized America and put cars at the disposition of criminals and police alike, police used bicycles to respond rapidly to crimes in progress. A century later, the bicycle is once again being pressed into service. Phoenix, Arizona, Seattle, Washington, and other cities find that bicycle patrols are an ideal combination of the popular touch of foot patrols and the mobility of car patrols.[51] The success of bicycle patrols depends on special bikes, special equipment for the officer, special training, and the appropriate area or terrain.

BENEFITS OF POLICE AND
EMERGENCY MEDICAL SERVICES (EMS) BIKE UNITS

- *Bicycles can easily penetrate crowds.* In highly congested areas police and EMS personnel on bikes can move more quickly and safely than those in golf carts, in Gators (utility vehicles), or on foot, and can reach areas that are not accessible to police cruisers and ambulances.
- *Response time in heavy traffic is improved.* During their trial period in Orlando, bike medics responded in less than one minute 55 percent of the time, less than two minutes 83 percent of the time, and less than three minutes 95 percent of the time, contrasted with an average of four minutes for motorized rescue units.
- *Bicycles give officers the "stealth advantage."* Because they are silent, cops on bikes can ride right up to the scene of a crime before they are noticed.
- *Police and EMS cyclists lead by example.* They promote helmet use and bike safety to the community and its children.
- *Bicycles are great for public relations.* A police officer or a medic on a bike is much more approachable than one in a police cruiser or ambulance.
- *Bicycle use promotes good health.* Departments benefit from decreased health care costs.
- *Bicycles are enjoyable.* Even occasional bike duty improves morale.
- *Bike units are cost effective.* The average cost per bike is approximately $1,200—a fraction of the cost of a cruiser, an ambulance, or any other motorized vehicle.

SOURCE: International Police Mountain Bike Association, http://www.ipmba.org/facts.htm.

Evaluating Traditional Techniques

The ability to respond as quickly as possible to citizen-initiated calls to the police has been considered one of the more important police techniques. Undoubtedly, a swift response can save lives in many fire and medical situations. This appears to be less true with respect to order maintenance or law enforcement calls. Studies in several cities conducted within the last fifteen years demonstrate that rapid response has very little likelihood of increasing the probability of arrest.

The reason has to do with the nature of most crimes and the time it takes to report a crime. Crimes like murders and burglaries often occur long before they are discovered. Quick arrival on the scene by the police does not improve the probability of finding the perpetrator. Even with index crimes such as rape and robbery, any delay in reporting the crime significantly reduces the probability of arrest. For example, in one four-city study published in 1981, the police had only a 10 percent chance of making an arrest if the crime was reported even one minute after it occurred. Arrest probabilities were highest for crimes reported while in progress, but even then the probability of an arrest was only 35 percent.[52]

To test the effectiveness of traditional police techniques, an experiment was conducted between October 1972 and September 1973, funded by the Police Foundation. The Kansas City Preventive Patrol Experiment measured the effectiveness of different levels of patrol presence on crime. With the cooperation of the Kansas City police, various strategies were tried in different sections of the city. Police presence was (1) increased through intensified patrol, (2) reduced by limiting it to responses to citizen calls, or (3) left unchanged. The results were surprising. Crime did not go down in areas of intensified patrol, nor did reduced patrol result in an increase of either crime or fear among residents.[53] The Kansas City experiment led to a reassessment of policing, especially with respect to the most productive use of a patrol officer's time. Administrators began to question the use of traditional preventive patrol as a crime deterrent.

New Policing Strategies

Taken together, the findings of many studies have highlighted the limitations of traditional techniques. It is clear that new strategies can benefit both the police and the public. Moreover, tightened police budgets have prompted a search for more cost-effective responses. During the last few decades American policing has moved through various phases of emphasis: from "professional" policing, to "community" policing, to "hot-spot" policing. Now it has reached the phase of "smart" policing, "scientific" policing, or, as Lawrence W. Sherman aptly calls it, "evidence-based" policing, meaning law enforcement strategies and guidelines resting on a solid research basis.[54]

Differential Response.   Some alternatives to rapid response were tried in a field experiment conducted in three cities (Garden Grove, California; Greensboro, North Carolina; and Toledo, Ohio) in the early 1980s. The tests involved both the creation of a new means of classifying calls and the implementation of **differential responses.** Among the possible means of responding to calls were these:

- Taking reports by phone.
- Delaying the mobile response for thirty to sixty minutes.
- Referring calls to other agencies.
- Scheduling appointments for report-taking.
- Asking the caller to come into the station to make a report or to mail in a report form provided by the police.

The results were very encouraging. Proper screening of calls allowed the police to respond quickly when needed, and the use of mobile units to respond to nonemergencies was reduced significantly. In one city, one-fifth of all calls were handled with a nonpatrol response, usually with a telephone report. Another 27 percent of calls were eligible for a delayed response. The use of the alternative responses enabled the patrol units to devote more time to crime

differential response
Response strategy that involves classifying calls for service and using various responses.

Careers

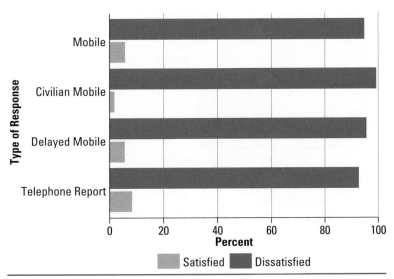

FIGURE 6.1 Alternative Response: Citizen Satisfaction

SOURCE: J. Thomas McEwen, Edward F. Connors III, and Marcia I. Cohen, *Evaluation of the Differential Police Response Field Test* (Washington, DC: National Institute of Justice, 1984), p. 102.

prevention activities and to other patrol strategies. More than 90 percent of the citizens involved in the test were dissatisfied with the alternative responses (Figure 6.1).[55] Cities around the country are now considering ways to implement differential response strategies in their police operations.

New Kinds of Patrol. In addition to alternate forms of response, other techniques can optimize the use of patrol time. One is **directed patrol,** in which patrol officers are assigned to specific activities chosen after an analysis of crime patterns. For example, an officer may be directed to spend a certain amount of time in particular high-crime areas known as "hot spots." Hot spots were discovered as a result of an analysis of the distribution of 911 calls for police assistance in Minneapolis. Three percent of the addresses and intersections in the city were the subject of 50 percent of the calls received.[56] Hot spots, then, are a natural target for directed patrol. Although some evidence indicates that directed patrol may reduce the incidence of certain targeted crimes in target areas, further study is required to determine whether crimes are actually being prevented or merely displaced to another location where the police are less in evidence.[57]

Problem-Oriented Policing. **Problem-oriented policing** is the creation of University of Wisconsin Law School professor Herman Goldstein. It seeks to identify the underlying problems within a community that create the specific problems police are called on to solve. Once the problems are identified, the police plan and implement solutions, usually with input from the community, although not necessarily. Problem-oriented policing has been tried in only a few locations. The best-known programs are those in Baltimore, Maryland, and Newport News, Virginia.[58] In 1982 the Baltimore County Police Department created three teams of officers to solve recurring problems. The teams, called COPE (Citizen-Oriented Police Enforcement), worked with local patrol officers to pinpoint conditions that appeared to be creating problems. For example, a neighborhood park was not being used by community residents. This was because rowdy youths had erected a treehouse in a vacant lot adjacent to the park and were using it as a hangout and drinking place. Fearful neighborhood residents did not want their own children exposed to the treehouse boys. The police, unable to enlist the help of other city agencies, finally tracked down the owner of the lot, who agreed to have the treehouse removed. Two police officers went out and demolished the treehouse, and the park soon filled with children.[59]

directed patrol
Patrol officers assigned to specific activities, such as patrolling a high-crime area, chosen after an analysis of crime patterns.

problem-oriented policing
Strategy that seeks to identify the underlying problems within a community so that community and police can work together to solve them.

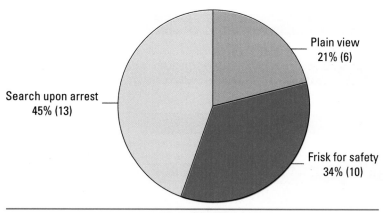

FIGURE 6.2 How Hot Spot Patrols Seized Guns

SOURCE: Lawrence W. Sherman, James W. Shaw, and Dennis P. Rogan, *The Kansas City Gun Experiment* (National Institute of Justice, U.S. Department of Justice, January 1995), p. 5.

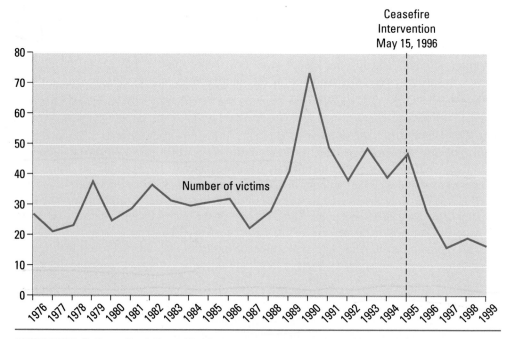

FIGURE 6.3 Youth Homicide Victims Ages 24 and Under in Boston, 1976–1999

SOURCES: David M. Kennedy, Anthony A. Braga, and Anne M. Piehl, "Developing and Implementing Operation Ceasefire," and Anthony A. Braga, David M. Kennedy, Anne M. Piehl, and Elin J. Waring, "Measuring the Impact of Operation Ceasefire," in *Reducing Gun Violence: The Boston Gun Project's Operation Ceasefire* (Washington, DC: U.S. Department of Justice, National Institute of Justice, September 2001).

Studies in Kansas City and Boston have evaluated new policing strategies to get guns off the street. In Kansas City, police focused traffic enforcement and field interrogations on gun crime hot spots, with the goal of seizing illegally carried weapons. Gun seizures in the target areas rose by 60 percent, and gun crimes dropped by 49 percent (see Figure 6.2).[60] In Boston, the police tried to discourage gun carrying in public by gang members and probationers. Gun carrying by the high-risk groups was substantially reduced, as were juvenile gun homicides (Figure 6.3).[61]

The Law Enforcement Function

Police officers are sworn to enforce the law. This aspect of police work is probably the best known and most widely publicized, although not necessarily the task to which most police time is devoted. The primary object in law enforcement is the apprehension of law breakers and the collection of evidence that will lead to conviction in a court proceeding.

Criminal Investigation

Criminal investigation conjures up the image of pipe-smoking Sherlock Holmes, deer-stalker hat on his head and magnifying glass in his hand. Television has done much to perpetuate a romanticized version of the detective. Their counterparts do exist in real life, but the modern detective may easily be someone who sits at a computer screening hundreds of MOs (*modus operandi*—characteristic methods used in commission of a crime) or who tests saliva samples for DNA identification. Most detectives are trained in modern investigative techniques and in the laws of evidence and criminal procedure.[62] They spend most of their time on routine chores involving lots of paperwork, hours of interviewing, and not much excitement.

The Initial Investigation.   When a crime is reported to the police, patrol officers are usually the first to arrive on the scene. That scene may be a shopping mall where a store security officer has just caught a person shoplifting or a remote area in the woods where a body has been found. Patrol officers perform the initial investigation; fill out the forms, such as the complaint; interview witnesses; make an arrest if there is a suspect; and appear in court with the arrestee. If a crime is not "cleared by arrest" by the patrol officer or if it requires expert investigation, detectives are called in. One analysis showed that, with the exception of rape, at least two-thirds of all arrests were made by the patrol division.[63]

The detective's first task usually is to examine the facts in order to determine whether a crime has actually been committed and whether further investigation is warranted. If a full investigation is initiated, the detective collects evidence, interviews witnesses and victims, contacts informants, and follows up on new leads, all with the purpose of making an arrest, securing evidence, and, where appropriate, recovering stolen property. In homicide cases, medical examiners are summoned.

Preparing a Case for Court.   After an arrest is made, investigative work is extremely important to the outcome of a court case. It is the principal means by which evidence is gathered in preparation for prosecution.[64] The investigator gathers all the evidence and appears in court to testify to its legality.[65] Case preparation includes reviewing and evaluating all evidence and reports on the case; determining whether physical evidence was properly obtained, transported, and safeguarded; reinterviewing witnesses and assisting in their preparation for court appearances; and preparing the final report.[66]

Careers

Law Enforcement Priorities Today

Each era has its own law enforcement concerns and priorities. Three priority areas of the 1980s and 1990s that have carried over into the twenty-first century demonstrate an aggressive approach to policing. These areas are:

- Narcotics
- Domestic violence
- Drunk driving

Narcotics: Aggressive Enforcement.   Illegal drugs have been a major focus of law enforcement for years. The current federal "war on drugs" continues the tradition established by previous administrations of mounting or at least attempting to mount a strong criminal justice response to the problem.[67] The rapid spread of crack cocaine in urban areas, the emergence of a new generation of young opiate abusers, and the violence associated with the drug trade continue the urgent call for the government to "do something" about the drug problem. As a

ELLIOT M. GROSS, M.D., INTER-COUNTY MEDICAL EXAMINER, COUNTIES OF CAPE MAY AND CUMBERLAND, NJ; CHIEF MEDICAL EXAMINER, CITY OF NEW YORK, 1979–1987; CHIEF MEDICAL EXAMINER, STATE OF CONNECTICUT, 1970–1979

The call to a homicide scene will result in my second case today. I have just completed an ME (medical examiner) autopsy on a 36-year-old male migrant worker found in his rooming house. The police had reported the death as "suspicious, possible OD," and had vouchered controlled drugs found in a washroom for laboratory submission. The "bruises" and bloody fluid about the victim's face, however, concerned them and it had been my job to see if the death was more than an OD.

The two-hour post-mortem procedure and subsequent testing comprised a familiar routine:

1. Examining the clothed body; checking the eyes for petechial hemorrhages—the fine blood spots seen in an asphyxial death.

2. Photographing and recording a description of the body's appearance—unique characteristics, signs of abusive treatment and injuries. (The blood-tinged foam in mouth and nose due to fluid accumulation in the lungs and left forearm "track-marks" tended to confirm the first police impression. The forehead and right-sided nose abrasions or scrapes were consistent with a face forward fall and unlikely "bruises" inflicted with a blunt instrument.)

3. Weighing and examining each vital organ for evidence of disease and injury; dissecting the larynx for fractures of the hyoid bone or its other components, lest a strangulation be overlooked. (Scarring with evidence of hemorrhage more than twenty-four hours old about forearm veins was not unexpected. Severe narrowing of arteries supplying the heart and "damage" to its muscle had surprised me. Did this farm worker die of a heart attack or an OD?)

4. Submitting body fluids for toxicological analysis. (These would detect a low blood cocaine level and cannabinoids [marijuana metabolites] as well as cocaine breakdown products in the urine.)

5. Saving tissue fragments for microscopic examination. (I would find minute crystals—"sparkling" under special light—lodged about lung vessels where they have traveled in the circulation from repeat injections of street drugs; recent death of heart muscle and a blood clot in a severely narrowed coronary artery.)

The cause of death will be later finalized as cocaine-related heart disease and confirmed to the police as not suspicious. The second case poses different challenges.

A small business owner has been found shot, facedown on the floor of his ransacked shop where he also lives. The Prosecutor's Crime

result, arrests for drug-related offenses increased 154 percent through the period of 1980–1995. Cocaine and heroin arrests increased an astonishing 741 percent during the same period. Arrests for the sale and/or manufacture or possession of illegal narcotics totaled 1.5 million in 1997—the highest ever.[68] Between 1991 and 1997 drug offenders in state and federal prisons grew by nearly 90,000.[69] In recent years, arrests for drug abuse violations decreased slightly, but drug offenders continue to densely populate our prisons (Table 6.3).

Policymakers at all levels of government have designed and implemented a variety of strategies intended to control the availability of illegal substances. One approach is to reduce the supply of drugs; the other is to reduce the demand.[70] Controlling supply begins at the international level and follows the production-shipment-distribution path to the local level.

Scene Unit is there, videotaping the scene, taking photographs, and finding casings (three) and spent bullets (two). After a look at the body, first as it was found, and then turned over, I observe a "bullet hole" in the back and bruises about the eyes. I have many questions:

- How long has he been dead? Was death instantaneous?

- How many bullet wounds? Did they all exit? Where did they enter and exit? From what range were the bullets fired? Did all the bullets fired enter the body? Did any bullet ricochet off a wall before entering the body? Did some just pass through clothing? Were bullets fired from more than one weapon? What paths did the bullets take?

- Are there other injuries besides gunshot wounds? From the firearm? From a fall? From another weapon? From grappling with the assailant?

Taking a body and room temperature and checking for the signs of death—the pooling of blood (lividity) and stiffening of muscles (rigor mortis)—allows me to give a range of time of death: late evening into early morning hours. The wound in the back is an exit, but I can't tell which one of the chest entries caused it or how close they were fired. The eyes are black and blue, but I can't tell if this was caused by facial blows or a skull fracture from a fall or a bullet to the head. The hands are placed in paper bags so trace evidence won't be lost. Finding such particles and definite answers to the questions must wait for the autopsy.

This procedure takes four hours. When the clothing is removed I see four bullet wounds, three entries (one in the head in addition to two in the right chest), and an exit in the back. Three bullets have been fired. X-rays show one in the head and a second in the spine just above the diaphragm.

Stippling (hemorrhages from powder grains pointing to close range) on the left arm indicates a fourth bullet. The location of this "tattooing" is beyond the proximity of the entries, one of which is "contact" and the other, close range. Before the internal examination and after the hands have been inspected (no hair fibers or smoke from a revolver are seen), the wounds are cleaned and photographed with rulers for test-fire and gun-muzzle comparison.

At autopsy, I identify the paths the bullets have taken, the one in the head fracturing the skull with resulting hemorrhage into soft tissues about the eye sockets and the bruised eyelids, first thought to have been caused by punches. I mark the non-jacketed bullet, which has entered the brain from the front, leaving the "rifling" intact.

Like the bullet in the head, the missile entering at contact range also traveled a "fatal" course—through the left lung and aorta and into the spine. The direction [of] this bullet, as well as that which has passed through the body, is easy to describe. Entry location and bullet location in the vertebra can be measured in relation to anatomical landmarks. Recovering the "slug" poses a problem, since it is lodged in dense bone and I don't want to mar the rifling. It is retrieved and given to the police.

I complete the autopsy, finding no other injuries or evidence but able to give the police the bullets and one more clue. With recognizable full stomach contents, the time of death is closer to the late evening than the early morning hours. It is up to the police to trace this victim's steps and find the weapon as well.

11:00 P.M.: Time to catch some sleep. After all, the phone may ring anytime. Death does not respect office hours.

Activities related to the importation of drugs from abroad are typically the responsibility of federal law enforcement agencies such as the Drug Enforcement Administration (DEA), the U.S. Coast Guard, and the Customs Service; they involve local law enforcement resources only occasionally.[71]

At the street level, police officers use many tactics to reduce local availability. Among the most common is the buy-and-bust, in which police simply buy some drugs from a dealer and then make an arrest. A recent variation on this technique is sell-and-bust. Working undercover, police pretend to be dealers and then arrest those who buy from them. Other tactics available include undercover operations, electronic surveillance, the use of informants to obtain information about large-scale dealers from smaller dealers in exchange for leniency

TABLE 6.3
Federal Prison Population
and Number and Percent
Sentenced for Drug Offenses
United States, 1970–2004

	Total Sentenced and Unsentenced Population	Sentenced Population		
			Drug Offenses	
		Total	Number	Precent of Total
1970	21,266	20,686	3,384	16.3%
1971	20,891	20,529	3,495	17.0
1972	22,090	20,729	3,523	16.9
1973	23,336	22,038	5,652	25.6
1974	23,690	21,769	6,203	28.4
1975	23,566	20,692	5,540	26.7
1976	27,033	24,135	6,425	26.6
1977	29,877	25,673	6,743	26.2
1978	27,674	23,501	5,981	25.4
1979	24,810	21,539	5,468	25.3
1980	24,252	19,023	4,749	24.9
1981	26,195	19,765	5,076	25.6
1982	28,133	20,938	5,518	26.3
1983	30,214	26,027	7,201	27.6
1984	32,317	27,622	8,152	29.5
1985	36,042	27,623	9,491	34.3
1986	37,542	30,104	11,344	37.7
1987	41,609	33,246	13,897	41.8
1988	41,342	33,758	15,087	44.7
1989	47,568	37,758	18,852	49.9
1990	54,613	46,575	24,297	52.2
1991	61,026	52,176	29,667	56.9
1992	67,768	59,516	35,398	59.5
1993	76,531	68,183	41,393	60.7
1994	82,269	73,958	45,367	61.3
1995	85,865	76,947	46,669	60.7
1996	89,672	80,872	49,096	60.7
1997	95,513	87,294	52,059	59.6
1998	104,507	95,323	55,984	58.7
1999	115,024	104,500	60,399	57.8
2000	123,141	112,329	63,898	56.9
2001	131,419	120,829	67,037	55.5
2002	139,183	128,090	70,009	54.7
2003	148,731	137,536	75,801	55.1
2004[a]	154,706	143,864	77,867	54.1

Note: These data represent prisoners housed in Federal Bureau of Prisons facilities; prisoners houses in contract facilities are not included. Data for 1970–76 are for June 30; beginning in 1977, data are for September 30. Some data have been revised by the Source and may differ from previous editions of *Sourcebook*.

[a]As of November 2004.

SOURCE: U.S. Department of Justice, Federal Bureau of Prisons, *Sourcebook of Criminal Justice Statistics 2003* [Online], http://www.bop.gov/fact0598.html [Sept. 9, 2003]; and data provided by the U.S. Department of Justice, Federal Bureau of Prisons.

in case of prosecution, and community-based intelligence gathering, which includes hotlines for reporting drug dealing and collaboration with community groups to identify drug problems. Some narcotics units may decide to target large-scale dealers, whereas others may go after users and street-level dealers, sometimes through street sweeps, which utilize a large police presence on the street to drive dealers away. Another strategy is to mount a focused crackdown on a particular area or type of drug.[72] These tactics can be used alone or combined in different strategies, depending on the needs and resources of the community and the police.

Evaluations of these strategies show mixed results.[73] New York City's Operation Pressure Point, a crackdown focused on one area of the city, boasts some success in making significant reductions in street-level dealing and in recorded rates of arrests for burglary and robbery, assuming that these property crimes are directly related to drug use. Considerable improvement in the quality of life in several neighborhoods was also achieved. However, the lower-income neighborhoods within the target area did not record significant decreases in drug traffic; dealers simply changed their methods.[74]

Aggressive drug law enforcement costs the federal government $16 billion annually.[75] At the street level it has clogged the nation's courts and resulted in severe overcrowding of jails and prisons, while drug abuse in some jurisdictions appears unaffected.[76] Police officials around the country acknowledge the limits of their efforts at controlling the problem.

Policing Domestic Violence. Tracey Thurman had repeatedly requested police assistance because she feared her estranged husband. Even after he threatened to shoot her and her son, the police merely told her to get a restraining order. Eventually, the husband attacked Thurman, inflicting multiple stab wounds that caused paralysis from the neck down and permanent disfigurement. The police had delayed in responding to her call on that occasion and the city of Torrington, Connecticut, was held liable for having failed to provide her with "equal protection" under the law. In the suit that followed, Ms. Thurman was awarded $2.3 million in damages.[77] That 1985 case helped to change the American pattern of policing domestic violence.

The traditional response in the past had been nonintervention: Police often refused to make an arrest even when the victim appeared to be in danger and requested that the assailant be arrested.[78] An arrest usually was made only if the assailant was drunk, had caused serious injury, and/or assaulted the officers.[79] The arrest typically was classified as a misdemeanor unless it was for infliction of serious injury.[80]

Today we view domestic violence as a major social problem. Family disturbance calls now represent the largest single category of calls received by the police.[81] The police response began to change during the 1980s for several reasons. First, feminists successfully pressed their case that domestic violence must be seen as a criminal matter. Second, the huge damage award in *Thurman v. Torrington* sent a clear message: If law enforcement agencies fail to protect victims of domestic violence, the cost will be high. In addition, studies conducted in the late 1970s had shown a relationship between domestic-related homicides (and assaults) and calls for police intervention in disputes. In a Kansas City study of these domestic violence cases, researchers found that the police had been previously called to the address at least once in 85 percent of the cases, and at least five times in 50 percent of the cases. Furthermore, threats preceded physical violence in nearly 80 percent of the cases.[82] Similar findings about threats as predictors of violence were also made in Detroit.[83]

Drunk-Driving: Aggressive Enforcement. Concern over drunk driving has increased markedly during the last several years, with groups like Mothers Against Drunk Driving (MADD) making the public aware of the seriousness of the problem. The result has been an enhanced police effort to combat drunk driving, coupled with legislatively mandated increased penalties for those convicted of the offense. The various techniques used to catch and deter drunk drivers include increasing the number of officers assigned to the traffic unit, creating incentives for making more arrests, launching media campaigns, and using roadblocks and checkpoints to stop and question all drivers. (See Table 6.4.)

Scandinavian countries impose punishment when a driver's blood level exceeds a statutory level; sanctions are severe and include imprisonment, heavy fines, and temporary or permanent loss of license. This approach is credited with having significantly reduced the

State	2006 Total Traffic Deaths	2006 Alcohol-Related Deaths	Percent Alcohol-Related	2006 Fatalities Involving a .08+ BAC Driver	Percent of 2006 Fatalities Involving a .08 + BAC Driver
Alabama	1,208	475	37%	384	32%
Alaska	74	23	31	20	27
Arizona	1,288	585	45	409	32
Arkansas	665	254	38	197	30
California	4,236	1,779	42	1,250	30
Colorado	535	226	42	177	33
Connecticut	301	129	43	109	36
Delaware	148	57	39	43	29
District of Columbia	37	18	48	12	32
Florida	3,374	1,376	41	959	28
Georgia	1,693	604	36	464	27
Hawaii	161	84	52	63	39
Idaho	267	106	40	84	31
Illinois	1,254	594	47	444	35
Indiana	899	319	36	247	27
Iowa	439	148	34	122	28
Kansas	468	170	36	135	29
Kentucky	913	272	30	222	24
Louisiana	982	475	48	364	37
Maine	188	74	39	51	27
Maryland	651	268	41	193	30
Massachusetts	430	174	40	137	32
Michigan	1,085	440	41	332	31
Minnesota	494	183	37	151	31
Mississippi	911	375	41	320	35
Missouri	1,096	500	46	380	35
Montana	263	126	48	103	39
Nebraska	269	89	33	70	26
Nevada	432	186	43	142	33
New Hampshire	127	52	41	47	37
New Jersey	772	341	44	224	29
New Mexico	484	186	38	136	28
New York	1,456	558	38	397	27
North Carolina	1,559	554	36	420	27
North Dakota	111	50	45	41	37
Ohio	1,238	488	39	377	30
Oklahoma	765	263	34	231	26
Oregon	477	196	41	148	31
Pennsylvania	1,525	600	39	487	32
Rhode Island	81	42	51	29	37

(continued)

SOURCE: National Highway Traffic Safety Administration, 2007. Available at http://www.madd.org/stats/11921.

TABLE 6.4   State-By-State Traffic Fatalities, 2006

State	2006 Total Traffic Deaths	2006 Alcohol-Related Deaths	Percent Alcohol-Related	2006 Fatalities Involving a .08+ BAC Driver	Percent of 2006 Fatalities Involving a .08 + BAC Driver
South Corolina	1,037	523	50	420	33
South Dakota	191	80	42	69	36
Tennessee	1,287	509	40	408	32
Taxas	3,475	1,677	48	1,354	39
Utah	287	69	24	54	19
Vermont	87	29	33	26	30
Virginia	963	379	39	300	31
Washington	630	294	47	225	36
West Virginia	410	161	39	129	31
Wisconsin	724	364	50	305	42
Wyoming	195	80	41	67	34
National	42,624	17,602	41	13,470	32
Puerto Rico	507	215	42	144	28

TABLE 6.4 (Continued)

frequency of drunk driving, with a lesser impact on drunk-driving accidents. For several countries it has been shown that cultural factors, including social disapproval and publicity, are more effective in controlling drunk driving than police-enforced deterrence.[84]

New Challenges: Post-9/11

Municipal police departments are increasingly being asked to join in the war against domestic terrorism. The challenge to police departments has been one of information sharing. There is a long-standing view that local police departments have been excluded from information sharing that takes place regularly across federal agencies. Joint counterterrorism tasks forces, including local police, are changing their view. Now federal agencies are looking to local police departments for leads from law enforcement and nonlaw enforcement data. In fact, much of the 9/11 commission's report turns on a far more strategic approach to agency integration, coordination, and the sharing of intelligence.

Controversial Law Enforcement Techniques

Some aggressive law enforcement activities, such as crackdowns, roadblocks, decoys, undercover work, reliance on informants, and "zero tolerance" have generated controversy and raised legal and ethical problems.

Crackdowns are an intensified effort by the police to deal with a problem in a particular area or to reduce the incidence of a particular crime. Targets include drunk driving, drug dealing, prostitution, and even illegal parking or bicycle riding. Research on the results of crackdowns indicates that they may result in an initial decrease in crime, but that the effect may be short-lived. The question is whether such a short-term benefit outweighs the risk of violations of civil liberties that are inherent in any operation that arbitrarily stops people in a targeted area. Philadelphia's Operation Cold Turkey, for example, stopped 1,000 people over a four-day period, yet only eighty narcotics arrests were made. The public outcry—and a lawsuit—forced the department to stop the operation abruptly.[85]

Another police strategy—the use of roadblocks and sobriety checkpoints to catch drunk drivers—has also been challenged. When the police stop drivers without any suspicion

crackdown
Intensified effort by the police to deal with a problem in a particular area, or to reduce the incidence of a particular crime.

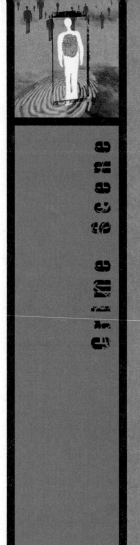

ROAD RAGE

It has been known for years as aggressive driving. It is a factor in 28,000 highway deaths per year. Road rage is a disorder that is said to affect over half of all drivers. Symptoms include speeding, tailgating, weaving in and out of busy traffic, passing on the right, making unsafe or improper lane changes, running stop signs and red lights, flashing lights or high beams at other drivers, using obscene gestures, swearing and yelling insults, honking or screaming at other drivers, throwing items at other vehicles, and shooting other drivers or passengers. "The symptoms are incredibly commonplace, and sometimes boil over into actual assault and life-threatening situations," explains John Hagerty of the New Jersey State Police.[1]

Road rage now results in more highway deaths than drunk driving. A national study by the AAA Foundation for Traffic Safety found that the majority of aggressive drivers were men ages eighteen to twenty-six, but that dangerous driving behavior is present in women also, and across age levels and economic classes.

Psychiatrists look to deep-seated personal causes such as stress disorders, which result in impaired judgment. Sociologists see a connection between problems in society and aggressive driving. Others say that the car shields drivers, in effect making them anonymous. This anonymity allows those who become frustrated while driving to ignore society's rules for proper behavior and to behave recklessly. Some claim that drivers see the car as an extension of themselves, and they react angrily when cut off, passed on the highway, or forced to slow down.

Two eerily similar accidents happened as a consequence of young men "dueling" with their cars. The first occurred on the George Washington Memorial Parkway in the nation's capital region. As the two cars raced each other along the parkway, one car crossed the median and hit an oncoming car. Three people were killed. Two of them were drivers not involved in the duel.[2] The second happened as two cars on the New Jersey Turnpike chased each other at speeds of up to 100 miles per hour. The cars wove in and out of lanes of traffic, until the occupant of one of the vehicles allegedly threw an object at the other

> "It is a factor in 28,000 highway deaths per year."

car. This caused the car to slam into a tree and resulted in the death of two men.[3]

Ricardo Martinez is head of the National Highway Traffic Safety Administration. He blames aggressive driving on a combination of an increase in a "me first" philosophy and reduced levels of traffic enforcement arising from budget cuts, as well as increased congestion and traffic in urban areas. Since 1987, traffic has increased by 35 percent, but new road construction has only increased 1 percent. Likewise, Pam Fischer, spokeswoman for the New Jersey Automobile Club, sees congestion

---

decoy
Police officer disguised as a potential crime victim to attract criminal attacks precipitating an arrest.

sting operation
Deceitful but lawful technique in which police pretend to be involved in illegal activities to trap a suspect.

entrapment
Illegal police practice of persuading an initially unwilling party to commit an offense.

that the particular person has committed an offense, it may well be argued that such a stop is an unreasonable—though very temporary—search and seizure. Yet, in several cases the Supreme Court has upheld the right of states to conduct roadblocks and sobriety checkpoints.[86]

In a number of cities the police have deployed **decoys** (officers disguised as potential victims) in an effort to attract and then arrest criminals thought to be responsible for crime problems in a given area.[87]

Sting operations, in which the police pretend to be involved in illegal activities to trap a suspect, have become highly controversial because of their resemblance to entrapment.[88] **Entrapment,** by which the police actually prompt an originally unwilling person to commit a crime, has been held to be an illegal police practice.[89] The police feel strongly that, to conduct effective investigations of crimes that are not likely to be reported because they involve consensual transactions, they must rely on methods of entrapment as well as on informants. These people frequently are criminals themselves. But the practice is not new: Investigators have always had to rely on criminals as sources of information.[90] Typically the police use criminals to obtain information in exchange for some form of lenient treatment, such as reduced charges for a crime. In some cases police will even pay for the information.

on the roadways as a contributing factor. "Anytime there is an accident or construction that slows down traffic, people tend to get more aggravated, and normal and rational people do some dumb things because they are running late or just don't want to sit there."[4]

What can be done to prevent this carnage on our highways? In New Jersey, state troopers and municipal police use plainclothes officers in unmarked cars to cruise dangerous highways during rush hours and spot aggressive drivers. Then they relay the information to police in marked cars, who stop the deviant motorists and give them tickets.[5] In the District of Columbia, Maryland, and Virginia, police have a program called Smooth Operator. In two one-week periods in the spring of 1997, they issued 28,958 summonses and warnings, including nearly 12,000 for speeding, 3,300 for failing to obey traffic signals, 2,000 for failing to wear a seat belt, and 1,800 for failing to obey a traffic sign.[6]

Another approach calls for making roads bigger. The reasoning is that wider roads reduce traffic congestion and the resulting frustration. But, as noted by Congressman Earl Blumenauer, a Democrat from Oregon, building more roads is "the equivalent of giving a wife beater more room to swing." Instead, he advocates building bicycle lanes and planting trees. These are "features that soften the streets and let drivers know they have to share the road."[7]

America has faced a deadly threat on its roadways before—drunk driving. Emphasis was placed on changing the laws and making it socially unacceptable to drink and drive. The experts say aggressive driving should be treated the same way. "We have to enforce the law, take bad drivers off the road and make them pay for their mistakes," urged Colonel Peter J. O'Hagan, director of the New Jersey Division of Highway Safety. The time has come to address aggressive driving through better education, better enforcement, and a get-tough policy. Dr. Martinez warns that "aggressive drivers must get the message that their behavior will not be tolerated, and that they will be prosecuted."[8] (See Figure 6.4 for ways to deal with an aggressive driver.)

Questions for Discussion

1. Have you ever been directly involved in an incident of aggressive driving? What do you think led to the behavior? How could it have been prevented?

2. Picture the area around your campus. Are there any problems with aggressive driving? What concrete steps could the university and local police take to address these problems?

3. What is a suitable punishment for someone who speeds? How about someone who screams obscenities at other drivers? Do you think it is possible to reduce or eliminate these behaviors through law enforcement?

SOURCES
1. Daniel B. Rathbone and Jorg C. Huckabee, "Controlling Road Rage: A Literature Review and Pilot Study" (Washington, DC: The AAA Foundation for Traffic Safety, 1999); Robert Cohen, "Road Rage' Replacing DWI as Top Problem," *The Star-Ledger,* July 28, 1997, pp. 1, 7.
2. Ibid.
3. Cohen, "Road Rage," pp. 1, 7.
4. Ibid.
5. Ibid.
6. Wald, "Temper·Cited as Cause."
7. Ibid.
8. Cohen, "Road Rage," pp. 1, 7.

<u>**Zero tolerance**</u> is the latest buzzword in policing. It has five key components: (1) a lowering of tolerance to crime and deviance; (2) a use of punitive, sometimes drastic, measures to achieve this; (3) a return to perceived past levels of respectability, order, and civility; (4) the awareness of the continuum between incivilities and crime with both minor "quality of life" offenses and serious crimes considered as problems; and (5) the belief that incivilities left unchecked give rise to crime.[91] It is widely believed that zero tolerance was the reason for the drastic drop in crime experienced recently in New York City, although, as discussed elsewhere in this book, other factors also may be responsible. In fact, the architects of the change in the NYPD that preceded the drop in crime, former Police Commissioner William Bratton and policing scholar George Kelling, both maintain that what has been going on in New York is not zero tolerance policing. Zero tolerance suggests that line officers have no discretion. Critics primarily point to the second element—"a use of punitive, sometimes drastic, measures" as a cause for concern. They conjure up images of police cracking heads and kicking butts, all in the name of zero tolerance policing. Others argue that zero tolerance policing is the exact opposite of community policing.[92] Yet it is possible to control "quality of life" offenses, after negotiating acceptable standards of behavior with the community.

zero tolerance
A new approach to policing that is characterized by a lowering of tolerance to crime and deviance and the use of punitive measures to achieve this goal.

185

What Is Aggressive Driving?

Aggressive driving is the operation of a motor vehicle in an unsafe and hostile manner without regard for others. Aggressive driving behavior may include: making frequent or unsafe lane changes, failing to signal or yield the right of way, tailgating, and disregarding traffic controls.

- -

What should you do when confronted by an aggressive driver?

▶ Stay calm and relaxed.

▶ Make every attempt to get out of the way safely. Don't escalate the situation.

▶ Put your pride in the back seat. Do not challenge an aggressive driver by speeding up or attempting to hold your position in your travel lane.

▶ Wear a seat belt and encourage your passengers to do the same.

▶ Avoid eye contact.

▶ Ignore harassing gestures and refrain from returning them.

▶ Report aggressive drivers to appropriate authorities by providing a vehicle description, location, license plate number, and direction of travel.

▶ If an aggressive driver is involved in a crash, stop a safe distance from the crash scene. When police arrive, report the driving behavior you witnessed.

Remember...
▶ You can control your reactions to other drivers.
If someone drives aggressively, do not retaliate...
Steer Clear of Aggressive Driving.

FIGURE 6.4   What Is Aggressive Driving?

SOURCE: New York State Governor's Traffic Safety Committee, George E. Pataki, Governor, Richard E. Jackson, Jr., Chair.

high-speed chase
The pursuit of a suspect at high speeds.

High-speed chases have come under scrutiny in the light of disturbing statistics (see Table 6.5). On average, about 1 to 3 percent of all pursuits end in death. Between 5 percent and 24 percent end in injuries; 18 percent to 44 percent end in auto accidents. Interestingly, even though between 68 percent and 82 percent of high-speed chases end in arrests, only 9 percent to 30 percent of all pursuits are initiated for felonies. Traffic violations are the most common offenses that bring on a high-speed chase.

TABLE 6.5
When Police Officers Say They Would Engage in Pursuits

Violation	Level of Risk*	
	Low	High
Traffic violation	43%	10%
Property crime: misdemeanor	42	17
Property crime: felony	64	34
Stolen vehicle	65	37
DUI	70	43
Violent felony: no death	87	80
Violent felony: with death	96	95
Officer shot	96	95

*Risk was defined by level of traffic congestion, weather conditions, type of road (e.g., whether surface street, highway, or interstate), and area of pursuit (e.g., whether urban, rural, or commercial). In filling out the questionnaire, respondents themselves determined whether they felt their risk was high or low.

SOURCE: Data from Metro-Dade, Florida; Omaha, Nebraska; Aiken County, South Carolina; and Mesa, Arizona. Geoffrey P. Alpert, *Police Pursuit: Policies and Training* (National Institute of Justice, U.S. Department of Justice, May 1997), p. 4.

Critics of high-speed chases argue that suspects and criminals cannot outrun a police radio. Communications between and among law enforcement agencies make the need for high-speed chases nearly obsolete. Supporters counter by arguing that police radios do not capture criminals, and so police must have the discretion to engage in high-speed chases that are reasonable in light of the circumstances. Yet many departments have moved to no-pursuit policies. Others have issued extensive guidelines that consider the nature and seriousness of the felony a suspect has committed; the danger that the suspect poses to the community; the likelihood of later capturing the suspect if he or she is allowed to escape; and the time of day and the location of the pursuit.[93] No one disputes the loss of lives by the continued practice of police pursuits (Table 6.6).

Changing Composition of the Police Force

The political and social crises of the 1960s challenged Americans to reaffirm their commitment to equality before the law. Title VII of the Civil Rights Act of 1964 prohibited the private sector from discrimination in employment on the basis of race, gender, religion, or national origin. In 1972, the Equal Employment Opportunity Act amended the Civil Rights Act to include the public sector. The 1972 act also required that federal agencies develop affirmative action programs. Besides federal legislation, state and local laws prohibit discrimination on the basis of race, national origin, religion, gender, and, most recently, sexual preference. Now that gays and lesbians can no longer be excluded, they are increasingly "coming out of the closet." Moreover, some cities—such as Boston, Philadelphia, Los Angeles, New York, Minneapolis, Seattle, Portland, and Atlanta—have actively recruited them.

These social and legal changes have had a major impact on the composition of the police force. Women make up 10 percent of all local police officers, blacks make up 11 percent, and Hispanics 7.8 (Figure 6.5). First, the law made it easier for individuals to bring employer discrimination suits against police agencies. Many did. In fact, over the last twenty years, most of the largest police departments in the country have been sued. Second, to comply with federal guidelines, police departments had to make an effort to attract minority and female applicants.[94] And third, the community has continued to put pressure on the police administration to make policy changes. There is widespread understanding that a police force can do its job best when all population groups are represented on the force.

Minority Groups in Policing

The first minority police officer was hired in Washington, District of Columbia, in 1861.[95] In 1940, only 1 percent of all sworn police officers in the United States came from minority groups; in 1950, only 2 percent. The percentage increased to 3.6 in 1960 and to 6.5 in 1973.[96] By the mid-1990s the figure had more than doubled. By 2003, nearly 25 percent of all police officers were racial and ethnic minorities. See Figure 6.5. Civil unrest in the 1960s showed that if police officers were recruited from only a limited segment of the population, there was a risk of alienating groups that were not represented in law enforcement. The contention was that officers from different backgrounds would have different attitudes and therefore would behave differently in their contact with the public. In 1973, the National Advisory Commission on Criminal Justice Standards and Goals adopted the following standard:

> Every police agency shall engage in positive efforts to employ ethnic minority group members. When a substantial ethnic minority population resides within the jurisdiction, the police agency should take affirmative action to achieve a ratio of minority group employees in approximate proportion to the makeup of the population.[97]

Since then, "positive efforts" to enlist minorities include the creation of specialized internal recruitment teams; advertisements on TV, radio, and even highway billboards specially

TABLE 6.6
Fatalities in Crashes Involving
Police in Pursuit, 2001 Fatality
Analysis Reporting System
(FARS)—Annual Report File
(ARF)

State	Occupant of Police Vehicle	Occupant of Chased Vehicle	Occupant of Other Vehicle	Nonoccupant	Total
Alabama	0	5	1	0	6
Alaska	0	0	4	0	4
Arizona	0	5	9	1	15
Arkansas	0	3	0	0	3
California	0	27	22	2	51
Colorado	0	4	2	1	7
Connecticut	0	4	0	0	4
Delaware	0	1	0	0	1
District of Columbia	0	2	0	0	2
Florida	0	10	4	1	15
Georgia	0	11	7	0	18
Hawaii	0	1	0	0	1
Idaho	0	1	0	0	1
Illinois	0	6	2	2	10
Indiana	1	4	3	0	8
Iowa	0	1	1	0	2
Kansas	0	2	2	0	4
Kentucky	0	1	1	0	2
Louisiana	0	8	1	0	9
Maine	0	3	0	0	3
Maryland	0	2	1	0	3
Massachusetts	0	3	2	2	7
Michigan	0	8	8	4	20
Minnesota	0	1	0	0	1
Mississippi	0	3	0	0	3
Missouri	0	4	7	0	11
Nebraska	0	1	0	0	1
Nevada	0	1	0	0	1
New Jersey	0	2	7	1	10
New Mexico	0	4	0	0	4
New York	0	2	6	1	9
North Carolina	2	13	0	0	15
Ohio	0	3	5	0	8
Oklahoma	0	6	0	0	6
Oregon	0	4	4	0	8
Pennsylvania	0	8	1	0	9
Rhode Island	0	0	3	0	3
South Carolina	0	6	2	0	8
South Dakota	0	2	0	0	2
Tennessee	0	8	4	1	13
Texas	0	23	3	4	30
Vermont	0	0	1	0	1
Virginia	0	6	3	0	9
Washington	1	5	2	0	8
West Virginia	0	2	0	0	2
Wisconsin	0	4	1	0	5
Wyoming	0	1	0	1	2
Total	4	221	119	21	365

SOURCE: Adapted from the PursuitWatch.org website, http://www.pursuitwatch.org/stats/2001.htm.

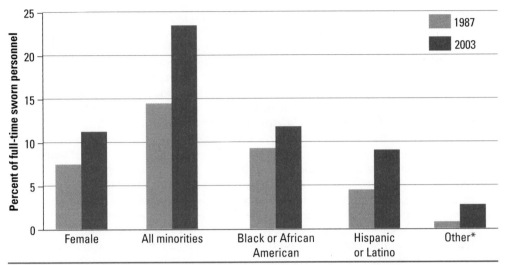

FIGURE 6.5 Female and Minority Local Police Officers, 1987 and 2003

*Includes Asians, Pacific Islanders, American Indians, and Alaska Natives.

SOURCE: Matthew J. Hickman and Brian A. Reeves, *Local Police Departments, 2003* (U.S. Department of Justice, Bureau of Justice Statistics: Washington, DC, 2006), p. iii.

targeting minority candidates; and outreach programs in minority neighborhoods. As of today, the majority of police departments had launched recruitment programs aimed at minorities. Even so, minorities remain disproportionately represented.

Women in Policing

In many ways, women in policing have had parallel experiences to black and Hispanic males. Despite the increasing acceptance of women in law enforcement, there are still problems concerning their number and duties. For example, Lucille Burrascano, one of the first women in the New York City Police Department, reported the following incident:

> During training, I rode as the third person with two men. We're on a robbery run, the siren's blaring, and we pull up right in front of the door. We're supposed to come out with guns drawn but, instead, one of the cops jumps out and opens the door for me. I said, "What are you doing? This is not a date."[98]

THE STATUS OF WOMEN IN POLICING

- Women currently comprise 13.0% of all sworn law enforcement positions among municipal, county, and state law enforcement agencies in the United States with 100 or more sworn officers. Women of color hold 4.9% of these positions.

- Over the last nine years, the representation of women in sworn law enforcement ranks has increased from 9% in 1990 to 13.0% in 2000—a gain of only 4%, or less than 1/2 of 1 percent each year. This underrepresentation of women is striking, given that women account for 46.5% of the adult labor force.

- The gains for women in policing are so slow that, at the current rate of growth, women will not reach equal representation or gender balance within the police profession for at least another seventy years, and many experts caution that time alone is insufficient to substantially increase women's numbers.

(continued)

- Women currently hold 7.3% of sworn Top Command law enforcement positions, 10.3% of Supervisory positions, and 13.7% of Line Operation positions.[1] Women of color hold 1.7% of sworn Top Command law enforcement positions, 3.2% of Supervisory positions, and 5.3% of Line Operation positions.
- More than half (57%) of the agencies surveyed reported no women in Top Command positions and 88% of the agencies reported no women of color in their highest ranks. This is a clear indication that women continue to be largely excluded from the essential policymaking positions in policing.
- State agencies trail municipal and county agencies by a wide margin in hiring and promoting women. Specifically, state agencies report 6.8% sworn women law enforcement officers, which is significantly lower than the percentage reported by municipal agencies (14.5%) and county agencies (13.5%).
- Consent decrees mandating the hiring and/or promotion of women and/or minorities are a significant factor in the gains women have made in law enforcement. Of the twenty-five agencies with the highest percentage of sworn women, ten are subject to this type of consent decree. In sharp contrast, only four of the twenty-five agencies with the lowest percentage of sworn women are under such a consent decree.
- On average, in agencies *without* a consent decree mandating the hiring and/or promotion of women and/or minorities, women comprise 9.7% of sworn personnel, whereas those agencies with a consent decree in force average 14.0% women in their ranks. The percentage of women of color is 6.3% in agencies *without* a consent decree and 11.7% in agencies operating under a consent decree.

[1]For this study, the sworn law enforcement positions have been grouped as follows: Top Command includes Chiefs, Deputy/Assistant Chiefs, Commanders/Majors, and Captains, or their equivalent; Supervisory includes Lieutenants and Sergeants, or their equivalent; and Line Operation includes Detectives and Patrol Officers, or their equivalent.
SOURCE: National Center for Women & Policing (NCWP), Equality Denied: The Status of Women in Policing: 2000 (2001), p. 4.

The first American woman to serve as a sworn police officer was Lola Baldwin, who joined the Portland, Oregon, police department in 1905. Like the police matrons of the nineteenth century, she dealt primarily with women and children. In fact, she was originally granted police power so that she could take care of children at the Ohio State Exposition. Five years later, in Los Angeles in 1910, Alice Stebbin Wells became the first officially classified policewoman, assigned to "supervising and enforcing laws concerning dance halls, skating rinks, and theaters; monitoring billboard displays; locating missing persons; and maintaining a general bureau for women seeking advice on matters within the scope of the police department."[99]

Recruitment of Women.   More than 60 police departments had women on their staffs by 1919; 145 had women by 1925. But the police roles of the women remained restricted; women did not attain patrol officer status until the 1960s. There were no female sergeants until 1965, after a successful lawsuit against New York City.[100] With the resurgent drive for women's rights in the late 1960s and early 1970s and the passage of the 1972 Equal Employment Opportunity Act, many departments began to recruit women. Others resisted. Serious obstacles and stereotypes had to be overcome: that women were physically weak, irrational, and illogical; that they lacked the toughness to work on the streets. Some critics argued that the association of female with male officers would cause complications in both job and family life.

By 1980 the number of policewomen was still low—less than 4 percent of all officers. By early 2000s that proportion had more than tripled. Most recent surveys of personnel practices have found that eligibility criteria and mechanisms used to recruit, screen, and select candidates have changed dramatically, thus enlarging the pool of eligible women. (Figure 6.6).

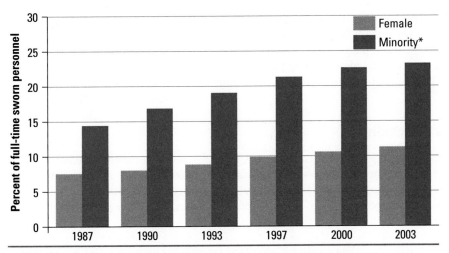

FIGURE 6.6   Female and Minority Local Police Officers, 1987–2003

*Includes blacks or African Americans, Hispanics or Latinos, Asians, Native Hawaiians or other Pacific Islanders, American Indians, Alaska Natives, and any other racial or ethnic minority.

SOURCE: Matthew J. Hickman and Brian A. Reeves, *Local Police Departments, 2003* (U.S. Department of Justice, Bureau of Justice Statistics: Washington, DC, 2006), p. 7.

The Police Subculture

Police officers stick together when they work the streets because of the constant stress and anxiety that go with the job. These working conditions, plus daily interaction with an often hostile public, combine to produce a set of norms and values that govern police behavior. This is called a **police subculture.**[101]

Socialization of New Recruits

Recruits learn the norms of the subculture during training and in the field.

> On his first day as a policeman a rookie may capture an armed felon, be cracked on the head with a rock, be offered sexual favors, free food, or money; he may be confronted by a naked woman, screaming hysterically, or a belligerent drunk who outweighs him by 50 pounds; or if he begins on "last out," he may spend the entire tour trying to fight off the desire to sleep. He has no control over what he will learn first, and when he will learn it. . . . Regardless of what occurs, he is obliged to be immediately what he has chosen to become, although his colleagues know he has only the vaguest appreciation of what that is.[102]

All states have a Police Officer Standards and Training (POST) commission that sets mandatory minimum requirements for training, although there is a great deal of difference among the states. Some states mandate sixteen weeks of training; others mandate three weeks. Depending on the length of the time, training programs range from basic training (handling of weapons) to academic courses.[103]

The process of socialization into the culture begins as soon as new recruits enter the academy. They get to know not only the formal rules of policing but also the informal norms a person must observe to be accepted into the group. They learn very quickly that loyalty—the obligation to support another officer—is the first priority. Respect for police authority, honor, individualism, and group solidarity also rank high. But there is much more to policing than what is learned at the academy.

In 1972 a police recruit from the San Jose, California, police department negligently operated a police car, causing an accident in which a passenger in the car was killed and the officer received serious injuries. A follow-up investigation demonstrated serious inadequacies in the department's training program. In 1972—the year of the accident—San Jose

police subculture
Set of norms and values that govern police behavior, brought about by stressful working conditions plus daily interaction with an often hostile public.

initiated what appears to be the earliest Field Training Program.[104] After graduation from the Police Academy, field training officers teach rookies that police work on the street may be quite different from police work learned in the classroom. According to one Illinois police department commander: "It was not unheard of for the experienced officers to tell the rookie, 'Forget what you learned in the academy, kid. I'll show you how it's done on the street.'"[105]

The Police Personality

In the same way doctors, janitors, lawyers, and industrial workers develop unique ways of looking at, and responding to, their work environment, so too do police officers. This effect of work on a person's outlook on the world is called the **working personality.**[106] The working personality of the police officer is molded by two elements of the police role: danger and authority.

working personality
Effect of police work on an officer's outlook on the world. Danger and authority are important factors.

Danger and Authority.   Police officers are often viewed as suspicious and authoritarian. Police work is potentially dangerous, so officers need to be constantly aware of what is happening around them. At the academy they are warned about what happens to officers who are too trusting. They learn about the many officers who have died in the line of duty because they did not exercise proper caution. On the street they need to stay alert for signals that crimes may be in progress: an unfamiliar noise, someone "checking into" an alleyway, a secret exchange of goods. Under these conditions, it would be surprising if officers did *not* become suspicious.

The working environment also demands that officers gain immediate control of potentially dangerous situations. They are routinely called on to demonstrate authority. Uniforms, badges, nightsticks, and guns signify authority—but officers soon learn that this authority is often challenged by a hostile public. Public hostility, coupled with other factors—a belief that courts are too lenient on criminals; the realization that it is often wiser for an officer to "look the other way" if he or she becomes aware of corrupt practices among peers on the force; and an awareness of the part that favoritism may play in promotions—leads to yet another trait that characterizes the police officer's working personality: cynicism.

Cynicism.   In the classic study of 220 New York City police officers, Professor Arthur Niederhoffer, himself a former police officer, found that 80 percent of the new recruits believed that the department was a smoothly operating, effective organization. Within a couple of months on the job, fewer than one-third still held that belief. They had become cynical about police work, supervisors, and the operating policies of the department. Moreover, cynicism increased with length of service and among the more highly educated who were not promoted.[107]

Styles of Policing

There are many styles of policing. One expert presents four types: the "tough cop," the "problem solver," the "rule applier," and the "crime-fighter."[108] Another distinguishes between "street cops" (who are attracted to job security and benefits, good salary, and so forth), "action seekers" (who focus on the excitement of crime-fighting), and "middle-class mobiles" (who enjoy the professional status of policing and the opportunity for upward mobility).[109] Los Angeles Police Department officers use the term "hardchargers" to describe many of their fellow officers who become "police warriors."[110] They willingly rush into dangerous situations, volunteer for high-risk assignments, enjoy displaying great courage, and proudly recount stories of their "heroic" actions. Aggressive and militaristic, they are labeled "ghetto fighters" and victims of the "John Wayne syndrome."

Whatever style police officers may prefer, experts agree that officers should be "generalists" who can readily adapt to all aspects of their role as a police officer. Their responses vary between situations and in like situations, at different times.

Stress

Crime and crime-fighting have always captured the imagination, and the media have always capitalized on the heroic crime-fighter. TV networks offer reality-based police shows in prime time. The emphasis in these shows is on reality, action, excitement, and good guys versus bad guys.

Flying bullets are in fact a rare event during the ordinary shift. But other stresses are more pervasive: danger, boredom, the negative attitudes of citizens, unfavorable press, threats of civil suits, departmental rules, frustration with court processing, anger over the early release of offenders, and daily exposure to a range of human tragedies. Police officers' personal lives are disrupted by irregular working hours and regular rotation through different shifts. These days, they fear increasing exposure to serious diseases, such as hepatitis B, tuberculosis, and acquired immune deficiency syndrome (AIDS). Encounters with broken glass, the jagged metal of wrecked cars, knives, razor blades, hypodermic needles, and attacks (including bites) from angry suspects are not uncommon at crime scenes. Officers are constantly aware of the dangers. For example, at a Washington, DC, demonstration, officers used yellow gloves to handle demonstrators, claiming that they were taking precautions in case the protest became violent.

POLICE POST-TRAUMATIC STRESS[1]

I am a (10 plus)-year police veteran and (30 plus)-years of age. I have become seriously concerned with some of the events that have been taking place in my life for the past two years. I have started having nightmares frequently and have great difficulty going to sleep at night. There is always a feeling of uneasiness at night, and I have started to develop some unnatural habits associated with these uneasy feelings. At the slightest sound, I have to get out of the bed and check every room in the house.

I have two children who live with me and my wife and I have gotten to the point that I almost always make them come into my room at night because of the feelings I have. If I am the first one in the house to go to sleep, I am OK, but otherwise, the feelings surface about midnight. I usually end up passing out somewhere between 3 and 5 A.M. I get up for work at 7 A.M. and this has started causing me a great deal of problems in my job. I often find myself in a trance thinking about traumatic events that have taken place in my career and always find myself in a very disheartened state afterward. During the recollection of these events, I often experience a shortness of breath and fear. I feel sad often and one specific event makes me feel very guilty. I know that I could have stopped a murder if I had taken other steps at the time of this incident. I often think about things while driving and end up going in the wrong direction before I realize where I am at.

Certain events that I have experienced cause me a great deal of emotional distress when I think or communicate about them. My hands are shaking here at 1:06 A.M. as I write this letter. I have recently found myself to be very irritable, and my wife and I often argue because I don't want to go to social gatherings with her. I am not being antisocial; I just don't like to be around people. I just like being with my kids and taking care of them. I feel bad about some things that are happening to me. My daughter came into my room four nights ago and kissed me on the cheek while I was sleeping. I jumped and scared her to death. My wife came to bed one night and when she walked up to the bed, I drew my fist back to hit her. I get up all hours of the night and check the house over and over. I don't even know what I am looking for. I was asleep about a month ago, and I just knew that someone had fired a gun in my living room. I hear people pound on my door in the middle of the night, when in fact there was never anyone there to my knowledge. One night I got up out of the bed and got my gun. I was about half-asleep. I don't know what I was looking for, but on my way through the house, I cocked my weapon. On the way through the house, the .357 discharged and shot a hole through my floor.

(continued)

> Some of the incidents that I remember the most seem vague. I remember every aspect of a shooting where I held the victim as he died. I can't remember what he looked like. We do not have counselors to speak to about these things and I feel that the average doctor would not be able to understand what I am talking about. I know I need help, but I have dealt with it for the past two years. It is getting harder to deal with.

[1]Hal Brown, "The Effects of Post Traumatic Stress Disorder (PTSD) on the Officer and the Family" (available at http://www.geocities.com/~halbrown/ptsd-family.html).

Additional stress factors are emerging. Community policing, with its many benefits, has nevertheless proven stressful to some officers. Community police officers are sometimes looked down on by coworkers as not doing "real police work"; others find that supervisors' high expectation that they can solve community problems results in fast burnout. Another stress factor is the increasing negative publicity and lawsuits (civil and criminal) that have followed in the wake of the Rodney King beating in Los Angeles and the fire at the Branch Davidians' Waco compound in Texas. Many believe that the constant media emphasis on what is "politically correct" interferes with doing legitimate police work. Finally, the prime perk of job security has been changed by budget cuts, promotional freezing, and downsizing of departments.[111]

Among the many factors contributing to stress among officers, none is as important as the constant threat of danger, including the threat of serious bodily injury or even death.

The number of line-of-duty deaths had been decreasing for many years—until 2001. Lower crime rates, improved bulletproof vests, and more restrictive deadly force policies had a definite effect on the number of officers killed in the line of duty. But, as Table 6.7 shows, the terrorist attacks on New York took their toll.

The threat of injury or death is an ever-present source of stress for police officers.

TABLE 6.7
Line of Duty Deaths, 2006–2007

2007 Total Line of Duty Deaths: 134			
Accidental:	1	Gunfire (Accidental):	3
Aircraft accident:	3	Heart attack:	5
Animal related:	1	Heat exhaustion:	1
Automobile accident:	34	Motorcycle accident:	5
Boating accident:	1	Struck by vehicle:	5
Bomb:	2	Vehicle pursuit:	6
Drowned:	3	Vehicular assault:	6
Exposure to toxins:	1	Weather/Natural disaster:	2
Gunfire:	55		

2006 Total Line of Duty Deaths: 146			
9/11 related illness:	1	Gunfire (Accidental):	3
Aircraft accident:	3	Heart attack:	11
Assault:	2	Motorcycle accident:	8
Automobile accident:	35	Stabbed:	1
Bomb:	1	Struck by vehicle:	11
Duty related illness:	1	Vehicle pursuit:	3
Gunfire:	49	Vehicular assault:	17

SOURCE: Officer Down Memorial Page, Statistics for 2007 and 2006, http://www.odmp.org/year.php?=2007; http://www.odmp.org/year.php?year=2006.

Behind the Blue Curtain

Two other characteristics of the police subculture are solidarity and isolation.

> Hackensack, New Jersey, Jan. 31—The manslaughter trial of a Teaneck police officer was thrown into an uproar today for the second time in two weeks when a former New York City officer who was paralyzed by a 15-year-old gunman's bullet was wheeled into the courtroom while the defendant was being cross-examined.[112]

Officer Gary Spath, thirty-one, was on trial for the manslaughter (by recklessness) of sixteen-year-old Phillip Pannell. Spath testified that he had shot and killed the boy as the boy reached into his jacket pocket. In a show of solidarity for Officer Spath, Steven McDonald, paralyzed from the neck down, was brought into the courtroom in an elaborate wheelchair equipped with a life-support system and chin-operated controls. McDonald, a thirty-four-year-old former New York City officer, was shot in the neck in Central Park in 1986 by a teenager he believed was stealing a bike. Similarly, in March 1999, hundreds of fellow police officers demonstrated in support of four of their colleagues indicted for the murder of a suspect (the Diallo Case), seeking to counteract a civil rights demonstration against the New York police department.

One of the primary reasons for the existence of a subculture that is characterized by very strong in-group ties, loyalty, secrecy, and isolation is the nature of police work.[113] Officers often view the external community as hostile and threatening.[114] They are caught in a bind: The job calls for them to discipline the people they serve, and they are allowed to use force to do it. Given the nature of their assignment, citizen complaints about threats to their civil liberties are often perceived by police as a challenge to their authority.

The uniform also isolates officers. Easily recognizable, they are constantly approached on the beat by people who know what is going on (door attendants, bartenders, servers) or who want to complain. When they are off duty, police officers also tend to isolate themselves from the community; they spend most of their time with other officers and their families.[115] Shared life among fellow officers has many advantages, including good communication, mutual support and respect, and shared pride. Nevertheless, all in all there is something that separates the society of the police from the rest of the community. This screen is called the **blue curtain.**[116]

Corruption

In the early 1970s, in the course of their work New York City police lieutenant David Durk and his partner Detective Frank Serpico discovered massive corruption among fellow officers and superiors. Durk and Serpico collected the evidence and reported it to higher authorities within the department. Neither there nor at the highest level of the department was any action taken. They ultimately reported their findings directly to the mayor. Still, nothing happened. In frustration, they released the information to the press. Durk and Serpico were attacked by other officers for "dirtying their own nest," "washing dirty laundry in public," and "tarnishing their shields." The result of their revelations was the creation of the Knapp Commission (1969–1972). Initiated by the mayor of New York City, this commission unraveled the existing police corruption in the city and recommended measures to avoid it in the future.[117]

The Range of Corrupt Activities

The term *corruption* covers a wide range of conduct. The Knapp Commission itself distinguished (in typical police jargon) between **meat eaters,** who solicit bribes or actually cooperate with criminals for personal gain, and **grass eaters,** who accept payoffs for rendering police services or for looking the other way when action is called for. The commission found a distinct pattern of corrupt activities. Officers assigned to enforce gambling and vice laws routinely collected graft payments of up to $3,500 a month from each location. Officers

blue curtain
Screen that separates police from civilians in society; isolation of police who spend time only with other police officers and their families.

meat eaters
Officers who solicit bribes or cooperate with criminals for personal gain.

grass eaters
Officers who accept payoffs for rendering police services or for looking the other way when action is called for.

received shares of $300 to $1,500 a month. Those higher in rank—supervisors, sergeants, and lieutenants—received more. New officers had to wait two months before their payoffs could begin. Uniformed officers received much less than plainclothes officers. The payoffs came from bars, construction sites, grocery stores, after-hour clubs, motorists (for traffic violations), prostitutes, parking lot operators, and others.[118]

The most frequent corrupt activity involves receiving gratuities, such as free meals, goods, or services. Business owners often offer gratuities in return for favors, such as extra patrol coverage of the premises. While the practice may appear harmless, it can lead to active solicitation of favors on the part of the officer for his or her service (extortion).

Bribes involve offering money to the police to ensure that they do not enforce the law. (See Figure 6.7.) Drivers, for instance, may use this technique to avoid getting

bribes

Offers of money, goods, or services to police to ensure that they do not enforce the law.

Case 1.	A police officer runs his [or her] own private business in which he sells and installs security devices, such as alarms, special locks, etc. He does this work during his off-duty hours.
Case 2.	A police officer routinely accepts free meals, cigarettes, and other items of small value from merchants on his beat. He does not solicit these gifts and is careful not to abuse the generosity of those who give gifts to him.
Case 3.	A police officer stops a motorist for speeding. The officer agrees to accept a personal gift of half of the amount of the fine in exchange for not issuing a citation.
Case 4.	A police officer is widely liked in the community, and on holidays local merchants and restaurant and bar owners show their appreciation for his attention by giving him gifts of food and liquor.
Case 5.	A police officer discovers a burglary of a jewelry shop. The display cases are smashed, and it is obvious that many items have been taken. While searching the shop, he takes a watch, worth about two days' pay for that officer. He reports that the watch had been stolen during the burglary.
Case 6.	A police officer has a private arrangement with a local auto body shop to refer the owners of cars damaged in accidents to the shop. In exchange for each referral, he receives payment of 5 percent of the repair bill from the shop owner.
Case 7.	A police officer, who happens to be a very good auto mechanic, is scheduled to work during coming holidays. A supervisor offers to give him these days off, if he agrees to tune up his supervisor's personal car. Evaluate the *supervisor's* behavior.
Case 8.	At 2:00 a.m., a police officer, who is on duty, is driving his patrol car on a deserted road. He sees a vehicle that has been driven off the road and is stuck in a ditch. He approaches the vehicle and observes that the driver is not hurt but is obviously intoxicated. He also finds that the driver is a police officer. Instead of reporting this accident and offense, he transports the driver to his home.
Case 9.	A police officer finds a bar on his beat that is still serving drinks a half-hour past its legal closing time. Instead of reporting this violation, the police officer agrees to accept a couple of free drinks from the owner.
Case 10.	Two police officers on foot patrol surprise a man who is attempting to break into an automobile. The man flees. They chase him for about two blocks before apprehending him by tackling him and wrestling him to the ground. After he is under control, both officers punch him a couple of times in the stomach as punishment for fleeing and resisting.
Case 11.	A police officer finds a wallet in a parking lot. It contains an amount of money equivalent to a full day's pay for that officer. He reports the wallet as lost property but keeps the money for himself.

FIGURE 6.7   *Case Scenarios*

SOURCE: From Carl B. Klockars, Sanja Kutnjak Ivkovich, William E. Harver, and Maria R. Haberfeld, "The Measurement of Police Integrity" (Washington, DC: National Institute of Justice, May 2000), p. 4.

traffic violations. Business owners may bribe officers to "overlook" double-parked delivery trucks. Some bribes are given for selling information about criminal investigations, for destroying evidence, or for alerting testimony of witnesses. More serious corruption stems from bribes offered on a regular basis— guarantees that the police will ignore various gambling, narcotics, or prostitution of-fenses. In 1998, twenty-one officers were implicated in a sex scandal in the Times Square area of New York City. In exchange for protecting the illegal businesses, officers, in uniform and while on duty, would relax, make personal calls, have free sex, and even hold parties. The brothel's

madam was so concerned about the frequency of these visits that she made her own apartment available to them as a "coop" (police slang for a place to hide during working hours).[119]

The 70th Precinct became the focus point of civil rights protests with the torture of Abner Louima by police officers.

Acts of theft and burglary may be isolated acts by lone officers (e.g., taking money from someone, such as an arrestee who is drunk) or well-planned acts by groups of officers. In Chicago, Denver, and Omaha, several officers formed burglary rings composed of those who committed the burglaries and those who patrolled the neighborhood to cover for them. Another not uncommon corrupt practice is stealing money or property from departmental property rooms.

Despite the efforts of the Knapp Commission in 1972 and the National Advisory Commission on Criminal Justice Standards and Goals in 1973, corruption continues. According to experts, corruption may be even more serious now than it was in the 1970s.[120]

One of the more remarkable aspects of the expansion of the drug trade has been its effect on criminal justice officials. Miami police officer Armando Garcia made it to the FBI Ten Most Wanted poster when he was accused of acting in concert with other officers to "rip off" drug dealers, steal two 400-kilogram shipments of cocaine, and then push the drug dealers overboard. The illicit drug market poses a potential for corruption among officers, in general, and especially among those officers who abuse drugs. Many police departments have instituted drug-testing programs. The issue of drug testing is complex, and cases are still being resolved in the courts. In *Turner v. Fraternal Order of Police* (1985), drug testing, based on a reasonable suspicion that drug use is occurring, was supported by the District of Columbia Court of Appeals. In 1986 the New York State Supreme Court banned random drug testing in *Caruso v. Benjamin Ward, Police Commissioner.* Of major consideration in the drug-testing issue is its threat to the personal rights and dignity of individuals.[121]

FBI Ten Most Wanted poster, September 1990. Miami police officer Armando Garcia, accused of acting in concert with other officers to "rip off" drug dealers, steal two 400-kilogram shipments of cocaine, and then push the drug dealers overboard. Garcia was taken into custody by the FBI on January 25, 1994.

Controlling Corruption

Over half of the nation's fifty largest cities have **civilian police review boards** to provide external control. Although they function well in some municipalities, police departments rely primarily on internal controls to police themselves. If internal controls are to be effective, experts argue, law enforcement professionals need to change their thinking about self-policing.

civilian police review boards
External control mechanism composed of persons usually from outside the police department.

In the past, departmental whistleblowers were regarded with derision. The claim is made that this attitude needs to be replaced by one of intolerance toward those who abuse the public trust and the power of the shield by engaging in abuses, corruption, and other forms of criminality. Studies indicate, however, that officers are usually unwilling to report misconduct by fellow officers. Robert Daley's *Prince of the City* describes the emotional struggle the New York City Detective Robert Leuci went through when he had to testify against his corrupt partners.[122]

Half a century ago, O. W. Wilson argued that even a free cup of coffee could put police officers in a compromising position. Several decades later, Patrick Murphy, former police commissioner of New York City, made it clear to his officers: "Except for your paycheck there is no such thing as a clean buck."[123] Experts predict that increased professionalism of police forces will become the major factor in corruption control.

Review

Since police forces are relatively rigidly constructed hierarchies, following the military model, police departments have been criticized for separating themselves from the community. During the last two decades, administrators have been searching for more effective and acceptable forms of organizational functioning. Such innovations as community policing have been tried. There are three categories of police functions. The service function is as old as American policing itself. The soup kitchens and night shelters that the police operated a century or more ago have their modern counterparts. The police, as government's uniformed front-line service, are called on by people in trouble—people who are homeless, injured, sick, and mentally ill.

The order maintenance function is traditionally performed through patrolling and, more recently, by innovative improvements in, and substitutes for, traditional patrols. These include preventive patrol, differential response techniques, directed patrol, saturation patrol, and aggressive patrol. Not all of these have proved effective, and some raise civil liberties issues. To counteract community objections, community policing and problem-oriented policing were instituted.

The best-known police function is law enforcement. Responding to a crime call and readying a case for prosecution are the most traditional law enforcement functions. They are reactive, a response to a crime having been observed or reported. Modern law enforcement functions, however, include a variety of proactive or aggressive means of dealing with crime. The new approaches, while enthusiastically embraced by some departments, are not necessarily cost beneficial. Some are particularly controversial: for example, the use of crackdowns, roadblocks (and sobriety checkpoints), decoys, sting operations, undercover work, the reliance on informants, and zero tolerance policing.

How does one become a police officer? What qualifications are typically required for the job? Until the 1960s, policing had been a largely male occupation. The equal rights movement opened police careers to minorities and women. Their numbers have been increasing steadily, yet the battle for full acceptance has not yet been won.

The police have developed and live in their own subculture, marked by loyalty to each other, respect for police authority, honor, and group solidarity. The police subculture is separated from the general culture by what some have called the blue curtain. All officers have their own style of policing: tough cop, problem-solver, rule applier, crime-fighter. Officers are constantly subjected to levels of stress not experienced in other professions. Such stress produces personal and family problems, which many departments now try to meet with counseling and other services. The authority and power of police officers subject them to the temptation of abuse of power through corruption. Some officers yield, especially those assigned to drug law enforcement. Effective control of police corruption remains a problem.

Police unions, at one time nonexistent, indeed outlawed, now have become important in collective bargaining, criminal justice legislation, and improving the lot of those in this very difficult profession.

Thinking Critically about Criminal Justice

1. Many community groups are concerned about the apparent move in some jurisdictions to a type of policing that focuses on "quality of life" issues. Should these groups be concerned? What dangers, if any, are there to civil rights if police departments adopt a strategy addressing quality of life issues?

2. Is it a good use of taxpayers' money to increase the number of police "on the streets" (one of the goals of the 1994 Crime Bill)? How could the money be spent in other ways to increase police efficiency or effectiveness?

3. Evaluations consistently show that some of the most popular programs, such as DARE and Neighborhood Watch, have no impact on crime. Why do so many police departments continue to support these programs?

4. Recruitment of women and minorities was meant to overcome inequality and segregation within the police force. In police departments, however, there are gender, racial, and ethnic-based societies. Do these societies have the reverse effect of driving groups apart? How can we justify membership in such societies?

5. The mayor and the police commissioner of a major city have come under attack for deteriorating police/community relations. Could improved recruitment practices help the situation? How?

Internet Connection

Note: While all of the URLs listed were current as of the printing of this book, these sites often change. Please check our website (http://www.mhhe.com/socscience/crimjustice/adlercj) for updates.

Municipal police departments are often complex, bureaucratic organizations. Consider the extensive structure of the Los Angeles Police Department (**http://www.lapdonline org/**). How does this compare with the organization of the police department in your city or town? Is it as specialized? What role does the FBI play in combating police corruption? See: **http://www.fbi.gov/press-rel/police.htm**

Notes

1. Egon Bittner, "The Functions of Police in Modern Society," in *Thinking About Police*, ed. Carl B. Klockars and Stephen D. Mastrofski (NY: McGraw-Hill, 1991), pp. 44, 45.

2. Albert J. Reiss, Jr., "Shaping and Serving the Community: The Role of the Police Chief Executive," in *Police Leadership in America: Crisis and Opportunity*, ed. William A. Geller (Chicago and NY: American Bar Foundation, 1985), pp. 3–19. See also Dennis Jay Kenney, "Strategic Approaches in Police Management: Issues and Perspectives," ed. L. Hoover (Washington, DC: Police Executive Research Forum, 1992).

3. James Q. Wilson, *Varieties of Police Behavior: The Management of Law and Order in Eight Communities* (Cambridge, MA: Harvard University Press, 1968).

4. Ibid.

5. Ibid.

6. William G. Archambeault and Charles R. Fenwick, "A Comparative Analysis of Japanese and American Police Organizational Management Models: The Evolution of a Military Bureaucracy to a Theory Z Organization," in *Police and Law Enforcement* 4, ed. Daniel B. Kennedy and Robert J. Homant (NY: AMS Press, 1987), p. 151.

7. Samuel Walker, *The Police in America: An Introduction*, 2nd ed. (NY: McGraw-Hill, 1992), p. 359.

8. Robert C. Wadman and Robert K. Olson, *Community Wellness: A New Theory of Policing* (Washington, DC: Police Executive Research Forum, 1990). See also Mark H. Moore, "Problem-Solving and Community Policing," in *Crime and Justice: A Review of Research* 15, ed. M. Tonry and N. Morris (Chicago: University of Chicago Press, 1992), pp. 99–158.

9. Gary W. Cordner and Robert C. Trojanowicz, "Patrol," in *What Works in Policing? Operations and Administration Examined*, ed. Gary W. Cordner and Donna C. Hale (Highland Heights, KY, and Cincinnati, OH: Academy of Criminal Justice Sciences and Anderson, 1992), p. 11.

10. V. M. del Buono, "Policing within the Concept of Community Policing," in *Policing the Future*, ed. A. B. Hoogenboom, M. J. Meiboom, D. C. M. Schoneveld, and J. W. M. Stoop (The Hague, the Netherlands: Kluwer Law International, 1997), p. 23.

11. Jerome H. Skolnick and David H. Bayley, *Community Policing: Issues and Practices Around the World* (Washington, DC: National Institute of Justice, May 1988).

12. Lawrence W. Sherman, "Policing for Crime Prevention," in *Preventing Crime: What Works, What Doesn't, What's Promising* (Washington, DC: U.S. Department of Justice, Office of Justice Programs 1997), pp. 8–25, 8–28.

13. See Office of Community Oriented Policing Services, U.S. Department of Justice, http://www.cops.usdoj.gov. See also Robert Trojanowicz and Hazel Hardin, *The Status of Contemporary Community Policing Programs* (Ann Arbor, MI: National Neighborhood Foot Patrol Center, Michigan State University, 1985).

14. Jerome H. Skolnick and David H. Bayley, *The New Blue Line: Police Innovation in Six American Cities* (NY: Free Press, 1986). See also Lee P. Brown, "Neighborhood-Oriented Policing," *American Journal of Police* 9 (1990), pp. 197–207; and Michael E. Buerger, "Problems of Redefining Police and Community," in *Police Innovation and Control of the Police*, ed. David Weisburd and Craig Uchida (NY: Springer Verlag, 1993).

15. George James, "Having to Sell as New an Old Idea: The Cop on the Beat," *The New York Times*, October 10, 1991, pp. B1, B7.

16. Jack Greene and Ralph Taylor, "Community-Based Policing and Foot Patrol: Issues of Theory and Evaluation," in *Community Policing, Rhetoric or Reality*, ed. Jack R. Greene and Stephen Mastrofski (NY: Praeger, 1988).

17. See David H. Bayley, "Community Policing: A Report from the Devil's Advocate," in *Community Policing,* ed. Greene and Mastrofski, pp. 225–237.

18. N. R. Kleinfeld, "Bias Crimes Hold Steady, but Leave Many Scars," *The New York Times,* January 27, 1992, pp. B1, B2.

19 James R. Davis, "A Comparison of Attitudes Toward the New York City Police," *Journal of Police Science and Administration* 17 (1990), pp. 233–243.

20. See Earl M. Sweeney, *The Public and the Police: A Partnership in Protection* (Springfield, IL: Charles C. Thomas, 1982).

21. Thomas A. Johnson, Gordon E. Misner, and Lee P. Brown, *The Police and Society: An Environment for Collaboration and Confrontation* (Englewood Cliffs, NJ: Prentice Hall, 1981).

22. Sherman, "Policing for Crime Prevention," pp. 8–25, 8–28.

23. Jerome H. Skolnick and Candace McCoy, "Police Accountability and the Media," in *Police Leadership in America,* ed. William A. Geller, pp. 102–135.

24. Ibid. See also Gerald W. Garner, *The Police Meet the Press* (Springfield, IL: Charles C. Thomas, 1984).

25. John P. Kenney and Dan G. Pursuit, *Police Work with Juveniles and the Administration of Juvenile Justice,* 5th ed. (Springfield, IL: Charles C. Thomas, 1975).

26. Lisa D. Bastian and Bruce M. Taylor, *School Crime: A National Crime Victimization Survey Report* (Washington, DC: Bureau of Justice Statistics, 1991).

27. Denise C. Gottfredson, "School-Based Crime Prevention," in *Preventing Crime: What Works, What Doesn't.*

28. Lt. Lew Archer, Assistant Chief of the San Antonio, Texas, School District's Police Department, cited in Arthur G. Sharp, "Is DARE a Sacred Lamb?" *Law and Order* 46 (April 1998), pp. 42–47.

29. Eamon Clifford, "Taking a Bite Out of DARE: Why Not More Cops in Clown Suits?" *Law and Order* 46 (April 1998), p. 51.

30. Arthur G. Sharp, "Is DARE a Sacred Lamb?" *Law and Order* 46 (April 1998), pp. 42–47.

31. Gary T. Marx, "Commentary: Some Trends and Issues in Citizen Involvement in the Law Enforcement Process," *Crime and Delinquency* 35 (1989), pp. 500–519.

32. James Garofalo and Maureen McLeod, "The Structure and Operations of Neighborhood Watch Programs in the United States," *Crime and Delinquency* 35 (1989), pp. 326–344.

33. Martin Alan Greenberg, "Volunteer Police: The People's Choice," *The Police Chief* 58 (1991), pp. 42–44.

34. See Georgia Smith and Steven P. Lab, "Urban and Rural Attitudes Toward Participating in an Auxiliary Policing Crime Prevention Program," *Criminal Justice and Behavior* 18 (1991), pp. 202–216.

35. Susan Pennell, Christine Curtis, Joel Henderson, and Jeff Tayman, "Guardian Angels: A Unique Approach to Crime Prevention," *Crime and Delinquency* 35 (1989), pp. 378–400.

36. Dennis P. Rosenbaum, Arthur J. Lurigio, and Paul J. Lavrakas, "Enhancing Citizen Participation and Solving Serious Crime: A National Evaluation of Crime Stoppers Programs," *Crime and Delinquency* 35 (1989), pp. 401–420.

37. Scott A. Nelson, "Crime-Time Television," *FBI Law Enforcement Bulletin* 58 (1989), pp. 1–9.

38. Albert J. Reiss, Jr., *The Police and the Public* (New Haven, CT: Yale University Press, 1971), pp. 70–72. For a discussion of the homeless, see Candace McCoy, "Policing the Homeless," *Criminal Law Bulletin* 22 (1986), pp. 263–274.

39. Cheryl L. Maxson, Margaret A. Little, and Malcolm W. Klein, "Police Response to Runaway and Missing Children: A Conceptual Framework for Research and Policy," *Crime and Delinquency* 34 (1988), pp. 84–102.

40. John A. Webster, "Police Task and Time Study," *Journal of Criminal Law, Criminology, and Police Science* 61 (1970), pp. 94–100.

41. J. Robert Lilly, "What Are the Police Now Doing?" *Journal of Police Science and Administration* 6 (1978), pp. 51–60.

42. Theodore M. Hammett, *AIDS and the Law Enforcement Officer: Concerns and Policy Responses* (Washington, DC: U.S. Department of Justice, 1987).

43. Daniel B. Kennedy, Robert J. Homant, and George L. Emery, "AIDS Concerns Among Crime Scene Investigators," *Journal of Police Science and Administration* 17 (1990), pp. 12–19.

44. *Year in Review 1995,* Monterey Park, CA: County of Los Angeles Sheriff's Department, 1996, p. 51.

45. Steven P. Lab, "Police Productivity: The Other Eighty Percent," *Journal of Police Science and Administration* 12 (1984), pp. 297–302. See also David H. Bayley and James Garofalo, "The Management of Violence by Police Patrol Officers," *Criminology* 27 (1989), pp. 1–25.

46. Gary W. Cordner, "Police on Patrol," in *Police and Policing: Contemporary Issues,* ed. Dennis J. Kenney (NY: Praeger, 1989), pp. 60–71.

47. Brian A. Reaves, *Police Departments in Large Cities, 1987* (Washington, DC: Bureau of Justice Statistics, 1989).

48. Lee A. Daniels, "How Many Does It Take to Staff a Squad Car?" *The New York Times,* December 8, 1991, p. 18.

49. See Police Foundation, *The Newark Foot Patrol Experiment* (Washington, DC: Author: 1981).

50. See Robert C. Trojanowicz, "An Evaluation of a Neighborhood Foot Patrol Program," *Journal of Police Science and Administration* 11 (1983), pp. 410–419.

51. Carl Ent, "Bicycle Patrol: A Community Policing Alternative," *The Police Chief* 58 (1991), pp. 58–59.

52. William Spelman and Dale K. Brown, *Calling the Police: Citizen Reporting of Serious Crime* (Washington, DC: National Institute of Justice, 1984).

53. See George L. Kelling, Tony Pate, Duane Dieckman, and Charles E. Brown, *The Kansas City Preventive Patrol Experiment: A Summary Report* (Washington, DC: Police Foundation, 1974).

54. Lawrence W. Sherman, *Evidence-Based Policing* (Washington, DC: Police Foundation, 1998).

55. J. Thomas McEwen, Edward F. Connors III, and Marcia I. Cohen, *Evaluation of the Differential Police Response Field Test* (Alexandria, VA: Research Management Associates, 1984).

56. Lawrence W. Sherman, Patrick R. Gartin, and Michael E. Buerger, "Hot Spots of Predatory Crime: Routine Activities and the Criminology of Place," *Criminology* 27 (1989), pp. 27–55.

57. Cordner and Trojanowicz, "Patrol."

58. John E. Eck and William Spelman, *Problem-Solving: Problem-Oriented Policing in Newport News* (Washington, DC: National Institute of Justice, 1988).

59. See Gary Cordner, "A Problem-Oriented Approach to Community-Oriented Policing," in *Community Policing,* ed. Greene and Mastrofski, pp. 135–152.

60. Lawrence W. Sherman, James W. Shaw, and Dennis P. Rogan, *The Kansas City Gun Experiment: Research in Brief* (Washington, DC: National Institute of Justice, 1995).

61. David M. Kennedy, Anne M. Piehl, and Anthony A. Braga, *Youth Gun Violence in Boston: Gun Markets, Serious Youth Offenders, and a Use Reduction Strategy* (Washington, DC: National Institute of Justice, 1996).

62. See Elizabeth M. Watson and William A. Young, "Criminal Investigation Trends," in *Issues in Policing: New Perspectives,* ed. John W. Bizzack (Lexington, KY: Autumn Press, 1992).

63. Reiss, *The Police and the Public,* p. 104.

64. For an example of the importance of the police report in the success of prosecutions, see John R. Snortum, Paul R. Riva, Dale E. Berger, and Thomas W. Mangione, "Police Documentation of Drunk-Driving Arrests: Jury Verdicts and Guilty Pleas as a Function of Quantity and Quality of Evidence," *Journal of Criminal Justice* 18 (1990), pp. 99–116.

65. Peter W. Greenwood, Jan M. Chaiken, Joan Petersilia, and Linda Prusoff, *The Criminal Justice Investigation Process, vol. 3: Observation and Analysis* (Santa Monica, CA: Rand Corporation, 1975).

66. Wayne W. Bennett and Karen M. Hess, *Criminal Investigation* (St. Paul, MN: West, 1981).

67. Some commentators have questioned the integrity of the administration's commitment to this war. Others have discussed the war in political terms, questioning the motivations of its supporters.

68. *Crime in the United States 1997* (Washington, DC: U.S. Department of Justice, Bureau of Justice Statistics, 1998), p. 222.

69. Christopher J. Mumola, *Substance Abuse and Treatment, State and Federal Prisoners, 1997* (Washington, DC: Bureau of Justice Statistics, January 1999).

70. See Jan Chaiken, Marcia Chaiken, and Clifford Karchmer, *Multijurisdictional Drug Law Enforcement Strategies: Reducing Supply and Demand* (Washington, DC: National Institute of Justice, 1990).

71. See Mark H. Moore, "Supply Reduction and Drug Law Enforcement," in *Drugs and Crime,* ed. Michael Tonry and James Q. Wilson (vol. 13 of *Crime and Justice,* ed. Michael Tonry and Norval Morris) (Chicago: University of Chicago Press, 1990), pp. 109–157. For a look at the domestic problem, see Ralph Weisheit, "The Intangible Rewards from Crime: The Case of Domestic Marijuana Cultivation," *Crime and Delinquency* 37 (1991), pp. 506–527. For the role of the military on the war on drugs, see Harry L. Marsh, "Law Enforcement, The Military and the War on Drugs: Is the Military Involvement in the War on Drugs Ethical?" *American Journal of Police* 10 (1991), pp. 61–75.

72. Mark A. R. Kleiman, "Crackdowns: The Effects of Intensive Enforcement of Retail Heroin Dealing," in *Street-Level Drug Enforcement: Examining the Issues,* ed. Marcia R. Chaiken (Washington, DC: National Institute of Justice, 1988), pp. 3–34.

73. David W. Hayeslip, Jr., and Deborah L. Weisel, "Local Level Drug Enforcement," in *What Works in Policing?* ed. Cordner and Hale, pp. 35–48.

74. Lynn Zimmer, "Proactive Policing Against Street-Level Drug Trafficking," *American Journal of Police* 9 (1990), pp. 43–74.

75. *Crime in the United States 1996* (Washington, DC: Department of Justice, Bureau of Justice Statistics, 1997), p. 280.

76. Thomas C. Castellano and Craig D. Uchida, "Local Drug Enforcement, Prosecutors and Case Attrition: Theoretical Perspectives for the Drug War," *American Journal of Police* 9 (1990), pp. 133–162.

77. *Thurman v. Torrington,* 596 F. Supp. 1521 (1985).

78. Eve S. Buzawa and Carl G. Buzawa, *Domestic Violence: The Criminal Justice Response* (Newbury Park, CA: Sage, 1990); J. David Hirschel, Ira W. Hutchinson, Charles W. Dean, and AnneMarie Mills, "Review Essay on the Law Enforcement Response to Spouse Abuse: Past, Present, and Future," *Justice Quarterly* 9 (1992), pp. 247–283.

79. J. David Hirschel and Ira W. Hutchinson III, "Female Spouse Abuse and the Police Response: The Charlotte, North Carolina Experiment," *Journal of Criminal Law and Criminology* 83 (1992), pp. 73–119.

80. G. A. Goolkasian, *Confronting Domestic Violence: A Guide for Criminal Justice Agencies,* for U.S. Department of Justice (Washington, DC: U.S. Government Printing Office, 1986).

81. Delbert S. Elliott, "Criminal Justice Procedures in Family Violence Crimes," in *Crime and Justice: An*

Annual Review of Research 11, ed. Michael Tonry and Norval Morris (Chicago: University of Chicago Press, 1989), pp. 427–480.

82. Ronald K. Breedlove, John W. Kennish, Donald M. Sandker, and Robert K. Sawtell, *Domestic Violence and the Police: Studies in Detroit and Kansas City* (Washington, DC: Police Foundation, 1977), pp. 22–33.

83. G. Marie Wilt and James D. Bannon, "Conflict-Motivated Homicides and Assaults in Detroit," in *Domestic Violence and the Police,* pp. 34–44.

84. See articles in Michael D. Laurence, John R. Snortum, and Franklin E. Zimring, eds., *Social Control of the Drinking Driver* (Chicago: University of Chicago Press, 1988).

85. Kleiman, "Crackdowns."

86. *Michigan v. Sitz,* 496 U.S. 444 (1990); and *Delaware v. Prousse,* 440 U.S. 648 (1979).

87. Gary T. Marx, "The New Police Undercover Work," *Urban Life* 8 (1990), pp. 399–446, reprinted in *Thinking About Police,* ed. Klockars and Mastrofski, pp. 242–243.

88. Robert H. Langworthy, "Do Stings Control Crime? An Evaluation of a Police Fencing Operation," *Justice Quarterly* 6 (1989), pp. 27–45.

89. *Sherman v. United States,* 356 U.S. 369 (1958).

90. Jerome Skolnick, *Justice without Trial: Law Enforcement in Democratic Society,* 2nd ed. (NY: Wiley, 1975). Also see Peter K. Manning, *The Narcs' Game: Organizational and Informational Limits on Drug Law Enforcement* (Cambridge, MA: MIT Press, 1980).

91. Jock Young, "Zero Tolerance: Back to the Future," in *Planning Safer Communities,* ed. Alan Marlow and John Pitts (Dorset, UK: Russell House Publishing, 1997), pp. 60–83.

92. Joseph D. McNamara, "Zero Tolerance, Infinite Repercussions," *News and Record,* November 9, 1997, pp. F1, F6.

93. David N. Falcone, Michael T. Charles, and Edward Wells, "A Study of Pursuits in Illinois," *The Police Chief* (July 1994), pp. 59–64.

94. Candice McCoy, "Affirmative Action in Police Organizations: Checklist for Supporting a Compelling State Interest," *Criminal Law Bulletin* 20 (1984), pp. 245–254.

95. Jack L. Kuykendall and David E. Burns, "The Black Police Officer: An Historical Perspective," *Journal of Contemporary Criminal Justice* 1 (1986), pp. 4–12.

96. Samuel Walker, *The Police in America: An Introduction,* 2nd ed. (NY: McGraw-Hill, 1992), pp. 246, 313.

97. National Advisory Commission on Criminal Justice Standards and Goals, *Report of the Commission* (Washington, DC: U.S. Government Printing Office, 1973), p. 329.

98. As quoted in Tom Seligson, "How Good Are Women Cops?" *Parade,* March 31, 1985, pp. 4–7.

99. Daniel J. Bell, "Policewomen: Myths and Reality," *Journal of Police Science and Administration* 10 (1982), pp. 112–120.

100. Samuel S. Janus, Cynthia Janus, Leslie K. Lord, and Thomas Power, "Women in Police Work—Annie Oakley or Little Orphan Annie?" *Police Studies* 11 (1988), pp. 124–127.

101. William A. Westley, *Violence and the Police: A Sociological Study of Law, Custom, and Morality* (Cambridge, MA: MIT Press, 1970), p. 11.

102. Jonathan Rubinstein, *City Police* (NY: Farrar, Straus, and Giroux, 1973), pp. 127–128.

103. Bruce L. Berg, "Who Should Teach Police: A Typology and Assessment of Police Academy Instructors," *American Journal of Police* 9 (1990), pp. 79–100.

104. Michael S. McCampbell, "Field Training for Police Officers: State of the Art," in *Critical Issues in Policing: Contemporary Readings,* ed. R. G. Dunham and G. P. Alpert (Prospect Heights, IL: Waveland, 1989), p. 111.

105. See James T. Haider, *Field Training Police Recruits: Developing, Improving and Operating a Field Training Program* (Springfield, IL: Charles C. Thomas, 1990), p. 3.

106. Jerome H. Skolnick, *Justice without Trial: Law Enforcement in Democratic Society* (NY: Wiley, 1966), p. 42.

107. Arthur Niederhoffer, *Behind the Shield* (Garden City, NY: Doubleday, 1967), pp. 216–220.

108. Susan O. White, "A Perspective on Police Professionalism," *Law and Society Review* 7 (1972), pp. 61–85.

109. James Leo Walsh, "Career Styles and Police Behavior," in *Police and Society,* ed. David H. Bayley (Beverly Hills, CA: Sage, 1977), pp. 149–167.

110. Steve Herbert, "Police Subculture Reconsidered," *Criminology* 36 (1998), pp. 343–369.

111. Peter Finn and Julie Esselman Tomz, *Developing a Law Enforcement Stress Program for Officers and Their Families,* National Institute of Justice (Washington, DC: U.S. Department of Justice, March 1997).

112. Robert Hanley, "Officer's Trial in Teaneck Is Disrupted," *The New York Times,* February 1, 1992, p. 23.

113. Michael K. Brown, *Working the Street* (NY: Sage, 1981), p. 82.

114. Albert Reiss, *The Police and the Public* (New Haven, CT: Yale University Press, 1971), p. 51. For juvenile attitudes, see Michael J. Leiber, Makesh K. Nalla, and Margaret Farnworth, "Explaining Juveniles' Attitudes Toward the Police," *Justice Quarterly* 15 (1998), pp. 151–174.

115. Margie T. Britz, "The Police Subculture and Occupational Socialization," *American Journal of Criminal Justice* 21 (1997), pp. 127–146.

116. Westley, *Violence and the Police,* p. 226.

117. *Knapp Commission Report on Police Corruption* (NY: George Braziller, 1973).

118. Harry W. More, *Special Topics in Policing* (Cincinnati, OH: Anderson, 1992), pp. 257, 258.

119. Dan Barry, "Police Used Brothel So Often, Madam Got Worried," *The New York Times,* July 18, 1998, pp. A1, B3.

120. Robert J. McCormack, "Confronting Police Corruption: Organizational Initiatives for Internal Control," in *Managing Police Corruption: International Perspectives,* ed. Richard H. Ward and Robert McCormack (Chicago: Office of International Criminal Justice, University of Illinois at Chicago, 1987), pp. 151–165.

121. *Police Officers for Equal Rights et. al. v. City of Columbus,* 644 F. Supp. 393 (S. D. Ohio, 1985); *In re Phil Caruso v. Benjamin Ward,* 133 Misc. 2d 544, 506 N. Y. S. 2d 789 (1986).

122. Robert Daley, *Prince of the City: The Story of a Cop Who Knew Too Much* (Boston: Houghton Mifflin, 1978).

123. Herman Goldstein, *Police Corruption: A Perspective on Its Nature and Control* (Washington, DC: Police Foundation, 1975), p. 29.

CHAPTER

7

The Rule of Law in Law Enforcement

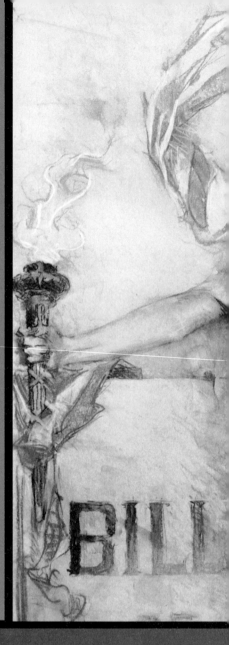

BILL

FREEDOM of SPEECH

FREEDOM of ASSEMB

Federal agents suspected that Danny Kyllo of Florence, Oregon, was growing marijuana in his home. Because growing marijuana indoors usually requires high-intensity lamps, agents used a thermal imager to scan Kyllo's home. Thermal imagers detect infrared radiation that is invisible to the naked eye. The scan of Kyllo's home took only a few minutes and was performed from the passenger seat of an agent's car across the street from the front of the house. The scan revealed that the roof over Kyllo's garage and a side wall were hotter than other parts of his home and that his home was warmer than other nearby homes. Agents concluded Kyllo was using heat lamps. Based on tips from informants, utility bills, and the thermal imaging, a federal magistrate issued a warrant to search Kyllo's home. The agents subsequently found an indoor growing operation involving more than 100 marijuana plants.

• Kyllo challenged the constitutionality of the search, claiming that it violated his Fourth Amendment rights against unreasonable searches and seizures. The case was decided by the United States Supreme Court in June 2001. Citing the sanctity of the home, and raising concerns with technology that reveals, or may potentially reveal, intimate details of a suspect's home, the Court found the agents' use of the thermal imaging device unconstitutional. Justice Scalia observed: "While it is certainly possible to conclude from the videotape of the thermal imaging that occurred in this case that no 'significant' compromise of the homeowner's privacy has occurred, we must take the long view, from the original meaning of the Fourth Amendment forward. . . . Where, as here, the Government uses a device that is not in general public use, to explore details of the home that would previously have been unknowable without physical intrusion, the surveillance is a 'search' and is presumptively unreasonable without a warrant."[1]

• The case of Mr. Kyllo is far from typical. Most searches and seizures do not amount to unreasonable invasions of privacy, just as most confessions elicited by police interrogation are not coerced and therefore not found by courts to have been involuntary. But the Kyllo case is important because it demonstrates the importance of placing limits on police conduct, especially in light of increasingly sophisticated technology. It reminds us that there is a rule of law and that it binds everyone, including those sworn to enforce it. Law is enforced within a context that sets definite boundaries, standards, and procedures. In this chapter we will focus on the police role in the law enforcement process. It is their job to uphold and enforce the law by preventing lawbreaking, responding to lawbreaking, and apprehending lawbreakers. But this does not mean that police can use any means they wish to prevent, fight, or solve crime. The Bill of Rights, part of the United States Constitution, curbs the police power of the state at all levels of government.

Criminal Justice under the Constitution

The story of how American criminal procedure was shaped by the Constitution is the focus of this chapter. It is an exciting story that shows the power of the courts to fashion and direct criminal justice procedures. It also shows how the courts can influence, shape, and sometimes constrain the role the police play performing their important functions.

Federal Criminal Justice: The Bill of Rights

The Bill of Rights was passed in 1791, but it had to wait a century to be awakened. What finally brought it to life was the U.S. Supreme Court. For over a hundred years, federal courts exercised little control over the procedures used in federal cases.[2] But this changed in 1897. In a case in which the voluntariness of a confession was challenged *(Bram v. United States)*, the U.S. Supreme Court ruled that extorting a confession violates the Fifth Amendment's privilege against self-incrimination.[3] From then on, the Bill of Rights set the outer limits of permissible (federal) police conduct in the federal criminal process.

State Criminal Justice: Selective Incorporation of the Bill of Rights

due process of law
According to the Fourteenth Amendment, a fundamental mandate that a person should not be deprived of life, liberty, or property without reasonable and lawful procedures.

selective incorporation
Supreme Court practice of incorporating the Bill of Rights selectively, by identifying federal rights that are "implicit in the concept of ordered liberty" and applying them to states through the Fourteenth Amendment's due process clause.

At the turn of the twentieth century, the Bill of Rights limited only the federal government. But the Fourteenth Amendment provides that no *state* shall "deprive any person of life, liberty, or property without due process of law." Many defense attorneys argued that **due process** includes such rights as protection against unreasonable searches and seizures (Fourth Amendment), freedom from self-incrimination (Fifth Amendment), or right to counsel (Sixth Amendment). The U.S. Supreme Court rejected these arguments until 1925. In that year, in the landmark case *Gitlow v. New York*,[4] the Supreme Court ruled that the First Amendment rights to freedom of speech and of the press are fundamental personal rights and liberties, guaranteed by the due process clause of the Fourteenth Amendment to the U.S. Constitution.[5] This was a momentous ruling: Due process, guaranteed by the Fourteenth Amendment to all citizens in both state and federal cases, *does* include some of the guarantees of the Bill of Rights. The implications were far-reaching: Potentially all of the due process guarantees in criminal justice that heretofore had obligated only the federal government might now also obligate the states.

Twelve years after *Gitlow*, in *Palko v. Connecticut* (1937),[6] the Supreme Court ruled that the Fourteenth Amendment prohibits all state action that "offends some principle of justice so rooted in the traditions and conscience of our people as to be ranked as fundamental."[7] With this case, the Court agreed to incorporate the Bill of Rights selectively by identifying federal rights that were "implicit in the concept of ordered liberty" and applying them to the states through the Fourteenth Amendment's due process clause. This was called the doctrine of **selective incorporation.** As Table 7.1 illustrates, most of the provisions in the

	Year	Right	Case
TAFT Court	1925	Freedom of speech.	*Gitlow v. New York,* 268 U.S. 652, 45 S. Ct. 625.
HUGHES Court	1931	Freedom of the press.	*Near v. Minnesota,* 283 U.S. 697, 51 S. Ct. 625.
	1932	Fair trial.	*Powell v. Alabama,* 287 U.S. 45, 53 S. Ct. 55.
	1934	Free exercise of religion.	*Hamilton v. Regents of the University of California,* 293 U.S. 245, 55 S. Ct. 197.
	1937	Freedom of assembly.	*D. Jonge v. Oregon,* 299 U.S. 353, 57 S. Ct. 255.
STONE Court	1942	Right to counsel in capital cases.	*Betts v. Brady,* 316 U.S. 455, 62 S. Ct. 1252.
VINSON Court	1947	Separation of church and state: right against the establishment of religion.	*Everson v. Board of Education,* 330 U.S. 1, 67 S. Ct. 594.
	1948	Public trial.	*In re Oliver,* 333 U.S. 257, 68 S. Ct. 499.
	1949	Right against unreasonable searches and seizures.	*Wolf v. Colorado,* 338 U.S. 25, 69 S. Ct. 1359.
WARREN Court	1961	Exclusionary rule as a deterrent to unreasonable searches and seizures.	*Mapp v. Ohio,* 367 U.S. 643, 81 S. Ct. 1684.
	1962	Right against cruel and unusual punishments.	*Robinson v. California,* 370 U.S. 660, 82 S. Ct. 1417.
	1963	Right to counsel in felony cases.	*Gideon v. Wainwright,* 372 U.S. 335, 83 S. Ct. 792.
	1964	Right against self-incrimination.	*Malloy v. Hogan,* 387 U.S. 1, 84 S. Ct. 1489; *Murphy v. Waterfront Com'n of New York Harbor,* 387 U.S. 52, 84 S. Ct. 1594.
	1965	Confrontation of witnesses.	*Pointer v. Texas,* 380 U.S. 300, 85 S. Ct. 1065; *Griswold v. Connecticut,* 381 U.S. 479, 85 S. Ct. 1678.
	1967	Right to speedy trial.	*Klopfer v. North Carolina,* 386 U.S. 213, 87 S. Ct. 988.
BURGER Court		Compulsory process to obtain witnesses.	*Washington v. Texas,* 388 U.S. 14, 87 S. Ct. 1920.
	1968	Jury trial for all serious crimes.	*Duncan v. Louisiana,* 391 U.S. 145, 88 S. Ct. 1444.
	1969	Right against double jeopardy.	*Benton v. Maryland,* 395 U.S. 784, 89 S. Ct. 2056.
	1972	Right to counsel for all crimes involving a jail term.	*Argersinger v. Hamlin,* 407 U.S. 25, 92 S. Ct. 2006.

SOURCE: Adapted from Craig R. Ducat and Harold W. Chase, *Constitutional Interpretation* (St. Paul, MN: West, 1983), p. 264.

TABLE 7.1   The Process of Selective Incorporation

Bill of Rights have by now been made applicable to the states under the Fourteenth Amendment. The practical effect is that all of us now enjoy a host of additional constitutional protections against the actions of *both* federal and state law enforcement officials.

The impact of all of these Supreme Court rulings has been immense. In effect, the criminal procedures of the fifty states have been unified to conform to the Bill of Rights, as interpreted by the U.S. Supreme Court. We call this the American criminal justice revolution. It is the legacy of the Warren Court—the U.S. Supreme Court under the leadership of Chief Justice Earl Warren, who served from 1953 to 1969.[8]

Fourth Amendment: Unreasonable Searches and Seizures

Let us look next at how the U.S. Supreme Court used the Fourteenth Amendment to incorporate the provisions of the Bill of Rights and fashion criminal justice procedures for all the states. We start with the Fourth Amendment and the all-important police power to search and arrest (Table 7.2).

Search and Seizure

The right of the people to be secure in their persons, houses, papers, and effects, against unreasonable searches and seizures, shall not be violated; and no Warrants shall issue but upon probable cause, supported by oath or affirmation, and particularly describing the place to be searched, and the persons or things to be seized.

In the seventeenth and eighteenth centuries, homeowners throughout England had the right to defend their "castles" against any unlawful entry—including by agents of the king. Even a cardboard box in which a homeless person lives is a castle in that sense: It is inviolable. Yet until 1949, this limitation bound only federal police forces and courts in the United States. The states were left to fashion their own procedures. In 1949 the Supreme Court handed down its decision in *Wolf v. Colorado.*[9] It held that the Fourth Amendment protection against unreasonable searches and seizures is a fundamental right implicit in the concept of ordered liberty and therefore covered by the Fourteenth Amendment due process clause and binding on the states.

search
Any governmental intrusion upon a person's reasonable expectation of privacy.

seizure
Exercise of control by a government official over a person or thing.

The Right to Privacy.   What do we mean by the terms "search" and "seizure"? A **search** is any governmental intrusion upon a person's reasonable expectation of privacy. A **seizure** is the exercise of control by a government official over a person or thing. The Fourth Amendment simply requires that both searches and seizures be "reasonable." Who judges what is reasonable? Courts consider the expectations of privacy of the person searched, and the extent to which society would consider the expectations to be reasonable.

The Warrant Requirement.   So far we have been describing searches and seizures without a warrant. But the Fourth Amendment requires, with the exceptions noted below, that searches be conducted according to the terms of a warrant issued by a neutral and detached magistrate or judicial officer. The warrant must be based on probable cause, and it must describe with reasonable certainty the place to be searched and the items to be seized. As we noted earlier, probable cause simply means a reasonable belief that certain pieces of evidence connected with a crime that has been or is being committed may be found on a particular person or in a particular place. The warrant requirement shifts the decision (regarding the reliability of an informant's affidavit, the extent of probable cause, and ultimately whether to engage in the search) from the law enforcement officer, who has a definite interest, to the disinterested judge. As a result, searches conducted with a warrant find easy acceptance at trial and offer far greater protection for officers against civil and/or criminal liability.[10] Whenever possible, therefore, law enforcement officers must obtain a judicial warrant to search and seize, with the following exceptions.

Warrantless Searches

Soon after Mark Knights was placed on probation for a drug charge, police in Napa County conducted a search of his home and found bomb-making material—evidence that clearly linked him to arson attacks aimed at a local electric company. Knights argued that the warrantless search violated his Fourth Amendment rights.

On December 10, 2001, the United States Supreme Court, in an opinion written by Chief Justice William H. Rehnquist, ruled that the probation order obviated the need for a search warrant, giving broad search authority to "any" law enforcement officer. According to Rehnquist, "Just as other punishments for criminal convictions curtail an offender's freedoms,

- **Brendlin v. California, 551 U.S. _____ (2007)**

Facts of the Case
Police stopped Karen Simeroth's car for having expired registration tabs. Bruce Brendlin, who had a warrant out for his arrest, was riding in the passenger seat. Police found methamphetamine, marijuana, and drug paraphemalia in the car and on Simeroth's person. In a California trial court, Brendlin filed a motion to suppress the evidence obtained at the traffic stop, claiming that the stop was an unreasonable seizure in violation of the Fourth Amendment. The trial court found that Brendlin had never been detained or "seized" within the meaning of the Fourth Amendment. It denied the motion, and Brendlin pleaded guilty to manufacturing methamphetamine. A California Court of Appeal reversed, holding that a traffic stop necessarily results in a Fourth Amendment seizure.

The California Supreme Court reversed the Court of Appeal and ruled for California. The court held that the driver of the car is the only one detained in a traffic stop. The movement of any passengers is also stopped as a practical matter, but the court considered this merely a necessary by-product of the detention of the driver. The court held that Brendlin had been free to leave the scene of the traffic stop or to simply ignore the police. Since he was never "seized," however, he could not claim a violation of the Fourth Amendment.

Question
When a vehicle is subject to a traffic stop, is a passenger in the vehicle "detained" for purposes of the Fourth Amendment?

Conclusion
Yes. In a unanimous opinion written by Justice David Souter, the Court held that when a vehicle is stopped at a traffic stop, the passenger as well as the driver is seized within the meaning of the Fourth Amendment. The justices said, "We resolve this question by asking whether a reasonable person in Brendlin's position when the car stopped would have believed himself free to 'terminate the encounter' between the police and himself." The Court held that Brendlin would have reasonably believed himself to be intentionally detained and subject to the authority of the police. Thus, he was justified in asserting his Fourth Amendment protection against unreasonable seizure. The Court noted that its ruling would not extend to more incidental restrictions on freedom of movement, such as when motorists are forced to slow down or stop because other vehicles are being detained. To accept the state's arguments, however, would be to "invite police officers to stop cars with passengers regardless of probable cause or reasonable suspicion of anything illegal."

- **United States v. Grubbs, 547 U.S. 90 (2006)**

Facts of the Case
On federal trial for possessing child pornography, Grubbs asked the judge to suppress evidence officers seized from his home. Grubbs said the search violated the Fourth Amendment because the officers showed him an "anticipatory warrant," something valid only after triggering events take place, with no mention of the triggering conditions. The condition set on this warrant was that officers could search Grubbs' house only after he received a pornographic video in the mail. The judge denied Grubbs' motion because the trigger was set forth in an affidavit that the officers carried during the search and that the warrant referenced. The Ninth Circuit reversed and said officers had to show the triggering events for an anticipatory warrant to the person being searched.

Question
Did the Fourth Amendment require suppression of evidence seized during a search that had been authorized by an anticipatory warrant, when the warrant's triggering events were not shown to the person searched?

Conclusion
No. Justice Antonin Scalia, in the majority opinion, wrote that under the Fourth Amendment's particularity requirement a warrant need not set out the conditions that trigger it, only the place to be searched and the persons or things to be searched for. The fact that the triggering conditions were included in the affidavit, even if they were never showed to Grubbs, was therefore sufficient.

- **Muehler v. Mena 544 U.S. 93 (2005)**

Facts of the Case
Police detained Mena and others in handcuffs while they searched the house they occupied. During the detention they asked Mena about her immigration status. The police had a search warrant to search the premises for deadly weapons and evidence of gang membership. Mena sued the officers in federal district court for violating her

(continued)

Adapted from the OYEZ Project of Northwestern University, *Recent Fourth Amendment Cases Before the United States Supreme Court,* http://oyez.nwu.edu (October 2007).

TABLE 7.2 Recent Fourth Amendment Cases before the United States Supreme Court

Fourth Amendment right to be free from unreasonable seizure. The district court ruled for Mena. The Ninth Circuit affirmed, holding that using handcuffs to detain Mena during the search violated the Fourth Amendment and that the officers' questioning of Mena about her immigration status also violated the Fourth Amendment.

Question
(1) Did police violate the Fourth Amendment right to be free from unreasonable seizure by detaining Mena in handcuffs while they executed a search warrant for contraband on the premises she occupied? (2) Did police violate the Fourth Amendment by questioning Mena about her immigration status during the detention?

Conclusion
No and no. In a 9–0 judgment delivered by Chief Justice William H. Rehnquist, the Court held that Mena's detention did not violate the Fourth Amendment. Officers with a search warrant for contraband had authority to detain occupants of the premises during the search, in order to minimize any risk to officers. Handcuffing Mena while police searched for weapons and a wanted gang member was also justified by officer safety concerns and because officers had to deal with detaining multiple occupants. The Court further held that the officers' questioning of Mena about her immigration status during her detention did not violate the Fourth Amendment. The officers did not need to have reasonable suspicion to question Mena. Moreover, the Court had held repeatedly that mere police questioning did not constitute a seizure.

TABLE 7.2   (*Continued*)

a court granting probation may impose reasonable conditions that deprive the offender of some freedoms enjoyed by law-abiding citizens."[11]

There are an additional eight exceptions to the general rule that a warrant is required to conduct a search. With each it should be clear that the willingness of courts to pass on the need for a warrant reflects their perception of a diminished expectation of privacy, due perhaps to the timing of the search (conducted during the "hot pursuit" of a suspect), the location of the search (conducted in an automobile that has been stopped on the side of a public highway), or the social relationships involved in the search (conducted in a shared dorm room after consent is given by a roommate).

1. Border Searches.   Fourth Amendment rights are severely restricted at international borders or their "functional equivalent," such as international airports. Customs agents and immigration officials have significant discretion at borders to conduct searches that range from superficial to invasive, without probable cause or a search warrant and with perhaps no reason other than mere suspicion. This was precisely the case in *United States v. Montoya de Hernandez* (1985). The defendant, who arrived at Los Angeles Airport from Bogotá, Colombia, fit a drug courier profile. Customs agents suspected that she had swallowed balloons filled with drugs, which were concealed in her alimentary canal. Reasonable suspicion was sufficient to justify a thorough search and sixteen-hour detention.[12]

Most recently, in *United States v. Flores-Montano* (2004), the U.S. Supreme Court wrestled with a border search of a car's gas tank. U.S. Customs inspectors noticed that Manuel Flores-Montano's hands were shaking when he stopped at the U.S.–Mexico border. After examining the outside of his vehicle, an inspector tapped Mr. Flores-Montano's gas tank with a screwdriver. The tank sounded solid. A mechanic was brought in to disassemble the car's fuel tank. He found 37 kilograms of marijuana bricks in the tank.

Flores-Montano tried to have the marijuana suppressed on Fourth Amendment grounds, arguing that the search was intrusive and nonroutine. It required reasonable suspicion. The Supreme Court held that an automobile's fuel tank may be inspected without suspicion at the border. Such an inspection "is justified by the Government's paramount interest in protecting the border. . . . Complex balancing tests," according to the Court, "have no place in border searches of vehicles."[13]

2. Automobile Searches.   The U.S. Supreme Court has repeatedly held that there is a diminished expectation of privacy in automobiles. Three reasons have been given: (1) the mobility of cars creates circumstances that make a warrant requirement impractical; (2) automobiles are regulated, licensed, and inspected on a regular basis by the government, resulting in a lesser expectation of privacy; and (3) cars move on public roads and highways, where the contents of the automobile as well as the occupants are in plain view. Even so, police officers must have probable cause to search a vehicle—but they can develop the belief that the car contains incriminating evidence while they question the driver! In the case of *Colorado v. Bannister* (1980),[14] a police officer, while writing a speeding ticket, noticed tools and steel parts on the back seat of the car. The driver and another occupant fit the description of suspects wanted for the theft of auto parts. A full search of the car was upheld by the U.S. Supreme Court.

3. Consent Searches.   A warrantless search may be conducted where the party to the search provides "voluntary and intelligent consent." The ultimate test of the **consent search** is voluntariness. As one Supreme Court decision states: "Two competing concerns must be accommodated . . . —the legitimate need for such searches and the equally important requirement of assuring the absence of coercion."[15] Police may seek consent for a variety of reasons. Perhaps they have little evidence and cannot get a search warrant. Perhaps they feel there may be insufficient time to get the warrant, given the nature of the criminal activity. Often they will ask the suspect to sign a consent form.

Police may also attempt to gain consent from a "third party," a person who has the right to consent but is not the suspect or object of the search. Third-party consent has been upheld by the Supreme Court where it is demonstrated that (1) the third party had mutual use or joint access and control over property or premises (called "common authority") and (2) the object of the search (the target) assumed the risk that the co-occupant, for example, might permit the search.[16] This means, for example, that spouses or roommates can give consent for each other; it also means that employers can give consent for employees.[17]

4. Hot Pursuit.   Police are permitted to engage in a warrantless search and seizure when they are in **hot pursuit** of a suspect believed to be dangerous. Police may enter a suspect's house without a warrant if they are in hot pursuit and have reason to believe that he or she is on the premises. The scope of the search can be as extensive as necessary to prevent escape or apprehend the suspect.[18]

5. Plain View.   Police need not obtain a warrant where the fruits or instrumentalities of a crime are in **plain view.** Such warrantless searches and seizures are upheld so long as the police are lawfully on the premises and they inadvertently see objects in plain view.[19] Consider what might happen if campus police arrive at a friend's door during a loud party and, when the door is opened, see illegal substances or objects on the dining room table. Would the police need a warrant? If they remove the substances from the table, would that be an unconstitutional seizure? Because of the plain view exception to the warrant requirement, the answer in both cases is no!

6. Stop and Frisk.   Police do not need probable cause to stop a person who is reasonably suspected of criminal activity, whether in a car or on foot. Moreover, they do not need a warrant to engage in a search of that person. They must, however, have a **reasonable suspicion** that the suspect is armed and presently dangerous in order to **frisk,** or pat down the outer clothing, for concealed weapons.[20] This reasonable suspicion may be based on the "totality of the circumstances," a consideration of the whole picture.[21]

Short of a **stop and frisk** police have the right to stop a person and ask for identification or perhaps ask if assistance is needed.[22] In such cases, all that is required is "articulable suspicion"—the police must be able to say why they stopped the person. But the standard situation is that of an *arrest*, for which police must have probable cause to believe that a crime has been committed (Table 7.3).

7. Exigent Circumstances.   Certain emergencies that call for immediate action do not allow time to obtain a search warrant; they are **exigent circumstances.** Two different kinds of emergencies qualify: (1) an ongoing physical event, such as a fire or the taking of hostages,[23] and (2) cases where physical evidence would disappear (e.g., due to the disposal of the substance) well before officers could obtain a warrant.[24]

consent search
Warrantless search conducted when the party to the search provides "voluntary and intelligent consent" to police.

hot pursuit
Exception to the rule requiring police to have a warrant to conduct a search; applies to cases of pursuit of vehicles and of suspects on foot.

plain view
No warrant is needed to conduct a search when the fruits or instrumentalities of a crime are in plain view.

reasonable suspicion
Suspicion (short of probable cause) that a person has been or may be engaged in the commission of a crime.

frisk
Patting down a suspect's clothing to search for concealed weapons, under reasonable suspicion.

stop and frisk
Technique used by police to "pat down" a person suspected of being armed or in possession of the instrumentalities of a crime.

exigent circumstances
Certain emergencies that call for immediate action and therefore do not allow time for a search warrant to be obtained.

A DIME'S WORTH OF PRIVACY GOES A LONG WAY

Until the 1960s, courts that considered search and seizure cases had been principally concerned with physical intrusions into houses, clothing, luggage, automobiles, and other so-called "constitutionally protected areas." But with *Katz v. United States* (1967), a dramatic change occurred.

Katz's Phone Booth Business

Charles Katz was a bookie, and he ran his betting business out of a public telephone booth. The FBI knew this and attached a "bug" to the outside of the booth. At Katz's trial, the government introduced into evidence recordings of phone conversations in which Katz and others discussed the placing of bets. The Supreme Court had to decide whether the government's recording of conversations constituted an unreasonable search and seizure in violation of the Fourth Amendment.

In *Katz v. United States,* the majority found that such recording did in fact violate Katz's Fourth Amendment rights, because the Fourth Amendment "protects people—and not simply 'areas.'" Katz thus had a legitimate and reasonable expectation of privacy, whether or not the public telephone booth was a constitutionally protected area. In effect, Charles Katz had bought himself a dime's worth of privacy in a public phone booth. After the Katz case, search and seizure questions could no longer be decided solely on the basis of the place or area that was searched; decisions would rest on the reasonableness of the privacy expectation held by the person searched. The real legacy of this case is found in a two-part opinion written by Supreme Court Justice John M. Harlan. The following words from Justice Harlan's opinion have appeared in hundreds of state and federal search and seizure decisions since *Katz.*

> My understanding of the rule that has emerged from prior decisions is that there is a twofold requirement, first that a person have exhibited an actual (subjective) expectation of privacy and, second, that the expectation be one that society is prepared to recognize as "reasonable."

Deciding What Is Reasonable

Note that the Constitution nowhere mentions the concept of "privacy." The Supreme Court fashioned the concept by interpreting the provisions of the Constitution. That, in our system, is the prerogative of the Supreme Court. In essence, the Constitution says what the Supreme Court says it does.

Having created privacy as a constitutionally protected right, the Court was then confronted with a number of issues that raised the question of whether a privacy expectation is reasonable. Here are some of the Supreme Court's answers:

In one case the Court decided that when a person leaves trash for collection, there is no longer any reasonable expectation of privacy, and when the police find incriminating evidence in that trash, it may be used against the defendant at trial (*California v. Greenwood,* 108 S. Ct. 1625, 1988).

In another case the police suspected a mobile home, parked in downtown San Diego,

Search and seizure in a Miami drug case.

TABLE 7.3
Stop and Frisk and Arrest

	"Stop and Frisk"	"Arrest"
1. Degree of certainty	"Reasonable suspicion"	"Probable cause"
2. Scope	Very limited—only pat down for weapons	Full body search
3. Purpose	Stop—to prevent criminal activity	To take person into custody
4. Warrant	Not needed	May or may not need

SOURCE: Rolando del Carmen, *Criminal Procedure: Law and Practice* (Pacific Grove, CA: Brooks/Cole, 1991), p. 109.

was being used as a sex-for-drugs swap shop. They asked one of the customers to knock at the door. When it was opened the police entered and searched the mobile home, seizing drugs. The Supreme Court ruled: A road vehicle parked downtown does not offer the same expectation of privacy as a brick and mortar building. The evidence seized was ruled admissible (*California v. Carney,* 105 S. Ct. 2066, 1985).

In a third case, the police had picked up a person bleeding from a gunshot wound and transported him to a hospital emergency room. He was immediately identified as a suspect in the shooting of a store owner during an attempted robbery. The police requested surgical removal, under anesthesia, of the bullet. The Court ruled that this removal of the evidence (the bullet) violated the defendant's reasonable expectation of privacy (*Winston v. Lee,* 105 S. Ct. 1611, 1985).

The Expectation of Privacy and New Technologies

The very idea of privacy expectations is put to the challenge by new technologies. What will the Supreme Court do when asked to consider expectations of privacy claimed by users of the Internet? The Internet poses a tremendous challenge for law enforcement officers to police unlawful money laundering, gambling, and pornography. The challenge is just as significant for courts in balancing an unfettered right to enjoy interstate commerce with the legitimate need for business regulation, as well as the balance between freedom of expression and speech that borders on obscenity. The technology is so new that courts have not even addressed the extent to which one may enjoy privacy on something as public as the Internet. There is no doubt, however, that the very technology that permits this wonderful form of communication encourages abuses and illegal activity for which no one should enjoy privacy.

Consider that a significant percentage of Internet activity is connected to the adult entertainment industry, with literally thousands of sites offering images, video clips, and interactive chat rooms catering to tastes ranging from bestiality to pedophilia. While the vast majority of the activity is legal, unlawful images of children, for example, lurk in the background of "teen," "family nudism," "Japanese school girl," anime (Japanese cartoons), and "Lolita" sites. Images of children that violate both state and federal obscenity laws are also posted in a vast array of teen and preteen newsgroups within computers (servers) located around the world. The few arrests that have been made through the coordinated efforts of the U.S. Postal Service, the U.S. Customs Service, Federal Bureau of Investigation, and specialized task forces of United States Attorneys reveal a global trading ground for pedophiles.

How to police this new technology, how to protect the rights of free speech among users, and how to honor legitimate expectations of privacy "online" will be just a few of the significant criminal justice challenges in years to come.

Questions for Discussion

1. How strictly should the Internet be regulated by state and federal authorities?
2. What balancing test would you use to determine the need for legal intervention?
3. How do you define "privacy"?

8. Incident to an Arrest. There is no need for police to secure a warrant for a search incident to (part of) an arrest. For the safety of the officers and to prevent the concealment or destruction of evidence, police can conduct a full search of a person once that person has been lawfully arrested. This search includes the areas within his or her immediate control, such as furniture within reach of the arrestee.[25]

Arrests

The Bill of Rights does not use the term "arrest," but when it speaks of seizures, it includes seizures of the person, or what we call arrest. Consequently, the Fourth Amendment is largely applicable to arrest as well, with some exceptions.

An **arrest** is the act of taking a person into custody by restricting that person's right to leave.[26] The grounds for a lawful arrest are straightforward—police must have probable cause.

arrest
Seizure of the person; the taking of a person into custody.

Cocaine smugglers known as "mules."

COKIE AND ROSA—FAMOUS BALLOON SWALLOWERS

Who could forget the sight of Cokie (also called Coke or Coco), the cute sheep dog that in December 1994 was used by drug dealers as a container to smuggle drugs into the United States? Ten condoms filled with cocaine were placed in Cokie's abdomen in a crude operation. Was this the first time that "balloons" of cocaine were swallowed in order to smuggle drugs across international borders? Certainly not. In fact, Cokie followed in a grand tradition of famous balloon swallowers. Perhaps the most famous was Rosa Elvira Montoya de Hernandez.

Shortly after midnight on March 5, 1983, Rosa arrived at Los Angeles International Airport on Avianca flight 080 from Bogotá, Colombia. She quickly passed through immigration and went to the customs desk. There she met Customs Inspector Talamantes who noticed from her passport that she had traveled to Miami and Los Angeles over eight times in recent months. When asked several questions about these trips, Rosa said that she did not understand or speak English. Further, she claimed to have no friends or family in the United States. The purpose of her trips to the United States was to purchase merchandise for her husband's store in Bogotá. She had $5,000 in her possession which, she claimed, would be used to buy goods from J. C. Penney and Kmart. Rosa did not have any checks, credit cards, or letters of credit.

Customs officials and inspectors became increasingly suspicious. Rosa had no hotel reservations and did not have any appointments with merchandise vendors. She did not know how much her airplane ticket cost. Her valise had four changes of "cold weather" clothing. Talamantes suspected that Rosa was attempting to smuggle drugs into the United States. His strong suspicions, based on years of experience with at least 12 other passengers on Avianca flights, was that Rosa was a balloon swallower—a drug smuggler who hides cocaine and other narcotics by swallowing balloons filled with drugs. Drug balloons become lodged in the alimentary canal, sometimes for days, until such time as a bowel movement occurs. Balloon swallowers often lose their lives when a balloon bursts before it is passed.

---

probable cause
Set of facts that would lead a reasonable person to believe that an accused person committed the offense in question; the minimum evidence requirement for an arrest, according to the Fourth Amendment.

arrest warrant
Written order from a court directing the police to effect an arrest.

In this context, **probable cause** amounts to facts that would lead a reasonable person to believe that the suspect had committed or was committing a crime. Common law placed certain limitations on the ability of police to act without an **arrest warrant**—an order from a court directing the police to effect an arrest. The person arrested must have committed a felony in the presence of the officer. Alternatively, there must be knowledge that a felony has been committed and probable cause to believe that the suspect committed it. Arrests for misdemeanors were limited to a breach of the peace committed in the presence of the officer.

Most arrests take place without a warrant, and here is one of the legal differences between seizures of property and seizures of the person. While law enforcement officers must obtain a warrant to search unless there is an exception to the general rule, when it comes to seizure of the person police need not obtain a warrant.[27] Most street arrests take place without a warrant, although under federal law and the law of some states, a judicial warrant must later be issued.[28] Warrantless arrests in a home, on the other hand, may be made only when there is danger in delay.[29]

Talamantes asked for a female customs inspector to frisk Rosa and conduct a strip search. The inspector noticed that she was wearing two pairs of elastic underpants with a paper towel lining. She also felt a "firm fullness" in Rosa's abdomen. Rosa was given three options:

- Return to Colombia on the next flight.
- Consent to an x-ray of her abdomen.
- Remain in custody until a bowel movement confirms either the presence or absence of drugs.

Rosa decided to return to Colombia, but unfortunately she was denied passage to Bogotá through Mexico City because she did not have a Mexican visa. Without any other option available, Rosa was told that she would be detained until she agreed to an x-ray or moved her bowels. Rosa remained under observation in the customs office curled up in a chair. She refused to eat, drink, or go to the bathroom. Nearly 24 hours after Rosa had landed in Los Angeles, customs officials finally obtained a court order from a federal magistrate to perform a pregnancy test, an x-ray, and a rectal examination. Rosa was taken to a hospital where a physician, after examining her rectum, removed a balloon containing cocaine. Rosa was placed under arrest. Over the next four days, Rosa passed ninety-four additional balloons, a total of more than 530 grams of 80 percent pure cocaine hydrochloride.

Rosa's experience in detention, and the plight of balloon swallowers more generally, was highlighted in the Supreme Court case *United States v. Montoya de Hernandez* (1985), in which Rosa challenged the reasonableness of her detention and the constitutionality of the resulting search. Justice Rehnquist sympathized with the uncomfortable circumstances surrounding Rosa's detention but nevertheless held that:

Under the circumstances, [Rosa's] detention, while long, uncomfortable, and humiliating, was not unreasonably long. Alimentary canal smuggling cannot be detected in the amount of time in which other illegal activity may be investigated through brief stops. When [Rosa] refused an x-ray as an alternative to simply awaiting her bowel movement, the customs inspectors were left with only two practical alternatives: detain her for such time as necessary to confirm their suspicions or turn her loose into the interior of the country carrying the reasonably suspected contraband drugs. Moreover, both the length of [Rosa's] detention and its discomfort resulted solely from the method that she chose to smuggle illicit drugs into this country. And in the presence of an articulable suspicion of alimentary canal smuggling, the customs officials were not required by the Fourth Amendment to pass [Rosa] and her cocaine-filled balloons into the interior.

Questions for Discussion

1. In your opinion, did the search and seizure of Rosa's person violate the Fourth Amendment?

2. What is the best case that you can make in support of Rosa's contention that the conduct of law enforcement in this case violated her rights?

3. What policy should officials at international borders adopt to protect against the illegal importation of drugs into this country?

The Right to Privacy Post-9/11

Within 45 days of the September 11 attacks, Congress passed the USA Patriot Act. This legislation was designed, at least in part, to facilitate the investigation and apprehension of known and would-be terrorists. According to civil libertarians, the Patriot Act undermines existing checks on law enforcement and, in doing so, threatens cherished rights and freedoms, including Fourth Amendment protections. This new legislation, when combined with technologies that allow for the combining of personal databases and records, poses a significant threat to ordinary citizens—or so we are told. In the excerpt from a recent report on the growth of the "American surveillance society," the American Civil Liberties Union outlines its concerns with this threat to privacy rights. How serious is the threat? Perhaps the only satisfactory answer is that this question is often debated and that reasonable people very often disagree.

Privacy and liberty in the United States are at risk. A combination of lightning-fast technological innovation and the erosion of privacy protections threatens to transform Big Brother from an oft-cited but remote threat into a very real part of American life. We are at risk of turning into a Surveillance Society.

The explosion of computers, cameras, sensors, wireless communication, GPS, biometrics, and other technologies in just the last 10 years is feeding a surveillance monster that is growing silently in our midst. Scarcely a month goes by in which we don't read about some new high-tech way to invade people's privacy, from face recognition to implantable microchips, data-mining, DNA chips, and even "brain wave fingerprinting." The fact is, there are no longer any *technical* barriers to the Big Brother regime portrayed by George Orwell.

Even as this surveillance monster grows in power, we are weakening the legal chains that keep it from trampling our lives. We should be responding to intrusive new technologies by building stronger restraints to protect our privacy; instead, we are doing the opposite—loosening regulations on government surveillance, watching passively as private surveillance grows unchecked, and contemplating the introduction of tremendously powerful new surveillance infrastructures that will tie all this information together.

A gradual weakening of our privacy rights has been under way for decades, but many of the most startling developments have come in response to the terrorist attacks of September 11. But few of these hastily enacted measures are likely to increase our protection against terrorism. More often than not, September 11 has been used as a pretext to loosen constraints that law enforcement has been chafing under for years.

It doesn't require some apocalyptic vision of American democracy being replaced by dictatorship to worry about a surveillance society. There is a lot of room for the United States to become a meaner, less open and less just place without any radical change in government. All that's required is the continued construction of new surveillance technologies and the simultaneous erosion of privacy protections.

It's not hard to imagine how in the near future we might see scenarios like the following:

- An African-American man from the central city visits an affluent white suburb to attend a coworker's barbeque. Later that night, a crime takes place elsewhere in the neighborhood. The police review surveillance camera images, use face recognition to identify the man, and pay him a visit at home the next day. His trip to the suburbs where he "didn't belong" has earned him an interrogation from suspicious police.
- A tourist walking through an unfamiliar city happens upon a sex shop. She stops to gaze at several curious items in the store's window before moving along. Unbeknownst to her, the store has set up the newly available "Customer Identification System," which detects a signal being emitted by a computer chip in her driver's license and records her identity and the date, time, and duration of her brief look inside the window. A week later, she gets a solicitation in the mail mentioning her "visit" and embarrassing her in front of her family.

Such possibilities are only the tip of the iceberg. The media faithfully reports the latest surveillance gadgets and the latest moves to soften the rules on government spying, but rarely provides the big picture. That is unfortunate, because each new threat to our privacy is much more significant as part of the overall trend than it seems when viewed in isolation. When these monitoring technologies and techniques are combined, they can create a surveillance network far more powerful than any single one would create on its own.

(continued)

The good news is that these trends can be stopped. As the American people realize that each new development is part of this larger story, they will give more and more weight to protecting privacy, and support the measures we need to preserve our freedom.

SOURCE: Jay Stanley and Barry Steinhardt, *Bigger Monster, Weaker Chains: The Growth of an American Surveillance Society* (New York: American Civil Liberties Union, 2003), pp. 1–2.

Fifth Amendment: Self-Incrimination

The relevant part of the Fifth Amendment reads: "nor shall any person . . . be compelled in any criminal case to be a witness against himself."

The Self-Incrimination Privilege

It was not until well over a century after the promulgation of the Bill of Rights that the U.S. Supreme Court invoked the Fifth Amendment in a federal case.[30] In the century since, the Court has seldom applied this amendment against the states. The process of broadening the use of the Fifth Amendment started with a case that truly shocked the conscience of the Court and of the nation: Three young black men were arrested in Mississippi and charged with murder. They were beaten, brutalized, and tortured into a confession of having committed a crime for which there was no other evidence. The Mississippi trial court hurriedly convicted them. The Supreme Court in 1936 reversed the conviction as "revolting to the sense of justice."[31] But it did not rest its reversal on the Fifth Amendment's self-incrimination privilege (see Table 7.1); rather, it ruled that the brutalization of the defendants violated their entitlement to "due process of law" (in general), under the Fourteenth Amendment.

In the years that followed, state convictions resting on a claim of violation of due process were generally based on psychological pressure rather than physical torture. In 1957 the Supreme Court, after reviewing some thirty of its own previous decisions, proposed the "totality of the circumstances test."[32] Suppose a suspect, a member of an ethnic minority, confessed after a prolonged interrogation with psychological pressure (or even deceit) and the withholding of food, drink, and sleep. The "totality of the circumstances" may be deemed to have broken down the suspect's power to resist. Any confession obtained in such a manner will be considered involuntary, and thus in violation of Fourteenth Amendment due process, just as if it had been beaten out of the suspect.

Next, the Supreme Court was to find help in its own "right to counsel" decisions. In 1963, in the famous *Gideon v. Wainwright* case, the Court had made the Sixth Amendment's right to counsel applicable to state criminal proceedings (again by the process of incorporation through the Fourteenth Amendment).[33] It was then logical for the Court to find that when defendants are made to incriminate themselves while being deprived of right to counsel, any such statements or confessions also violate the Sixth Amendment.[34] The link to the Fifth Amendment came with the *Miranda* case.

The *Miranda* Warnings

Miranda v. Arizona (1966) is the one Supreme Court decision every law enforcement officer remembers by name. Ernesto Miranda, an indigent with an eighth-grade education and a history of psychological problems, had confessed to a kidnap and rape after interrogation in police custody for less than two hours. The Court "did not find the defendant's statements to have been involuntary in the traditional sense," but found them to have been induced in a "menacing police interrogation procedure," in violation of the defendant's Fifth Amendment self-incrimination privilege. The Supreme Court was quick to add that Miranda's Sixth Amendment right to counsel was also violated.[35] If an attorney had been brought in, either the defendant would not have incriminated himself, or at least the "menacing police interrogation procedure" would not have taken place. The Court took one additional step by requiring that

> **Miranda Warnings**
> 1. You have the right to remain silent.
> 2. Anything you say can and will be used against you in a court of law.
> 3. You have the right to talk to a lawyer and have him present with you while you are being questioned.
> 4. If you cannot afford to hire a lawyer, one will be appointed to represent you before any questioning, if you wish one.
> 5. You may stop answering questions at any time.
> 6. Do you understand each of these rights I have explained to you?
> 7. Having these rights in mind, do you wish to talk to us now?

FIGURE 7.1   The *Miranda* Warnings

from here on, as soon as a suspect is taken into custody, the officer must advise the arrestee of his or her rights under the Constitution—that is, the officer must read the *Miranda* warnings (Figure 7.1).

The *Miranda* decision was truly a first. Never before had the Supreme Court provided such a clear rule in the area of law enforcement or influenced the criminal justice system so significantly. And never before had the Supreme Court created so much controversy in the field of criminal justice. Before reviewing the impact of *Miranda*, we need to consider the ways in which courts have interpreted this landmark case. When does *Miranda* apply? And when are the warnings not required?

custody
Suspect under arrest or deprived of freedom in a significant way.

interrogation
Explicit questioning or actions that may elicit an incriminating statement.

Miranda warnings must be given whenever a suspect is taken into **custody** (when the suspect is placed under arrest or is deprived of freedom in a significant way) and may be subjected to **interrogation** (explicit questioning or actions that may elicit an incriminating statement). Generally, *Miranda* warnings are given when there is (1) questioning of a suspect at a police station, (2) questioning of a suspect in a police car, (3) questioning of a suspect who is not free to leave, and (4) questioning of a defendant who is in custody for another offense.[36] On the other hand, *Miranda* warnings may not be necessary (1) with roadside questioning of a motorist during a routine traffic stop, (2) when police do not intend to ask the suspect questions, (3) with nonspecific on-the-scene questioning by the police, and (4) when a statement is actually volunteered by the suspect.[37]

Miranda still stands, but as Table 7.4 reveals, the strength of the *Miranda* decision has been undercut by a series of Supreme Court cases that allow the use of confessions after some defect in the administration of the warnings[38] and that limit *Miranda*'s reach to custodial interrogations only. Moreover, several decisions allow pretrial statements obtained in violation of *Miranda* to be used to impeach or discredit subsequent testimony. Cases supporting *Miranda* have a more narrow focus. Typically, these cases concern attempts to continue questioning once counsel has been requested. That said, in the U.S. Supreme Court's most recent *Miranda* decision, a majority of the court demonstrated a strong commitment to its constitutionality. *Dickerson v. United States* is perhaps the strongest signal from the court that *Miranda* is here to stay.

Miranda is a constitutional rule that may not be trumped by acts of Congress.

DICKERSON V. UNITED STATES

530 U.S. 428; 120 S. Ct. 2326; 147 L. Ed. 2d 405 (2000)

In *Miranda v. Arizona*, 384 U.S. 436, 16 L. Ed. 2d 694, 86 S. Ct. 1602 (1966), we held that certain warnings must be given before a suspect's statement made during custodial interrogation could be admitted in evidence. In the wake of that

(*continued*)

Cases Affirming Miranda: *Evidence Ruled Not Admissible*

	Factual Situation
1. *U.S. v. Henry* (1979)	Questioning of defendant without a lawyer after indictment.
2. *Edwards v. Arizona* (1981)	No valid waiver of right to counsel.
3. *Smith v. Illinois* (1985)	After invocation of right to counsel during questioning.
4. *Michigan v. Jackson* (1986)	Right to counsel invoked at arraignment.
5. *Arizona v. Roberson* (1988)	Invoking *Miranda* for one offense, admissible for second offense?
6. *Minnick v. Mississippi* (1990)	When counsel is requested, the suspect has the right to have an attorney present during the interrogation.
7. *Dickerson v. United States* (2000)	Failure to give warning before interrogation.
8. *Missouri v. Seibert* (2004)	*Miranda* rights to make a second confession.

Cases Eroding Miranda: *Evidence Ruled Admissible*

	Factual Situation
1. *Harris v. New York* (1971)	Impeachment of credibility.
2. *Michigan v. Tucker* (1974)	Collateral derivative evidence.
3. *Michigan v. Mosley* (1975)	Questioning on an unrelated offense.
4. *New York v. Quarles* (1984)	Threat to public safety.
5. *Berkemer v. McCarty* (1984)	Roadside questioning of a motorist pursuant to routine traffic stop.
6. *Oregon v. Elstad* (1985)	Confession obtained after warnings given following earlier voluntary but unwarned admission.
7. *Moran v. Burbine* (1986)	Failure of police to inform suspect of attorney retained for him.
8. *Colorado v. Connelly* (1986)	Confession following advice of God.
9. *Connecticut v. Barrett* (1987)	Oral confession.
10. *Colorado v. Spring* (1987)	Shift to another crime.
11. *Arizona v. Mauro* (1987)	Officer recorded conversation with defendant's wife.
12. *Pennsylvania v. Bruder* (1988)	Curbside stop for traffic violation.
13. *Duckworth v. Eagan* (1989)	Variation in warning.
14. *Michigan v. Harvey* (1990)	Impeachment of testimony.
15. *Illinois v. Perkins* (1990)	Officer posing as inmate.
16. *Pennsylvania v. Muniz* (1990)	Routine questions and videotaping DWI.
17. *McNeil v. Wisconsin* (1991)	Invoking a suspect's Sixth Amendment right to counsel does not amount to an invocation of the right to counsel derived by *Miranda*.
18. *United States v. Pantane* (2003)	Physical evidence found as a result of un-Mirandized but voluntary testimony can be used in court.
19. *Chavez v. Martinez* (2003)	Coercive statements made while in custody that were not used against the suspect do not violate the Fifth Amendment.
20. *Yarborough v. Alvarado* (2004)	Deciding when a suspect is in custody and, thus, entitled to a *Miranda* warning.

SOURCE: Adapted and updated from Rolando del Carmen, *Criminal Procedure: Law and Practice* (Pacific Grove, CA: Brooks/Cole, 1991), p. 307.

TABLE 7.4 Cases Affirming and Eroding *Miranda*

decision, Congress enacted 18 U.S.C. § 3501, which in essence laid down a rule that the admissibility of such statements should turn only on whether or not they were voluntarily made. We hold that *Miranda,* being a constitutional decision of this Court, may not be in effect overruled by an Act of Congress, and we decline to overrule *Miranda* ourselves. We therefore hold that *Miranda* and its progeny in this Court govern the admissibility of statements made during custodial interrogation in both state and federal courts.

Petitioner Dickerson was indicted for bank robbery, conspiracy to commit bank robbery, and using a firearm in the course of committing a crime of violence, all in violation of the applicable provisions of Title 18 of the United States Code. Before trial, Dickerson moved to suppress a statement he had made at a Federal Bureau of Investigation field office, on the grounds that he had not received "*Miranda* warnings" before being interrogated. The District Court granted his motion to suppress, and the Government took an interlocutory appeal to the United States Court of Appeals for the Fourth Circuit. That court, by a divided vote, reversed the District Court's suppression order. It agreed with the District Court's conclusion that petitioner had not received *Miranda* warnings before making his statement. But it went on to hold that § 3501, which in effect makes the admissibility of statements such as Dickerson's turn solely on whether they were made voluntarily, was satisfied in this case. It then concluded that our decision in *Miranda* was not a constitutional holding, and that therefore Congress could by statute have the final say on the question of admissibility. 166 F.3d 667 (1999).

Because of the importance of the questions raised by the Court of Appeals' decision, we granted certiorari, 528 U.S. 1045 (1999), and now reverse. *Miranda* has become embedded in routine police practice to the point where the warnings have become part of our national culture. If anything, our subsequent cases have reduced the impact of the *Miranda* rule on legitimate law enforcement while reaffirming the decision's core ruling that unwarned statements may not be used as evidence in the prosecution's case in chief.

The disadvantage of the *Miranda* rule is that statements which may be by no means involuntary, made by a defendant who is aware of his "rights," may nonetheless be excluded and a guilty defendant go free as a result. But experience suggests that the totality-of-the-circumstances test which § 3501 seeks to revive is more difficult than *Miranda* for law enforcement officers to conform to, and for courts to apply in a consistent manner. ***In sum, we conclude that *Miranda* announced a constitutional rule that Congress may not supersede legislatively. Following the rule of *stare decisis,* we decline to overrule *Miranda* ourselves.

Enforcing Constitutional Rights: The Exclusionary Rule

Throughout the 1960s and 1970s, the Supreme Court continued to expand the reach of the Fourth, Fifth, and Sixth Amendments to the states in offering protection to the accused. The landmark decision that started this criminal justice revolution was *Mapp v. Ohio,* which extended the exclusionary rule to state criminal proceedings.

Mapp v. Ohio (1961)

Dolree Mapp was a Cleveland landlord. On May 23, 1957, police officers knocked at her door and demanded entry. When entrance was denied, they entered forcefully, waving a piece of paper they claimed was a search warrant. Dolree grabbed the paper and shoved it down her blouse. A struggle ensued and the officers retrieved the paper. (In all probability, so the courts noted, it was not a search warrant.) They then searched the house, including her dresser drawers and a boarder's locked suitcase in the basement. In it they found "incriminating evidence"—obscene magazines. It appears that neither Mrs. Mapp nor the police knew of the presence of these magazines; the police apparently had been looking for something else.

Mrs. Mapp was convicted of the crime of possession of obscene publications. Her case wound its way through the Ohio appeals process until it reached the Supreme Court of the United States. Most observers were expecting a decision to the effect that the states cannot punish innocent people—Mrs. Mapp did not possess obscene publications (they were her boarder's), nor did she have any criminal intent (*mens rea*) to possess obscene publications. But the Supreme Court ignored substantive issues and decided the case on a procedural question: The search was unreasonable and therefore illegal. The Court did not stop there. It delivered the constitutional bombshell that became the **exclusionary rule:** "We hold that all evidence obtained by searches and seizures in violation of the Constitution is, by that same authority, inadmissible in a state court."[39]

exclusionary rule
Rule prohibiting use of illegally obtained evidence in a court of law.

Until that time every state had been left free to devise its own means of enforcing constitutional rights, including those of the Fourth, Fifth, and Sixth Amendments. Theoretically, the state systems had at their disposition:

- Criminal law remedies against police officers violating the law (criminal trespass, assault, and battery).
- Civil remedies against offending officers and their employers, such as city and state governments.
- Administrative remedies, such as departmental disciplinary proceedings.
- "Bonding" law enforcement officers and forfeiting the bond for the benefit of aggrieved parties and possibly other remedies.[40]

The fact is, as the Supreme Court noted, none of these remedies had ever been seriously tried, and in any case, they did not work. The Court noted that by then (1961), most of the states had switched to the one remedy the federal courts had used since the *Weeks* case of 1914: exclusion of evidence obtained by unconstitutional methods.[41] "Other means of protection," said the Court in *Mapp,* have not worked. It felt compelled "to close the only courtroom door remaining open to evidence secured by official lawlessness in flagrant abuse" of the Constitution.

More particularly, there were two considerations. First, courts should not "dirty" their hands by making decisions on the basis of dirty evidence, procured in violation of law. Second, excluding illegally obtained evidence, reasoned the Court, punishes the police for violating the law by depriving them of the fruits of their labor—a conviction. Police abide by the law, just as potential criminals will not offend for fear of punishment. This is the deterrence rationale, and it involves a big assumption: that deterrence works to stop people from committing offenses. Yet to this day we know that only some would-be offenders are deterred from committing some types of crime, under some circumstances. Even less is known about the effect of the exclusionary rule on the conduct of individual police officers.[42] Studies have shown inconclusive results.[43] One thing is certain: By forcing the exclusion of illegally obtained evidence, the Supreme Court provided a significant incentive to the law enforcement community to intensify training programs for law enforcement officers. In the long run, improved education and training may lead to greater adherence to the law on the part of the police.

The exclusionary rule typically comes into play prior to trial, when the attorney for the accused makes a motion to suppress or exclude illegally obtained evidence, such as an illegally obtained confession, or the instruments of a crime (the tools used by a burglar or an auto thief) or other evidence suggesting the defendant's guilt (blood-stained clothing). If a court fails to exclude illegally obtained evidence and the evidence is used at trial, its use may constitute an error and require reversal of a conviction.

But the reach of the exclusionary rule does not stop there. Any additional evidence that police acquire, directly or indirectly, as a result of the illegal search, arrest, or confession, also may be excluded (see Figure 7.2). Courts have called this additional or secondary

JOE WATERS, CAPTAIN (RETIRED), PHILADELPHIA POLICE DEPARTMENT

From my days as a rookie officer to my retirement last year as a captain in the Philadelphia Police Department, I never once used my gun. This may be surprising and almost inconceivable to those who regularly watch overscripted and densely choreographed police dramas on network television. For those academics who study the police,

and for the family and friends of officers, it is far less surprising.

A police officer's weapon represents a very special symbol of social control. Strange as it might seem, a Glock, a SIG Sauer, or a Beretta serves as a powerful symbol of authoritarian rule. Police wear a uniform and a badge and carry a gun as part of a state-sanctioned wardrobe that conveys authority and, importantly, the community's consent to enforce that authority. Imagine a police force where officers serve without badges or uniforms. Imagine law enforcement in any major city in the United States without weapons to enforce their words; to support their judgment; to move the unmovable to act.

Beyond the notion of social control, a police officer's gun can be a lifeline as a last resort and, most frequently, a place where one's hand goes when suspicions exceed a level of comfort, when the only thing certain about a possibly dangerous situation is uncertainty. Police work can be lonely, challenging, boring, and then, in seconds, exhilarating. Its monotony can be interrupted by an

---

evidence "fruit" and the illegal search or arrest "the poisonous tree." Thus, in legal terms, evidence that is obtained from illegally obtained evidence is excluded from trial because it is tainted—it is **fruit of the poisonous tree.**[44]

Exceptions to the Rule

In a number of exceptional circumstances the Supreme Court has permitted illegally obtained evidence to be presented at trial. Most notable is the **good faith exception**—where police officers acted in good faith on what they believed to be a lawful warrant, evidence so obtained is admissible, even though the warrant never was, or no longer is, valid.[45]

fruit of the poisonous tree
Evidence obtained through illegally obtained evidence, inadmissible because it is tainted by the illegality of the initial search, arrest, or confession.

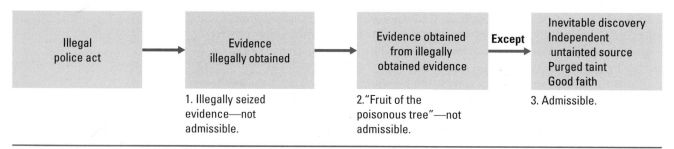

Illegal police act	→	Evidence illegally obtained	→	Evidence obtained from illegally obtained evidence	**Except** →	Inevitable discovery Independent untainted source Purged taint Good faith
		1. Illegally seized evidence—not admissible.		2. "Fruit of the poisonous tree"—not admissible.		3. Admissible.

FIGURE 7.2 How Evidence Becomes Inadmissible and the Exceptions That Make It Admissible

SOURCE: Adapted from Rolando del Carmen, *Criminal Procedure: Law and Practice* (Pacific Grove, CA: Brooks/Cole, 1991), p. 61.

adrenaline rush. Throughout your career, the gun by your side is a stable, consistent, and reliable part of your person, no matter how often or how infrequently you reach for it. Its virtue, some might say, is that it is always there through times of loneliness, challenge, boredom, and exhilaration.

What police rarely discuss, and academics miss entirely, is that most officers—more than one might surmise—have at once a healthy respect and fear of their weapon. Few want to use it. Even fewer want to explain why they felt justified to do so. Once used, there is often more suspicion than congratulations. Once used, there are always more that will second-guess what for you required a second's judgment; a brief encounter in the middle of the night after five hours of work with a momentary, fleeting image. Frequently, the discharge of your gun brings a career change. Not so infrequently, it can end your career.

Perhaps most important, the justice that guns impart is instant and final. Legislatures can en-

gage in debates over the requirements of due process. Courts can patiently adjudicate claims. Prisons can dispense a cold-hearted regime of custody and control over time. Police, though, do not have such a luxury. The use of a weapon on duty results in an instant judgment that can deprive a person of his or her life. That judgment is framed in a simple-minded utility analysis that legislatures and courts may respect and endorse, but one in which legislators and judges have no real understanding.

When determining the reasonableness of the use of force either legislatively or judicially, few discuss or attend to the sense of vulnerability that police have on the less-than-receptive streets of our cities; the ease with which feelings of idealism, caring, and altruism that accompany one's early years of policing may be turned around by rejections and insults from those whom we are asked to serve and protect. No one discusses how very easy the decision is to use deadly force; how very difficult it is to determine when and where deadly force is justified; and how hard it can be to live with the decision once made. I join many of my colleagues in being fortunate never to have once discharged my gun.

The Demise of *Mapp v. Ohio?*

The increasing number of exceptions to the exclusionary rule may signal that the rule itself is on its way out, at the hands of a far more conservative Supreme Court. The battle lines have been drawn and the arguments on both sides of the issue have been marshaled along political and ideological lines.[46] Opponents of the exclusionary rule argue that it:

good faith exception
Exception to the exclusionary rule in which evidence obtained by police acting in good faith with a search warrant issued by a neutral and detached magistrate is admissible, even though the warrant is ultimately found to be invalid.

- Encourages plea bargains and reduced charges through the perception by prosecutors that a case may be lost due to suppressed evidence.
- Excludes reliable evidence and thus undermines the "truth seeking" function of the judiciary.
- Diminishes respect for and perception of legitimacy of the system of justice.
- Vindicates the rights of the accused, but provides no remedy for the victims of crime.
- Fails to deter police misconduct and may actually promote other tactics of questionable constitutional validity, such as raids and sting operations.
- Distorts the allocation of criminal justice resources given the time and money necessary to dispose of the many efforts to suppress evidence.[47]

Whether or not the Supreme Court abandons the exclusionary rule, it cannot be claimed that the rule has severely handicapped the police. Nor has it resulted in the wholesale discharge of obviously guilty parties. Indeed, several studies have found that only between 0.5 and 0.8 percent of felony cases resulted in nonconviction due to the exclusionary rule.[48]

Alternatives to the Rule

There are alternatives to the exclusionary rule if it is ever to be abandoned.[49] There have been proposals for police–civilian review boards to examine allegations of police illegality.[50] Other proposals suggest that the evidence in question should be allowed at trial, but that a separate hearing on the police officer's conduct should take place as well. And then there are those proposals that have not worked well before: criminal actions, civil suits, and administrative sanctions against offending officers.[51]

Illegally Seized Persons

We cannot end the discussion of the exclusionary rule without describing a significant oddity in the law. Illegally seized evidence (mostly personal property) may be excluded at trial, but an illegally seized person may not be excluded. This results from a Supreme Court decision well over a century old, and never overturned. In 1883 an agent of the U.S. government (Henry G. Julian) went to Lima, Peru; kidnapped Frederick Ker, a thief and embezzler under indictment in Illinois; and brought him back to Illinois for trial.

The U.S. Supreme Court ruled that it makes no difference how a defendant's presence at trial is secured (in this case by kidnapping); the court has jurisdiction, no matter what. In other words, an illegally seized person cannot be "excluded" from trial.[52] This rule was applied in subsequent cases. The Supreme Court of Israel relied on the U.S. Supreme Court ruling when it found that its courts had jurisdiction over the infamous Nazi mass murderer Adolf Eichmann, who had been forcibly taken by Israeli agents in Argentina.[53] Most recently, a Mexican resident was kidnapped from his home, flown to Texas, and arrested for his participation in the murder and kidnapping of a Drug Enforcement Administration agent. He subsequently challenged the abduction on the grounds that it violated international law. The U.S. Supreme Court did not agree. In an opinion by Chief Justice Rehnquist, the Court ruled that international law does not prohibit forcible abductions for the purposes of securing a person accused of violating U.S. law.[54] You may recall as well that the United States invaded Panama in 1989 and arrested General Manuel Noriega on U.S. drug charges. He was subsequently convicted in federal court in Miami and is now serving his sentence in federal prison.[55]

Questions about "illegally seized persons" have been raised recently with the indeterminate detention of hundreds of terrorists and suspected terrorists at a maximum-security facility on a U.S. Navy base at Guantanamo Bay, Cuba. Over the past several years of their detention, allegations have surfaced that nearly 10 percent of the detainees are not in any way affiliated with Al Qaeda or the Taliban. According to press reports, many are considered to be of no intelligence value and some were simply low-level Taliban fighters drawn into the conflict immediately before the collapse of the ruling Afghan regime.

The Use and Abuse of Force

In 1829, Sir Robert Peel gave officers of the first police in England the advice that we here quote from the Metropolitan Police Force *Instruction Book* (1829) as still valid: "Remember, that there is no qualification more indispensable to a police officer than a perfect command of temper, never suffering himself to be moved in the slightest degree, by any language or threats that may be used." But when force becomes necessary, how do police officers regulate its use and avoid its abuse? We examine two current issues in law enforcement: the use of deadly force, and the abuse of nondeadly force.

The Ultimate Seizure of the Person: Deadly Force

In *Tennessee v. Garner* (1985), the Supreme Court decided a case in which a father sued a Memphis police officer, as well as governmental agencies, for the loss of life of his seventeen-year-old son. The son, according to undisputed facts, had burglarized a home, and the police had responded instantly to the homeowner's call. An officer spotted the suspect fleeing across the backyard and ordered him to stop. The officer saw that the suspect was unarmed. The youngster made an effort to jump over a high fence. The officer shot and killed him. The common-law rule of England and the United States, as well as the law of Tennessee, had always been that the police may use deadly force to stop a fleeing felon whether or not he or she is in possession of a weapon. The officer had acted properly, according to existing state law and departmental policies, when he shot and killed the suspect; the Supreme Court found that the officer could not be sued for wrongful death.

The Court reached a different conclusion, however, with respect to governmental liability. The Court reasoned that in England when all felonies were capital crimes, perhaps such a rule on the use of deadly force made sense, because an offender found guilty of a felony could be sentenced to death. But taking the life of a suspect who, if convicted, might receive only a relatively short prison sentence makes no sense and constitutes an unreasonable seizure of the person in violation of the Fourth Amendment. The Supreme Court therefore overturned the common-law rule as violating the due process clause of the Fourteenth Amendment. Deadly force may not be used unless it is necessary to prevent the escape of a suspect who, the officer has probable cause to believe, poses a significant threat of death or serious injury to the officer or others.[56] The law in *Garner* has been upheld and distinguished in a host of cases before the United States Supreme Court. Most recently in *Brosseau v. Haugen* (2004), the Court deliberated over whether police used excessive force by shooting a felony suspect in the back as he attempted to flee in an automobile. Given risk the posed by the suspect to persons in the immediate area, the Court held that the officer did not violate the Fourth Amendment's deadly-force standards.[57]

The Police Foundation was allowed to file an *amicus curiae* (friend of the court) brief in which it supported abandonment of the harsh common-law rule. The brief demonstrated through research that the shoot-to-kill rule for fleeing felons does not prevent crime or enhance the protection of police officers, and thus is unreasonable as a law enforcement tool (Table 7.5).

Use of deadly force by police officers has been a major issue in police–minority relations. One commentator has observed, "As most police recruits learn in the academy, the cop on the street . . . carries in his holster more power than has been granted the chief justice of the Supreme Court."[58] Used improperly, this power can lead to riots, needless deaths, litigation against the police, and the downfall of entire city administrations. During and after the urban unrest of the 1960s, the issue was confronted by two presidential commissions, the Commission on Civil Disorders (1968) and the President's Commission on Law Enforcement and the Administration of Justice (1967). Both suggested that use of deadly force was the immediate cause of urban riots.

Even with improved training and clearly articulated guidelines (Table 7.5), controversial incidents will still happen, often polarizing an entire county or city. For example, a New Milford (Connecticut) police officer was charged with murder for shooting a convicted

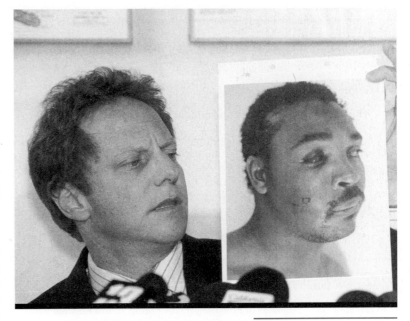

Rodney King's lawyer during a press conference in Los Angeles in March 1991, holding a photo of King showing the injuries inflicted on him by police. Both criminal and civil cases resulted from the beating incident made famous by an amateur videotape.

Use of Force

1. General Policy

- Law enforcement agencies must recognize and respect the value and dignity of every person. In vesting law enforcement officers with the lawful authority to use force to protect the public welfare, a careful balancing of all human interests is required.

- Courtesy in all public contacts encourages understanding and cooperation. The most desirable method for effectuating an arrest is where a suspect complies with simple directions given by an officer. When officers are confronted with a situation where control is required to effect arrest or protect the public safety, officers should attempt to achieve control through advice, warnings and persuasion. Where such verbal persuasion has not been effective, is not feasible, or would appear to be ineffective, an officer may use force that is reasonably necessary.

- Policing requires that at times an officer must exercise control of a violent, assaultive, or resisting individual to make an arrest, or to protect the officer, other officers, or members of the general public from a risk of imminent harm. Police officers should use only an amount of force that is reasonably necessary to effectively bring an incident under control, while protecting the lives of the officers and others.

2. Deadly Force

- Law enforcement officers are authorized to use deadly force only when it is reasonable and necessary to protect the officer or others from an imminent danger of death or serious physical injury to the officer or another person. If nondeadly force reasonably appears to be sufficient to accomplish an arrest or otherwise accomplish the law enforcement purpose, deadly force is not necessary.

- Agencies should develop use of force policies that address use of firearms and other weapons and particular use of force issues such as: firing at moving vehicles, verbal warnings, positional asphyxia, bar arm restraints, and the use of chemical agents.

3. Nondeadly Force

- Law enforcement officers are authorized to use agency-approved nondeadly force techniques and agency-issued equipment where reasonable and necessary to resolve incidents; to protect themselves or another from physical harm; to restrain or subdue a resistant individual; or to bring an unlawful situation safely and effectively under control.

- Where nondeadly force is authorized, officers should assess the incident to determine which nondeadly technique or weapon will best de-escalate the incident and bring it under control in a safe manner.

4. Continuum of Force

- When the use of force is reasonable and necessary, officers should, to the extent possible, use an escalating scale of options and not employ more forceful means unless it is determined that a lower level of force would not be, or has not been, adequate. The levels of force that generally should be included in the agency's continuum of force include: verbal commands, use of hands, chemical agents, baton or other impact weapon, canine, less-than-lethal projectiles, and deadly force.

- Each situation is unique. Good judgment and the circumstances of each situation will dictate the level on the continuum of force at which an officer will start. Depending on the circumstances, officers may find it necessary to escalate or de-escalate the use of force by progressing up or down the force continuum. It is not the intent of this policy to require officers to try each of the options before moving to the next, as long as the level of force used is reasonable under the circumstances.

SOURCE: Excerpt from U.S. Department of Justice, *Principles in Promoting Police Integrity*, http://ojp.osobj.gov/lawenforcement/policeintegrity/welcome.html (June 11, 2002).

TABLE 7.5　Examples of Promising Police Practices and Policies
January 2001 Principles for Promoting Police Integrity

felon whom he was trying to arrest. The suspect was on his knees with his back to the officer.[59] In one of the most controversial cases of deadly force in years, four white New York City police officers were charged with second-degree murder in the fatal shooting of Amadou Diallo, an unarmed West African immigrant. (Figure 7.3) Diallo was shot more than twenty times in a hail of forty-one shots, as he stood in front of his Bronx apartment. The officers were subsequently acquitted of all charges.[60]

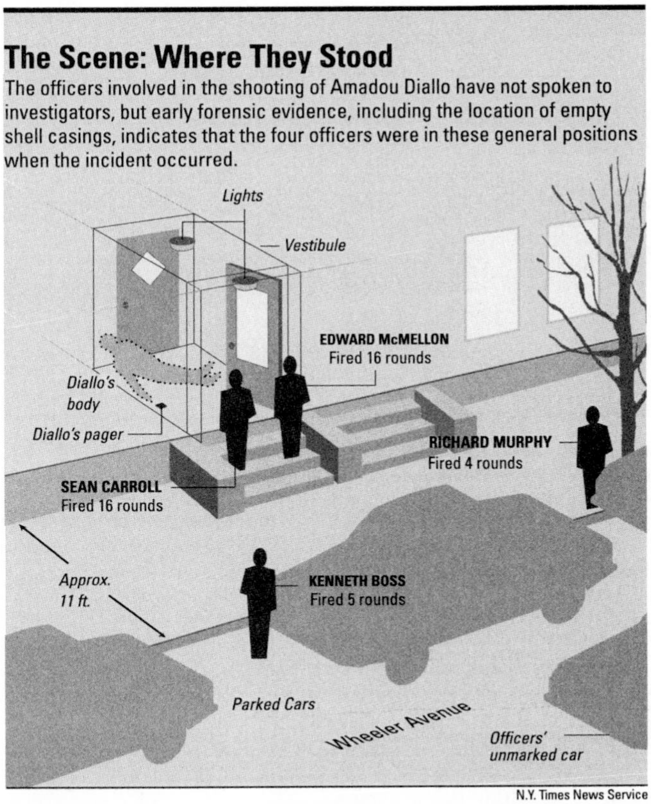

The Scene: Where They Stood

The officers involved in the shooting of Amadou Diallo have not spoken to investigators, but early forensic evidence, including the location of empty shell casings, indicates that the four officers were in these general positions when the incident occurred.

Lights

Vestibule

EDWARD McMELLON
Fired 16 rounds

Diallo's body

Diallo's pager

RICHARD MURPHY
Fired 4 rounds

SEAN CARROLL
Fired 16 rounds

Approx. 11 ft.

KENNETH BOSS
Fired 5 rounds

Parked Cars

Wheeler Avenue

Officers' unmarked car

N.Y. Times News Service

FIGURE 7.3   Diagram of "The Scene: Where They Stood," showing the locations of the officers involved in the Amadou Diallo shooting in the Bronx, New York, in February 1999. Diallo, a twenty-two-year-old West African immigrant, who was unarmed, was killed in the vestibule of his home by a barrage of forty-one bullets, leaving a number of unanswered questions and a strained relationship between the Police Department and the city's many minority groups.

Abuse of Force

The use of overwhelming force against persons, frequently suspects, who are deemed not to respect the power of the police is what we call **police brutality.** Who can forget the image of Rodney King being beaten mercilessly, without any apparent reason, by four Los Angeles police officers?[61] Who can forget the horrific case of Abner Louima, a Haitian immigrant who while in police custody in a Brooklyn (New York) precinct was handcuffed, stripped naked below the waist, and sodomized with a broken broomstick.[62]

How often is excessive force used? Several studies reveal that while excessive force is rarely used if one considers all police–civilian contacts, "improper force" is employed in approximately 35 percent of all encounters involving force. Survey research of police officers also reveals some tolerance for excessive use of force (see Tables 7.6 and 7.7).[63]

Force must be used in law enforcement, but democracies always put limits on that use. In this chapter we have examined the constitutional restrictions on the abuse of force. The best-known abuse historically was probably the "third degree"—torture for the purpose of extracting a confession. Torture by police may be rare in the United States today, but it remains a significant problem in many countries around the world.

police brutality
Use of excessive physical force against another person (usually a suspect) by law enforcement officers.

TABLE 7.6
General Attitudes toward the
Use of Force (in Percent)

	Strongly Agree	Agree	Disagree	Strongly Disagree
Police are not permitted to use as much force as is often necessary in making arrests. (n = 912)[a]	6.2[b]	24.9	60.5	8.4
It is sometimes acceptable to use more force than is legally allowable to control someone who physically assaults an officer. (n = 912)	3.3	21.2	55.2	20.3
Always following the rules is not compatible with getting the job done. (n = 919)	3.8	39.1	49.6	7.6

a. Numbers in parentheses represent valid responses.

b. The frequencies are weighted to reflect the population parameters. The 95 percent confidence intervals for responses in this exhibit range between plus or minus 1.0 percent and 4.0 percent for the frequencies reported. Such confidence intervals are commonly noted as the margin of error or sampling error of the survey findings.

NOTE: Totals may not equal 100 percent due to rounding.

SOURCE: David Weisburd and Rosann Greenspan with Edwin E. Hamilton, Hubert Williams, and Kellie A. Bryant, *Police Attitudes Toward Abuse of Authority: Findings From a National Study* (Washington, DC: National Institute of Justice, 2000), p. 2.

TABLE 7.7
Use of Force Behavior in Officers' Departments (in Percent)

	Never	Seldom	Sometimes, Often, or Always
Police officers in [your department] use more force than is necessary to make an arrest. (n = 922)[a]	16.0[b]	62.4	21.7
Police officers in your department respond to verbal abuse with physical force. (n = 922)	31.8	53.5	14.7

a. Numbers in parentheses represent valid responses.

b. The frequencies are weighted to reflect the population parameters. The 95 percent confidence intervals for responses in this exhibit range between plus or minus 1.0 percent and 4.0 percent for the frequencies reported. Such confidence intervals are commonly noted as the margin of error or sampling error of the survey findings.

NOTE: Totals may not equal 100 percent due to rounding.

SOURCE: David Weisburd and Rosann Greenspan with Edwin E. Hamilton, Hubert Williams, and Kellie A. Bryant, *Police Attitudes Toward Abuse of Authority: Findings From a National Study* (Washington, DC: National Institute of Justice, 2000), p. 3.

Review

The Bill of Rights of 1791, as interpreted by the Supreme Court of the United States, determines the powers of law enforcement at both the federal and the state levels. But it took a century until the federal courts subjected the federal criminal process to the Bill of Rights, and it took more than another half century until the Supreme Court, by a process of selective incorporation, made the principal provisions of the Bill of Rights binding on the states: the Fourth Amendment's protection against unreasonable searches and seizures and the Fifth Amendment's privilege against self-incrimination; and the Sixth Amendment's right to counsel. In doing so, the Supreme Court engaged in judicial legislation by requiring police officers

to give the *Miranda* warnings to arrested persons and by mandating the exclusion of all evidence obtained illegally.

A growing number of exceptions to the original rulings could signal a change: The Supreme Court may abandon its insistence on the exclusionary rule as a "constitutional" requirement. Empirical evidence seems to indicate that constitutional restraints have not handicapped law enforcement—but they have led to improved police training. A troubling issue remains, that of the abuse of force by law enforcement officers. Although the Supreme Court has laid down definite limits on the use of deadly force by such officers, instances of abuse continue to occur.

Thinking Critically about Criminal Justice

1. What are the strongest arguments in favor of abandoning the exclusionary rule? Do you support this rule, or do you feel that it unfairly restricts legitimate police action, letting otherwise guilty criminals go free? If you were asked to write a set of rules for police use of deadly force, would the final product resemble the Supreme Court's ruling in *Tennessee v. Garner?* How would it differ?

Internet Connection

Note: While all of the URLs listed were current as of the printing of this book, these sites often change. Please check our website (http://www. mhhe.com/socscience/crimjustice/adlercj) for updates.

Consider the facts in the tragic shooting death of Malik Jones on April 14, 1997. What conclusions do you come to about the way in which police handled the Jones case? See **http://www.yaledailynews.com/article.asp?AID-1420.**

How many police officers were killed in the line of duty last year? See **http://www.odmp.org/year.php.**

Notes

1. *Kyllo v. United States,* 533 U.S. 27 (2001).
2. See *Hopt v. Utah,* 110 U.S. 574 (1884); and B. James George, *Constitutional Limitations on Evidence in Criminal Cases* (NY: Practicing Law Institute, 1969), pp. 257–258.
3. *Bram v. United States,* 168 U.S. 532 (1897).
4. *Gitlow v. New York,* 268 U.S. 652 (1925).
5. See, e.g., Raoul Berger, *Government by Judiciary: The Transformation of the Fourteenth Amendment* (Cambridge, MA: Harvard University Press, 1977).
6. *Palko v. Connecticut,* 302 U.S. 319 (1937).
7. Ibid., at 325.
8. See *The Criminal Law Revolution and Its Aftermath (1960–1977)* by the editors of *Criminal Law Reporter* (Washington, DC: Bureau of National Affairs, 1972).
9. *Wolf v. Colorado,* 338 U.S. 25 (1949).
10. See John N. Ferdico, *Criminal Procedure for the Criminal Justice Professional* (St. Paul, MN: West, 1985), p. 139.
11. Charles Lane, "Supreme Court Upholds Warrantless Searches: Justices Say California Law Allows Criminals to Sign Away Protections to Gain Probation," *The Washington Post,* December 11, 2001, p. A10.
12. *United States v. Montoya de Hernandez,* 473 U.S. 531 (1985).
13. *United States v. Flores-Montano,* 124 S. Ct. 1582 (2004).
14. *Colorado v. Bannister,* 449 U.S. 1 (1980).
15. *Schneckloth v. Bustamente,* 412 U.S. 218 (1973).
16. *United States v. Matlock,* 415 U.S. 164 (1974); see also Dorothy Kagehiro and William S. Laufer, "The Assumption of Risk Doctrine in Third Party Consent Searches," *Criminal Law Bulletin* 26 (1990), p. 195; and Dorothy Kagehiro and William S. Laufer, "*Illinois v. Rodriguez* and the Social Psychology of Consent," *Criminal Law Bulletin* 27 (1991), p. 42.
17. See Wayne R. LaFave and Jerold H. Israel, *Criminal Procedure* (St. Paul, MN: West, 1985), p. 213.
18. See *Warden v. Hayden,* 387 U.S. 294 (1967).
19. See *Coolidge v. New Hampshire,* 403 U.S. 443 (1971); and *Texas v. Brown,* 460 U.S. 730 (1983).
20. *Terry v. Ohio,* 392 U.S. 1 (1968).
21. See *United States v. Cortez,* 449 U.S. 411 (1981).
22. See *Kolender v. Lawson,* 461 U.S. 352 (1983).
23. See, e.g., *Michigan v. Tyler,* 436 U.S. 499 (1978).
24. See, e.g., *Schmerber v. California,* 384 U.S. 757 (1966). Also see Max DeBerry and G. O. W. Mueller, "Pending Peril and the Right to Search Dwellings," *West Virginia Law Review* 58 (1956), pp. 219–240.
25. See *Chimel v. California,* 395 U.S. 752 (1969).
26. See *Dunaway v. New York,* 442 U.S. 200 (1979).
27. *Carroll v. United States,* 267 U.S. 132 (1925).
28. *Payton v. New York,* 445 U.S. 573 (1980).
29. See *Welsh v. Wisconsin,* 446 U.S. 740 (1984); and *Payton v. New York,* 445 U.S. 573 (1980).
30. *Bram v. United States,* 168 U.S. 532 (1897).
31. *Brown v. Mississippi,* 297 U.S. 278 (1936).
32. *Fikes v. Alabama,* 352 U.S. 191 (1957).
33. *Gideon v. Wainwright,* 372 U.S. 335 (1963).
34. See *Spano v. New York,* 360 U.S. 315 (1959); *Massiah v. United States,* 377 U.S. 201 (1964); and *McLeod v. Ohio,* 381 U.S. 356 (1965).
35. *Miranda v. Arizona,* 384 U.S. 436 (1966).
36. These categories are found in Rolando del Carmen, *Criminal Procedure: Law and Practice,* 2nd ed. (Pacific Grove, CA: Brooks/Cole, 1991).
37. Ibid.
38. See Jill Adler, "The U.S. Supreme Court's 'Harmless Error': An Essay on *Arizona v. Fulminante,*" *Tilburg Foreign Law Review* 1 (1991), p. 15.
39. *Mapp v. Ohio,* 367 U.S. 643 (1961).
40. See B. James George, Jr., *Constitutional Limitations on Evidence in Criminal Cases* (NY: Practicing Law Institute, 1969), pp. 119–132.
41. *Weeks v. United States,* 232 U.S. 383 (1914).
42. See Yale Kamisar, "Does (Did) (Should) the Exclusionary Rule Rest on a 'Principled Basis' Rather Than an 'Empirical Proposition'?" *Creighton Law Review* 16 (1983), p. 565.
43. Craig D. Uchida and Timothy S. Bynum, "Search Warrants, Motions to Suppress and 'Lost Cases': The Effects of the Exclusionary Rule in Seven Jurisdictions,"

Journal of Criminal Law and Criminology 81 (1991), pp. 1034–1066.

44. See *Nardone v. United States,* 308 U.S. 338 (1939); and *Wong Sun v. United States,* 371 U.S. 471 (1963).

45. See *Massachusetts v. Sheppard,* 468 U.S. 981 (1984); *United States v. Leon,* 468 U.S. 897 (1984); and *Arizona v. Evans,* U.S., 63 USLW 4179 (1994).

46. See K. E. Goodpaster, "An Essay on Ending the Exclusionary Rule," *Hastings Law Journal* 33 (1984), p. 1065.

47. These arguments are based on those presented in *Report to the Attorney General: Search and Seizure—Exclusionary Rule* (Washington, DC: Department of Justice, 1986) and found in del Carmen, *Criminal Procedure.*

48. Peter Nardulli, "The Societal Cost of the Exclusionary Rule: An Empirical Assessment," *American Bar Foundation Journal* (1983), p. 585.

49. Indy Hails Keci, "Improving the Exclusionary Rule: A Remedial Education Model," *American Journal of Criminal Justice* 12 (1988), pp. 147–166.

50. See James Hudson, "Police Review Boards and Police Accountability," *Law and Contemporary Problems* 36 (1971), p. 515.

51. William A. Schroeder, "Deterring Fourth Amendment Violations: Alternatives to the Exclusionary Rule," *Georgetown Law Journal* 69 (1981), p. 1361.

52. *Ker v. Illinois,* 119 U.S. 436 (1886).

53. See Michael H. Cardozo, "When Extradition Fails, Is Abduction the Solution?" in *International Criminal Law,* ed. G. O. W. Mueller and Edward M. Wise (South Hackensack, NJ: Fred B. Rothman, 1965), pp. 465–475.

54. *United States v. Humberto Alvarez-Machain,* 112 S. Ct. 2188 (1992).

55. See San Vincent Meddis, "Noriega Defense Team Chips Away," *USA Today,* February 17, 1992, p. 2.

56. *Tennessee v. Garner,* 471 U.S. 1 (1985). For an examination of police shootings subsequent to *Tennessee v. Garner,* see Terry R. Sparger and David J. Giacopassi, "Memphis Revisited: A Reexamination of Police Shootings After the Garner Decision," *Justice Quarterly* 9, no. 2 (1992), pp. 211–225.

57. *Brosseau v. Haugen,* 125 S. Ct. 596 (2004).

58. James J. Fyfe, "Police Use of Deadly Force: Research and Reform," *Justice Quarterly* 5 (June 1988), pp. 165–205; see also Geoffrey P. Alpert and Lorie A. Fridell, *Police Vehicles and Firearms: Instruments of Deadly Force* (Prospect Heights, IL: Waveland Press, 1992).

59. Jill Storms, "Officer Can't Challenge Probable Cause Finding," *The Hartford Courant,* March 27, 1999, p. B2.

60. Laurle P. Cohen, "System Set to Protect Police," *Newsday,* April 11, 1999, p. A8.

61. Carl E. Pope and Lee E. Ross, "Race, Crime and Justice: The Aftermath of Rodney King," *The Criminologist* 17 (1992), pp. 1–10.

62. Dan Barry, "2 More Officers Held in Attack on Haitian Man," *The New York Times,* August 19, 1997, p. A1.

63. David Weisburd and Rosann Greenspan with Edwin E. Hamilton, Hubert Williams, and Kellie A. Bryant, *Police Attitudes Toward Abuse of Authority: Findings from a National Study* (Washington, DC: National Institute of Justice, 2000).

The Courts

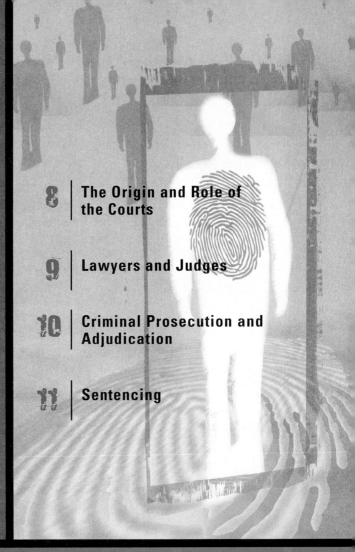

The Origin and Role of the Courts

Lawyers and Judges

10 **Criminal Prosecution and Adjudication**

11 **Sentencing**

• Courts, the heart of the criminal justice system, have had the same function throughout recorded history: to adjudicate cases and controversies. The American court system grew out of the English system, which in turn grew out of earlier systems. In CHAPTER 8, we discuss the contemporary American judicial system and its origins, noting the diversity of federal and state courts, their hierarchical structure (trial and appellate courts), and their interrelationships (especially when federal constitutional issues arise). CHAPTER 9 makes clear that there is much more to courts than judges. Prosecutors and defense attorneys, too, are officers of the court, as are the many administrators and officials who ensure the day-to-day functioning of the judicial machinery.

• CHAPTER 10 focuses on the judicial process, from the defendant's first appearance before a judge through the bail decision, arraignment, and trial. In this chapter, we consider the participation of lay people, the grand and petit jurors, in the trial process, as well as the rights of appeal.

• The final chapter of this part, CHAPTER 11, deals with sentencing—including the many considerations that go into a judicial decision to impose a sentence. The options available and the limitations on judicial discretion, sentencing guidelines, that are one kind of limit, are an outgrowth of the just desserts movement that has shaped sentencing goals and practices during the last two decades. The chapter ends with a discussion of the arguments surrounding the imposition of the death penalty.

CHAPTER

The Origin and
Role of the Courts

It's 3 A.M. on Saturday. Half of New York is still celebrating the start of the weekend and the rest of the city is fast asleep. But not Richard Lawrence. With tears in his eyes, the thirty-seven-year-old Brooklyn electrician is leaving Manhattan's criminal court after more than twenty-eight hours in a cell he shared with pimps, drug addicts, wife beaters, drunks, graffiti artists, and petty crooks.

• Hours after the trial of Sean "Puffy" Combs on weapons and bribery charges wound down for the day, the wheels of justice are still turning in what court officers call the "lobster shift." "I was on the subway and I had to go to the bathroom real bad," said Lawrence. "So I went between the cars and an undercover policewoman arrested me for public urination."

• Lawrence, who was released without a fine, was just one of the 300 cases that were waiting to be processed by prosecutors from the New York County District Attorneys office who work around the clock from Wednesday to Saturday and from 9 A.M. to 1 A.M. every other day. So heavy is their caseload that judges here don't even take time off for Christmas Day.

• A visit to court in the dead of night shows the criminal justice system at its most depressing. Water leaking from the roof drips onto the linoleum floor, pregnant teenagers wait with very young children for relatives to be bailed, and all officials except the judges carry guns. Most of those arrested meet their lawyer for the first time in a glass cubicle for about five minutes while the case ahead of theirs is heard.

• Lawyer Bob Zuflacht, who has been representing legal aid clients for twenty-five years, said the lack of preparation and the pressure to move cases through can be worrying. "Just five minutes in front of a judge in the middle of the night is the difference here between a man returning to his wife and kids or going off to Rikers Island prison," he said.

• Yet for a system that is meant to work through the backlog of people in custody, the lobster shift works slowly. Frequent breaks mean an average of three cases may be heard an hour, and every time a suspect who has jumped bail is brought in or the police need a warrant issued, proceedings are broken off while the judge deals with them. Senior court clerk Bob Smith said every conceivable sort of criminal passes through the nighttime arraignment court.

- "I've seen everything from babies boiled in oil to sixteen-year-olds raping eight-year-olds, beheadings, the lot. Then you'll get a guy who has been brought in without a bell on his bicycle and he'll have to sit in the cells for hours with psychos who are under observation as suicide risks."

- However, Judge Mathew Cooper insists that the system may not be pretty but it is effective. "There is very little glory here, but without this people would wait for days. I try my best to deliver justice," he said. "At 1.30 A.M. I feel the same as when I start at 9 A.M. or 5 P.M. Every case is important and there's no tendency to say, 'It's late, let's just get out of here.' Everyone who passes through the twenty-four-hour court is glad of it because it represents at least the hope of freedom."

- Ronald Beckwith Brown claims he borrowed a friend's car and drove to New York from Ohio but was arrested for car theft. He was bailed after spending thirty-five hours in the cells.

- "It's bad back there," he said. "I only came for a look at the Big Apple and I ended up with no toothbrush, no toilet paper, no soap, people drunk and bleeding laying on the floor. At least when I saw the judge it was over."[1]

Some courts, particularly in large, congested, urban areas, find it a great challenge to dispense justice fairly, impartially, and promptly. Why? There are many reasons.

Let's consider one of the least offered explanations. In their exuberance over "getting tough" on crime, Washington and California voters passed referenda in December 1993 and March 1994 that (1) send third-felony convicts (even those convicted for a nonviolent third felony) away for twenty-five years to life, and (2) give double sentences for second-felony convicts (Table 8.1). It is doubtful that voters considered the full impact of such a law. Had criminal justice specialists been consulted, they would have predicted that many offenders, affected by the new law, would no longer plead guilty. (Under the old law, an average of 94 percent did.) In fact, recent data show that only 14 percent of two-strike defendants and 6 percent of third-strike offenders plead guilty. The others demand a jury trial and so courts in Washington and California gasp for air and money—in addition to independence, impartiality, and fairness. Local jails and detention facilities have felt the effects as well. Pretrial detention populations have risen dramatically.

In this chapter we trace the history of our state and federal court system. We examine the extent to which court systems can administer justice fairly, equitably, and expeditiously under a host of pressures including that from legislation that may satisfy an important political purpose.

TABLE 8.1
Three Strikes and You're Out in California

Examples of qualifying convictions: murder, rape, robbery, attempted murder, assault with intent to rape or rob, any felony resulting in bodily harm, arson, kidnapping, mayhem, burglary of occupied dwelling, grand theft with firearm, drug sales to minors, any felony with deadly weapon.

	Required Prior Record	Current Offense	Enhancement
Second strike	One qualifying conviction	Any felony	Twice the current offense term with no release before serving 80% of that term.
Third strike	Two qualifying convictions	Any felony	25 years to life with no release before serving 80% of the 25-year term.

SOURCES: Adapted from California Penal Code S. 667; Franklin E. Zimring, Gordon Hawkins, and Sam Kamin, *Punishment and Democracy: Three Strikes and You're Out in California* (New York: Oxford University Press, 2001).

Origin of America's Courts

Throughout history, emperors, kings, dukes, and other nobles had estates or castles that were referred to as "courts"—the court of the king of England, the court of the queen of Spain, and so on. Important business was conducted at the court, including the business of resolving disputes and adjudging the guilt or innocence of persons accused of crime by means of a trial. Trial was a game at the court, very much like games played on basketball courts and tennis courts.

What all these court games had in common was the fact that they were: (*a*) played in established public places in accordance with a set of agreed-upon rules, and (*b*) judged by referees or judges in the presence of the public. Over the centuries, changes have been made in the procedures used to judge the guilt of an accused, but the basic idea still holds. A criminal trial is a game played in court by competitors; it is an adversarial contest in which combatants defend opposing positions. At least, such is the English-American view of a trial.

Colonial Courts

Colonial courts started modestly. Perhaps Thomas Olive, the governor of the colony of West Jersey, summed up the prevailing view. He said that he was "in the habit of dispensing justice sitting on a stump in his meadow."[2] As the population of the colonies grew, however, formal courts of law appeared in Virginia, Plymouth, Massachusetts Bay, Maryland, Rhode Island, Connecticut, and New Haven. Drawing on the example set by the English Parliament, the colonial legislatures became the highest courts.[3] The Massachusetts Bay Colony established a powerful body known as the General Court that acted as both a legislature and the highest court of the colony.[4]

Beneath the legislatures were the superior courts, with the same jurisdiction as the Kings Bench and the courts of assize. Examples were the Court of Assistants in the Massachusetts Bay Colony, the General Court in Virginia, and the Court of Tryals in Rhode Island. These courts heard both civil and criminal cases. Over time, some colonies established trial courts headed by a chief justice and several associate justices. Appeals from the trial courts were heard by the governor and his council in what were often called "courts of appeals."[5]

Courts established at the county level played a key role in both the government and the social life of the colonies. In addition to having jurisdiction in both civil and criminal cases, county courts fulfilled many administrative duties: setting and collecting taxes, supervising the building of roads, and licensing taverns.

"The Trial of George Jacobs, August 5, 1692," by J. H. Matteson, 1855. George Jacobs, a patriarch of Salem, Massachusetts, was accused, tried, and executed as a witch.

Courts for a New Nation

The founders of the new republic had profound concerns about the distribution of power between courts and legislatures, and between the states and the federal government. For good and obvious reasons they feared the tyranny that flows from the concentration of governmental power. After all, they were living in the shadow of their experience with English rule. On the other hand, they were also living with the problems associated with a weak centralized government. This conflict prompted the delegates to the Constitutional Convention (1787) to create a separate federal judiciary—separate from the legislative branch. As a result, there are two legal systems in America, one implemented by the state courts (inherited directly from the Crown of England) and another artificially created by the Congress and entrusted to the federal courts.

State Courts: Organization and Role

We begin our examination with the state court system, since it began at the moment of independence and simply continued the pre-Revolutionary (royal) system but under republican auspices. Moreover, there is far more activity in the state courts than in federal courts. In 2002, for example, over 96.2 million cases were filed in the trial courts of the 50 states, the District of Columbia, and Puerto Rico, including 15.4 million criminal and 16.3 million civil cases. Juvenile cases accounted for 2 million cases, domestic cases summed 4.6 million, but the great majority concerned traffic and other local law violations, which numbered 57.6 million. Most states have a three-tier system of courts: courts of limited or special jurisdiction, courts of general jurisdiction, and a double tier of appellate courts (Figure 8.1).

Courts of Limited or Special Jurisdiction

Dimmit County, Texas, has been called "an easy target" and "the land that law forgot," because the judge who presides over the local court has had no trials in fourteen years. According to friends, the former service-station clerk is simply "nervous" about the trial process. As a nonlawyer, he may feel at a distinct disadvantage.[6]

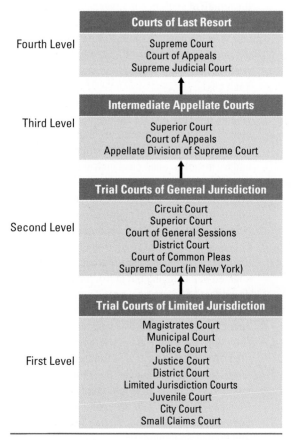

	Fourth Level	**Courts of Last Resort**

Fourth Level

Courts of Last Resort
Supreme Court
Court of Appeals
Supreme Judicial Court

Third Level

Intermediate Appellate Courts
Superior Court
Court of Appeals
Appellate Division of Supreme Court

Second Level

Trial Courts of General Jurisdiction
Circuit Court
Superior Court
Court of General Sessions
District Court
Court of Common Pleas
Supreme Court (in New York)

First Level

Trial Courts of Limited Jurisdiction
Magistrates Court
Municipal Court
Police Court
Justice Court
District Court
Limited Jurisdiction Courts
Juvenile Court
City Court
Small Claims Court

FIGURE 8.1   State Court Systems

SOURCE: Adapted from Abraham S. Blumberg, *Criminal Justice: Issues and Ironies* (New York: New Viewpoints, 1979), p. 150.

But while nonlawyer judges may feel disadvantaged, at least they are not alone. Almost every town or city has a court with a **justice of the peace,** magistrate, or judge, who is not necessarily trained in law, who handles minor criminal cases (misdemeanors or violations), less serious civil suits (involving small sums of money), traffic and parking violations, and health law violations. These courts are variously called municipal courts, justice of the peace courts, and magistrate's courts. They are known more generally as **courts of limited jurisdiction.**

Courts of limited jurisdiction have been called the "workhorses of the state judiciary." This is a well-deserved name. There are more than 14,000 courts of limited jurisdiction in forty-four states, with nearly 20,000 magistrates, district judges, and justices of the peace. Courts of limited jurisdiction process more than half of the cases tried in state courts. The balance of the cases are traffic and local law violations. **Courts of special jurisdiction** include courts that specialize in certain areas of law: family courts, juvenile courts, and probate courts (which deal with the transfer of the property and money of a deceased).

Courts of General Jurisdiction

At the next level are the major trial courts—**courts of general jurisdiction.** Such courts have regular jurisdiction over all cases and controversies involving civil and criminal law. Courts of general jurisdiction are typically county courts but, in less populated states, they

justice of the peace
Originally a judicial officer, normally not learned in the law, assigned to investigate and try minor cases. Presently a judge of a lower local or municipal court with limited jurisdiction.

courts of limited jurisdiction
Courts (with a justice of the peace, magistrate, or judge presiding) that handle minor criminal cases, less serious civil suits, traffic and parking violations, and health law violations.

courts of special jurisdiction
Courts that specialize in certain areas of law: family courts, juvenile courts, and probate courts (transfer of property and money of deceased).

courts of general jurisdiction
Major trial courts that have regular, unlimited jurisdiction over all cases and controversies involving civil and criminal law.

MICHAEL HARWIN, SUPERIOR COURT JUDGE, NORTHWEST DISTRICT, LOS ANGELES COUNTY, CALIFORNIA

When I first began law school, becoming a lawyer was my only goal. That years later I would become a judge never occurred to me. Movies and television focus on the lawyers, police, witnesses and in criminal cases the accused. Law school focuses more on appellate rulings than actual courtroom procedure.

Nothing prepared me for the first time on a Monday when I walked into a courtroom to preside over an arraignment calendar. There were almost a hundred people in custody for driving under the influence, several bailiffs, prosecutors, public defenders and private defense lawyers. All were having conversations at once.

Even harder to get used to was having every word you say written down by an ever present court reporter. No other profession keeps track verbatim of everything said the entire working day.

Most plead guilty for "time served" instead of demanding a trial. Their main concern is "will I get out today?" It was my responsibility to make sure each defendant understood their constitutional rights and wanted to waive or give them up by pleading guilty. With one or two defense lawyers taking only a minute or two to discuss each case with their client, that meant I had to explain their rights when accepting their pleas in such a way that I could certify that's what they really wanted to do.

After misdemeanor arraignments I graduated to a master calendar assignment where I directed three hundred cases per day. I was told by a *New York Times* reporter it was the busiest courtroom in America at the time. Master calendar courts send cases out to trial courts when they are ready to start trial, take guilty pleas from some cases that had entered not-guilty pleas at arraignment, and postponed or "continued" cases not ready for trial.

With only a limited number of courtrooms to try cases, it is easy to calculate that if most do not plead guilty, the system could not provide speedy trials for all cases. How do we maintain the balance? Both sides have to be reasonable, as does the judge. The prosecution may not get the length of sentence it always wants and the defense may have to agree to a sentence more stiff than it wants. The judge often must rely on the parties to best know the strengths and weaknesses of their case (and know when to back off).

There is a possibility that with the large amount of cases and the small amount of time able to be devoted to each case that an assembly line mentality can develop. We strive against that and try to look at each case individually.

I once had a homeless man on probation for arson. This was not a case of burning down a house or building but a slight charring caused by a fire he started in a trash bin outside a building. Those on probation are required to return periodically to check on their progress. The man seemed to be staying out of trouble and so I ordered that he return on a specific day in the future. I asked him, "Do you want a paper with the next date?" He said, "No, it's my birthday." I responded, "Well we will have to have a party then." Most defendants don't realize that I write down on the case file any statement, excuse or fact of note. This is so a defendant is precluded from saying, "I didn't do my community service because my grandmother died in Texas, in May and then in September use the same excuse. I wrote down "Defendant's birthday next appearance."

Generally the judge reviews the case files the day before or that day in a mass court as opposed to a trial court where you have fewer cases and more advance time. The day before the probationer's next appearance I saw my birthday note. I bought a cake the next morning on the way to court. When he came into court I had reviewed the probation report and he was in compliance. I said, "We won't need to see you for six months." He said, "You forgot my birthday, didn't you judge." I took the cake out from under the bench, without candles since he was a convicted arsonist, and this grown man started to cry. He said no one had remembered his birthday since he was a little child. The entire staff had a slice. A bailiff told me he took what was left and walked to the probation department and gave a slice to his probation officer.

When I was assigned to felony preliminary hearings, I heard about 5–10 cases per day. Generally only the prosecutor calls witnesses who can then be cross-examined by the defense lawyer. The judge's job is to decide if there is a sufficient case to go to trial. This is a "mini-trial" usually without a defense case. The prosecutor calls only enough witnesses to convince the judge to "hold the defendant to answer" or go to trial. When several "prelims" are set for the morning calendar we call each case only when all the witnesses are present. Consequently, some victims and witnesses arrive on time and may have to sit all day if a defense lawyer is late, a defendant who is being transported in custody is delayed or crucial other prosecution witnesses are not present.

I had a commercial burglary case where the alleged victim owned a small furniture store that had been burglarized. The owner had sat and waited all day and his case was not ready. When I ordered him to come back the next day he said, "Judge, I had to close my store all day today. I lost more today by closing than was taken in the burglary. I feel as if I'm being victimized twice." I arranged to have him placed "on call," meaning he could go to work and agreed to come in within one hour after we called him and told him we would be ready for him.

When I began hearing felony trials, I presided over numerous murder trials. On one case I was assigned to re-try a man whose murder conviction in front of another judge years before had been reversed due to the prior jury having heard an improperly obtained confession. He had been convicted of throwing acid in the face of a woman law student who swallowed some of the acid and died. He and another man had been convicted. This time he decided to represent himself. As a judge I told him, among other things, it was dangerous for him to be his own

lawyer and that he would be held to the same standards as an experienced lawyer. He said, "No one else knows my case like I do and no one else cares as much and I do not want another lawyer." The first witness called was a former prostitute who had been with the defendant and her pimp when they planned the crime. He cross-examined her and committed the biggest trial mistake possible; he asked a question to which he was not certain of the answer. He said, "How do you know I threw the acid and not your boyfriend?" She said, "I was in the police station and I heard you confess." He was convicted and is still in prison.

The saddest cases a judge hears are those involving child abuse. In child murder cases there are often gruesome autopsy photos. The judge has discretion under the evidence code to decide if the jury should be allowed to see them. Generally the prosecution tries to introduce them and the defense objects. The judge conducts a balancing test to determine if the probative value is outweighed by the prejudicial effect. In one case where the mother and her boyfriend were charged with killing her child and then burning the body, I did not allow the photo. The body was so badly and thoroughly burned it did not depict anything which would help a jury decide the case since the coroner said the burning was after death. The prejudicial effect would have been too great. The boyfriend was found guilty. The jury hung 11–1 for guilty on the mother. The holdout juror later said she did not believe a mother could have done such a thing to her child.

Having been on the bench over 22 years, I have heard thousands and thousands of cases, some very minor, some horrendous. I will occasionally have someone approach me on the street or in a restaurant and say, "You're a judge, aren't you?" It is virtually impossible to remember if a particular person was a witness, victim or defendant from years ago. The person asking could be someone I sentenced to years in prison now released or a family member. I always respond, "Before I answer your question, tell me if you were treated fairly in the courtroom." So far no one has said they weren't.

DRUG COURTS

The "war on drugs" may not have stemmed the tide of illegal drug trafficking in the United States, but it has had a dramatic impact on the number of drug-related arrests, prosecutions, and imprisonments. Drug offenders clog state and federal court systems throughout the United States and have contributed to the worst prison-crowding problem in our nation's history. Many factors, including the effectiveness of drug courts, will determine how serious this problem will be in the next millennium.

The Emergence of Specialized "Drug Courts"

In 1989, the Florida Supreme Court gave Associate Chief Judge Herbert M. Klein a one-year leave of absence to arrive at a solution to the devastating effects that drug offenses were having on the Dade County Court.[1] After much study, Judge Klein concluded that a whole new approach to drug crime was desperately needed. The key to addressing the problem of drug-related court delays and prison overcrowding was reducing the number of drug users, not finding new ways of processing more drug arrestees through the courts.

How is it possible to do this? Klein proposed a community-based diversion program for a select number of arrestees—specifically, those charged with possessing or purchasing drugs who do not have a history of violent crime, drug trafficking, or prior nondrug felonies. The program is based on a simple carrot-and-stick approach: Your case will be dismissed and the record will be sealed if you agree to be treated for drug addiction and then complete treatment. If you do not agree to be treated or fail to complete treatment, the criminal case against you

will be prosecuted. It is better, Klein argues, to invest in a year of drug treatment and close surveillance than to deal with the costs of years of drug-related offending.

At the center of the program is a drug court. After deciding who will be included in the program, the drug court monitors the progress of participants and determines when cases should be dismissed. In contrast to traditional criminal courts, defendants must talk directly to the drug court judge. Defense counsel, the prosecutor, and the judge all join together on one team with two clear objectives: successful drug treatment and diversion out of the criminal justice system.

The treatment phase of the program has three phases: detoxification, stabilization, and aftercare. Detoxification consists of developing a treatment plan, regularly scheduled acupuncture sessions, group and individual counseling, and inpatient residential treatment. After successfully attending all scheduled sessions, and after seven consecutive negative urine tests, clients are evaluated by counselors and the judge for the fourteen- to sixteen-week stabilization phase. Here clients maintain abstinence, attend one-to-one substance abuse counseling sessions, and engage in group therapy. Placement in aftercare, the third phase of the program, takes place after an overall assessment of client readiness. In this final phase, which lasts thirty-six weeks, the focus is on education (community college) and gaining the vocational skills necessary for employment. Following an assessment that the client no longer needs further monitoring, counselors make a discharge recommendation to the judge, and all charges are dropped. If the client is not re-arrested within a twelve-month period, the arrest record is sealed.

may be courts of a region that includes several counties. They may be called superior courts or district courts, and their judges are law school graduates, often with extensive experience at the bar. They are either elected or appointed.

Appellate Courts

James Cecil Law, Jr., decided to purchase a $39 shotgun. Why? He and his wife had recently moved into a new neighborhood and were burglarized within two weeks of their arrival. The shotgun, along with special locks on the windows, would protect the home. Several weeks after the purchase of the shotgun, a neighbor of Law's called the police to investigate a strange light that appeared to come from Law's home. The police arrived and first checked all doors. They started looking at the condition of the windows and found a broken pane of glass on a door. An officer removed the pane and stuck his hand through the opening to see whether he could open the door. As the officer reached inside, Law, suspecting another burglary, fired his shotgun through the door, killing the officer.

Miami's drug court has been a great success. Between 1989 and 1993, over 4,500 arrestees have entered the program (nearly 20 percent of all arrestees charged with drug offenses). Before the drug court, up to 60 percent of all drug offenders in the county were rearrested. For the first twelve months after program completion, only 11 percent of the graduates of the drug court were rearrested. Remarkably, of those drug court defendants who were rearrested, the length of time to their first rearrest was two to three times longer than comparable non-drug court offenders.[2] The success of Miami's drug court is reflected in a growing number of drug courts and court-ordered drug treatment programs, including: the Los Angeles County Drug Court; Multnomah County's Sanction Treatment Opportunity Progress Program in Portland, Oregon; and Kings County's Drug Treatment Alternative-to-Prison Program in Brooklyn, New York.

The Future of Drug Courts

As of May 2001, more than 229,000 drug-dependent offenders have made their way through 688 drug courts around the United States.[3] What makes these courts so important in the "war" against drugs? There have been many creative proposals to combat drug-related violence, as well as the use, sale, and distribution of drugs.

Few, however, have met with the success of drug courts in achieving reductions in recidivism and drug usage, not to mention the birth of hundreds of drug-free babies, the re-unification of countless families, the successful vocational and educational training of a sizable percentage of drug court participants, and the active endorsement of the drug court judiciary who, in spite of the burdensome job, wholeheartedly endorse the value of specialized courts for drug offenders.

After only a few years as a criminal justice specialist, you too will celebrate programs that offer real solutions to the most difficult problems complicating the entire criminal justice system—drugs and drug violence. This makes drug courts one of the few notable successes to bring with us into the future.

Questions for Discussion

1. Are you convinced of the need for specialized courts?

2. Would the legalization and legal regulation of drugs be a more reasonable and preferable alternative to drug courts?

SOURCES
1. Peter Finn and Andrea K. Newlyn, "Miami Drug Court Gives Drug Defendants a Second Chance," *National Institute of Justice Journal* (November 1993).
2. John S. Goldkamp and Doris Weiland, *Assessing the Impact of Dade County's Felony Drug Court* (Washington, DC: NIJ, 1993).
3. Steven Belenko, *Research on Drug Courts: A Critical Review 2001 Update* (New York: The National Center on Addiction and Substance Abuse at Columbia University, 2001).

A jury found Law guilty of second-degree murder and assault with intent to murder. He was sentenced to two concurrent ten-year prison sentences. Law appealed: He asked the Maryland Court of Appeals to consider if (1) there was sufficient evidence to sustain a conviction, (2) the trial court's instructions to the jury unfairly shifted the burden of proof, and (3) the degree of force used by Law was justifiable in light of the circumstances. You may be disappointed to learn that Judge Lowe of the Maryland Court of Appeals affirmed Law's conviction, ruling that he had failed to establish the necessity of his conduct.[7]

Maryland, like all other states, has developed elaborate procedures of appeal for parties who are unsuccessful at trial. In criminal cases this refers exclusively to those claiming to be unjustly convicted. In some states the only **appellate court** is the state's supreme court; others provide an intermediate court of appeals. A person convicted of a crime has the right to appeal to an appellate court and ultimately to the court of last resort, usually the state supreme court, whenever the trial court is alleged to have erred on a point of law. Some appeals are mandatory—the appellate court is required to hear the case (death

appellate court
Court with the power to review the judgment of a trial court, examining errors of law.

241

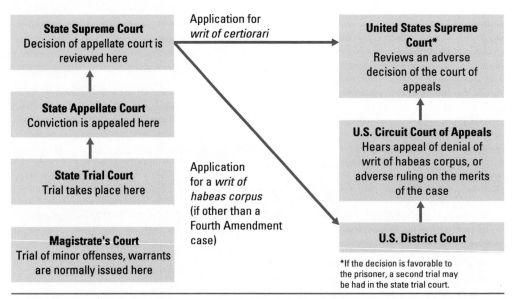

FIGURE 8.2   Path of Criminal Cases through State and Federal Appeals Processes with Crossover in Constitutional Cases

sentences often result in mandatory appeals). States can also permit their appellate courts to choose which appeals they will hear in certain categories of cases. These are known as discretionary appeals.

Intermediate Appellate Courts and Supreme Courts

The majority thirty-two of states have one intermediate appellate court and a single court of last resort, which is usually called the **state supreme court** but in some states is known as the supreme judicial court or the court of appeals. Texas and Oklahoma have two separate courts of last resort, one for civil and one for criminal appeals. Supreme courts consist of five to nine justices, usually sitting together (*en banc*) to hear a case, although in some states they will divide into panels for certain cases.

In most states with intermediate appellate courts, appeals from trial courts normally lie with that court before going to the state's court of last resort (Figure 8.2). Only a small percentage of intermediate appeals decisions are reviewed by the courts of last resort, thus making the intermediate appellate court the final arbiter in many cases.[8] What are the chances of a successful appeal? In reviewing the work of a sample of state supreme courts over a 100-year period, Stanton Wheeler and his colleagues found that an average of 60 percent of lower-court rulings were affirmed by the supreme courts. Of the criminal appeals filed during this time frame, the government was far more successful than individuals in its appeals: The government was successful in 68 percent of the criminal appeals filed between 1935 and 1970, the latest period Wheeler examined.[9]

state supreme court
State court of last resort (except in certain jurisdictions, where the supreme court is a trial court of unlimited jurisdiction).

Federal Courts: Organization and Role

federal courts
Courts of the federal system, applying federal law, with power to test the constitutionality of state law and adjudicate controversies arising between residents of two or more states.

The primary function of the **federal courts** is to apply and enforce all federal laws created by Congress. These laws, in the form of statutes or codified law, include a large body of federal criminal laws that range from violations of environmental laws to treason and piracy. Most of the federal criminal laws can be found in one title (Title 18) in the comprehensive collection of federal statutes called the U.S. Code. But there are more than

1,700 non–Title 18 federal statutes that have criminal penalties. All of these crimes have been created to protect the powers of the federal government to carry out both domestic and foreign policy.

The federal courts have a second and perhaps even more important function: They are continually called on to test the constitutionality of federal and state legislation and of court decisions. Let us begin with an example. Can a state pass and enforce a statute making it a criminal offense for black and white citizens to intermarry? In *Loving v. Virginia* (1967), the Supreme Court of the United States resoundingly said no.[10] The states cannot create such a crime because it violates the equal protection clause of the Fourteenth Amendment to the Constitution. In other words, the United States Supreme Court (a federal court) has the power to hold as a matter of law that a state cannot enact a statute that violates the United States Constitution. Consider another example, this time one of criminal procedure. Can a state court receive in evidence at trial an object seized by state or local law enforcement officers in violation of the Fourth Amendment, which protects citizens against unreasonable searches and seizures? No, said the Supreme Court in *Mapp v. Ohio:* The Fourth Amendment, under the due process guarantee of the Fourteenth Amendment, protects all people in the United States.[11]

Federal Magistrates

At the lowest level of jurisdiction are the federal magistrates, formerly called United States commissioners. The magistrates not only have trial jurisdiction over minor federal offenses, but they also have the important task of issuing warrants of arrest or search warrants to federal law enforcement officers, such as agents of the Federal Bureau of Investigation and the Drug Enforcement Administration. Congress expanded the power of the federal magistrates by allowing them to "undertake virtually any task performed by district judges, except for felony trials and sentencing."[12]

United States District Courts

The trial courts in the federal system, called United States **district courts,** have both civil and criminal jurisdiction. There are ninety-four federal district courts, including those in Guam, the Virgin Islands, the northern Marianas, and Puerto Rico. Every state has at least one such court, and the populous states have more than one.

During 2005 criminal cases were commenced against 68,996 defendants in federal district courts. Nearly 90 percent of these cases were against felony defendants.

Drug cases represent the single largest category of criminal cases filed (34 percent of all criminal filings in 2005). These figures probably fail to reveal the full extent of drug-related cases brought before the district courts. The Anti-Drug Abuse Act of 1988 designated drug crimes as "crimes of violence" and enabled the United States to wage a "war on drugs" with weapons of war and immigration laws. In 1991, the attorney general announced "Operation Triggerlock," an enforcement effort aimed at finding and prosecuting individuals and drug gangs that violate federal weapons laws.[13] The result: In one year, a 15 percent increase in immigration cases and a 20 percent increase in weapons and firearms cases. Another "hidden" area of drug-related cases are the civil suits filed to seize assets in criminal drug cases.

district courts
Trial courts in the federal and in some state systems.

Fired Arthur Andersen auditor David Duncan, right, listens to his attorney Robert Giuffra on Capitol Hill Thursday, January 24, 2002, before a House Energy subcommittee hearing on the destruction of Enron-related documents. Duncan cited his Fifth Amendment rights, declining to testify to Congress about anything he knows or anything he did in the destruction of Enron documents.

In 1974, Congress passed the Speedy Trial Act, which requires that all criminal cases be brought to trial within 100 days or be dismissed. Quite obviously, criminal cases are now given priority over civil cases in the district courts. But this has resulted in civil suits having to wait years to be heard. District Court Judge Charles Richey has lamented: "I'm a drug judge five days a week and a civil judge at night and on the weekend."[14]

United States Circuit Courts of Appeal

circuit courts of appeal
Federal appellate courts with the power to review judgments of federal district courts. See also *appellate court*.

An appeal of a conviction in a federal district court is heard by a United States **circuit court of appeal.** There are 13 appeals courts: one in each of 11 circuits, plus one in the District of Columbia and another (since 1982), also in Washington, District of Columbia, called the federal circuit (see Figure 8.3). The last handles appeals that originate anywhere in the country when they pertain to such matters as patents and copyrights, some tax disputes, and suits against the federal government. There are 167 federal appeals court judges.

The original designation of states included within the federal circuits was made when most of the business of the federal courts was on the heavily populated East Coast and in the Midwest. Because the West Coast has since become very populous, the Ninth Circuit, which covers a vast area, has more business than any of the other courts.

The Supreme Court of the United States

The Supreme Court of the United States occupies a unique position in our system of government. It represents the highest echelon of the third branch of government, the judiciary. The power of the Court is not equaled by courts of any other country. The chief

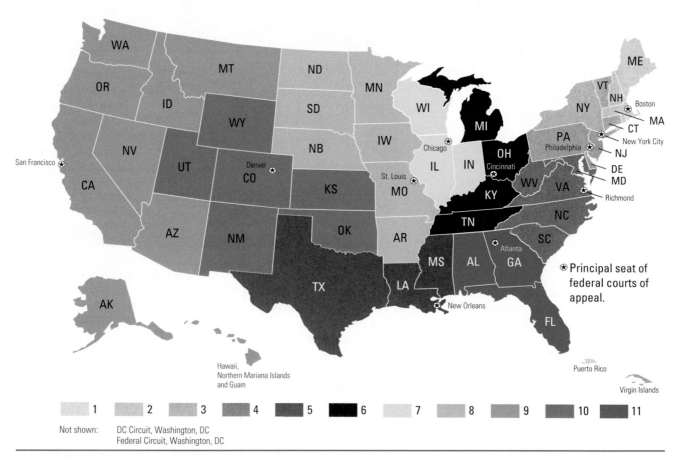

FIGURE 8.3   United States Circuit Courts of Appeal

**Courtroom Seating of the Justices,
Marshal, Clerk, and Counsel**

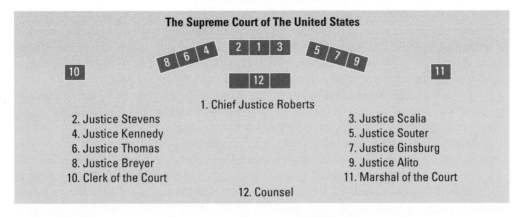

The Supreme Court of The United States

1. Chief Justice Roberts

2. Justice Stevens
4. Justice Kennedy
6. Justice Thomas
8. Justice Breyer
10. Clerk of the Court

3. Justice Scalia
5. Justice Souter
7. Justice Ginsburg
9. Justice Alito
11. Marshal of the Court

12. Counsel

FIGURE 8.4   The Supreme Court of the United States, 2007–2008 Term

justice is not just the chief justice of the Supreme Court but the chief justice of the United States. The chief justice and the eight associate justices are appointed by the president of the United States, with the advice and consent of the Senate (Figure 8.4).

Each year more than 7,000 cases are filed in the Supreme Court asking for review. The justices hear approximately 100 (or fewer) cases. These cases deal with significant areas of the law and interpretations of the Constitution. Over the years, the Court has focused on specific areas. Earlier this century, for example, the Court issued an extensive number of rulings that dealt with economic regulation. Beginning at midcentury, the Court's attention shifted to civil rights, an area in which the Court has led the way for the other branches of government in instituting important social changes.

The **United States Supreme Court** is the ultimate authority in interpreting the Constitution as it applies to both federal and state law. It also is the final authority in interpreting federal law. Thus, both federal and state cases may reach the Supreme Court.

**United States
Supreme Court**
Federal court that has ultimate authority in interpreting the Constitution as it applies to federal and state law; the final authority in interpreting federal law.

Interaction between State Courts and Federal Courts

It is important not to view the state and the federal court systems as wholly independent or mutually exclusive. A legal controversy that arises in a state court may raise federal constitutional questions. In such a case, a federal court may be asked to resolve the federal constitutional question, as it did in *Loving v. Virginia* and *Mapp v. Ohio*.

Suppose, for example, that on the tip of an anonymous informer, with no corroborating evidence, a local magistrate issues a search warrant authorizing the search of a college dormitory room for marijuana. Suppose further that marijuana is found in the drawer of a desk that is used by two students. Both are arrested, tried in a local court, and convicted of the crime of possession of a controlled substance. Defense counsel claims that the search warrant was illegally issued, because it was not based on the constitutionally required "probable cause" that a crime was committed. Therefore, the evidence should never have been admitted in court. Suppose the state trial judge does not agree with this defense.

Appeal and the *Writ of Certiorari*

writ of certiorari
Document issued by a higher court directing a lower court to prepare the record of a case and send it to the higher court for review.

The students decide to appeal their conviction, claiming that the trial judge has committed a legal error by not excluding the evidence. Suppose the state court of appeals (if there is one) rules against the students. They next appeal to the state supreme court. If the state supreme court rejects the argument as well, the next option is to appeal to the United States Supreme Court. The basis of this appeal is the violation of a federal constitutional right to be free from unreasonable searches and seizures, guaranteed by the Fourth Amendment. This option is exercised by an application for a **writ of certiorari,** a document issued by a higher court (in this case the United States Supreme Court) directing a lower court (the state supreme court) to forward the records of the case.

The Supreme Court may accept this case because it has established the rule that a search warrant issued on the basis of an unreliable informant's tip does not meet the reasonableness test and probable cause requirements of the Fourth Amendment.[15] But, as we noted earlier, the Supreme Court receives thousands of appeals and applications for *writs of certiorari* every year; it can consider only a few. Normally the Court chooses to review a case only if the case involves a substantial unresolved constitutional question, particularly one on which the findings of the various federal courts of appeals have diverged (Figure 8.2).

Habeas Corpus

habeas corpus
Writ requesting that a person or institution detaining a named prisoner bring him or her before a judicial officer and give reasons for the detention.

Having been denied a writ of certiorari by the Supreme Court, the students may apply for a writ of **habeas corpus** at the federal district court. Historically, under the common law of England, a prisoner's detention could be tested by a judicial writ (command) to a jailer for an inquiry. Written in Latin, the writ contained the crucial words **habeas corpus**, which means "you have the body (person) of. . . ." The text of the writ concluded with a request to produce the prisoner before the reviewing judge and to explain by what lawful authority the prisoner is being detained. Used in Anglo-American law since the seventeenth century, such inquiries still determine whether the Constitution was violated during the trial that resulted in the conviction that led to imprisonment.

In our hypothetical case, until 1976 the students could indeed have applied to the federal district court for a writ of *habeas corpus*. But in that year the United States Supreme Court held that the writ was no longer available in Fourth Amendment search-and-seizure cases because the federal courts were so flooded with applications they could not manage the caseload.[16] Whenever the alleged constitutional violation pertains to issues other than search and seizure, the writ is still legally available. If the district court denies the writ of *habeas corpus,* the prisoner can appeal that decision to a United States Court of Appeal. If that court does not overrule the district court, the prisoner can appeal again to the United States Supreme Court (Figure 8.2). However, legislation is pending which would restrict the availability of the writ of *habeas corpus.*

The Future of the Courts: Issues

If you were to ask judges and court administrators what single issue has most affected the judiciary at both the federal and the state levels in recent years, they would answer: caseloads. For example, at the federal level, the number of cases filed in the district courts has more than tripled over the last thirty years.[17] At the state level, cases filed at the trial and appellate level have increased nearly as fast.[18] The caseload increases in both state and federal courts have far outpaced the growth in population. The Administrative Office of the United States Courts predicts that filings in the federal district courts will certainly triple in the next twenty-five years, and caseloads in the courts of appeal will nearly triple during this time.[19]

Federal Issues

The chief justice of the United States, William Rehnquist, characterized the federal courts as "an exhaustible resource."[20] The supply of judges has not kept up with the demand. The problem is exacerbated by the fact that partisan politics make judicial nominations and confirmations problematic. The reasons for the shortage are many and include delays in screening, selection, and confirmation; inadequate salaries; and an increased scrutiny of a candidate's political orientation. According to Conrad Harper, president of the New York City Bar Association: "It is simply unconscionable for us to have this number of vacancies, and it needs prompt remedy. . . . It has a decisive and terrible influence upon the prompt dispatch of justice."[21]

State Issues

State courts face similar pressures as they look toward the twenty-first century. A few states, such as Virginia, Arizona, Michigan, Utah, Maine, and Colorado, have appointed commissions to study and plan for the future of the courts. The recommendations issued thus far show diversity in their approaches to handling existing and emerging problems. Arizona's commission, for example, recommended the creation of a three-level court system, while Virginia's commission advocated reorganizing its courts into a single-level system with divisions.[22]

The federal war on drugs campaign has had a significant impact on state court caseloads (Figure 8.5). Many courts have been so overwhelmed that they have had to institute

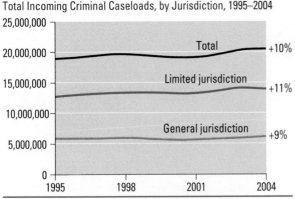

Total Incoming Criminal Caseloads, by Jurisdiction, 1995–2004

FIGURE 8.5   Criminal Cases Filed in State Courts, 1995–2004.

SOURCE: National Center for State Courts, *Examining the Work of State Courts, 2005* (Williamsburg, VA: National Center for State Courts, 2003), p. 47.

THE SUPREME COURT AND PUBLIC OPINION

- Should young offenders receive the death penalty?
- Should people who are mentally disabled who commit murder be executed?
- Do sobriety checkpoints constitute an unreasonable search and thus violate the Constitution?
- Should flag burning be allowed?

It is nearly impossible for many Americans to avoid taking a position every time the Supreme Court decides a case, and public opinion polls conducted by Roper, Gallup, Harris, and various news media often include questions about Supreme Court decisions. Over the last decade, the Court has grown increasingly conservative. Do citizens' views match those of the justices? Let us compare your opinions with Court decisions and with public opinion poll data for seven recent Supreme Court cases ranging from death penalty decisions to decisions on abortion.

Performing Drug Tests

The Case: National Treasury Employees Union v. Von Raab, 489 U.S. 656 (March 21, 1989).

The Supreme Court: Upheld the right to perform reasonable drug tests.

Public Opinion: "Would you favor (drug testing) for those responsible for the safety of others, such as surgeons, airplane pilots, and police officers, or would that be an unfair invasion of privacy?"

Yes, favor—83 percent

No, unfair—11 percent

Depends—3 percent

No opinion—3 percent

SOURCE:
CBS, *The New York Times* poll, August 18–21, 1986.

Using Checkpoints

The Case: Michigan Department of State Police v. Stitz, 496 U.S. 444 (June 14, 1990).

The Supreme Court: Upheld the right to use checkpoints to stop cars and check for drunk drivers.

Public Opinion: "Do you favor or oppose the use of random police checks at toll booths to check drivers for signs of alcohol and drug intoxication?"

Yes, favor—74 percent

No, oppose—25 percent

Not sure—1 percent

SOURCE:
Harris poll, January 11–February 11, 1990.

Raising the Drinking Age

The Case: South Dakota v. Dole, 483 U.S. 203 (June 23, 1987).

The Supreme Court: Upheld the power of Congress to raise the drinking age to 21 across the country but indirectly, under Congress's spending powers.

Public Opinion: "Would you favor or oppose having the federal government start withholding funds from these states if they fail to raise their drinking age to 21 by October 1?"

Yes, favor—64 percent

No, oppose—32 percent

No opinion—4 percent

SOURCE:
Gallup poll, June 9–16, 1988.

No Abortions in Public Hospitals

The Case: Webster v. Reproductive Health Services, 492 U.S. 490 (July 3, 1989).

The Supreme Court: Gave any state the right to prohibit public employees or public hospitals from performing abortions except to save the mother's life.

Public Opinion: "Are you in favor of that part of the decision, or are you opposed to it?"

Yes, favor—56 percent

No, oppose—40 percent

Not sure—4 percent

SOURCE:
Los Angeles Times poll, July 3, 1989.

> "The Supreme Court upheld the right to use checkpoints to stop cars and check for drunk drivers."

Yes, approve—29 percent

No, disapprove—63 percent

No opinion—8 percent

SOURCE:
Gallup poll, April 10–13, 1987.

Executing 16-Year-Olds

The Cases: Wilkins v. Missouri and Stanford v. Kentucky, 106 L. Ed. 2d 306 (June 26, 1989).

The Supreme Court: Upheld the right to execute 16-year-olds.

Public Opinion: "In many states, one of the criminal punishments that is available is the death penalty. Some people think that persons convicted of murder committed when they are under 18 years old should never be executed, while other people think it is right to execute those who are under the age of 18 at the time the crime was committed. Which is closer to the way you think, that young people who are convicted of murder committed when they are under 18 years old should never be executed, or is it right to execute young people for a murder they committed before they were 18?"

Never execute—49 percent

Right to execute—44 percent

Not sure—7 percent

SOURCE:
Harris poll, June 3–September 12, 1988.

Reverse Discrimination

The Case: Johnson v. Transportation Agency of Santa Clara County, 480 U.S. 616 (March 25, 1987).

The Supreme Court: Ruled that employers may sometimes favor women and minorities over better-qualified men and whites in hiring and promoting to achieve better balance in their workforces.

Public Opinion: "Do you approve or disapprove of this decision?"

Executing Defendants Who Are Mentally Disabled

The Case: Penry v. Lynaugh, 492 U.S. 302 (June 26, 1989).

The Supreme Court: Upheld the right to execute defendants with mental retardation.

Public Opinion: "Some people think that persons convicted of murder who have a mental age of less than 18 (or the 'retarded') should not be executed. Other people think that 'retarded' persons should be subject to the death penalty like anyone else. Which is closer to the way you feel, that 'retarded' persons should not be executed, or that 'retarded' persons should be subject to the death penalty like anyone else?"

Should not be executed—71 percent

Should be executed—21 percent

Depends—4 percent

Not sure—3 percent

SOURCE:
Harris poll, June 3–September 12, 1988.

Questions for Discussion

1. Would you expect the Supreme Court rulings to be consistent with public opinion?

2. Do you think that the nomination process for Supreme Court justices should include an examination of the political or ideological orientation of the nominee?

3. Is there any consistency in the unpopular versus popular decisions?

SOURCE:
Thomas R. Marshall, "Public Opinion and the Rehnquist Court," *Judicature* 74, no. 6 (April-May 1991), pp. 324-325.

special case-processing procedures to deal with drug cases. Some states, like New Jersey, have reassigned trial court judges to do nothing but dispose of drug cases.[23] Finally, as discussed, other jurisdictions have created specialized courts to deal exclusively with drug offenses.

Despite the vast number of cases added to the courts by the onslaught of drug arrests, the effect on court delay is still unclear. Researchers examining the caseloads of twenty-six urban trial courts from 1983 to 1987 found that most had experienced increases in the number of drug cases filed. Boston had the largest increase: Its caseload of drug cases rose 175 percent over a four-year period. The courts with the largest increases and the largest total percentage of drug-related cases tended to be the slowest in terms of the average length of time it took to process a case from indictment to disposition. These same courts also tended to be the slowest in overall handling of all types of cases. It is possible, therefore, that delays may simply be the result of a particular court's caseload management, rather than the infusion of additional drug cases.[24]

Courts will continue to be affected by shifting social and political currents as more and more groups use them as the arena in which to air their grievances or enforce their policies. Technology is also a likely source of change. Increasingly, courts are using technological innovations to conduct their business; for example, fax machines are used to file court papers; satellite and closed circuit television hookups are used to conduct various court proceedings with people not present in the courtroom; and videotape cameras have replaced the traditional court stenographer as the recorder of what happens in the courtroom.[25]

Review

Since earliest times society has had processes to resolve disputes arising under its rules, or laws. With the emergence of centralized government under strong rulers, the establishment of courts became a sovereign prerogative. In colonial times there was a definite shift away from the use of legislatures as courts. Local and state-level courts were created according to English models. With the achievement of their independence, state courts simply took over the powers of the courts of the Crown of England. Soon thereafter, the Congress established a system of federal courts.

In the United States, criminal cases are tried in state courts when the crime is a violation of state law, and in federal courts when it is a violation of federal law. Each state has its own court system, with courts of limited and special jurisdiction, courts of general jurisdiction, an intermediate appellate court (in most states), and courts of last resort. In the federal system, the trial courts are called district courts, the appellate courts are courts of appeal, and the highest court is the Supreme Court. Both state and federal convictions may be appealed within their respective systems. Federal review of state cases may take place when federal constitutional issues are raised.

Both state and federal courts face many challenges. The most significant are related to caseloads. Drug cases, in particular, have had a significant impact on state and federal court caseloads.

Thinking Critically about Criminal Justice

1. Very few cases are actually argued before the United States Supreme Court. Most petitions for review are denied. What does it mean when the United States Supreme Court decides not to hear a case from an inferior court? Does this mean that the judgment of the Supreme Court concurs with that of the inferior court? Or has the Supreme Court merely expressed a preference not to hear a particular claim at this time?

Internet Connection

Note: While all of the URLs listed were current as of the printing of this book, these sites often change. Please check our website (http://www. mhhe.com/socscience/crimjustice/adlercj) for updates.

Examine the number of cases heard by the United States Supreme Court. Do you see a trend? **http://www.albany. edu/sourcebook/pdf/t570.pdf.**

Notes

1. Adapted from Molly Watson, "New York Keeps the Wheels of Justice Turning through the Night; As the Government Considers Introducing 24-Hour Courts..." *The Evening Standard,* February 20, 2001, p. 17.

2. Erwin C. Surrency, "The Courts in the American Colonies," *American Journal of Legal History* 11 (1967), p. 258.

3. Kermit L. Hall, *The Magic Mirror: Law in American History* (NY: Oxford University Press, 1989).

4. Lawrence M. Friedman, *A History of American Law* (NY: Simon and Schuster, 1973).

5. Surrency, "The Courts in the American Colonies," p. 258.

6. Robert Elder, Jr., "The Land That Law Forgot: With No Trials for 14 Years, Court May Break Streak," *Texas Lawyer,* November 18, 1991, p. 1.

7. *Law v. State,* 31 8 A.2d 859 (Maryland, 1974).

8. National Center for State Courts, *Intermediate Appellate Courts: Improving Case Processing* (Williamsburg, VA: National Center for State Courts, 1990).

9. Stanton Wheeler, Bliss Cartwright, Robert A. Kagan, and Lawrence M. Friedman, "Do the 'Haves' Come Out Ahead? Winning and Losing in State Supreme Courts, 1870–1970," *Law and Society Review* 21 (1987), pp. 403–445.

10. *Loving v. Virginia,* 388 U.S. 1 (1967).

11. *Mapp v. Ohio,* 367 U.S. 643 (1961).

12. Christopher E. Smith, *United States Magistrates in the Federal Courts: Subordinate Judges* (NY: Praeger, 1990).

13. See Michael deCourcy Hinds, "Bush's Aides Push Gun-Related Cases on Federal Courts," *The New York Times,* May 17, 1991, pp. A1, B16.

14. Garry Sturgess, "Another Clash over Criminal Caseload," *Legal Times,* April 1, 1991, p. 7.

15. See, e.g., *Illinois v. Gates,* 462 U.S. 213 (1983).

16. See *Stone v. Powell,* 428 U.S. 465 (1976).

17. U.S. Federal Courts Study Committee, *Report of the Federal Courts Study Committee,* April 2, 1990 (Philadelphia, PA).

18. Ibid., note 5.

19. U.S. Federal Courts Study Committee, *Report of the Federal Courts Study Committee.*

20. William K. Slate II, "Congress Needs to Get to Work on Judicial Workloads; Courts Have Already Reached Outer Limits of Their Capacity," *Connecticut Law Tribune,* March 2, 1992, p. 21.

21. Constance L. Hays, "Shortage of Judges Slows Cases," *The New York Times,* August 6, 1991, p. B1.

22. National Center for State Courts Information Service, "Special Report: Trends in the State Courts," *State Court Journal* 15 (Winter 1991), pp. 4–12.

23. Ibid.

24. John A. Goerdt and John A. Martin, "The Impact of Drug Cases on Case Processing in Urban Trial Courts," *State Court Journal* 13 (Fall 1989), pp. 4–12.

25. Selwyn Raab, "New York City Plans a TV Network to Link Jails and Courts," *The New York Times,* September 15, 1991, p. A33.

Lawyers and Judges

PROSECUTION

DEFENSE COUNSEL

JUDGES

OTHER COURT PERSONNEL

REVIEW

THINKING CRITICALLY ABOUT
CRIMINAL JUSTICE

INTERNET CONNECTION

NOTES

BOXES

Crime Scene: A Day in the Life of a Rookie DA

In Their Own Words: Delores D. Jones-Brown, Assistant Professor, John Jay College of Criminal Justice, City University of New York, and Former Assistant Prosecutor, Monmouth County, Freehold, New Jersey

21st Century Challenge: Black Robes and White Justice

Long before the coaches jarred to a halt in the shadow of the Langtry water tank, the greenhorns in the smoking car would have full information, some of it true, about the law west of the Pecos, as Roy Bean called himself. With their curiosity already on edge they would take in the handful of adobe buildings which was Langtry, the little station and the big water tank, and finally the small frame shack twenty steps north of the tracks with a covered porch in front and signs plastered over it: THE JERSEY LILLY: JUDGE ROY BEAN NOTARY PUBLIC. LAW WEST OF THE PECOS.

• Someone would say, "There he is!" And there he would be—a sturdy, gray-bearded figure with a Mexican sombrero on his head and a portly stomach mushrooming out over his belt, waiting on his porch for the swirl of business and excitement which always came at train time. You could see at a glance that he was as rough as a sand burr and tough as a boiled owl, but you realized also that he was a genuine character with plenty of salt in him.

• For a while he lived the epic he imagined. He really was the Law in those parts for a few years. It was 200 miles to the nearest justice court and naturally he had things his own way. Before long, civilization and lawyers moved in on him, but by that time his saga was started and his position was assured. He became in the minds of other men a sort of Ulysses of West Texas—a man of craft and action combined—a figure of colorful peculiarities and great resourcefulness. His fame was no surprise to him, though it was to a great many other people, for he had been convinced all along that he was no ordinary citizen. He probably thought his recognition was, if anything, considerably overdue.

• And so when the train pulled into Langtry, there he was on his porch. He always exposed himself at train time so people could see him. He was sure they would want to.[1]

Texas and the rest of the country have come a long way since Roy Bean held court in Langtry 100 years ago. During the twentieth century "the law" covered the countryside. In fact, over the last forty years alone, the number of lawyers has more than tripled to over 1 million.[2] Today the United States has nearly 50 percent of all of the world's practicing and nonpracticing lawyers. There are also thousands of state and federal judges, supported by court administrators, clerks, and administrative staff.

In this chapter we examine the professional and social roles of attorneys and judges and the many organizational and personal constraints that defense and prosecuting attorneys experience in providing representation. We then consider the qualifications and selection of judges. Finally, we discuss the other key players in the courtroom, including court administrators, court clerks, and court personnel.

Throughout the chapter we will be describing personnel in both state and federal courts. As we discovered in Chapter 8, state and federal courts differ considerably. These differences include:

- The law that governs (federal law in federal courts and state law in state courts).
- The jurisdiction of the courts (the power of state and federal courts to hear certain kinds of cases differs).
- The procedure followed in the courts (in federal courts there are uniform rules of procedure and evidence, while procedures vary among state courts).
- The caseload of the courts (state courts hear a vast majority of court cases).

So it is not surprising that the tasks and roles of state and federal court functionaries differ as well. Let us begin with a discussion of the government's attorney, the prosecutor. Attorney General Robert H. Jackson, who later became a United States Supreme Court justice, once said: "The prosecutor has more control over life, liberty, and reputation than any other person in America."[3]

Prosecution

Some prosecutors become well-known figures. For example, District Attorney Michael Bradbury became an outspoken symbol of law and order in Ventura County, California. Other district attorneys, such as Robert Morgenthau (New York County), maintain a less visible public image but act aggressively and decisively in the prosecution of violent, property, and white-collar offenders. But most prosecutors do not have the high profile or prominent reputation of Bradbury or Morgenthau, even though they have considerable decision-making powers within their county or district.[4]

Roles and Duties

Prosecutors are government lawyers, public officials, who represent the people of a particular jurisdiction (county, city, state, or federal district) in a criminal case. When a crime is committed the "people of the state," acting through the prosecutor, proceed in court against the suspected criminal. Today prosecution is almost exclusively the responsibility of an elected or appointed prosecutor.[5] More than 8,000 state and local government agencies are involved in prosecution, as is the federal government.[6]

Prosecutors have many duties. Once an arrest has been made, the prosecutor:

- Screens cases to determine which should be accepted for further processing.
- Decides with what specific offenses to charge a suspect.
- Coordinates the investigation of a case, including the gathering of evidence and interviewing of witnesses.
- Issues an information—charging the defendant with a crime—when the law allows initiation of a criminal case by information.
- Presents the facts to the grand jury when so required by law, acting as the grand jury's counsel, in order to obtain an indictment against the defendant.
- Makes recommendations about whether a defendant should be released on bail and how much the amount of bail should be.
- Responds to any pretrial motions filed by the defense.
- Decides which cases might be amenable to a plea bargain and then negotiates the settlement with the defense attorney.
- Prepares the case for trial, if necessary.
- Participates in the selection of a jury for those cases that go to trial.
- Argues the case on behalf of the government at trial.
- Makes recommendations about sentencing.

The duties and roles we have described vary with the organization of each prosecutorial office and the jurisdiction. The differences are most apparent in comparing federal and state prosecutorial offices. As you may imagine, federal and state (or local) prosecutors differ in responsibilities and often in degrees of specialization. Federal prosecutors' agencies are divided into divisions, offices, and bureaus according to an area of federal law (civil, criminal, tax, or antitrust). They often become highly specialized, focusing on the prosecution of offenses falling within a single body of law. State or local prosecutors, for example, could never combat a nationwide problem like the S&L fraud. They have neither the resources nor the legal power to deal with national problems. And except for large district attorneys' offices in urban centers (for example, Los Angeles and New York), they are rarely as well staffed or as specialized as their federal counterparts.

Federal Prosecutors

Prosecutions at the federal level are carried out by **United States attorneys.** Each federal judicial district has one U.S. attorney with a large staff of assistant attorneys, who carry out most of the day-to-day work of the office. United States attorneys are appointed by the president and subject to Senate confirmation. Assistant U.S. attorneys are formally appointed by the **United States attorney general,** the highest-ranking official in the U.S. Department of Justice (Figure 9.1). Usually the U.S. attorneys select their own assistants and pass the names on to the attorney general for official appointment. In practice, most U.S. attorneys are from the same political party as the president, who may use this appointment as a reward for political support. The position of U.S. attorney can be a highly visible one that some see as a stepping stone to a prominent political office. In the 1980s, the local law enforcement

prosecutor
Attorney and government official who represents the people against persons accused of committing criminal acts.

United States attorney
Attorney and government official who prosecutes cases at the federal level.

careers

United States attorney general
Highest-ranking official in the United States Department of Justice.

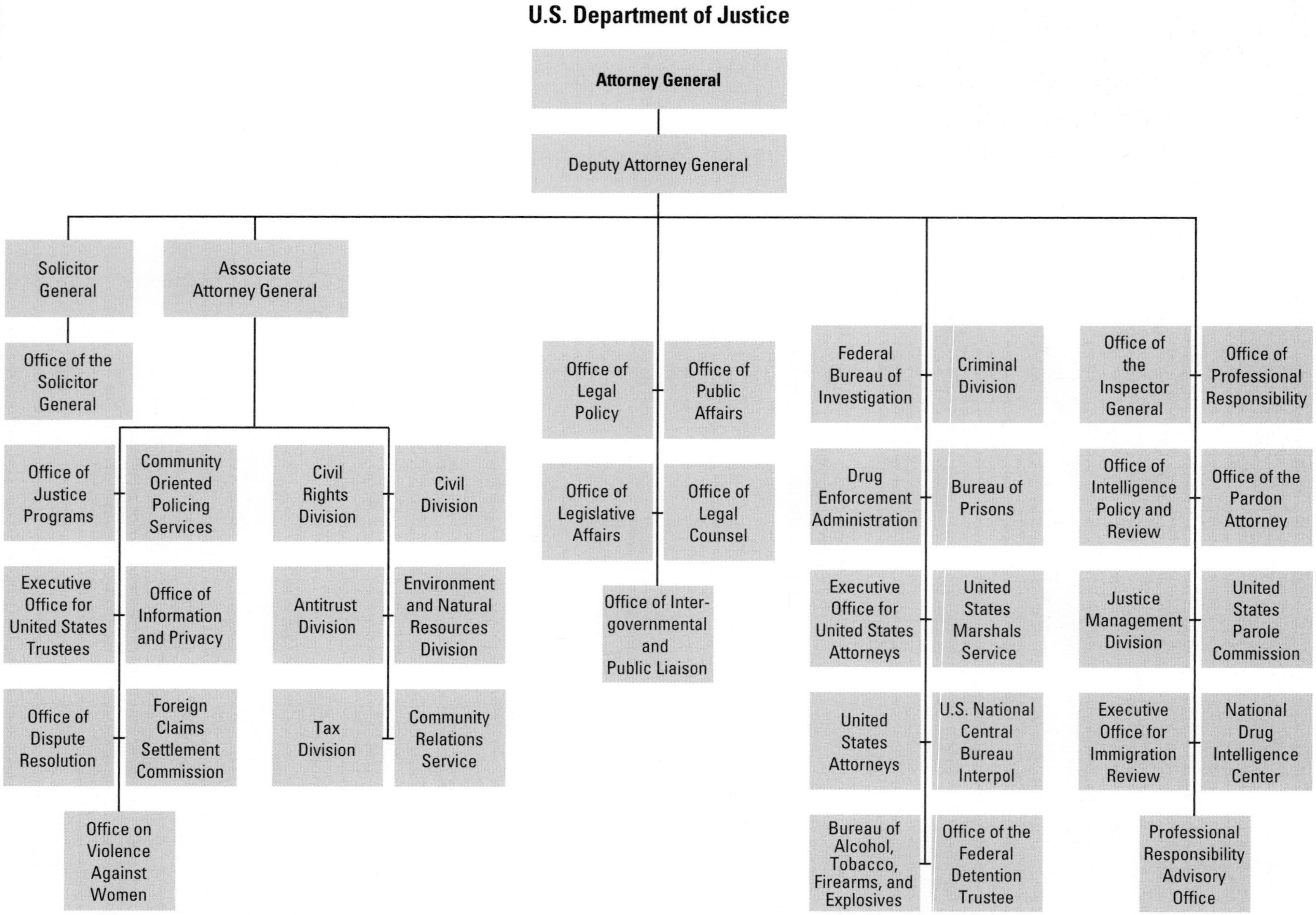

U.S. Department of Justice

FIGURE 9.1 Organization of the U.S. Department of Justice

SOURCE: U.S. Department of Justice, http://www.usdoj.gov/dojorg.htm.

hero in Manhattan was Rudolph W. Giuliani, the U.S. attorney for the Southern District of New York. Giuliani's much publicized prosecutions of organized crime figures earned him great praise, as well as some controversy. In 1994, he became mayor of New York City. His administration was credited with a dramatic reduction in crime rates in and around the city.

While federal criminal law spans a wide range of offenses, all of which U.S. attorneys have the power to prosecute, the focus of investigations changes frequently. Antitrust violations were the focus at one time, organized crime at another. Today, national policy, as interpreted by the attorney general, has called for an emphasis on prosecuting terrorists, narcotic drug traffickers, and white-collar criminals (see Figure 9.2).

State Prosecutors

The State Attorney General. The state counterpart to the attorney general of the United States is the **state attorney general.** Like the U.S. attorney general, the state attorneys general are the chief legal officers of their jurisdictions. But here the analogy ends. State attorneys general are, for the most part, elected officials. They normally do not have the same power over the local prosecutors in their state that the U.S. attorney general has over the federal prosecutors (Figure 9.3).

State attorneys general, assisted by staff, are not concerned with local criminal prosecutions. Most of the work of this office concerns civil cases; most violations of the state criminal code are handled at the local level. State attorneys general, however, often play an important role in the investigation of statewide criminal activities (e.g., consumer, health care, and financial fraud). They may work closely with federal and local prosecutors to prepare the criminal cases resulting from such investigations.

Former Attorney General John Ashcroft testifying before the Senate Judiciary Committee on Capitol Hill during a hearing on President Bush's executive order to hold military tribunals, and Justice Department policy in the U.S. war on terrorism.

state attorney general
Chief legal officer of the state; state counterpart to the U.S. attorney general.

Politics and Policy

"We are going to make the streets hot in Teaneck," said the Reverend Al Sharpton in February 1992. "The process has not been completely fair and thorough," said Keith Jones, president of the New Jersey Chapter of the NAACP.[7] Earlier, Sharpton and Jones, along with other community leaders, had joined the U.S. attorney for New Jersey in calling for federal charges to be brought against Officer Gary Spath in the Teaneck Police Department. Spath, a white police officer, had just been acquitted of manslaughter in the killing of Phillip Pannell, a sixteen-year-old black youth whom the officer was chasing. Spath testified at trial that he fired in self-defense. Medical experts testified that Pannell had his hands raised in surrender at the time he was shot to death. An all-white jury acquitted Spath.[8]

The Pannell case, like countless others, suggests the obvious—that prosecutors' offices face significant political pressures from the community. But these pressures may be minor or insignificant compared with pressures brought to bear from other sources. Prosecutors function within a larger system with many other "players." They interact constantly with police, judges, and defense attorneys and must be ready to work in a cooperative way to achieve the goals of the office. This is not an easy task given the many roles that prosecutors play.[9]

Prosecutors can be used as a tool of regulatory policy. For example, in 2002 President Bush created the Corporate Fraud Task Force led by the deputy attorney general. This task force of attorneys and investigators from the Department of Justice and other federal agencies aggressively pursue white-collar and corporate criminals. Former Deputy Attorney General Thompson explained the objective of the task force in simple terms: the

FIGURE 9.2

Highlights of Federal Prosecution, Fiscal Year 2006

SOURCE: Executive Office for
the United States Attorneys,
*Annual Statistical Report, Fiscal
Year 2006* (Washington, DC: U.S.
Department of Justice, 2007),
pp. 5–8.

FISCAL YEAR 2006 STATISTICAL HIGHLIGHTS

Overall Criminal Prosecutions
- 58,702 cases filed against 81,088 defendants—case filings down 2 percent
- 60,393 cases against 82,343 defendants terminated—case terminations up 3 percent
- 75,650 defendants convicted
- 92 percent conviction rate
- 83 percent of convicted defendants sentenced to prison
- 52 percent of prison sentences greater than 3 years
- 31 percent of prison sentences greater than 5 years

Violent Crime
- 10,908 cases filed against 12,904 defendants—case filings down 4 percent
- 11,479 cases against 13,415 defendants terminated—case terminations up 3 percent
- 12,179 defendants convicted
- 91 percent conviction rate
- 92 percent of convicted defendants sentenced to prison
- 70 percent of prison sentences greater than 3 years
- 47 percent of prison sentences greater than 5 years

Overall Narcotics
- 15,408 cases filed against 29,051 defendants—case filings down 4 percent
  - *15,498 cases filed against 29,171 defendants–case filings down 4 percent– when drug cases included under the Government Regulatory/Money Laundering Program Category are included*
- 16,023 cases against 29,569 defendants terminated—case terminations up 4 percent
- 27,128 defendants convicted
- 92 percent conviction rate
- 92 percent of convicted defendants sentenced to prison
- 71 percent of prison sentences greater than 3 years
- 48 percent of prison sentences greater than 5 years

OCDETF
- 2,529 cases filed against 8,182 defendants—case filings up 1 percent
- 2,783 cases against 8,305 defendants terminated—case terminations up 2 percent
- 7,391 defendants convicted
- 89 percent conviction rate
- 91 percent of convicted defendants sentenced to prison
- 81 percent of prison sentences greater than 3 years
- 58 percent of prison sentences greater than 5 years

Non-OCDETF
- 12,879 cases filed against 20,869 defendants—case filings down 5 percent
  - *12,969 cases filed against 20,989 defendants–case filings down 5 percent– when drug cases included under the Government Regulatory/Money Laundering Program Category are included*
- 13,240 cases against 21,264 defendants terminated—case terminations up 5 percent

(continued)

FIGURE 9.2
(*Continued*)

- 19,737 defendants convicted
- 93 percent conviction rate
- 92 percent of convicted defendants sentenced to prison
- 68 percent of prison sentences greater than 3 years
- 44 percent of prison sentences greater than 5 years

Immigration

- 17,686 cases filed against 19,215 defendants—case filings down 3 percent
- 18,165 cases against 19,526 defendants terminated—case terminations up 5 percent
- 18,794 defendants convicted
- 96 percent conviction rate
- 86 percent of convicted defendants sentenced to prison
- 24 percent of prison sentences greater than 3 years
- 5 percent of prison sentences greater than 5 years

Organized Crime

- 156 cases filed against 459 defendants—case filings down 33 percent
- 217 cases against 634 defendants terminated—case terminations up 5 percent
- 550 defendants convicted
- 87 percent conviction rate
- 77 percent of convicted defendants sentenced to prison
- 57 percent of prison sentences greater than 3 years
- 37 percent of prison sentences greater than 5 years

Official Corruption

- 503 cases filed against 731 defendants—case filings up 14 percent
- 501 cases against 706 defendants terminated—case terminations up 4 percent
- 635 defendants convicted
- 90 percent conviction rate
- 56 percent of convicted defendants sentenced to prison
- 26 percent of prison sentences greater than 3 years
- 13 percent of prison sentences greater than 5 years

White-Collar Crime

- 5,745 cases filed against 8,036 defendants—case filings up 5 percent
- 5,805 cases against 8,146 defendants terminated—case terminations up 7 percent
- 7,309 defendants convicted
- 90 percent conviction rate
- 61 percent of convicted defendants sentenced to prison
- 26 percent of prison sentences greater than 3 years
- 11 percent of prison sentences greater than 5 years

Asset Forfeiture Litigation

- Asset forfeiture counts filed in 4,053 criminal cases—up 7 percent
- A total of 2,181 civil asset forfeiture actions filed—down 3 percent
- Estimated recoveries of $703,280,200 in forfeited cash and property—up 18 percent

(continued)

FIGURE 9.2
(*Continued*)

Overall Civil Litigation

- 71,402 cases filed or responded to—down 9 percent
- 68,858 cases terminated—case terminations down 12 percent
- 23,026 judgments, or 76 percent, were in favor of the United States
- 13,698 settlements—20 percent of all cases terminated

Affirmative Civil Litigation

- 7,109 cases filed—case filings down 10 percent
- 7,507 cases terminated—case terminations down 6 percent
- 4,719 judgments, or 98 percent, were in favor of the United States
- 850 settlements—11 percent of all cases terminated

Affirmative Civil Enforcement

- 1,887 cases filed—case filings down 3 percent
- 1,843 cases terminated—case terminations up 12 percent
- 382 judgments, or 92 percent, were in favor of the United States
- 463 settlements—25 percent of all cases terminated

Defensive Civil Litigation

- 49,701 cases responded to—down 8 percent
- 46,631 cases terminated—case terminations down 13 percent
- 17,407 judgments, or 72 percent, were in favor of the United States
- 2,616 settlements—6 percent of all cases terminated

Civil Litigation Where the United States Is Otherwise Designated

- 14,592 cases filed or responded to—down 12 percent
- 14,720 cases terminated—down 12 percent
- 900 judgments, or 90 percent, were in favor of the United States
- 10,232 settlements—70 percent of all cases terminated

Criminal and Civil Appeals

- 15,275 appeals filed—down 7 percent
- 10,786 criminal appeals filed—down 2 percent
- 4,489 civil appeals filed—down 16 percent
- 81 percent of all criminal appeals terminated in favor of the United States
- 78 percent of all civil appeals terminated in favor of the United States
- 5,948 post-sentencing motions filed by incarcerated defendants—down 28 percent

restoration of the integrity of our markets to once again earn the trust and confidence of the country. In 2003 the task force obtained more than 500 corporate fraud convictions or guilty pleas and charged more than 900 defendants, including over 60 corporate CEOs and presidents.[10]

Prosecutors play a number of roles not necessarily made explicit by law. In smaller communities they may collect and dispense money to cover debts, such as those due to missing family support payments or from the issuing of bad checks, or those arising from fraud. They also dispense justice by weighing the available penalties provided for certain crimes and then using their discretion to "do justice," perhaps by not prosecuting.

As "political enforcers," prosecutors may aggressively prosecute or fail to prosecute a case for reasons and purposes other than a desire to achieve justice—perhaps to make a

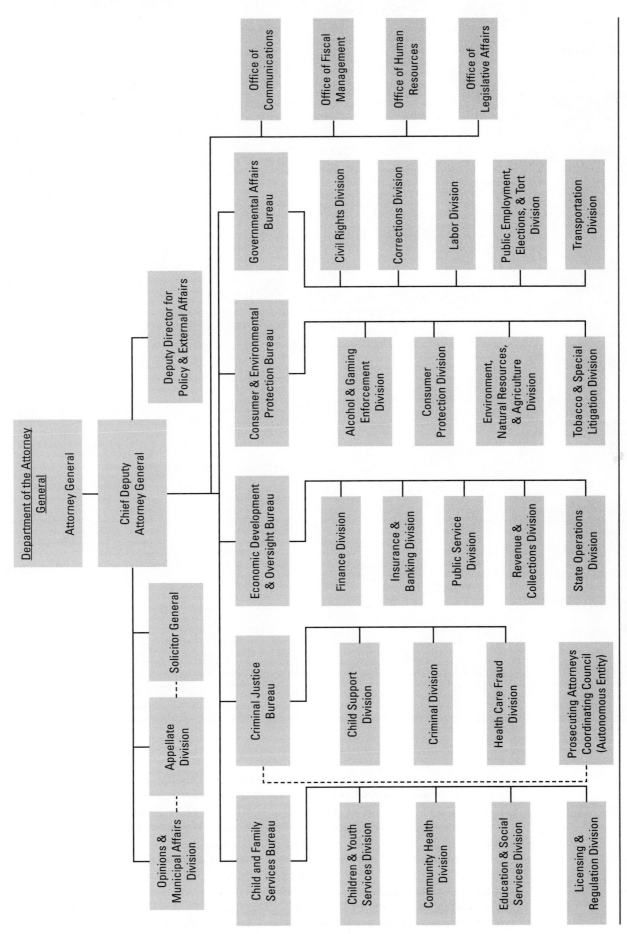

FIGURE 9.3 Michigan Attorney General's Organizational Structure

SOURCE: www.michigan.gov/documents/AGorg01-11-05_117507.pdf.

A DAY IN THE LIFE OF A ROOKIE DA

At age twenty-eight, John F. Kennedy, Jr., was one of sixty-four rookie prosecutors hired in 1989 by the New York County district attorney's office, one of the nation's most prestigious prosecutors' offices. Perhaps it was Kennedy who took the place of David Heilbroner, an assistant district attorney who had retired in 1988 after a three-year stint. Heilbroner's recollections of his work reveal some of the frustrations and realities of the life of a rookie district attorney.

Doing Justice

Heilbroner retired after only three years because he lacked the zeal that seemed to fuel his colleagues' efforts—the zeal for "locking up the scum" who prey on innocent New Yorkers. Heilbroner reports about the people with whom he worked:

> Questions about social injustice or the fact that jails only made defendants more deeply embittered brought unencouraging answers: "The slimeballs shouldn't have been there in the first place." "You know what they say: 'Don't do the crime if you can't do the time.'"[1]

> Oliver W. Holmes, Jr., once remarked, "I don't do justice. I merely apply the law." Heilbroner, however, had hoped to "do justice"; he soon became disabled by compassion and disillusioned by the never-ending constraints on the system. Some of these feelings are recorded in his descriptions of courtroom interactions:

> David Middleton, a sixteen-year-old felon with three aliases, had been arrested for beating the subway fare. *Manipulating a turnstyle:* $24.00. The case, like all farebeats, was probably a winner. When Middleton's name was run through a computer, a bench warrant "dropped." It had been issued in a shoplifting case when Middleton skipped out. Judges usually gave teenagers the benefit of every doubt, since the more time kids spend inside, the less likely they are to

reform. But Middleton had worn out his welcome. In only three years, he had amassed a felony conviction for robbery and two drug-related misdemeanors, not to mention the open shoplift case. He wasn't old enough to drink legally, yet he probably knew the arraignment process better than I did.

> Middleton had served first 15 and then 45 days on his two drug convictions and he was still on probation for the robbery. He faced up to one year or a $1,000 fine on the farebeat alone. Our class had recently been instructed that, as a matter of policy, sentences should increase with every new arrest. Sixty days, therefore, seemed about right.

> One of the court officers announced, "The people versus David Middleton, Docket Number 5N078546," and Middleton, a handsome, well-built youth, got up off the defendant's bench and strutted over to the defense table. Expensive basketball sneakers. Padded leather jacket. The usual.

> "Your honor," said Middleton's legal aid lawyer, "may we approach to discuss a disposition?"

> "Gentlemen, step up," said the Honorable Louis Friedland. Friedland, a heavy-set man with a shock of black hair, was a seasoned jurist who prided himself on running a tight ship. Cases proceeded quickly in his court, so quickly, in fact, that he often requested that overflow cases from secondary arraignment parts be added to the day's work. He was known as the Tsar of Arraignments.

> "Mr. DA," he asked the moment I arrived at the bench, "what are you looking for to cover the farebeat?"

> "Well, Judge," I answered nervously, "the defendant got 15 days for his first misdemeanor and 45 days for his last offense. It seems to me the penalties should go up with each subsequent—"

> "Cut the crap, Mr. DA, just tell me what you're looking for to cover the farebeat." I should have known I didn't have to explain sentencing policy to a judge with 20 years on the bench.

> "Sixty days," I answered.

> Friedland froze for a moment. Then he pounced: "Sixty days for a farebeat? Listen, Mister, you better get it together or you'll be practicing law in Poughkeepsie. You don't give two months to a 16-year-old kid for beating unless you're out of your _ _ _ _ ing mind. Who the hell

political point, to deter certain conduct, or to damage a reputation. To get the conviction of General Manuel Antonio Noriega on eight of ten counts of cocaine trafficking, racketeering, and money-laundering charges in April 1992, three prosecutors spent over two years exclusively preparing and presenting this case. Was this case more of a political statement than an attempt to "do justice"? Critics have strongly debated this point.[11]

Prosecutors can also take on the role of "overseer of police" when they monitor the work of a department.[12] They influence law enforcement by focusing on certain types of criminals. To target a particular type of offender, such as a "career criminal," the prosecutor needs the cooperation of the police. In many cities around the United States, special police–prosecutor teams work together toward such common goals.[13]

told you a kid should go to jail for two months over a $1 token? You're lucky I don't tell your bureau chief."

"Sir," Friedland turned to the tired-looking legal aid lawyer, who, decently enough, had stepped back, "tell Mr. Middleton that the offer is 30 days—to cover the shoplifting case as well."

As I turned to the prosecution table, I felt as if I had just committed an unpardonable error in judgment. For the rest of the morning the word echoed in my ears: "Poughkeepsie."[2]

Doing Rough Justice

These interactions expose only a small piece of a much larger, complex, and disturbing puzzle in urban courts around the nation. Heilbroner describes the administration of a "rough justice," a justice that reflects accommodations and compromises in the name of caseload management or system efficiency. It was not the kind of justice he felt comfortable with.

And in every direction innumerable aspects of the justice system cried out for reform: police misconduct, defense attorneys' delays, meaningless paperwork, the rubber-stamp grand jury, rigid strictures on sentencing, incarceration of psychiatric patients, insufficient numbers of judges and courtrooms, to name just a few of the egregious problems.

The crisis of the courts, itself the result of too many cases, was also the product of broader social injustices: the inequitable distribution of wealth, the legacy of racism, bleak opportunities for minorities and the poor. None of these were any less a problem for my having spent three years as an agent of the system.[3]

Looking Back

In the end, Heilbroner looked back at the system of criminal justice with some concrete suggestions:

- Rookies should be encouraged to dismiss more marginal cases (e. g., prostitution and marijuana possession).
- The distinction between felonies and misdemeanors should be reformed so that sentencing decisions are not hampered by artificial distinctions.
- The grand jury should be abolished—it is a waste of resources and accomplishes little.
- Police officers should be fined every time they engage in illegal searches and arrests.
- Lawyers should be disciplined for delays and misrepresentations.

Heilbroner admits, however, that the work associated with prosecution does not "lend itself" to reform or analysis. Unfortunately, all energy is expended on keeping pace and maintaining some perspective.

Questions for Discussion

1. Why do you think law students are interested in working as prosecutors?
2. What changes to the criminal justice system would allow rookie prosecutors to remain idealistic and committed to "justice"?
3. Perhaps lawyers' disillusionment as they begin work in "the real world" is just a normal part of gaining experience. Do you think they should remain idealistic, or is it better that they fit into the system?

SOURCES:
1. David Heilbroner, *Rough Justice: Days and Nights of a Young DA* (New York: Pantheon, 1990), p. 76.
2. Ibid., pp. 41–42.
3. Ibid., pp. 284–285.

Discretion

On paper, the rules for the administration of the criminal law provide that all offenders should be treated equally—no defendant should receive more or less punishment than another who has committed a similar offense and the rich and powerful should be prosecuted as vigorously as the poor and weak. Actually, however, whether or not a particular offender is prosecuted depends very largely upon the personal reactions (or judgment) of the prosecutor.[14]

These are the words of Newman Baker, author of a series of classic articles in the 1930s about the American prosecutor, at a time when the public was first learning about the role that prosecutorial discretion plays in the administration of criminal justice. Of course, there is nothing inherently bad about discretion, properly used: Charles Breitel, then a justice of the New York Supreme Court (later chief judge of the New York Court of Appeals), noted some years ago that

> [i]f every policeman, every prosecutor, every court, and every postsentence agency performed his or its responsibility in strict accordance with rules of law, precisely and narrowly laid down, the criminal law would be ordered but intolerable. . . . [T]he presence and expansion of discretion in crime control are both desirable and inevitable in a modern democratic society.[15]

Prosecutors cannot pursue every case. Decisions have to be made—and most often these decisions are guided by the strength of the evidence. After all, a weak case is less likely to result in a conviction. But, as we shall see, strength of evidence is not the *sole* criterion.

Extent of Discretion.   At each stage in the processing of a case, discretion is used in arriving at a decision. Among the most important decisions are the following:

- Does a case warrant further action beyond the arrest? Should it be rejected for prosecution?
- If a decision is made to file charges, what specific charges should they be?
- What recommendations should be made regarding bail?
- Should the case be resolved through a plea bargain or a trial?

Figure 9.4 shows the probability of being convicted and sentenced for a felony. Many variables contribute to the likelihood of remaining in the criminal justice system—including race.

Of course, discretion varies significantly from jurisdiction to jurisdiction and from district attorney to district attorney. Some prosecutors attempt to eliminate weak cases before

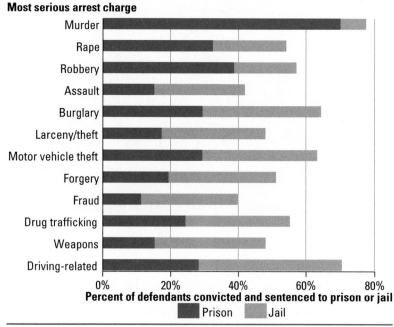

Most serious arrest charge

FIGURE 9.4   Probability of Being Convicted and Sentenced to Incarceration for Felony Defendants in the 75 Largest Counties, 2002

SOURCE: Thomas H. Cohen and Brian A. Reaves, *Felony Defendants in Large Urban Counties, 2002* (Washington, DC: Bureau of Justice Statistics, 2006), p. iv.

charges are even filed; others file charges and then have cases weeded out at later stages. For example, in New York County, only 2 percent of all cases presented by the police are rejected before the filing of criminal charges, whereas Los Angeles County rejects 35 percent of cases before charges are filed. However, 40 percent of New York's cases are dismissed following the filing of charges, compared with only 10 percent of Los Angeles's cases.[16] Another study of Los Angeles prosecutors asked about the standards of proof used in deciding whether to file a criminal complaint against a suspect. One-fifth of the prosecutors said they would file a complaint even if they thought the case would go no further than a preliminary hearing, while another 30 percent said they would file the complaint even though they thought the case would be lost at trial. Half said they would file the complaint only if they thought the case would probably be won at trial.[17]

Decision to Prosecute.   Among the most important of the case-related factors that affect the decision to prosecute are the seriousness of the offense and the amount of harm that may have resulted, in terms of injury to a victim or loss involved in property offenses.[18] The strength and amount of evidence against a suspect,[19] whether a weapon was used in the commission of the offense,[20] whether a suspect has confessed,[21] and the prior criminal record of the suspect[22] have been identified as additional factors that are taken into account in the decision to file charges, reduce charges, or continue prosecution after the initial charges have been filed.

These case-related factors seem like perfectly appropriate criteria to use in prosecutorial decisions. But consider some of the other factors that have been identified as determinants of prosecutors' decisions. Prosecutors must consider whether the victim wants prosecution to proceed. A recent study that examined 200 domestic assault cases in which charges were not filed against the offender found that "victim wishes" accounted for nearly half the decisions not to file charges.[23]

Victims have been shown to have an effect on the prosecutor's decision making in other ways as well. A study of New York County prosecutors found that district attorneys often judge the victim's credibility and use this assessment in weighing prosecution decisions. Less-than-credible victims may have their cases rejected, since prosecutors are always interested in maximizing the number of convictions obtained.[24]

Factors such as the relationship between the victim and the accused, whether the victim took action that might be considered provocation, and whether the victim participated in the crime may also play a role. Victim provocation and participation in the crime appear to decrease the likelihood that a case will be prosecuted, perhaps because the prosecutor believes that the victim is more blameworthy in such cases and less likely to be believed.[25]

Many personal characteristics are used by prosecutors to evaluate whether to prosecute a suspect. Women suspects, for example, are less likely to be prosecuted than men.[26] Surprisingly, some studies have shown that African Americans and other minorities are less likely to be prosecuted than whites,[27] and that charges against African Americans are more likely to be reduced than those against whites (Table 9.1).[28] Research examining prosecutorial discretion in requesting the death penalty, on the other hand, has consistently shown that prosecutors are more likely to request the death penalty in cases where the murder victim is white.[29]

Controlling Discretion.   Concerns about discretion are magnified by the fact that prosecutorial decisions are rarely subjected to review. Courts simply give great deference to prosecutors.[30] Advocates of discretion argue that a trial effectively serves as a review of the prosecutor's actions. If the prosecutor has acted improperly or brought charges without justification, the defendant will be acquitted. But this is small consolation to the innocent person who has been charged with a crime and possibly placed in a detention facility while awaiting trial.

Calls for the control of discretion have prompted proposals such as:

• Decision-making guidelines—Written guidelines that would provide specific criteria for decision making.[31]

• Intraoffice reviews—The simple practice of having a superior check the work of those under his or her supervision can be an effective means of oversight.

Most Serious Arrest Charge	Number of Defendants	Percent of Felony Defendants in the 75 Largest Counties		Most Serious Additional Charge		
		Total	No Other Charges	Total	Felony	Misdemeanor
All offenses	56,147	100%	42%	58%	40%	18%
Violent offenses	13,683	100%	36%	64%	48%	16%
Murder	475	100	35	65	61	4
Rape	1,002	100	29	71	65	6
Robbery	3,036	100	29	71	59	12
Assault	7,123	100	38	62	42	20
Other violent	2,048	100	41	59	41	18
Property offenses	17,021	100%	46%	54%	42%	13%
Burglary	4,544	100	35	65	51	14
Larceny/theft	4,930	100	49	51	40	10
Motor vehicle theft	1,869	100	53	47	33	14
Forgery	1,734	100	42	58	46	13
Fraud	1,727	100	42	58	52	7
Other property	2,218	100	57	43	22	21
Drug offenses	20,073	100%	42%	58%	38%	20%
Trafficking	9,618	100	28	72	58	14
Other drug	10,455	100	54	46	20	26
Public-order offenses	5,370	100%	48%	52%	27%	26%
Weapons	1,501	100	36	64	43	21
Driving-related	1,788	100	43	57	27	30
Other public-order	2,081	100	60	40	15	25

NOTE: Data for the most sarious arrest charge and the next most serious arrest charge were available for all cases. Detail may not add to total because of rounding.

SOURCE: Thomas H. Cohen and Brian A. Reaves, *Felony Defendants in Large Urban Counties, 2002* (Washington, DC: Bureau of Justice Statistics, 2006), p. 9.

TABLE 9.1   Level of Second Most Serious Charge of Felony Defendants, by Most Serious Arrest Charge, 2002

- Limiting the number of decision makers—The horizontal model of prosecution that assigns specific duties to experienced prosecutors may help control discretion. Seemingly arbitrary variations among prosecutors are also minimized by this method.
- Periodic review of charging policies and decisions.

Of course, discretion is not likely to be eliminated. The real issue of concern is not how to "do away" with discretion but rather, in the words of Chief Judge Charles Breitel, "how to control it so as to avoid the unequal, the arbitrary, the discriminatory, and the oppressive."[32]

Defense Counsel

The typical TV image of defense lawyers are from *The Practice*—brilliant legal detectives, and strategists, often with questionable morals. Scripts call for flamboyant, publicity-seeking, and often unscrupulous attorneys who may well use legal technicalities to help their clients go free. Yet another image is the idealistic and bumbling public defender who, due to time and budgetary constraints, can barely afford to become acquainted with each impoverished defendant prior to trial. But, as we shall see, none of these popular images is a fair representation of the defense attorney.

Defense attorneys occupy a critical place in our adversarial system of justice. They ensure that the legal rights of an accused person are fully protected at every stage in the criminal justice process, and that those accused of crime receive zealous representation. Fewer than 5 percent of all lawyers today practice criminal law on a regular basis, and only 1.2 percent of all practicing lawyers may be found in legal aid or public defender offices. The number of single-practitioner defense lawyers is also declining—they have been properly called an "endangered species" and a "dying breed."[33]

Roles and Duties

Manhattan Criminal Court Judge Harold J. Rothwax, formerly a Legal Aid attorney, once described the "typical day" in his court:

> The prosecutor and the Legal Aid attorney, respectively and hurriedly, begin to look through the large pile of papers in front of them; the judge sits and waits; having found the paper they begin their preparation by glancing at it quickly; the judge waits; the prosecutor then turns to his witnesses, ascertains who they are, and discusses the case with them; the Legal Aid attorney turns to the defendant, introduces himself if they have not previously met, and discusses the case with him; the judge waits, reads, or shouts for quiet in the courtroom; having concluded their preparation the prosecutor and the Legal Aid attorney begin to negotiate with each other to see if they can agree upon a disposition; the judge waits. The case is then either disposed or adjourned.[34]

But there is more. The complaint that the defendant has received reveals little information, other than the charge and its alleged time and place of occurrence. Thus, the defendant is often ill-informed and sometimes lacks an appreciation of the nature and consequences of the proceedings that are taking place.

In considering the roles and duties of defense lawyers, it is important to remember the distinction between theory and practice. Much of what is presented here is theoretical. In many urban criminal courts around the United States, theory is overridden by limited budgets and resources, overcrowded dockets, and inadequately trained personnel. In fact, the New York State Judicial Commission on Minorities reported that the state's court system is "infested with racism," and that it doles out "basement justice."[35] According to its final report, there are two systems of justice in New York, one for whites and one for blacks and the poor. One important recommendation for change is the proposed requirement of attorney certification (above and beyond the admission to the bar) for all legal aid and contract attorneys, to ensure minimal levels of competence.[36]

Defense Attorney Roles. All persons accused of a crime for which jail or prison is the possible penalty have a right to counsel under the Sixth Amendment to the United States Constitution.[37] The person who represents the accused is called a **defense attorney.** In theory, defense attorneys fulfill three roles.[38] First, they are advocates for the accused. It is important to remember that an accused is presumed innocent until such time as guilt may be proven in a court of law. Even if an accused admits guilt, the person is still entitled to the full protection of the law, that is, advice and representation of counsel. Defense attorneys are there to ensure that the interests of the accused are fully protected.

A second role is that of an intermediary. The language used in criminal court may be confusing to those not educated in law. Many criminal defendants are poorly educated and may be intimidated by the nature of criminal proceedings. They may be unable to fully or adequately express themselves or to assist in the presentation of their own defense. The defense attorney becomes a spokesperson for the accused.

A third function is that of a learned friend. The defense attorney is also a counselor, offering advice and assistance in explaining the risks and benefits of alternative courses of action. Together, attorney and client formulate an agreement as to the best steps to take at each juncture of the process.

Defense Attorney Duties. The defense attorney has duties to perform at the various stages in the criminal process. For example, defendants have a right to have an attorney present at police interrogations, lineups, preliminary hearings, and probation and parole

defense attorney (in criminal cases)
Lawyer retained by an individual accused of committing a crime or assigned by the court if the individual is unable to pay.

In Their Own Words

DELORES D. JONES-BROWN, ASSOCIATE PROFESSOR, JOHN JAY COLLEGE OF CRIMINAL JUSTICE, CITY UNIVERSITY OF NEW YORK, AND FORMER ASSISTANT PROSECUTOR, MONMOUTH COUNTY, FREEHOLD, NEW JERSEY

For three years I introduced myself to judges and juries as follows: "My name is Delores D. Jones and I represent the people of the State of New Jersey." In that three-year period, I found that my original image of prosecutors was both accurate and inaccurate.

As a woman and a racial minority, the role of prosecutor in the American justice system proved to be riddled with conflicts and contradictions. It was a position in which I felt both powerful and powerless. I had the power to indict and convict; the power to persuade juries or allow a defendant to avoid one. It was a position where showmanship was important, but sincerity was ethically required. It was a position which allowed one individual to hold the keys to the liberty or confinement of another.

Yet, in many ways, the role of the prosecutor was without power. The final decisions (such as guilt, sentencing, and sometimes the charge) were made by judges and/or juries with only some constrained by input from the prosecution (rules of evidence, court rules, and professional ethics).

While I always attempted to maintain a level of compassion and empathy for victims (and sometimes even defendants), the demands and constraints of the profession were often frustrating. I wasn't allowed to investigate why the majority of the defendants arraigned on any given day were black or Hispanic, while the majority of all the courtroom personnel were nonminority.

Court rules and professional rules of ethics would not allow me to speak with individual defendants to attempt to get their side of the story before aggressively pursuing the case against

revocation proceedings. The defense attorney's first and foremost duty in the proceedings is to protect the accused. This includes informing the client of the rights guaranteed by law and determining what procedural steps should be taken to ensure those rights. These may include:

- Seeking the pretrial release of the accused.
- Filing motions to suppress illegally obtained evidence.
- Moving to have the client's case separated from the cases of others if several people have been jointly accused of the same offense.
- Seeking to have the charges dismissed.

One of the first duties of a defense attorney upon agreeing to represent a client is to investigate the circumstances of the case by securing information held by the prosecutor or police and interviewing witnesses. On conclusion of an investigation, the attorney advises the accused about all aspects of the case and provides an assessment of the probable outcome. This consultation allows both the attorney and the accused to make three important decisions about the case:

268

them. I had to rely instead on representations from other individuals and agencies and hope that in the end, "justice would be done." Most disheartening, I left the prosecutor's office without being able to change the "assembly line" quality of justice being meted out under the current system.

The volume of cases being handled by the court system on any one day made it nearly impossible for any single case to be handled carefully and individually. Fridays were particularly bad. In most jurisdictions, Fridays are motion and sentencing day. Defendants who are asking to have evidence excluded on constitutional grounds, for example, and defendants who have pleaded guilty or who have been found guilty in previous weeks, are lined up to argue or hear their fate. In some courtrooms, the number of cases listed, and the speed with which the cases were handled, caused me to adopt the phrase "the justice factory" to describe what I observed and was required to participate in.

I learned that judges weren't always fair and impartial. And that they were being "graded" on how quickly they moved the cases that came before them. The more cases they handled, the better the grade that they received. Justice and individual attention appeared secondary to "moving" the cases. To keep pace, the prosecutor's role became affected by similar concerns.

Contrary to the television versions of trials depicting weeks or months of preparation time and numerous high-paid experts and investigation teams, there were times when cases had to be prepared over one weekend, and once, like the stories told about public defenders, I was handed a case that had to be tried the very same morning that I received the file.

When referring to my time in the prosecutor's office, I often say that "I used to send people to jail for a living." I then quickly add, "only if they deserved to go." While I am fairly confident that that is an accurate statement, there is no way to know for sure. The way the system is structured, it is easy to become more concerned with winning cases than securing accurate and just verdicts. Maintaining an ethical stance in the face of time constraints, uncooperative witnesses, unsavory defendants, *and* victims (and other factors) is no small feat. A commitment to doing the best job possible, with a focus on just outcomes (in spite of numerous limitations), is a necessary and difficult element in becoming a successful and *respectable* prosecutor.

- What plea to enter in response to the charges filed.
- Whether to waive the right to a jury trial.
- Whether the accused should testify on his or her own behalf.

If the defense attorney concludes that a conviction is probable, the accused may be asked to consider entering a discussion with the prosecutor about a negotiated plea or plea bargain. If the defendant chooses to go to trial, the defense attorney, together with the prosecutor, is responsible for *voir dire,* or selection of the jury members. During the trial, the defense counsel and the prosecutor perform essentially the same duties: presentation of evidence, examination of witnesses, and raising of objections to any questions or evidence by the other side considered inadmissible. If the defendant is convicted, the defense counsel has an important role to play in sentencing.[39]

Private Defense Counsel

Famous celebrity defense lawyers, like Alan Dershowitz, Gloria Allred, Mark Geraogs, and F. Lee Bailey, thrive on cases that generate a lot of publicity. They command high fees for their professional expertise, often with the justification that such fees will allow them to represent clients with lesser means. Not surprisingly, the number of criminal defendants who can afford the services of attorneys like these is very small.[40]

Besides "celebrity lawyers," private criminal lawyers can be grouped into three other categories. The first group consists of those who represent frequently arrested clients, such as gamblers, drug dealers, and prostitutes. Among them are also lawyers who serve as "in-house counsel" on a regular basis to members of organized crime. This group is quite small. The second group, "occasionals," are attorneys who, from time to time, agree to handle a criminal case.[41] The experience of representing a defendant charged with a criminal offense may represent a diversion from their regular practice. Their livelihood is not dependent on these cases, and concerns about fees and the cost of time consumed while waiting for a case to be called in the courtroom will not cause them to modify their style of representation or strategy. The third category, "regulars," by contrast, depend on criminal cases for a sizable portion of their income. Most of the defendants they work with, however, are able to pay only small fees. Thus the regulars must carefully monitor their time to be sure they are adequately compensated for the services they perform.[42]

Public Defenders

> Life in the fast lane of the law can be observed on the fourth floor of the municipal court building each morning beginning at 9:00 A.M. Columbus, OH, defense attorney Madelon Rosenfeld was at work only 15 minutes one recent Monday morning and she already had a standing-room-only string of clients. She would confer with one client, move down a long table to talk with another, hurry to comfort a third, pause for a minute to consult with a legal colleague, then return to the first client ready to make a careful legal recommendation.
>
> About 100 Columbus men and women would seek Rosenfeld's legal skills that Monday, not an unusual daily workload for her. Rosenfeld is a public defender, one of 17 attorneys assigned to the municipal court division of the Franklin County Office—the largest criminal defense law office in the state.[43]

After reading this, it may come as a surprise that the poor—at least in theory—are entitled to the same legal rights as the rich.

The Constitutional Right to Counsel.   In 1932, the Supreme Court ruled that the Fourteenth Amendment of the Constitution required that defense counsel be provided for poor defendants on trial for a capital offense.[44] Six years later, the right of indigent defendants to be represented in all criminal proceedings in federal courts was established.[45] Not until the landmark case of *Gideon v. Wainwright* was decided in 1963 did the court extend the right to appointed counsel to indigent defendants charged with felonies in state courts, ruling that "lawyers in criminal courts are necessities, not luxuries."[46] Nine years later, the Supreme Court's decision in *Argersinger v. Hamlin* expanded the right to counsel to include all cases, including misdemeanors, that may result in sentences of imprisonment.[47]

Types of Public Defense.   Attorneys now work in three types of arrangements for the defense of persons charged with crime: public defender, assigned counsel, and contract systems. These systems are funded primarily by state and county governments and have become a significant resource in, and burden on, the justice system. Counties have the sole responsibility for providing indigent defense systems in twenty-four states, while seventeen states have statewide systems.

Each state and county may utilize more than one type of system, although within each jurisdiction there is a primary system. **Assigned counsel systems** are the most frequently used. Here the judge appoints a private lawyer selected from a list of attorneys. Assigned counsel systems are favored in rural areas, so even though most counties use this type of system, assigned counsel programs actually serve less than one-third of the population. **Public defender systems,** consisting of public or nonprofit organizations with staff that provide defense services, are used by most of the largest counties in the country, which by themselves account for one-third of the nation's population.[48] There is considerable variation in the types of programs

assigned counsel system
Judge appoints a private lawyer selected from a list of attorneys to represent indigent defendants in criminal proceedings.

public defender system
Public or nonprofit organizations (with staff) provide defense services to indigent defendants.

(see Figure 9.5). In the Northeast, for example, nearly all of the counties use public defender systems, whereas in the South almost all of the counties use assigned counsel systems.[49] Finally, **contract systems,** under which private attorneys from law firms or local bar associations contract to provide defense services, are used in significantly fewer counties.

Evaluations of Public Defense. Federal District Judge Ann Williams does not mince words. For the second time in a month, in November 1986, Judge Williams overturned a conviction in Cook County Court due to attorney incompetence—the first time by a state's attorney, the second by a Cook County public defender. In her words: "This case teaches the lesson that sloppy lawyering can undermine individual rights and drain judicial resources. The inferior counseling of a defendant means that the efforts of many participants in the judicial process have been wasted and may mean that an individual has been unjustly incarcerated for eight years."[50]

contract system
Private attorneys from law firms or local bar associations provide defense services to indigent defendants.

FIGURE 9.5
Types of Indigent Criminal Defense Services in the Nation's 100 Largest Counties in 1999

County/State	Total 1999 Population	Public Defender Services	Assigned Counsel Services	Contract Services
Los Angeles, CA	9,329,989	■	■	■
Cook, IL	5,192,326	■	■	
Harris, TX	3,250,404		■	■
Maricopa, AZ	2,861,395	■		■
San Diego, CA	2,820,844	■	■	
Orange, CA	2,760,948	■		■
Kings, NY	2,268,297	■	■	■
Dade, FL	2,175,634	■	■	
Wayne, MI	2,106,495	■	■	
Dallas, TX	2,062,100	■	■	
Queens, NY	2,000,642	■	■	■
San Bernardino, CA	1,669,934	■	■	■
King, WA	1,664,846	■	■	
Santa Clara, CA	1,647,419	■	■	
New York, NY	1,551,844	■	■	■
Broward, FL	1,535,468	■		■
Riverside, CA	1,530,653	■	■	■
Middlesex, MA	1,426,606	■	■	
Philadelphia, PA	1,417,601	■	■	
Alameda, CA	1,415,582	■	■	
Suffolk, NY	1,383,847	■	■	■
Tarrant, TX[a]	1,382,442		■	
Bexar, TX	1,372,867		■	
Cuyahoga, OH	1,371,717	■	■	
Nassau, NY	1,305,057	■	■	■
Allegheny, PA	1,256,806	■	■	
Clark, NV	1,217,155	■	■	■
Bronx, NY	1,194,099	■	■	■
Sacramento, CA	1,184,586	■	■	
Oakland, MI	1,179,978	■	■	
Hennepin, MN	1,064,419	■	■	

(continued)

FIGURE 9.5
(*Continued*)

County/State	Total 1999 Population	Public Defender Services	Assigned Counsel Services	Contract Services
Palm Beach, FL	1,049,420	■	■	■
Franklin, OH	1,027,821	■	■	
St. Louis, MO	996,181	■	■	
Fairfax, VA	945,717	■	■	
Hillsborough, FL	940,484	■	■	
Contra Costa, CA	933,141	■	■	
Erie, NY	925,957	■	■	■
Milwaukee, WI	906,248	■	■	■
Westchester, NY	905,572	■	■	■
DuPage, IL	892,547	■	■	
Pinellas, FL	878,499	■	■	
Shelby, TN	873,000	■	■	
Honolulu, HI	864,571	■	■	
Bergen, NJ	857,052	■	■	
Montgomery, MD	852,174	■	■	
Salt Lake, UT	850,243	■	■	
Fairfield, CT	841,334	■	■	■
Hamilton, OH	840,443	■	■	
Hartford, CT	829,671	■	■	■
Orange, FL	817,206	■	■	■
Marion, IN	810,946	■	■	■
Pima, AZ	803,618	■	■	■
New Haven, CT	793,208	■	■	■
Macomb, MI	792,082		■	
Prince George's, MD	781,781	■	■	
Fresno, CA	763,069	■	■	■
Essex, NJ	747,355	■	■	
San Francisco, CA	746,777	■	■	
Ventura, CA	745,063	■		■
Fulton, GA	744,827	■	■	■
Worcester, MA	738,629	■	■	
Duval, FL	738,483	■	■	
Travis, TX	727,022	■	■	
Montgomery, PA	724,087	■	■	
Baltimore,MD	723,914	■	■	
Middlesex, NJ	717,949	■	■	
Monroe, NY	712,419	■	■	■
Essex, MA	704,407	■	■	
San Mateo, CA	702,102			■
El Paso, TX	701,908	■	■	
Pierce, WA	688,807	■	■	■
Jefferson, KY	672,900	■	■	

(*continued*)

FIGURE 9.5
(Continued)

County/State	Total 1999 Population	Public Defender Services	Assigned Counsel Services	Contract Services
Jefferson, AL[b]	657,422		■	■
Jackson, MO	654,484	■	■	
Mecklenburg, NC	648,400	■	■	■
Norfolk, VA	643,580	■	■	
Kern, CA	642,495	■	■	
Suffolk, MA	641,695	■	■	
Oklahoma, OK	636,539	■	■	■
Multnomah, OR[b]	633,224		■	■
Baltimore City, MD	632,681	■	■	
Lake, IL	617,975	■		■
Monmouth, NJ	611,444	■	■	
DeKalb, GA	596,853	■	■	■
Snohomish, WA	596,598	■	■	
Bucks, PA	594,047	■	■	■
Wake, NC	586,940		■	■
Cobb, GA	583,541		■	■
Providence, RI	574,108	■	■	
Montgomery, OH	565,866	■	■	
San Joaquin, CA	563,183	■		■
Hudson, NJ	552,819	■	■	
Kent, MI	550,388	■	■	■
Tulsa, OK	548,296	■	■	
Delaware, PA	541,502	■	■	
Summit, OH	537,856	■	■	
Davidson, TN	530,050	■	■	
Bernalillo, NM	523,472	■		■
District of Columbia	519,000	■	■	

NOTE: Categories were assembled for illustrative purposes. Local indigent criminal defense providers may use different categories.

[a]The small public defender program identified in Tarrant County during the 1982 BJS study was not located in this 1999 study.

[b]Includes a public defender program primarily funded by an awarded contract.

SOURCES: 1999 population estimates for each county came from the Census Bureau website, http://www.census.gov/population/www/estimates/countypop.html.

Carol J. Defrances and Marika Litras, *Indigent Defense Services in Large Counties, 1999* (Washington, DC: Bureau of Justice Statistics, 2001), p. 10.

Defense attorneys, both private and public, have frequently been the target of accusations of incompetence. One observer of the courts has remarked that "incompetence is more the rule than the exception. . . . Whether public defender, court-appointed attorney, or counsel retained by the defendant, defense lawyers frequently are inexperienced, incompetent, unprepared, and uninterested in their clients' interests and needs."[51] Defendants—the clients of the indigent defense bar—sometimes share a dim appraisal of the effectiveness of the assistance they receive. Their views are perhaps best summed up by the oft-quoted remark recorded by Jonathan Casper:

"Did you have a lawyer when you went to court?"
"No, I had a public defender."[52]

This remark is troubling because the public defender's office was once viewed as a solution to the problems associated with the private defense bar.[53] The defendants discussed in Casper's study, however, felt that they would have been better represented by private attorneys than by public defenders. Much of their dissatisfaction with public defenders stemmed from the perception that any attorney who is paid by the state, in effect, works for the state, not the defendant. Some depictions of the way in which public defenders operate have tended to confirm this view of the defender as negotiator and conciliator, interested in helping the system to dispose of cases rather than being a zealous and rigorous advocate for the defendant.[54]

Several guidelines attempt to specify competence standards for the criminal defense bar.[55] However, guidelines do not ensure that defense attorneys will provide competent assistance in the face of the realities of the criminal courtroom. Studies of indigent defense systems over the last several years have concluded that the poor are not always well served by the private or public defense bar. Generally, these studies have found that the systems are underfunded and understaffed and, as a result, there is enormous pressure to simply get the defendant to "cop a plea," that is, accept a plea bargain.[56] Defendants in some jurisdictions are treated to a sort of "assembly-line justice," in which they may not meet their defense attorney until they arrive at the courtroom, only to find the attorney suggesting that they plead guilty.[57]

Ethical Issues

When defense lawyers attend social functions they are invariably asked: "How can you defend people who you know are guilty?" To most people, it seems that lawyers who defend criminals must have to compromise their own values. However, most members of the criminal defense bar will respond with a little lesson in civics, explaining that under the United States Constitution every person is entitled to a fair trial, that every person is to be presumed innocent until proven guilty, and that everyone is entitled to be represented by counsel. Defense attorneys see themselves as performing a function that is a fundamental part of our Constitution. As one veteran public defender put it: Representing an indigent criminal defendant is all about duty. When a case is assigned, that duty arises, and it remains until the defendant is sentenced after a plea of guilty, he is freed after a successful trial, or his case is appealed after an unsuccessful one. Because your client is poor and can't afford anyone else, the duty owed him is the highest duty a lawyer can have.[58]

ABA TEN PRINCIPLES OF A PUBLIC DEFENSE DELIVERY SYSTEM

Black Letter

1. The public defense function, including the selection, funding, and payment of defense counsel, is independent.
2. Where the caseload is sufficiently high, the public defense delivery system consists of both a defender office and the active participation of the private bar.
3. Clients are screened for eligibility, and defense counsel is assigned and notified of appointment, as soon as feasible after clients' arrest, detention, or request for counsel.
4. Defense counsel is provided sufficient time and a confidential space within which to meet with the client.
5. Defense counsel's workload is controlled to permit the rendering of quality representation.
6. Defense counsel's ability, training, and experience match the complexity of the case.
7. The same attorney continuously represents the client until completion of the case.

(continued)

8. There is parity between defense counsel and the prosecution with respect to resources and defense counsel is included as an equal partner in the justice system.
9. Defense counsel is provided with and required to attend continuing legal education.
10. Defense counsel is supervised and systematically reviewed for quality and efficiency according to nationally and locally adopted standards.

SOURCE: American Bar Association, *ABA Ten Principles of a Public Defense Delivery System* (Chicago: American Bar Association, 2002), p. 5.

The American Bar Association's Model Code of Professional Responsibility contains a provision that states that "*a lawyer should represent a client zealously within the bounds of the law.*"[59] That does not mean that a defense attorney must go beyond the limits of his or her own conscience, nor does it mean that the attorney has license to do whatever might be necessary to win a case. As with the prosecutor, the defense counsel's paramount obligation is to the administration of justice. But he or she is also an advocate who must make sure that all legal mechanisms available to the defense are utilized. Sometimes this may result in attacks based on seeming technicalities, which can create anger on the part of the public, especially if a client ends up "getting off" on a technicality. It can also lead defense attorneys to cross-examinations of victims and witnesses that may make these persons feel as though they are the ones who are on trial.

The bounds of "zealous representation" are not clearly articulated, although the ABA's standards, along with its Model Code of Professional Responsibility and Model Rules of Professional Conduct, attempt to provide guidance to defense attorneys by defining specific behaviors as unprofessional conduct. Examples include counseling a client to engage in conduct the lawyer knows to be illegal, using illegal means to obtain evidence, paying a witness (other than an expert witness) for testimony, and knowingly entering false evidence.

Judges

> At 5 A.M. he wakes to down a bowl of cold cereal in an otherwise sleeping house in the remote northern suburbs. By 6:05 he is on the Metro-North train, another harried commuter balancing legal briefs and statute books on his lap. A little more than an hour later he is waiting on the Grand Central subway platform for a No. 4 or No. 5 express to Brooklyn Bridge, and by 7:30 he is at his desk on the fifth floor of the columned United States Courthouse on Foley Square, sipping from a container of steaming tea.[60]

Another day in the life of a judge. After the commute, a judge may hear motions; listen to testimony; instruct a jury; and write opinions. What do judges do besides sit in court? What roles do they assume? What duties do they perform? Who are they? How are they selected? We will address these questions next.

Roles and Duties

Judges are the supreme officers of the court. They preside over courtroom proceedings and interpret and decide questions of law. In doing so they play a prominent role in ensuring that justice is served—sometimes at great expense. As decision makers and arbiters, judges exert control over criminal cases at each stage of the criminal process. Judges are called on to decide questions presented to the court. While each side in a case may present arguments asking for a ruling in its favor, the judge must weigh both sides and make a decision. Rulings are required about whether to detain a defendant pending trial. If the defendant is to be released, the judge must determine if bail is required or if the defendant can be released on his own recognizance. The judge also sets the dollar amount of bail

judge
Public officer lawfully instituted (by appointment or election) to decide litigated questions according to law, presiding in a court of law.

BLACK ROBES AND WHITE JUSTICE

Not one black judge sat on the bench in any of the federal courts—district courts, courts of appeal, or the U.S. Supreme Court—for the first 145 years of our nation's history. The first, William H. Hastie, was appointed by President Harry S Truman in 1949.[1]

Until only recently there have been policies of racial discrimination in the United States that prevented African Americans from attending most of the nation's law schools. In addition, many blacks have been deprived of the high school education that would afford them a chance to go on to college and then to law school. Others have been discouraged by the strong sense that justice in America is distributed along racial lines—that black lawyers and judges would bear an extra burden in all-white courts.

Times have changed—but not enough for most and, for many, not much at all. Today there are approximately 36,000 African-American lawyers in the United States. Of the 24,000 judges nationwide, 895 are black.

The fear that black judges would "bear an extra burden" in American courts is well founded. In a report of the New York State Judicial Commission on Minorities, white judges and nonwhite judges rated the extent to which the treatment of judges is affected by racial and ethnic differences.[2] Essentially, white judges do not think judges are treated any differently if they are not white, but minority judges feel that other judges, attorneys, and courtroom personnel treat white judges one way and minority judges another. These differences appear in judges'

perceptions of the importance of cross-cultural sensitivity training for judges as well. Minority judges feel that it is more important than do white judges.

The New York commission listed a host of conclusions, including the following four:

1. There is a perception that minorities are underrepresented in the state judiciary in comparison with their share of the overall population.

2. There is a particular need for more minority judges in upstate districts.

3. There is a pool of minority applicants for judgeships who have been rated as qualified but who have not been appointed.

4. By any measure, minorities are grossly underrepresented in supervisory and other high-level administrative positions within the judiciary.

Justice Wright's Experience

The plight of the black judge has been chronicled by the late New York State Supreme Court Justice Bruce McM. Wright. Justice Wright, once a judge in the Manhattan Criminal Court and the New York Civil Court, had felt the pain associated with rejection by colleagues, ridicule by the press, and harassment from the public. According to Justice Wright, the differential treatment of black judges—by white defendants, judges, and politicians—reflects the racism found within the structure of American society. As Justice Wright has written:

> Racism inside the courts is but a reflection of what goes on in society in general. This was brought home

required. Defense attorneys may file pretrial motions requesting, for example, the suppression of evidence that allegedly has been obtained illegally. The judge must rule on all pretrial motions. Before setting a case for trial, the judge may be called on to rule on the competence of a defendant to stand trial. If the defense attorney and prosecutor negotiate an agreement in which the defendant will plead guilty, the judge still has to decide whether to accept that agreement.

Trials.   If a case does proceed to trial and the defendant opts to have the case heard before a jury, the judge oversees the jury selection and controls the presentation of evidence. During the trial, the judge must maintain the decorum of the courtroom and rule on any motions and objections. Avoiding legal errors during a trial is extremely important because such errors can form the basis of an appeal that may result in reversing the decision. At the conclusion of the presentation of evidence and arguments, the judge must formulate instructions advising the jurors how to apply the law to the facts presented.

In cases where the defendant chooses to waive the right to a jury trial, the judge becomes the trier of facts and decides the guilt or innocence of the defendant. If a defendant is found guilty by a judge or jury, the judge determines the sentence given to the defendant.

Other Judicial and Nonjudicial Functions.   Of course, judges perform many other duties besides their critical trial role. Judges are responsible for the functioning of their courts.

forcefully to me with a kind of grim humor in 1974. At that time I was teaching a course at The New School for Social Research in the evenings, as well as an early morning one at Staten Island Community College. This called for some tense traveling in order not to be late in reporting to court. After leaving Staten Island, I would speed across the Verrazano Bridge to be in my courtroom by 10 A.M.

One afternoon, during a trial, I felt so faint and weak I could not carry on. The clerks, with affectionate concern, feared that I was having a heart attack. I was taken out of the courthouse lashed to a stretcher. It was an embarrassment to be so helpless and publicly exhibited.

In the emergency room of the hospital, I was placed in a curtained-off area where there [were] two beds some distance apart. On one was a white man, obviously one of the poor derelicts now and then brought in from the Bowery. He appeared to be in a state of joyous alcoholic bewilderment. He needed a shave; neither soiled sneakers nor his socks matched; he drooled a bit and sang softly in garbled syllables.

As I watched him from my bed, I felt pangs of pity. He seemed much worse off than I. I felt guilty for being dressed in a three-piece suit and clean shirt.

I heard a nurse outside the curtained area say, "Hurry, doctor, we have a judge who is ill." A white doctor parted the curtains, paused at the entrance, looked at me and then at the white derelict. He hurried to the side of the white man, lifted his wrist as though to test his pulse, and said, "Judge, what seems to be the matter?"

It was a bracing experience, wholly therapeutic, and I began to recover without delay.

The most remarkable aspect of the hospital experience was the reinforcement of my view that whites almost automatically have a "place" reaction to the color of dark skin. Compared with a poor, ragged, homeless white unfortunate, unshaven and drooling, a well-dressed black simply could not be the judge. What a sadness, I thought, and how appropriate was the observation of an unknown who had said that America was the only country in the world to suffer a decline and fall in its civilization without first becoming civilized.[3]

Race remains one of the greatest challenges to the judicial system as we chart the progress of the next century.

Questions for Discussion

1. How does the lack of minority judges affect American justice?

2. Devise a strategy to increase the representation of African Americans and Hispanics on our nation's courts.

3. How would you go about ensuring equal and fair treatment for all judges, regardless of race?

SOURCES
1. Franklin Edwards, *The Negro Professional Class* (Glencoe, IL: Free Press, 1959), p. 155.
2. New York State Judicial Commission on Minorities, *Report of the New York State Judicial Commission on Minorities 4* (New York: Author, 1991).
3. Bruce Wright, *Black Robes, White Justice* (Secaucus, NJ: Lyle Stuart, 1987), pp. 24–25.

Fewer than half preside at a trial on an average day, but nearly three-quarters report that they spend time on administrative duties.

The administrative functions of the judge include being responsible for support staff, lending assistance in the preparation of the budget, and managing the case flow within the court. Case-flow management, extremely important because of concerns over backlogs, has been given added importance because of the passage of "speedy trial laws" at the federal and state levels. These laws require that a defendant in a criminal case be brought to trial within a specified time, usually within four to six months.

Management of case flow involves control over what is called the court calendar. Each case that is filed in a court is entered into the records and is then placed on the court calendar for a hearing. In jurisdictions with many judges, courts may organize themselves in different ways for calendar management. Two primary methods of calendar management are used. In the individual calendar system, a case is randomly assigned to whichever judge is free. That judge is then responsible for the case from beginning to end. In the master calendar system, judges are assigned to hear particular kinds of cases. Thus, one judge may hear all the pretrial issues of a case while another judge may be responsible only for trials. Not surprisingly, some courts also utilize a modification of these systems.

Types of Judges

In federal courts, there are four different types of judges:

- *Magistrates,* whose responsibility is to hear such matters as pretrial motions and whose duties may include the trial and disposition of minor federal offenses.
- *District judges,* who are the trial judges of the federal courts.
- *Judges of the court of appeal,* who hear appeals from district courts.
- *Justices of the Supreme Court,* who review a small number of cases and render definitive opinions binding all federal courts and, in constitutional matters, all state courts as well.

In addition to these, the federal system also has nearly 300 bankruptcy court judges. Moreover, a variety of administrative law judges, tax court judges, and judges of other specialized courts deal primarily with matters of administrative law.

Careers

In state courts, justices of the peace and magistrates are found at the lowest level of the state court systems, typically in courts of limited jurisdiction and often at the municipal level. Trial judges are found in both courts of general jurisdiction and courts of limited jurisdiction. Appellate court judges and the justices of a state's court of last resort hear appeals on points of law and render final judgments.

Approximately 60 percent of the nation's trial court judges have general assignments in which they handle all types of cases that come before them, while 13 percent handle only criminal cases. About one-quarter of trial judges are assigned to hear only civil cases. Depending on the operation of the court in which they serve, judges may also be assigned to handle a particular aspect of cases, such as bail hearings or preliminary hearings.

Qualifications and Background

What are the formal requirements for a person who wishes to become, say, a U.S. Supreme Court justice? There are none! The Constitution, which authorizes the establishment of the Supreme Court, confers on the president the power to appoint judges to the highest court, subject to approval by the Senate. Congress has established the same selection process for lower court federal judges. However, there is no mention in the Constitution or elsewhere of any particular qualifications for federal judgeships. Candidates need have no special educational backgrounds, meet no minimum age requirements, or even be lawyers. There is no stipulation that a judge be a citizen of the United States or a legal resident. Interestingly, however, qualifications for U.S. magistrates *have* been set forth: A full-time magistrate must be a lawyer and a member of the state bar.

Federal Judges.   In practice, of course, qualifications for federal judges exist by custom. Most important is professional competence.[61] Despite the lack of a requirement that judges be lawyers, virtually all appointments are of distinguished attorneys. Virtually all of the nominees of recent presidential administrations have come directly from another level of the judiciary, the practice of law, or the teaching of law. From two-thirds to three-quarters have had prior judicial or prosecutorial experience.[62] It is worth noting that the extent of prior prosecutorial experience has disturbed some members of the defense bar. The late William M. Kunstler had gone so far as to say: "It is a little short of infantile to expect that any former prosecutor could possibly, by exchanging a dress or business suit for a black robe, suddenly become an impartial administrator of the law."[63]

A second factor is political affiliation. With the exception of President Ford, at least 90 percent of every president's judicial nominees in the last thirty years have been in the same political party as the president who made the appointment.[64] Political affiliation does not mean that a nominee has been especially active in politics, but, in the words of one commentator, "partisan political activism has always been considered to be a great boon to a judgeship candidacy."[65]

State Judges.   At the state level, qualifications are more clearly articulated. With the exception of New Hampshire, every state stipulates minimum requirements for judges of

Clarence Thomas appearing before the Senate in 1991, immediately before being confirmed.

the appellate courts and the courts of general jurisdiction. Criteria vary from state to state, but most require (1) a minimum age, (2) a number of years of residence within the state, and (3) membership in the state bar.[66] Most states do not require that magistrates or justices of the peace have law degrees or bar membership.

Selection

Federal Judges. Under the Constitution, the president of the United States has the responsibility of selecting nominees for judges at all levels of the federal judiciary. After selection, their names are presented to the Senate for confirmation or approval. Most presidents have traditionally taken a good deal more interest in personally selecting the nominees to the U.S. Supreme Court than to the lower courts. This may be due to the importance of the Court, and the fact that a tradition has been established regarding district court appointments: Senators from the president's party tend to exercise virtual veto power over nominees to district judgeships in their state. Should the home-state senator object to the nominee, the members of the Senate Judiciary Committee, who review and make recommendations about all judicial nominees, will simply not recommend the nomination to the full Senate. In view of this tradition, presidents tend to leave the selection of district judges to members of the White House staff and high-ranking officials of the Department of Justice.[67] The great majority of a president's nominees are approved by the Senate.

One important factor in the selection of federal judges has been the rating given to them by the American Bar Association's Committee on the Federal Judiciary. This committee, composed of members from each of the federal circuits, carefully evaluates all potential candidates for the federal bench and gives them one of four possible ratings: "exceptionally well qualified," "well qualified," "qualified," or "not qualified." A rating of "not qualified" by the ABA committee makes appointment extremely unlikely.[68] But clearly, the most important criterion for selection is political party affiliation.

State Judges. State judiciaries use one of five methods to choose their judges: (1) partisan elections (in which judges' party affiliations appear on the ballot); (2) nonpartisan elections; (3) merit selection; (4) gubernatorial appointment; and (5) appointment by the legislature. Partisan elections are used in nine states, and another thirteen states use nonpartisan elections. This makes the elective process the most popular form of selection at the state level.[69] Research has shown that voters are often unfamiliar with judicial candidates and therefore do not make informed choices when they vote.[70]

One alternative to elections that has become extremely popular is merit selection. First adopted in Missouri in 1940, and known ever since as "the Missouri Plan," merit selection is intended to provide a means of selecting well-qualified candidates untainted by political influence. Under the typical plan, a state nominating commission will select several candidates and submit their names to the governor, who then appoints one from among them. After a short period, the judge must stand for election, which usually takes the form of a question on the ballot that asks, "Shall Judge X be retained in office?" As in other judicial elections, the voters tend to vote "yes" even though they may know nothing about the judge. Merit selection has grown steadily in popularity and is now used in twenty-one states.

Other Court Personnel

It would be a mistake to assume that judges manage the entire operation of the courts. It would be a mistake as well to assume that courts run by themselves. They are complex organizations requiring day-to-day management, administrative assistance, and support. Figure 9.6 depicts the continuum of administrative-judicial action, revealing the full range of activities that transcend the adjudicatory function.

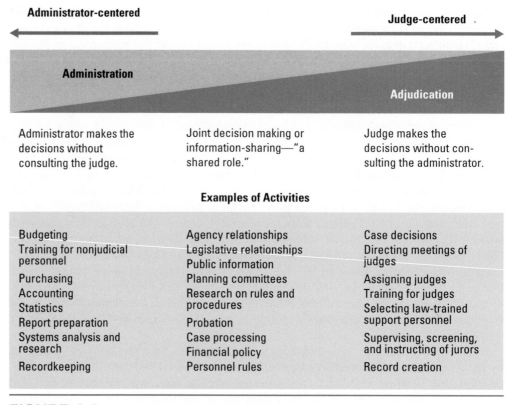

Administrator-centered

Judge-centered

Administrator makes the decisions without consulting the judge.

Joint decision making or information-sharing—"a shared role."

Judge makes the decisions without consulting the administrator.

Examples of Activities

Budgeting	Agency relationships	Case decisions
Training for nonjudicial personnel	Legislative relationships	Directing meetings of judges
Purchasing	Public information	Assigning judges
Accounting	Planning committees	Training for judges
Statistics	Research on rules and procedures	Selecting law-trained support personnel
Report preparation	Probation	
Systems analysis and research	Case processing	Supervising, screening, and instructing of jurors
	Financial policy	
Recordkeeping	Personnel rules	Record creation

FIGURE 9.6   Continuum of Administrative-Judicial Activities

SOURCE: E. Keith Stott, Jr., "The Judicial Executive: Toward Greater Congruence in an Emerging Profession," *The Justice System Journal,* Fall 1982.

court administrator
Chief administrative officer of the court, usually appointed by the state court of last resort, the chief justice of the court of last resort, or a judicial council.

Most state court systems today use the services of a **court administrator** to execute the many nonjudicial, administrative duties. The court administrator is usually appointed by the state court of last resort, the chief justice of the court of last resort, or a judicial council. Despite the presence of the court administrator, the judges retain the primary responsibility for the way in which the court functions. The court administrator may be properly considered the chief operating officer of the court, and the chief judge its executive officer.

The day-to-day affairs of all federal courts are the responsibility of the Administrative Office of the U.S. Courts. The Administrative Office, created by Congress in 1939, serves as the management arm of the federal courts. It also collects and disseminates statistics and information on federal cases. More recently, the Administrative Office has served as an advocate for the federal judiciary before Congress, the White House, professional groups, and the general public.[71]

The same office in smaller, local state courts is held by the clerk of the court—who is sometimes called a register of probate or a prothonotary. Clerks docket cases, collect fees and court costs, maintain records, and manage jury selection. Their position and role should not be confused with those of the law clerks. Law clerks, both in the state and federal courts, are graduates of law school who spend one or two years in an apprenticeship position to a judge. Law clerks review motions and draft legal memoranda and judicial opinions.

Many other court employees perform useful tasks, including:

court officers and marshals
Persons who provide courtroom security and maintain order. See also *bailiff.*

bailiff
Officer of the court who administers formal procedures, keeps order, announces a judge's arrival, and administers oaths.

- **Court officers and marshals,** who provide courtroom security and maintain order.
- **Bailiffs,** who administer formal procedures, keep order in the court, announce a judge's arrival, and administer oaths.
- Deputy clerks, who, along with secretaries, maintain, type, and duplicate records and legal documents.[72]

Review

Lawyers and judges play different roles, carry out different duties, and operate under different constraints. Prosecutors are government attorneys who represent the people of their jurisdiction. They are responsible for some of the most important initial responses to crime, such as deciding what offenses to charge a suspect with, obtaining an indictment or filing an information against a defendant, and trying the criminal case. The different types of prosecutors include district attorneys, state attorneys general, and United States attorneys. Prosecutors are elected at the local and state level, and they are appointed at the federal level.

Both private defense counsel and public defenders represent the interests of those accused of crimes. They are advocates for their clients, and they act as intermediaries and as counselors. Defense attorneys, whether private or public, may face significant ethical dilemmas in their attempt to provide zealous representation for those who cannot afford to retain private counsel. Caseload pressures add to the problem.

Judges are the supreme officers of the court. They preside over proceedings, interpret and decide questions of law, and ensure that justice is served. In the federal courts there are four different kinds of judges: magistrates, district court judges, judges of the courts of appeals, and U.S. Supreme Court judges. In state courts there are justices of the peace, trial judges, appellate court judges, and justices of the court of last resort. Federal judges are appointed by the president with the advice and consent of the Senate. At the state level, most judges are elected.

Other court personnel include court administrators, who execute nonjudicial administrative duties; clerks of the court, who collect fees and maintain records; law clerks, who occupy an apprenticeship position to a judge; and court officers, marshals, and bailiffs, who manage the day-to-day operations of a particular courtroom.

Thinking Critically about Criminal Justice

1. Do you feel that prosecutors have too much discretion? What danger is there, if any, that prosecutors may be capricious, arbitrary, or discriminatory if given too much discretionary power?

Internet Connection

Note: While all of the URLs listed were current as of the printing of this book, these sites often change. Please check our website (http://www. mhhe.com/socscience/crimjustice/adlercj) for updates.

Examine the *Second Year Report to the President: Corporate Fraud Task Force* created by President Bush. How many corporations have been indicted, prosecuted, and convicted? **http://www.usdoj.gov/dag/cftf/2nd_yr_ fraud_report.pdf.**

What role does gender bias play in federal courts? See: **http://www.fjc.gov.**

Notes

1 C. L. Sonnichsen, *Roy Bean: Law West of the Pecos* (NY: Macmillan, 1943).

2. Barbara A. Curran and Clara N. Carson, *The Lawyers Statistical Abstracts* (Chicago: American Bar Association, 1944); Laurence H. Silberman, "Will Lawyering Strangle Democratic Capitalism?: A Retrospective," *Harvard Journal of Law and Public Policy* 21 (1998) p. 607; American Bar Foundation, *Supplement to the Lawyer Statistical Report: The U.S. Legal Profession in 1988* (1989). See http://www.ABANET.ORG.

3. John Jay Douglass, *Ethical Issues in Prosecution* (Houston, TX: National College of District Attorneys, 1988), p. 9.

4. Ibid.

5. For a view of the historical evolution of prosecution from private to public responsibility, see Joan E. Jacoby, *The American Prosecutor: A Search for Identity* (Lexington, MA: Lexington Books, 1980); Allen Steinberg, "From Private Prosecution to Plea Bargaining: Criminal Prosecution, the District Attorney, and American Legal History," *Crime and Delinquency* 30 (1984), pp. 568–592.

6. Marianne W. Zawitz, ed., *Report to the Nation on Crime and Justice,* 2nd ed. (Washington, DC: Bureau of Justice Statistics, 1988).

7. Charles Strum, "Federal Prosecutor Urged to Take up Teaneck Case," *The New York Times,* February 14, 1992, p. B7.

8. Ibid.

9. Martin H. Belsky, "On Becoming a Prosecutor," *The Prosecutor* 12 (1981), pp. 22–39.

10. See http://www.USDOJ.GOV/DAG/CFTF.

11. Larry Rohter, "Victory in Noriega Case Stunned Even Prosecutors," *The New York Times,* April 17, 1992, p. B16.

12. Abraham S. Blumberg, *Criminal Justice: Issues and Ironies* (NY: New Viewpoints, 1979), p. 123.

13. See, e.g., J. Buchanan, "Police–Prosecutor Teams: Innovations in Several Jurisdictions," *National Institute of Justice Reports No. 214* (Washington, DC: National Institute of Justice, 1989).

14. Newman F. Baker, "The Prosecutor-Initiation of Prosecution," *Journal of Criminal Law and Criminology* 23 (1933), p. 770.

15. Charles D. Breitel, "Controls in Criminal Law Enforcement," *University of Chicago Law Review* 27 (1960), pp. 427–435.

16. Barbara Boland, *The Prosecution of Felony Arrests, 1987* (Washington, DC: U.S. Department of Justice, Bureau of Justice Statistics, 1989).

17. Comment, "Prosecutorial Discretion in the Initiation of Criminal Complaints," *Southern California Law Review* 42 (1969), pp. 519–545.

18. See, e.g., Janell Schmidt and Ellen Hochstedler Steury, "Prosecutorial Discretion in Filing Charges in Domestic Violence Cases," *Criminology* 27 (1989), pp. 487–510; Huey-Tsyh Chen, "Dropping In and Dropping Out: Judicial Decision Making in the Disposition of Felony Arrests," *Journal of Criminal Justice* 19 (1991), pp. 1–17; Martha A. Myers and John Hagan, "Private and Public Trouble: Prosecutors and the Allocation of Court Resources," *Social Problems* 26 (1979), pp. 439–451; and Celesta A. Albonetti, "Criminality, Prosecutorial Screening, and Uncertainty: Toward a Theory of Discretionary Decision Making in Felony Case Processings," *Criminology* 24 (1986), pp. 623–644.

19. See David W. Neubauer, "After the Arrest: The Charging Decision in Prairie City," *Law and Society Review* 8 (1974), pp. 495–517.

20. See Malcolm D. Holmes, Howard C. Daudistel, and Ronald Farrell, "Determinants of Charge Reductions and Final Dispositions in Cases of Burglary and Robbery," *Journal of Research in Crime and Delinquency* 24 (1987), pp. 233–254; and Chen, "Dropping In and Dropping Out."

21. See Holmes, Daudistel, and Farrell, "Determinants of Charge Reductions"; and Myers and Hagan, "Private and Public Trouble."

22. See, e.g., Albonetti, "Criminality, Prosecutorial Screening, and Uncertainty"; and Chen, "Dropping In and Dropping Out."

23. Schmidt and Steury, "Prosecutorial Discretion." See, e.g., Maureen McLeod, "Victim Noncooperation in the Prosecution of Domestic Assault," *Criminology* 21 (1983), pp. 395–416.

24. Elizabeth Anne Stanko, "The Impact of Victim Assessment on Prosecutors' Screening Decisions: The Case of the New York County District Attorney's Office," *Law and Society Review* 16 (1981–82), pp. 225–239; and Kristen M. Williams, "The Effects of Victim Characteristics on the Disposition of Violent Crimes," in *Criminal Justice and the Victim,* ed. William F. McDonald (Beverly Hills, CA: Sage, 1976), pp. 177–213.

25. See Williams, "The Effects of Victim Characteristics."

26. See Albonetti, "Criminality, Prosecutorial Screening, and Uncertainty"; and Chen, "Dropping In and Dropping Out."

27. See Chen, "Dropping In and Dropping Out."

28. See Holmes, Daudistel, and Farrell, "Determinants of Charge Reductions."

29. For examples, see Thomas J. Keil and Gennaro F. Vito, "Race, Homicide Severity, and Application of the Death Penalty: A Consideration of the Barnett Scale," *Criminology* 27 (1989), pp. 511–535; and Raymond Paternoster, "Prosecutorial Discretion in Requesting the Death Penalty: A Case of Victim-based Racial Discrimination," *Law and Society Review* 18 (1984), pp. 437–478.

30. *Oyler v. Boles,* 368 U.S. 448 (1962).

31. See Charles W. Thomas and W. Anthony Fitch, "Prosecutorial Decision Making," *American Criminal Law Review* 13 (1976), pp. 507–559.

32. Breitel, "Controls in Criminal Law Enforcement."

33. Paul B. Wise, *Criminal Lawyers: An Endangered Species* (Beverly Hills, CA: Sage, 1978). See http://www.BIS.GOV/OCO/OCOS053.htm.

34. Harold J. Rothwax, "The Criminal Court: Problems and Proposals," unpublished manuscript (Biddle Law Library, University of Pennsylvania, 1970).

35. Edward A. Adams, "State Commission Finds Racism in Courts; 70 Suggestions Proposed to Eliminate 2-Tier System," *New York Law Journal,* June 5, 1991, p. 1.

36. Ibid.

37. *Gideon v. Wainwright,* 372 U.S. 335 (1963); *Argersinger v. Hamlin,* 407 U.S. 25 (1972).

38. American Bar Association Project on Standards for Criminal Justice, *Standards Relating to the Prosecution Function and the Defense Function* (NY: American Bar Association, 1970).

39. Benson B. Weintraub, "The Role of Defense Counsel at Sentencing," *Federal Probation* 51 (March 1987), p. 27.

40. Paul B. Wise, *Chaos in the Courthouse: The Inner Workings of the Urban Criminal Courts* (NY: Praeger, 1985).

41. James Eisenstein and Herbert Jacob, *Felony Justice. Organizational Analysis of Criminal Courts* (NY: McGraw-Hill, 1977).

42. The white-collar-crime defense attorney differs significantly from the courthouse regulars just described. See Kenneth Mann's study, *Defending White Collar Crime: A Portrait of Attorneys at Work* (New Haven, CT: Yale University Press, 1985).

43. Dick Kimmins, "Public Defenders—Shock Troops of the Legal Profession," *Business First—Columbus* 2 (33, Sec. 1), May 19, 1986, p. 1.

44. *Powell v. Alabama,* 287 U.S. 45 (1932).

45. *Johnson v. Zerbst,* 304 U.S. 458 (1938).

46. *Gideon v. Wainwright,* 372 U.S. 335 (1963).

47. *Argersinger v. Hamlin,* 407 U.S. 25 (1972).

48. Robert L. Spangenberg, Beverly Lee, Michael Battaglia, Patricia Smith, and A. David Davis, *National Criminal Defense Systems Study: Final Report* (Washington, DC: Bureau of Justice Statistics, NCJ-94702, 1986).

49. Bureau of Justice Statistics, *Criminal Defense for the Poor, 1986* (Washington, DC: Bureau of Justice Statistics, 1988). See also Steven K. Smith and Carol J. DeFrances, *Indigent Defense* (Washington, DC: Bureau of Justice Statistics, 1996).

50. "Lawyers Fumble, but Citizens Pay," *Chicago Tribune,* Business Section, November 11, 1986, p. 1.

51. Charles E. Silberman, *Criminal Justice, Criminal Violence* (NY: Vintage Books, 1980), p. 410.

52. Jonathan D. Casper, "'Did You Have a Lawyer When You Went to Court?' 'No, I Had a Public Defender,'" *Yale Review of Law and Social Action* 1 (1971), pp. 4–9.

53. See, e.g., Robert Wayne Gordon, "Defense of Indigents in Texas: A Mockery of Justice," *Baylor Law Review* 30 (1978), pp. 739–764.

54. See, in particular, David Sudnow, "Normal Crimes: Sociological Features of the Penal Code in a Public Defender Office," *Social Problems* 12 (1965), pp. 255–276.

55. See, e.g., American Bar Association, *Standards Relating to the Defense Function, Model Code of Professional Responsibility, and Model Rules of Professional Conduct.*

56. Norman Lefstein, *Criminal Defense Services for the Poor: Methods and Programs for Providing Legal Representation and the Need for Adequate Financing* (American Bar Association Standing Committee on Legal Aid and Indigent Defendants, 1982).

57. Casper, "'Did You Have a Lawyer When You Went to Court?'"

58. Milton Chivizzani, "A Former Public Defender Proudly States His Case," *Seattle Times,* March 23, 1992, p. A7.

59. American Bar Association, *Model Code of Professional Responsibility* (1979).

60. Ralph Blumenthal, "The View from the Bench: Once a Prosecutor, Now a Federal Judge: A Harried but Happy Life in the Law," *The New York Times,* March 11, 1992, p. B1.

61. Robert A. Carp and Ronald Stidham, *Judicial Process in America* (Washington, DC: CQ Press, 1990).

62. Kathleen Maguire and Timothy Flanagan, eds., *Sourcebook of Criminal Justice Statistics—1990* (Washington, DC: Bureau of Justice Statistics, 1991), pp. 53–54.

63. William M. Kunstler, "The Prosecutor–Judge," *New York Law Journal,* March 31, 1992, p. 2.

64. Ibid.

65. Elliot E. Slotnick, "The Paths to the Federal Bench: Gender, Race, and Judicial Recruitment Variation," *Judicature* 67 (1984), p. 378.

66. Ibid.

67. Carp and Stidham, *Judicial Process in America.*

68. See Henry J. Abraham, *Justices and Presidents: A Political History of Appointments to the Supreme Court* (NY: Oxford University Press, 1974).

69. Maguire and Flanagan, *Sourcebook of Criminal Justice Statistics—1990.*

70. Ibid., p. 17. See also Anthony Champagne and Greg Thielemann, "Awareness of Trial Court Judges," *Judicature* 74 (1991), pp. 271–276.

71. Robert A. Carp and Ronald Stidham, *The Federal Courts* (Washington, DC: CQ Press, 1985).

72. Ibid.

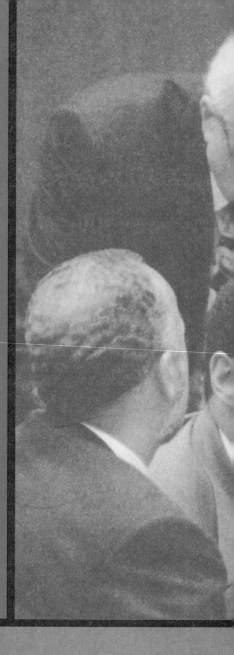

10

Criminal Prosecution and Adjudication

In March 1995, a radio commentator presented to his listeners an update on the O.J. Simpson trial from the year 2018. Judge Ito was still presiding, although approaching retirement. The jury was down to two members. All but one of the defense attorneys had since passed away, though the prosecution was still going strong. By then countless books had been published on O.J.'s trials and tribulations, and most of the attorneys and witnesses that played a part in this "trial of the twentieth century" had become wealthy from book contracts and movie rights.

- The O.J. Simpson trial for a double murder held the world in its grip as trial testimony unfolded. The defense team was composed of the very best of the defense bar. Everything was done that conceivably could be done in a criminal case. If this same—allowable—process were used in every criminal case, justice would come to a standstill, the national debt would increase vastly within a few years, potential jurors would have to be swept from their places of employment, and the business of the nation would suffer. The cost of O.J.'s case was enormous.[1]

- No case before or after O.J. Simpson captured the public's attention in the same way, including the trials of Robert Blake, Kobe Bryant, Michael Jackson, Scott Peterson, Andrea Yates, Martha Stewart, Jayson Williams, Phil Spector, Michael Vick, and Warren Jeffs.

- And interest in his guilt (or innocence) continues—rekindled recently when O.J. was arrested in Las Vegas and charged with committing armed robbery of sports memorabilia at a casino hotel.

- To an ordinary citizen charged with a crime, the experience of going to court is vastly different. Trials are rarely well-attended media events. Only a select few attract even local attention. An accused may find a trial confusing, frightening, and often frustrating. Courts follow legal rules and procedures that only lawyers and judges fully understand.

- Without a legal education it is difficult to grasp the subtleties of the proceedings. Defendants may be frightened because they experience a loss of control over their own destiny. The experience can be frustrating because courts seldom function as effectively or efficiently as they should. Delay is inevitable. Bargains and deals made by prosecutor and defense counsel are common. So are charges of bias, discrimination, and arbitrariness.

In this chapter we examine the key decisions made during the process that begins after a person is brought into the court system, from the first stages through postconviction procedures. But first we consider the ways in which some defendants avoid going to trial.

No Trial

Policies about charging decisions vary by jurisdiction. Some prosecutors prefer to screen cases carefully before deciding whether to file charges against a suspect. Others make such decisions after charges have been filed. In any event, many of those arrested are never charged. Of those charged, many do not proceed to trial: The prosecutor may reject a case in which the quality of the evidence is poor or witnesses are reluctant to cooperate. Other cases may be dismissed in court either before or after indictment. After all decisions are made, what percentage of all cases are actually dropped? A recent survey of thirty large urban jurisdictions revealed that 45 percent of all felony arrests do not go past the indictment phase.[2] Figures for the federal courts are a bit more conservative: In 2003, U.S. attorneys chose to decline slightly more than one-third of the 115,976 criminal matters received.[3] Let us see how and why so many cases leave the system at an early stage (see Figure 10.1).

1955–2003			
	Total Terminated		**Total Terminated**
1955	38,580	1981	30,221
1956	32,053	1982	31,889
1957	29,826	1983	33,985
1958	30,781	1984	35,494
1959	30,377	1985	37,139
1960	29,864	1986	39,333
1961	29,881	1987	42,287
1962	30,013	1988	42,115
1963	31,546	1989	42,810
1964	31,437	1990	44,295
1965	32,078	1991	42,788
1966	30,644	1992	44,147
1967	30,350	1993	44,800
1968	31,349	1994	45,129
1969	32,406	1995	41,527
1970	36,819	1996	45,499
1971	39,582	1997	46,887
1972	48,101	1998	51,428
1973	43,456	1999	56,511
1974	41,526	2000	58,102
1975	43,515	2001	58,718
1976	43,675	2002	60,991
1977	44,233	2003	65,628
1978	37,288	2004	64,621
1979	33,411	2005	66,561
1980	29,297		

FIGURE 10.1   Criminal Cases Filed, Terminated, and Pending in U.S. District Courts

SOURCE: Kathleen Maguire and Ann L. Pastore, eds., *Sourcebook of Criminal Justice Statistics 2007* [Online], http://www.albany.edu/sourcebook/pdf/t59/2005.pdf.

Diversion

William Douglas Teisher's crime was minor compared with the many drive-by shootings, muggings, and drug-related homicides in Washington, District of Columbia. Teisher, a young college student, went on a one-man drunken rampage through the Mount Zion United Methodist Church in Georgetown, soaking the sanctuary with a fire extinguisher and nearly destroying the church basement. The property damage amounted to nearly $7,000. As a first-time offender, Teisher was given a nontrial option: He agreed to apologize directly to the congregation, perform forty hours of community service, and repay the church for the cost of repairing the damage.[4]

Nearly 5 percent of all criminal cases that are not prosecuted in the United States are referred to **diversion** programs like the District of Columbia Superior Court program. Such programs remove an accused like Teisher from the court system in order to address a special problem, such as a drug or alcohol addiction. The value of diversion programs was recognized in the report of the President's Commission on Law Enforcement and the Administration of Justice (1967). The commission found that many defendants were in need of treatment or supervision, and that the criminal justice system was too harsh a means of providing such services. It endorsed the establishment of programs to which prosecutors might divert certain offenders in order to avoid formal prosecution.

diversion
Removal of the defendant from the normal path of the criminal justice process to an alternative path (for example, a treatment program).

Today diversion programs attempt to deal with the problems that may have led to criminal behavior, with the goal of preventing future involvement in crime. Those arrested for public intoxication or certain drug offenses, for example, may be diverted to an alcohol or drug abuse treatment program. Others may be sent to programs like the Manhattan Court Employment Project in New York and Project Crossroads in Washington, District of Columbia, which provide vocational and educational training.[5] Some programs arrange and oversee community service and restitution to victims.

Diversion can occur before or after charges are filed.[6] But once a decision to divert is made and an accused has agreed to participate in the diversionary program, formal prosecution is suspended pending program completion. If the offender completes all program requirements, the charges are usually dismissed. Noncompliance can result in the resumption of formal prosecution.

Evaluation of Diversion Programs

Diversion programs appear to benefit the offender, the criminal justice system, and the community. The offender avoids the stigma of being labeled a criminal, as well as the harshness of incarceration. Treatment or assistance focuses on the problem that led to the criminal behavior in the first place. The system benefits by avoiding the costs associated with prosecution, detention, trial, probation, incarceration, and parole. Diversion also relieves pressures on court caseloads and jail or prison populations. Finally, the community may benefit when offenders learn the job skills necessary for gainful employment.

Evaluations of diversion programs show that offenders who go through such programs generally have very low rates of subsequent offending. The question is: Are these low rates due to the selection of particular offenders? Or are they due to the effects of the program? Critics argue that the highly selective process used to choose participants may in fact result in the selection of people who are unlikely to commit new offenses under any circumstances. Moreover, they claim that since many of the cases might have been dismissed if no diversion programs existed, the benefit in terms of cost reduction to the criminal justice system is unclear.[7] In terms of the offender, the programs may even be harmful, because people who might not have been prosecuted anyway are processed by the system.

Pretrial

If a case is not diverted, a number of important decisions have to be made. Should an accused be detained or released prior to trial? At what level should bail be set? Should the defendant plead guilty or not guilty? Should the prosecutor and defense attorney engage in plea negotiations? If there is a plea bargain, should the court accept it as having been voluntarily made?

Pretrial Release

Following an arrest, an accused makes an appearance before a magistrate, where a decision is made about whether he or she will be released pending final disposition of the case. The consequences of this decision are obvious. A released defendant can live with, and support, a family; maintain ties to the community; and prepare or assist in the preparation of the defense. A pretrial prisoner, on the other hand, lives in the squalor of jail, perhaps for a crime never to be proved; others may spend a lengthy period there before trial, only to be found guilty and released on probation.[8]

How does an accused end up back on the street pending trial? In this section we will examine the traditional forms of pretrial release, including bail and release on personal recognizance, and the risks associated with release.

bail
Security given to ensure the reappearance of a defendant, in order to obtain his or her release from imprisonment.

Right to Bail.   The word **bail** refers to a court-imposed requirement for the posting of a security to obtain release of a defendant pending disposition of a criminal case. Bail serves as a kind of insurance policy against the defendant's failure to appear. The U.S. Constitution does not grant a specific right to bail, but the Eighth Amendment prohibits excessive bail. What is excessive?

Years of experience have shown that excessive is, indeed, a relative word. What might seem like an insignificant amount of bail to some may be well beyond the reach of others. Studies have repeatedly demonstrated that a significant number of defendants whose bail is set at amounts of $500 or less are unable to post it.[9]

The U.S. Supreme Court dealt with the question of what constitutes "excessive" bail in 1951 in *Stack v. Boyle.*[10] Bail must be set at an amount no greater than would reasonably ensure the presence of the defendant at required court proceedings, ruled the Court. This, of course, is the underlying purpose of bail. Rather than establishing specific amounts, the Court left that determination to individual judges, based on their evaluation of the risk of flight. Each defendant's case is to be judged individually, taking into account such factors as the defendant's character, the weight of evidence against her or him, the nature and circumstances of the offense, and the person's financial ability to pay cash bail.[11]

bail bond agent
Private business operators, paid by the defendant, who post the amount required by the court to secure the release of the defendant.

Bail Bond Agents.   Many states retain a commercial bail system that uses **bail bond agents,** private business operators who act as a type of insurance agent for defendants. In exchange for a fee paid by the defendant—usually 10 percent of the bail amount—the bond agent posts the amount required to secure the defendant's release and therefore guarantees to the court that the defendant will appear as required. Should the defendant fail to appear, the agent may have to forfeit the bond.[12]

Commercial bonding systems have been criticized over the years, especially since the bail reform movements of the 1960s. Some of the major criticisms are:

- Freedom of an accused defendant becomes contingent on a business decision made by a bond agent.
- Kickbacks, bribery, and payoffs are prevalent in the bail bond industry.
- Bond agents have used unscrupulous means to apprehend "bail jumpers."[13]

Critiques of the commercial bail bonding system, coupled with the unsavory reputation of some bail bond agents, have led a number of states to eliminate bonding.

Bail Reform.   The movement to ensure fairness in bail decisions that began in the early 1960s emerged in response to perceptions of racial or other discrimination in the decision-making process. The Manhattan Bail Project, sponsored by the Vera Institute of Justice (a privately funded criminal justice research and reform organization), was an important catalyst in this movement. It demonstrated that it is possible to minimize "no-shows" and to predict with reasonable accuracy whether an accused will return to court on the basis of that person's history, family and community ties, and employment record. The project's early findings revealed a surprisingly low default rate.

In 1966, the federal government enacted the first statute since 1789 that significantly modified bail procedures in federal courts. The Bail Reform Act of 1966 was notable for creating a presumption in favor of releasing defendants simply on their promise that they would return to court as required, a practice known as **release on recognizance (ROR).** It also emphasized that courts should release defendants under the least restrictive conditions needed to ensure their return to court. Another feature of the act was the authorization of a cash deposit with the court of 10 percent of the bail amount, returnable upon the defendant's appearance in court. Since the enactment of this legislation, many states have adopted similar statutes.[14] As a result, a wide variety of options for pretrial release now exist (Table 10.1).

release on recognizance (ROR) Release of a defendant on his or her promise to return to court as required.

Risk of Pretrial Release. How do judges determine the risk of releasing a defendant pending trial? In the case of *United States v. Patriarca* (1991), Judge Mark L. Wolf made a decision on the basis of a single statement by the accused: "The only thing I have to give you is my word as a man."[15] Not surprisingly, the accused, former reputed Mafia boss Raymond J. (Junior) Patriarca, was denied bail.

Judge Wolf, and other magistrates and judges who hear bail applications, face two major problems about releasing defendants: the risk that (1) they will fail to appear for subsequent court proceedings (historically this was the sole legitimate question), and (2) they will commit crimes while on release (a question, permissible or not, that judges will always examine). National studies reveal that approximately 15 percent of all felony defendants on pretrial release were rearrested for a felony offense committed while they were on release. About one-quarter of the released defendants failed to make all required court appearances.[16]

Judges share the public's concern about the risks posed by these defendants. The ideal solution, some believe, would be to find a means of accurately predicting who is

TABLE 10.1
Current Pretrial Release Options

Financial Bond	Alternative Release Options
Fully secured bail: The defendant posts the full amount of bail with the court.	**Release on recognizance (ROR):** The court releases the defendant on the promise that he or she will appear in court as required.
Privately secured bail: A bond agent signs a promissory note to the court for the bail amount and charges the defendant a fee for the service (usually 10 percent of the bail amount). If the defendant fails to appear, the agent must pay the court the full amount. Frequently, the bond agent requires the defendant to post collateral in addition to the fee.	**Conditional release:** The court releases the defendant subject to his or her following specific conditions set by the court, such as attendance at drug treatment therapy or staying away from the complaining witness.
Deposit bail: The courts allow the defendant to deposit a percentage (usually 10 percent) of the full bail with the court. The full amount of the bail is required if the defendant fails to appear. The percentage bail is returned after disposition of the case but the court often retains 1 percent for administrative costs.	**Third-party custody:** The defendant is released into the custody of an individual or agency that promises to assure his or her appearance in court. No monetary transactions are involved in this type of release.
Unsecured bail: The defendant pays no money to the court but is liable for the full amount of bail should he or she fail to appear.	**Citation release:** Arrestees are released pending their first court appearance on a written order issued by law enforcement personnel.

SOURCE: Bureau of Justice Statistics, *Report to the Nation on Crime and Justice,* 2nd ed. (Washington, DC: Department of Justice, 1988), p. 58.

most likely to engage in criminal behavior while on pretrial release and to adjust the release decision accordingly. Research has identified certain factors associated with the risk: the length of time the defendant is at liberty between release and case disposition; the defendant's age, employment status, and prior criminal record; and whether the defendant is supervised during release.[17] Unfortunately, many of these factors have not proved to be reliable predictors of who actually fails to appear in court or who commits another crime.[18]

Pretrial Detention

In view of the conflicting evidence on the use of bail as an alternative to jail, and with the return of the country to a more punitive approach to crime and justice, both practice and law on the use of bail have become more conservative. As the data in Table 10.2 show, there has been a steady increase in pretrial detention and confinement.[19] This does not, however, tell the whole story. If you took a snapshot of defendants in state courts of the seventy-five most populous counties in the United States in May 2000, you would see just how complex the criminal justice system is before and during trial.

- An estimated 62 percent were released by the court prior to the disposition of their case. Thirty-eight percent were detained until case disposition, including 7 percent who were denied bail.

- Released defendants were most likely to be released on commercial surety bond (37 percent) or their own recognizance (26 percent).

- Murder defendants (13 percent) were the least likely to be released prior to case disposition, followed by defendants whose most serious arrest charge was robbery (44 percent), motor vehicle theft (46 percent), burglary (49 percent), or rape (56 percent).

- Less than half of defendants with an active criminal justice status, such as parole (23 percent) or probation (41 percent), at the time of arrest were released, compared to 70 percent of these with no active status.

- About a third of released defendants were either rearrested for a new offense, failed to appear in court as scheduled, or committed some other violation that resulted in the revocation of their pretrial release.

- Of the 22 percent of released defendants who had a bench warrant issued for their arrest because they did not appear in court as scheduled, about a fourth, representing 6 percent of all released defendants, were still fugitives after one year.

- An estimated 16 percent of all released defendants were rearrested while awaiting disposition of their case. About three-fifths of these new arrests were for a felony.[20]

Preventive Detention. In *Stack v. Boyle,* the U.S. Supreme Court underscored the notion that the purpose of bail is to ensure the subsequent appearance in court of a defendant released from custody. The risk of flight posed by a defendant has been the only official basis of pretrial release decisions. Recently, however, twenty-five states have enacted laws that allow for the consideration of danger to others in these decisions and

The conditions in many detention facilities, police lockups, and court holding are notoriously poor.

Confinement Status and Type of Program	Persons under Jail Supervision											
	1995	1996	1997	1998	1999	2000	2001	2002	2003	2004	2005	2006
Total	541,913	591,469	637,319	664,847	687,973	687,033	702,044	737,912	762,672	784,538	817,214	826,232
Held in jail	507,044	518,492	567,079	592,462	605,943	621,149	631,240	665,475	691,301	713,990	747,529	766,010
Supervised outside a jail facility[a]	34,869	72,977	70,239	72,385	82,030	65,884	70,804	72,437	71,371	70,548	69,685	60,222
Electronic monitoring	6,788	7,480	8,699	10,827	10,230	10,782	10,017	9,706	12,678	11,689	11,403	10,999
Home detention[b]	1,376	907	1,164	370	518	332	539	1,037	594	1,173	1,497	807
Day reporting	1,283	3,298	2,768	3,089	5,080	3,969	3,522	5,010	7,965	6,627	4,747	4,841
Community service	10,253	17,410	15,918	17,518	20,139	13,592	17,561	13,918	17,102	13,171	17,193	14,667
Weekender programs	1,909	16,336	17,656	17,249	16,089	14,523	14,381	17,955	12,111	11,589	14,110	11,421
Other pretrial supervision	3,229	2,135	7,368	6,048	10,092	6,279	6,632	8,702	11,452	14,370	10,858	6,409
Other work programs[c]	9,144	14,469	6,631	7,089	7,780	8,011	5,204	5,190	4,498	7,208	6,519	8,319
Treatment programs[d]	NA	10,425	6,693	5,702	8,500	5,714	5,219	1,256	1,891	2,208	1,973	1,486
Other	887	517	3,342	4,493	3,602	2,682	7,729	9,663	3,080	2,513	1,385	1,273

NOTE: Some data have been revised by the Source and may differ from previous editions of *Sourcebook*.

[a]Excludes persons supervised by a probation or parole agency.

[b]Includes only those without electronic monitoring.

[c]Includes persons in work release programs, work gangs, and other work alternative programs.

[d]Includes persons under drug, alcohol, mental health, and other medical treatment.

SOURCE: U.S. Department of Justice, Bureau of Justice Statistics, *Prison and Jail Inmates at Midyear 2000*, Bulletin NCJ 185989, p. 6; *2003*, Bulletin NCJ 203947, p. 7; *2005*, Bulletin NCJ 213133, p. 7: *2006*, Bulletin NCJ 217675, p. 21 (Washington, DC: U.S. Department of Justice). Table adapted by *Sourcebook* staff.

TABLE 10.2 Persons under Jail Supervision
By Confinement Status and Type of Program, United States, 1995–2006

HUMAN RIGHTS WATCH PRISON PROJECT

Excessive Pretrial Detention

In numerous countries—including Bangladesh, Chad, the Dominican Republic, Ecuador, El Salvador, Guatemala, Haiti, Honduras, India, Mali, Nigeria, Pakistan, Paraguay, Peru, Rwanda, Uganda, Uruguay, and Venezuela—unsentenced prisoners make up the majority of the prison population. Such detainees may in many instances be held for years before being judged not guilty of the crime with which they were charged. They may even be imprisoned for periods longer than the sentences they would have served had they been found guilty. This state of affairs not only violates fundamental human rights norms, but contributes significantly to prison overcrowding, a problem that is itself at the root of numerous additional abuses.

The lengthy detention of unsentenced prisoners has its origins in two common phenomena: the denial of pretrial release to criminal defendants, and the excessive duration of criminal proceedings. Both of these ingredients in themselves violate international human rights norms, but combined they constitute a grievious affront to justice.

Consistent with the presumption of innocence, defendants should normally be granted release pending trial. Articulating this principle, Article 9(3) of the International Covenant on Civil and Political Rights (ICCPR) provides in relevant part that "it shall not be the general rule that persons awaiting trial shall be detained in custody, but release may be subject to guarantees to appear for trial." In interpreting this provision, the U.N. Human Rights Committee has ruled that detention before trial should be used only to the extent it is lawful, reasonable, and necessary. Necessity is defined narrowly: "to prevent flight, interference with evidence or the recurrence of crime" or "where the person concerned constitutes a clear and serious threat to society which cannot be contained in any other manner."[1] The weighing of the relevant criteria for a finding of necessity requires an individualized determination.

The laws of many countries, either as they are written or as they are applied, do not satisfy these criteria. Some countries simply lack a mechanism for granting pretrial release. In other countries, large categories of prisoners—such as persons charged with drug crimes or crimes of violence, or recidivists—may be disqualified from obtaining relief under the terms of provisional liberty laws. In such countries, accordingly, the large majority of pretrial detainees may not be eligible for provisional release. Moreover, judges are often hostile to the idea of pretrial release, leading them to refuse to apply provisional liberty laws even to eligible defendants.

Particularly when defendants are detained, the long delays associated with criminal trials in many countries are also inconsistent with international human rights norms. Such delays violate two provisions of the ICCPR, Articles 9(3) and 14(3)(c), which prohibit unreasonably protracted criminal proceedings. Although the U.N. Human Rights Committee has emphasized that long criminal proceedings must be assessed on a case-by-case basis, in the absence of unusual circumstances it has found that trial proceedings of more than a few years constitute a violation of these rights. Notably, in making such determinations, the committee has stressed that "[t]he lack of adequate budgetary appropriations for the administration of criminal justice . . . does not justify unreasonable delays in the adjudication of criminal cases."

There is no dearth of authoritative pronouncements that unduly prolonged pretrial detention is a human rights violation. Instead, what is lacking is government attention to the issue, broad-based study of possible reforms, and international assistance in implementing them.

(*continued*)

Solving the problem of excessive pretrial detention will require innovative thinking. In some countries, the needed reforms may include amending or overhauling the code of criminal procedure; strengthening the judiciary and, in particular, increasing its size and efficiency; adopting provisional release laws; and establishing a bail system or other effective substitute for detention. The precise nature of these reforms will require careful examination and analysis in order for them to fit comfortably within a country's existing legal framework.

SOURCE: Human Rights Watch, available at http://www.hrw.org/advocacy/prisons/pretrial.htm.

permit **preventive detention** and the denial of bail to defendants charged with certain serious offenses.[21] Among those states that have a constitutional provision guaranteeing a right to bail, ten have amended their constitutions to permit the detention of arrestees.[22] The federal Bail Reform Act of 1984 permits preventive detention where "no condition or combination of conditions will reasonably assure the appearance of the person as required and the safety of any other person, and the community."[23] It may well be argued that such new laws simply have enacted what had always been judicial practice.

Preventive detention has been harshly criticized because it is a deprivation of liberty for those whose guilt has not been proved. Proponents counter that the interests of the community far outweigh those of the individual defendant. In *United States v. Salerno* (1987),[24] the Supreme Court upheld the constitutionality of the preventive detention provisions of the Bail Reform Act of 1984. This decision was based at least in part on the understanding that preventive detention was intended not as a form of punishment but rather as a legitimate means of attempting to prevent harm to the community.

Impact of Preventive Detention.   Preventive detention has had an impact on the patterns of pretrial release. But what effect does preventive detention have on defendants? Defendants held in jail are suddenly cut off from families and friends at a time when social support is critical. They may face the loss of a job, a situation that has severe financial consequences, and their standing in the community may be jeopardized. Added to this is the fact that detainees have a distinct disadvantage with respect to the ultimate disposition of their case. In one study, 79 percent of detained felony defendants in the nation's largest jurisdictions were ultimately convicted, compared with 66 percent of those who were released before the disposition of their case. Of those who were convicted, sentences of incarceration were given to half the released defendants and to 83 percent of the detainees.[25]

The Plea

Defendants in jail or on bail are willingly or unwillingly participating in a process that ultimately leads them before the trial judge. A preliminary hearing may be conducted, various motions may be made by defense counsel, and the prosecutor will ready the case for trial, either on the basis of an **information** (accusation by the prosecutor) or an **indictment** (accusation by the grand jury). The proceedings that follow depend entirely on the defendant's response to the accusation, known as the **plea.** No matter how serious the alleged crime, all defendants must enter a plea.

In January 2004, Martha Stewart went to the federal courthouse near New York City's financial district. She waved to several supporters outside and gave a nod to prospective jurors inside the courthouse.[26]

Appearing in court before U.S. District Court Judge Miriam Goldman Cedarbaum, Stewart had to enter a plea. In a barely audible voice, she said "not guilty." With this plea, and that of her codefendant, the judge replied, "Very well, I will enter your pleas. You may be seated."[27] The script is a very familiar one. It is the same for everyone with the misfortune of standing before a judge, charged with a crime. More than a decade ago, in May 1990,

preventive detention
Pretrial incarceration of an accused deemed dangerous.

information
Accusation against a criminal defendant prepared by a prosecuting attorney.

indictment
Accusation against a criminal defendant rendered by a grand jury on the basis of evidence constituting a *prima facie* case.

plea
Response to a criminal charge. Traditional pleas are guilty, not guilty, *nolo contendere,* and not guilty by reason of insanity.

arraignment
First stage of the trial process, at which the indictment of information is read in open court and the defendant is requested to respond thereto.

Michael R. Milken appeared in the same courthouse before U.S. District Court Judge Kimba M. Wood on charges of racketeering, insider trading, and fraud. Judge Wood quizzed the defendant: "Is your mind clear today?" Milken replied, "Yes." "Mr. Milken, how do you plead to the charges set forth?" asked the judge. "Guilty, your honor," replied the ex-financier.[28] Both Stewart and Milken appeared at the procedural stage known as the **arraignment,** a proceeding where a person named in the indictment or information is asked to plead to the charge. Milken pleaded "guilty"; Stewart maintained her innocence by pleading "not guilty." These are two of the four pleas available to all defendants.

Guilty.   When Milken pleaded guilty, he admitted all the facts alleged to have occurred, as well as their legal implications. Of course, such a plea means that no trial need take place. The trial judge must make sure that the plea has been voluntarily entered, that the defendant understands the implications of the plea, and that, indeed, there is a factual basis for the plea. Such a determination could amount to a mini-minitrial. The judge then accepts the plea of guilty and, as did Judge Wood, schedules a date for sentencing.

As we have seen, the overwhelming majority of convictions result from guilty pleas. Typically, people assume that these pleas are the result of a negotiation in which the prosecutor offers leniency to the defendant in return for a guilty plea, an exchange referred to as plea bargaining. (We will examine plea bargaining in detail in the next section.) Not all observers agree that the prevalence of guilty pleas is the result of "bargained justice." The facts and evidence of most cases make it obvious to both sides that going to trial would serve no purpose, and both often agree on the plea.

Not Guilty.   The defendant may plead not guilty, like Stewart, denying the allegations and placing on the prosecution the burden of proving beyond a reasonable doubt all the facts alleged in the indictment. If the defendant enters a plea of not guilty, the judge will set a date for trial. In some cases, a defendant may enter a not guilty plea at the arraignment but later arrange to plead guilty in exchange for some leniency offered by the prosecution.

Despite the importance we attach to the idea that each citizen accused of a crime has the right to a trial by jury, few defendants choose to exercise that right. A recent survey revealed that only 6 percent of all felony arrests that led to a misdemeanor or felony charge went to trial. The balance resulted in diversion or referral elsewhere (6 percent), dismissal (21 percent), or a guilty plea (67 percent).[29] Pleas of not guilty are more common among defendants charged with serious violent crimes such as murder or rape than among those charged with less serious property or drug offenses.

nolo contendere
Defendant pleads no contest (admits criminal liability for purposes of this proceeding only).

Nolo Contendere.   In many jurisdictions the defendant may plead no contest, or ***nolo contendere,*** with the approval of the court and, in some jurisdictions, the prosecution. By this plea the defendant admits criminal liability for purposes of this proceeding only. Such a plea has the practical advantage of avoiding implications of guilt in other proceedings (a civil suit for damages, for example). It also provides the defendant with a face-saving mechanism because he or she can claim that there was no guilty verdict, even though a *nolo* plea does result in a conviction and the defendant can be given the same sentence that would have resulted from a guilty plea.[30]

Not Guilty by Reason of Insanity.   Psychiatrists who evaluated Milwaukee serial murderer Jeffrey Dahmer in 1992 gave many reasons for his bizarre behavior: "The drugging [was done] to satisfy his sexual need for a not-fully-cooperative partner"; "Death was an unintended byproduct of his efforts to create a zombie"; "Dismembering was a disposal problem." But it was Dahmer who summed it up best, "I carried it too far, that's for sure."[31]

Defendants who enter a plea of not guilty by reason of insanity are claiming that they cannot be held criminally responsible for their acts. The issue in the insanity defense is whether an event that looks like a crime can be attributed to the defendant as his or her (rational) act and whether the defendant had the requisite guilty mind—or whether it was obliterated by mental illness. Defendants found not guilty by reason of insanity are, with few exceptions, committed to a psychiatric facility for treatment for an indefinite period. In some jurisdictions they can be discharged upon certification of fitness for release; in others, the trial judge must approve any motion for discharge.

Opposition to the insanity defense has grown so strong in recent years that three states have even eliminated the defense. Others, led by Michigan in 1975, have added an alternative disposition, "guilty but mentally ill." That verdict usually results in a sentence to a correctional facility, with mandatory mental health treatment. Legislatures that enacted such laws hoped to reduce the number of insanity acquittals and prevent what was perceived as the premature release of individuals acquitted by reason of insanity. Research in Michigan has yet to show a reduction in insanity acquittals since the guilty-but-mentally-ill plea was adopted.[32] Like the insanity defense itself, the plea is seldom used.[33]

Plea Bargaining

"Punch $200 into the machine or I'll blow you away." With these words Curtis K. Taylor would approach customers at automated teller machines throughout California. Taylor was prolific, perhaps the most prolific of all teller-machine bandits in the United States. When apprehended in 1988, he pleaded guilty to thirty-seven robbery and attempted robbery charges. Taylor faced over sixty-five years in prison if convicted on all charges. Under a plea-bargain agreement, the district attorney recommended twenty-eight years.[34]

The idea arose centuries ago that both sides of a criminal case—the prosecution and the defense—could benefit if they were to agree on a plea. This would save the government the expense of a trial and the defendant the risk of a very stiff sentence. Certainly it has always been clear that trial could take place only "if the issues were joined," meaning that both prosecution and defense had to agree on the precise nature of the issues before the court. The prosecution presented its views in the indictment, the defense in its response to the indictment, or the plea. That necessitated a discussion of what was contained in the indictment, with the resulting need for a trial only on issues not agreed upon. If, for example, the defendant pleads guilty to one count of larceny and not guilty to a second count, trial is necessary only on the second count.

By the mid-twentieth century it became an openly recognized (and not just secretly tolerated) practice in the United States for prosecutors and defense attorneys to engage in **plea bargaining**—to discuss the criminal charges against defendants and to agree on a reduced or modified sentence that would spare the state the cost of a trial and guarantee the defendant a reduced term of imprisonment.

Types. Plea bargaining, or plea negotiation, may be explicit or implicit.[35] Explicit bargaining involves overt negotiations between two or more parties in the case (prosecutor, defense counsel, judge) that result in an agreement on the terms under which the defendant will plead guilty. The concessions made by the state can relate to the charges against the defendant or to the sentence. Implicit bargaining, on the other hand, means that the defendant simply understands that a more severe sentence is likely to result if the case goes to trial.

Plea bargains may be desirable, from a defendant's point of view, for a number of reasons. A bargain may result in:

- **Charge reduction.** As we saw in Chapter 9, the prosecutor has significant discretion in charging a defendant. In some jurisdictions, the prosecutor's office may choose to file the most serious charges warranted by the facts and evidence of the case. A prosecutor can then afford to lower the charge to one that carries a less severe penalty, in exchange for a guilty plea.

- **Removal of charges.** In some cases the prosecutor may agree to drop other charges pending against a defendant who pleads guilty. This typically occurs in one of two ways. In the first type of bargain, if an offender is charged with a number of different offenses arising from the same incident, he or she may plead guilty to one of the lesser offenses in exchange for dropping the more serious ones. For example, a person using a stolen credit

plea bargaining
Agreement made between defense and prosecution for certain leniencies in return for a guilty plea.

STACKING THE DECK—USING SCIENCE TO PICK THE RIGHT JURY

Early in the fall of 1994, there were 900 people available for a jury of twelve, and eight alternates who were to try O.J. Simpson on two murder charges in Los Angeles County. Here was their profile:

- 53.1 percent were over forty.
- 48.6 percent were married.
- 58.6 percent were in managerial professional jobs.
- 52.2 percent were men, and 47.8 percent were women.
- 37.9 percent were white; 28.1 percent were black; and 17 percent were Hispanic.
- 37 percent were college graduates; 36.3 percent had some college education; and 3 percent were college students.
- 36.6 percent earned more than $50,000 a year.[1]

The Sixth Amendment to the United States Constitution speaks of an "impartial jury." But what kind of a jury did the defense want for Mr. Simpson, and what were the prosecution's preferences?

By early November, twelve jurors had been selected. They did not at all reflect the composition of the original pool. Of the twelve, eight were black, two were Hispanic, one was white, and one listed himself as half Native American and half white. Only two of the jurors had any education beyond high school. What had happened?

Experts offered these explanations:

- **For the defense:** "The defense wanted less-educated jurors because they will be more easily confused by the inevitable battle of DNA experts." Inevitably, this may lead at least to a hung (deadlocked) jury.

- **For the prosecution:** "African Americans are going to potentially judge O.J. by a higher standard," and it's "wrong to assume that women would be less likely to convict an attractive man."[2]

But a lot more than mere guesswork had gone into the jury selection process. The defense and prosecution had each picked prestigious jury consultants from among 1,200 firms nationwide, firms that net $100 million annually[3]—firms with

> "The defense wanted less-educated jurors because they will be more easily confused by the inevitable battle of DNA experts."

---

card might be charged with theft, forgery, and possession of a stolen credit card. The prosecutor might be willing to drop the theft and forgery charges if the defendant pleads guilty to possession of a stolen credit card. The second type of bargain occurs when there are a number of indictments pending for the same type of crime, committed on different occasions. For instance, a person arrested on a burglary charge may have a number of other burglary charges pending. Should the defendant agree to plead guilty to one of these burglary charges, the other outstanding charges may be dropped by the prosecutor.

- **Sentence negotiation.** Negotiations about sentences typically involve an agreement by the prosecutor to recommend a lighter sentence in consideration for a guilty plea. The agreement is not binding on the judge. In practice, however, the judge will usually accept the recommendation.

Trial

It is the function of the trial court to find and express the communal judgment, under law, as to the guilt or innocence of an accused person. The public in whose name the judgment is rendered participates actively in the process. Indictments read "The People of the State of . . . versus John Doe (or Jane Roe)." What specifically is meant by "the people"? One answer is that the judge, who is elected by the people or appointed by somebody who was elected by the people, represents the people of the community. Furthermore, when an indictment is handed down and a trial is held, the people are directly represented by a cross section of the community participating in

such names as DecisionQuest, JuriLink International Corp., Jury Dynamics, Inc., Jury Research Institute, Jury Think, and Trial Practices. Such firms engage in jury simulations, focus groups, witness preparation, change of venue studies, and jury profiling/jury selection. It is this last category that has raised concerns. Jury consultants argue that there are far better ways to pick a jury than the orthodox means of determining a juror's fit (demographics, body language, appearance, and personality) that attorneys tend to rely on. The answer comes in the form of in-depth questionnaires with mock jurors, so that picking a jury becomes a social science.

The jury consultants in the Simpson case had jointly prepared an eighty-page questionnaire, with 294 questions for potential jurors to answer. There were such queries as: "Have you ever asked a celebrity for an autograph?" "Does playing sports build an individual's character?" "Are there any charities or organizations to which you make donations?"[4] On the basis of the answers, the consultants recommended removal from the list. One surprising common characteristic stood out: Seemingly all wanted to serve on the jury in this case. Their answers were usually "politically correct." It seems Mark Twain was mostly wrong when he wrote 120 years ago that we "swear in juries composed of fools and rascals, because the system rigidly excludes honest men and men of brains."

The type of jury selection that we see in famous cases on Court TV is the exception. After all, most indicted defendants plead guilty in a plea bargain, and most of those going to trial before a jury could not afford the $200,000 consultant's fee William Kennedy Smith paid in *his* trial on rape charges. The fact is, however, that jury consultants are playing an increasing role in the outcome of complex civil and well-reported criminal cases. Whether such firms are retained for state-of-the-art courtroom exhibits, multimedia presentations, computer-animated imagery, or empirical testing, jury selection will never be the same. In the coming years, indigent criminal defendants without such assistance may be at a distinct disadvantage—perhaps they already are.

Questions for Discussion

1. Why do some claim that jury consultants make trials less fair?
2. Should states pass restrictions on the use of jury consultants?

SOURCES
1. Hayer El Nasser and Gale Holland, "Simpson Hearing Keys on Leaks," *USA Today,* October 14, 1994, p. 31.
2. "Experts Debate Composition of Simpson Jury," *The New York Times,* November 4, 1994, p. 9.
3. Sally Ann Stewart, "Out of the Pool," *USA Today,* October 13, 1994, p. 3A.
4. Jeffery Toobin, "Juries on Trial," *The New Yorker,* October 31, 1994, pp. 42–47.

the grand jury that indicts the defendant and the **trial jury** that tries the defendant. The public is allowed into the courtroom to witness the proceedings. Indeed, in pioneer days, trial day at the county seat was a major social event. Everybody would be there to see justice administered.

trial jury
Body of persons legally selected and sworn to inquire into any matter of fact and to give their verdict according to the evidence.

Voir Dire

After a plea of not guilty, the first step is the impaneling of the jury (which is called the *petit* or *petty jury* in contrast to the grand jury). Twelve is the traditional number of trial jurors. Some states use fewer than twelve for trials involving crimes of lesser seriousness. Ordinarily, several alternate jurors are selected to take the place of any jurors who might become disabled during the trial. The process of selecting the jury is called ***voir dire,*** Norman French for "to see and to speak," meaning a visual-oral process for qualifying summoned citizens to serve as jurors in a particular case.

Jury Selection: Objectives. Jury selection is usually guided by three objectives. Attorneys have to:

voir dire
Process in which lawyers and a judge question potential jurors to select those who are acceptable.

- Determine whether prospective jurors meet the minimum qualifications to sit as jurors (e.g., age and residency requirements).
- Determine the impartiality of prospective jurors.
- Obtain sufficient information on prospective jurors to enable them to exclude "for cause" any who may be prejudiced for or against the defendant.

circling their prey. The major networks saw an opportunity to boost ratings with the O.J. Simpson case, for example, and quickly erected a multimillion dollar media complex across the street from the courthouse. The "O.J. case" was the most blanketed network TV news story in recent history. While networks scrambled to get coverage of O.J.'s grimaces, the sad faces of Lyle and Erik Menendez, the deadpan expression of Jeffrey Dahmer, the still-frightening Charles Manson, the denials of William Kennedy Smith, the scars on Rodney King's face, the graphic description of Lorena's surgical technique, and the defensive testimony of Woody Allen, it was just another broadcast day for a cable service called Court TV.

Some have called it luck. First Woody Allen, then the Menendez brothers, the Bobbitts, Rodney King, Tonya Harding, O.J., the nanny trial, the Oklahoma Bombing trial, Marv Albert's trial, the Unabomber, the Scott Peterson case, Robert Blake's trial, and Michael Jackson's trial. Over the last five years, the Courtroom Television Network (Court TV), a 24-hour cable service that broadcasts directly from the courtroom, has become a cult hit. Over 15 million households receive it. Nielsen surveys place Court TV as the

COURT TV

What do money, prestige, and ratings have to do with the criminal cases of the Unabomber, Louise Woodward (of "the nanny murder trial"), broadcaster Marv Albert, Lorena Bobbit, Rodney King, Tonya Harding, O.J. Simpson, and the Menendez brothers? Everything. CBS, ABC, NBC, and CNN vie for dramatic courtroom testimony like vultures

> "CBS, ABC, NBC, and CNN vie for dramatic testimony like vultures circling their prey."

---

peremptory challenges
Challenges (limited in number) by which a potential juror may be dismissed by either the prosecution or the defense without assignment of reason. See also *challenge for cause;* voir dire.

challenge for cause
Challenge to remove a potential juror because of his or her inability to render a fair and impartial decision in a case. See also *peremptory challenges;* voir dire.

298

The process by which lawyers and the judge examine a prospective juror to determine acceptability extends further. Counsel for both the defense and the prosecution have certain strategic considerations. Attorneys for each side attempt to pick jurors who might be just a little more understanding or sympathetic to their arguments. They can exclude people they think will be unsympathetic by means of **peremptory challenges,** or objections for which no explanation is required. Each side has a certain number of such challenges; usually the defense has more than the prosecution. Either side may use an unlimited number of **challenges for cause,** which are intended to keep persons with a conflict of interest or bias off the jury. A person related by birth or by marriage to any of the parties connected with the case, for example, would almost certainly be challenged for cause.

Jury Selection: Issues.   Jury selection has been the subject of controversy. The expectation is that a defendant is to be tried by an impartial jury of peers, although this does not mean that the jurors must be like the defendant in all characteristics. The representativeness of juries has been called into question because most jurisdictions rely on voter registration rolls for their juror pool and such rolls are not representative of the total population. As a result, juror pools tend to have a disproportionately high number of middle-class, employed, educated persons. Racial and ethnic minorities tend to be underrepresented in some areas.

fourth-ranked daytime show among cable viewers. And some in its legion of followers have become true addicts to the real-life soap opera of criminal justice. In fact, many viewers have reported that they become tremendously involved in each case, doing everything—including postponing surgery, missing appointments, and showing up late for work—not to miss an episode.

Court TV was developed by Steven Brill, the owner of *American Lawyer,* a popular lawyer's magazine. The idea came to him while riding in a taxi in New York: "[T]he way to make law very dramatic and accessible to people is through video, not print."[1] Brill joined forces with the late Steve Ross (chair, Warner Communications) to produce a "mix of C-Span televised debates in Congress and long, dull but important conference speeches and soap operas."[2] Brill reasoned, "If you present people with the entire story and explain to them what is going on, it is undeniably a good way to learn about a misunderstood branch of government."[3] Brill considers Court TV to be an antidote to the crime docudrama and the "tabloidisation" of courtroom testimony. After airing the Menendez case, Brill commented: "There'll probably be 58 docudramas about the Menendez brothers' trial. But [the producers] will probably be a little more honest because they know so many people have watched the real thing."[4]

In reflecting on the decision to carry the Bobbitt trial live, Brill observed: "When I watched her testify, I was very glad we decided to carry it because it really brought home the issue of spousal abuse. And with us and CNN carrying the whole trial, as opposed to people talking about the worst 10 seconds or so of sound bites... I'm utterly convinced that our coverage made that case a serious case, which is what it deserved to be.[5]

Not everyone is pleased with the way Court TV selects cases. Critics, such as Harvard Law School Professor Alan Dershowitz, express concerns over sensationalizing criminal justice. According to Dershowitz, "Coverage of trials is a good idea. The way Court TV does it is a bad idea. Virtually all they cover is sex, gore and pornography."[6] This kind of criticism does not seem reasonable to Brill, given the fact that most of Court TV cases are unspectacular cases. "We could do a rape and grisly murder trial every minute of our 24 hours if we wanted to," claims Brill. "That's not what I want to do for a living."[7]

Questions for Discussion

1. Has Court TV changed our popular culture?

2. Are you a critic or supporter of Court TV?

SOURCES
1. Peter Pringle, "The Channel Where the Stars Are Behind Bars," *The Independent,* October 11, 1994, p27.
2. Ibid.
3. Ibid.
4. Massimo Calabresi, "Swaying the Home Jury," *Time,* January 10, 1994, p. 56.
5. Ibid.
6. Ibid.
7. Ibid.

Critics of peremptory challenges have maintained that attorneys have used such challenges to exclude minorities from juries. In 1986, the Supreme Court held that the prosecution's use of peremptory challenges to exclude blacks from a jury solely on the basis of race constituted a violation of the equal protection clause of the Fourteenth Amendment.[36] Peremptory challenges are thought by their very nature to make a mockery of the notion of an impartial jury, since attorneys for both sides use these challenges to try to get a jury that will be partial to their side.[37]

Opening Statements

Once a jury has been chosen, or the defendant has waived a jury trial and consented to a trial by the judge alone, the trial proceedings begin. The prosecution makes an opening statement, outlining the case and previewing what it proposes to prove and how. The defense may then make or postpone its opening statement. Long opening statements are more common in jury trials where prosecution and defense know that they will be presenting their cases before people unfamiliar with the law. Both sides hope that well-presented and clear opening statements will make it easier for the jury to follow what happens during the trial and to remain focused on the important points they hope to prove, rather than on the technicalities of the legal process.

The Prosecution's Case

After the opening statements, the prosecution introduces the evidence against the defendant. There are two types of evidence. Physical evidence includes such things as guns, knives, bullets, pieces of clothing, confiscated drugs, fingerprints, blood specimens, and urine analyses. Such evidence is used to establish proof that the crime was committed by the defendant. DNA tests, which attempt to show a sort of genetic fingerprint, are the latest innovation in forensic evidence available to law enforcement. Testimony by witnesses is the other principal form of evidence presented at trial (see Table 10.3).

The prosecution will call witnesses to testify about their knowledge of the crime and the defendant's role in it. Their testimony is elicited by questions posed by the prosecutor. After each prosecution witness testifies, the defense has an opportunity to question the witness in a process called cross-examination. The defense hopes to cast doubt on the witness's testimony, either by raising questions about the person's credibility or by demonstrating some alternative interpretation of the events that does not implicate the defendant. Once cross-examination has been completed, the prosecution may question the witness again in a redirect examination. This examination allows the prosecution to clarify or correct statements made by the witness, which can help to counter points made by the defense during cross-examination of the witness.

TABLE 10.3

DNA Evidence Admission in Criminal Trials by State: *Number of Cases Received and Analyzed by Publicly Operated DNA Crime Laboratories*

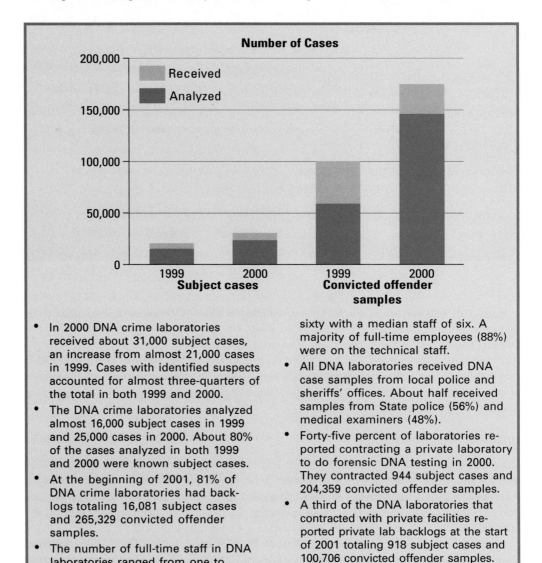

- In 2000 DNA crime laboratories received about 31,000 subject cases, an increase from almost 21,000 cases in 1999. Cases with identified suspects accounted for almost three-quarters of the total in both 1999 and 2000.
- The DNA crime laboratories analyzed almost 16,000 subject cases in 1999 and 25,000 cases in 2000. About 80% of the cases analyzed in both 1999 and 2000 were known subject cases.
- At the beginning of 2001, 81% of DNA crime laboratories had backlogs totaling 16,081 subject cases and 265,329 convicted offender samples.
- The number of full-time staff in DNA laboratories ranged from one to sixty with a median staff of six. A majority of full-time employees (88%) were on the technical staff.
- All DNA laboratories received DNA case samples from local police and sheriffs' offices. About half received samples from State police (56%) and medical examiners (48%).
- Forty-five percent of laboratories reported contracting a private laboratory to do forensic DNA testing in 2000. They contracted 944 subject cases and 204,359 convicted offender samples.
- A third of the DNA laboratories that contracted with private facilities reported private lab backlogs at the start of 2001 totaling 918 subject cases and 100,706 convicted offender samples.

SOURCE: Greg W. Steadman, *Survey of DNA Crime Laboratories,* 2001 (Washington, DC: Bureau of Justice Statistics, 2002), p. 1.

All evidence necessary to prove the case must be introduced in court directly and in compliance with the laws and rules of evidence. One prominent rule requires that certain out-of-court statements, known as hearsay, not be used. This rule is based on the fact that when information is repeated, relayed from person to person, it tends to become distorted. The authenticity of such information is doubtful if the person who made the statement or the source of the information cannot be examined under oath in court. Thus, it is unsafe to trust secondhand or thirdhand renditions of out-of-court statements.

In modern times the exclusionary rule has also been used for public policy purposes. As explained in Chapter 7, the U.S. Supreme Court has used the exclusionary rule for a century to prohibit law enforcement from introducing at trial evidence obtained in violation of the Constitution.[38] Thus, for example, if a suspect is not given the *Miranda* warning, any evidence obtained through police-initiated questioning after arrest may be excluded from trial. The exclusionary rule for unconstitutionally obtained evidence has become a standard of constitutional law that binds not only the federal courts but all state courts as well.[39]

During the entire evidentiary stage of the trial, the defense listens and watches carefully; the defense objects immediately when it appears that one of the rules of evidence may have been violated to the detriment of the defendant. If the breach of the rule is so grave that the defendant's chance of a fair trial has been prejudiced, the defense may even move for a mistrial. A mistrial is an invalid trial, one in which a fundamental requirement of justice is lacking, including lack of jurisdiction or an error in the selection of jurors. If the defense's **motion** is granted, the prosecution has the option of starting over again before a new jury. The judge rules on all motions and objections. If the judge rules against the defense, defense counsel will have the ruling placed on record as a potential cause to appeal a verdict and judgment of guilty. After presentation of all the evidence, the prosecution rests its case.

The Defense's Case

When the prosecution has completed its case, the defense has several options. If the evidence against the defendant is so weak that there can be only one verdict as a matter of law, the defense may move for a directed verdict of **acquittal** or a motion to dismiss. A directed verdict will be pronounced by the judge if the evidence, before a reasonable jury, could not possibly lead to a verdict of guilty. Here the judge simply takes the case away from the jury by directing the verdict in favor of the defendant. A motion to dismiss is a request that the proceedings be terminated. Most cases are not dismissed or terminated at this stage. More likely the defense will now present its own evidence—alibi witnesses, expert witnesses, and character witnesses. The defendant, however, is under no obligation to testify. Of course, if the defendant does testify, he or she is subject to cross-examination by the prosecution just as any other witness is.

After the defense has rested its case, the prosecution has another opportunity to present evidence to refute the case presented by the defense. This part of the trial is known as a rebuttal. Following a rebuttal, both sides make their closing arguments.

Closing Arguments and Instructions

In their closing arguments, the two opposing lawyers present a summary of their case to the jury, emphasizing the evidence that is most favorable to their side. New evidence may not be presented during this phase of the trial. Closing arguments are usually an occasion for lawyers to display whatever oratorical skills they possess as they try to impress the jury with the cogency of their arguments. The prosecution will normally stress that it has demonstrated the guilt of the defendant beyond a reasonable doubt and will call on the jury to return a verdict of guilty. The defense will take the opposite position, pointing out weaknesses in the case that call the defendant's guilt into doubt. If there seems to be little room for doubt about the defendant's involvement, the defense may attempt to sway the jury toward a lenient verdict.

After the closing arguments, the jurors must apply the law to the facts they have heard and determine whether the prosecution has fulfilled its task of proving guilt beyond a

motion
Oral or written request to a judge, asking the court to make a specified ruling, finding, decision, or order; may be presented at any appropriate moment from arrest until the end of the trial.

acquittal
Judicial finding or jury verdict finding the defendant not guilty of the crime charged.

TERRI KOPP, COUNSEL (RETIRED), LEGAL AID SOCIETY, NEW YORK

The question I got at parties when I told people I was a Public Defender was always the same: "How can you represent guilty people?" Over the years I played with the answer. "I get a warm, fuzzy feeling every time I put a criminal back out on the street" or "Easily" or "Criminals are people too." The truth is that my job was extremely difficult—but not for the reason you might think, and certainly not because most of my clients were guilty.

I remember my decision to leave a law firm to go to the Legal Aid Society. I had always wanted to be a Public Defender and had gotten sidetracked by real concerns about paying off my student debt. But after nine months of pushing paper I sat at my desk thinking I want to cross-examine witnesses, I want courtroom drama. I want action.

Well, I certainly got action, although it wasn't the kind I expected. I dealt with DAs who, when a line-up was ruled unduly suggestive and was suppressed, never thought, "My God, maybe we have an innocent person here." Instead they thought, "How can I get over this?" I dealt with clients who thought I got paid by the guilty plea and who didn't trust me because I looked just like a DA. And I dealt with court officers who treated my clients like they

> "The question I got at parties when I told people I was a Public Defender was always the same: 'How can you represent guilty people?'"

---

reasonable doubt. To ensure that they do so responsibly, the judge presents the law to the jury in the form of instructions. Often both prosecution and defense will propose instructions to the judge. If the defense counsel objects to the proposed instructions, these objections are noted for a potential appeal.

The judge's instructions amount to a minicourse in criminal law. After all, jurors are usually not familiar with the law they are called on to apply. The crime of which the defendant is accused must be defined for the jury, along with any other legal concepts relevant to the case, such as **burden of proof.** The judge reminds the jury that the defendant is considered not guilty and must be acquitted unless the state has proved its case beyond a reasonable doubt. Finally, the judge will provide the jury with procedural instructions about such matters as contacting the judge during deliberations if its members have any questions, or the order in which they must consider charges if the accusation includes more than one charge. Once the jury has been instructed, it retires to a private room to begin its deliberations.[40]

burden of proof
In criminal cases, the legal obligation of the prosecution to prove the charges against the defendent beyond a reasonable doubt.

were widgets on a conveyer belt instead of human beings: in and out, as many as possible as quickly as possible. What? You didn't speak to your lawyer? Too bad.

Even the judges were unsympathetic. When I first started at Legal Aid I had a mentally retarded client who was accused of taking pictures of some young schoolgirls. Not dirty pictures. He'd just been given a camera for his birthday so he hung around on the street and took pictures of kids as they passed by. He hadn't committed a crime. It simply isn't a crime to take pictures of people.

On the day I handed the motion up to the judge I asked for another court date, assuming she'd need time to read my twenty-page opus. Instead, she took it in her hands, flipped through the pages in fifteen seconds and said, without looking up, "Denied." When I pointed out that it was a serious and rather lengthy motion and perhaps we could adjourn the case for her to actually read it, she glared at me. "Counselor, I said denied."

It was a constant battle. Most of the players in the system are so jaded and used to seeing people come and go that they see the person standing before them and think "guilty" before bail has even been set. Not that most of my clients aren't guilty. Most of them are. But for the system to work properly, for the people who are innocent to be protected, the rules should be followed.

And some of my clients actually were innocent. I had a guy charged with robbery who spent eight months in jail awaiting trial. At the suppression hearing, we discovered that the victim had looked at a photo spread and picked out someone else. When she did that, the detective pointed at my client's photograph and said, "Why don't you look at him and remember your original description." So she changed her mind. The DA had known about all this. He just didn't bother to tell me about it—he didn't think it was really exculpatory evidence. And even after this all came out, the judge was totally unoffended by it, refusing to release my client for another week, until the DA finally agreed to dismiss the case.

I had come from a Wall Street law firm, where motions were read and people suing people for money were taken seriously. Judges cared about the law; procedure was followed; the law was applied. In criminal court very few people actually cared about the law or justice. And no one cared about my clients. My job became being the one to stand there and remind everyone that they were dealing with a human being and that somehow the law should matter.

At times it was overwhelming. I dealt with kids accused of selling drugs because their mother had been arrested for smoking crack and they didn't have any money. I represented men who hit their wives and didn't see what the problem was. "She's my woman. I didn't break no law." I fought for robbers, thieves, rapists, burglars and drug addicts. And I loved it. I loved it because, believe it or not, I liked my clients. They were funny or sad or pathetic. They were hapless or hopeless or they had a great sense of humor. They had families who loved them or hated them. They were people. And they deserved not to be ground up by the system.

In the end I left the PD's office to move to Hollywood and write for television. Another unreal place. I made the change because I figured maybe if I write enough about the system, more people will want to get involved. But I miss my old job. I miss the action. I miss the drama. But mostly I miss my clients.

Jury Deliberations

Deliberations inside the jury room are guided by a foreperson—a juror selected (or elected) to preside over the deliberations. The jurors may look at items that were entered into evidence during the trial and ask to review portions of the transcript. Beyond that, however, they receive no assistance. They remain in the jury room in complete privacy. If they do not reach a verdict by the end of the day, they go home, with an admonition from the judge not to discuss the case with anyone and not to read anything about it. In cases that have attracted a good deal of media attention, the judge may order the jury to be sequestered, which means they will be kept apart from family, friends, and the general public, until the end of the trial. Instead they will spend the night (or a series of nights) in a hotel at state expense, where they can be shielded from outside influences and kept under guard.

Once the jurors have reached a decision, they will return to the courtroom where their verdict will be announced. Occasionally, the defense or prosecution will ask that the jury be polled—that jurors be asked if they agree with the verdict. This process is intended to ensure that all jurors know and agree with the verdict. If the polling reveals that a juror does not agree with the verdict, the jury may be sent back for further deliberations or a mistrial might be called. In that case, a new trial would be required.

Sentencing

After the verdict is pronounced, the proceedings enter the penalty phase, in which the sentence is determined. In most states and in federal cases, the sentence is decided by the judge alone. Before delivery of the sentence, posttrial motions may be filed and a presentence investigation may be conducted. This investigation is carried out by a probation officer who examines the defendant's record and background and prepares a report making a recommendation of a sentence. In Chapter 11 we will examine sentencing in detail.

Posttrial

An appeal to a higher court from a conviction obtained in a lower court is a relatively recent right in Anglo-American law. Even though the Constitution does not guarantee the right to an appeal in a criminal case, the right exists.

Rights to Appeal

Every state and the federal government have now provided some form of review to convicted defendants. Although all defendants have this right, in reality most do not exercise it. A voluntary guilty plea eliminates most grounds upon which a defendant could base an appeal. Since a large percentage of all convictions are the result of guilty pleas, the vast majority of cases will not be appealed.

It is a fundamental concept of our system of justice that the prosecution has no right to appeal an adverse ruling in a criminal case unless the legislature has specifically authorized it by statute. The Supreme Court has stated that appeals by the government in criminal cases are something unusual, exceptional, and not favored.[41] Virtually all of the states and the federal government now have provisions that do allow appeals by the prosecutor, but they generally contain restrictions as to the conditions under which the prosecution may exercise this option, and generally appeals are not allowed when a defendant has been acquitted.

Appellate Review

Reviews by appeals courts are restricted to procedural questions and questions of law. Examples include questions concerning the adequacy of a judge's instructions to a jury; evidence that was inappropriately revealed to the jury; and failure by the prosecution to disclose material evidence favorable to the defendant. Appellate review rarely considers facts relating to a defendant's guilt or innocence. In most states, the length of a defendant's sentence is also not subject to appeal, as long as the sentence is within the limits allowable by law.[42]

In filing an appeal, the defendant is asserting that some error was made during the process by which the conviction was obtained. For a successful appeal, the alleged error must be reversible—an error that has affected the outcome of the case. (An error that had no effect on the outcome is called a harmless error.) For example, a defendant may assert that evidence presented at trial was illegally obtained, that the jury selection process was such that the trial was decided by a biased jury, or that the judge's instructions to the jury were faulty in some way and liable to influence the jurors to decide on a conviction. These are matters related to constitutional protections and due process of law.

Preeminent constitutional law scholar and lawyer, Lawrence Tribe of Harvard Law School, appears on the steps of the United States Supreme Court after arguing on behalf of Vice President Al Gore.

Appellate Process

An appeal in a criminal case is initiated by the losing side, which becomes known as the *appellant;* the opposing side is referred to as the *appellee.* The first step in the process is to file a notice of appeal with the trial court that heard the original case. This normally must be done within a month or two of the trial. The court then sends a copy of the notice to the appellee. During the next several weeks, the appellant is responsible for getting all the records of the trial court, including a transcript of the trial, to the appeals court. The appellant's lawyer must submit a legal brief setting forth the reasons for the appeal. The appellee prepares a brief that responds to the appellant's arguments, normally asking that the lower-court decision be upheld. In some cases the court will allow the two sides to make an oral presentation. After the presentation of the arguments, the court decides the case and issues a written opinion.

Appellate courts have at least five options in deciding an appeal. They may:

- Affirm, or uphold, the lower-court ruling.
- Modify the lower-court ruling (change a part of the ruling but not reverse it).
- Reverse the lower-court ruling (the trial decision is set aside and no further court action is required).
- Remand the case, or send it back down to the lower court without overturning the original ruling (in such cases, the appellate court will often instruct the lower court to conduct a new trial).
- Reverse and remand the case (overturn the lower-court ruling while at the same time requiring further action by the lower court, such as conducting a new trial).

In most cases, lower-court rulings are not simply reversed. Even a successful appeal usually does not mean that the defendant goes free. More often, the case is remanded to the lower court and the prosecution must then decide whether or not to pursue the case in a second trial. If the appeal has not been successful, the defendant can request review in the state supreme court (or highest court in the state) and, if a federal constitutional question is involved, in the federal courts.

Review

The trial segment of the criminal justice process has pretrial, trial, and posttrial stages. For all cases that are not diverted, a host of critical decisions must be made concerning the detention of the defendant, the amount of bail to be imposed (if any), what plea to enter, whether to plea bargain, what jurors to choose, what evidence to present, what motions to file, what instructions to recommend, what kind of closing argument to make, whether to file an appeal, and whether to seek a retrial.

The process is complex, and research on it is still in its early stages. Preliminary findings reveal that persons sent to diversion programs show low rates of recidivism, that bail guidelines may be effective in minimizing judicial discretion, and that certain factors—such as age, drug use, and employment status—are associated with pretrial flight or misconduct.

Significant problems exist at virtually every stage of the criminal process. Inequities in the setting of bail, the pretrial detention of indigents, and the composition of juries are but a few of the challenges facing criminal justice professionals.

Thinking Critically about Criminal Justice

1. What is the justification for pretrial detention? Do you feel that pretrial detention unfairly discriminates against the poor? If pretrial detention were ruled unconstitutional, do you think that most defendants would not appear on their court dates? Would crime rates rise?

Internet Connection

Note: While all of the URLs listed were current as of the printing of this book, these sites often change. Please check our website (http://www. mhhe.com/socscience/crimjustice/adlercj) for updates.

Can you name the top 10 prosecutors' offices by size? For the answer to this question go to http://www.ojp.usdoj. gov/bjs/abstract/psc01.htm.

How many death row inmates have been executed since 1976? See http://www.deathpenalty.info.org/.

Notes

1. Attributable to a CBS broadcast, March 1995.

2. Barbara Boland, Paul Mahanna, and Ronald Stones, *The Prosecution of Felony Arrests, 1988* (Washington, DC: Bureau of Justice Statistics, NCJ-130914, 1992).

3. United State Attorneys, *Annual Statistical Report, Fiscal Year 2003* (Washington, DC: U.S. Department of Justice, 2004).

4. Alison Howard, "A Vandal Finds Forgiveness at the Scene of the Crime: A NJ Man Apologizes to DC Church for $7,000 Rampage," *The Washington Post,* October 7, 1991, p. B3.

5. Roberta Rovner-Pieczenik, *Pretrial Intervention Strategies: An Evaluation of Policy-Related Research and Policymaker Perceptions* (Chicago: American Bar Association, 1974).

6. Peter Zablotsky, "An Analysis of State Pretrial Diversion Statutes," *Columbia Journal of Law and Social Problems* 15 (1979), pp. 1–32.

7. Franklin Zimring, "Measuring the Impact of Pretrial Diversion from the Criminal Justice System," *University of Chicago Law Review* 41 (1974), pp. 224–241.

8. President's Commission on Law Enforcement and the Administration of Justice, *Task Force Report: Courts* (Washington, DC: U.S. Government Printing Office, 1967).

9. See Chris W. Eskridge, *Pretrial Release Programming: Issues and Trends* (NY: Clark Boardman, 1983).

10. *Stack v. Boyle*, 342 U.S. 1 (1951).

11. See Ilene H. Nagel, "The Legal Extra-legal Controversy: Judicial Decisions in Pretrial Release," *Law and Society Review* 17 (1983), pp. 481–515.

12. Forrest Dill, "Discretion, Exchange and Social Control: Bail Bondsmen in Criminal Courts," *Law and Society Review* 9 (1975), pp. 639–674.

13. Andy Hall, *Pretrial Release Program Options* (Washington, DC: National Institute of Justice, 1984).

14. Michele Sviridoff, "Bail Bonds and Cash Alternatives: The Influence of "Discounts on Bail-making in New York City," *Justice System Journal* 11 (1986), pp. 131–147.

15. John H. Kennedy, "Patriarca Pledges Honor for His Freedom on Bail," *Boston Globe,* May 14, 1991, p. 19.

16. Brian A. Reaves, *Pretrial Release of Felony Defendants, 1992* (Washington, DC: Bureau of Justice Statistics, 1994).

17. Christy A. Visher and Richard L. Linster, "A Survival Model of Pretrial Failure," *Journal of Quantitative Criminology* 6 (1990), pp. 153–184. See also James Austin, Barry Krisberg, and Paul Litsky, "The Effectiveness of Supervised Pretrial Release," *Crime and Delinquency* 31 (1985), pp. 519–537.

18. See Michael R. Gottfredson and Don M. Gottfredson, *Decision Making in Criminal Justice: Toward the Rational Exercise of Discretion,* 2nd ed. (NY: Plenum Press, 1988).

19. Kathleen Maguire and Ann L. Pastore, eds., *Sourcebook of Criminal Justice Statistics 2002* [Online], http:// www.albany.edu/sourcebook/.

20. See Bureau of Justice Statistics Online, http://www. ojp.usdoj.gov/bjs/pretrial.htm.

21. Barbara Gottlieb, *Public Danger as a Factor in Pretrial Release: A Comparative Analysis of State Laws* (Washington, DC: National Institute of Justice, 1985).

22. Marc Miller and Martin Guggenheim, "Pretrial Detention and Punishment," *Minnesota Law Review* 75 (1990), pp. 335–426.

23. Bail Reform Act of 1984, 18 U.S.C. Secs. 3141–3150 (1984).

24. *United States v. Salerno*, 481 U.S. 739 (1987).

25. Reaves, *Pretrial Release of Felony Defendants.*

26. For a detailed chronology of Martha Stewart's trial, see http://www.courttv.com/trials/stewart/012003_stewart_ap.html.

27. Ibid.

28. Michele Galen, "Guilty, Your Honor," *Business-Week,* May 7, 1990, p. 33.

29. Boland, Mahanna, and Stones, *The Prosecution of Felony Arrests, 1988.*

30. Adam Gelb, "Georgia's DUI Scandal," *Atlanta Journal and Constitution,* November 4, 1991, p. E1.

31. Joan Ullman, "'I Carried It Too Far, That's For Sure'; Report from Jeffrey Dahmer Trial," *Psychology Today* 25 (May 1992), p. 28.

32. Henry J. Steadman, "Empirical Research on the Insanity Defense," *Annals of the American Academy of Political and Social Science* 477 (1985), pp. 58–71.

33. Hugh McGinley and Richard A. Pasewark, "National Survey of the Frequency and Success of the Insanity Plea and Alternate Pleas," *Journal of Psychiatry and Law* 17 (1989), pp. 205–221.

34. Josh Meyer, "Prolific ATM Robber Scheduled to Get Prison Term," *Los Angeles Times,* January 29, 1991, p. 3.

35. See Robert A. Weninger, "The Abolition of Plea Bargaining: A Case Study of El Paso County, Texas," *UCLA Law Review* 35 (1987), pp. 265–313.

36. *Batson v. Kentucky,* 476 U.S. 79 (1986). For a study of the selection of more representative juries, see Hiroshi Fukurai, Edgar W. Butler, and Richard Krooth, "Cross-sectional Jury Representation or Systematic Jury Representation? Simple Random and Cluster Sampling Strategies in Jury Selection," *Journal of Criminal Justice* 19 (1991), pp. 31–48.

37. See Marvin B. Steinberg, "The Case for Eliminating Peremptory Challenges," *Criminal Law Bulletin* 27 (1991), pp. 216–229; James J. Gobert, "In Search of the Impartial Jury," *Journal of Criminal Law and Criminology* 79 (1988), pp. 269–327; and William S. Laufer, "The Rhetoric of Innocence," *Washington Law Review* 70 (1995), pp. 329–421.

38. *Mapp v. Ohio,* 367 U.S. 643 (1969).

39. The *Mapp* decision made the Fourth Amendment's exclusionary rule applicable to the states through the Fourteenth Amendment's due process clause.

40. See Geoffrey P. Kramer and Dorean M. Koenig, "Do Jurors Understand Criminal Jury Instructions? Analyzing the Results of the Michigan Juror Comprehension Project," *University of Michigan Journal of Law Reform* 23 (1990), pp. 401–437.

41. *Carroll v. United States,* 354 U.S. 394 (1957).

42. G. O. W. Mueller, "Penology on Appeal: Appellate Review of Legal but Excessive Sentences," *Vanderbilt Law Review* 15 (1962), pp. 671–697.

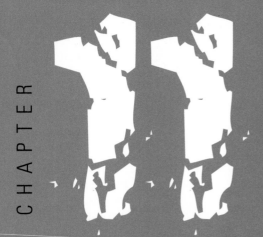

CHAPTER

Sentencing

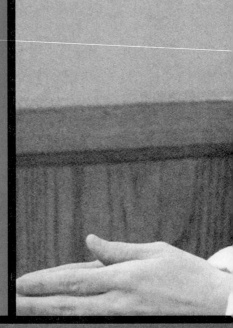

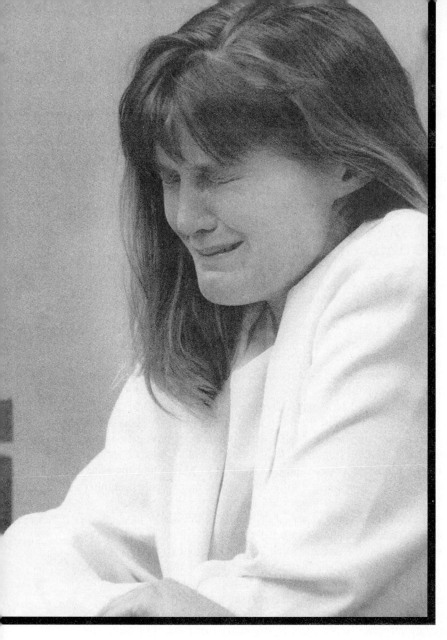

—Ninety Days for a Swordfish Steak; Life for a Slice of Pizza. Gangaram Mahes looks fairly presentable in his donated suit. So he has no problem getting seated for dinner at a nice restaurant. He will start with a cocktail, choose a delicious appetizer, follow with a respectable main course— swordfish steak, for example. He finishes his meal with black coffee. The dinner invariably ends with the police taking him away, since Mr. Mahes can't pay. He is a homeless person without money. There usually follows a ninety-day jail sentence during which, Mr. Mahes says, he enjoys a routine life, a roof over his head, a clean bed, and three regular meals every day. These are not quite up to his standards so, immediately upon release, he chooses another fine restaurant. Mr. Mahes, dubbed "the serial eater," has done it at least thirty-one times, on record, at an estimated overall cost to the restauranteurs of between $1,500 and $2,000. His jail terms have cost the county more than $250,000 over five years.

• And then there is Jerry Dewayne Williams, who stole a slice of pizza from a group of children dining in a pizza parlor. His sentence: twenty-five years to life. Under California's new strict "three strikes and you're out" law, the judge had no alternative but to send Jerry away, for good, because he had three previous felony convictions. Cost to the California taxpayers: somewhere between $700,000 and $1 million.

These two cases raise many issues. First, what are appropriate sentences for Mr. Mahes and Mr. Williams? Are the sentences proportional to the criminal acts committed? Should judges fashion a special "nonprison" sentence for serial eaters? Should prior convictions result in stiff sentences for acts as minor as pizza theft? Second, should sentences consider the likelihood of future arrests and convictions? And, perhaps most important, do you feel the resources of the criminal justice system are being used wisely by the imprisonment of Mr. Mahes and Mr. Williams?

Purposes and Goals of the Criminal Sanction

Four traditional philosophies have molded the types of sentences in use today: retribution, deterrence, incapacitation, and rehabilitation. Another—mixed goals—combines elements of several philosophies.

Retribution

retribution
"Eye for an eye" philosophy of justice, now known as just desserts.

Three elements—a proportionate penalty, a penalty that is deserved, and a penalty that expresses the moral condemnation of society—capture the essence of the concept of **retribution.**

The recent sentencing of teen sniper Lee Boyd Malvo provides a good illustration of how the notion of retribution challenges and, at the same time, guides juries in their deliberations over a just and proportional punishment. Malvo was convicted of killing FBI analyst Linda Franklin on October 14, 2002, in front of a Home Depot in Falls Church, Virginia. Franklin was but one victim of a host of sniper attacks attributed to Malvo and his older accomplice, John Allen Muhammad. These attacks killed ten people and wounded another three in the Washington, DC, area.

After nine hours of intense deliberations over a period of two days, the Malvo jury agreed on a sentence of life without parole, even though jurors were sharply divided. Five jurors favored a death sentence, with the balance concluding that he was too young to be executed.

As with other murder cases, jurors weighed many aggravating and mitigating factors. A juror recounted, "This case was both mentally challenging and emotionally exhausting. Deep thought and consideration has gone into our deliberations and the decisions that we reached."[1] Ultimately, the sentence of life without parole was said to reflect the consensus of the jury as to an appropriate response by the state to the murder of Linda Franklin. The jury's verdict, in a very real sense, reflects the community's response to the devastating harm coming from this loss of life and its meaning to society. It is *our* proportionate response. Retribution, frequently referred to as "just desserts," simply requires a punishment proportionate to the harm done.

Just Desserts

just desserts
Philosophy of justice that asserts that the punishment should fit the crime and the culpability of the offender.

Underlying the concept of **just desserts** is the proposition that the punishment must be based on the gravity of the offense and the culpability or blameworthiness of the perpetrator. Just desserts advocates argue that courts simply do not have the capacity to determine who can be successfully deterred or reformed and who cannot. Parole boards are not prepared to make sound decisions as to which offenders are good risks for release and which are not. Finally, the notion of rehabilitation was premised on the ability of prisons—"correctional" institutions—to correct or rehabilitate; but they do not have the resources or the mission to do so, and most often they fail to do anything more than "warehouse" inmates. Therefore, it is argued, there are few choices but to return to a system of retribution, which at the bare minimum guarantees like sentences for like crimes. Any rehabilitative efforts in prisons should be made only within the terms of a proportionate sentence, and with the full consent of the inmate.

The just desserts approach has been successful in minimizing disparities in sentences and in curbing judicial arbitrariness. But it has problems as well. It has been blamed for prison overcrowding. It has been attacked for its insensitivity to the social problems that lead a large percentage of offenders to crime. It has been criticized for its refusal to acknowledge the fact that education or reeducation, in the broadest sense, can affect values, attitudes, and behavior. It also has been called unscientific because of its rejection of scientific efforts to identify and selectively incapacitate habitual or chronic offenders. Critics have characterized the concept as superficial—both for its rejection of the rehabilitative ideal and its refusal to recognize the fact that rehabilitation has been condemned on the basis of inadequate or flawed evaluations.

Just desserts theorists have reasonable answers to these criticisms. They are not insensitive to the social problems that promote crime but feel strongly that defendants should be sentenced on the basis of the crime they have committed, rather than their social background. They are not insensitive to the utility of education, but they contend that a defendant's ability to grow intellectually should not influence the sentencing decision. Why should judges be forward-looking in fashioning a sanction, when the sentence must reflect a crime that was committed in the past? Finally, theorists have not condemned rehabilitation on the basis of flawed evaluations. Rather, they have dismissed rehabilitation on the basis of its irrelevance to the nature of the crime that was committed and the culpability of the offender at the time of the crime.[2]

Deterrence

What would happen if there were no costs associated with illegal activity? According to some scholars, if we disbanded all law enforcement agencies and removed all sanctions from the penal laws, the result would be "a crime wave of unprecedented proportions."[3] The very existence of the criminal justice system, it has been argued, has a strong general deterrent effect, ensuring obedience in those who otherwise would resort to crime. Thus, the basic principle underlying **deterrence** theory is that people will refrain from engaging in criminal activity because of the consequences associated with detection.

Types of Deterrence. A distinction is often made between two types of deterrence. **General deterrence** refers to the effect that the criminal law with its punishments has on people in general. Those considering whether to commit a crime will be deterred by knowing that a law prohibits certain behavior and that those who have broken the law have paid a penalty for it. **Special deterrence,** sometimes called specific deterrence, reflects punishment that deters an offender from engaging in additional criminal behavior because of the disagreeable experience of a past punishment.

Effectiveness. If the advocates of deterrence are correct, potential offenders should be affected by the relative certainty that punishment will result from the commission of a crime. Indeed, research has shown that certainty of punishment is more important than either the severity or swiftness of a sanction in achieving the goal of deterrence.[4] For punishment to be certain, however, the criminal must first be caught. For common street crimes, then, a police presence increases the chances of capture and supplies an important component of deterrence. A would-be burglar might decide not to break into a house on a block where a patrol officer is stationed. (Of course, the burglar may then decide to move to another block without police presence, which means that the crime has merely been displaced.) One way to evaluate the effectiveness of deterrence, therefore, is to examine the degree to which a police presence affects the extent of crime. Research in the 1970s on the effect of police strikes on the crime rates of eleven American cities provided very little support for the hypothesis that removal of the police presence raises crime rates.[5] The evidence on the effects of intensified policing is no clearer. In 1982, New York City's transit police force was strengthened to combat subway crime. Additional officers were posted in subway stations and on virtually all trains between 8 P.M. and 4 A.M. The results were inconclusive.[6]

What about the deterrent effect of criminal sanctions? Researchers have studied the effects of increasing the threatened punishments for some crimes. Massachusetts mandated

deterrence
Theory of punishment that holds that potential offenders will refrain from committing crimes for fear of punishment (sometimes called general prevention).

general deterrence
Threat of punishment intended to induce the general public not to engage in criminal acts.

special deterrence
Threat of punishment that deters an offender from engaging in any additional criminal behavior, based on the disagreeable experience with a past punishment.

CORPORAL PUNISHMENT—A TALE OF TWO CITIZENS

In 1994 two young Americans were sentenced to the punishment of whipping (caning, flogging) for relatively minor offenses. One of the cases made the headlines of most major newspapers and magazines. The other, when mentioned at all, was buried in the back pages. In the first of these cases, the president of the United States intervened with the government that had imposed the sentence—Singapore. In the second case, there was no intervention—that sentence was executed by a Native American tribal court, one supposedly subject to the U.S. Constitution.

There are detailed accounts of the caning of the American youngster, Michael Fay, in Singapore: being stripped, and tied, the forceful and well-aimed hits of the cane, the ripping of the flesh of the buttocks, the intense pain, and the repeat strokes—though the government of Singapore reported that, after the execution, the convict smiled, shook hands with his executioner, sat through a post-sentence interview, and was given medical attention.[1]

No account of the other flogging, that of a young American tribal woman, is available and since, oddly, the case gained no favor with the media, there was no public reaction to the American whipping. What explains the difference in attention? Is it differential bias? Do we expect more of others than we are willing to render to our own?

Surprisingly, while the media condemned the Singapore caning—even calling for a boycott of Singapore-made products—the American public reacted otherwise. Mail and phone calls to talk shows and other media by far favored caning as a punishment for graffiti spraying. Why? Is it disgust with America's high crime rate, revulsion against graffiti, or envy of Singapore, that highly prosper-

a minimum prison term of one year for carrying a firearm without a permit. This law had a measurable deterrent effect,[7] although studies in both Michigan and Florida, which likewise imposed mandatory sentences for firearm law violations, indicate that such penalties did not lead to declining incidences of the violent crimes measured, such as homicide or robbery.[8] The severity of possible sanctions also does not appear to deter people from drinking and driving. In recent years, several jurisdictions have enacted statutes calling for mandatory jail sentences for those convicted of drinking and driving offenses. Evaluations of the effect of these laws reveal that drivers are not deterred by the threat of jail,[9] although the threat of a lesser formal sanction, such as license suspension,[10] or even moral disapproval[11] may deter some people from drinking and driving.

Overall, research results are still inconclusive, largely because the opportunities for making controlled studies are extremely limited. Early studies tended to support the hypothesis that crime rates will be lower in places where the threat of punishment is great. Subsequent work, which focused on individuals' perceptions of the risk of sanctions, found that certainty

ous and practically crime-free (by our standards) little island country? Or is it that not so long ago, caning was a legal punishment in Delaware (abolished in 1972), flogging of sailors ended only in 1874, and slaves and former slaves had been whipped both before and after the 1863 Emancipation Proclamation? In fact, in the United States, paddling apparently is still a legal form of school discipline in twenty-three states.

What Is the Goal of Punishment?

The U.S. Constitution (Eighth Amendment) prohibits the infliction of "cruel and unusual punishment," as does the Universal Declaration of Human Rights. Yet, we permit the capital execution of youngsters aged sixteen, which is contrary to international standards (which posit a minimum age of eighteen). Suppose that caning were proven to be an effective deterrent to vandalism (which is unproven) and that capital punishment were proven an effective deterrent to juvenile murderers (which is unproven): Should we embrace such punishments?

As recently as 1984, a distinguished—indeed highly respected—American criminologist published a reasoned argument for a return to flogging as the principal punishment for all offenders except for incorrigibles and the like who, he posited, should be given one of only two alternate punishments: either fifteen years or life in prison.[2]

His book had rather mixed reactions. For one thing, controlled studies about the effectiveness of flogging are not available and are hard to construct. For another, there is a widespread revulsion against physical corporal punishments (even in a society as physical as our own, as evidenced by our predilection for contact sports, violent entertainment, and everyday physical reactions to conflict situations). An American legal philosopher once posited the case of a defendant "convicted of treasonable utterances by which he successfully sought to impair the morale and obedience of combat soldiers in time of war. The sentence of the court [was] that he be compelled to submit to a surgical operation on his vocal cords so that thereafter he [could] only bark like a dog."[3]

Where should we draw the line on what is cruel and unusual? And whose conscience should prevail on legislators?

Questions for Discussion

1. Why do Americans sense injustice in corporal punishment when the methods of capital punishment (e.g., electrocution or the use of a gas chamber) are as cruel as can be imagined?

2. Do you think that corporal punishment deters criminals from committing future offenses?

SOURCES
1. "I Tried to Ignore the Pain," Melinda Liu interview of Michael Fay, *Newsweek,* July 4, 1994, p. 36; and "Singapore: After the Caning, 'Mike's in Pain,' " *Newsweek,* May 16, 1994, p. 41.
2. Graeme Newman, *Just and Painful: A Case for the Corporal Punishment of Criminals* (London: Macmillan, 1984).
3. Edmond Cahn, *The Sense of Injustice* (New York: New York University Press, 1949), p. 17.

is more important than severity of punishment in people's decision making about engaging in criminal acts.

Incapacitation

How many times have you heard the expression, "Lock' em up and throw away the key"? It captures the frustration that law-abiding people feel about the problem of crime in America. It reflects a belief that society is best off when criminals are housed in prisons, or **incapacitated,** for long periods. This strategy has an obvious appeal—locking up offenders prevents them from committing additional crimes in the community, at least during the course of their confinement. Yet, according to some scholars, long sentences imposed for the purpose of incapacitation may be unjust, unnecessary, counterproductive, and inappropriate:

- Unjust—if other offenders who have committed the same crime receive shorter sentences.
- Unnecessary—if the offender is not likely to offend again.

incapacitation
Preventing persons from committing crime by physical restraint, for example, incarceration.

- Counterproductive—whenever prison increases the risk of subsequent or habitual criminal behavior.
- Inappropriate—if the offender has committed an offense entailing insignificant harm to the community.

Some believe that a policy of **selective incapacitation,** or the targeting of high-risk, repeat offenders for rigorous prosecution and incarceration, may be worth pursuing.[12]

Rehabilitation

As a sentencing rationale, **rehabilitation** is based on the notion that through a correctional intervention (e.g., educational programs, vocational training, and psychological therapies), an offender may be changed. This change should result in the offender's ability to return to society in some productive, meaningful capacity. Consequently, sentences must be individualized or tailored to the needs of the offender. A judge might select a sentence that includes probation or imprisonment of indeterminate length. The parole board decides when the convict should be released and under what conditions.

In the 1970s, rehabilitation came under attack. The dramatic rise in crime rates at the end of the 1960s led conservatives to point to rehabilitation as a failed policy that treated offenders too leniently and did nothing to deter them. Liberals objected to a coercive treatment strategy intended to "habilitate" people so that they would conform to the dominant culture's values and norms. Researchers attacked the rehabilitative ideal as a colossal practical failure. An examination of some 400 evaluations of treatment programs, published in an article entitled "What Works?" concluded that "with few and isolated exceptions, the rehabilitative efforts that have been reported so far have had no appreciable effect on recidivism."[13] In short, the answer to the question, "What works?" was "Nothing." After this devastating analysis of rehabilitation, other scholars published similar findings and conclusions, although the picture they painted was a bit less bleak.[14]

There is still no agreement on the effectiveness of rehabilitation, but more recent analyses of treatment evaluations conclude that some programs do in fact work—if only for a select number of offenders. But successful programs require a careful matching of individual needs and program attributes, and that is very difficult to achieve in practice.[15]

Mixed Goals

Judges often employ a combination or mix of sentencing philosophies in justifying their selection of a sanction. When Judge Kimba M. Wood sentenced legendary junk-bond trader Michael R. Milken in November 1990, she turned the courtroom into a classroom.[16] Judge Wood defended her choice of a ten-year prison sentence, significant fines, and a sentence of community service by explaining a series of goals that would be achieved by this sentence:

- Special deterrence—achieved by barring Mr. Milken from working in the securities industry and by the significant fines imposed.
- General deterrence—achieved by the imposition of a long prison term.
- Retribution—achieved by the combination of a prison term and a fine.
- Rehabilitation—achieved by requiring community service.

Judge Wood's sentence, which she later reduced to two years, was a well-crafted effort. It is fair to say that most sentences are not nearly as well tailored, for lack of time and talent.

The Choice of a Sanction

In all jurisdictions, the forms of criminal sanctions at the disposition of the sentencing judge are specified by legislation. These forms include institutional sanctions—time to be served in prison or jail; and noninstitutional sanctions—fines and forfeiture of the proceeds of

---

selective incapacitation
Targeting of high-risk and recidivistic offenders for rigorous prosecution and incarceration.

rehabilitation
Reformation of an offender through interventions such as educational and vocational programs and psychotherapy.

crime, and service of the sentence in the community in the form of probation or parole. Recently the arsenal of punishments has been considerably enlarged by the creation of mixed sanctions and alternatives to either institutional or noninstitutional sanctions. Judges now have a variety of options:

- **Death penalty.** In thirty-six states (as well as the federal courts), courts may impose a sentence of death for any offense designated a capital crime, for example, first-degree murder.

- **Incarceration.** The defendant may be sentenced to serve a term in a local jail, state prison, or federal prison.

- **Probation.** The defendant may be sentenced to a period of probationary supervision within the community.

- **Split sentence.** A judge may split the sentence between a period of incarceration and a period of probation.

- **Restitution.** An offender may be required to provide financial reimbursement to cover the cost of a victim's losses.

- **Community service.** An offender may be required to spend a period of time performing public service work.

- **Fine.** An offender may be required to pay a certain sum of money as a penalty and/or as an alternative to or in conjunction with incarceration.

What factors determine the choice of a sanction? Within the range of options imposed by the legislature, judges are given discretion guided by their preference for one or more of the sentencing philosophies discussed earlier. But judges often subscribe to different philosophies for different offenders. Faced with an offender with a long record of felony arrests and convictions, a judge may place greater emphasis on the incapacitative function of punishment and sentence the offender to a long period of incarceration. The same judge may decide that an offender with no prior record may very well succeed in being "rehabilitated" and therefore order a sentence that involves some type of treatment program.

Research has shown that the most important factors affecting a judge's sentencing decisions are the severity of the offense and the criminal history of the offender.[17] Offense severity is usually measured not only by the statutory classification (for instance, classes of felonies) but also by nonstatutory aspects of the crime, such as the amount of harm inflicted, the value of property lost or damaged, the motive of the offender, and whether a deadly weapon was used in the commission of the crime. A first-time offender who has committed a relatively minor offense is likely to get a more lenient sentence than a repeat offender. Judges receive information about the nature of the offense and the offender in a **presentence investigation report** prepared by a probation officer.[18] In this report, a probation officer will provide details of the crime and information about the offender, including a history of any prior offenses. The presentence investigation report may also contain a recommendation of an appropriate sentence.[19]

A recent innovation growing out of the victims' rights movement in the sentencing process is the consideration of a statement by the victim, known as a victim impact statement (VIS). Twenty-six states have mandated the use of VIS in criminal cases, while another twenty-two states have adopted so-called victim bills of rights that include recognition of the right of a victim to present a VIS. In the VIS, the victim provides a statement about the extent of economic, physical, or psychological harm suffered as a result of the victimization. The victim also can make a recommendation about the type of sentence an offender should receive. Usually the VIS is incorporated into the presentence investigation report written by the probation officer. Research has revealed that a judge's choice of a sentence is influenced much more by legal considerations than by victim preferences in cases where a VIS has been presented.[20]

The third judge's suggestion is "restorative justice."[21] Restorative justice has been a feature of justice systems for a long time, though it was little used until a group of criminologists in the United States and the Commonwealth countries brought the idea back to life.

---

incarceration
Sanction that requires a defendant to serve a term in a local jail, state prison, or federal prison.

split sentence
Sentence that requires the convicted criminal to serve time in jail followed by probation.

restitution
Sanction that requires an offender to cover the cost of a victim's losses.

community service
Sanction that requires an offender to spend a period of time performing public service work.

fine
Sum of money paid as a penalty and/or as an alternative to or in conjunction with incarceration.

presentence investigation report
Report prepared by the probation department for a judge; contains information about the offense, the offender, and the history of prior offenses and may include a recommendation of a sentence.

TABLE 11.1
Retributive versus Restorative
Justice

The Retributive Paradigm	The Restorative Paradigm
Crime	**Crime**
is a violation of law, and the state is the victim.	is a violation or harm to people and relationships.
The aim of justice	**The aim of justice**
is to establish blame (guilt) and administer pain (punishment).	is to identify obligations, to meet needs, and to promote healing.
The process of justice	**The process of justice**
is a conflict between adversaries in which the offender is pitted against state rules, intentions outweigh outcomes, and one side wins while the other loses.	involves victims, offenders, and the community in an effort to identify obligations and solutions, maximizing the exchange of information (dialogue, mutual agreement) between them.

SOURCE: Howard Zehr, "Justice as Restoration, Justice as Respect," in *The Justice Professional* 11, nos. 1–2 (1998), pp. 71–87, Taylor & Francis, Ltd., http://www.tandf.co.uk/journals. This special issue was edited by Dennis Sullivan and Larry Tifft, under the general editorship of Roslyn Muraskin.

restorative justice
Model of justice, as opposed to retributive justice, aiming at the offender's contribution to offset the harm done, including reconciliation with victims.

The term **restorative justice** was virtually unknown a decade ago, and it is still in search of a commonly accepted meaning. Yet, the literature related to this subject has grown rapidly, so that we venture to define it in terms offered by Howard Zehr, published in a symposium of *The Justice Professional*, entitled "Criminology as Peacemaking."[22] Zehr provides contrasting paradigms between the traditional, retributive sense of justice and the newly emerging (or reemerging) restorative sense of justice (Table 11.1).

At first glance these two conflicting paradigms seem little more than the traditional difference between criminal law and private law. But there is more to it. For one, it is a return to the justice administered when societies were simpler. The concept of restorative justice is appealing because it combines obligations that the victimizer incurred (blame) with the

Restorative justice in action: two convicts shoveling snow for the benefit of the community they harmed—instead of serving a costly jail term.

idea of having to meet one's obligations (in lieu of purely retributive punishment). We must also note that the processes under the two paradigms differ vastly. Under retributive justice, the process is purely controversial; under restorative justice, it aims at conflict resolution.

If the proposed paradigm of restorative justice were adopted, where would that leave us with respect to the traditional "aims" or "justifications" of criminal justice?

1. As to *retribution* (or just desserts), we would still be limited to never imposing an obligation (sanction) that outweighs the harm done.
2. As to *incapacitation,* even the staunchest advocates of restorative justice recognize that some offenders are far too dangerous to be returned to the community and that their separation from the community is necessary. But the prison population could be vastly reduced.
3. As to *resocialization or rehabilitation,* the very idea is built into restorative justice, which aims at restoring the community.

A multitude of programs that aim at making restorative justice a reality have been established and tested over the years. There are victim–offender reconciliation programs like the Minneapolis Mediation Program, the Vermont Reparative Probation Program, and other, mostly local, restitution and mediation projects.[23] Restorative justice programs, an alternative to handling juvenile crime, as pioneered by the Hudson Institute in Indianapolis, have shown particular promise.[24]

The course from (mostly) retributive to (mostly) restorative criminal justice is not charted. There are many obstacles,[25] not the least of which is the question of the public sentiment, the political will, and the energy needed to generate both. Many experts believe that on the basis of historical developments the switch to restorative justice is likely. The acceptance of restorative justice in the United Kingdom, Australia, and elsewhere supports this belief.

careers

THE NEW CONVENTIONAL WISDOM ON RESTORATIVE JUSTICE

John Braithwaite:

The ideal of responsibility in restorative jurisprudence is different from the responsibility ideal in traditional criminal law. Traditional criminal law holds wrongdoers responsible. This is a passive conception of responsibility.

Restorative justice has an active conception of responsibility. It is something taken rather than something to be held to.

Responsibility is the virtue of wanting to make amends in the future for something done in the past. When citizens take active responsibility for their wrongs, it is good to give them the gift of mercy.

Restorative justice gives citizens who have done nothing wrong the opportunity to take active responsibility for repairing the harm from the wrongs of others.

SOURCE: Excerpted from John Braithwaite and Declan Roche, "Responsibility and Restorative Justice," in *Restorative Community Justice: Repairing Harm and Transforming Communities,* ed. G. Bazemore and M. Schiff (Cincinnati, OH: Anderson, 2001).

Lawrence W. Sherman:

As I watched the World Trade Center towers collapse, I began to see the broader implications of our experiments in "restorative justice." For thousands of years, local communities have tried to prevent endless cycles of violence by repairing the harm caused by violent crime. Reparation agreements were the

(continued)

basis of English law until the Norman Conquest. Modern England will go back to the future with us in testing meetings between victims and offenders with their respective friends and families. These efforts to find voluntary ways to restore crime victims are designed to reduce repeat offending, as well as victim retaliation.

The theory draws on research showing that many criminals believe they are acting morally. Change their morality, and you may reduce crime. Our Australian experiment with restorative justice reduced repeat crime by 38 percent in a randomized controlled trial, one of the strongest tests in science.

Criminology has found increasing evidence that strong moral beliefs may cause as much crime as weak moral beliefs. Yet my field has done little to apply these findings to the moral beliefs of terrorists. When 20 people are willing to commit suicide to attack our "evil" country, the rational choice explanation of crime must be carefully reassessed.

SOURCE: Excerpted from Lawrence W. Sherman, "In Search of Restorative Justice: The Road Ahead," *The Daily Pennsylvanian*, October 1, 2001, p. 1.

Structuring Sentences

Legislators have devised a number of different methods to structure sentencing decisions. Strategies differ from state to state, and some states even have different sentencing structures to cover different types of offenses.

Indeterminate Sentences

In 1977, Johnny Arafiles fatally stabbed Eddie Leroy Anderson, a witness who had testified against his brother in a drug case. He was convicted of murder in a California court and received a term of seven years to life in prison. With such a sentence, Arafiles could have served as little as seven years (minus time off for good behavior) or an entire life sentence. Thirteen years after his conviction, Arafiles appeared before the State Board of Prison Terms (the parole board) and convinced its members that he was a changed man. He had taken educational courses, enlisted in vocational training programs, and participated in psychological therapy. Moreover, he had turned to religion. The board granted Arafiles parole in March 1990.[26]

indeterminate sentence
Sentence for which the legislature allows the judge to impose a minimum and/or a maximum term, the actual length of service depending on the discretion of corrections officials.

Arafiles's **indeterminate sentence** had a fixed minimum (seven years), but no fixed or predetermined end. However, indeterminate sentence statutes may allow the judge to fix a maximum or both a minimum and a maximum. The important aspect of the indeterminate sentence is that the prisoner's actual prison term is undetermined above the minimum and below the maximum and depends entirely on the discretion of the correctional authorities, especially the parole board. Members of a parole board periodically review the record of an offender's behavior while the offender is under correctional supervision to decide if, in their opinion, release is appropriate.

While indeterminate sentences may accommodate goals of retribution, deterrence, and incapacitation, the guiding principle behind them is rehabilitation: The indeterminance of a sentence provides flexibility for the offender to demonstrate that he or she has been rehabilitated, at which time the parole board will, at least in theory, authorize a release. Rather than the sentence being the same for every offender, indeterminate sentencing is said to have the advantage of allowing for individualized sentencing on the basis of the offender's background, the circumstances of the crime, and the offender's behavior while incarcerated.

Indeterminate sentences were subjected to extensive criticism during the 1970s, fueled by prisoner uprisings that demonstrated their discontent with the conditions of their imprisonment and, particularly, the widely varying length of sentences for like crimes. In 1970 the American Friends Service Committee published a report entitled *Struggle for Justice*[27] that galvanized opposition to indeterminate sentences and led eventually to a reconsideration of sentencing practices that had been used throughout the country.[28] Chief among the complaints were the following:

- Individualized sentences based on the characteristics of the offender instead of the crime have led to variations in sanctions that many believe are attributable to extralegal factors such as the offender's gender, ethnic origin, or socioeconomic status.

- Indeterminate sentences represent a particularly cruel injustice to prisoners, suspending them in a nether world of uncertainty, dependent on what many believe are the arbitrary decisions of parole boards. The uncertain release date is depicted not as an incentive to reform, but as a technique designed to frustrate inmates.

- The emerging research on rehabilitation programs indicates that they are ineffective in achieving their goals. Furthermore, the underlying assumption behind rehabilitation— that criminals are "sick" and need "treatment"—is ill-conceived and arrogant, especially since correctional officials have no effective means of treating the supposed sickness.

- Indeterminate sentencing in many cases means that sentences are really given not by judges but by parole boards, a questionable shifting of authority.[29]

The solution, as many saw it, was to switch to definite, or determinate, sentences based on the amount of harm inflicted by the offense. The result was widespread change in sentencing structures. In fact, over the past decade all fifty states and the District of Columbia have passed or considered legislation to change their existing indeterminate sentencing structures.[30] Some states have sought to limit indeterminate sentences by giving parole boards guidelines to follow in making release decisions. Others have turned to determinate sentences.

Determinate Sentences

In 1975 Maine became the first state to abolish its parole board, thereby removing the support for indeterminate sentencing.[31] For nearly thirty years, judges in Maine have sentenced offenders to prison terms of fixed length, called **determinate** (or **flat**) **sentences.** All offenders sentenced under such a scheme must serve the entire length of the sentence, less any "good time" accrued while in prison. Early release on parole is unavailable. Since Maine replaced its indeterminate system, at least nine other states—California, Connecticut, Florida, Illinois, Indiana, Minnesota, New Mexico, North Carolina, and Washington—have adopted plans where all or most sentences are determinate.

Determinate sentencing plans vary from state to state. In Maine, as stated, the legislature simply eliminated parole. The result: Judges resorted to what has been referred to as "judicial parole," a practice in which an offender is given a split sentence consisting of a period of incarceration followed by probationary supervision upon release. Revocation of probation rests with the judge, who thus fulfills the role previously held by the parole board.[32] Other states, such as California and North Carolina, have specific standards for sentences set by the legislature, including aggravating and mitigating factors that must be taken into account in sentencing.[33]

determinate sentence
Sentence to prison that has a fixed term; also called a flat sentence.

Mandatory Sentences

Determinate sentences should be distinguished from **mandatory sentences,** meaning sentences for given crimes that are fixed by the legislature, from which the judge may not deviate. Laws that require mandatory sentences for certain offenses have been passed in forty-nine states. Most commonly they are used for violent and serious offenses; crimes involving the use of a firearm; violations of drinking and driving statutes; and increasingly, certain drug offenses. Most mandatory sentencing statutes prescribe a minimum period of incarceration for offenders whose crimes and prior record fall within specific categories (although some require incarceration even for first-time offenders).

Mandatory sentences have been justified on the basis of their deterrence value. But such sentences do not appear to have a significant deterrent effect. Furthermore, the severity of

mandatory sentence
Sentence prescribed by the legislature, which a judge has no choice but to impose.

DEBORAH W. DENNO, PROFESSOR OF LAW, FORDHAM UNIVERSITY SCHOOL OF LAW; DEATH PENALTY RESEARCHER

On June 30, 1997, I saw a metal bowl electrocuted at Florida State Prison. This is my story about how and why I was asked to witness such a peculiar and disturbing event and what my experiences say about this country's death penalty process.

The story starts with a Florida trial court judge who ordered the metal bowl's electrocution to determine if "Old Sparky," Florida's 74-year-old electric chair, was a cruel or unusual method of punishment. Presumably, an upside-down metal bowl and adjoining pipes best simulated a real human's head and legs. The electric chair's sponge and head piece were strapped on top of the bowl and the leg electrodes were attached to the pipes. Expert witnesses, such as myself, were asked to view the results when the generator was activated in the same way it would be with the electrocution of an inmate. Yet, the judge also

ordered death row inmate Leo Jones to watch the simulated execution. Mr. Jones was the Florida inmate next under warrant to die.

Why now the need to test Old Sparky? The test was prompted by the horribly botched electrocution of Florida inmate Pedro Medina on March 25, 1997. Immediately after the executioner applied electricity, Mr. Medina's face mask burst into flames "up to a foot long" and the "the smell of burnt flesh filled the witness room." A panicked maintenance supervisor snuffed out the flames on Mr. Medina's head, while others aired the room of smoke.

Prison officials could not explain the botch. Some claimed Mr. Medina felt no pain. Others depicted his pain as unbearable. Moreover, journalists reminded the public of the 1990 Florida electrocution of Jesse Joseph Tafero, whose face mask also erupted into flames in an eerily identical fashion.

According to Mr. Jones's attorneys, these incidences indicated that Old Sparky could cause Mr. Jones excruciating pain, grotesque mutilation, and a torturous, lingering death. Their challenge to the constitutionality of electrocution started with an evidentiary hearing to review all the evidence of electrocution's effects. The testing of Old Sparky was one component of the hearing.

But a perplexing question remains. Why was Mr. Jones ordered to watch the testing of the very electric chair that would soon kill him? Neither Jones nor his attorneys approved of this mandate. Presumably, the judge thought Mr. Jones personally should see the device function properly. Yet, this decision instigated a troubling series of

the sentences is such that police, judges, and prosecutors have been found to alter their practices to avoid the possibility of a mandatory sentence in cases where they believe the sentence would be too harsh for the crime involved.[34] Finally, new evidence suggests that mandatory sentences may disproportionately affect minorities.

Sentencing Guidelines

sentencing guidelines
System for the judicial determination of a relatively firm sentence based on specific aggravating or mitigating circumstances.

Sentencing guidelines provide a relatively fixed punishment that corresponds with prevailing notions of harm and allows for the upward or downward adjustment of a sentence on the basis of specific aggravating or mitigating circumstances.[35] In the United States, the movement toward sentencing guidelines began with a plea by Federal District Judge Marvin E. Frankel in 1972 for an independent sentencing commission to study sentences and assist in the formulation and enactment of detailed guidelines for use by judges.[36] Since then a number of states have adopted guidelines and several have created sentencing commissions authorized by state legislatures to create guidelines. The best-known state sentencing commissions are those of Minnesota, Washington, and Pennsylvania. In

events on a day of electric chair testing that will haunt me forever.

In Florida State Prison, the execution chamber is separated in half by a large clear panel. The electric chair occupies the left half of the chamber, and seats for witnesses occupy the right half. When I entered the witnesses' side of the room on the day of the test, prison officials were busily preparing the chair that I viewed through the panel. The state's expert who devised the test, Michael Morse, was providing the officials with guidance.

The most striking person in the witness room, however, was Mr. Jones. He sat in the middle, close to the clear panel that separated him, by only several feet, from the instrument of his death.

After what seemed like hours, officials indicated that the "electrocution" was ready to begin. About two dozen of us sat silently while 2,000 volts of electricity surged through the makeshift inmate. We knew the generator switch had been activated, yet there was no sound or sight that would have suggested it. After all, we were watching the electrocution of a metal bowl, not a human being.

Amazingly, however, it soon became clear to us that prison officials would have to conduct yet a second test! Although the first test showed that the amps and volts peaked the way they were expected, the paper in the small printing machine recording this activity had become stuck and was unable to print out the results. I was wondering what Mr. Jones thought as he sat so impassively staring at the commotion. The sole device that truly resembled a "real" execution (the printer recording amps and volts) did not work properly, even though all officials were doing their utmost to perfect this highly scrutinized procedure. Finally, the printer worked for the second test.

Months later, the trial court upheld the constitutionality of Florida's electric chair following a four-day evidentiary hearing that introduced substantial evidence that even a properly performed electrocution could cause pain and suffering. On October 20, 1997, the Supreme Court of Florida affirmed this outcome, one vote short of finding electrocution unconstitutional (*Jones v. State,* 701 So.2d 76 [Fla. 1997]).

Mr. Jones was executed on March 24, 1998. Witnesses filed affidavits documenting that Mr. Jones's body smoked and was badly burned. Regardless, Florida remains one of only four states that provide an inmate no other execution method.

No one could read Mr. Jones's mind during that day of testing in Florida. Perhaps no one would have wanted to. Who could rest knowing the mental torture that he must have felt? I could think only that there would soon be a live human being, the man sitting just inches away from me, taking the place of that ridiculous metal bowl. In time, other inmates would follow Mr. Jones— all assured by the state that their deaths would be carried out humanely because electrocution had worked so well with a metal bowl.

1984 the United States Sentencing Commission was established by Congress, and in 1987 it delivered its guidelines for the sentencing of individual defendants. In November 1991, Congress adopted guidelines proposed by the Sentencing Commission for organizations, especially for corporations.[37] After the United States Supreme Court case of *U.S. v. Booker* (2005), the federal sentencing guidelines were ruled discretionary, not mandatory. Thus, judges in federal court may, at their discretion, use or depart from prescribed guidelines for sentencing.

At the crux of all guidelines is a sentencing grid, most often in the form of a matrix, in which a ranking of the severity of the offense is combined with a defendant's criminal history or other characteristics to arrive at a recommended sentence or sentence range (Figure 11.1). Guidelines usually allow for mitigating or aggravating circumstances associated with the specific offense. They typically indicate which offenses should be sanctioned by a prison term (the "in/out" decision) and the length of the sentence. A judge simply calculates a defendant's history and the severity of the offense, plus or minus mitigating or aggravating circumstances (where allowed), and, with the exactness of a

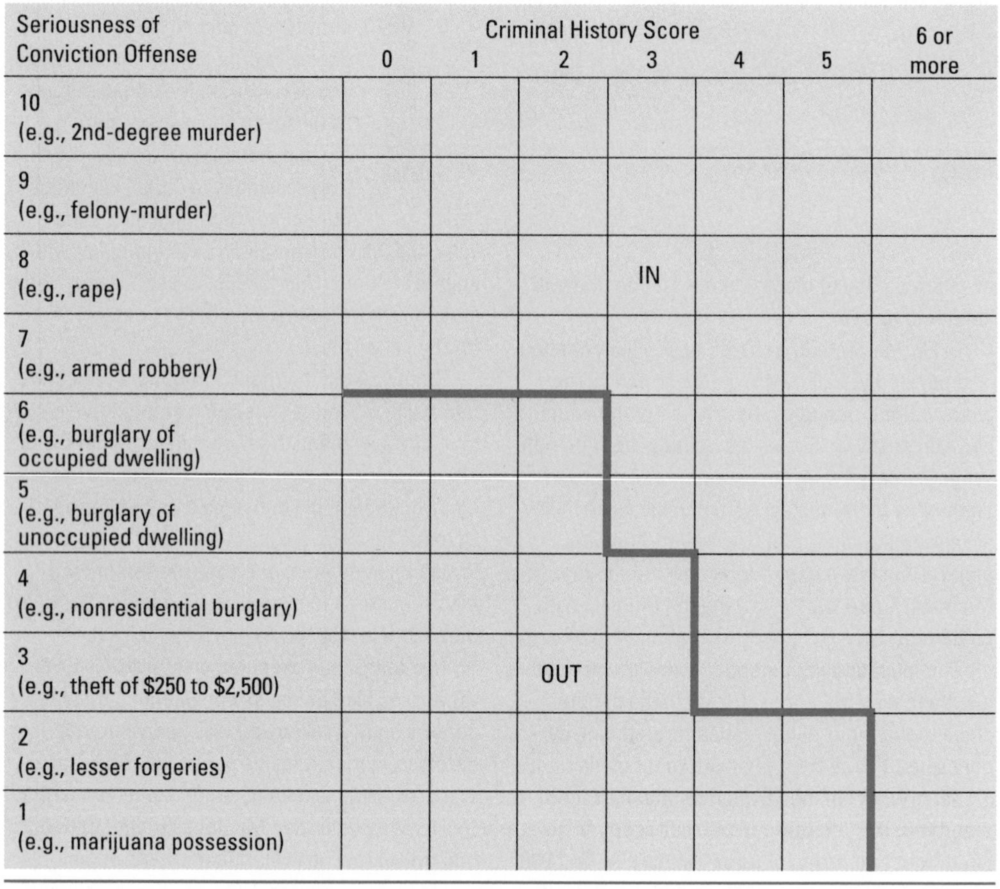

Seriousness of Conviction Offense	Criminal History Score						6 or more
	0	1	2	3	4	5	
10 (e.g., 2nd-degree murder)							
9 (e.g., felony-murder)							
8 (e.g., rape)				IN			
7 (e.g., armed robbery)							
6 (e.g., burglary of occupied dwelling)							
5 (e.g., burglary of unoccupied dwelling)							
4 (e.g., nonresidential burglary)							
3 (e.g., theft of $250 to $2,500)			OUT				
2 (e.g., lesser forgeries)							
1 (e.g., marijuana possession)							

FIGURE 11.1   The Dispositional Line on Minnesota's Sentencing Grid

SOURCE: Andrew von Hirsch, Kay A. Knapp, and Michael Tonry, *The Sentencing Commission and Its Guidelines* (Boston: Northeastern University Press, 1987), p. 91.

computer, has a sentence to impose. In practice, some guidelines can be fairly complicated to use because of the number of factors that must be included in calculating the sentence. Every U.S. probation office and U.S. attorney's office has been provided with a computer program to assist in calculating recommended sentences in accordance with the federal sentencing guidelines.[38]

Types of Guidelines.   There are two types of sentencing guidelines: voluntary and presumptive. Voluntary guidelines are created by the judiciary rather than mandated by the legislature. They are sometimes referred to as descriptive guidelines because they describe, rather than prescribe, recommended sentences.

The other form of sentencing guideline is referred to as presumptive because the appropriate sentence for an offender is presumed to fall within the range of sentences specified by the guidelines. Judges are expected to choose from a range of available sentences, and all deviations from the guidelines must be documented in writing. The Minnesota, Pennsylvania, and Washington guidelines are all considered presumptive schemes. The federal guidelines, as noted earlier, are voluntary.

Criticisms.   Sentencing commissions and sentencing guidelines have both met with significant resistance, perhaps because the state sentencing commissions are independent of the judicial and the legislative branches. Some proposed guidelines or recommendations simply have been rejected by the legislatures.[39] The Connecticut commission developed a guidelines system but went on record as strongly opposed to its adoption and instead recommended statutory determinate sentences.[40] At the federal level, before *U.S. v. Booker*

(2005), opposition to individual guidelines came chiefly from the judges themselves. The guidelines for individuals took effect on November 1, 1987, but many judges found them unconstitutional. They reasoned that, since the U.S. Sentencing Commission was created by Congress, the guidelines represented a violation of the separation of powers between the judicial and legislative branches of government.[41]

Like statutory determinate sentencing schemes, guidelines represent an attempt to overcome the inequities and uncertainties associated with indeterminate sentences. Critics of presumptive sentencing guidelines, however, fear that their implementation will lead to harsher sentences and make the already serious problem of prison overcrowding worse. Others suggest that discretion in sentencing will simply move from the judge to the prosecutor. Defendants will seek charge bargains that move their charges to the "out" side of the "in/out" line or to a location on the sentencing grid that carries a more lenient sentence. The pressure to bargain will also lead defendants to avoid trials. Finally, some are concerned that judges will simply ignore the guidelines as compromising their discretion and as being inappropriate.

Capital Punishment

A judge's most awesome sentencing alternative for those convicted of a capital crime is the imposition of the death sentence. Capital punishment is a controversial issue and one that poses particular challenges to the judiciary. After all, it is the only sentence that is irreversible and final: It deprives the convicted person of an ultimate appeal.

Daniel Frank's execution in 1622 was the first on record in America. He was executed in the colony of Virginia for the crime of theft.[42] Scholars have estimated that since that year, between 18,000 and 20,000 people in America have suffered state-sanctioned execution for crimes including train wrecking, aggravated murder, and rape[43] (although the latest estimate puts the total at 15,285).[44] Countless others have died at the hands of lynch mobs.[45] During the last century, Western countries have employed six methods of execution: firing squad, lethal gas, hanging, decapitation by ax or guillotine, electrocution, and lethal injection. Decapitation is the only one of these methods that has never been used in the United States (Table 11.2).

Since 1976, when the death penalty was reinstated in the United States after a short moratorium, 1,099 convicted criminals have been executed. In 2006 there were 53 executions (Figure 11.2). Thirty-six states and the federal government now have death penalty laws in effect.

The arguments surrounding capital punishment are deceptively simple. What makes them deceptive is that abolitionist or retentionist views of the death penalty often influence assessments of the penalty's utility and effectiveness. Abolitionists find little empirical evidence of a deterrent effect, and retentionists claim that sophisticated studies can be conducted only after executions have been resumed at a steady pace. They argue, in other words, that it is impossible to tell whether deterrence is fact or fiction until we execute, as a matter of course, all inmates sentenced to death.

The Deterrence Argument

Social scientists have long debated whether and to what extent executions deter murder. The debate focuses on two questions: Do would-be murderers decide not to kill out of fear of being put to death? If the threat of execution is in fact a deterrent, would the threat of life imprisonment be just as effective?

The results of studies designed to answer these questions are inconclusive. Most scholars have found little evidence that homicide rates are affected by executions.[46] On the other hand, one researcher, an economist, has found what does appear to be a deterrent effect; specifically, that each execution prevents between eight and twenty murders.[47] His study, however, has been criticized on a number of methodological grounds. Recent

TABLE 11.2
Authorized Methods of
Execution by Method

Method	Number of Executions by Method since 1976	Number of States Authorizing Method	Jurisdictions That Authorize
Lethal Injection	924	**37 states + U.S. Military and U.S. Gov't**	Alabama, Arizona, Arkansas, California, Colorado, Connecticut, Delaware, Florida, Georgia, Idaho, Illinois, Indiana, Kansas, Kentucky, Louisiana, Maryland, Mississippi, Missouri, Montana, Nevada, New Hampshire, New Jersey, New Mexico, New York*, North Carolina, Ohio, Oklahoma, Oregon, Pennsylvania, South Carolina, South Dakota, Tennessee, Texas, Utah, Virginia, Washington, Wyoming, U.S. Military, U.S. Government ***New York's Death Penalty was declared unconstitutional on June 24, 2004.**
Electrocution	154	**10 states (Nebraska is the only state that requires electrocution)**	Alabama, Arkansas, Florida, [Illinois], Kentucky, Nebraska, [Oklahoma], South Carolina, Tennessee, Virginia
Gas Chamber	11	**5 states (all have lethal injection as an alternative method)**	Arizona, California, Maryland, Missouri, [Wyoming]
Hanging	3	**2 states (all have lethal injection as an alternative method)**	New Hampshire, Washington
Firing Squad	2	**2 states (all have lethal injection as an alternative method)**	Idaho, [Oklahoma], Utah** **** Utah offers the firing squad only for inmates who chose this method prior to its elimination as an option.**

NOTE: States in brackets authorize the listed method only if a current method is found unconstitutional.
SOURCE: Death Penalty Information Center, http://www.deathpenaltyinfo.org/article.php?scid=8&did=245.

research on the deterrent effect of the death penalty has focused on the relationship between publicity about executions and homicide rates. If deterrence works, the argument goes, then publicized executions should result in lower numbers of murders because of a heightened perception of the risks of being sentenced to death. Here again, the results of research are equivocal, with some showing that publicity does have some deterrent effect (albeit much weaker than other factors associated with the homicide rate),[48] and others

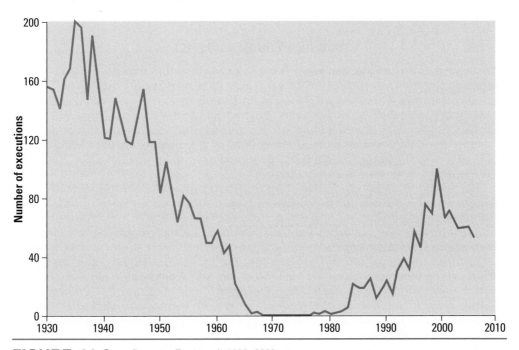

FIGURE 11.2   Persons Executed, 1930–2006

SOURCES: Tracy C. Snell, *Capital Punishment 2000* (Washington DC: BJS, 2007); http://www.deathpenaltyinfo.org.

concluding that neither newspaper nor television coverage of executions has had any deterrent effect.[49]

One scholar has noted that it is extremely difficult to design methodologically sound deterrence studies. How can we estimate the number of people who did not commit murder in a jurisdiction with a death penalty or in one without a death penalty? How can we know that a would-be killer decided against the act of murder?[50]

The Discrimination Argument

In the early 1970s researchers identified a problem in the use of the death penalty. Since the 1950s it had become clear that death sentences in some southern states fell disproportionately on blacks who had been convicted of the rape of white women. They noted, "Of the 3,859 persons executed for all crimes since 1930, 54.6 percent have been black or members of other racial minority groups. Of the 455 executed for rape alone, 89.5 percent have been nonwhite."[51]

Though the discrimination question has been at the core of legal challenges to the constitutionality of many death sentences, it remained in the background until a comprehensive and methodologically sound analysis of discrimination in capital sentencing in Fulton County, Georgia, was conducted.[52] This study, which clearly and unequivocally demonstrated that a black defendant is eleven times more likely to be sentenced to death for killing a white person than a white for killing a black, was presented to the United States Supreme Court in *McKlesky v. Kemp* (1985).[53] Warren McKlesky asked the Supreme Court to invalidate the Georgia capital punishment statute because of this proven discrimination. The Court refused to do so because defense attorneys had not shown that McKlesky himself had been discriminated against. Further, the Court ruled that if there is such racial bias, it is at a tolerable level. But a level that is tolerable is difficult to specify. For over fifty years research on sentencing disparity has found racial discrimination in both capital and noncapital cases. This is not to suggest that all judges discriminate. Rather, as it has been said, some judges discriminate and some do not.[54] Furthermore, differences based on race are

CHOOSING EQUAL INJUSTICE?

The legacy of Ernest van den Haag is captured by a simple maxim that was repeated throughout much of his career: Unequal justice is preferable to equal injustice.[1] Borrowed from the writings of Immanuel Kant, this was van den Haag's rallying cry in countless debates with abolitionists of capital punishment. No matter how much racial discrimination is documented, the dispositive question is whether the death penalty is deserved in light of the offender's guilt. "Maldistribution of any punishment among those who deserve it," argues van den Haag, "is irrelevant to its justice or morality."[2]

Those who challenged van den Haag in debates over abolishing the death penalty found it difficult to win concessions with mounting evidence of racial inequities in its application. In a wonderfully crafted rebuttal to the fiery rhetoric of death penalty lawyers about the racial nature of capital sentencing, van den Haag stubbornly questions its moral and practical relevance. If only blacks were selected for the death penalty, for example, and all white offenders who deserved the death penalty were given life sentences, this fact would not mean that capital punishment is in any way unjust. True there are inequalities, but the problem here is discrimination in favor of whites, not discrimination against blacks. "Discrimination must be abolished," argues van den Haag, "by abolishing discrimination—not by abolishing penalties."[3]

Van den Haag, to be clear, did not dismiss the importance of equality. It is simply that in the case of punishment, matters of equality and distribution are incidental to the principles of retributive justice. Even if many escape a date with the executioner for reasons having more to do with race and class than culpability, according to van den Haag, "the guilt of the executed convicts would not be diminished, nor would their punishment be less deserved."[4] Guilt is personal, and thus, claims of maldistribution and disproportionality in punishment should not in any way compromise the delivery of deserved punishment.

Van den Haag concludes that it is only rational that society should prefer the unequal application of deserved punishments (unequal justice) to the abandonment of deserved punishments where some, for whatever reasons, do not get their just desserts (equal injustice). Until his recent death, van den Haag challenged anyone to defy his logic that rationality assumes a definitive preference for unequal justice over equal injustice, no matter how unequal that justice.

What are the best arguments against van den Haag's position and in favor of choosing "equal injustice"?

NOTE: This feature is excerpted from William S. Laufer and Nein-hê Hsieh, "Choosing Equal Injustice," *American Journal of Criminal Law* 30 (2003), pp. 343–361.

SOURCES

1. See Ernest van den Haag, The Ultimate Punishment: A Defense, *Harvard Law Review* 99 1662 (1986) (making the case that "justice is independent to distributional inequalities"); Ernest van den Haag and John P. Conrad, The Death Penalty: A Debate 224 (1983) (repeating the maxim that unequal justice is preferred over equal injustice)
2. See van den Haag, *supra* note 2 at 1663.
3. See van den Haag, *supra* note 2 at 223.
4. See van den Haag, *supra* note 2 at 224.

not solely the result of judicial decision making. Research has found evidence that prosecutors are more likely to request the death penalty for black killers of white people.[55]

Other Arguments

Other arguments have been advanced for and against the death penalty. They are based on everything from religious concerns to a calculation of the cost of imprisonment. Table 11.3 lists these arguments and gives the rationale for them.

TABLE 11.3
Arguments against and for
the Death Penalty

Arguments	Rationale
Against	
Arbitrary use argument	With over 3,600 inmates on death row, the process by which an inmate is selected to die is entirely arbitrary; it is not determined by the seriousness of the crime committed or any other objective measure.
Mistakes argument	Studies have documented cases in which individuals were wrongly convicted and thus executed in error.* It is impossible to be entirely certain that a person is truly guilty. Are we willing to permit mistakes?
Religious argument	Organizations representing most of the major religions have called for an end to the death penalty. Interreligious task forces have voiced concern over issues of ethics and guilt in the putting to death of fellow human beings.
Cost–benefit argument	The cost of appeals and maintenance of a person on death row is higher than the cost of maintaining a prisoner sentenced to life imprisonment—approximately $3 million.
Risk argument	Convicted murderers behave well in prison and, if paroled, rarely commit violent offenses.
Morality argument	Examinations of the relation between moral development and attitudes toward capital punishment show that the more developed one's sense of morality, the less likely one is to favor the death penalty.
For	
Economic argument	The cost of maintaining an inmate in prison for life places an unfair burden on taxpayers and the state.[†]
Retribution argument	Any individual who kills another human being must pay for the crime.
Community protection argument	It is always possible that a person on death row may escape and kill again, or may kill another inmate or correctional officer. Thus the community cannot be fully protected unless the person is executed.[‡]
Public opinion argument	Standards of decency, the criteria by which courts judge the humaneness of a punishment, are continually evolving. Two decades ago public opinion was not in favor of the death penalty. Today three-quarters of Americans favor capital punishment.

*Hugo Adam Bedau and Michael L. Radelet, "Miscarriages of Justice in Potentially Capital Cases," *Stanford Law Review* 40, no. 1 (1987), pp. 21–129.

[†]Actually, the cost of appeals and maintenance of a person on death row is far higher than the cost of maintaining a prisoner sentenced to life imprisonment—approximately $3 million. See Andrew H. Malcolm, "Capital Punishment Is Popular, but So Are Its Alternatives," *The New York Times,* September 10, 1989, p. E4.

[‡]Thorsten Sellin's research demonstrated that this argument is specious. Convicted murderers behave exceedingly well in prison and if released have very good parole records. Repeat homicides are statistically rare. See Thorsten Sellin, *The Death Penalty* (Philadelphia: American Law Institute, 1959), pp. 69, 79.

A NEW CRIME—HATE; A NEW PUNISHMENT— SENTENCE ENHANCEMENT

- Gay college student Matthew Shepard was tied to a fence and beaten to death by his attackers.

- Self-identified neo-Nazis killed two African-American residents of Fayetteville, North Carolina, for kicks.

- Two African-American men killed a white father of three in Lubbock, Texas, in their search for a white victim.

- Two men in Houston, Texas, killed a gay man by stabbing him thirty-five times.

The murder of gay student Matthew Shepard.

- A Brooklyn real estate office was firebombed for showing properties to African Americans.

- A North Hollywood school was painted with swastikas and slurs against Jews by young vandals.

The stories are as chilling as the headlines. In Hillsborough County, Florida, two white males kidnapped a black man from a shopping center, forced him at gunpoint to drive sixteen miles to an isolated spot, poured gasoline over him, and then lit four matches. When the matches went out they continued with a cigarette lighter to ignite the fire that burned 40 percent of the victim's body. Charles Rourk, thirty-three, and Mark Kahut, twenty-seven, two friends from Illinois who shared an interest in hard rock music, motorcycles, and action movies and lived in a trailer park with their pet dog, Caesar, a pit bull, were sentenced to life-plus for the horrific attack.

An eighteen-year-old leader of a skinhead gang, the S.S. Action Group, became disenchanted with racism, dropped out of the New Jersey group, and fed information on its activities to the authorities. He described how the skinheads thrived on hostility against minorities, the sounds of racist music from Britain and Germany, known as oi, and fascist demonstrations where members dressed in military fatigues and, with arms raised straight in the Nazi salute, taunted spectators with a call for white supremacy.[1]

Four whites were charged with breaking into a home and badly beating a deaf black mother and her teenage son with baseball bats. It was not the first racially motivated attack on the

The Future of the Death Penalty

Given the public support for the death penalty and the increasing calls for politicians to "get tough" on crime, the death penalty in America is likely to continue for the foreseeable future.[56] Furthermore, recent Supreme Court decisions indicate a growing impatience with the number of appellate reviews traditionally granted a death-row inmate, presaging a willingness to consider restrictions on the number of such appeals. Legislation has been introduced in Congress to limit the number of appeals available for a death sentence.

Of the world's major industrialized nations, only the United States and Japan retain the death penalty. Much of the rest of the world has shown the opposite trend. Between 1965 and 1990, twenty-five countries abolished the death penalty altogether and ten abolished it for "ordinary crimes" (i.e., crimes other than those under military codes or

family of this thirty-nine-year-old substitute teacher at a school for the deaf. Shortly after they had moved into their new home, eighteen months earlier (they were the only black family on the street), a Molotov cocktail had been tossed into a window.

Destruction of property, arson, vandalism, assault, and attempted homicide—all fit the definition of "hate crime," or "bias crime": crimes committed against a person or property because of the race, religion, color, disability, sexual orientation, national origin, or ancestry of the victim. The National Hate Crime Statistics Act of 1990 mandates comprehensive reports on bias crimes, and in early 1993 the first such report was issued by the FBI. Although fewer than a fifth of the nation's law enforcement agencies contributed data for the report, 4,558 hate-crime incidents reported in 1991 were included in the study. The FBI found that blacks are the targets of most hate crimes (36 percent), followed by whites (19 percent), and Jews (17 percent). Religious bias motivated two of every ten incidents reported, with ethnic and sexual-orientation bias accounting for one of every ten. Racial bias was responsible for the greatest number of incidents by far—six of every ten. By 1997 the number of reported hate crimes rose to 9,861, with more than 60 percent motivated by racial bias. Most of the prosecutions have been initiated under state criminal laws.[2]

Two trends will continue, posing a great challenge to legislators, judges, and criminal justice specialists. First, jurisdictions around the United States are adding sentence enhancements to hate-crime statutes. Such amendments either allow or require judges to add additional prison time for those convicted of hate crimes. Second, jurisdiction for prosecuting hate crimes is expanding rapidly. For example, under current federal law, hate crimes may be prosecuted only if there is a crime motivated by bias based on religion, national origin, or color. With the Hate Crimes Prevention Act of 1998, however, Congress is debating the expansion of the definition of a "hate crime" to include a violent act causing death or bodily injury "because of the actual or perceived race, color, religion, national origin, sexual orientation, gender, or disability" of the victim. This expansion of federal jurisdiction will no doubt increase the number of prosecutions—at a time when we are made increasingly aware of the vulnerability of diversity in our very own neighborhoods.

Questions for Discussion

1. Are the acts that we characterize as hate crimes increasing in frequency?

2. Is there a definite need for a new class of federal hate crimes?

SOURCES
1. Clifford J. Levy, "Crusading for Harmony as a Skinhead Spy," *The New York Times,* April 4, 1994, pp. B1, B8.
2. David Van Biema, "When White Makes Right," *Time,* August 9, 1993, p. 40.

those enforced in time of war). The only country in the region of western Europe that retains the death penalty in practice is Turkey (Belgium, Ireland, and Greece also retain the death penalty but do not use it in practice), and the trend in the eastern European countries is toward abolition.[57] The lessons learned from those countries where capital punishment has been abolished might be useful in this country when the future of the death penalty is discussed. The deterrence argument would hold that homicide rates should go up when the death penalty is abolished. However, an analysis of murder rates in fourteen abolitionist nations shows that homicide rates actually have declined more often than not after abolition.[58]

In March 2005, the United States Supreme Court departed from prior case law in considering the death penalty practices of the international community. In *Roper v. Simmons* the Court forbade imposition of the death penalty on offenders who were under

TABLE 11.4
Emerging National Consensus on the Juvenile Death Penalty: The States before *Roper v. Simmons*

No Death Penalty for Juveniles (31 States)	No Juveniles Executed since 1976 (43 States)	No Juveniles Currently on Death Row (38 States)	No Death Penalty (12 States*)
California	EXCEPTIONS:	EXCEPTIONS:	Alaska
Colorado	Texas	Texas	Hawaii
Connecticut	South Carolina	Alabama	Iowa
Illinois	Louisiana	Louisiana	Maine
Indiana	Missouri[†]	Arizona	Massachusetts
Kansas	Georgia	Mississippi	Michigan
Maryland	Virginia	North Carolina	Minnesota
Missouri	Oklahoma	Florida	North Dakota
Montana		Georgia	Rhode Island
Nebraska		South Carolina	Vermont
New Jersey		Pennsylvania	West Virginia
New Mexico		Virginia	Wisconsin
New York		Nevada	
Ohio			
Oregon			
South Dakota			
Tennessee			
Washington			
Wyoming			
PLUS: 12 states with no death penalty			

*Also included are Washington, DC, and Puerto Rico.
[†]Now banned.
SOURCE: Adapted from the Death Penalty Information Center, http://www.deathpenaltyinfo.org/article.php?did=205&scid=27.

eighteen years of age when their crimes were committed (Table 11.4). The death penalty for juvenile offenders violates the Eighth Amendment and is unconstitutional. The Court had struggled with this issue for years—with *Eddings v. Oklahoma, Thompson v. Oklahoma,* and then *Stanford v. Kentucky*. Armed with a tradition of benchmarking our death penalty practices against "evolving standards of decency," the juvenile death penalty's time had come.

As Justice Kennedy reasoned

> Our determination that the death penalty is disproportionate punishment for offenders under 18 finds confirmation in the stark reality that the United States is the only country in the world that continues to give official sanction to the juvenile death penalty. This reality does not become controlling, for the task of interpreting the Eighth Amendment remains our responsibility. Yet at least from the time of the Court's decision in *Trop,* the Court has referred to the laws of other countries and to international authorities as instructive for its interpretation of the Eighth Amendment's prohibition of "cruel and unusual punishments."[59]

As of January 1, 2007, more than 3,350 adults await the execution of their death sentence around the United States (Figure 11.3).

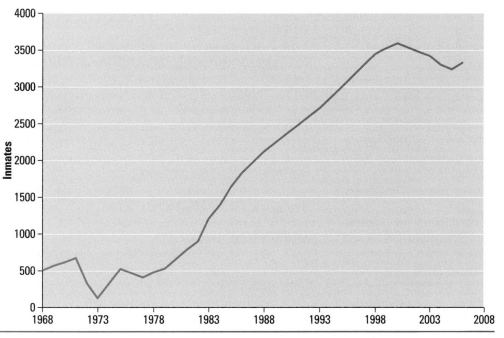

FIGURE 11.3 Size of Death Row by Year, 1968–2006

SOURCE: Death Penalty Information Center, http://www.deathpenaltyinfo.org/article. php?scid=9&did=188#state.

Review

Criminal sanctions are shaped by four philosophical traditions: retribution, deterrence, incapacitation, and rehabilitation. Three elements capture the essence of the modern concept of retribution—a proportionate penalty, a penalty that is deserved, and a penalty that expresses the moral condemnation of society. Today retribution is frequently referred to as just desserts. The basic principle underlying deterrence is that people will refrain from engaging in criminal activity because of the consequences of detection. Incapacitative strategies require the use of imprisonment to remove offenders from the community. Rehabilitation promises meaningful changes in offenders following appropriate correctional interventions. Finally, a mixed-goals approach allows for a combination of different philosophical rationales.

Legislative and judicial policies in sentencing convicted offenders are in a state of turmoil. Evidence of disproportionate sentences for like offenders has led to a wide abandonment of the rehabilitative ideal and a return to retributive and incapacitative approaches. But sentencing continues to be in a state of flux, with some signs of a rebirth of the rehabilitative goal. Many states operate sentencing guidelines that seek to curb abuses of judicial discretion, incorporate just dessert ideals, and allow some flexibility for considering aggravating and mitigating circumstances.

Capital punishment as a sentencing option preoccupies the thinking of policymakers and the general public. The United States is the last major democratic country to have retained capital punishment without any clear evidence that it promotes public safety.

Thinking Critically about Criminal Justice

1. Why is it that the United States remains the only Western country in the world to retain the death penalty? Why is there such great public support for capital punishment? Do you predict a downturn in support over the next decade? Why or why not?

Internet Connection

Note: While all of the URLs listed were current as of the printing of this book, these sites often change. Please check our website (http://www. mhhe.com/socscience/crimjustice/adlercj) for updates.

What is the average length of a sentence given in state court for violent, property, drug, and weapon offenses? For an answer to this question, see **http://www.ojp.usdoj.gov/ bjs/sent.htm.**

How will the *Booker* case change the way in which sentencing guidelines are used in federal courts? See **http://sentencing.typepad.com/sentencing_law_and_policy/booker_and_fanfan_commentary/**.

Notes

1. CNN.com, "Jury Sharply Split in Sparing Sniper Malvo," December 24, 2003, http://www.cnn.com/2003/LAW/12/24/sprj.dcsp.malvo.trial/index.html.

2. See Andrew von Hirsch, *Doing Justice: The Choice of Punishment* (NY: Hill & Wang, 1976).

3. Philip Cook, "The Demand and Supply of Criminal Opportunities," in *Crime and Justice: An Annual Review of Research,* vol. 7, ed. Michael Tonry and Norval Morris (Chicago: University of Chicago Press, 1986).

4. Scott H. Decker and Carol W. Kohfeld, "Certainty, Severity, and the Probability of Crime: A Logistic Analysis," *Policy Studies Journal* 19 (1990), pp. 2–21.

5. Edwin H. Phuhl, Jr., "Police Strikes and Conventional Crime," *Criminology* 21 (1983), pp. 489–503.

6. Ari L. Goldman, "In Spite of Dip, Subway Crime Nears a Record," *The New York Times,* November 20, 1982, pp. 1, 26.

7. James A. Beha II, "And Nobody Can Get You Out: The Impact of a Mandatory Prison Sentence for the Illegal Carrying of a Firearm on the Administration of Criminal Justice in Boston," *Boston University Law Review* 57 (March 1977), pp. 96–146.

8. See Colin Loftin and David McDowall, "'One with a Gun Gets You Two': Mandatory Sentencing and Firearms Violence in Detroit," *Annals of the American Academy of Political and Social Science* 455 (1981), pp. 150–167; and Colin Loftin and David McDowall, "The Deterrent Effects of the Florida Felony Firearm Law," *Journal of Criminal Law and Criminology* 75 (1984), pp. 250–259.

9. See H. Laurence Ross, Richard McCleary, and Gary LaFree, "Can Mandatory Jail Laws Deter Drunk Driving? The Arizona Case," *Journal of Criminal Law and Criminology* 81 (1990), pp. 156–170.

10. See Dennis M. Donovan, "Driving While Intoxicated: Different Roads to and from the Problem," *Criminal Justice and Behavior* 16 (1989), pp. 270–298.

11. Lonn Lanza-Kaduce, "Perceptual Deterrence and Drinking and Driving among College Students," *Criminology* 26 (1988), pp. 321–341.

12. See, e.g., Peter Greenwood with Allan Abrahamse, *Selective Incapacitation* (Santa Monica, CA: Rand Corporation, 1982).

13. Douglas R. Lipton, Robert Martinson, and Judith Wilks, *The Effectiveness of Correctional Treatment: A Survey of Treatment Evaluation Studies* (NY: Praeger, 1975).

14. Lee Sechrest, Susan O. White, and Elizabeth D. Brown, eds., *The Rehabilitation of Criminal Offenders: Problems and Prospects* (Washington, DC: National Academy of Sciences, 1979), pp. 5–6.

15. See Ted Palmer, "The Effectiveness of Intervention: Recent Trends and Current Issues," *Crime and Delinquency* 37 (1991), pp. 330–346; and John T. Whitehead and Steven P. Lab, "A Meta-analysis of Juvenile Correctional Treatment," *Journal of Research in Crime and Delinquency* 26 (1989), pp. 276–295.

16. "The Milken Sentence: Excerpts from Judge Wood's Explanation of the Milken Sentencing," *The New York Times,* November 22, 1990, p. 1.

17. See Alfred Blumstein, Jacqueline Cohen, Susan E. Martin, and Michael H. Tonry, eds., *Research on Sentencing: The Search for Reform* 1 (Washington, DC: National Academy Press, 1983).

18. See Robert O. Dawson, *Sentencing: The Decision as to Type, Length, and Conditions of Sentence* (Boston: Little, Brown, 1969).

19. See Anthony Walsh, "The Role of the Probation Officer in the Sentencing Process: Independent Professional or Judicial Hack?" *Criminal Justice and Behavior* 12 (1985), pp. 289–303.

20. Edna Erez and Pamela Tontodonato, "The Effect of Victim Participation in Sentencing on Sentence Outcome," *Criminology* 28 (1990), pp. 451–474. See also Edna Erez, "Victim Participation in Sentencing: Rhetoric and Reality," *Journal of Criminal Justice* 18 (1990), pp. 19–31; and William E. Hellerstein, "The Victim Impact Statement: Reform or Reprisal," *American Criminal Law Review* 27 (1989), pp. 391–430.

21. For a general introduction to restorative justice, see Martin Wright, *Justice for Victims and Offenders—A Restorative Response to Crime,* 2nd ed. (Winchester, UK: Waterside Press, 1996); Aleksander Fatic, *Punishment and Restorative Crime-Handling: A Social Theory of Trust* (Aldershot, UK: Avebury, 1995); Gordon Bazemore and Mark Umbreit, "Rethinking the Sanctioning Function in Juvenile Court: Retributive or Restorative Responses to Youth Crime," *Crime and Delinquency* 41 (1995), pp. 296–316; Sally Merry and Neal Milner, eds., *The Possibility of Popular Justice: A Case Study of Community Mediation in the United States* (Ann Arbor: University of Michigan Press, 1995); Kayleen M. Hazelhurst, ed., *Popular Justice and Community Regeneration: Pathways of Indigenous Reform* (Westport, CT: Praeger, 1995); Daniel W. Van Ness and Andrew Ashworth, "New Wine and Old Wineskins: Four Challenges to Restorative Justice," *Criminal Law Forum* 4, no. 2 (1993), pp. 251–306.

22. Howard Zehr, "Justice as Restoration, Justice as Respect," in *The Justice Professional* 11, nos. 1–2 (1998), pp. 71–87. This special issue was edited by Dennis Sullivan and Larry Tifft, under the general editorship of Roslyn Muraskin.

23. Mark S. Umbreit, "Crime Victims Confront Their Offenders: The Impact of the Minneapolis Mediation

Program," *Research on Social Work Practice* 4, no. 4 (1994), pp. 436–447; Lynne Walther and John Perry, "The Vermont Reparative Probation Program," *ICAA Journal on Community Corrections* 8, no. 2 (1997), pp. 13–50; John F. Gorczyk and John G. Perry, "What the Public Wants; Market Research Finds Support for Restorative Justice," *Corrections Today* 59, no. 7 (1997), pp. 78–83.

24. Edmund F. McGarrell, *Restorative Justice Conferences* (Indianapolis, IN: Hudson Institute, 1999); Edmund F. McGarrell, "Cutting Crime through Police-Citizen Cooperation," *American Outlook,* Spring 1998, pp. 65–67.

25. Van Ness and Ashworth, "New Wine and Old Wineskins, pp. 251–276; Andrew Ashworth, "Some Doubts About Restorative Justice," *Criminal Law Forum* 4, no. 2 (1993), pp. 277–299; Daniel W. Van Ness, "A Reply to Andrew Ashworth," *Criminal Law Forum* 4, no. 2 (1993), pp. 301–306.

26. California Governor Pete Wilson overturned the board's decision. See Philip Hager, "High Court Asked to Void Wilson Veto of Parole for Killer," *Los Angeles Times,* July 4, 1991, p. 3.

27. American Friends Service Committee, *Struggle for Justice: A Report on Crime and Punishment in America* (NY: Hill and Wang, 1971).

28. See also Marvin E. Frankel, *Criminal Sentences: Law without Order* (NY: Hill and Wang, 1972); Morris, *The Future of Imprisonment;* and von Hirsch, *Doing Justice: The Choice of Punishment.*

29. American Friends Service Committee, *Struggle for Justice.* For a recent study of race disparities in sentencing, see Cassia Spohn and Jerry Cederblom, "Race and Disparities in Sentencing: A Test of the Liberation Hypothesis," *Justice Quarterly* 8 (1991), pp. 305–327.

30. Sandra Shane-DuBow, Alice P. Brown, and Erik Olsen, *Sentencing Reform in the United States: History, Content, and Effect* (Washington, DC: National Institute of Justice, 1985).

31. See Andrew von Hirsch and Kathleen Hanrahan, "Determinate Penalty Systems in America: An Overview," *Crime and Delinquency* 27 (1981), pp. 289–316.

32. See Donald F. Anspach and S. Henry Monsen, "Determinate Sentencing, Formal Rationality, and Khadi Justice in Maine: An Application of Weber's Typology," *Journal of Criminal Justice* 17 (1989), pp. 471–485.

33. See von Hirsch and Hanrahan, "Determinate Penalty Systems in America."

34. See Michael Tonry, "Structuring Sentencing," *Crime and Justice: A Review of Research* 10 (Chicago: University of Chicago, 1988), p. 267.

35. Contemporary sentencing guidelines are neither novel nor unique. Mosaic law *(lex talionis)* in Exodus 21 graded the punishment in accordance with the harm done.

36. Frankel, *Criminal Sentences: Law without Order.*

37. Sally S. Simpson and Christopher S. Koper, "Deterring Corporate Crime," *Criminology* 30 (1992), pp. 347–373; also

see Andrew von Hirsch, Kay A. Knapp, and Michael Tonry, eds., *The Sentencing Commission and Its Guidelines* (Boston: Northeastern University Press, 1987); and William S. Laufer, "Culpability and the Sentencing of Corporations," *Nebraska Law Review* 71 (1992), pp. 1049–1094.

38. See Eric Simon, Gerry Gaes, and William Rhodes, "ASSYST—The Design and Implementation of Computer-Assisted Sentencing," *Federal Probation* 55 (1991), pp. 46–55.

39. Pamala L. Griset, *Determinate Sentencing: The Promise and the Reality of Retributive Justice* (Albany: State University of New York Press, 1991).

40. Michael Tonry, "Sentencing Guidelines and Their Effects," in *The Sentencing Commission and Its Guidelines,* pp. 16–43; and Laura Lein, Robert Rickards, and Tony Fabelo, "The Attitudes of Criminal Justice Practitioners toward Sentencing Issues," *Crime and Delinquency* 38 (1992), pp. 189–203.

41. *Mistretta v. U.S.,* 488 U.S. 361 (1989).

42. Sara T. Dike, "Capital Punishment in the United States. Part I: Observations on the Use and Interpretation of the Law," *Criminal Justice Abstracts* 13 (1981), pp. 283–311; Hugo A. Bedau, *The Death Penalty in America* (NY: Oxford University Press, 1984).

43. William Bowers, *Executions in America* (Lexington, MA: Lexington Books, 1974).

44. Death Penalty-Information Centers http:www.deathpenaltyinfo.org/article.php?scid=8&did=146 and http://www.deathpenaltyinfo.org/article.php?scid=8&did=269.

45. Sandra Nicolai, Karen Riley, Rhonda Christensen, Patrice Stych, and Leslie Greunke, *The Question of Capital Punishment* (Lincoln, NE: Contact, 1980).

46. Thorsten Sellin, *The Death Penalty* (Philadelphia: American Law Institute, 1959); Thorsten Sellin, *Capital Punishment* (NY: Harper and Row, 1967); and Ruth D. Peterson and William C. Bailey, "Murder and Capital Punishment in the Evolving Context of the *Post-Furman* Era," *Social Forces* 66 (1988), pp. 774–807.

47. Isaac Ehrlich, "The Deterrent Effect of Capital Punishment: A Question of Life and Death," *American Economic Review* 65 (1975), pp. 397–417; Gennaro F. Vito, Pat Koester, and Deborah G. Wilson, "Return of the Dead: An Update on the Status of *Furman*-Commuted Death Row Inmates," in *The Death Penalty in America: Current Research,* pp. 89–99.

48. See Steven Stack, "Publicized Executions and Homicide, 1950–1980," *American Sociological Review* 52 (1987), pp. 532–540.

49. Ruth D. Peterson and William C. Bailey, "Felony Murder and Capital Punishment: An Examination of the Deterrence Question," *Criminology* 29 (1991), pp. 367–395.

50. Charles L. Black, *Capital Punishment: The Inevitability of Caprice and Mistake* (New Haven, CT: Yale University Press, 1984).

51. Marvin Wolfgang and Mark Riedel, "Race, Judicial Discretion, and the Death Penalty," *Annals of the American Academy of Political and Social Sciences* 407 (1973), pp. 119–133. See also Joseph E. Jacoby and Raymond Paternoster, "Sentencing Disparity and Jury Packing: Further Challenges to the Death Penalty," *Journal of Criminal Law and Criminology* 73 (1982), pp. 379–387.

52. David Baldus, Charles Pulaski, and George Woodworth, "Comparative Review of Death Sentences: An Empirical Study of the Georgia Experience," *Journal of Criminal Law and Criminology* 74 (1983), pp. 661–678.

53. *McKlesky v. Kemp,* 478 U.S. 109 (1985). For a recent study, see Thomas J. Keil and Gennaro F. Vito, "Race and the Death Penalty in Kentucky Murder Trials: An Analysis of Post-*Gregg* Outcomes," *Justice Quarterly* 7 (1990), pp. 189–207.

54. Abraham S. Blumberg, *Criminal Justice: Issues and Ironies* (NY: New Viewpoints, 1979).

55. Michael L. Radelet and Glenn L. Pierce, "Race and Prosecutorial Discretion in Homicide Cases," *Law and Society Review* 19 (1985), pp. 587–621; Paige H. Ralph, Jonathan R. Sorensen, and James W. Marquart, "A Comparison of Death-sentenced and Incarcerated Murderers in Pre-*Furman* Texas," *Justice Quarterly* 9 (1992), pp. 185–209.

56. Robert M. Bohm, Louise J. Clark, and Adrian F. Aveni, "The Influence of Knowledge on Reasons for Death Penalty Opinions: An Experimental Test," *Justice Quarterly* 7 (1990), pp. 175–188.

57. Roger Hood, *The Death Penalty: A Worldwide Perspective* (NY: Oxford University Press, 1989).

58. See Dane Archer, Rosemary Gartner, and Marc Beittel, "Homicide and the Death Penalty: A Cross-National Test of a Deterrence Hypothesis," *Journal of Criminal Law and Criminology* 74 (1983), pp. 991–1013.

59. *Roper v. Simmons,* S.Ct., 2005 WL 464890 (2005).

Corrections

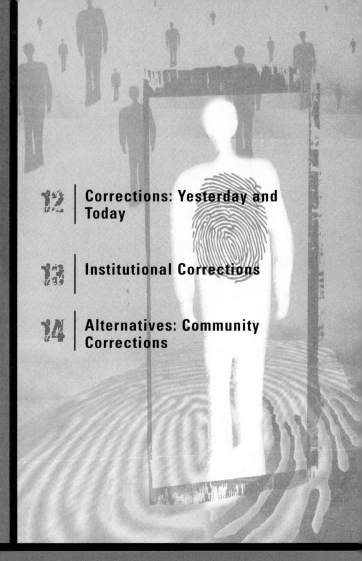

• Burdened by a history of inhumanity and brutality, corrections acquired its name less than a century ago, when it was believed that offenders should and could be corrected. Chapter 12 focuses on the history of corrections in the United States, with special attention to efforts at reform, the prisoners' rights movement, and the Supreme Court's subsequent recognition of constitutional guarantees for prisoners. The chapter also describes the variety of contemporary correctional facilities and the variety of problems the system faces at all levels.

• CHAPTER 13 is devoted to contemporary American institutional corrections, how the system deals with its clients, how these clients (prisoners) behave in prison, how they interact with corrections personnel, and how these officers perceive and fulfill their functions. The chapter examines special problems, like the increasing number of women prisoners and of violent and addict offenders in confinement, as well as contemporary prison health problems such as AIDS and TB.

• CHAPTER 14 focuses on the topic of noninstitutional corrections, which has been and continues to be shaped by imaginative reformers. Probation and parole, a century and a half old, are now being supplemented by other alternatives to incarceration, among them the increased use of fines, restitution to victims, intensive supervision programs, halfway houses, shock programs (boot camps), house arrest, and, particularly, community service.

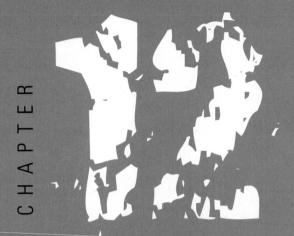

Corrections: Yesterday and Today

—In 1584, Balthazar Geraerts assassinated King Willem of Orange (Holland). His punishment, inflicted before a cheering multitude, consisted of unspeakable cruelties and finally decapitation.[1] These atrocities took place at a time of great advances: the worldwide voyages of discovery; the expansion of scientific knowledge; and the flourishing of art, literature, and music. Human life, however, was still cheap. Cruelty was a way of life, and death was usually early and sudden, whether from marauding armies, disease, or an executioner's axe.

• Today we pride ourselves on the progress we have made and the barbarities we no longer practice. We pride ourselves on our extraordinary advances in many fields: the exploration of space, great leaps in technology, the conquest of many diseases. And yet human life is still cheap. The inner-city ghettoes are hard, cruel places where life is often cut short suddenly and violently. We still execute prisoners. To some, going to jail is regarded as a rite of passage. Tattoos acquired in prison are badges of honor, and the returning offender may be a hero in the community. The prospect of prison for some, far from being a deterrent, has turned into the opposite—an acceptable alternative, a respite for street warriors, a time to build muscles and connections, a period of rest and preparation for the next battle.[2]

Institutional corrections has had a long history, from the workhouses (or houses of corrections) of Holland, England, and colonial Pennsylvania to the penitentiary movement, the reformatory movement, the medical model of confinement, and the contemporary prison and jail. As we will see, the treatment of prisoners has also evolved from a rule of terror and brutality to a rule of law.

In this chapter we focus on the evolution and contemporary state of the system that currently bears the name "corrections." In the early twentieth century, Americans adopted this term with the expectation that offenders could be corrected by the system, just as nearsightedness is corrected by eyeglasses. The personnel who run this system consist of corrections officers, corrections administrators (superintendents and wardens), and administrative staff.

The History of Institutional Corrections

Can you imagine a world without prisons? Impossible? Such a world did exist, until the very end of the Middle Ages. There always had been jails, but only to detain defendants pending trial or awaiting execution of sentence. The punishments used were brutal, such as banishment, capital punishment by hanging, burning at the stake, drawing and quartering, disemboweling, boiling, breaking on the wheel, stoning to death, impaling, pressing to death in spiked containers, and being torn by red-hot tongs. Noncapital corporal punishments included branding, dismembering, flogging, and torturing. Yet there also was another type of punishment, namely public labor, by work in mines, on construction projects, rowing galleys, or performing other tasks for the benefit of the public treasury. Such labor was performed under the most inhumane conditions so that convicts often preferred death.

The Workhouse

By the end of the sixteenth century, England and Holland increasingly replaced older forms of punishment with incarceration in "workhouses," where inmates spent the days at hard labor and the nights in communal squalor. Although these institutions initially had rehabilitative aims, overcrowding and deteriorating conditions soon transformed them into dangerous places whose only recognizable purpose was punishment. There was no separation of prisoners by gender, age, or severity of offense. Prisoners had to pay for provisions, and illness spread quickly—"jail fever" (typhus) was especially common in the cramped quarters. The worst conditions were found on **prison "hulks,"** decommissioned naval ships used as floating prisons starting in 1775. Able-bodied convicts were frequently sent overseas, first to the American colonies as slave labor, and then to Australia. Over 135,000 convicts were sent to Australia from 1787 to 1875.

prison "hulks"
Decommissioned ships converted into prisons.

Enlightenment Reform

The appalling conditions of incarceration drew the scrutiny of Enlightenment thinkers in the mid-eighteenth century, who advocated more humane methods of punishment. A young Italian, Cesare Beccaria, became one of the most influential writers of the time when he published *An Essay on Crimes and Punishment* in 1764. Beccaria's novel ideas made waves in Europe: the importance of prevention over punishment, the abolition of torture and the death penalty, the presumption of innocence, the right to cross-examine witnesses in one's defense, and many others. Sound familiar? These ideas provided inspiration for future reformers, including America's founding fathers.

The writings of Beccaria and other philosophers were influential, but none had the immediate reformatory impact of John Howard's *The State of Prisons in England and Wales*, published in 1777. Howard was horrified at the conditions of incarceration, particularly the hulks, when he was appointed as a sheriff in 1773. He traveled Europe examining others' penal institutions, finding similar conditions. His reformatory efforts pushed the British

Parliament to pass the Penitentiary Act in 1779, which prioritized security, sanitation, abolition of fees, and systematic inspection.

During his travels, Belgium's Maison de Force particularly impressed Howard. It was among the first institutions to classify prisoners, separating women from men and minor offenders from dangerous felons, as well as housing inmates in individual cells rather than common areas. It also relied upon the withholding of food rather than corporal punishment for discipline, unlike the harsh rule in England's workhouses.

The Penitentiary

Under British rule, America's penal system reflected the strict Anglican system of hard labor, corporal punishment, and capital punishment for numerous crimes. Connecticut first attempted a state prison for felons at an abandoned copper mine in 1773. This was the site of the first prison riots one year later. Pennsylvania Quakers built the first modern correctional institution in 1790 as an addition to Philadelphia's Walnut Street Jail. The addition's U-shaped corridor of cells housed prisoners in solitary confinement to encourage reflection and repentance, although a shortage of cells meant that convicts often cycled in and out of the solitary confinement. The prison pioneered education within prison walls, establishing a school in 1798; proper health care, providing weekly doctor's visits; vocational training, requiring inmates to occupy their time with small industries usually of their choosing; and a sophisticated classification system similar to that which so impressed John Howard in Belgium.[3]

Pennsylvania continued its leadership in penal construction with the addition of Eastern **Penitentiary** in 1829. Similar in philosophy to the Walnut Street Jail, it enforced a strict regime of solitary confinement, silence, biblical study, and handicraft work in the hope of encouraging repentance and reform. Its wheel and spoke construction, whose small cells attached to even smaller outdoor "yards," introduced a new style of penitentiary. The "Pennsylvania system," or "separate system," attracted international fame and replication abroad.[4]

It also faced competition. New York had established it own state penitentiary at Auburn in 1819, which featured extremely small, inward facing cells intended only for sleeping. Days were spent in silent congregate labor. Discipline was strictly enforced with the whip. The "Auburn system," or "congregate system," became the more popular model, largely because it was much less expensive and group labor generated more income. There was also increasing evidence that solitary confinement encouraged insanity rather than reform. "Auburn" penitentiaries grew in size and number throughout the country. However, by the mid-nineteenth century it had become clear that penitence could not be achieved in these fortresses of cruelty.

The Reformatory

Reform-minded prison administrators developed a new type of correctional institution, specifically aimed at the reform of first-time offenders aged 16 to 30. These **reformatories** emphasized education and vocational training in a military environment. Influenced by reforms in Australia and Ireland, they adopted indeterminate sentences and a grading system based on marks, which determined when an inmate would be released on parole. The first reformatory, built in Elmira, New York, in 1876, served as a popular model for other states.

Reformatories did not live up to their promise. They were seen as little more than junior prisons by the early twentieth century. The emphasis on education and use of indeterminate sentencing lived far longer than the institutions that popularized these reforms.

Major Developments in American Corrections

Few could have predicted the major changes that would shake the foundations of America's corrections system during the second half of the twentieth century. Rapid growth in prison populations followed 50 years of stability, extraordinary judicial involvement compelled significant reforms and professionalization, and prison administrators faced unprecedented political and public scrutiny.[5]

penitentiary
Prison or place of confinement and correction for persons convicted of criminal acts; originally a place where convicts did penance.

reformatory
Institution designed to reform criminals through individualized treatment, education, and vocational training.

Attica Prison in the aftermath of the 1971 uprising: Inmates were ordered to lie down in a yard, prior to a skin search. As the area became crowded, they were made to crawl away from the door on their bellies, hands locked behind their heads, to make room for more.

The Rise and Fall of Prison Labor

Labor had always been a centerpiece of penitentiary life. It prevented idleness, provided vocational skills, and most importantly, offered a source of income to the state. Some states produced finished goods in prison factories, while others contracted with private parties for labor or piecework. The South took this practice to cruel heights after the Civil War, establishing a leasing system that relinquished all responsibility for prisoners to private contractors. Prisoners became a source of income for the insolvent state governments, rather than a cost burden. Convicts, predominantly African-American, replaced the newly freed slaves as an exploited source of cheap labor. Through such arrangements, chain gangs, housed in rolling cages, built thousands of miles of railroad during the last half of the nineteenth century.[6]

Contractors had little incentive to care for their convict laborers. Physical abuse and inhumane conditions prompted widespread public outrage at the turn of the century. The fatal beating of Martin Tabert, a white man arrested for hopping a freight train and put to work in Florida's swamps stripping turpentine, helped put an end to leasing. Alabama was the last state to abolish the practice in 1924.[7]

Opposition to more traditional forms of prison labor also gained strength in the late nineteenth century. Organized labor objected loudly to the competition free-market goods faced from prisoner-made goods. Their overtures resulting in a steady erosion of the industrial prison, which culminated in the federal government's 1935 Ashurst-Sumners Act, effectively banning the interstate transport of prison-made goods. Prisoners were limited to making license plates and other such good for state consumption. More often than not, for the first time in America's correctional history, most inmates sat idle.[8]

The Rehabilitation Model

The rehabilitation model emerged as the dominant penal philosophy in the first half of the twentieth century, promoting indeterminate sentencing, careful classification, and treatment. Advocates argued that all offenders, independent of the nature of their offense, should be sentenced for a term ranging from a very short period to life in prison. Release would depend on when the criminality was cured. Classification was an elaborate, systematic diagnosis and prescription. On classification, inmates would be assigned to programs involving psychotherapy, vocational training, and education.[9] Offenders would be retrained, resocialized, rehabilitated, and reintegrated as socially skilled citizens.

The medical approach to dealing with criminality flourished until the 1970s. California was the leader in the therapeutic approach, but nearly all states instituted group and individual therapy programs, counseling services, and behavior modification programs of various sorts. Conditions in the prisons, however, actually changed very little. Underfunded and inadequately staffed rehabilitative programs reached only a small number of inmates.

The Prisoners' Rights Movement

The "Hands-Off" Doctrine   The U.S. Constitution dictates a separation of powers: the legislature makes laws, the executive executes laws, and the judiciary adjudicates any controversies arising under these laws. Until the 1960s, courts were quite willing to test laws made by legislatures, but they declined to supervise or review the execution of these laws by the executive branch, including the execution of corrections. With rare exception, the courts refused to hear prisoner complaints about the terms and conditions of their confinement. This "hands-off" doctrine was clearly articulated in 1954 by a federal appeals court: "[C]ourts are without power to supervise prison administrators or to interfere with the ordinary prison rules or regulations."[10]

But in the 1960s, society experienced rapid social change. Minority groups demanded equality in voting rights, housing, education, and employment. Women strove for equal treatment in public and private domains. Students rebelled against complacent and conservative political and social systems. Prisoners, too, demanded their rights. During these years, the extraordinary efforts of the National Prison Project of the American Civil Liberties Union, the NAACP Legal Defense and Educational Fund, the legal services branch of the federal government's Office of Economic Opportunity, public defenders and legal aid lawyers, as well as countless volunteers from the legal profession and hundreds of self-trained jailhouse lawyers, succeeded in overturning the longstanding "hands-off" doctrine. But it took some very dramatic events to get the prisoners' rights movement under way.

Riots in Attica   Social discontent within prison walls had made itself known in the early 1950s. Thirty riots took place between April 1952 and September 1953, more than the entire preceding quarter-century.[11] Encouraged by the unrest outside prison walls, such uprisings continued into the 1960s. A member of the Maryland state legislature blamed the civil rights movement in the wake of a large prison riot in Baltimore in 1966: "It stems from people on the outside. If they don't stop telling these prisoners about their rights it is going to get worse."[12] See Table 12.1.

TABLE 12.1
Attica Demands

Attica Demands
- Adequate food and water.
- Protection from administrative reprisals and amnesty for deaths.
- Minimum wage for all inmate labor and provision of wage records.
- Establishment of an Ombudsman and inmate grievance commission.
- The right to be politically active.
- "True" religious freedom.
- Removal of restrictions on outside communications.
- "Realistic, effective rehabilitation programs."
- "Modernization" of the education system, including Spanish language resources.
- "Adequate legal assistance."
- Better recreational facilities and more time to use them.
- Adequate medical treatment, including drug treatment.
- Recruitment of minority corrections officers.
- Revise resentencing rules for violation of parole (i.e., for traffic violations).
- 30-day maximum for punitive segregation.

SOURCE: Adapted from Douglas. J. Besharov and Gerhard O. W. Mueller. "The Demands of the Inmates of Attica State Prison and the United Nations Standard Minimum Rules for the Treatment of Prisoners: A Comparison." *Buffalo Law Review* 21 (1971–1972), pp. 839–854.

Indeed, five years later, it got much worse. On September 9, 1971, a riot broke out in New York's Attica prison, an institution then holding 2,200 inmates. Prisoners took over most of the facility and held forty corrections officers hostage. Three inmates and one guard lost their lives that morning. After four days of unsuccessful negotiations, Governor Nelson Rockefeller ordered the state police to take the prison back by force, which they did during fifteen minutes of tear gas and gunfire that left 80 wounded and 39 dead, including one-quarter of the hostages. It was the bloodiest one-day encounter between Americans since the Civil War.[13]

The events at Attica drew unprecedented attention to the inhumane conditions of the nation's prisons and the lack of basic rights afforded to its prisoners, opening the floodgates to lawsuits testing not only the right of access to the courts, but also the particular conditions of confinement. A former director of the federal Bureau of Prisons went as far as to claim that "[m]uch of the way we administer our prisons today is predicated on our reaction to the events at Attica in 1971."[14]

The Role of the Supreme Court.   Any analysis of the prisoners' rights movement must acknowledge the crucial role of the United States Supreme Court. To begin with, the prisoners' rights movement required a symbolic "shot in the arm" from the Supreme Court.[15] *Cooper v. Pate* (1964) was the opening.[16] Ninety-three years after passage of the Civil Rights Act (1871), prisoners could finally sue a warden for a violation of their civil rights. The old "hands-off" doctrine was dead.

Many legal victories followed *Cooper v. Pate,* and each contributed to the strength, self-confidence, and momentum of the prisoners' rights movement. A high-water mark was reached in 1974 with *Wolff v. McDonnell,*[17] a case that resolved issues about the procedural protections to which prisoners are entitled at disciplinary hearings. In *Wolff,* the Supreme Court provided the statement that served as a rallying call for prisoners' rights advocates. Speaking for the Court, Justice White said:

> [The State of Nebraska] asserts that the procedure for disciplining prison inmates for serious misconduct is a matter of policy raising no constitutional issue. If the position implies that prisoners in state institutions are wholly without the protections of the Constitution and the Due Process Clause, it is plainly untenable. Lawful imprisonment necessarily makes unavailable many rights and privileges of the ordinary citizen, a "retraction justified by the considerations underlying our penal system." But though his rights may be diminished by the needs and exigencies of the institutional environment, a prisoner is not wholly stripped of constitutional protections when he is imprisoned for crime. There is no iron curtain drawn between the Constitution and the prisons of this country.[18]

Since *Wolff,* prisoners have won several important victories in the Supreme Court.[19] For example, the Court in *Estelle v. Gamble* (1976) found that "deliberate indifference to serious medical needs" constitutes cruel and unusual punishment.[20] In *Hutto v. Finney* (1978) it approved a wide-ranging structural injunction against certain practices and conditions in the Arkansas prisons.[21] In *Hudson v. McMillian* (1992) the Court ruled that the beating of a prisoner by officers may constitute cruel and unusual punishment even if it did not result in serious injury[22] (see Table 12.2).

Recent cases have narrowly expanded the rights of prisoners including, for example, their right to file *habeas* petitions (*Stewart v. Martinez-Villareal* (1998)); the evidentiary standards in prisoners' lawsuits (*Crawford-El v. Britton* (1998)); the right to an evidentiary hearing (*Williams v. Taylor* (2000)); the right to challenge prison disciplinary charges (*Muhammad v. Close* (2004)); and the practice of temporary racial segregation (*Johnson v. California* (2005)).

The Impact of the Prisoners' Rights Movement

The prisoners' rights movement has had an enormous impact on American corrections. The developmental stage in which it was necessary for the U.S. Supreme Court to set policy for correctional institutions is over; now federal district courts are busy implementing these mandates. Over the past decade, more than forty states, not including the District

TABLE 12.2
Selected Constitutional Rights of Inmates

First Amendment

Communication

Do inmates have the right to freedom of communication?
Yes, with significant limitations. Procunier v. Martinez, 416 U.S. 396 (1974) (censorship of inmate mail with members of the general public is allowed only where there is a substantial government interest in maintaining security)

Do inmates have the right to correspond with counsel and the courts?
Yes, with limitations. Bounds v. Smith, 430 U.S. 817, 825–826 (1977) (prison administration may not place undue restrictions or otherwise interfere with mail given an inmate's otherwise limited access to courts)

Do inmates have an unlimited right to access the media?
No, prison rules prohibiting access are legal if other avenues of expression exist.

Do inmates have an unlimited right to read what they choose?
No, courts have upheld prison rules approving only certain publications.

Political Rights

Do inmates retain any political rights?
Possibly, but limited to the restrictions of prison administrators. Jones v. North Carolina Prisoners Labor Union, Inc., 433 U.S. 199 (1977) (prison officials may bar inmate membership in prisoners' union and restrict union meetings)

Can inmates be punished for political expression?
Possibly, where such expression creates a danger to the orderly administration of the prison.

Are persons convicted of felonies entitled to vote?
The Constitution allows states to deny this right to those convicted of felonies.

Religious Rights

Can prison officials restrict an inmate's free expression of religion?
Prison policies that restrict religious expression are constitutional if reasonably related to legitimate penal objectives (O'Lone v. Estate of Shabazz, 107 S.Ct. 2400 (1987); Religious freedom, however, must be granted equally to inmates of all faiths. Cruz v. Beto, 405 U.S. 319 (1972))

Can prison officials restrict inmates of Muslim and Buddhist faiths from the practice of their religion?
Prison officials cannot deny inmates the right to practice these religions, but can restrict or limit the practice of all religions.

Association

Do inmates have a constitutional right to marry?
Yes, with some narrow limitations, male inmates may marry female inmates, and male or female inmates may marry non-prisoners. (Turner v. Safley, 107 S.Ct. 2254 (1987))

Fourth Amendment
Privacy Expectations

Do inmates have any legitimate expectations to privacy?
Generally, no.

Do prison authorities have an unlimited right to search an inmate's living area?
Without limitation for both pretrial detainee and prison inmate. The Fourth Amendment's prohibition against unreasonable searches and seizures is inapplicable in prison. (Hudson v. Palmer, 468 U.S. 517 (1984) (inmates); Bell v. Wolfish, 441 U.S. 520 (1979) (pretrial detainees))

Can prison authorities conduct searches, even "strip" searches, without restriction?
Yes, but all searches must be conducted in a reasonable manner. Courts have placed some restrictions, however, on body cavity searches and "visual" body cavity

(continued)

TABLE 12.2
(*Continued*)

searches. (*United States v. Lilly*, 576 F. 2d 1240 (5th Cir. 1978) (officials bear the burden of proving the reasonableness of such searches); *Lee v. Downs*, 641 F. 2d 1117 (4th Cir. 1981))

Sixth Amendment

Right to Counsel and Legal Assistance

Do inmates have a right to meet and correspond with counsel?
Yes. Johnson v. Avery, 393 U.S. 499 (1969) (inmates have a right to assistance from jailhouse lawyers)

Do inmates have the right to meet privately with counsel?
No. Conversations between inmates and counsel can be monitored, at the discretion of prison officials. O'Brien v. United States, 386 U.S. 345 (1967); *Weatherford v. Bursey*, 429 U.S. 545 (1977)

Must inmates have access to a law library?
Yes, prisons must grant inmates reasonable access to adequately staffed law libraries. (*Bounds v. Smith*, 430 U.S. 817 (1977))

Eighth Amendment

Cruel and Unusual Punishment

Can prison overcrowding amount to cruel and unusual punishment?
Generally not. Four factors must be considered in such cases: (1) The actual level of crowding, (2) the location of beds, (3) times away from living quarters, and (4) in the case of pretrial detention, its duration. See, e.g., *Rhodes v. Chapman*, 452 U.S. 337 (1981); Claudia Angelos and James B. Jacobs, "Prison Overcrowding and the Law," *Annals* 478 (1985) pp. 100–112.

Can solitary confinement violate the Cruel and Unusual Punishment clause?
Generally not, although some lower courts have found conditions to fall below standards of civilized society and, thus, constitute cruel and unusual punishment. Other courts have found an Eighth Amendment violation in the length of confinement, and the absence of a justification for its use. Hutto v. Finney, 437 U.S. 678 (1978)

Do any specific forms of punishment or restrictions in prison constitute cruel and unusual punishment?
Yes, for example, the use of mechanical restraints, restricting any exercise, and diets of bread and water have been found unconstitutional.

Can deliberate indifference to medical treatment constitute cruel and unusual punishment?
Yes, particularly when and where a serious medical condition exists.

Can prison officials authorize corporal punishment?
No, most prisons have regulations prohibiting the use of straps, whips, chains, and handcuffs. Further, the Eighth Amendment prohibits most if not all forms of corporal punishment.

Is the beating of an inmate by correctional officers prohibited by the Eighth Amendment?
The Constitution prohibits the use of excessive force in controlling inmate behavior. (*Hudson v. McMillian*, 112 S.Ct. 995 (1992))

Is it cruel and unusual punishment to deprive an inmate of conjugal visits?
No.

Fourteenth Amendment

Due Process

Do inmates have a right to due process in prison disciplinary proceedings?
Yes, certain procedural due process guarantees (e.g., right to notice of charges and right to call witnesses) attach in cases of serious disciplinary actions. (*Wolff v. McDonnell*, 418 U.S. 539 (1974))

(*continued*)

TABLE 12.2
(*Continued*)

Can prison officials rule arbitrarily at inmate disciplinary hearings?
Courts have ruled that there are some limits. For example, the Supreme Court has determined that a decision revoking good time credit has to be supported by at least some evidence of wrongful conduct. (*Superintendent v. Hill;* 472 U.S. 445 (1985))

Are inmates entitled to due process during classification or in transfer decisions?
Generally not.

Can prison officials take or destroy an inmate's personal property?
Courts do not find a due process violation where state remedies are available, e.g., prison grievance mechanisms. (*Parratt v. Taylor,* 451 U.S. 527 (1981); *Hudson v. Palmer,* 468 U.S. 516 (1984))

Equal Protection

Is racial discrimination permitted in prison?
Generally, discrimination on the basis of race is constitutionally impermissible. (*Lee v. Washington,* 390 U.S. 333 (1968)

SOURCE: Adapted from David Rudovsky, Alvin J. Bronstein, Edward I. Koren, and Julia Cade, *The Rights of Prisoners,* 4th ed. (Carbondale: Southern Illinois University Press, 1988).

of Columbia, Puerto Rico, and the U.S. Virgin Islands, have been under court order (or consent decree) to limit populations and/or improve conditions of confinement. Some of these court orders were applicable to the entire correctional system, others to major institutions only.[23] In many states the federal courts have appointed special masters or monitors who supervise the management of institutions as they move toward compliance with court orders.

Unfortunately, conditions in jails have been even worse than those in prisons. Jail systems are regularly under court order to limit jail populations. The impact of these orders has been immense. They have:

- Contributed to the bureaucratization of the prison.
- Produced a new generation of administrators.
- Expanded the procedural protections available to prisoners.
- Heightened public awareness of prison conditions.
- Politicized prisoners and heightened their expectations.
- Demoralized prison staff.
- Made it more difficult to maintain control over prisoners.
- Contributed to a professional movement within corrections to establish national standards.[24]
- Vastly increased prison construction by attacking prison overcrowding.

The Rebirth of Retribution Philosophy

The prisoners' rights movement was one of two factors that changed the nature of American corrections. The other was the rebirth in the mid-1970s of retribution in the form of the just desserts model (see Chapter 11). As sentencing became oriented toward proportionate prison sentences, corrections became more punitive and custodial. Most rehabilitative programs in prisons, already discredited, were abandoned. Prisoners were "doing time" in proportion to the seriousness of their crime; they were not there to be rehabilitated or reformed. This more punitive attitude had an unfortunate consequence: Legislators passed more punitive sentencing laws, and parole boards became more reluctant to grant parole or were abolished altogether. The result was a steep increase in prison populations, filling the prisons that had been constructed as a consequence of prisoners' rights suits.

Institutional Corrections Today

detention facility
Facility that houses persons arrested and undergoing processing, awaiting trial, or awaiting transfer to a correctional facility.

correctional facility
Facility where convicted offenders serve their sentence; includes county jails and state and federal prisons.

Today there are two categories of prison facilities—detention and correctional. **Detention facilities** normally do not house convicted inmates and are not technically correctional facilities. They house persons arrested and undergoing processing, awaiting trial, or awaiting transfer to a correctional facility after conviction. **Correctional facilities,** where convicted offenders serve their sentence, include county jails and state and federal prisons. Those convicted of misdemeanors normally serve sentences of not more than one year in county jails. But there are exceptions to the rule. Many jails operated by counties and cities serve two purposes: They house those awaiting trial or transfer and also hold convicts serving misdemeanor sentences. Moreover, because of overcrowding in state prisons, many states have found it necessary to house inmates sentenced for felony offenses in county jails. Local variations cloud the distinction even further. Rikers Island in New York City serves not only as the jail for all the boroughs of the city but also as a prison for those serving longer state sentences. A few states call some of their prisons "houses of detention," but the basic differences remain: County jails are intended for the temporary detention of prisoners and for persons serving sentences for misdemeanors; federal and state prisons are intended for felons, whose sentences are for longer than one year. Remarkably, at the end of June 2006, 1 in every 133 U.S. residents were incarcerated in a correctional facility.[25]

Jails

Careers

jail
Place of confinement administered by local officials and designed to hold persons for more than forty-eight hours but usually less than one year.

Jails are generally defined as facilities administered by local officials and designed to hold persons for more than forty-eight hours but usually less than one year. There are thousands of jails of various sizes in the United States. A jail in one state may be as large as the entire prison system of another state. The men's central jail of Los Angeles can house more inmates (6,800) than 16 state prison systems.[26] And that's just one facility—the entire Los Angeles jail system holds about 20,000.[27] Many jails in rural counties, by contrast, house but a few prisoners and operate with a fee system, under which the county government pays a modest amount of money for each prisoner per day, rather than providing a fixed operating budget. Almost 40 percent of local jurisdictions have an average daily jail population of less than fifty inmates.[28]

The number of inmates held in jails has grown approximately 3.5 percent each year. Between 2000 and 2006, the number of inmates in jails rose from 621,149 to 766,010, and the jail incarceration rate rose from 220 inmates per 100,000 residents to 256.[29] Since jails often serve as detention centers, a majority of inmates are often defendants awaiting trial. This population has been rising, from 56 percent of all jail inmates in 2000 to 62.1 percent in 2006.[30] Of the convicted population, roughly 25 percent are state or federal prisoners whose care has been contracted out to local jails due to overcrowding in prisons.[31] Louisiana houses 45 percent of its state prisoners in jails, rather than state correctional facilities.[32]

The movement to deinstitutionalize mental patients in the 1960s created an additional burden for the entire criminal justice system. Thanks to poor classification systems and minimal programs or services, jails especially struggle with handling the mentally ill population. An estimated 64 percent of jail inmates had a mental health problem in 2005, in contrast to 56 percent state inmates and 45 percent federal inmates. However, only 17.5 percent of mentally ill jail inmates received treatment after admission, in contrast to 24 percent of state inmates and 33.8 percent of federal inmates. Almost a quarter of jail inmates had symptoms of a psychotic disorder (hallucinations or delusions) and 5 percent reported hospitalization in the past year for a mental health problem.

Jail staff, whether law enforcement or corrections employees, cannot be expected to have the expertise to deal with such significant mental health problems, but the problem is not only a lack of capacity and expertise in jails. For the severely mentally ill, there's just not enough beds in secure state psychiatric wards. Perpetually short on beds, Florida had routinely broken state law by keeping inmates found incompetent to stand trial in jail for longer than 15 days, rather than sending them to a psychiatric hospital. It was only after several inmates died, one schizophrenic gouged out his eye, and a judge threatened the head of the state's Department of Children and Families with jail time and fines that the state finally committed the resources necessary to transfer all such inmates within the 15-day window.[33]

Prisons

Prisons are federal or state penal institutions in which offenders serve sentences in excess of one year. For the most part, both state and federal prisons have been blessed with better management than jails and often with better education, recreation, and employment training programs.[34] But this is not too surprising. After all, prisons are larger, have many more inmates, and thus have much bigger budgets. A prison normally has three distinct custody levels for inmates, based on an assessment of their perceived dangerousness: maximum danger, medium danger, and minimum danger. Maximum security prisons are designed to hold the most violent, dangerous, and aggressive inmates. They have high concrete walls or double-perimeter razor wire fences, gun towers with armed officers, and strategically placed electronic monitors. Every state has one or several maximum security prisons. There are only a handful of supermax prisons, including the federal supermax prison at ADX Florence (Colorado), and Pelican Bay (California) and Tamms (Illinois)—two state supermax facilities.

Medium security prisons house inmates who are considered less dangerous or escape prone than those in maximum security facilities. These structures typically have no high outside wall, only a series of fences. Many medium security inmates are housed in large dormitories rather than cells.

Minimum security prisons hold inmates who are considered the lowest security risks. Very often these institutions operate without armed officers and without perimeter walls or fences. The typical inmate in such an institution has proved trustworthy in the correctional setting, is nonviolent, and is serving a short prison sentence.

careers

prison
Federal or state penal institution in which offenders serve sentences longer than one year.

Federal Prison System

Federal prisons were first built at the end of the nineteenth century, but they did not become a professionally run system until 1929, when Sanford Bates, a Massachusetts corrections official, was appointed director (he served until 1937). He was charged with reorganizing an institutional system long troubled by political domination, official incompetence, and corruption. He reconstituted the federal correctional system as the Federal Bureau of Prisons in 1930. At that time there were only five federal institutions: three penitentiaries and two reformatories, one for men and one for women. Today there is a federal system of more than 90 institutions responsible for almost 200,000 federal inmates. Although the formidable high-security U.S. Penitentiaries are the best known federal facilities, they house only 11 percent of federal inmates. Most live in low security (38 percent) or medium security (28 percent) federal correctional institutions. Nearly 20 percent are housed in minimum security "camps."[35]

Due to the nature of criminal law, prisoners in federal institutions have different profiles than those in state institutions. Federal prisons house more white-collar offenders. Drug offenders make up the majority of prisoners. Public order offenses, including immigration and weapons offenses, are more common in federal prisons. Increases in drug, immigration, and weapons offenders accounted for almost 90 percent of the federal prison population's increase between 1995 and 2003. Despite the increased public attention, immigration offenders have remained about 10 percent of all federal prisoners since 2000.

State Prison System

At the end of June 2006, there were 1.36 million prisoners under the jurisdiction of state correctional authorities. Approximately half of state prisoners are violent offenders, compared to only one-tenth of federal prisoners. Property and drug offenders each make up one-fifth of the population.

LOCKUPS AND JAILS—CONDITIONS WORSEN

Russian novelist Fyodor Dostoyevski commented that "The degree of civilization in society can be judged by entering its prisons." Anyone observing conditions in many of America's jails and lockups would question just how civilized we really are. At the Erie County Holding Center, the second largest jail in New York State, inmates are jammed in so tight, sometimes 300 men must sleep on the floor. Wherever a mattress can be thrown, an inmate may be sleeping, even next to toilets.[1] Overcrowding conditions similar to those in Erie County have given rise to a number of lawsuits in recent years, from such varied places as Kenton County, Ohio; Onondaga and Broome counties in New York; and Blount County, Tennessee.

An investigative reporter described in hair-raising detail the situation in New York City's police lockups and holding pens:

There are no mattresses, no bedding, no clean clothing, and no showers. The toilets, where there are toilets at all, are open bowls along the walls and often encrusted and overflowing. Meals usually consist of a single slice of baloney and a single slice of American cheese on white bread.

People who have been through the system say it is not easy to forget. Some were threatened by other prisoners. Others were chained to people who were vomiting and stinking of the streets. With few phone privileges, many felt as if they were lost in a hellish labyrinth far from the lives they had been plucked from.[2]

Lockups and holding pens were designed to hold arrested persons for a few hours. They are detention facilities meant to house, not to punish, those accused or convicted of crimes. They are meant to be temporary facilities for persons in transit from one part or stage of the criminal justice system to another. Nowadays, the clients of the criminal justice system are confined there often for at least several days before they are taken to court. Rather than the few hundred persons originally envisaged, thousands are occupying the dingy, dark cells in the basements of police stations and courthouses. There are no national statistics on the flow through the lockups, but it is estimated that only one-third of those who receive this "pretrial punishment" are ultimately sentenced to prison.

The situation is virtually out of control. Officials alerted to the chaos in the lockups and pens have promised to look into the situation, and a consultant has been engaged to suggest solutions to the problem. Meanwhile, inhumane conditions

As with local jails, state prisons vary greatly in their size and conditions.

Size: At the end of June 2006, the two largest state systems, California and Texas, incarcerated 175,115 and 172,889 sentenced prisoners, respectively. This was only slightly less than the entire federal correctional system's 191,080 prisoners. On the other hand, nine states had less than 5,000 prisoners.[36]

Incarceration Rate: At the end of June 2006, the median state incarceration rate was 400 inmates per 100,000 residents. Louisiana more than doubled the median (835), followed by Texas (687), Mississippi (661), and Oklahoma (658). Three states incarcerated individuals at less than half the median rate: Maine (141), Minnesota (189), and Rhode island (195).

Crowding: As discussed in this chapter's boxes, overcrowding has persistently plagued state correctional facilities. Thirty state prison systems exceeded 100 percent of their intended capacity in 2005. California, with a notoriously troubled corrections system and some of the country's strictest sentencing laws, operated at almost double its design capacity (193 percent). Illinois, Alabama, and Hawaii also operated at more than 150 percent capacity.

still exist for thousands trapped underneath New York City's police stations and courthouses.

Things may not be much better in the thousands of lockups and jails across the nation. Most of them are overcrowded, underfunded, unsanitary places that throw together dangerous and nondangerous offenders.[3] In many, there is little accountability. Take, for example, the Baltimore City Jail. When in July 1991 the state of Maryland took control of the jail, state investigators were in for a surprise. They found more than 100 lost inmates—inmates who once were charged with a crime or assigned a court date but who were forgotten, as well as inmates everyone thought had been released but were still imprisoned. The examples are hair-raising:

- A man charged with shoplifting was held for more than 500 days without a trial date.
- A man was held for thirteen months on arson charges without a scheduled court appearance because jailers thought he had been released.
- A man was held five months on traffic charges without a scheduled court date.
- A woman was held for 1,210 days thinking that she was there awaiting trial for theft, when she was actually serving an indefinite term for contempt of court in a child custody case.
- A man whom jail administrators thought was awaiting trial on robbery and assault charges for over two years was actually not in the jail at all; he was living in a mental hospital over twenty miles away.[4]

Given that the number of arrested persons going through the criminal justice system is increasing, it appears that we have a long way to go before lockups and jails are places where people are cared for rather than abandoned.

Questions for Discussion

1. What are the alternatives to putting arrested persons in lockups and jails?

2. Do you think it is possible that the horror of being confined in a lockup or jail, even for a short period of time, might serve as a deterrent to potential offenders?

3. Do you think it is reasonable to take money from schools, welfare, or support for the elderly in order to improve conditions in lockups? Why or why not?

SOURCES
1. Bernie Zolnowski, Jr., "Overcrowding at the Erie County Holding Center: A Third World Gulag in Our Backyard" (ALT/Alternative Press, October 1995).
2. William Glaberson, "Trapped in the Terror of New York's Holding Pens," *The New York Times*, March 23, 1990, pp. A1, B4.
3. Michael T. Charles, Sesha Kethineni, and Jeffrey L. Thompson, "The State of Jails in America," *Federal Probation 56* (1992), pp. 56–62.
4. ArLynn Leiber Presser, "Lost and Found: Baltimore Jail Officials Find Forgotten Inmates," *ABA Journal*, November 1991, p. 42.

Cost per Prisoner: The median cost per prisoner in 2001 was just under $23,000. Alabama had a shockingly low outlay per prisoner of $8,128, followed by Mississippi ($12,795), Missouri ($12,867), and Louisiana ($12,951).

Penal Institutions for Women

Female convicts have traditionally been a small, overlooked minority. Until the early nineteenth century, they were often housed with male prisoners in institutions designed for male prisoners. New York established the first penal facility for women in 1835, opening Mount Pleasant Female Prison as an administrative attachment to Sing Sing, a prison for men. Other states followed suit during the great era of prison construction in the late 1900s.

During the twentieth century, women inmates were incarcerated in designated women's prisons. These institutions tended to be smaller and less threatening in appearance and operation than male prisons (for example, there were no high walls or guard towers). Yet, being smaller, they lacked many programs and amenities of their male counterparts. Female prisoner lawsuits have challenged these inequitable conditions, but federal courts have regularly ruled that women prisoners do not have constitutional claims to equal treatment.[37]

In Their Own Words

P. F. McMANIMON, JR., WARDEN (RETIRED), MERCER COUNTY DETENTION CENTER

7:00 A.M. I place a call to the shift commander . . . "What's the count this morning, Lieutenant?"

"We have 561 in-house, one at the hospital, and twenty-one in the bullpen from last night. We expect another eight from Trenton, and there are five discharges planned for today. Total will be 585, with one in the hospital. (The jail was built for 196 inmates.) "What's your pleasure, Warden?"

"Call the other municipalities and find out what they have waiting. I'll be in at 8:00 A.M. and we'll get together in my office with the record office personnel and figure out where to send these people."

It's now 7:04 A.M. The process of management starts with where we are going to house these inmates. Before a shower, breakfast, or a glimpse at the newspaper, the day begins with a major problem that is typical of the daily operation of the detention center.

7:45 A.M. I arrive at the jail, to find the internal affairs investigator waiting for me in the parking lot. He advises me that there was a fight on the medium security unit involving two rival street gangs.

7:50 A.M. I get the reports from yesterday and begin to review the events. There were four fights on the evening shift the night before and all isolation cells are occupied with the combatants from those incidents. The midnight shift had to call in additional overtime to increase the staffing levels as a result of the fights and also had to guard an inmate at the hospital. He was admitted for a possible heart attack. Also, the midnight shift admitted twelve inmates from a drug raid, which explains the high number of inmates awaiting placement on a living unit.

8:05 A.M. The shift commander advises that there are five additional persons awaiting transfer from other municipalities, and the Correctional Center (the other county facility) can only take ten inmates. We are left with nineteen inmates that must be housed. The records personnel advise that we have thirty-one inmates that can be transferred to the Department of Corrections, but when a call was placed to DOC, they stated that they could not take inmates today.

8:45 A.M. I called the criminal case manager for the Superior Court, and requested some expedited bail reviews for inmates whose bail was set at $500 or lower.

9:30 A.M. I began to conduct disciplinary hearings for staff misconduct. The charges range from abuse of sick leave to insubordination.

11:30 A.M. Internal affairs reports that there are rumors of at least ten large shanks on the unit, and the

Inferior medical care is particularly problematic because incarcerated women tend to need more medical services than men. More women than men report medical problems at admittance.[38] They have a significantly higher incidence of HIV (7.9 versus 3.9 percent in the Northeast).[39] Female inmates have an incidence of cancer almost 8 times greater than men (831 per 10,000 inmates, compared to 108 per 10,000 inmates).[40] A higher proportion of women have a history of substance abuse and dependence (60 percent, compared to 53 percent), despite the comparatively fewer treatment resources women's facilities offer.[41] Female inmates also suffer from mental health problems to a greater degree than men (73 percent versus 55 percent in state prisons).[42] More than half have experienced past physical or sexual abuse.[43]

Unfortunately, sexual abuse also occurs within prison walls. The sexual exploitation of female inmates by male corrections officers ranges from verbal harassment to forcible rape. It is difficult to estimate the prevalence of sexual misconduct because many women, embarrassed and fearful of retaliation, keep quiet, but anecdotal evidence suggests it is a pervasive problem. A successful class-action lawsuit by the District of Columbia's women prisoners in 1993 exposed a system of widespread harassment and sexual assault, whose complaining victims faced retaliation and indifference.[44] Michigan settled similar lawsuits filed by female

suming process. Luckily the inmates are not combative and the search moves along without a problem.

3:30 P.M. The court has ROR'd 10 inmates and this enables all inmates to have a cell for sleeping purposes. There are six spaces available.

inmate informants state that participants of the fights were trying to get to the weapons, but that the staff reaction to the incident prevented their use. The unit is locked down since the incident this morning and remains in that status. I call the shift commander and the captain in to discuss the plan of action we should take given the information developed by internal affairs. All parties agree that the unit must be searched and, because of the danger to staff, the Emergency Response Team should be activated. I authorize the activation of the team, and advise the public safety director of the situation. He informs me that the Department of Corrections will accept fifteen inmates from the detention center, but the jail will have to transport the inmates to reception. I advise the shift commander to begin the process of transfer to the state. Only four more inmates need housing.

12:45 P.M. A code 6 is called. A code 6 indicates that an officer is in need of help. The location is the maximum security unit. All parties respond to the area, where two inmates in a blind area of the unit have attacked an officer. The officer is bleeding from his head and lip and the two inmates are in handcuffs and are being escorted to the already-full isolation area when I arrive.

2:00 P.M. The Emergency Response Team began a cell-to-cell search on the medium security unit, looking for the weapons used in the morning gang assault. The team is divided into six three-man squads, alternating between searching the cells and controlling the inmates during the cell search. This is a time-con-

4:10 P.M. Internal affairs radios for me to report to the medium security unit. Upon arrival, there are ten homemade knives in the control booth.

6:20 P.M. The Emergency Response Team completes the search of the medium security unit. They find an additional five shanks.

7:00 P.M. I attend a Board of Freeholders Meeting (the legislative branch of county government in New Jersey). The topic of the meeting, a special session, is to discuss the closing of the detention center, because of physical plant problems that require $43 million to repair.

8:08 P.M. I receive a page from the detention center. I call the facility, and the shift commander advises that an inmate committed suicide. I immediately report to the jail to find the inmate lying dead on the floor.

9:22 P.M. All initial reports were completed and the coroner removed the body to the morgue for an autopsy the next day.

10:15 P.M. I finally returned home. I am haunted by the suicide, as I never understood what would bring a young person to such depths of hopelessness. I have experienced four suicides over my twenty-five-year career. I have never forgotten their names, their faces, and the anguish of the families who are left behind to deal with this act.

inmates and the U.S. Department of Justice's Civil Rights Division in 1999 and 2000. But the effectiveness of court remedies appears to be limited. Subsequent lawsuits in D.C. reveal the entrenched nature of sexual exploitation in women's penal institutions.[45] The protections Michigan promised in 2000 have been only partially implemented, and reports of sexual abuse have increased.[46]

Addressing these problems becomes both more important and more difficult as the number of female prisoners rapidly increases. In June 2006, 111,403 women were incarcerated in state or federal prison and 70,414 in local jails, a respective 62 percent and 35 percent increase from 1995, and more than 4 times the number of women incarcerated in 1985. Women now make up 13 percent of jail inmates and 7.2 percent of state and federal prisoners.[47] Most are drug or property offenders; their growing presence is partly due to the increase in mandatory sentencing rules.

Co-correctional Facilities

It seemed like a step backward when, in 1971, the Federal Correctional Institute (Fort Worth, Texas) became the first co-correctional institution. But in this institution men and women were not haphazardly thrown together; a structured program had been worked out.

Men and women, segregated at night, participated in joint daytime programs of work, education, recreation, and meals. Infraction of the rules led to transfer to a separate institution. Observers have credited co-correctional institutions with creating an atmosphere more like the one to which the inmates will return upon release. Yet, most of the state co-correctional institutions have now been closed. Both custodial and treatment staff have experienced difficulty creating and administering rules. Ensuring reasonable restraints on physical contacts has been a consistent problem. Notwithstanding the problems, the federal prison system continues to play a leading role in operating co-correctional institutions. Most women inmates in the federal system serve their sentences in such facilities.[48] Yet, co-correctional facilities offer women few, if any, economic, educational, vocational, or social advantages.[49]

The Size and Cost of the Corrections Enterprise

When politicians and citizens call for longer prison sentences to control the "crime epidemic," they rarely consider the resulting burden on the taxpayer. The American correctional system is an incredibly costly enterprise. "Tough on crime" rhetoric comes and goes, but it can leave lasting impacts on the overcrowded prison system and creates long-term financial obligations for government budgets.

The Size of the System

America's correctional system is a vast enterprise, in terms of the number of people it processes and services; the number of employees required for inmate care, custody, and control; the cost of outside contracting required to maintain and constantly enlarge facilities; and the burden to the taxpayer.

The Incarcerated Population.   The number of people incarcerated in America has steadily increased. Over a century ago, in 1880, the imprisonment rate was 61 per 100,000 citizens.[50] Today, about 750 persons per 100,000 citizens are incarcerated at any moment (see table above), and almost three times that number have previously been incarcerated.[51]

From 1995 to 2005, the prison population grew most rapidly in the West (42 percent). The Midwest grew 32 percent. The South, which has the highest incarceration rate of all regions, grew 30.5 percent. The Northeast, including two states who decreased their prison populations (New York and Massachusetts), grew only 5 percent.

The Nonincarcerated Population   The majority of offenders in the corrections system are sentenced to noninstitutional or community corrections, rather than prison (see Tables 12.3 and 12.4). At the end of 2005, there were more than 4.1 million people on

TABLE 12.3
State and Federal Prisoners Held in Local Jails, by Jurisdiction, Year End 2000 to 2005

Number of State and Federal Inmates Held in Local Jails			
	Total	State	Federal	Percent of All Inmates
2005	73,097	72,053	1,044	4.8%
2004	74,445	73,246	1,199	5.0
2003	73,440	70,162	3,278	5.0
2002	72,550	69,173	3,377	5.0
2001	70,681	67,760	2,921	5.0
2000	63,140	60,702	2,438	4.5

SOURCE: Paige M. Harrison and Allen J. Beck, *Prisoners in 2005* (Bureau of Justice Statistics: Washington, DC, 2006), p. 6.

Year	Total Inmates in Custody	Prisoners in Federal Custody	Prisoners in State Custody	Inmates in Local Jails	Incarceration Rate	Total Estimate Correctional Population	Probation	Parole
1990	1,148,702	58,838	684,544	405,320	458	4,350,343	2,670,234	531,407
1995	1,585,596	99,538	989,004	507,044	601	5,342,878	3,077,861	679,421
2000	1,937,482	133,921	1,176,269	621,149	684	6,487,589	3,826,209	723,898
2001	1,961,247	143,337	190,155	631,240	685	6,625,311	3,931,731	732,333
2002	2,033,022	151,618	1,209,331	665,475	701	6,808,023	4,024,067	750,934
2003	2,081,590	161,673	122,135	691,301	712	6,971,527	4,120,012	769,925
2004	2,135,335	170,535	1,243,745	713,990	723	7,050,653	4,143,466	771,852
2005	2,193,798	179,220	1,259,905	747,529	737	7,140,742	4,162,536	784,408
2006	2,245,189	181,622	1,290,200	766,010	750	n/a	n/a	n/a
Average annual change		12/31/95–6/30/06					6/30/95–6/30/05	
	3.4%	7.0%	2.6%	3.8%		2.90%	3.10%	1.40%

SOURCE: Sourcebook of Criminal Justice Statistics, 2002, table 6. 1. 2005.

TABLE 12.4 Correctional Population, 1990–2006

probation and almost a quarter million on parole, constituting about 70 percent of the total correctional population.[52]

Incarceration Rates Worldwide. In 1991, *New York Times* columnist Tom Wicker bestowed the "Iron Medal" on the United States, for being the world's leader in rates of imprisonment.[53] The United States has consistently led the pack (750 per 100,000), with Russia in second place (611), followed by Belize (487) and Belarus (426). The substantially smaller incarceration rates of our neighbors and allies arouse questions as to why the United States incarcerates such a relatively large number of its residents. The incarceration rates of Canada (107), the United Kingdom (146), Germany (95), and Japan (62) are less than 20 percent of the U.S. rate.

These comparisons may make the United States look bad. But if we were to base comparative prison rates not on population (per capita), but rather on the volume of crime (measured by arrest rates), we may not deserve the "Iron Medal" after all, for then our imprisonment rate is more or less on a par with those of the comparable Western countries like Canada and England (see Table 12.5).

The Cost of the System

The correctional system requires nearly one-third of all the resources allocated to the criminal justice system, in terms of employment[54] and expenditures.[55] Annually, it costs over $64 billion to operate the correctional systems of the fifty states, the District of Columbia, and the federal government.[56] This is a very large public expenditure. But keep in mind that this sum amounts to only 1 percent of all government spending, and is dwarfed by spending for other criminal justice systems. (see Table 12.6).

Costs per Prisoner. While there is considerable variation among the states, on average prison officials report that it costs about $20,000 per year to house, feed, clothe, and supervise a prisoner.[57] Because this estimate does not include indirect costs, the real annual expenditure probably exceeds $30,000 per prisoner. The other significant cost is construction. We divide the total construction cost of any one institution by the number of prisoners it houses to get the cost per "bed." This cost is on average as low as $31,000 per year for a minimum security prisoner to as high as $80,000 for a maximum

TABLE 12.5
World Prison Population and
Rates, 2005

	Africa	
	Prison Population Total (No. in Penal Institutions Incl. Pretrial Detainees)	**Prison Population Rate (per 100,000 of National Population)**
Northern Africa		
Algeria	38,868	121
Egypt	c.80,000	c.121
Libya	11,790	207
Morocco	54,200	174
Sudan	c.12,000	c.36
Tunisia	23,165	252
Western Africa		
Benin	4,961	81
Burkina Faso	2,800	23
Cape Verde	755	178
Cote d'Ivoire	10,355	62
Gambia	450	32
Ghana	11,379	54
Guinea (Conakry)	3,070	37
Mali	4,040	34
Mauritania	1,185	41
Niger	c.6,000	c.52
Nigeria	39,153	31
Senegal	5,360	54
Togo	3,200	65
Central Africa		
Angola	6,008	44
Cameroon	20,000	125
Central African Rep.	4,168	110
Chad	3,883	46
Congo (Brazzaville)	918	38
Dem. Repub. Congo	c.30,000	c.57
Sao Tome e Principe	130	79
Eastern Africa		
Burundi	7,914	116
Comoros	c.200	c.30
Djibouti	384	61
Ethiopia	c.65,000	c.92
Kenya	55,000	169
Madagascar	c.19,000	c.109
Malawi	8,566	70
Mauritius	2,565	214
Mazambique	8,812	50
Rwanda	112,000[*]	–[*]
	[*](Prison population total includes 103,134 held on suspicion of participation in genocide.)	
Seychelles	149	186
Tanzania	43,244	116

(continued)

TABLE 12.5
(*Continued*)

	Africa	
	Prison Population Total (No. in Penal Institutions Incl. Pretrial Detainees)	Prison Population Rate (per 100,000 of National Population)
Uganda	c.21,900	c.89
Zambia	13,200	122
Zimbabwe	c.20,000	c.155
Mayotte (France)	161	85
Réunion (France)	1,054	137
Southern Africa		
Botswana	6,105	339
Lesotho	3,000	143
Nemibia	4,814	267
South Africa	186,739	413
Swaziland	3,245	324

Figures not available **Western Africa:** Guinea Bissau, Liberia, Sierra Leone.
Central Africa: Equatarial Guinea, Gabon.
Eastern Africa: Eritrea, Somalia.

	Americas	
North America		
Canada	36,389*	116
	*Average daily population, including young offenders, 1/4/2002-31/3/2003)	
USA	2,085,620	714
Bermuda (UK)	343	532
Greenland (Denmark)	107	190
Central America		
Belize	1,074	420
Costa Rica	7,619	177
El Salvador	12,117	184
Guatemala	8,307	68
Honduras	11,236	158
Mexico	191,890	182
Nicaragua	5,610	100
Panama	10,630	354
Caribbean		
Antigua & Barbuda	184	269
Bahamas	1,280	410
Barbados	992	367
Cuba	c.55,000	c.487
Dominica	243	337
Dominican Republic	13,836	157
Grenada	237	265
Haiti	3,519	42
Jamaica	4,744	176
St Kitts & Nevis	195	415
St Lucia	460	287

(*continued*)

TABLE 12.5
(*Continued*)

	Americas	
	Prison Population Total (No. in Penal Institutions Incl. Pretrial Detainees)	Prison Population Rate (per 100,000 of National Population)
St Vincent & Grenadines	397	339
Trinidad & Tobago	3,991	307
Aruba (Netherlands)	231	324
Cayman Islands (UK)	187	429
Guadeloupe (France)	767	173
Martinique (France)	671	169
Neth. Antilles (Netherlands)	780	364
Puerto Rico (US)	15,046	386
Virgin Islands (UK)	43	215
Virgin Islands (US)	559	490
South America		
Argentina	56,313	148
Bolivia	6,768	76
Brazil	330,642	183
Chile	33,098	212
Colombia	68,545	152
Ecuador	13,045	100
Guyana	1,295	169
Paraguay	4,088	75
Peru	32,129	114
Suriname	1,933	437
Uruguay	7,100	209
Venezuela	21,342	83
French Guiana/ Guyane (France)	691	358
	Asia	
Western Asia		
Bahrain	911	155
Iraq	c.15,000	c.60
Israel	13,603	209
Jordan	5,448	106
Kuwait	c.3,700	c.148
Lebanon	5,375	145
Oman	2,020	81
Qatar	570	95
Saudi Arabia	23,720	110
Syria	14,000	93
United Arab Emirates	c.6,000	c.250
Yemen	14,000[*]	83[*]
	*(government managed prisons only)	
Central Asia		
Kazakhstan	58,300	386
Kyrgyzstan	19,500	390
	(*continued*)	

TABLE 12.5
(*Continued*)

	Asia	
	Prison Population Total (No. in Penal Institutions Incl. Pretrial Detainees)	**Prison Population Rate** (per 100,000 of National Population)
Tajikistan	c.10,000	c.159
Turkmenistan	c.22,000	c.489
Uzbekistan	48,000	184
South Central Asia		
Bangladesh	74,170	50
India	313,635	29
Iran	133,658	194
Maldive Is.	1,098*	414*
		*(sentenced prisoners only)
Nepal	7,132	29
Pakistan	86,000	55
Sri Lanka	20,975	110
South Eastern Asia		
Brunei Darussalam	463	127
Cambodia	6,778	47
Indonesia	84,357	38
Malaysia	43,424	174
Myanmar (Burma)	c.60,000	c.120
Philippines	70,383	94
Singapore	16,835*	392*
		*(does not include those in drug rehabilitation centres run by the Singapore Prison Service)
Thailand	168,264	264
Timor-Leste	c.320	41
Vietnam	55,000	71
Eastern Asia		
China	1,548,498*	118*
		*(sentenced prisoners only)
Japan	73,734	58
Korea (Republic of)	57,902	121
Mongolia	6,400	246
Taiwan	57,037	251
Hong Kong (China)	13,226	189
Macau (China)	875	197

Figures not available **South Central Asia:** Afghanistan, Bhutan.

South Eastern Asia: Laos.

Eastern Asia: Korea (Democratic People's Republic of North Korea).

	Europe	
Northern Europe		
Denmark	3,774	70
Estonia	4,571	339
Finland	3,719	71

(*continued*)

TABLE 12.5
(*Continued*)

	Europe	
	Prison Population Total (No. in Penal Institutions Incl. Pretrial Detainees)	Prison Population Rate (per 100,000 of National Population)
Iceland	115	39
Ireland	3,417	85
Latvia	7,796	337
Lithuania	8,063	234
Norway	2,975	65
Sweden	6,755	75
United Kingdom		
–England & Wales	75,320	142
–Northern Ireland	1,275	72
–Scotland	6,742	132
Faeroe Is. (Denmark)	14	30
Guernsey (UK)	107	164
Isle of Man (UK)	62	83
Jersey (UK)	168	185
Southern Europe		
Albania	3,778	105
Andorra	61	90
Bosnia & Herzegovina		
–Federation	1,509	58
–Republika Srpska	1,052	75
Croatia	3,010	68
Greece	8,760	82
Italy*	57,046	98

*(by agreement with Italy, persons imprisoned by San Marino and Vatican City are held in Italian prisons.)

Macedonia (F Yug Rep)	1,598	78
Malta	278	72
Portugal	13,498	128
Serbia & Montenegro		
–Serbia	7,487	92
–Montenegro	734	108
–Kosovo	1,182	62
Slovenia	1,129	56
Spain	59,899	140
Gibraltar (UK)	19	68
Western Europe		
Austria	8,700	106
Belgium	9,245	88
France	55,028*	91

*(metropolitan France, excluding departments and territories in Africa, the Americas and Oceania)

(*continued*)

TABLE 12.5
(*Continued*)

	Europe	
	Prison Population Total (No. in Penal Institutions Incl. Pretrial Detainees)	Prison Population Rate (per 100,000 of National Population)
Germany	79,329	96
Liechtenstein*	18	53

*(by agreement with Austria, some persons imprisoned by Liechtenstein are held in Austrian prisons.)

Luxembourg	655	144
Monaco*	13	39

*(by agreement with France, some persons imprisoned by Monaco are held in French prisons.)

Netherlands	19,999	123
Switzerland	6,021	81
Europe/Asia		
Armenia	2,866	92
Azerbaijan	16,345	198
Cyprus	355*	50

*(does not include the internationally unrecognised Turkish Republic of Northern Cyprus (TRNC). Including TRNC the population of Cyprus is estimated at about 809,000 in 2003, plus about 100,000 Turkish settlers.)

Georgia	7,091	165
Russian Federation	763,054	532
Turkey	67,772	95
Central and Eastern Europe		
Belarus	52,500	532
Bulgaria	11,060	143
Czech Republic	18,830	184
Hungary	16,700	165
Moldova	10,729*	297

*(does not Include the internationally unrecognised Transdniestria. Including Transdniestria the national population of Moldova is estimated at 4.3 millions.)

Poland	79,087	209
Romania	39,015	180
Slovakia	8,891	165
Ukraine	198,388	416

	Oceania	
Australia	23,362	117
Fiji	1,083	128
Kiribati	81	80
Marshall Is.	23	44
Micronesia, Fed States of	39	34
Nauru	6	48
New Zealand	6,802	168

(*continued*)

TABLE 12.5
(*Continued*)

	Oceania	
	Prison Population Total **(No. in Penal Institutions** **Incl. Pretrial Detainees)**	**Prison Population Rate** **(per 100,000 of** **National Population)**
Palau	103	523
Papua New Guinea	3,302	66
Samoa	281	158
Solomon Is.	275	56
Tonga	116	105
Tuvalu	6	56
Vanuatu	93	44
American Samoa (US)	174	301
Cook Is. (NZ)	19	90
French Polynesia (France)	327	131
Guam (US)	579	353
New Caledonia (France)	286	122
Northern Mariana Is. (US)	136	173

NOTE: Footnotes have been removed.
For exact figures, see source.
SOURCE: Roy Walmsley, *World Prison Population List*, 6th ed. (London: Home Office, 2005), pp. 2–6.

Large corrections conglomerates around the United States grew significantly through the mid-1990s, both in the number of prisons they operated and in their profits.

security prisoner.[58] (The comparable cost fifty years ago was between $4,000 and $6,000.) Of course, the annual cost of incarcerating just one offender varies from state to state.

Impact on State Budgets.　The enormous cost of imprisonment is just beginning to be felt by the states. For example, Florida recently completed the construction of a 336-person death row and two 900-inmate prisons—yet it has no operating budget to run these facilities.[59] In California, a $300 million state deficit, caused in part by uncontrolled rising costs of the prison system, resulted in a cutback in funds for public education and medical services for the poor. Budgetary battles have begun in which important state services for children, the elderly, the sick, and the poor are being cut back to pay for prisons.[60] While it may be too early to discern any particular trends, it is notable that in some states new political alliances have been formed between liberal and conservative legislators. Liberal legislators, in general, support humane correctional policies and have been less punitive. Conservative legislators, on the whole, have supported more punitive imprisonment policies. Yet with the enormous budget increases required for new prison construction and prisoner maintenance, some conservative legislators, ever intent on cutting costs, have joined their liberal colleagues in opposing new prison construction.

Privatization of Corrections

Frustration over high rates of recidivism and spiraling prison maintenance costs has prompted policymakers to search for alternatives to government-operated prisons. One such alternative is to contract with private firms that administer "for profit" prisons.[61]

Expenditure (in millions)	Federal				State				Local			
	Total	Police Protection	Judicial and Legal	Corrections	Total	Police Protection	Judicial and Legal	Corrections	Total	Police Protection	Judicial and Legal	Corrections
1982	$4,458	$2,527	$1,390	$541	$11,602	$2,833	$2,748	$6,020	$20,968	$14,172	$3,784	$3,011
1987	7,496	4,231	2,271	994	20,157	4,067	4,339	11,691	33,265	21,089	6,230	5,947
1992	17,423	7,400	7,377	2,646	33,755	5,593	7,723	20,439	50,115	29,659	10,052	10,404
1997	27,065	12,518	10,651	3,896	46,444	7,501	9,903	29,141	67,083	40,976	13,101	13,007
2000	27,820	13,999	9,353	4,467	58,165	9,787	13,249	35,129	78,995	48,219	14,842	15,934
2001	30,443	15,014	10,290	5,199	63,372	10,497	14,444	38,432	83,377	50,718	15,938	16,721
2002	34,346	17,626	11,013	5,707	65,508	11,081	15,365	39,062	90,485	55,086	17,042	18,358
2003	35,323	20,422	9,356	5,545	66,114	11,144	15,782	39,197	93,877	57,503	17,718	18,658
Percent change												
1982–2003	692.4%	702.2%	579.1%	925.0%	469.9%	293.4%	474.3%	550.9%	347.7%	305.8%	389.2%	519.6%
Average annual percent change, 1992–2002	9.9%	10.0%	9.1%	11.2%	8.2%	6.4%	8.3%	8.9%	7.1%	6.6%	7.3%	8.6%

NOTE: Detail may not add to total because of rounding.
SOURCE: Kristen Hughes, "Justice Expenditures and Employment in the United States, 2003," Bureau of Justice Statistics Bulletin, April 2006, NCJ.

TABLE 12.6 Total Expenditure of Federal, State, and Local Governments for Each Justice Function, and Percent Change, Fiscal Years 1982–2003

PRISON VIOLENCE—PROTECTION IN A DANGEROUS ENVIRONMENT

When a battle erupted in an exercise yard at Arizona State Prison,

—one inmate was stabbed to death and two others were critically injured before guards brought the melee under control.

About 200 of the unit's 598 inmates reportedly were involved in the disturbance.

—[T]he melee began after a black inmate was stabbed outside the Ira Hayes Dormitory. The fighting escalated when whites on one side of an exercise yard charged a group of blacks on the other side.

Corrections Director Sam Lewis arrived at the prison during the morning … but Lewis is leaving it up to leaders of race-based prison gangs to stop the bloodshed.

Officials said the fighting Friday was in retaliation for the death of Paul Engle, twenty-six, of Phoenix, whose throat was slashed Thursday. Engle was a member of the Aryan Brotherhood, a white supremacist prison gang.[1]

Since they began tracing membership in 1993, jail officials have identified 1,200 members of the Ñetas and the Latin Kings in New York City jails. Gang members show their affiliation by wearing black and gold beads for Latin Kings; and white, red, and black for the Ñetas. They use hand signals to communicate—a tactic that allows them to defy corrections officers. There were 60 stabbings with homemade knives in one year among inmates in the 450-bed high-security unit at Rikers Island.[2]

Over the past thirty years prison gangs have evolved from small groups of inmates associated for mutual protection into self-perpetuating criminal gangs with the characteristics of organized crime syndicates. The first prison gang, the Gypsy Jokers, started at Washington State Penitentiary, Walla Walla, in 1950. In the 1960s, racial turmoil in American society spilled into the prisons, sometimes resulting in inmate race wars. Gangs provided protection for their members. At California's San Quentin, for example, there were the Aryan Brotherhood, supposedly created to protect white inmates; the Black Guerrilla Family, a militant gang associated with the Black Panther Party; the Mexican Mafia, with members from East Los Angeles; and their bitter rivals, the Nuestra Familia, consisting of rural Chicanos. Gangs appeared in Illinois in the late 1960s, and by the 1970s and 1980s prison gangs had spread throughout the country. A recent report indicates that there are prison gangs in the federal system and in thirty-two state jurisdictions.[3] Most gang members are in Illinois (5,300), Pennsylvania (2,400), and California (2,050).

Gangs typically are organized in paramilitary fashion. The Texas Syndicate, for example, has an elected president and vice president, along with unit chairmen, vice chairmen, captains, lieutenants, sergeants at arms, and soldiers. Many gang officials are elected, usually on the basis of their criminal record working for the gang. Prison gangs have codes of conduct ("once a member, always a member," for

This is a rather revolutionary concept if you consider that, since the Middle Ages, the punishment of offenders has been viewed as the sole prerogative of the sovereign, or the people, whose laws the offender has violated. In modern times the sovereign (the state) exercises this prerogative through the correctional system (the executive branch of government). Can the sovereign (the state) delegate any of its functions to private enterprise? The state can let private entrepreneurs sell postage stamps and deliver mail. It can, and does, let private security firms perform functions that heretofore were the prerogative of the government police force—always subject to a certain amount of control or supervision by government.[62] And now privatization has entered corrections.[63]

At this point, the private sector is performing a series of functions in the correctional sector:

• Financing and constructing prisons.
• Operating facilities for juveniles.
• Operating facilities for adults.
• Providing work for prisoners.
• Providing specific contractual services to prisons, for example health care and vocational education for the inmates and training for the staff.[64]

more and more street gang members wind up in prison. For example, the Bloods and Crips, two well-publicized Los Angeles–based street gangs, will eventually add many from their ranks to the prison gang population—and to the wars with other dominant prison gangs.

example), and the penalty for violating rules may well be death. Organized along racial and ethnic lines, gangs serve many purposes. They protect members in a dangerous environment. They provide goods and services. They give psychological support.

Members stay in the gang when they get back to their neighborhoods—and they continue a liaison with gang members inside the walls. Some gangs even require released inmates to work for them by expanding illegal enterprises and sharing the profits. Youngsters on the street offer their services in return for a place in the prison gang at some point in their lives.

It is estimated that the United States now has about 13,000 prison gang members. While they account for a small proportion of all inmates, they create over half the problems. Among the many problems prison gangs present for prison officials are violence, drug trafficking, gang wars, contract murders, rapes, co-opting of guards, confrontation between gang members and nonmembers, and the difficulties in gaining information about secret activities. Gang-related problems may increase as

Questions for Discussion

1. What concrete steps could a prison administration take to prevent gang-related violence?
2. Why would an inmate who was never before involved in a gang decide to join one in prison?
3. How do gangs serve some sort of useful purpose in prisons?

SOURCES
1. "Arizona Prison Racial Conflicts Leave Two Dead," Associated Press, Los Angeles Times, October 25, 1986, p. 2.
2. Mireya Navarro, "The Inmate Gangs of Rikers Island," The New York Times, May 8, 1994, pp. 29, 36.
3. George M. Camp and Camille Graham Camp, Prison Gangs, U.S. Department of Justice (South Salem, NY: Criminal Justice Institute, 1985).

The first private "for profit" prison was established in 1975 when RCA, under contract with the Commonwealth of Pennsylvania, opened a training school for delinquents in Weaversville. When James O. Finckenauer evaluated this facility, he found it "better staffed, organized, and equipped than any other program of its size."[65] In 2003, approximately 93,000 adults were incarcerated in over 140 privately run prisons. Private juvenile facilities were in operation in 18 states.[66]

Effectiveness of Privatization

A report prepared for the National Institute of Justice, based on a survey of private-sector corrections in all states, is optimistic about the future of private prisons. It was found that idleness is reduced, prison administration has access to private-sector economic expertise, the prison environment is improved, prisoners may earn real wages and obtain vocational training useful after their release, taxpayers benefit because the wages of prisoners help offset the cost of incarceration, and victims have a better chance of obtaining compensation from prisoners' earnings.[67] A study of privatization that explored how inmates perceived the effectiveness of one private institution in Tennessee found that, by and large, prisoners do not care who runs the institution. Their paramount interest is in the quality of conditions and decent treatment of prisoners.[68]

Trends in Privatization

In recent years there has been a growth in correctional contracting to private agencies. A study for the National Institute of Corrections that included responses from fifty-two agencies, representing fifty-four jurisdictions, found twenty-nine juvenile and thirty-seven adult agencies purchasing thirty-three types of services and/or programs from the private sector. The management of prisons was not in the top ten most frequently used services or programs. Rather, human services were ranked first among those most frequently purchased from private sources, including physicians, health care, mental health care, community treatment centers, education, drug treatment, college programs, staff training, vocational training, and counseling. Construction of correctional facilities ranked number five for private contracting. Most highly rated for private sector growth in the future are food services, canteen and commissary, vocational training, drug treatment, health services, and recreational therapy.[69]

The move toward privatization of corrections raises some troubling questions that to date have not been entirely resolved.[70] Experts agree that the most disturbing and basic question is whether the sovereign right of the people, as represented by their government, to punish those found guilty of violating laws should ever be transferred to private hands. The question is whether the authority to deprive others of their liberty and to coerce them ought to be delegated to nongovernmental entities, not whether such persons or groups ought to profit financially from their services. Thus, in the unlikely event that private prison firms were to offer their services free, the ethical case against privatization would not be affected in the least.[71]

Other troubling questions include:[72]

- What standards will govern the operation of the institution?
- Who will monitor the implementation of the standards?
- Will the public have access to the facility?
- Who will be responsible for maintaining security if the private personnel go on strike?
- Where will the responsibility for prison disciplinary procedures lie?
- Will the company be able to refuse servicing certain inmates, such as those who have contracted AIDS?
- What options will be available to the government if the corporation substantially increases its fees?
- What will happen if the company declares bankruptcy or simply goes out of business because there is not enough profit?

The general reluctance to accept the concept of private correctional institutions may perhaps be offset by a reminder that American corrections, institutional and noninstitutional, owe their origin largely to private entrepreneurship, private concern for convicts, and community action in caring for convicted offenders.

Review

Institutional corrections is only 450 years old. It was meant to be a humane alternative to the brutal punishments of old. The first institutions were the houses of correction (workhouses) of Holland, England, and Pennsylvania. But it was soon apparent that houses of correction did not correct. Penitentiaries were invented, but it was clear that these did not produce penitence. Reformatories replaced penitentiaries, but reformatories did not reform. Nor did the medical-therapeutic model prove to be a cure for the crime problem. Thus, in the 1970s punishment returned to the classic form of being a just dessert—retribution.

The bright light in the history of American corrections is the extension of due process guarantees to inmates by the Supreme Court, a result of the prisoners' rights movement.

American corrections today is a vast enterprise. One in every 155 Americans is incarcerated on any given day, and 1 in 51 adult residents is under some form of correctional control. No other country has a system of this scope and size. The staggering cost of maintaining such a pervasive apparatus has put pressure on political leaders to search for more cost-beneficial ways of dealing with the corrections problem.

Thinking Critically about Criminal Justice

1. What are some reasons for the extremely high incarceration rate in the United States?

2. Has the Supreme Court gone too far in protecting the rights of prisoners, or not far enough?

3. What do you think accounts for the rapid increase in the female prison population over the last decade?

Internet Connection

Note: While all of the URLs listed were current as of the printing of this book, these sites often change. Please check our website (http://www. mhhe.com/socscience/crimjustice/adlercj) for updates.

Amnesty International is an organization that monitors apparent violations of human rights around the world. Read the section on the United States in Amnesty International's report (http://www.amnesty.org). What are the corrections-related incidents that concern Amnesty International? Did any of these incidents violate the constitutional rights of inmates?

What patterns do you see in global incarceration rates? See **http://www.homeoffice.gov.uk/rds/pdfs2/r188.pdf** (Roy Walmsley, *World Prison Population List,* 4th ed. [London: Home Office, 2003]).

Notes

1. John Lothrop Motley, *Rise of the Dutch Republic III* (NY: Harpers, 1880), pp. 612–613. See also Harry Elmer Barnes and Negley K. Teeters, *New Horizons in Criminology,* 2nd ed. (Englewood Cliffs, NJ: Prentice Hall, 1951), p. 344.

2. Don Terry, "Prisons as Usual," *The New York Times,* September 13, 1992, Section A, p. 1.

3. Rex A. Skidmore, "Penological Pioneering in the Walnut Street Jail, 1789–1799," *Journal of Criminal Law and Criminology,* 39:2 (July–August 1948), pp. 167–180.

4. U.R.Q. Henriques, "The Rise and Decline of the Separate System of Prison Discipline," *Past and Present,* No 54 (February 1972), pp. 61–93.

5. Chase Riveland, "Prison Management Trends, 1975–2025," *Crime and Justice,* Vol. 26 (1999), pp. 163–203.

6. Christopher Adamson, "Punishment after Slavery: Southern State Penal Systems, 1865–1890," *Social Problems,* 30:5 (June 1983), pp. 555–569.

7. Henry Theodore Jackson, "Prison Labor," *Journal of the American Institute of Criminal Law and Criminology,* Vol. 18 (1927–1928), 218, 230–235.

8. Stephen P. Garvey, "Freeing Prisoners' Labor," *Stanford Law Review,* Vol 50 pp. 339, 367–369.

9. J. Michael Oliverio and James B. Roberts, "The United States Federal Penitentiary at Marion, Illinois: Alcatraz Revisited," *New England Journal on Criminal and Civil Confinement* 16 (1990), pp. 21–51.

10. 194 F.2d 32 (8th Cir. 1952) at 34.

11. Austin H. MacCormick, "Behind the Prison Riots," *Annals of the American Academy of Political and Social Science* 293 (May 1954), p. 17.

12. Associated Press, "1,000 Riot 2 Hours in Baltimore Prison," *New York Times* (July 9, 1966), p. 9.

13. William Wilbanks, "Report of the Commission on Attica," *Federal Probation* 37 (1973), pp. 3–7.

14. Chase Riveland, "Prison Management Trends, 1975–2025," *Crime and Justice,* Vol. 28 (1999), pp. 163–203. Adapted from Douglas J. Besharov and Gerhard O. W. Mueller, "The Demands of the Inmates of Attica State Prison and the United Nations Standard Minimum Rules for the Treatment of Prisoners: A Comparison," *Buffalo Law Review* 21 (1971–1972), pp. 839–854.

15. James B. Jacobs, "The Prisoners' Rights Movement and Its Impacts, 1960–80," in *Crime and Justice: An Annual Review of Research* 2, ed. Norval Morris and Michael Tonry (Chicago: University of Chicago Press, 1980).

16. *Cooper v. Pate,* 378 U.S. 546 (1964).

17. *Wolff v. McDonnell,* 418 U.S. 539 (1974).

18. Ibid., at 555.

19. For the impact of the Supreme Court decisions, see Jacobs, "The Prisoners' Rights Movement."

20. *Estelle v. Gamble,* 429 U.S. 97 (1976).

21. *Hutto v. Finney,* 437 U.S. 678 (1978).

22. *Hudson v. McMillian,* 112 S. Ct. 995 (1992).

23. The National Prison Project, "Status Report: State Prisons and the Courts," *Corrections Digest,* March 19, 1992, pp. 3–9; April 1, 1992, pp. 2–6.

24. Jacobs, "The Prisoners' Rights Movement"; Alfred Blumstein, "American Prisons in a Time of Crisis," in *The American Prison: Issues in Research and Policy,* ed. Lynne Goodstein and Doris Layton MacKenzie (NY: Plenum Press, 1989).

25. William Sabol, Todd Minton, and Paige Harrison, "Prison and Jail Inmates at Midyear 2006," Bureau of Justice Statistics Bulletin, June 2007, NCJ 217675.

26. Calculations from Paige Harrison and Allen Beck, Prisoners in 2005, " Bureau of Justice Statistics Bulletin, November 2006, NCJ 215092.

27. William Sabol, Todd Minton, and Paige Harrison, "Prison and Jail Inmates at Midyear 2006," Bureau of Justice Statistics Bulletin, June 2007, NCJ 217675.

28. Ibid.

29. Ibid.

30. Ibid.

31. Calculations from Paige Harrison and Allen Beck, "Prisoners in 2005," Bureau of Justice Statistics Bulletin, November 2006, NCJ 215092 (73,097 state/federal prisoners in local jails, 2005; and William Sabol, Todd Minton, and Paige Harrison, "Prison and Jail Inmates at Midyear 2006," Bureau of Justice Statistics Bulletin, June 2007, NCJ 217675 (38% of 747,529 inmates convicted, 2005).

32. Paige Harrison and Allen Beck, "Prisoners in 2005," Bureau of Justice Statistics Bulletin, November 2006, NCJ 215092.

33. Alisa Ulferts, "Turnaround for Mentally Ill," *St. Petersburg Times* May 10, 2007; and Abby Goodnough, "Officials Clash Over Mentally Ill in Florida Jails," *New York Times,* November 16,2006.

34. See Richard Hawkins and Geoffrey P. Alpert, *American Prison Systems: Punishment and Justice* (Englewood Cliffs, NJ: Prentice Hall, 1989).

35. Federal Bureau of Prisons, "Prison Types & General Information," Federal Bureau of Prisons Website, http://www.bop.gov/locations/institutions/index.jsp (accessed April 15, 2008).

36. William J. Sabol, Tod D. Minton and Paige M. Harrison, "Prison and Jail Inmates at Midyear 2006," *Bureau of Justice Statistics Bulletin,* June 2007.

37. Male and Female Prisoners Are Not "Similarly Situated." See *Klinger v. Department of Corrections,* 31 F.3d 727 (8th Cir. 1994); and *Pargo v. Elliott,* 69 F.3d 280 (8th Cir. 1995).

38. Laura Maruschak, "Medical Problems of Jail Inmates," Bureau of Justice Statistics Special Report, November 2006, NCl 210696.

39. Laura Maruschak, "HIV in Prisons, 2004," Bureau of Justice Statistics Bulletin, November 2006, NCl 213897.

40. Laura Maruschak, "Medical Problems of Jail Inmates," Bureau of Justice Statistics Special Report, November 2006, NCl 210696.

41. Christopher Mumola and Jennifer Karberg, "Drug Use and Dependence, State and Federal Prisoners, 2004," Bureau of Justice Statistics Special Report, October 2006, NCl 213530.

42. Doris James and Lauren Glaze, "Mental Health Problems of Prison and Jail Inmates," Bureau of Justice Statistics Special Report, September 2006, NCl 213600.

43. Ibid.

44. *Women Prisoners of the District of Columbia Department of Corrections v. District of Columbia*, 877 F. Supp. 634 (D.D.C. 1994).

45. *Jacquelyn Newby v. The District Of Columbia,.* 59 F. Supp. 2d 35 (1999). Also, *Daskalea v. District of Columbia,* 227 F.3d 433, 441 (D.C.Cir.2000).

46. Melvin Claxton, Ronald J. Hansen, and Norman Sinclair, "Guards Assault Female Inmates," *The Detroit News,* May 22, 2005.

47. William Sabol, Todd Minton, and Paige Harrison, "Prison and Jail Inmates at Midyear 2006," Bureau of Justice Statistics Bulletin, June 2007, NCJ 217675. Also, Paige Harrison and Allen Beck, "Prisoners in 2005," Bureau of Justice Statistics Bulletin, November 2006, NCJ 215092.

48. Kathleen Maguire and Timothy J. Flanagan, eds., *Sourcebook on Criminal Justice Statistics* (Washington, DC: Government Printing Office, 1991), Table 1.87, pp. 107–108.

49. John Ortiz Smykla and Jimmy J. Williams, "Co-corrections in the United States of America, 1970–1990: Two Decades of Disadvantages for Women Prisoners," *Women and Criminal Justice* 8 (1994), pp. 61–76.

50. U.S. Department of Justice, Correctional Populations in the U.S. (Washington, D.C.: DOJ, 1991).

51. Thomas Bonczar, "Prevalence of Imprisonment in the U.S. Population, 1974–2001," Bureau of Justice Statistics Special Report, August 2005, NCJ 197976. (Rate 2,068 previously imprisoned in 2001)

52. CJS Sourcebook, Table 6.1., 2005.

53. Tom Wicker, "In the Nation; The Iron Medal," *The New York Times,* January 9, 1991.

54. Bureau of Justice Statistics, *Justice Expenditure and Employment, 1993* (Washington, DC: U.S. Department of Justice, July 1995).

55. Ibid.

56. *The Corrections Yearbook, 1997,* p. 70–71; see also Chiquita A. Sipos, "The Corrections Workforce: Professionalism in a Thankless Profession," *Vital Statistics in Corrections* (Laurel, MD: American-Correctional Association, 1991).

57. *The Corrections Yearbook, 1997,* p. 74.

58. *The Corrections Yearbook, 1997,* p. 69.

59. Peter Katel, "New Walls, No Inmates," *Newsweek,* May 18, 1992, p. 63.

60. Irwin and Austin, "It's About Time," p. 7.

61. Alexis M. Durham III, "Origins of Interest in the Privatization of Punishment: The Nineteenth and Twentieth Century American Experience," *Criminology* 27 (1989), pp. 107–139.

62. Harold W. Demone, Jr., and Margaret Gibelman, "Privatizing the Treatment of Criminal Offenders," *Clinical Treatment of the Criminal Offender* 15 (1990), pp. 7–26.

63. For a general overview, see "Privatization of Corrections," *Corrections Today* 50 (Special Issue) (1988). See also Byron R. Johnson and Paul P. Ross, "The Privatization of Correctional Management: A Review," *Journal of Criminal Justice* 18 (1990), pp. 351–358.

64. E. S. Savas, "Privatization and Prisons," *Vanderbilt Law Review* 40 (1987).

65. Quoted in Kevin Krajick, "Punishment for Profit," *Across the Road* 21 (1984), p. 25.

66. Kathleen Maguire and Ann L. Pastore, eds., *Sourcebook of Criminal Justice Statistics 2002* [Online], http://www.albany.edu/sourcebook.

67. Barbara J. Auerbach et al., *Work in American Prisons: The Private Sector Gets Involved,* for National Institute of Justice (Washington, DC: U.S. Government Printing Office, 1988).

68. Samuel Jan Brakel, "Prison Management, Private Enterprise Style: The Inmates' Evaluation," *New England Journal on Criminal and Civil Confinement* 14 (1988), pp. 175–244.

69. Camille Camp and George Camp, "Correctional Privatization in Perspective," *The Prison Journal* (1985), pp. 14–31.

70. See, e.g., John Dijulio, Jr., "Prisons, Profits and the Public Good: The Privatization of Corrections," *Criminal Justice Research Bulletin,* no. 1 (Sam Houston State University, 1986).

71. Ibid.

72. Ira P. Robbins, "Privatization of Corrections: Defining the Issues," *Federal Probation* 50 (1986), pp. 24–30.

CHAPTER 13

Institutional Corrections

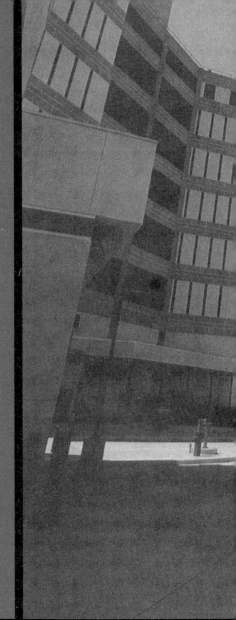

On December 16, 1937, the second escape attempt [from Alcatraz] ended in the death of two inmates . . . at the merciless hands of the swift, icy, turbulent, racing waters of the bay. Theodore Cole (AZ258) was serving fifty years for kidnapping, and Ralph Roe (AZ260) ninety-nine years for bank robbery. On this cold and extremely foggy day, with a strong eight mph outgoing tide, Cole and Roe engaged in what they had considered their well-planned escape. . . .

• After the guard had left at 1:00 P.M., Roe and Cole wrenched loose the cut bars, dropped to the ground below, and proceeded to a locked gate in the fence. This particular gate was used to dump useless parts of tires from the mat shop into the bay. Here, they used a wrench to break the gate lock, after which they climbed down to a ledge twenty feet below. They were now at the water's edge. Each inmate carried a sealed five gallon can with straps attached to act as a life preserver, and a knife. Not taken into account in all their well-laid plans were the treacherous, menacing waters on which they depended for transportation to freedom.

• Shortly after entering these waters, the two men were grabbed by the swift, moving current and swept outward toward the ocean. As they approached "Little Alcatraz," a tiny island off the end of Alcatraz, they were torn loose from their supportive cans. They both disappeared beneath the surface of the water—first Roe, then Cole—never to be seen again. Their cans raced away to vanish in the now heavy fog.[1] Alcatraz juts out of the sea about a mile and a quarter from shore and is swept by treacherous currents and enveloped by a soupy fog most of the time. Guards are forced to wear overcoats many days throughout the summer. This old establishment was renovated and turned into the most scientific prison in the world. It had for its objectives: maximum security, minimum privileges, complete isolation of dangerous convicts from the outside world, and 100 percent "humane" treatment. . . . From the moment the convict entered, he became a victim to all the mechanical gadgets that science has perfected to depersonalize not only him but the administrative officers as well. He was frisked at the entrance by a steel detector, known by the convicts as a "mechanical stool pigeon" or "snitch box." In the dining room, the inmate was ever conscious of the large metal cylinders above him filled with tear gas and ready upon a moment's notice to be opened to hurl down upon him this terrible punishment.[2]

Alcatraz, "The Rock," once America's most secure and most dreaded prison.

San Francisco's Alcatraz penitentiary, the "Rock," epitomized the American preoccupation with security. On March 21, 1963, twenty-nine years after Alcatraz opened in 1934, it was abandoned. To optimists, the closing was a sign of a new direction in American corrections. The aim would now be to socialize convicts rather than "asocialize" them by totally withdrawing them from society. The President's Commission on Law Enforcement and the Administration of Justice (1967) emphasized such innovations as small-unit institutions for community-based treatment, rehabilitation programs administered jointly by staff and inmates, the upgrading of education and vocational training for inmates, the improvement of prison industries, and gradual release and furlough programs.[3] Just a few years later, in 1973, the National Advisory Commission on Criminal Justice Standards and Goals focused on the rights of prisoners. Its report included plans for education, recreation, counseling, and other prison reforms.[4]

During the 1960s and early 1970s, the rehabilitative approach dictated the direction of American corrections. But the "lock 'em up' philosophy was never totally replaced, and when rehabilitation was abandoned in the late 1970s, it made a near-complete comeback. The spirit of Alcatraz was resurrected in the 1980s with the opening of the super-maximum security Marion (Illinois) Federal Penitentiary. At Marion there are, in addition to the general population units, two less restrictive units, one high-control unit, and a special basement unit for high-profile inmates, among them a spy, Jonathon Pollard. A federal court described conditions at Marion as "horrible":

> [E]ach inmate at Marion is confined to a one-man cell (there are no female inmates in the prison) round the clock, except for brief periods outside the cell for recreation (between 7 and 11 hours a week), for a shower, for a visit to the infirmary, to the law library, etc. (Some inmates have more time outside the cell. . . .) Recreation means pacing in a small enclosure—sometimes just in the corridor between the rows of cells. The inmate is fed in his cell, on a tray shoved in between the bars. The cells are modern and roomy and contain a television set as well as a bed, toilet, and sink, but there is no other furniture and when an inmate is outside his cell he is handcuffed and a box is placed over the handcuffs to prevent the lock from being picked; his legs may also be shackled. Inmates are forbidden to socialize with each other or to participate in group religious services. Inmates who throw food or otherwise misbehave in their cells are sometimes tied spread-eagled on their beds, often for hours at a stretch, while inmates returning to their cells are often (inmates of the control unit, always) subjected to a rectal search.[5]

Human Rights Watch recently investigated super-maximum security prisons and found that here, too, prisoners spend nearly all of their time in locked cells that are usually badly ventilated. It is like living in a tomb. They cannot participate in classes, outdoor exercises, or recreation. More than 20,000 prisoners are housed in super-maximum prisons in the United States.[6]

Given the high priority of custody security in institutional corrections, we focus first on institutional control and on the corrections officers charged with maintaining orderly and safe jails and prisons. Then we describe prison life and how that life has changed since the

1960s with the influx of a younger, more heterogeneous population that often forms racial and ethnic power blocks. We examine rehabilitation and the intervention strategies used in various institutions. Last, we look at programs aimed at the well-being of prisoners.

Custody/Security

Nearly all correctional institutions have security as their first priority. This includes not only **maximum security** but also **medium security** and **minimum security** prisons. Annually, an average of more than 1,000 prisoners escape from locked institutions, from among a population of more than 1 million.[7] Critics claim that officials regard an escape as an incredible blemish on the whole system, a far bigger blemish than the many crimes committed by those discharged after serving their time. European administrators see their American counterparts as too little concerned with the reintegration of convicts into the community and overly concerned with security.

The focus on security is evident not only from the construction of prisons, with their security perimeters, high walls, guard towers, TV scanners, and electronic signals and alarms, but also from internal, management-designed procedures ranging from classification to examination of mail (or anything or anybody entering the security perimeter) to constant inmate counts, cell-locks, passes, and the harsh communal punishment of lockdowns for all inmates whenever an escape has been rumored or has taken place. This concern with security also appears in the training of correctional officers, which is devoted more to security than to the long-range prevention of crime through socialization.

In 1995, a $60 million ultra-maximum security prison opened in Florence, Colorado, to house the most dangerous men in America. It is called an administrative maximum facility (Admax or ADX). Closed-circuit television pipes orders directly into cells and remote controlled steel doors channel inmates through the institution. The prison houses such notorious criminals as Terry Nichols (Oklahoma City bombing), Richard Reid (shoe bomber), Eyad Ismoil (World Trade Center bombing), Ted Kaczynski (the Unabomber), Ramzi Yousef (planner of the 1993 World Trade Center attack), and Luis Felipe (head of the Latin Kings street gang). In fact, they get to see each other twice a week when they are allowed to exercise within the confines of wire enclosures.

Rules and Regulations

Prisons have been and continue to be run by the rule, within a strictly hierarchical system. Corrections officers are expected to apply the rules, and prisoners are expected to obey them. Every state system has its own set of rules, incorporating state law and directives from the governor and/or the state correctional administration, as well as staff directives from the chief executive officer, usually the warden or superintendent. To comply with the standards of the American Correctional Association, institutions must inform all incoming inmates of the rules and the penalties imposed for violations.[8] The rule book for the state of Kansas, for example, opens with this instruction: "You should read well this entire book and keep it available for quick reference."[9] Rules dictate all aspects of daily life.

If inmates commit acts covered by criminal law, their cases are referred to law enforcement or prosecutorial agencies. Prosecution by the outside agency does not preclude a disciplinary charge and proceeding by the institution for the infraction of its own rule. If inmates believe they have been treated unfairly they may file grievances using official procedures.[10]

Classification

Perhaps more important than rules and regulations in the smooth functioning of a correctional institution is a classification system that permits the organization of inmates into cohesive, manageable units. The **classification** process consists of regular procedures through which the custodial, treatment, vocational, and educational needs of each individual are determined. While program classifications are important, security classifications are the

maximum security prison
Penal institution designed and operated with the principal goal of preventing escape and avoiding violence on the part of prisoners, virtually to the exclusion of rehabilitation or other programs.

medium security prison
Penal institutions with emphasis on control and custody, but not to the exclusion of rehabilitative or other programs.

minimum security prison
Penal institution allowing inmates and visitors internal freedom of movement and program participation consistent with incarceration.

classification
Process that consists of regular procedures through which the custodial, treatment, vocational, and educational needs of each prisoner are determined.

number-one priority. Security requirements are necessary for the protection of the inmates themselves, for the safety of other persons within the institution, and for the protection of the public. Custodial classification is based on the inmate's behavior, mental health, attitude, and likelihood of attempting escape.

All new prisoners pass through a diagnostic or reception center where specialized personnel such as social workers, psychologists, and physicians make decisions about treatment and custodial needs.[11] Decisions on placement are made by classification committees, typically comprising the warden or deputy warden and the heads of various prison departments, including chaplains, vocational and recreational supervisors, medical officers, and others. Ideally, information from the diagnostic process, the presentence investigation report, police records, and an interview with the inmate should determine placement. In correctional institutions that are severely overcrowded, classification is often far less precise and orderly.

Corrections Officers

Careers

In the past, state prisons, located in little towns far from crime-prone urban centers, provided employment for generations of local youth. They needed no education past public schooling, and they filled the jobs their fathers had occupied. These civil service careers offered security (if the person played it right) and a pension to start a second career in town after retirement.[12] During the 1970s, however, changes began to take place in the correctional employment field. With the vast increase in correctional facilities, many states adopted proactive recruitment policies emphasizing education and qualifications. Salary levels began to go up, and officer training was somewhat upgraded. New affirmative action goals resulted in a slightly increased percentage of minorities and women working as correctional officers. Women officers now work in both men's and women's prisons.[13] There has also been a rise in membership in prison employee unions.

Despite the somewhat improved situation of the corrections officer, the job still has little prestige. Officers spend long hours in hostile surroundings with few contacts outside the walls. While they may move to higher ranks within the corrections hierarchy, they generally do not move into administrative positions. Turnover rates are high (11.9 percent nationally), salaries are still relatively low, and absenteeism reaches 15 percent at any one time in many prisons.[14]

The Corrections Officer Role. The popular perception of the corrections officer is that he or she controls prisoners by brute force. Yet officers rarely carry weapons inside the prison (because inmates would likely take them away). Officers survive by earning respect and resorting, whenever necessary, to unarmed coercion, or the granting of rewards.[15]

Officers' assignments have been classified into seven categories: block officers, work detail, supervisors, industrial shop and school officers, yard officers, and administration building assignments. Block officers have the most demanding assignments. Several studies have identified different types of officers. One divides new officers into three groups on the basis of their attitudes toward inmates and other officers: "Pollyannas" (positive to both groups), "white hats" (positive to inmates, negative toward other officers), and "hard asses" (negative toward inmates, positive toward fellow officers). With time, most officers become either "burnouts" (negative to both groups) or "functionaries" (indifferent to both groups).[16] Another study describes "John Waynes" (disciplinarians), "wishy-washies" (appear afraid of inmates), "lazy-laid-backs" (don't care), "all rights" (usually old-timers who accept the rules), and "dirty cops" (who do illegal favors for prisoners).

Job Satisfaction among Officers. Most corrections officers choose the job for security, for civil service benefits, or because it may be the only work available in the small towns and farm areas where most prisons are located. There are several negative factors associated with the work. According to one officer: "[The worst thing about the job] is the fear there might be a riot. That you might be dead, that you might not come out. It's there every day, but you just wonder if it will happen today."[17] In addition to their concern with danger, officers resent the "hostile" attitudes of inmates, their isolation behind walls, and the little input that they have into decisions that affect assignments and working conditions.[18] A recent study shows that the level of corrections officer job satisfaction is lower than that of any other occupational category.[19]

Living with Convicts

Corrections officers and administrators work with people whose lives are marked by poverty, lack of education, and violence and who live by very different rules in a very different kind of society.

Who Are the Inmates?

According to the Bureau of Justice Statistics, on June 30, 2006:

- A total of 2,245,189 prisoners were held in federal or state prisons or in local jails—an increase of 3.0 percent from midyear 2005, less than the average annual growth of 3.5 percent since year-end 1995.
- There were an estimated 497 prison inmates per 100,000 U.S. residents—up from 488 at midyear 2005.
- The number of women under the jurisdiction of state or federal prison authorities increased 4.8 percent from midyear 2005, reaching 111,403, and the number of men rose 2.7 percent, totaling 1,443,115.

At midyear 2005 there were 4,789 black male prisoners per 100,000 black males in the United States in prison, compared to 1,862 Hispanic male inmates per 100,000 Hispanic males and 736 white male inmates per 100,000 white males (Table 13.1).

Between 1995 and 2001, the increasing number of violent offenders accounted for 63 percent of the total growth of the state prison population; 15 percent of the total growth was attributable to the increasing number of drug offenders.[20]

The Deprivation Model

Inmates constitute a unique social group. They live together, but not voluntarily. They live in extremely close quarters, often sharing all space other than a bed. They must stay in the group even if they fear for their personal safety.

For over half a century social scientists have studied the prison as a social entity. Some experts argue that the traditions, norms, language, and roles that develop in prison result from

| | Number of Sentenced Prisoners | | | | | | | |
| | Males | | | | Females | | | |
Age	Total[a]	White[b]	Black[b]	Hispanic	Total[a]	White[b]	Black[b]	Hispanic
Total	1,362,500	459,700	547,200	279,000	98,600	45,800	29,900	15,900
18–19	26,300	7,200	11,800	5,600	1,200	500	400	200
20–24	218,700	62,700	94,200	50,400	11,900	5,300	3,600	2,300
25–29	244,800	67,000	106,600	59,600	15,300	6,700	4,700	2,900
30–34	224,200	69,800	92,000	51,100	17,400	8,100	5,100	2,900
35–39	207,200	72,300	81,600	41,600	19,400	9,000	6,000	3,000
40–44	185,200	70,900	71,000	31,600	16,500	7,800	5,100	2,400
45–54	189,800	76,300	71,100	29,500	13,800	6,500	4,300	1,800
55 or older	63,500	32,900	17,600	9,000	3,000	1,800	700	300

[a]Includes American Indians, Alaska Natives, Asians, Native Hawaiians, other Pacific Islanders, and persons identifying two or more races.
[b]Excludes Hispanics and persons identifying two or more races.
NOTE: Based on estimates by gender, race, Hispanic origin, and age from the 2004 Survey of Inmates in State Correctional Facilities and updated from jurisdiction counts by gender at yearend 2005. Estimates were rounded to the nearest 100.
SOURCE: Paige M. Harrison and Allen J. Beck, *Prisons in 2005* (Bureau of Justice Statistics: Washington, DC, 2006), p. 8.

TABLE 13.1 Number of Adults under Correctional Supervision by Gender, Race, Hispanic Origin, and Age, 2005

deprivation model
Explanation of prison subculture that suggests norms, language, roles, and traditions are developed in the prison to help prisoners adjust to the pains of imprisonment.

prisonization
Socialization process in which new prisoners learn the ways of prison society, including rules, hierarchy, customs, and culture.

inmate code
Informal set of rules that reflect the values of the prison society.

prison argot
Unique vocabulary used by prisoners.

hustling
Inmate activity that involves obtaining goods and services that are unavailable through legitimate channels.

the deprivations of prison life (the **deprivation model**).[21] Donald Clemmer, who has described the prison subculture and how inmates adapt to it, uses the term **prisonization** to describe the complex process by which new inmates learn the ways of the prison society and what is expected of them. Inmates are first reduced in status from civilians to anonymous figures, numbers in a common uniform, subject to institutional rules and the prison's rigid hierarchy. After a while they begin to accept the inferior role; to take on new habits of eating, sleeping, and working; and to learn that they do not owe anything to anybody for their subsistence.[22]

Building on Clemmer's work, Gresham Sykes has described how people respond to the deprivations they experience as inmates. According to him, a "society of captives" emerges as a response to imprisonment.[23] To cope with the "pains of imprisonment" that new inmates suffer, they become part of a society that has an **inmate code** (a set of rules that tells the inmate how to behave toward other inmates and toward custodial officers) and a set of social roles defined in terms of **prison argot** (a unique vocabulary used by prisoners).

The Pains of Imprisonment.   First, inmates are deprived of liberty and are cut off from friends and family. The results are lost emotional relationships, boredom, and loneliness.[24] Second, inmates are deprived of goods and services. While it is true that an inmate will get "three squares and clean sheets," the standard of living inside a jail or prison is very low. Prisoners have no chance to keep or to obtain material possessions. **Hustling,** obtaining goods and services that are unavailable through legitimate channels, is a basic inmate activity. The informal economy can supply drugs, alcohol, food, and sex. Cigarettes are a valued commodity. They are permitted in the institution, and they are popularly used for trading purposes.[25]

The third pain of imprisonment is the deprivation of heterosexual relations. Researchers have identified a number of psychological problems that result from this deprivation. The worst of these expresses itself in the homosexual enslavement of younger prisoners by aggressive older inmates. Few studies have been more shocking and revealing than an investigation of local corrections facilities by the Philadelphia district attorney's office and police department conducted nearly thirty years ago. It revealed that over a twenty-six-month period there were 2,000 sexual assaults involving 3,500 perpetrators and 1,500 victims. Furthermore, it found that almost all "slightly built" young men were sexually approached almost immediately upon admission. Many were raped repeatedly by gangs of inmates.[26] A 2001 Human Rights Watch report on male rape in U.S. prisons called for legal reforms to address a "wholesale disregard for prisoners' right to be free of violent rape."[27]

For heterosexual inmates the deprivation of a partner of the opposite sex is one of the worst forms of punishment. Precisely for that reason, a number of correctional systems—including California, Connecticut, Mississippi, New Mexico, New York, and Washington—have instituted programs that permit conjugal visits.[28] At the Eastern Correctional Facility in Napanoch, New York, for example, inmates are given the opportunity to stay with their spouse for forty-four hours every three or four months. Conjugal visits help maintain family relationships and reduce sexual frustration. There are no comparable programs for unmarried inmates.

The fourth pain of imprisonment is deprivation of personal autonomy. Inmates' lives are regulated and controlled twenty-four hours a day. Yet the control by corrections staff is selective. Staff are likely to look the other way when prisoners enforce, often brutally, their own code of conduct among themselves. The fifth pain of imprisonment is the deprivation of security. When a prisoner shares a small space with other inmates, some of whom are likely to be violent, aggression, violence, and sexual exploitation are inevitable. Inmates who are attacked and do not fight back suffer the contempt of the prison community and open themselves to further victimization.

The Convict Social System.   To cope with these pains of imprisonment, an inmate needs to live by the inmate code. "Don't inform on another convict" and "do your own time" are the two basic rules of the code. Among the others are "don't interfere with inmate interests," "don't quarrel with fellow inmates," "don't weaken," and "don't trust the guards or the things they stand for."[29]

The prison social system also defines various social roles in terms of prison argot. Some roles undermine group solidarity. There are "rats" and "snitches" who get inmates into trouble, "merchants" who deal in stolen goods (usually from the prison supply store), "gorillas" who use violence to get what they want, "wolves" who coerce other inmates into homosexual relations, and "centermen" who take the side of the custodians. The "real man," on the other hand, is loyal, maintains dignity, shares possessions, yet remains tough. The characteristics of the real man build a cohesive inmate society that provides the prisoner with a social group with which to identify—one that will support him in his struggle with captivity.[30]

The Importation Model

There are opposing explanations of prison cultures. According to one theorist, the values one finds within the prison are precisely those found on the streets from which the offenders come.[31] The **importation model** suggests that the inmate subculture is brought in from the outside. There are four major roles within the prison community—"square John," "right guy," "con politician," and "outlaw." This theory argues that these roles correspond to the life experiences of those brought into the institution. To other scholars, the prison subculture represents a combination of the "convict" subculture (those who spend most of their lives in foster homes, reform schools, jails, and prisons), the "straight" subculture (those—usually one-time offenders—who live by conventional social rules and want to avoid trouble in prison), and the "thief" subculture (professional criminals who keep to themselves). Only the convict subculture is unique to the prison; the others are imported from outside the walls.[32]

importation model
Explanation of prison subculture that suggests norms, language, roles, and traditions are brought into the prison from outside the walls.

A New Prison Society

Changes in the prison population since the 1960s have created a new prison society. Contemporary prisons now house a more heterogeneous group of inmates, and it appears that a single inmate code for the whole population no longer exists. Race plays the dominant role in inmate relationships.[33] In many state prison systems competition among black, Hispanic, Native American, and white power blocks often leads to alliances that resemble international treaties among nations. One researcher concludes:

> Whites, who represent the dominant race outside prison, find themselves [to be] a distinct minority group on the inside. Whites' apparent realization of their minority position seems to affect their perception of their living space, levels of aggression, and attitudes towards the dominant racial group—blacks.[34]

Prison Violence and Overcrowding

The new prison society is also characterized by more violence. On February 2, 1980, the New Mexico Penitentiary in Santa Fe exploded in the most violent and destructive riot since 43 inmates and hostages were killed at Attica in 1971. In Attica, the disturbance was tightly controlled by a small group of powerful inmates. By contrast, the New Mexico inmates were leaderless and out of control. Fourteen guards were held hostage while hundreds of prisoners roamed the prison smashing and burning everything in sight. At least seven of the hostages were severely beaten and several were repeatedly raped. But the inmates reserved the brunt of their rage for each other: 33 inmates were killed, some after being brutally tortured and mutilated. As many as 200 other inmates were beaten and raped. The terror was so pervasive and uncontrolled that the majority of the 1,136 inmates fled and sought safety among the state police and National Guard personnel ringing the penitentiary. The level of inmate-to-inmate violence was unprecedented.

When the riot was over, officials acknowledged that the New Mexico corrections system had long been neglected. Maximum-custody inmates, including some labeled psychotic, were mixed together with young and vulnerable first offenders, often in dormitories holding as many as 90 men each.[35]

The increasing violence in prisons has been attributed to the younger age of inmates, warring racial groups, and the transfer of the subculture of violence from the streets into the prison.[36] A study of four Virginia institutions found a prison assault rate of 9.96 attacks per 100 inmates each year.[37] Many inmates "spend years in fear of harm. Some inmates request segregation, others lock themselves in and some are hermits by choice."[38]

Inmates from Gatesville, Texas, women's prison at work in the fields.

Life in a Women's Prison

Most correctional facilities for women have better physical surroundings than institutions for men. Fortresslike walls and gun towers restrain male inmates who have little freedom of movement. Women are usually free to roam the grounds of their institutions. But, despite the more pleasant surroundings, according to many experts, the frustration of incarcerated women may be even greater than that of men. Because women represent only 6.9 percent of the state inmate population, women's facilities have been assigned a low priority.[39] Money spent for women's education, job training, or counseling would reach too few of the total prison population. Women are therefore offered little more than inexpensive programs that emphasize stereotypes of "women's work": cooking, sewing, cosmetology, and office work, to which more recently computer languages and programming have been added. Delaware provides a typical example. Amy Grossberg and Brian Peterson, young lovers who killed their newborn son in a Newark motel room and left his corpse in a dumpster, were sentenced in 1998 to terms of 2 1/2 and 2 years, respectively, after they each pleaded guilty to manslaughter. As an inmate at Delaware's only prison for women, Grossberg's training programs are limited for the most part to typically female occupations: sewing, tailoring, home economics, typing, food service, health care, cosmetology, clerical work, and furniture building. On the other hand, Peterson, as a male prisoner in Delaware, has many more training options, mostly for trades that pay quite well on the outside, such as auto repair, furniture restoration, electric motor repair, plumbing, drafting, carpentry, masonry, metal works, construction and renovation, upholstery, air conditioning repair, climate control, printing, farming, and animal husbandry. In addition, male prisoners in Delaware are also used as workers for highway beautification projects.[40]

The populations in women's prisons share many characteristics:

• Thirty-eight percent of women prisoners are African American and 17 percent are Latinas.

• Women in state prisons in 2001 were more likely than men to be incarcerated for a drug offense (32 percent vs. 20 percent) or property offense (25 percent vs. 19 percent) and less likely than men to be incarcerated for a violent offense (31 percent vs. 50 percent).

- Three-quarters of women in state and federal prisons report that they had used drugs regularly prior to their arrest; over 60 percent had used drugs in the month prior to their offense.

- In 1997, 65 percent of women in state prisons were parents of minor children, compared to 55 percent of men. Two-thirds of mothers incarcerated in state prison lived with their children prior to their arrest.

- Approximately 37 percent of women and 28 percent of men in prison had monthly incomes of less than $600 prior to their arrest.

- Nearly a quarter of women in state prisons have a history of mental illness.

- Nationally 3.6 percent of women in state and federal prisons were HIV positive in 2000, compared to 2 percent of men. The women's figures range as high as 18.2 percent in New York State and 41 percent in the District of Columbia.

- More than half of the women in state prisons have been abused, 47 percent physically abused, and 39 percent sexually abused (with many being survivors of both types of abuse).[41]

Mothers in Prison. More than 60 percent of women prisoners are mothers.[42] Many give birth in prison. At most institutions mothers may keep their newborns only for a few weeks. At the Federal Correctional Institution in Lexington, Kentucky, the home of approximately 1,400 female offenders, babies are born to incarcerated mothers at a local community contract hospital. Between the time the mother arrives at the prison and the baby's birth, the staff does extensive preparation. The woman is interviewed to determine her possible due date and her plans for the newborn. When labor begins, she is taken by correctional staff to a local hospital for delivery. Barring complications, the inmate and her baby stay at the hospital for three days. The baby is then transported to the designated family member.

The issue of babies delivered to incarcerated women is extremely complex. The incarcerated mother fears that her infant children will no longer need her or, in fact, recognize her upon her release.[43] Very few prisons allow mothers to keep their babies incarcerated with them. Some question whether a prison, under any circumstances, can provide safety and the proper emotional environment for a child. There are also those who take a strictly punitive view—a mother who commits a crime has lost the right to nurture and enjoy her baby.

A study of the effects of separation on 138 inmate mothers in Washington state and Kentucky showed that the women felt guilt and shame. Many of the drug abusers, drug-free in prison, began to realize for the first time the effects of their behavior on the family. Some inmate mothers wanted their experience to serve as an example to their older children of what can happen when you commit a crime; other mothers did not tell their children about their incarceration, fearing that the children would suffer ostracism among friends[44] (see Table 13.2).

Women in prison say that this separation from their children is their main stress factor. Most women's prisons are located in rural areas far from cities. This can make it hard for families with few resources to visit. In fact, only 9 percent of women in state prisons get visits from their minor children. Warden Roberta Richman, of the Rhode Island women's facility in Cranston, has observed the effects of this sometimes long-term separation from children. "When you lock a man up, the family unit usually stays intact. When you lock a woman up, you're destroying families."[45]

The vast majority of inmate mothers attempt to fulfill their maternal roles in spite of their incarceration. Mothers who are in prison manifest concern about the welfare of their children and generally attempt to maintain contact with them through prison visits, letters, telephone calls, and furloughs. Most inmate mothers lived with their children before their arrest and plan to reunite with them when released from prison.[46]

PRISON OVERCROWDING—WHAT ARE THE LIMITS?

Seven inmates were shot to death and forty-three wounded, between 1988 and 1994, at Corcoran Prison, one of California's thirty-three "correctional" institutions. Corcoran leads the pack, though some other California prisons are not far behind. Only now has California started an inquiry into its "brutal, deadly prisons."[1] Is prison violence the result of overcrowding in correctional facilities or hastily recruited and ill-trained officers?

One of the legacies of the "get tough" stance on criminal justice is prison systems that are dangerously overcrowded. The prison and jail population in this country is currently about 2 million. This represents a quadrupling of the inmate population since 1980. Mandatory sentences, parole abolition, and stricter sentences for drug offenses have resulted in prisons that have been compared to sardine cans. A prison is said to be "operating over capacity" if it holds more than 105 percent of the inmates who may be properly housed in the facility. In 2003, the prison systems of 22 states were operating over capacity. Alabama led this list with 109 percent over capacity. In addition, the federal system and the District of Columbia were operating over capacity.[2]

The typical response of states to overcrowding has been to build more prisons. California, which has spent over $7 billion on prison construction since the early 1980s, now spends more on building new prisons than it does on building new facilities for postsecondary education. As well, the additional cost to states of housing all these people cannot be understated. Howard Peters, Illinois' Director of Corrections, has commented that "You don't just lock them up and throw away the key. You lock them up and spend thousands of dollars on them."[3]

The policy of increasing prison beds is seen by some as shortsighted. "Building more prisons to address crime is like building more graveyards to address a fatal disease," explains Robert Gangi, the executive director of the Correctional Association of New York.[4] Others fear that plans for new construction may not be adequate to deal with the rapidly growing need for more space. Corrections professionals employ a number of options, such as putting two inmates in a cell (double-celling) and making requests for capacity increases. But this doesn't solve the problem, it just makes it easier to disguise in official monthly and year-end reports. Other alternatives include contracting with private prisons and placing inmates in local jails or out-of-state facilities. Throughout the country states now send some of their inmates to facilities out of state—and then not necessarily to adjoining states. For example, Alaska sends some of its prisoners to Arizona, inmates from Florida may be sent to California, and Texas receives prisoners from Colorado, Hawaii, Massachusetts, Missouri, North Carolina, Oklahoma, Oregon, and Virginia. This practice has been questioned in the courts by inmates concerned about the conditions of these correctional facilities. Also, moving a prisoner out of state can impose a burden on

TABLE 13.2
Percent of State and Federal Prisoners with Minor Children by Sex of Prisoners, United States, 1997

	State Prisoners			Federal Prisoners		
	Total	Male	Female	Total	Male	Female
Have minor children						
No	44.6%	45.3%	34.7%	37.0%	36.6%	41.2%
Yes	55.4	54.7	65.3	63.0	63.4	58.8
Number of minor children						
1	23.8	24.0	20.5	24.0	24.0	24.5
2	15.8	15.6	18.7	18.5	18.7	17.1
3	8.7	8.4	13.7	11.1	11.3	9.7
4	4.1	3.9	7.3	5.0	5.1	4.1
5	1.7	1.6	3.6	2.3	2.2	2.7
6 or more	1.3	1.3	1.6	2.1	2.2	0.7
Lived with children at time of admission	45.3	43.8	64.3	57.2	55.2	84.0

SOURCE: Kathleen Maguire and Ann L. Pastore, eds., *Sourcebook of Criminal Justice Statistics 2002* [Online], http://www.albany.edu/sourcebook/pdf/t636.pdf.

family members, who can no longer visit. Prison reform groups describe the practice as "psychological" punishment or "banishment." Out-of-state transfers have sometimes even resulted in inmate uprisings.[5]

Crowding in prisons has been linked to a number of problems: (1) prisoners housed in large dormitories are more likely to visit clinics and have high blood pressure than are prisoners in other housing arrangements such as single-bunked cells and small dormitories; (2) prisons that use dormitories have higher assault rates than those with cells; and (3) prisons housing significantly more inmates than design capacity based on sixty feet per inmate have higher assault rates than other prisons.[6]

Most people who work in corrections believe this upward spiral in the inmate population cannot continue. A number of solutions have been proposed, ranging from the increased use of intermediate sanctions to the decriminalization of drugs. But the public clamors for harsher punishments and longer sentences, ignorant of the consequences of such demands. It remains to be seen whether politicians will be able to resist these demands and stop passing legislation that seems destined to severely curtail government spending in virtually all areas but corrections.

Questions for Discussion

1. Are there alternatives to imprisonment for punishing people for their crimes? Are there alternatives to prison for keeping dangerous offenders away from the public?

2. Many people think building new prisons should be a priority. Where do you think cuts in government spending should be made to fund new prisons? Or would you support increasing taxes?

3. Do you think overcrowding in prison constitutes "cruel and unusual punishment"? Why or why not?

SOURCES

1. Evelyn Nieves, "California Examines Brutal, Deadly Prisons—Killings by Guards Prompt an Inquiry," *The New York Times,* November 7, 1998, p. A7.
2. Paige M. Harrison and Allen J. Beck, *Prisoners in 2003* (Washington, DC: Bureau of Justice Statistics, 2004).
3. Jill Smolowe, "Lock 'Em Up ... and Throw Away the Key," *Time,* February 7, 1994, pp. 54–56, 58–59.
4. Ibid.
5. Greg Wees, "Inmate Population Expected to Increase 43% by 2002," *Corrections Compendium* 21 (1996), pp. 1–4.
6. Gerald G. Gaes, "The Effects of Overcrowding in Prison," in *Crime and Justice: An Annual Review of Research,* ed. Norval Morris and Michael Tonry (Chicago: University of Chicago Press, 1985).

Beyond Custody and Control: Old and New Goals

To this point we have discussed the primary goal of prisons, namely custody and control, and the implications of this goal for the lives of inmates. But prisons were designed for more than just custody and control. Workhouse advocates expected that habituation to good work habits would turn the prisoner into a useful citizen (besides cutting down on the cost of imprisonment or even enriching the treasury). Penitentiary advocates expected convicts to become penitent and thus less crime-prone. Reformatory advocates hoped to reform inmates, and rehabilitation proponents hoped to rehabilitate or habilitate prisoners to function well in the mainstream society. Of course, accomplishing these goals requires effort by those with skills capable of producing the desired result.

The Rehabilitation Approach

Unlike rehabilitation programs of the 1970s and earlier, nearly all of today's programs are voluntary (except prison labor which, in many jurisdictions, is required). It seems that after a period of nearly twenty years during which the correctional approach was out of favor, the tide may have turned. An increasing number of criminologists and specialists in criminal justice and corrections now support a cost–benefit rehabilitative approach. It is, as some have called it, "the only justification of criminal sanctioning that obligates the state to care for an offender's needs or welfare."[47] It is a humanitarian approach. The reform-minded maintain that if we were not trying to change offenders into nonoffenders, we would systematically increase the offender population. They regard the principal objective of the correctional system to be **reformation,** the voluntary transformation of an individual lacking in social or vocational skills into a productive, well-socialized citizen. According to proponents, offenders are in need of rehabilitation. They may be psychologically disturbed, addicted to alcohol or drugs, or simply lacking in the basic skills necessary to survive in a complex society.

Among criminologists, there is a strong and honest split in views. Some have little faith in rehabilitation programs or are opposed to placing the primary emphasis on treating and correcting behavior. Moreover, integration of a treatment approach with the widely accepted just desserts model seems hard to achieve. But even those who do not support the rehabilitative model would not deny prisoners the right to participate in voluntary programs.

Rehabilitation has been broadly defined as the result of any social or psychological intervention intended to reduce an offender's potential future criminal activity.[48] By this standard, the true test of success is noninvolvement in crime following participation in an intervention program. Criminologists examine recidivism data for those who have and have not been exposed to intervention programs. **Recidivism** refers to repeated or habitual relapses into criminal behavior; it may be measured by rates of rearrest, reconviction, or reimprisonment. Supporters of rehabilitation hope to see lower recidivism rates for those who have been in rehabilitation programs. The three types of programs used most frequently are psychological (psychotherapy and behavior therapy), educational, and vocational.

Innovative rehabilitation programs usually start with great enthusiasm, but they typically fail to produce results. The most devastating evaluation was that by Douglas Lipton, Robert Martinson, and Judith Wilks, published in 1975, proclaiming that "nothing works."[49] As a result of these studies, the treatment philosophy was discredited, programs were dismantled, and the vacuum in corrections was filled by the just desserts approach.

Some criminologists who subsequently scrutinized Martinson's evaluations found them methodologically flawed.[50] Martinson himself later confirmed that some programs have had some success in curbing recidivism.[51] After a thorough review of treatment programs initiated between 1981 and 1987, researchers concluded it is downright ridiculous to say nothing works.[52] An analysis of biomedical, diversion, family intervention, education, get-tough, and work programs gives reason for hope. The expectation that appropriate rehabilitation efforts may yield some success in curbing recidivism rates has thus been rekindled, and the rehabilitation approach has been reborn.[53]

Vocational Training and Prison Industries

It is fair to say that the vast majority of inmates are "economic failures." They do not have the skills and work ethic to perform gainful legitimate employment in a highly competitive society.[54] The aim of vocational training programs, therefore, is to turn these economic failures into successes. Yet vocational training and the instilling of a work ethic have a sad history in American corrections, where the state's profit motive has ranked first and meaningful vocational training for prisoners a distant second.

In the nineteenth century, American convicts were farmed out to private entrepreneurs. In Alabama until 1862, Burrows, Holt & Company used prison labor for the manufacture of "sacks, blinds, doors, russet, brogans, cabinet furniture, wagons, wheat fans, well buckets and kegs."[55] Today more than thirty private-sector prison industry projects are in operation. These projects are called joint ventures (see Table 13.3). Companies such as Best Western International Hotels, Wahlers Company (office furniture), and Utah Printing

reformation
Voluntary, self-initiated transformation of an individual lacking in social or vocational skills into a productive, normally functioning citizen.

rehabilitation
Punishment philosophy that asserts that through proper correctional intervention, a criminal can be reformed into a law-abiding citizen.

recidivism
Repeated or habitual relapses into criminal behavior.

Model	Workers Employed By	Workers Supervised By	Workers Trained By	Benefits for Company	Benefits for Prison
Manpower[a]	Prison	Company	Prison	• Work force • Rent/utility • Money for equipment • Administrative support	• Employment • Overhead rate • Wage deductions • Payback on equipment
Employer[a]	Company	Company	Company	• Work force • Rent • Utilities	• Employment • Wage deductions
Customer[b]	Prison	Prison	Prison	• Product or service	• Payment for finished goods

[a]Risks and rewards shared by company and prison, with each partner giving significant resources.
[b]High risk for prison because the administrators must operate a competitive business within the constraints of a government bureaucracy. Low risk for companies that simply buy finished product.
SOURCE: Adapted from George E. Sexton, *Work in American Prisons: Joint Ventures with the Private Sector,* National Institute of Justice (Washington, DC: U.S. Department of Justice, November 1995), p. 11.

TABLE 13.3 Principal Characteristics of Three Types of Joint Ventures

and Graphics have set up shops in prisons around the United States. Prisoners manufacture such products as disk drives, airplane parts, light metal products, and condensing units. The wages, however, are less than those paid to free workers.[56] Other troublesome issues involve industrial safety, the absence of benefits, and labor union objections to competition from prisoners.

Educational Programs

Educational programs are promoted with great fervor in most prisons, yet there are continuous problems. Educational efforts in prison are far more complex than providing public school education. Many prisoner-students have disciplinary problems, learning disabilities, adjustment problems, and a history of failure. It is not easy to find devoted and courageous teachers. Most prison educational programs must be at the elementary school level, yet elementary school texts are hardly fit for teaching adults. Moreover, prison education programs are dogged by the consistent finding that such programs have no impact on recidivism rates.[57]

Still, there is a great need to provide prisoners with a basic education to make them functional in society, and such programs are very much alive. Most correctional facilities currently offer academic programs with courses for which inmates are credited in accordance with state requirements. In fact, all states offer some form of academic education. Many inmates avail themselves of high school, college, and vocational programs.

Prison administrators have long recognized the value of rehabilitative programs for the overall prison culture. They help maintain a more peaceful atmosphere and a certain comfort level in prison. Other programs are specifically aimed at the well-being of prisoners. These are recreational and health programs.

Recreation

Social life in prison is unimaginable without recreational programs. Prisoners need recreation to interrupt a dull routine. Recreation in prison may take many forms. At one time restricted to an hour's circular walk in the yard, then enhanced by music or individual radios, recreation now extends to television, handicrafts (and their sale), rap music, and hobby and interest sessions on any imaginable subject. Prisoners may use the

ROBERTA RICHMAN, WARDEN, RHODE ISLAND DEPARTMENT OF CORRECTIONS, WOMEN'S FACILITIES

In the midst of my eighth year as warden, no two days are ever quite the same. Managing an institution means making hundreds of decisions every day that have a significant impact on many lives.

- Arriving at the facility at about 8:00 A.M. after a 45-minute commute, I meet with shift commanders, a captain, and two lieutenants to be briefed and review reports recording activity occurring during the past day. As the manager of a twenty-four-hour institution, it is essential that I know everything of importance that occurred in my absence since the previous day.

- I then stop into the dispensary, one of the most critical hubs of activity in a women's prison. I check on daily medical emergencies, clinic schedules, and hospitalized inmates.

- By about 8:30 A.M., I arrive at my office where my first inmate interaction of the day is with a just-turned 16-year-old who has been waived to the adult system to serve a 45-year prison sentence for first-degree murder, a crime she committed at the age of 13. I have hired Jessica to work in my office to ensure that I see her daily to check on her behavior and problems. As the youngest juvenile in an adult facility by a full two years, she is a constant challenge. Managing to protect her from older inmates and, given her temperament, them from her, is an ongoing struggle that requires daily monitoring.

- At 9:00 A.M. I convene the weekly staff meeting. Our issue of the day is a need to cancel visits for minimum security inmates while asbestos wrapping on leaking pipes is removed.

- At 10:30 A.M. I am called on to testify at a hearing concerning the termination of a staff member who has been charged with staff/inmate sexual misconduct. In this case, involving a kitchen steward and a woman working in the kitchen, we have been unable to prove the relationship occurred but have been successful in proving that he has brought food in from the outside to use as bribes for women who cover for them as they conduct their relationship in hidden areas of the kitchen. He was disciplined and transferred to a male unit. Later, after the woman has been paroled, we are able to prove that he is visiting her in her

skills other inmates have to start new programs, and administrators generally favor any recreational program that does not create security risks. As in normal life, sports are of paramount interest to prisoners. When Mike Tyson was in the Indiana Youth Center his fellow inmates welcomed the ex-heavyweight champion and wanted his autograph. For them, Tyson was a role model. Most institutions have teams—softball, baseball, boxing, even football and soccer. Administrators like them: They take the steam out of the inmates, and they provide entertainment.[58]

home which is just cause for termination. He is appealing the termination on the grounds that it began after her release and her status as a parolee should not prevent him from dating her. We insist that the relationship began in prison, that she is still a client of the Department of Corrections and he is in violation of our code of ethics. We take the position that any staff/inmate intimate relationship is a violation of policy; that such relationships cannot be consensual, a common defense, in a prison setting where a strong power imbalance exists. Now, with legislation passed in 1994, staff/inmate sexual relationships are considered felonies subject to up to five years in prison and a $100,000 fine.

- My afternoon is devoted to touring the facility, interacting personally with inmates and staff. On this day one inmate asks that I help her contact her social worker at the Department of Children, Youth, and Families, who is preparing her for a termination of parental rights hearing; a second asks if I can get the doctor to see her roommate who appears to be ill; a third group of three women are concerned about an older woman who just came in with a hearing aid which has no batteries; and a fourth wants to tell me how well she is doing in her GED testing. In the Isolation Unit I stop to talk with two women who are waiting to be extradited back to their home state of Oregon. One is serving life without parole and the other is an ex-corrections officer she met while serving her sentence. They developed a relationship strong enough to make the officer resign, give up custody of her

thirteen-year-old, and aid the inmate to escape by breaking into the institution and breaking her out. Relationships among women are common in prison and difficult to manage.

- My last stop of the afternoon is the substance abuse treatment unit in minimum security, called the Discovery Program. This is an intensive residential treatment program that is operated on contract with a community-based nonprofit agency that can continue to treat women in the community after release. The director and four counselors work directly in the housing unit which serves twenty-eight women. Victims of sexual and domestic violence, mothers who need help learning how to parent, mental health issues, medical concerns, physical fitness and general wellness, the arts and education, job training—all receive attention as needed by each individual woman. This visit is the most pleasant of the day. I reflect on how positive the environment is, both physically, with wonderful murals painted by the women on all the walls, and psychologically, with positive, well-trained staff working a disciplined and very well-structured program guiding the activity of the day.

- It is now 5:40 P.M. and I am leaving to attend our annual Thanksgiving dinner celebration. The event is organized by our Mentoring Program which recruits and trains volunteers to mentor inmates and remain with them as they move out of prison and back into the community, for as long as they wish to stay together. Many of our mentors and mentees have been together for years and attend monthly support meetings together with women still incarcerated. This evening we expect about seventy-five women—inmates, ex-inmates, and their mentors—to share a special evening and give thanks together to each other for what they have accomplished. My presence at these events is important to the inmates, to the volunteers, and, not least, to me.

Health Problems

Apart from the routine medical problems everyone encounters, prisoners have special and more profound medical problems, caused by close living and confinement. In 2003, 14,847 inmates in state and federal prisons tested positive for tuberculosis (TB). The national rate for active TB cases is 5.1 per 100,000—the prison rate is nearly four times this.[59] It is such a serious health risk that the federal system and most states screen new prisoners for the disease at intake.[60] TB is a typical prison disease, as it is an airborne

GROWING OLD BEHIND GRAY WALLS

John Saxon expects to die in prison. For the better part of the 1990s, the fifty-six-year-old paraplegic has been serving a fifteen- to thirty-year sentence for killing a person and wounding two others. He is confined to a hospital bed and can't feed himself or go to the bathroom alone.[1] He is one of the nearly 40,000 prisoners aged fifty-five or older in state and federal prisons in this country.[2] The rapid growth of older inmates mirrors the increase in elderly in the nation as a whole and is expected to increase due largely to longer prison sentences, the widespread abolition of parole, and "three strikes and you're out" laws.

Elderly prisoners are a significant financial burden. Their medical expenses are estimated to be two to three times greater than those for younger prisoners. Inmates are not eligible for Medicaid or Medicare, and federal judges have ruled that failure to provide adequate care is a violation of the Eighth Amendment's ban on cruel and unusual punishment. Prison systems end up footing the entire bill for treatments of cancer, heart disease, prostate problems, strokes, Alzheimer's, and emphysema.[3] For example, one seventy-eight-year-old inmate, Dr. Charles Friedgood, who has been incarcerated since 1977 for murdering his wife, has racked up medical bills of $230,000 over the past few years. This includes routine care as well as treatment for cancer and heart disease. Dr. Lester Lewis, the medical director of the Pennsylvania Department of Corrections, observes that inmates age faster than other people. A lifetime of high-risk behaviors, such as smoking, drinking, drug use, poor diet, and a lack of medical care, takes its toll. Indeed, says Lewis, "often on admission an inmate will say it is the first time he has ever seen a doctor, except maybe in an emergency room."[4]

Many people think elderly inmates have been in prison for years, perhaps locked up decades earlier as lifers. But in reality, a quarter have been in prison for less than a year, and 68 percent for less than five years. Only one percent have been in prison longer than thirty years. Also, more than two-thirds of these inmates were incarcerated for violent crimes, 25 percent for murder or manslaughter, and 27 percent for rape or sexual assault.[5]

It is generally accepted, although for reasons not yet determined, that people "age out" of criminal behavior. This assumption, along with humanitarian concerns over the plight of older prisoners, and a need to free up cells and resources for younger, more dangerous offenders, has led to a movement to gain early release for some older inmates. The Project for Older Prisoners (POP) has won the release of 168 prisoners in various states. All these prisoners were selected after their disciplinary records and the severity of their crimes were checked, it was determined they had no

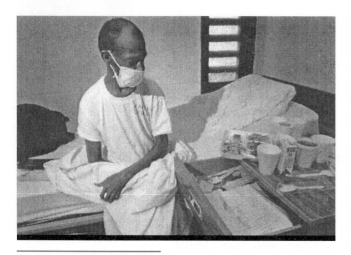

An inmate with AIDS in the infirmary, Limestone, Alabama.

infection that spreads through repetitious exposure in poorly ventilated spaces. Prisons are challenged to provide isolation wards for those affected and to improve ventilation for all prisoners. Still, most of those with active TB in federal and state prisons were being treated.[61] There is also the danger of infection for the community at large from released TB-infected convicts.

AIDS (acquired immune deficiency syndrome) poses an even greater danger and is proving to be a vast drain on prison budgets. According to the National Institute of Justice, by the end of 2005 there were 5,620 federal and state prisoners with AIDS and 22,480 prisoners who had HIV without manifesting symptoms of AIDS. New York has been hit particularly hard. In that one state alone, 4,440 prisoners under state jurisdiction tested positive for HIV/AIDS. The number of AIDS-related deaths declined significantly over the past decade. That said, controlling for New York (and its significant decline in HIV/AIDS cases), the number of cases has increased slightly.[62] (See Figure 13.1.) Coping with AIDS patients and controlling the spread of HIV infection in prison is a major problem.

3. Should elderly prisoners be housed in separate geriatric facilities, as some states have done, or kept in regular facilities? Are there benefits for the correctional system if elderly prisoners socialize with younger ones?

problems with drugs or alcohol, and the victims' families consented to their release. None of the 168 has been rearrested.[6]

The boom in elderly inmates is only just beginning. Experts are concerned with what will happen once the full impact of mandatory sentencing laws and "three strikes and you're out" are felt. Medical expenses are the fastest growing items in prison budgets, and expenditures on prisons are the fastest growing items in state budgets. The cost to states may well become too much to bear.

Questions for Discussion

1. Should elderly prisoners be released if they are too sick to be a danger to anyone, even if they have not served their sentences? Why or why not?

2. What duty does the government have to prisoners who are released after they are too old to support themselves economically (i.e., by getting a job)?

SOURCES

1. Fox Butterfield, "America's Aging, Violent Prisoners," *The New York Times,* July 6, 1997, p. E3.
2. Paige M. Harrison and Allen J. Beck, *Prisoners in 2002* (Washington, DC: Bureau of Justice Statistics, 2003), p. 9.
3. David C. Anderson, "Aging Behind Bars," *The New York Times Magazine,* July 13, 1997, p. 28.
4. Butterfield, "America's Aging, Violent Prisoners," p. E3.
5. Ibid.
6. Ibid.

Number of AIDS-related deaths in State prisons

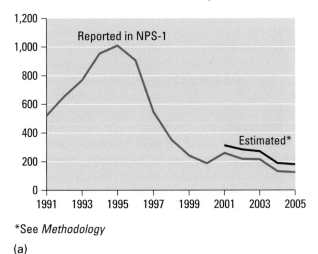

*See *Methodology*

(a)

Number of HIV/AIDS cases

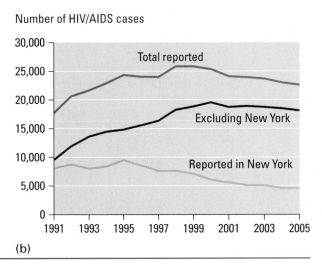

(b)

FIGURE 13.1   (a) Trends in AIDS-Related Deaths, 1991–2005 (b) HIV/AIDS Cases in State and Federal Prisons, 1991–2005

SOURCE: Laura M. Maruschuk, *HIV in Prison, 2005* (Bureau of Justice Statistics: Washington, DC, 2007), pp. 2, 5.   **385**

Most Serious Offense	State Prison		Federal Prison		Local Jail		Probation	
	Mentally Ill Inmates	Other Inmates	Mentally Ill Inmates	Other Inmates	Mentally Ill Inmates	Other Inmates	Mentally Ill Proba-tioners	Other Proba-tioners
All Offenses	100.0%	100.0%	100.0%	100.0%	100.0%	100.0%	100.0%	100.0%
Violent Offenses	52.9%	46.1%	33.1%	13.3%	29.9%	25.6%	28.4%	18.4%
Murder*	13.2	11.4	1.9	1.4	3.5	2.7	0.5	0.9
Sexual assault	12.4	7.9	1.9	0.7	5.2	2.8	6.8	4.1
Robbery	13.0	14.4	20.8	9.1	4.7	6.9	2.0	1.4
Assault	10.9	9.0	3.8	1.1	14.4	11.0	14.0	10.5
Property Offenses	24.4%	21.5%	8.7%	6.7%	31.3%	26.0%	30.0%	28.5%
Burglary	12.1	10.5	1.0	0.3	9.1	7.4	6.4	4.3
Larceny/theft	4.6	4.1	1.3	0.4	8.4	7.9	5.3	8.8
Fraud	3.1	2.6	5.0	4.9	5.2	4.4	11.7	9.2
Drug Offenses	12.8%	22.2%	40.4%	64.4%	15.2%	23.3%	16.1%	20.7%
Possession	5.7	9.4	3.9	11.9	7.3	12.3	7.2	11.0
Trafficking	6.6	12.2	35.7	46.6	7.0	9.6	6.7	9.2
Public-Order Offenses	9.9%	9.8%	17.0%	14.6%	23.2%	24.6%	24.7%	31.6%

NOTE: Detail does not sum to total because of excluded offense categories.

*Includes nonnegligent manslaughter.

SOURCE: Paula M. Ditton, *Mental Health and Treatment of Inmates and Probationers* (Washington, DC: Bureau of Justice Statistics, 1999).

TABLE 13.4   Most Serious Current Offense of Inmates and Probationers, by Mental Health Status

Mental Health

Mentally ill offenders pose a special and costly challenge for correctional services. Every state operates one or more facilities for mentally ill offenders (see Table 13.4 and Figure 13.2). Overall, there are 51,500 inmates in mental health programs in state and federal prisons. A small part of this population is made up of persons acquitted by reason of insanity. An even smaller number (about 10,000) are in sex offender programs. Nearly one-third of the patients are individuals unable to stand trial by virtue of mental illness, and over half are prisoners who have become mentally ill in prison.[63]

The nation's jails have been swelled by former or would-be mental patients who, under the deinstitutionalization policies in effect since the 1960s, are no longer cared for in mental hospitals. They are forced to live on their own, frequently become homeless, and are often in conflict with the law.[64] Prison and jail inmates often migrate between correctional and mental health facilities.[65] The cost to the public is considerable, and there are no promising cures on the horizon.

Drug and Alcohol Abuse

In addition to AIDS and mental health problems, inmates bring their drug and alcohol problems with them to jails and prisons.[66] Surveys of U.S. jails find a small percentage

	Estimated number of offenders*			
	State prison	Federal prison	Local jail	Probation
Identified as mentally Ill	179,200	7,900	96,700	547,800
Reported a mental or emotional condition	111,300	5,200	62,100	473,000
Admitted overnight to a mental hospital	118,300	5,000	60,500	281,200

*Based on midyear 1998 counts from the National Prisoner Statistics and Annual Survey of Jails and preliminary yearend 1998 counts from the Annual Probation Survey.

FIGURE 13.2   Estimated Number of Mentally Ill Inmates and Probationers, 1998
SOURCE: Paula M. Ditto, *Mental Health and Treatment of Inmates and Probationers* (Bureau of Justice Statistics: Washington, DC, 1999), p. 3.

of the average daily population of jail inmates are enrolled in drug treatment programs. Even in jails that have such programs, only about 10 percent receive daily treatment.[67] Things may be improving, however. A survey of all jail systems with over 200 prisoners found that all but one provided some sort of drug program, such as detoxification, drug education, individual or group counseling, therapeutic community, or community referrals.[68] According to one study, in the state and federal systems, 96,000 prisoners were in a drug treatment program—13.6 percent of the total inmate population.[69] The costs of operating an institutional drug treatment program are relatively modest, about $3.50 per day, per inmate, above and beyond the ordinary cost of incarceration. Enhanced treatment services would raise this cost to no more than $8 per day. Many criminal justice personnel believe that rehabilitative efforts aimed at substance-abusing offenders are relatively ineffective.[70]

Religion in Prison

Religion has been part of prison life since the establishment of prisons 450 years ago. It is surprising, however, that until recently not a single study documented the influence of religious experiences on prisoners.[71] Recent studies have revealed a modest to strong relationship between religiosity, religious commitment, and coping in prison.[72]

Furloughs

To soldiers and prisoners equally, a furlough and thus a break with boredom or stress is one of the most welcome privileges. Furloughs may be granted as a reward for good behavior, for purposes of participating in some outside program (education, or work-release), or for compassionate reasons such as a death in the family. During the 1970s, furloughs were increasingly granted. Only a very small proportion of prisoners on furlough did not return to the institution or did not return in a timely fashion.[73]

Furlough programs, like probation and parole, are strongly influenced by public opinion. It takes only one major failure to result in program curtailment or abandonment. The Willie Horton case is an example. Horton, a convicted murderer, committed rape and an assault while on furlough from a Massachusetts state prison. During the 1988 presidential campaign the Horton case became a major issue for liberal Democrats and conservative Republicans. The result was a sharp restriction of the federal furlough program: Whereas 4,610 federal furloughs had been granted in 1987, the number was down to 3,190 by 1991.[74]

Review

A very strong concern for security marks the U.S. prison today. Maximum security prisons are dedicated solely to that purpose. Medium security prisons have a somewhat more relaxed attitude but still emphasize security. Only minimum security prisons subordinate security to institutional programs.

Prisoners live "by the rules"; their assignments depend on their "classification" (profile). Corrections officers—predominantly custodial—have a difficult life in an environment that always seems threatening, yet their salaries and social prestige are low. Given the history of prison riots and attacks on officers, this fear is not exaggerated. The majority of inmates are young, black, undereducated, and largely aggressive. Aggressiveness is aggravated by prison overcrowding.

Women's prisons have their own distinct problems. Three-quarters of all imprisoned women are mothers. In some states mothers may keep their newborns with them for a while, but in most states children are placed with relatives in the community.

Correctional goals have changed somewhat over the last thirty years. Rehabilitation programs today are entirely voluntary, there are fewer of them, and enthusiasm has decreased ever since, in the 1970s, researchers demonstrated their overall ineffectiveness. But rehabilitation is making a comeback.

Vocational training and prison labor have likewise been transformed. Some correctional systems have formed their own prison industry organizations, and these are producing profits and creating skills and work discipline for inmates. Educational programs, provided by all federal and state correction systems, cover basic academic subjects as well as life skills.

Contemporary prison health problems are severe, particularly because of AIDS and TB. Programs designed to promote health, including mental health, through hygiene and recreation, are found in all prisons. Furlough programs, despite their positive effect on morale, have been decreasing for security reasons.

Thinking Critically about Criminal Justice

1. Should women in prison be allowed to keep their newborn babies with them? If so, for how long? If not, why not?

2. In some jurisdictions, married inmates are permitted conjugal visits. Should this privilege be extended to unmarried inmates as well? Why or why not?

3. There is debate over whether needles and condoms should be made available in prison. Advocates argue that drug use and sexual contact in prison are inevitable, and the goal should be reducing the harms of these behaviors (such as AIDS). But others say that giving out needles and condoms encourages and condones these illicit behaviors. Where do you stand on this issue?

Internet Connection

Note: While all of the URLs listed were current as of the printing of this book, these sites often change. Please check our website (http://www. mhhe.com/socscience/crimjustice/adlercj) for updates.

The Bureau of Justice Statistics (http://www.ojp.usdoj.gov/ bjs) collects data on prisons and inmates. Which states have the highest incarceration rates for females? Which have the lowest? What accounts for these great differences in the female incarceration rate across states?

What role does religion play in prison? See **http://www. youthandreligion.org/resources/ref_delinquency. html.**

Notes

1. Jim Quillan, *Alcatraz from Inside* (San Francisco: Golden Gate National Park Association, 1991), pp. 154, 155.

2. Harry Elmer Barnes and Neagley K. Teeters, *New Horizons in Criminology,* 2nd ed. (Englewood Cliffs, NJ: Prentice Hall, 1951), p. 456.

3. The President's Commission on Law Enforcement and the Administration of Justice, *Task Force Report: Corrections* (Washington, DC: U.S. Government Printing Office, 1967).

4. National Advisory Commission on Criminal Justice Standards and Goals, *Corrections* (Washington, DC: U.S. Government Printing Office, 1973).

5. *Bruscino v. Carlson,* 854 F.2d (7th Cir. 1988).

6. Human Rights Watch Report, "Out of Sight: Super Maximum Security Confinement in the United States," *Human Rights Watch* 12, February 2000.

7. Camille Graham Camp and George M. Camp, *The Corrections Yearbook, 1998* (Middletown, CT: Criminal Justice Institute, 1998), p. 19.

8. *Guidelines for the Development of Policies and Procedures, Adult Correctional Institutions* (College Park, MD: American Correctional Association, May 1981).

9. State of Kansas, *Inmate Rule Book* (May 1, 1986).

10. David R. Eichenthal and James B. Jacobs, "Enforcing the Criminal Law in State Prisons," *Justice Quarterly* 8 (1991), pp. 283–303.

11. Classification, which usually takes three to six weeks, is done either in a central recovery facility that serves the entire system or (in most states) in a reception center within each facility. For important classification factors, see Doris Layton MacKenzie and Robert A. Buchanan, "The Process of Classification in Prisons: A Descriptive Study of Staff Use of the System," *Journal of Crime and Justice* 13 (1990), pp. 1–26.

12. Lucien X. Lombardo, *Guards Imprisoned* (NY: Elsevier, 1981), p. 21.

13. Nicolette Parisi, "The Female Correctional Officer: Her Progress toward and Prospects for Equality," *Prison Journal* 64 (1984), pp. 92–109.

14. Kathleen Maguire and Ann L. Pastore, eds., *Source book of Criminal Justice Statistics, 1997* (Washington, DC: U.S. Government Printing Office, 1998), p. 88.

15. Gresham M. Sykes, *The Society of Captives: A Study of a Maximum Security Prison* (Princeton, NJ: Princeton University Press, 1958).

16. Kelsey Kauffman, *Prison Officers and Their World* (Cambridge, MA: Harvard University Press, 1988).

17. Lombardo, *Guards Imprisoned,* p. 115; Stephen C. Light, "Assaults on Prison Officers: Interactional Themes," *Justice Quarterly* 8 (1991), pp. 243–261. See also John R. Hepburn, "The Prison Control Structure and Its Effects on Work Attitudes: The Perceptions and Attitudes of Prison Guards," *Journal of Criminal Justice* 15 (1987), pp. 49–64.

18. Lombardo, *Guards Imprisoned,* pp. 113–140.

19. Francis Cullen, Bruce Link, John Cullen, and Nancy Wolfe, "How Satisfying Is Prison Work? A Comparative Occupational Approach," *Journal of Offender Counseling, Services and Rehabilitation* 14 (1989), pp. 89–108.

20. Bureau of Justice Statistics, http://www.ojp.usdoj.gov/bjs/prisons.htm.

21. Social scientists began to study inmate subcultures in 1934 with the publication of Joseph Fishman's *Sex in Prison* (NY: Padell Book Co., 1934).

22. Donald Clemmer, *The Prison Community* (NY: Holt, Rinehart and Winston, 1940). For adjustment to prison, see Kevin N. Wright, "A Study of Individual, Environmental, and Interactive Effects in Explaining Adjustment to Prison," *Justice Quarterly* 8 (June 1991), pp. 216–242.

23. For a full discussion of the "society of captives," the process of imprisonment, the inmate code, and the argot roles, see Sykes, *The Society of Captives.*

24. For a discussion of how prisoners deal with rejection from the free community, see Lloyd W. McCorkle and Richard Korn, "Resocialization within Walls," *Annals of the Academy of Political and Social Science* 293 (1954), pp. 88–98.

25. Susan Sheehan, *A Prison and a Prisoner* (Boston: Houghton Mifflin, 1978).

26. Alan J. Davis, "Sexual Assaults in the Philadelphia Prison System," in *Corrections: Problems and Prospects,* ed. David M. Peterson and Charles W. Thomas (Englewood Cliffs, NJ: Prentice Hall, 1975), pp. 64–75.

27. Human Rights Watch, No Escape: Male Rape in Prisons, available at: http://www.hrw.org/reports/2001/prison/

28. Camille Camp and George Camp, *The Corrections Yearbook, 1998,* p. 127; Ann Goetting, "Conjugal Association in Prison: Issues and Perspectives," *Crime and Delinquency* 28 (1982), pp. 52–71.

29. See Gresham M. Sykes and Sheldon L. Messinger, "The Inmate Social System," in *Theoretical Studies in the Social Organization of the Prison,* ed. Richard A. Cloward, Donald R. Cressey, George H. Gresser, Richard McCleery, Lloyd E. Ohlin, Gresham M. Sykes, and Sheldon L. Messinger (NY: Social Science Research Council, 1960), pp. 6–8.

30. Sykes, *Society of Captives,* p. 107.

31. Clarence Schrag, "Some Foundations for a Theory of Corrections," in *The Prison: Studies in Institutional Organization and Change,* ed. Donald R. Cressey (NY: Holt, Rinehart and Winston, 1961).

32. John Irwin and Donald R. Cressey, "Thieves, Convicts, and the Inmate Culture," *Social Problems* 10 (1962), pp. 142–155.

33. Frank S. Pearson, "Evaluation of New Jersey's Intensive Supervision Program," *Crime and Delinquency* 34 (1988), pp. 437–448.

34. R. G. Leger, "Perception of Crowding, Racial Antagonism, and Aggression in a Custodial Prison," *Journal of Criminal Justice* 16 (1988), pp. 167–181, 178.

35. Michael S. Serrill and Peter Katel, "New Mexico: The Anatomy of a Riot," *Corrections Magazine* 6 (1980), pp. 6–7. For causes of riots, see Randy Martin and Sherwood Zimmerman, "A Typology of the Causes of Prison Riots and an Analytical Extension to the 1986 West Virginia Riot," *Justice Quarterly* 7 (1990), pp. 711–737.

36. For a study of violence in female prisons, see Richard H. Anson and Barry W. Hancock, "Crowding, Proximity, Inmate Violence, and the Eighth Amendment," *Journal of Offender Rehabilitation* 17 (1992), pp. 123–132; Candace Kruttschnitt and Sharon Krmpotich, "Aggressive Behavior among Female Inmates: An Exploratory Study," *Justice Quarterly* 7 (1990), pp. 371–389.

37. Lee H. Bowker, *Prison Victimization* (NY: Elsevier, 1980), p. 25.

38. Hans Toch, *Peacekeeping: Police, Prisons, and Violence* (Lexington, MA: Lexington Books, 1976), pp. 47–48.

39. Camille Camp and George Camp, *Corrections Yearbook, 1997,* p. 6. For an historical study of the problems of female inmates, see Beverly A. Smith, "The Female Prisoner in Ireland, 1855–1878," *Federal Probation* 54 (1990), pp. 69–81.

40. Matthew Futterman, "Cold, Hard Life Awaits Grossberg, Peterson," *The Star-Ledger,* July 9, 1998, p. 17; Report on Delaware Corrections, 1981–1982 and 1986 (State of Delaware Department of Correction: Smyrna, DE, 1983, 1986).

41. *Fact Sheet, Women in Prison, The Sentencing Project,* December 2004, http://www.sentencingproject.org/pdfs/1032.pdf#search='women%20in%20prison%20and %20Bureau%20of%20justice%20statistics.

42. Ibid.

43. Joyce Carmouche and Loretta Jones, "Her Children, Their Future: Learning to Parent in Federal Prison," *Federal Prisons Journal* 1 (1989), pp. 23, 26, 27.

44. Phyllis Jo Baunach, *Mothers in Prison* (New Brunswick, NJ: Transaction, 1985); Phyllis Jo Baunach, "Critical Problems of Women in Prison," in *The Changing Roles of Women in the Criminal Justice System: Offenders, Victims, and Professionals,* ed. Imogene L. Moyer (Prospect Heights, IL: Waveland, 1992), pp. 99–112.

45. Nicole Gaouette, "Prisons Grapple with Rapid Influx of Women—and Mothers," *Christian Science Monitor,* May 19, 1997, pp. 1, 9–11.

46. B. McGowen and K. Blumenthal, "Children of Women Prisoners: A Forgotten Minority," in *The Female Offender,* ed. L. Crites (Lexington, MA: DC Heath, 1976).

47. Francis T. Cullen and Karen E. Gilbert, *Reaffirming Rehabilitation* (Cincinnati, OH: Anderson, 1982), p. 247.

48. D. Sechrest, S. O. White, and E. D. Brown, eds., *The Rehabilitation of Criminal Offenders: Problems and Prospects* (Washington, DC: National Academy of Sciences, 1979).

49. Douglas Lipton, Robert Martinson, and Judith Wilks, *The Effectiveness of Correctional Treatment: A Survey of Treatment Evaluation Studies* (NY: Praeger, 1975); Robert Martinson, "What Works?: Questions and Answers about Prison Reform," *Public Policy* 35 (1974), pp. 22–54.

50. Carl B. Klockars, "The True Limits of the Effectiveness of Correctional Treatment," *Prison Journal* 55 (1975), pp. 53–64; Ted Palmer, "Martinson Revisited," *Journal of Research in Crime and Delinquency* 12 (1975), pp. 133–152.

51. Robert Martinson, "New Findings, New Views: A Note of Caution Regarding Sentencing Reform," *Hofstra Law Review* 7 (1979), pp. 254–258.

52. Paul Gendreau and Robert R. Ross, "Revivification of Rehabilitation: Evidence from the 1980s," *Justice Quarterly* 4 (1987), pp. 395–407.

53. Carol J. Garrett, "Effects of Residential Treatment on Adjudicated Delinquents: A Meta-analysis," *Journal of Research in Crime and Delinquency* 22 (1985), pp. 287–308; Carol J. Garrett, *Treating the Criminal Offender,* 3rd ed. (NY: Plenum Press, 1988).

54. G. O. W. Mueller, "Economic Failures in the Iron Womb: The Birth of Rational Alternatives to Imprisonment," in *Sentencing: Process and Purpose,* 6 (Springfield, IL: Charles C. Thomas, 1977), pp. 110–143. See also William S. Laufer, "Vocational Interests of Criminal Offenders: A Typological and Demographic Investigation," *Psychological Reports* 46 (1980), pp. 315–324.

55. Thorsten Sellin, *Slavery and the Penal System* (NY: Elsevier, 1976), p. 143.

56. Todd Clear and George F. Cole, *American Corrections* (Pacific Grove, CA: Brooks/Cole, 1990), pp. 348–354.

57. Daniel Glaser, "The Effectiveness of Correctional Education," *American Journal of Corrections* 28 (1966), pp. 4–9.

58. Rick Telander, "Sports behind the Walls," *Sports Illustrated,* October 17, 1998, p. 82.

59. Centers for Disease Control and Prevention, *Tuberculosis Cases, Case Rates per 100,000 Population, Deaths, and Death Rates per 100,000 Population, and Percent Change: United States, 1953–2003,*http://www.cdc.gov/nchstp/tb/surv/surv2003/PDF/Table1.pdf.

60. Centers for Disease Control, *TB Transmission in Correctional Facilities 2002–2003,* numbers at www.cdc.gov.

61. Ibid.

62. Laura M. Maruschak, *HIV in Prisons and Jails, 2005* (Washington, DC: Bureau of Justice Statistics, 2005).

63. Camille Camp and George Camp, *The Corrections Yearbook, 1997,* p. 93; Bureau of Justice Statistics, *Report to the Nation on Crime and Justice* (Washington, DC: U.S. Government Printing Office, 1983), p. 68. On the extent of psychopathology in prison, as related to violence, see Deborah R. Baskin, Ira Sommers, and Henry H. Steadman, "Assessing the Impact of Psychiatric Impairment on Prison Violence," *Journal of Criminal Justice* 19 (1991), pp. 271–280.

64. Freda Adler, "Jail as a Repository for Former Mental Patients," *International Journal of Offender Therapy and Comparative Criminology* 30 (1986), pp. 225–236.

65. Henry J. Steadman and Joseph J. Cocozza, *Careers of the Criminally Insane* (Lexington, MA: Lexington Books, 1974), p. 17.

66. See Gerald Vigdal and Donald Stadler, "Controlling Inmate Drug Use: Cut Consumption by Reducing Demand," *Corrections Today,* June 1989.

67. M. Douglas Anglin and Yih-Ing Hser, "Treatment of Drug Abuse," in *Drugs and Crime: A Review of Research,* 13, ed. Michael Tonry and James Q. Wilson (Chicago: University of Chicago Press, 1990).

68. Camille Camp and George Camp, *The Corrections Yearbook, 1997,* pp. 226–228.

69. Ibid, p. 95.

70. Anglin and Hser, "Treatment of Drug Abuse."

71. See James M. Day and William S. Laufer, eds., *Crime, Values and Religion* (Norwood, NJ: Ablex, 1987);

Byron R. Johnson, "Religious Commitment within the Corrections Environment: An Empirical Assessment," in *Crime, Values and Religion,* ed. Day and Laufer. See also Harry Dammer III, *Prisoners, Prisons and Religion,* PhD dissertation, Rutgers University, 1992.

72. See Day and Laufer, *Crime, Values and Religion.* For a discussion of prison chaplains, see Bruce D. Stout and Todd Clear, "Federal Prison Chaplains: Satisfied in Ministry but Often Undervalued," *Federal Prisons Journal* 2 (1992), pp. 8–10.

73. Michael Isikoff, "Debate Rises on Prison Furlough Cuts; Critics Quiz Reasons behind the Crackdown," *The Houston Chronicle,* Star Edition, March 15, 1992, p. 2.

74. Camille Camp and George Camp, *The Corrections Yearbook, 1997,* p. 105.

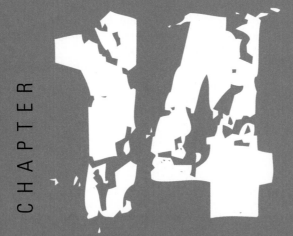

Alternatives: Community Corrections

Electronic ankle monitors may symbolize today's noninstitutionalized corrections. Obviously, it did not start that way. How did noninstitutionalized corrections get its start? John Augustus tells us: In the month of August 1841, I was in court one morning, when the door communicating with the lock-room was opened and an officer entered, followed by a ragged and wretched looking man, who took his seat upon the bench allotted to prisoners. I imagined from the man's appearance, that his offence was that of yielding to his appetite for intoxicating drinks, and in a few moments I found that my suspicions were correct, for the clerk read the complaint, in which the man was charged with being a common drunkard. The case was clearly made out, but before sentence had been passed, I conversed with him for a few moments, and found that he was not yet past all hope of reformation, although his appearance and his looks precluded a belief in the minds of others that he would ever become a man again. He told me that if he could be saved from the House of Correction, he never again would taste intoxicating liquors; there was such an earnestness in that tone, and a look expressive of firm resolve, that I determined to aid him; I bailed him, by permission of the Court. He was ordered to appear for sentence in three weeks from that time. He signed the pledge and became a sober man; at the expiration of this period of probation, I accompanied him into the courtroom; his whole appearance was changed and no one, not even the scrutinizing officers, could have believed that he was the same person who, less than a month before, had stood trembling on the prisoner's stand. The Judge expressed himself much pleased with the account we gave of the man, and instead of the usual penalty—imprisonment in the House of Correction—he fined him one cent and costs, amounting in all to $3.76, which was immediately paid. The man continued industrious and sober, and without doubt has been by this treatment saved from a drunkard's grave.

• This was truly encouraging, and before January 1842, I had bailed 17 persons for a similar offence, and they had severally been sentenced in the same manner, which in all amounted to $60.87. Eleven of this number paid the fine, but the other six being too poor to raise the amount, I paid it for them. (John Augustus)[1]

The community corrections movement of the 1960s emerged simultaneously with the growing concern for the rights of the accused in the criminal justice system. It was not coincidental that the decisions of the United States Supreme Court of the 1960s, notably cases that resulted in an expansion of the due process rights of defendants, had an effect on the corrections system. The use of alternatives to incarceration was consistent with the demand for more humane and effective methods of dealing with offenders who do not require imprisonment. More recently, a major challenge to the criminal justice system—prison overcrowding—has been the significant factor in rapid and politically motivated changes in corrections.[2] Probation, parole, and fines have always been regarded as cost-beneficial alternatives to imprisonment.[3] However, in an era when violent crime is increasing, policymakers and the public sometimes view these sanctions as inadequate solutions to the problem of prison overcrowding. Conservative legislators generally have been willing to fund the construction of new prisons, but construction costs and the frequency with which new facilities have to be built have put such a strain on state budgets that many conservatives have joined their liberal colleagues in opposing the expansion of the prison system. These circumstances have prompted the search for correctional alternatives consistent with the public demand for security, lower costs, and punishment (retribution). There are some promising possibilities, among them intensive supervision programs, shock programs, residential programs, home confinement, electronic monitoring, the use of volunteers in probation, and community service orders. We begin with the traditional alternative sanctions—probation and parole.

Probation

John Augustus was born in Woburn, Massachusetts, in 1784. He moved to Lexington at the age of twenty-one, learned the shoemaking trade, and by 1827 had become a successful shoemaker in Boston. Appalled by what he saw on his frequent visits to the courts—petty criminals jailed simply because they could not pay their fines—Augustus stepped forward and paid the fines himself. Nearly a century later, Sheldon Glueck described how John Augustus worked:

> His method was to bail the offender after conviction, to utilize this favor as an entering wedge to the convict's confidence and friendship, and through such evidence of friendliness as helping the offender to obtain a job and aiding his family in various ways, to drive the wedge home. When the defendant was later brought into court for sentence, Augustus would report on his progress toward reformation, and the judge would usually fine the convict one cent and costs, instead of committing him to an institution.[4]

probation
Alternative to imprisonment, allowing a person found guilty of an offense to stay in the community, under conditions and with supervision.

John Augustus promoted this new approach through his Washington Total Abstinence Society, and the Boston courts endorsed the idea. Thus was born the idea of **probation,** the release of a prison-bound convict into the community under the supervision of a trustworthy person and bound by certain conditions, such as not to violate the law, not to leave the jurisdiction, and to maintain employment.[5] Probation was a welcome alternative to prisons in the mid-nineteenth century, when the demand for prison space was greater than the supply, the first disenchantment about the capacity of penitentiaries to make inmates "penitent" had set in, and the exorbitant cost of imprisonment was first perceived.

The Benefits of Probation

The purpose of probation has always been to integrate offenders, under supervision, into law-abiding society.[6] By 1956 all states had a probation system. Most systems operate on the county level, but some are statewide.[7] Probation is now one of the most widely used correctional dispositions. In fact, approximately four times as many offenders are placed

Number of persons

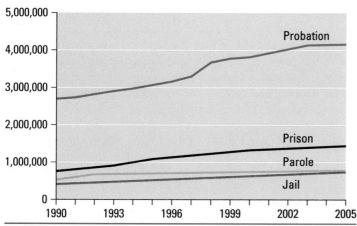

FIGURE 14.1 Number of Persons under Adult Correctional Supervision by Type of Supervision, 1995–2005

SOURCE: Lauren E. Glaze and Thomas P. Bonczar, *Probation and Parole in the United States, 2005* (Bureau of Justice Statistics: Washington, DC, 2006), p. 1.

on probation as are sent to prison. Probation serves the dual purpose of protecting the community through continued court supervision and attempting to rehabilitate the offender.

The benefits of probation are great: (1) Not all types of offenses are serious enough to require incarceration; (2) probationers can obtain or maintain employment and pay taxes; and (3) offenders can care for their families and meet their other financial responsibilities without becoming burdens on the state.

At year-end 2005, there were approximately 4,162,536 on probation; half (50 percent) had been convicted for committing a felony, 49 percent for a misdemeanor, and 1 percent for other infractions.[8] See Figure 14.1.

Revocation of Probation

Probation was often regarded as a favor bestowed by the judge on worthy prisoners. The court retained jurisdiction over probationers, reserving the right to revoke probation or to change probation conditions. With few restrictions on the court, judges used their discretion as to when and how to revoke or modify the original probation order. There was little concern for the normal due-process guarantees defendants enjoyed at their original trials. This situation began to change in 1967, when the Supreme Court ruled in *Mempa v. Rhay* that probationers are entitled to counsel at revocation proceedings.[9] *Gagnon v. Scarpelli* (1973) mandated the right to probation and parole revocation hearings, due-process guarantees during the probable-cause hearing, and a trial-like determination of the charges.[10]

The grounds for revocation have been somewhat softened over the years. Technical violations—including, in many cases, alcohol consumption—no longer routinely lead to revocation. Disciplinary hearings to determine revocations are based primarily on absconding, failing to maintain contact with the probation officer, arrest or conviction for a new offense, failure to pay fines or restitution, failure to attend or complete an alcohol or drug program, testing positive on a drug test, and failing to complete a community service requirement. Of probationers who have a disciplinary hearing, less than 30 percent are incarcerated in jail or prison. The majority are permitted to continue their probationary sentence, either with the original conditions or with the addition of new ones.[11]

Probation Officers

Probation officers are responsible for monitoring probationers' activities in the community. Treatment programs in general and probation programs in particular depend heavily on the personality and style of the person providing the service. The relative success of probation programs may be attributable to the professionals who have joined the probation service. An evaluation of the Massachusetts probation system found the quality of probation staff to be outstanding, officers having a strong and common desire to ensure public safety while providing rehabilitative support for offenders.[12] Generally they liked what they were doing, except for the endless administrative procedures.[13]

More than 80 percent of all probation departments in the United States require at least a bachelor's degree for initial appointment. In addition, many require specific courses of study (for example, criminal justice, sociology, or psychology), as well as varying levels of training and experience. Continuous in-service training is used in the majority of probation agencies to maintain and improve the skills of their personnel.

What Probation Officers Do.   Probation officers are employment agents, vocational counselors, marital counselors, school counselors, psychoanalysts, sheriffs, and moralists.[14] In short, probation officers are expected to help their clients comply with court orders, and this help calls for control (law enforcement functions) and treatment (social service functions).[15] Because caseloads now include an increasing number of high-risk probationers, the control law enforcement function has become dominant.[16] Other risk factors also have been changing the duties of probation officers, as this California example shows:

> Growing fears that violent crime is out of control in East Palo Alto have prompted San Mateo County to bar probation officers from making unannounced visits to the homes of clients in the beleaguered city.
>
> "We're trying to reduce our exposure to the volatile situation there," Rick Jones, deputy chief probation officer, said yesterday. . . .
>
> Jones said the probation department has been told that trouble between two street gangs has increased in recent weeks and that there have been reports of as many as 30 recent gunfire exchanges involving the gangs.[17]

Presentence Investigations.   The trial judge, in order to determine a convicted defendant's eligibility for probation, requests a presentence investigation (PSI) report (see Chapter 11).[18] However, PSIs are not prepared for all offenders who end up getting probation. Each year, only about 500,000 PSIs are written by probation officers in state systems.[19] Presentence reports are completed more often for felons than misdemeanants. Those with a past sentence of incarceration are more likely to have a PSI than those with no prior sentence.[20] This report is prepared by a probation officer, who focuses on such factors as the nature of the offense (violent or nonviolent), the defendant's version of the offense, previous criminal record, employment history, family background, financial situation, health, religious involvement, length of current residence, and community ties.[21] On the basis of the report, the judge decides whether to impose a prison sentence or probation.

The PSI report is a basic working document in judicial and correctional administration: (1) It aids the court in determining the appropriate sentence; (2) it aids the probation officer's rehabilitative efforts during probation supervision; (3) it assists prison staff in classification and in planning of treatment programs; (4) it furnishes the board of parole with pertinent information; and (5) it serves as a source of information for systematic criminal justice research.[22]

Some researchers have found that probation officer recommendations have a substantial effect on actual sentences.[23] Key factors used to make decisions about the perceived risk of probationers are information about previous record, seriousness of the offense, and negative attitudes about the consequences of the offense.[24] Some argue that the reason PSI reports have an impact on actual sentences is precisely because probation officers try to classify offenders according to the usual judicial considerations of offense and prior record. Moreover, even though other data, such as the defendant's attitudes and social history, are collected and included in the report, critics suggest probation officers give them much less weight in order to satisfy judicial expectations.[25]

The preparation of the presentence report is a complex process. Where appropriate, the information is verified through other sources. The massive amount of information that results from the investigatory process is then sorted, analyzed, and condensed into a written report. The investigator often encounters resistance, unclear leads, ambiguous information, and even misinformation. It takes a considerable amount of skill and experience to translate the mass of information into meaningful recommendations.[26]

Effectiveness of Probation

Probation as it works in practice has two major flaws:

1. Judges generally do not have the time, the information, or the ability to determine whether a given person is a good prospect for probation. They frequently view probation simply as a means to control the prison population by keeping less serious offenders out of prison or jail.

2. The probationer does not have the assistance and guidance that John Augustus considered essential for the success of probation.

There are other factors, as well, that affect the success of probation, for example, caseload. Officers performing regular supervision have a larger number of cases on average than those involved in intensive or electronic supervision.[27] The offenders being supervised are constantly changing. Under such circumstances, the officer has no chance to provide meaningful guidance and assistance. One would expect very high failure rates. It is not clear that this is the case. An examination of 19 studies reporting recidivism rates for probationers found failure rates ranging from 12 percent to 65 percent. The great difference in these rates is due to a number of factors: (1) no agreement on what constitutes probation "failure"; (2) different follow-up periods; and (3) differing study designs.[28] In general, recidivism rates are high for felony probationers, especially in areas where probation is used extensively. A low level of supervision is also related to recidivism.[29]

Probation programs are not keeping up with the rising prison population. As we begin the new millennium, the situation worsens, as most specialists deem community-based corrections inadequate for the young, aggressive, male offender whose numbers consistently rise.

Parole

Parole (from the French for "word" [of honor]) is a prisoner's conditional release under supervision after a portion of a sentence has been served. On the surface, parole may appear to be similar to probation. Both programs provide periods in which an offender lives in the community instead of serving time in a prison. Both programs require that the convict be under supervision to ensure good conduct. When the condition is violated, confinement results. But here the similarity ends (see Tables 14.1 and 14.2).

parole
Supervised conditional release of a convicted prisoner before expiration of the sentence of imprisonment.

Origins of Parole

The idea of parole was introduced in the United States at the first National Prison Association Congress in Cincinnati in 1870. Warden Zebulon Brockway of the Elmira Reformatory in New York began using parole in 1876. Promising convicts were released into the care of private reform groups before their terms had expired. Later on, corrections officers were assigned to supervise the parolees. By 1900, twenty states and the federal government had parole systems in place. Ultimately, all jurisdictions instituted parole (see Table 14.3). At present: There are approximately 784,408 adults under the supervision of parole agencies nationwide as of January 2006.[30]

TABLE 14.1
Probation versus Parole

Probation	Parole
A convict is sentenced to a period of probation *in lieu of prison.*	A prisoner is *released from prison* and placed on parole.
Probation is a front-end measure.	Parole is a tail-end measure.
The court imposes the sentence of probation.	A parole board grants release on parole.
The court retains jurisdiction.	A parole board retains jurisdiction.
A probation officer is an officer of the court and is employed by a county or district government.	A parole officer is a state officer employed by the state government.
Probation is an alternative sentence for less serious cases.	Originally, serious offenders earned parole through good conduct in prison.
Eligibility depends on a favorable PSI report.	Eligibility depends on successful service of a specific part of the prison sentence.

The Decision to Parole

parole board
Group of citizens, usually appointed by the governor of a state, who determine the eligibility of prisoners for release from prison and the dates for their release from prison and from parole.

The authority to release a prisoner on parole is usually vested in a **parole board** made up of respected citizens, usually appointed by the governor of the state. To provide professional input, governors have favored doctors, lawyers, educators, and psychologists in their appointments. Yet the boards do not present themselves as professional decision makers; they are there to represent the people of the state.

Members of the parole board serve for terms that range from two years to life. The average term is six years.[31] In some jurisdictions, the terms of the board members are staggered. Traditionally, it has been the function of parole boards to:

Year	Total Estimated Correctional Population[a]	Community Supervision		Incarceration	
		Probation	Parole	Jail	Prison
1995	5,342,900	3,077,861	679,421	507,044	1,078,542
2000	6,445,100	3,826,209	723,898	621,149	1,316,333
2001	6,581,700	3,931,731	732,333	631,240	1,330,007
2002	6,758,800	4,024,067	750,934	665,475	1,367,547
2003	6,883,200	4,073,987	774,588	691,301	1,390,279
2003 (revised)[b]	6,924,500	4,120,012	769,925	691,301	1,390,279
2004	6,995,200	4,143,466	771,852	713,990	1,421,911
2005	7,056,000	4,162,536	784,408	747,529	1,446,269
Percent change, 2004–2005	0.9%	0.5%	1.6%	4.7%	1.7%
Average annual percent change 1995–2005[c]	2.5%	2.5%	1.4%	3.9%	3.0%

NOTE: Counts of probationers, parolees, and prisoners are for December 31. All jail counts are for June 30. Jail and prison counts include inmates held in private facilities. Totals in 2000 through 2005 exclude probationers held in jail or prison.

[a]Because some offenders may have multiple statuses, totals were rounded to the nearest 100.

[b]Due to changes in reporting, total probation and parole counts include estimated counts for Massachusetts, Pennsylvania, and Washington based on reporting methods comparable to 2004.

[c]Percent change is based on comparable reporting agencies, excluding 226,192 probationers from agencies added since 1995.

Lauren E. Glaze and Thomas P. Bonczar, *Probation and Parole in the United States, 2005* (Bureau of Justice Statistics: Washington, DC, 2006), p. 1.

TABLE 14.2 Persons under Adult Correctional Supervision, 1995–2005

TABLE 14.3
Significant Developments in Parole

Year	Events
1840	Alexander Maconochie devises mark system for release of prisoners in Australian penal colony, a forerunner of parole.
1853	Sir Walter Crofton in Ireland establishes system under which prisoners can earn conditional freedom.
1869	New York State legislature passes enabling legislation and establishes indeterminate sentencing.
1870	American Prison Association endorses expanded use of parole.
1876	Parole release adopted at Elmira Reformatory, New York.
1931	Wickersham Commission criticizes laxity in use of early parole.
1944	Last state passes enabling legislation for parole.
1980s	Parole comes under attack as inconsistent with the just desserts model of sanctions. Twenty-nine states and the federal government abolish parole altogether or modify it severely by guidelines.
1993	Abolition and modifications have not created a decline in the number of parolees.

1. Determine the eligibility of prisoners for parole and place them on parole at their discretion.
2. Aid, supervise, and provide continuing control of parolees in the community.
3. Determine when the parole term has been completed and discharge a person from parole.
4. Determine whether parole revocation should take place if violation of conditions of parole occurs.[32]

Parole Hearings.   Members of the parole board meet to decide which prisoners will be granted parole at a **parole hearing.** Hearings are held in camera, meaning they are closed to the public, usually at penitentiaries, with only prisoners, attorneys, and witnesses in attendance. At the hearing, the board reviews information from many sources. The board thoroughly reviews the prisoner's file, which includes work reports from corrections officers, psychiatrists' reports on the "readiness" of the prisoner for release into the community, remarks the judge made at the time of sentencing, and, in some jurisdictions, statements submitted by victims of the crime. The prisoner may then be summoned to the hearing to argue why he or she is ready for release.

Parole boards are often faced with the difficulty of preferring to keep an inmate imprisoned, even though the individual is eligible for parole. Such a case may attract nationwide publicity because of the notoriety of the crime, such as that of Arthur Jackson, who attempted to kill the actress Theresa Saldana; or of Sirhan Sirhan, the assassin of Robert F. Kennedy; or of Charles Manson (and his followers), who massacred actress Sharon Tate and others. In many cases parole is strongly opposed by victims or victims' families, or by police groups, which routinely oppose the paroling of murderers of police officers.

Conditions of Parole.   Inmates granted parole are released into the community under supervision. As a prerequisite to release, the inmate must sign an agreement to adhere to the parole conditions—rules that prohibit, demand, or encourage certain behavior on the part of the parolee. The rules are meant to prevent the person from getting into trouble. Common conditions include abstinence from alcohol and drugs, restrictions on the people with whom the parolee can associate, curfew restrictions, and a prohibition against frequenting places the parole board deems a threat to the parolee's lawful behavior. Moreover, at least thirty-two states have enacted statutes that mandate the informing of local residents that a sex offender is living in their midst (see Figure 14.2). Usually, the parolee is required to report at frequent intervals to a parole officer and to notify the officer of any changes in place of residence or employment.

parole hearing
Meeting held by members of the parole board to decide whether prisoners will be granted parole.

SEX OFFENDER NOTIFICATION

The Thurston County Sheriff's Office is releasing the following information pursuant to RCW 4.24.550 which authorizes law enforcement agencies to inform the public when the release of information will enhance public safety and protection.

The individual who appears on this notification has been convicted of a sex offense that requires registration with the Sheriff's Office. Further, his previous criminal history places him in a classification level which reflects the potential to reoffend.

This individual has served the sentence imposed on him by the courts and has advised this office that he will be living in the location below. This notification is not intended to increase fear; rather, it is our belief that an informed public is a safer public.

NAME:
AGE:
RACE: White
SEX: Male
HEIGHT: 5-07
WEIGHT: 160
HAIR: Brown
EYES

RESIDENCE:

VEHICLES:

SYNOPSIS: In 1981 .... pled guilty in Clark County Superior Court to Indecent Liberties. This resulted from his sexual contact with an 8-year-old girl who was known to him. In 1988 .... again pled guilty to Indecent Liberties for multiple sexual contacts with a different 8-year-old girl, also known to him. In 1995 he pled guilty to Luring a Child for inviting another 8-year-old girl into his apartment. This girl was a stranger to him. After his release from custody, ... moved to Thurston County. He is under the supervision of the Washington State Department of Corrections and is not allowed unsupervised contact with juveniles.

For additional information, call Detective Jack Furey at 786-5—- or Detective Roland Weiss at 786-5—-.

FIGURE 14.2   Example of a Notification (All blank spaces have been blocked out.)

SOURCE: Peter Finn, Sex Offender Community Notification, National Institute of Justice (Washington, DC: U.S. Department of Justice, February 1997), p. 10.

Revocation of Parole

Technically still under the control of the corrections department while living in the community under "contract," parolees traditionally were returned to prison with few formalities when they violated the conditions of their contract. But since 1972, procedures for **revocation of parole** have undergone major changes. In a landmark decision *(Morrissey v. Brewer)* that changed parole agency procedures nationwide, the Supreme Court mandated that the Fourteenth Amendment requirement of due process of law applies to parole revocation proceedings.[33] While the Court did not call for the full range of rights due a defendant in a criminal proceeding, it set up procedural guidelines that states must follow before revoking an offender's parole.

Violations of parole conditions can be of two types: (1) commission of another crime, or (2) technical violation of a condition, such as breaking a curfew, leaving the jurisdiction, frequenting an off-limits place, or drinking alcohol. While commission of another crime may appear to be the major factor influencing decisions to revoke parole, studies reveal that two-thirds of all parolees released by decisions of the parole board, along with one-half of

revocation of parole
Return of a person on parole to prison for violation of a parole condition.

the mandatory releases, were returned to prison for technical violations of the conditions of their release (such as missing a curfew or a meeting with the parole officer). The parole-revocation process, it appears, cannot be fully understood without examining the strong influence of technical violations.[34]

Parole Officers

At the time of release, the parolee is assigned to a **parole officer** who is responsible for monitoring the parolee's activities and for providing him or her with help in readjusting to life in the community. This dual role makes the parole officer both a cop and a social worker. In the police officer's role, the parole officer has the duty to restrict the parolee's activities, to detect violations, to make an arrest, and to initiate revocation proceedings. As a social worker, the parole officer has to assist the parolee with adjustment and lend a helping hand when he or she is about to stumble. It is not easy to play both roles. A considerable body of research has tried to unravel the conflict between the roles to find practical solutions to the parole officer's predicament.[35] Georgia has experimented with assigning two officers to each case—one taking the role of the cop, the other the role of the social worker.[36] Who are these officers of which society expects virtual magic in the management of human behavior? For the most part they are college graduates with majors in relevant fields. A master's degree is frequently required for a supervisory position.

parole officer
Officer of the executive branch of government responsible for the supervision of convicts released from prison on parole.

Careers

An analysis of the workload allocation of parole officers, undertaken by the Adult Probation and Parole Services of Virginia, found that 36.4 percent of a parole officer's time was spent on supervising clients, 26.2 percent on investigations for courts and for the parole board, 11.2 percent on travel, 10.9 percent on administrative tasks, and the rest on training, public relations, and waiting.[37] The study also noted that time spent on investigatory activities had increased in recent years because of policy changes requiring a formal report on all persons entering supervision. Supervisory time had declined as a result of the increase in investigation activities.[38]

Effectiveness of Parole

Parole success rates have never been great.[39] In 2005, only 45 percent of parolees had completed their terms successfully.[40] The high failure rate is not the only reason parole has come under attack in recent years. First, parole is supposed to be a reward for rehabilitation in prison, yet prisons are generally not known for rehabilitating inmates. Thus prisoners are denied a reward because of the prison's failure. Second, the parole system has long been plagued by questions about the validity of the criteria used by parole boards in making parole decisions. Though nineteen jurisdictions have had guidelines for such decisions since federal guidelines were introduced in 1973, parole decision making nevertheless remains a mysterious and seemingly arbitrary process. Moreover, the system is subject to political manipulation and lobbying. For example, the governor may pressure the parole board to grant more releases when prisons are overcrowded. Lobbyists may exert pressure against a parole decision when a notorious inmate comes up for parole. The success of parole, like probation, depends on assistance and supervision. Yet caseloads are so great that such assistance is usually not available.[41] There is also the problem of changing release criteria every time the composition of the parole board changes.

Some scholars argue persuasively for the abolition of parole. The decision to release an offender, they argue, should not be based on questions of treatment or likelihood of offending again; rather, prison time should be correlated with degree of responsibility for the current offense. Most jurisdictions have terminated discretionary releases by parole boards and substituted release dates which are decided at the time of sentencing, so-called "determinate sentencing" (all but Hawaii, Kentucky, Montana, Nebraska, Pennsylvania, Utah, Vermont, Wyoming, and the District of Columbia). Some others have abolished parole altogether: Arizona, Delaware, Florida, Kansas, Maine, Minnesota, North Carolina, Ohio, Oregon, Virginia, Washington, and the federal system (Table 14.4).[42]

UNINTENDED CONSEQUENCES OF MEGAN'S LAW

In 1994, New Jersey became the first state to pass "Megan's Law," named after Megan Kanka, murdered by a neighbor who happened to be a recently released sex offender. The law calls for community notification when a sex offender moves into a neighborhood (see Figure 14.2). Opponents of the law argued that this notification would lead to harassment, threats, and vigilantism against parolees who are identified to neighbors and coworkers as convicted sex offenders. This, say detractors of the law, amounts to punishment on top of the punishment meted out by the court, and it is therefore unconstitutional. Litigation prevented application of the law for two years, but in February 1998 the United States Supreme Court declined to hear a constitutional challenge, and New Jersey began implementing the law.

Megan's Law is applied differently depending on the seriousness of the offense for which the offender was originally sentenced, estimations of his dangerousness, and where he ends up living. In some jurisdictions, information is widely distributed using material such as pamphlets, while in Connecticut and fourteen other states, citizens must ask police for the information without being told. This can create serious problems, as the residents of Willimatic, Connecticut, discovered. A convicted sex offender was charged there with murdering an eleven-year-old girl who delivered newspapers and lived in the same apartment complex. People claim Megan's Law failed them by not telling them about the rapist in their midst.[1]

Providing information about sex offenders living in the area is not without its consequences either. Frank Penna was convicted in July 1976 of kidnapping and raping two junior high school girls and was sentenced to ninety-nine years in prison. He was released in 1992 under stringent parole supervision. After six years of living a quiet life in Linden, New Jersey, his sleep was interrupted early in the morning of June 16, 1998, when someone fired five large-caliber bullets through the front window of his house. Earlier in the month, law enforcement officials had distributed fliers in the area identifying Penna as a high-risk sex offender. The fliers included information on Penna's name and address, as well as his description and photograph.[2]

For critics of Megan's Law, what happened to Frank Penna came as no surprise. John Furlong, a lawyer who helps parolees challenge their risk classifications, says the public hates sex offenders even more than murderers. He claims public notifications create scare-mongering and harassment—"I don't expect a rational response from a politicized public. The law appeals to the basest instinct in all of us to cast the demons out of our midst."[3]

Instances of vigilantism are not unique. In Warren County, New Jersey, a father and son broke

TABLE 14.4
States That Have Abolished Discretionary Parole, 2000

All Offenders		Certain Violent Offenders
Arizona	Minnesota	Alaska
California[a]	Mississippi	Louisiana
Delaware	North Carolina	New York
Florida[b]	Ohio[d]	Tennessee
Illinois	Oregon	Virginia
Indiana	Washington	
Kansas[c]	Wisconsin	
Maine		

[a]In 1976 the Uniform Determinate Sentencing Act abolished discretionary parole for all offenses except some violent crimes with a long sentence or a sentence to life.

[b]In 1995, parole eligibility was abolished for offenses with a life sentence and a twenty-five-year mandatory term.

[c]Excludes a few offenses, primarily first-degree murder and intentional second-degree murder.

[d]Excludes murder and aggravated murder.

SOURCE: U.S. Department of Justice, *Trends in State Parole, 1990–2000* (Washington, DC: Bureau of Justice Statistics, 2001).

sex offenders. "We understand society's desire to protect public safety and we sympathize with people who want to do something about sex offenders," she remarks. "But I wonder if this is the most effective manner."[5]

into the home where a paroled child molester was staying and then beat up the wrong man. Other sex offenders across the country have had repercussions directed toward them as well, such as threats, harassment, physical attacks, eviction, and loss of employment. Judges of the U.S. Court of Appeals considered these to be unintended consequences of Megan's Law and concluded they did not make the law an unconstitutional punishment.[4]

Others oppose laws identifying sex offenders, not because they lead to vigilantism, but because they violate privacy and aren't the best way to protect the community. A new law in Delaware requires the driver's licenses of sex offenders in that state to include the designation "y" on the license. The intent of the law is for sex offenders who leave Delaware to be identified as sex offenders in their new states when they apply for local driver's licenses. Judith Mellon, director of the American Civil Liberties Union in Wilmington, says she doesn't think the law will make much of a difference in tracking

Questions for Discussion

1. How can officials protect the community from released sex offenders, while at the same time not exposing them to the acts of vigilantes?

2. Some people say Megan's Law is unfair because it continues to punish sex offenders after they have "served their time." Do you agree with this argument? Why or why not?

3. Do sex offenders have a right to privacy after they are released? How about armed robbers, drug dealers, or white-collar offenders?

SOURCES
1. *Crime Prevention News,* September 10, 1998, p. 14.
2. Robert Hanley, "Shots Fired at the House of a Rapist," *The New York Times,* June 17, 1998, p. B1.
3. Robert Hanley, "Attorney General Seeks to Combat Vigilantism," *The New York Times,* June 18, 1998, p. B5.
4. Ibid.
5. Michael Janofsky, "Delaware Driver's Licenses to Note Sex Offenders," *The New York Times,* April 21, 1998, p. A15.

The **good time system** entails a procedure by which the length of the sentence is shortened by specific periods if the prisoner performs in accordance with the expectations of prison authorities. There may be many risks, especially to public safety, in the good time system, and much has to be learned about it before it can be considered an effective mechanism for alleviating prison overcrowding.[43] One survey from the 1980s found strong public approval for the use of good time and community-based corrections. Construction of more prisons received only moderate support, and shortening sentences and increasing parole boards' authority were disapproved.[44]

good time system
System under which time is deducted from a prison sentence for good behavior within the institution.

Intermediate Sanctions

Intermediate sanctions, such as fines, electronic monitoring, and intensive supervision, are designed to fill the gap between the two extremes of punishment—probation and incarceration. Sometimes intermediate sanctions are imposed along with a sentence of probation. The underlying assumption of intermediate sanctions is that community-based punishments can be as severe as prison sentences. It seems strange that an offender would find prison *less* punitive than intermediate sanctions, but keep in mind that the restrictions imposed on a person being intensively supervised or electronically monitored can seem quite daunting. One study found that inmates considered one year in prison to be as severe as three years

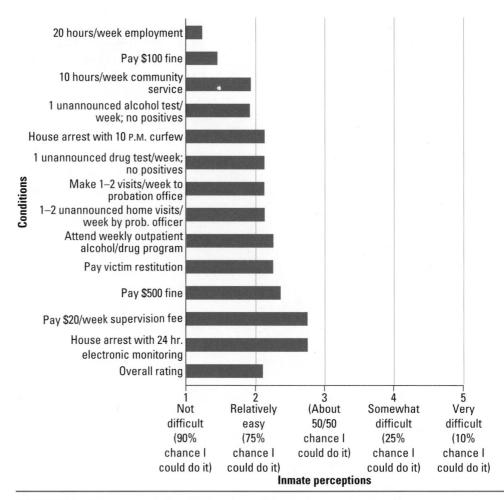

Conditions

- 20 hours/week employment
- Pay $100 fine
- 10 hours/week community service
- 1 unannounced alcohol test/ week; no positives
- House arrest with 10 P.M. curfew
- 1 unannounced drug test/week; no positives
- Make 1–2 visits/week to probation office
- 1–2 unannounced home visits/ week by prob. officer
- Attend weekly outpatient alcohol/drug program
- Pay victim restitution
- Pay $500 fine
- Pay $20/week supervision fee
- House arrest with 24 hr. electronic monitoring
- Overall rating

1	2	3	4	5
Not difficult (90% chance I could do it)	Relatively easy (75% chance I could do it)	(About 50/50 chance I could do it)	Somewhat difficult (25% chance I could do it)	Very difficult (10% chance I could do it)

Inmate perceptions

FIGURE 14.3 Inmate Perceptions of the Difficulty of Probation Conditions

SOURCE: Joan Petersilia and Elizabeth Piper Deschenes, "What Punishes? Inmates Rank the Severity of Prison versus Intermediate Sanctions" in *Community Corrections: Probation, Parole, and Intermediate Sanctions,* ed. Joan Petersilia (New York: Oxford University Press, 1998), pp. 149–159.

of intensive supervision or five years of regular probation. The key to making intermediate sanctions as unwelcome as prison is to manipulate the conditions. For example, a fine might not seem so bad, and most offenders think community service is easy. But combine a fine, community service, and unannounced drug testing for a period of three to five years, and some people think prison is preferable.[45] See Figure 14.3 for a look at how easy offenders thought it would be to comply with various intermediate sanctions.

There is a lot of variation in the types of intermediate sanctions available. New things are tried out by inventive judges, and changes in technology have led to many new developments. This section will look at pardons and monetary sanctions, restitution to victims, intensive supervision probation, shock programs, and residential and community-service programs.

Pardons and Monetary Sanctions

Probation and parole came into existence about 150 years ago. Yet two alternatives have been in use for almost 4,000 years: pardons and fines.

Pardons. Mechanisms resembling pardons existed in ancient legal systems, and they exist in all legal systems today. A **pardon** is the release from the legal penalties of an offense. Pardons are either full (absolute) or conditional. A pardon is **conditional** when its effectiveness

pardon
Release from the legal penalties of an offense.

conditional pardon
Pardon that depends on the fulfillment of specified conditions.

depends on the fulfillment of a condition (for example, serving a lesser sentence). A conditional pardon may be revoked for violation of the conditions imposed; a full pardon cannot be revoked. In 1867 the Supreme Court decreed that a pardon makes the offender "as innocent as if he had never committed the offense" *(Ex parte Garland),*[46] but in some states and for some purposes, a pardoned conviction may count as a previous offense.[47]

The power to pardon is exercised by the chief executive officer—the president of the United States in federal cases and the governor in state cases. In 1974 President Ford, for example, granted a pardon to ex-President Nixon, thereby sparing Nixon criminal prosecution. In 1992 President Bush granted Caspar Weinberger a pardon for his role in the Iran-Contra affair. President Clinton issued a series of controversial pardons as he left the White House. In state cases, pardons may be issued by the governor, usually acting through a state board of pardons, which is sometimes the parole board.

The pardoning power was originally seen as a method of righting legal wrongs, of freeing the innocent. Following this, a commutation of sentence, in the form of a pardon, became an acceptable way to correct unduly severe sentences, or to recognize mitigating circumstances that were not taken into consideration at the trial. When pardons are granted to an entire group of defendants, we speak of an amnesty. Although frequently used in other (especially Latin American) countries, and particularly in the case of political prisoners, neither pardons nor amnesties have played a significant role in the American criminal justice system. Nevertheless, the pardoning power remains important in individual cases, because it is the only available remedy—short of an act of the legislature—in the case of convicted persons whose innocence is discovered after all rights of appeal have expired.

Fines.   Until recently, fines were not used much in the American legal system, largely because it was felt that most offenders were unable to pay. Now the use of fines is increasing. A National Institute of Corrections report suggests that the increase has been prompted by financial pressure on the criminal justice system to demonstrate to the public that the "user" of the system must pay. Monetary sanctions include fines and also the payment of court costs and various types of fees including those for bail, public defender services, alcohol or drug assessment, urinalysis, and out-of-state transfers.[48] In traffic courts, fines are used almost exclusively.

In courts that handle serious felony offenses, fines are much less common.[49] There appear to be significant gender differences in the assessment of fines. In cases of violence against the person, for example, fines are imposed in 40 percent of cases with male defendants but only 25 percent of cases with female defendants. But for indictable traffic offenses, 73 percent of cases with females result in fines compared with 53 percent of male cases.[50]

Although monetary sanctions may seem an effective and cost-beneficial alternative to incarceration, many offenders are too poor to pay fines. A fixed sum of money has different meanings for people in high, medium, and low income brackets. To compensate for income differentials among offenders, the Nordic countries (Sweden, Denmark, Norway, Finland, and Iceland) have long used the "day fine" system: the amount of the fine is measured in days of earnings. For a drunk-driving offense, the fine may be ten days' earnings. For the corporate executive, the fine may amount to ten times $500, or $5,000. For a factory worker, it may amount to ten times $50, or $500. This scheme, which is like the graduated income tax, helps the treasury as well. The offender stays in the community and is able to meet other obligations, such as supporting a family and making the car payments.

Restitution to Victims

The concept of restitution by offenders to their victims is as old as that of punishment. In ancient legal systems we find the two side by side, either as sole or as alternative sanctions. In theory, victims of crime have always had some recourse against victimizers. Modern legal systems have permitted a civil suit by the victim against the offender, and in some European countries the crime victim may join the criminal prosecution and obtain a damage award in case of conviction.

Restitution is different from victim compensation. **Restitution** binds the offender to pay the victim; in victim compensation schemes it is the state that compensates crime victims.

restitution
Compensation (normally court-ordered) on the part of an offender to the victim, or a victim substitute, for any losses or harm inflicted, usually in money or services.

In recent years victim advocates have endorsed restitution as part of the sentence imposed on the convict. The purpose of restitution is to make up for some of the victim's financial losses and to begin the process of healing and recovery.[51]

An option for nonviolent offenders that takes restitution a step further is **restorative justice.** In addition to paying the victim, the offender has to apologize to the victim and others affected by the crime, repair the damage done to the victim (such as fixing damaged property), and take specific steps not to commit the crime again. The goal of restorative justice is to force offenders to acknowledge what they have done and make amends to the community (see Chapter 15).[52]

Intensive Supervision Programs

As originally conceived, probation programs were aimed at prison-bound convicts for whom it was thought that safety considerations did not require imprisonment and for whom association with other prisoners in confinement would do more harm than good. Traditional probation requires intensive supervision, and such supervision has become impossible because the number of probationers is so enormous.[53] Some states continue to use token or routine probation for low-risk cases, but many have also introduced **intensive supervision probation (ISP)** for convicts who do not qualify for routine probation.

The New Jersey Experience.   The experience of the New Jersey ISP program has been particularly encouraging. This program, directed by the Administrative Office of the Courts since 1983, is designed to handle 500 convicts, the equivalent of the population of one prison. Since only nonviolent offenders are eligible, the program excludes armed robbers, murderers, and all sex offenders. Inmates who want to be considered must apply between the first and second month of imprisonment. (This period is considered a desirable shock incarceration period.)

The Offender's ISP Plan.   Each applicant must develop a personal plan describing his or her own problems, available community resources, and contacts. A community sponsor must be identified with whom the offender will live during the early months after release and who will help the offender fulfill the program's objectives. Applicants must also identify several other people in the community who can be relied on for help. These people are called the "network team."

The offender's ISP plan and the persons identified in it are closely checked. All information is placed before the ISP screening board, which includes the ISP director, corrections staff, and community representatives. If the screening board's decision is positive, the application goes to a three-judge resentencing panel. A positive decision by this panel results in a ninety-day placement in the ISP program; the placement is renewable after ninety days. Each ISP participant must serve a minimum of one year in the program, including time on parole after release, during which period he or she is on a bench-warrant status (subject to immediate arrest should a violation occur).

Program Conditions.   The program conditions, focusing on employment and hard work, are punitive and onerous. They include the following:

- At least sixteen hours of community service per month.
- Multiple weekly contacts with the ISP officer and the community sponsor.
- Maintenance of a daily diary detailing accomplishments.
- Immediate notification of the ISP officer of any police contact or arrest.
- Participation in counseling activities, if ordered.
- Maintenance of employment or participation in a vocational training program.
- Participation in any treatment program (drug, alcohol) designated by the ISP officer.
- Adherence to curfew (normally 6 P.M. to 6 A.M.).
- Electronic monitoring, if ordered.

---

restorative justice
Model of justice, opposed to retributive justice, aimed at the offender's contribution to offset the harm done, including reconciliation with victims.

intensive supervision probation (ISP)
Alternative to prison for convicted nonviolent offenders who do not qualify for routine probation; probation subject to stringent supervision.

Alternative programs: Goree boot camp, an intensive supervision program, Huntsville, TX.

- Home visits by the ISP officer.
- Abstinence from illegal drugs and alcohol and gambling (including playing the lottery).
- Payment of all obligations, such as the cost of electronic monitoring ($5 to $18 daily), court costs, fines, victim compensation, and child support, to the extent ordered by the court.

Evaluation. The failure rate in the New Jersey ISP program has been far lower than anybody expected. As of 2006, the reconviction rate of those who graduate is 11 percent, compared to nearly 50 percent for state inmates.

Among the program's greatest benefits are these:

- Rather than costing the state $36,357 per year for incarceration, ISP costs $9,472, thus saving the state over $25,000 yearly per convict.
- The offender earns a living, pays taxes, and pays the cost of electronic monitoring, fines, fees, and other obligations.
- There is significant evidence that ISP participants do better after discharge than prison inmates.[54]

ISP Nationwide. New Jersey's program is particularly strict and demanding, and thus more costly than that of any other state. Yet by saving prison space it is cost effective.[55] The program in Illinois targets offenders who constitute a lesser risk and costs only $2,500 per convict. ISP programs in some other jurisdictions have proved to be similarly cost effective. In Georgia, ISP has proven to be an effective alternative to prison with little risk to the public. On the basis of the number of offenders diverted from prison to the program, it is estimated that Georgia's program has saved $20 million.[56] The ISP program in Montgomery County (Dayton), Ohio, has also been found to be cost effective.[57]

But not all research supports the use of ISP. A recent scathing attack suggests that ISP does not reduce recidivism rates, is not cost effective, and does not reduce rates of imprisonment.[58] It is not surprising, then, that some states seem reluctant to experiment with it.

Intensive Supervision of Parolees. Intensive supervision appears to be effective and cost beneficial for convicts who are eligible for parole but who might pose undue risks and are therefore denied release on routine parole. Release into an intensive supervision parole program, structured along the same lines as front-end programs, frees prison bed space and provides the same financial rewards to the community as front-end programs. New Jersey's Intensive Supervision and Surveillance Program (ISSP), operated by the Bureau of Parole, assigns high-risk offenders to ISSP for ninety days. Following a case evaluation, the parolee may be assigned to standard parole. Judgment as to the effectiveness of these types of programs awaits further research.

Shock Programs

Shock probation is probation granted after a short period of incarceration. Some corrections specialists believe that punishment should be measured not by time alone, but also by the punitiveness and severity of the experience. A short, sharp shock incarceration may be as intense as a longer, "easy-time" confinement in a prison. Moreover, the shorter incarceration may avoid the "prisonization effects" that longer prison sentences entail.

Shock incarceration attempts to "shock" offenders out of criminal behavior by subjecting them to short periods (90–180 days) of intense drills, hard work, and character-building exercises. Similar to Marine Corps or army training, these shock programs are sometimes referred to as "boot camp."

Shock Incarceration. There are many types of shock incarceration (SI) programs. They operate either inside prison or in separate facilities and focus on young prison-bound convicts, many with histories of alcohol and drug abuse. The first SI program, Oklahoma's

shock probation
Sentence that allows for brief incarceration followed by probation, in an effort to induce law abidance by shocking the offender.

shock incarceration
Short term of incarceration that subjects offenders to hard work, intense drills, and other character-building exercises.

JOHN LILLY, DIRECTOR, DAY REPORTING PROGRAM, ATLANTIC COUNTY CORRECTIONAL INSTITUTION, MAYS LANDING, NEW JERSEY

When I began in corrections as a line officer I was determined to be a contributor, to make a difference. I soon learned that there were insurmountable obstacles at every turn. And, incidentally, I am not talking about resistance from the inmate population. Albeit, there are always those who resist change even if it serves as a means of improvement. But the overall plan initiated by the "system" has to be correct, implemented properly, and maintained with unquestionable persistence. The big questions are "What works?" and "How much is it going to cost?" And to most people, any additional funding is too much.

On the surface, I may sound like a defeatist. Yet I firmly believe that some, not all, inmates are fully capable of being rehabilitated for reentry into society. I have been there in the trenches. I have been subjected to physical assaults and, unfortunately, I've been the recipient of stale, stinking urine and aged, disgusting feces. I have seen the results of gang rapes and I have witnessed uncontrolled violence, unimaginable bloodshed resulting from serious, life-threatening assaults, and the sad aftermath when an inmate has given up all hope—resigned to taking his or her precious life by suicide.

Let me add to this the constant verbal abuse that exists all around you at all times. The abuse and intimidation is like adding fuel to a flash fire. It produces extremely high stress levels that hover constantly like a dense fog that could be cut with a knife. Just imagine that you got up late for work one morning, which started raising your stress level. Add to this scenario that your children are "out of control." Now you arrive for work, already stressed out, and instead of your coworker or customer greeting you with "Hello," you are greeted with an obscenity. This is the way it really is. And it is damn hard not to let go and unleash that pent-up stress. But that poor judgment could cost you your life or, possibly, the life of someone else.

And still I have always believed that there is a chance for salvaging some inmate. You have to learn to rationalize what the offender is going through, what he or she is facing, in order to begin to understand how to intervene with a defined,

Regimented Inmate Discipline (RID) program, was established in 1983. Inmates who meet the criteria for eligibility (no previous prison term) may volunteer. Along with the usual strict discipline and drill of all SI programs, inmates of RID spend several hours daily in educational, vocational, drug-abuse, and counseling programs. After completing the 120-day program, the Oklahoma Department of Corrections recommends that judges resentence the inmates to probation or, in some cases, to a halfway house.[59]

The inmates of Georgia's Special Alternative Incarceration (SAI) programs spend eight hours a day at hard labor in addition to the usual boot camp activities. Except for drug-abuse education, SAI participants get little counseling or treatment. The "shock" component of the program is primary. After completion of the program, inmates are released to regular probation supervision.[60] Recent SI programs have more innovative goals than the older ones. The New York program, for example, created in 1987, features more extensive therapy programs (see Figure 14.4). Connecticut's program includes community service as part of the incarceration program.[61]

Evaluation of SI Programs. On the whole, shock incarceration programs do not reduce recidivism. There is no difference in the rate of reoffending of boot camp graduates and

disciplined program of reeducation, regardless of the number of government-funded programs. You have to give respect, be truthful, and demonstrate trust in order to earn respect and trust from the inmates. You must be honest at all times and never, ever agree to anything, no matter how trivial, that you can't see through. You have to get inside the inmates' heads and make them realize that they are individuals with the ability to change, to improve, and ultimately, to make a difference in their lives and their futures. Inmates have to realize that they are responsible for their own actions.

I have always had a strong, sincere belief that there exists some good in all of us, whether on the inside or outside. For that reason, I became instrumental in building a community release project limited in scope and designed specifically for inmates sentenced for nonviolent offenses. Guidelines are rigid with virtually no room for mistakes. Inmates are totally responsible for all of their own actions or inactions while in this program.

They are required to attend an initial orientation where they sign a written agreement to abide by all conditions of the program regardless of any inconveniences. While on the program, participants remain free from incarceration and abstain from all alcohol and drugs. They are required to report to the justice facility a minimum of two days a week, dressed to work outside, and bring their lunch. Agencies, municipalities, and non-profit organizations pick up the inmates and supervise them in the performance of work projects, such as but not limited to sweeping streets, lawn maintenance in cemeteries, construction of playgrounds, and distribution of food to the needy.

Noncompliance with the rules and regulations of the program suffices for the participant's removal from the program and immediate incarceration. Correspondingly, the sentencing court has the option of imposing additional jail time if the participant's violation included any involvement or conspiracy in a criminal act.

The project, called the Day Reporting Program (DRP), began in 1991 with 11 participants. As of December 31, 1998, there were 350 participants with a recidivism rate of less than 2 percent. The program received national recognition and has been the recipient of two national awards.

The program has satisfied the two major objectives anticipated during its initial implementation: (1) provide a manageable mechanism that would demonstrate a significant, measurable reduction in jail overcrowding; (2) create a platform for utilizing community agencies in a unified effort to improve the quality of life, appearance, and environment in the community without having to resort to increasing taxes to local citizens.

Now, fifteen years later, I have stepped outside the field of corrections and I look back. I weigh my accomplishments and any contributions that I may have made. I believe that I actually made a difference. Granted, working in the field of corrections is one of the most stressful, demanding careers. However, it can be a very rewarding professional experience.

those with similar profiles who have served time in prison. Shock incarceration programs are thought to be cost-effective in that they reduce prison overcrowding and save prison bed space. But this is only true if the programs target offenders who would otherwise have been sent to prison. If offenders are sent to boot camp when they would have otherwise received a lesser sentence such as probation, then the program can end up costing more. However, shock incarceration is successful in changing the attitudes of offenders. Unlike prison inmates, boot camp inmates develop more positive attitudes over time about the program and feel their participation has changed them for the better.[62]

Boot camp programs are politically attractive because they are cost-effective and they demonstrate to the public that offenders are undergoing an intense disciplinary experience. Their popularity has spread across the country.[63] The programs are almost always used only for young male offenders, but these men traditionally constitute two-thirds of all inmates. It may be too early to assess the value of boot camps to the parole and probation systems, but the legislatures of several states, including California, Delaware, Georgia, Idaho, Louisiana, Kansas, Maryland, Michigan, Montana, New Hampshire, North Carolina, Ohio, Texas, Virginia, Wisconsin, and Wyoming, have been willing to experiment with this alternative form

A.M.	
5:30	Wake up and standing count
5:45–6:30	Calisthenics and drill
6:30–7:00	Run
7:00–8:00	Mandatory breakfast/cleanup
8:15	Standing count and company formation
8:30–11:55	Work/school schedules
P.M.	
12:00–12:30	Mandatory lunch and standing count
12:30–3:30	Afternoon work/school schedule
3:30–4:00	Shower
4:00–4:45	Network community meeting
4:45–5:45	Mandatory dinner, prepare for evening
6:00–9:00	School, group counseling, drug counseling, prerelease counseling, decisionmaking classes
8:00	Count while in programs
9:15–9:30	Squad bay, prepare for bed
9:30	Standing count, lights out

FIGURE 14.4   Daily Schedule for Offenders in New York Shock Incarceration Facilities

SOURCE: Cherie L. Clark, David W. Aziz, and Doris L. MacKenzie, *Shock Incarceration in New York: Focus on Treatment* (Washington, DC: National Institute of Justice, 1994), p. 5.

of confinement.[64] It remains to be seen whether American boot camps will produce disciplined and productive members of the community.[65] In several European countries, similar treatment programs have had little success and have therefore been discontinued.[66]

Residential Programs

Mexico's Toluca Federal Prison has a number of cottages right outside the prison wall where inmates may spend the last portion of their sentence in relative freedom. They lead their own lives, they are not locked up, and they are bused to town for work. The prison wall behind the cottages reminds them of what will happen if they fail. At the same time, the social workers at the penitentiary are close enough to provide counseling and assistance. Toluca's cottages illustrate the worldwide search for a correctional strategy somewhere between prison and the community.

Halfway Houses.   In the United States, residential programs take a variety of forms, so that it is difficult to classify them. The most common form is the **halfway house.** Halfway houses are located in the community, have resident staff (social workers, clergy), typically offer drug and alcohol treatment, and are most often operated by private organizations under contract with the state. The average capacity of halfway houses is twenty-five residents, and individuals stay for an average of eight to sixteen weeks.[67]

Halfway houses often face objections from the community: No one wants "ex-cons" in their neighborhood. This is called the nimby attitude, short for "not in my back yard." To overcome this problem, a variation on the standard halfway house has been developed. For want of a better name one could call this variation the "economic opportunity group home." The group home leaders are social activists who want to change former inmates from economic failures to economic successes. Leading examples are House of Umoja in Philadelphia; Achievement Place in Lawrence, Kansas; Pyramid House in Newark, New Jersey; and the Delancy Street Foundation in San Francisco. Some of these group homes accept mostly juveniles (often violent and drug addicted); others target primarily adults. In the adult halfway

halfway house
Residential correctional facility in which an offender may have to serve the last portion of his or her sentence outside prison, but not yet in the community.

houses, all types of offenders live together—those who have committed street crimes and those involved in white-collar crimes. (Baseball hero Pete Rose spent three months in a halfway house in the same city where a street is named after him.)

Halfway houses rely on group therapy, education, training, and jobs to help the ex-cons adjust to life outside prison. Yet another and more recent version of halfway houses are restitution centers, designed to provide a basis for convicts to meet their financial obligations, including restitution.

Home Confinement and Electronic Monitoring

House Arrest.   In 1985, Federal District Court Judge Jack Weinstein imposed an unusual sentence on Maureen Murphy, who had been convicted of a large insurance fraud. Instead of being confined to prison, she was confined to her own home. The judge explained his departure from the traditional sentence as an effort to balance the competing aims of public safety, humaneness, and accountability against a backdrop of seriously crowded prisons. Probation did not seem severe enough; on the other hand, prison for a person with no previous criminal record seemed too severe.[68]

House arrest is a sentence imposed by the court whereby offenders are legally ordered to remain confined in their own residences for the duration of their sentence. House arrestees may be allowed to leave their homes for medical reasons, employment, and approved religious services. They may also be required to perform community service and to pay victim restitution and probation supervising fees. In selected instances, electronic monitoring equipment may be used to monitor an offender's presence in a residence where he or she is required to remain.[69]

The selection criteria for house arrest offenders are similar across all jurisdictions. Offenders are disqualified if they have:

- A history of violence.
- Chronic drug or alcohol problems.
- Unstable interpersonal relationships at home.
- Immigration problems.
- A prior criminal history, including a history of failure to appear.
- An unstable employment history.

In general, probation officers and judges look at the whole picture—prior record, age, health, substance abuse, circumstances of the current offense, home life, employment, and the attitude of the offender—to decide if home confinement is a "good bet."[70]

Michigan, Nevada, and Oklahoma have experimented with residential confinement programs with participants drawn from the prison population. Most states with such programs use them for front-end diversion from prison. In the Maryland program, which has operated successfully for several years, the sentencing judge and the Department of Corrections jointly make the decision to use the defendant's home rather than a prison cell as the place of confinement. This twofold approval is designed to ensure that dangerous or high-risk offenders are not placed in the program.

Evaluations of house arrest programs are generally favorable. In one evaluation in Florida, over half the people on house arrest would have gone to prison if the program did not exist. Some critics of house arrest fear the possible danger to the community, yet this study found the program did not constitute a threat to public safety. Further, only two-thirds of the house arrestees were arrested for new crimes, compared to 100 percent for a similar group of former prisoners. The research also concluded that the savings from the program may be close to $300 million annually.[71]

Electronic Monitoring.
Many house arrest programs incorporate a level of **electronic monitoring.** Electronic devices provide for computer-assisted checks on an offender to ensure that he or she is not moving about in the community in violation of restrictions ordered by the court.[72] Electronic

house arrest
Sentence in which convicts are confined to their own residence in lieu of imprisonment in an institution

electronic monitoring
Computer-assisted checks on offender's movement to ensure that he or she is not going to places in violation of restrictions.

PUBLIC HUMILIATION— AN EFFECTIVE FORM OF PUNISHMENT?

When it comes to sentencing, judges have long experimented with different combinations, such as jail and a fine, a fine and community service, community service and probation, and so on. Some of the sentences judges come up with are creative and are designed to help rehabilitate the offender as well as punish.

A case in Rockville, Maryland, resulted in sanctions against a parent. Timothy Rinehart, an unlicensed sixteen-year-old boy, drove his car head-on into Judith Flannery, fifty-seven, and killed her. She was a world-class triathlete out for bicycle training. Montgomery County Juvenile Court Judge Dennis McHugh sentenced Rinehart to perform 300 hours of community service, write an essay, and seek a judge's permission before applying for a driver's license. His father, who, after drinking several beers, was sitting in the passenger's seat at the time of the accident, was ordered not to drink around his son, nor to drink four hours before or after being in the presence of his son.[1]

A similar case involved Brandon Blenden, who was sentenced by Harrison County, Mississippi, Circuit Court Judge John Whitfield to twenty years after killing someone while he was driving drunk. As part of his sentence, he must write a check every Friday for ten years for $1 and send it to Mrs. Ann Lee, the mother of the 4-year-old child he killed. On each check, Blenden must write "for the death of your daughter, Whitney."[2]

Other jurisdictions are exploring sentences intended to cause public humiliation to the offender. Said Harris County, Texas, State District Judge Ted Poe, "Most of us care what people think of us. If we're held up for public embarrassment, we don't like it." Here are some examples of Poe's sentencing practices:

- A man who drove 100 mph without headlights on was told to carry a sign along a major highway which read, "I killed two people while I was driving drunk," and to keep pictures of his victims in his wallet for 10 years.

monitoring is used in conjunction with both home detention and intensive supervision programs as a way to monitor compliance with the conditions of a sentence.

There are two types of electronic monitoring systems—active and passive. Active systems (sometimes called "continuous signal systems") provide constant monitoring. A transmitting device, or "tag," strapped to the offender continuously signals either a central tracking computer or a portable receiver carried in the supervisor's vehicle. The transmitter signals a receiver–dialer. The receiver–dialer receives the signal and dials the central office computer when the transmitter is within a predetermined geographic range, indicating that the offender is at home. Passive systems (sometimes called "programmed contact systems") include less sophisticated techniques such as telephone verification. The offender must respond to a telephone call within a prescribed time period, or a failure reading is recorded.[73]

Global positioning satellites (GPS) are now being used in some places to track offenders wherever they go. This technology, first used for electronic monitoring in 1997, generates maps that indicate an offender's exact location. In addition to providing the same apparent benefits of active monitoring, this GPS system allows certain areas to be designated "off-limits" to offenders, such as the area around a wife's house for a spousal abuser, or playgrounds or schoolyards for pedophiles. Entering these forbidden zones sets off an alarm.[74]

- A man convicted of domestic violence was made to apologize to his wife in front of a crowd of 450 people.

- A teenaged graffiti writer had to apologize to students at all 13 schools he vandalized.[3]

As part of a probation sentence, Judge Thomas Brownfield of Pittsfield, Illinois, ordered the display of a sign declaring, "Warning: A Violent Felon Lives Here, Travel at Your Own Risk," at the end of a sixty-two-year-old farmer's driveway after he was convicted for bashing another farmer in the face with a fuel pump. It seems the defendant had previously been convicted of aggravated assault for stomping an insurance adjuster and acquitted of scuffling with a collection agent.[4]

In Rehoboth Beach, Delaware, bar patrons who urinate in public can expect to have their names sent to newspapers and local radio and television stations. They are also fined $100. The town's police chief, Creig Doyle, also relies on public humiliation to address other offenses such as loitering, drinking under age, and drinking and driving.[5]

Creative sentences are sometimes given to youthful offenders because they are seen as more easily rehabilitated and judges are hesitant to send them to jail or prison where they can learn more bad behavior. An example comes from Bucks County, Pennsylvania. Three teens vandalized a Jewish farmer's menorah. Instead of a prison term, Judge Kenneth Biehn sentenced them to community service and two years probation. In addition, the teens were ordered to watch the movie *Schindler's List*, write an essay on how Martin Markovitz must have felt when a baseball bat shattered his living room window and knocked over his electric menorah on the third night of Hanukkah, and send written apologies to Mr. Markovitz's family.[6]

Questions for Discussion

1. Is there a limit to the seriousness of offenses for which an offender can be sentenced using some form of public humiliation? What is it?

2. Is it possible that some people are not influenced by what others think of them? If so, is public humiliation likely to be a good sentence?

3. Do you think it is fair for a young offender's parents to be punished for their child's crime? Why or why not?

SOURCES

1. *Crime Prevention News,* January 22, 1998, p. 16.
2. *Crime Prevention News,* January 9, 1997, p. 15.
3. *Crime Prevention News,* September 10, 1998, p. 14.
4. *Crime Prevention News,* January 23, 1997, p. 17.
5. *Crime Prevention News,* July 9, 1998, p. 14.
6. *Crime Prevention News,* June 12, 1997, p. 17.

Cost–Benefit Analysis of House Arrest Electronic Monitoring. House arrest electronic monitoring sentences have come under criticism. The National Association of Probation Officers (NAPO) argues that the people selected for release subject to electronic monitoring are those who probably would normally be placed on bail.[75] The value of the deterrent component of the electronic monitoring of offenders is minimized when clients learn that there is a low certainty of detection and no swift response with more serious sanctions.[76] Research on electronic monitoring is scanty and, in general, does not support the effectiveness of the measure. One study found that electronic monitoring programs had higher technical violation and arrest rates than ordinary probation (around 35 percent).[77] Another study found that electronic monitoring increased correctional costs overall due to net-widening.[78] An Indiana study compared the effectiveness of electronic and human monitoring and found no real difference.[79] Marc Mauer of the Sentencing Project suggested a possible reason for the rapid growth of electronic monitoring:

> Tagging only expanded as it did, because, in truth, the supervision given by probation was sloppy, marginal or nonexistent. Since then it has been expanded on no real evidence at all and there has certainly been nothing sophisticated in terms of targeting or proper evaluation. It's been a rather collusive growth because, all too often, it has solved one of the probation officer's problems—they no longer have to meet up with difficult, dangerous clients; they can stay in the office and watch the computer.[80]

To some critics, the question as to whether electronic monitoring and house arrest are effective ignores the central question of their constitutionality. They suggest that house arrest and electronic monitoring interfere with First Amendment (freedom of speech and assembly) and Fourth Amendment (unreasonable search and seizure) rights.[81] These critics suggest that the law, having failed to keep pace with technological changes in punishment alternatives, does not provide adequate protection for offenders.[82] Others see the introduction of electronic monitoring as destroying the notion that one's home is the ultimate refuge from state authority.[83]

In contrast, advocates of house arrest programs using electronic monitoring devices argue that these do not infringe upon First or Fourth Amendment rights because the devices do not record any conversations or actions within the home. Additionally, advocates point out that the people who enter house arrest and electronic monitoring programs do so on a voluntary basis.[84] Home confinement is seen as punitive; the retribution and deterrence goals of punishment are satisfied; and the offender is still allowed to maintain employment as well as close family ties, which can be particularly important when the family includes young children who need the offender at home. But it is too early to claim that such programs are a total success.[85]

Community Service

community service order
Sanction in which the sentencing judge orders the convict to perform any of a range of services to the community.

The Vera Institute of Justice, in New York, has pioneered many improvements in corrections. In the 1960s it began experimenting with a novel alternative to incarceration in cases where imprisonment is not called for, because neither the offense nor the offender justifies its use, and where a fine is not appropriate, usually because the offender would have to commit another offense to get the money to pay it. The answer: a **community service order.** The sentencing judge orders the convict to perform any of a range of services to the community: driving a bus for disabled people, serving meals to the elderly, building a playground for kids, or landscaping a highway.[86]

One of the first jurisdictions in the United States to use community service orders was Alameda County, California. Judges there wanted to avoid fining low-income women for traffic offenses because they knew many would be sent to jail for nonpayment. In October 1966 the Alameda County Court agreed to permit those convicted of such misdemeanors to serve their sentences as volunteers for community organizations. Thereafter, community service programs proliferated around the country. The Law Enforcement Assistance Administration (LEAA) funded many projects in the late 1970s, but these programs died off as the funding dwindled in the 1980s. Yet judges liked the idea of sentencing offenders to unpaid labor; they saw it as cheap, punitive, and rehabilitative at the same time. According to Justice Charles Solomon, supervising judge of the Manhattan Criminal Court, "It's more meaningful to have someone do two weeks of real work than to sit in a jail cell for two weeks."[87]

Community service programs offer promises that:

- Offenders will have opportunities to engage in constructive activities.
- Offenders will likely undergo a change of attitude through the experience of volunteer work.
- Community service is a sentence uniquely appropriate to indigent offenders.
- Community service also can be an appropriate sentence for persons in higher income brackets whose offenses merit publicity and public shaming.

Community service is widely used in many countries as an alternative to incarceration for moderately severe crimes. In the United States, however, community service is used as a supplement to probation or a sentence for very minor offenses. It really has not caught on in this country and, consequently, there is little research on the effectiveness of the sanction.[88] But some researchers think that these are largely "unmet promises."[89]

Evaluation of Alternative Programs

In recent years, both liberal and conservative legislators have challenged criminologists to devise alternatives to incarceration. Some notable liberal thinkers argued that it is inhumane to house offenders in overcrowded jails and prisons. Some conservative thinkers could no longer justify spending ever-increasing portions of state budgets to build new jails and prisons for low-risk offenders. Since the late 1970s, the programs described in this chapter have proliferated throughout the United States and also abroad. Many were readily implemented because of their political appeal. An extensive assessment of the entire body of evaluation research undertaken on these alternative programs concludes that traditional probation is cost effective.[90] The claims made by advocates of intermediate sanctions, such as reduced recidivism, lower costs, and less prison use, have not been supported by research. But this may have more to do with the way participants are selected than with the sanctions themselves. Intermediate sanctions are most appropriate for mid-level, nonviolent offenders.[91]

Review

The first set of alternatives to imprisonment, probation and parole, were intended to humanize corrections. Probation and parole were the innovations of practical people, not scholars or jurists. John Augustus, who invented probation, was a cobbler, and Alexander Maconochie, who invented parole, was a naval officer. These two alternatives to prison (or continued prison confinement), now a century and a half old, are still widely in use, servicing a convict population three times the size of that incarcerated. Both sanctions are more cost beneficial than prison. The effectiveness of probation is considerable: Only 20 percent of probationers are rearrested for violent crime within three years. With parole, the failure rate is over 50 percent. While predicting the success of probationers and parolees is difficult (and failure has led to a movement to abolish or curtail parole), it is generally agreed that if officers' caseloads were reduced, the success rate would rise.

Because of rising crime rates and an increasingly punitive public attitude, we have recently witnessed the emergence of tough new programs designed to control and penalize even some of the more severe offenders by sanctions that are short of traditional imprisonment, yet more severe than traditional probation. Among them are intensive supervision programs which, in effect, were part of the original idea of probation and parole; shock programs in the form of Marine Corps–type boot camps emphasizing discipline and reeducation; and residential programs in the community aimed at teaching self-respect and the capacity to survive economically. Some of these programs rely on various forms of electronic monitoring, and all are meant to be tough alternatives, so as not to detract from the perceived severity of a sentence. Additional recent alternatives include volunteers in probation programs, restitution to victims (some programs with residential requirements), community service programs, and the greater use of fines.

The effectiveness of these innovative programs is not yet fully established. Some have proved cheaper than imprisonment and not less effective, as measured by recidivism rates. The danger is that they can be used to "widen the net" by subjecting more persons to control by the criminal justice system. All the new programs have political appeal. Whether they are an improvement over past penal practice, only evaluation research and time will tell.

Thinking Critically about Criminal Justice

1. Technological developments, such as the use of global positioning satellites in electronic monitoring, make it easier for probation and parole officers to track offenders' movements. Will this lead to more parole revocations and increased detection of violations of probation? If so, do you think this is a good or bad thing?

2. What would you find more daunting—one year in jail or three years on intensive supervision probation? Why? How about one year in jail versus a fine for the equivalent of three months' earnings?

3. Many states have done away with parole and moved to embrace a "truth in sentencing" philosophy. Is this a smart thing to do given what we know about prison overcrowding? Why is the availability of parole a valuable prison management tool?

Internet Connection

Note: While all of the URLs listed were current as of the printing of this book, these sites often change. Please check our website (http://www. mhhe.com/socscience/crimjustice/adlercj) for updates.

What purpose did electronic home monitoring serve in the case of Martha Stewart? In what ways is her situation ideally suited for this kind of community-based corrections? See **http://abcnews.go.com/Business/wireStory?id=582231.**

To what extent does the call to abolish parole reflect a politically liberal or conservative orientation? See **http:// www.senate.state.tx.us/75r/Senate/Members/Dist12/ pr97/p030497a.htm.**

Notes

1. *John Augustus—First Probation Officer (1852). John Augustus's Original Report of His Labors (1852),* with an introduction by Sheldon Glueck (Montclair, NJ: Patterson Smith, 1972), pp. 4–5.

2. Steven Dillingham and Lawrence Greenfield, "An Overview of National Corrections Statistics," *Federal Probation* 55 (1991), pp. 27–34.

3. This section is based on Kevin Krajick and Steven Gettinger, *Overcrowded Time: Why Prisons Are So Crowded and What Can Be Done* (NY: Edna McConnel Clark Foundation, 1982).

4. Sheldon Glueck, Introduction, *John Augustus—First Probation Officer,* p. *xvi.*

5. Charles Lindner and Margaret Saverese, "The Evolution of Probation: University Settlement and Its Pioneering Role in Probation Work," *Federal Probation* 68 (1984), pp. 3–13.

6. Harry Allen, Chris Eskridge, Edward Latessa, and Gennaro Vito, *Probation and Parole in America* (NY: Free Press, 1985).

7. Randall Guynes, "Difficult Clients, Large Caseloads Plague Probation Parole Agencies," *Research in Action* (Washington, DC: National Institute of Justice, 1988).

8. Bureau of Justice Statistics, http://www.ojp.usdoj.gov/bjs/pandp.htm.

9. *Mempa v. Rhay,* 389 U.S. 128 (1967).

10. *Gagnon v. Scarpelli,* 411 U.S. 778 (1973).

11. Thomas P. Bonczar, "Characteristics of Adults on Probation, 1995," *BJS Special Report* (Washington, DC: Bureau of Justice Statistics, December 1997), p. 10.

12. Robert L. Spangenberg et al., *Assessment of the Massachusetts Probation System* (Newton, MA: Spangenberg Group, 1987).

13. Robert L. Thomas, "Stress Perception among Select Federal Probation and Pretrial Services Officers and Their Supervisors," *Federal Probation* 52 (1988), pp. 48–58.

14. Thomas Ellsworth, "The Goal Orientation of Adult Probation Professionals: A Study of Probation Systems," *Journal of Crime and Justice* 12 (1990), pp. 55–76.

15. Lori Colley, Robert Culbertson, and Edward Latessa, "Probation Officer Job Analysis: Rural-Urban Differences," *Federal Probation* 50 (1986), pp. 67–71. See also D. Glaser, *The Effectiveness of a Prison and Parole System* (Indianapolis: Bobbs-Merrill, 1964).

16. Charles Lindner, "The Refocused Probation Home Visit: A Subtle but Revolutionary Change," *Journal of Contemporary Criminal Justice* 7 (1991), pp. 115–127.

17. Bill Workman, "Probation Cops in East Palo Alto Can't Drop in on Their Clients," *The San Francisco Chronicle,* December 18, 1991, p. A15.

18. Todd Clear, Val Clear, and William Burrell, *Offender Assessment and Evaluation: The Presentence Investigation Report* (Cincinnati, OH: Anderson, 1989).

19. Camille Graham Camp and George M. Camp, *The Corrections Yearbook, 1997* (South Salem, NY: Criminal Justice Institute, 1997), p. 155.

20. Bonczar, "Characteristics of Adults on Probation, 1995," p. 5.

21. Gennaro F. Vito, "Developments in Shock Probation: A Review of Research Findings and Policy Implications," *Federal Probation* 48 (1984), pp. 22–27.

22. Division of Probation, Administrative Office of the United States Courts, Washington, DC, "The Selective Presentence Investigation Report," *Federal Probation* (1974), pp. 47–54.

23. Anthony Walsh, "The Role of the Probation Officer in the Sentencing Process: Independent Professional or Judicial Hack?" *Criminal Justice and Behavior* 12 (1985), pp. 289–303.

24. Kriss A. Drass and J. William Spencer, "Accounting for Presentencing Recommendations: Typologies and Probation Officers' Theory of Office," *Social Problems* 34 (1987), pp. 277–293.

25. John Rosecrance, "Maintaining the Myth of Individualized Justice: Probation Presentence Reports," *Justice Quarterly* 5 (1988), pp. 235–256. For a dissenting opinion about the myth of presentence reports, see Joseph W. Rogers, "The Predisposition Report: Maintaining the Promise of Individualized Juvenile Justice," *Federal Probation* 54 (1990), pp. 43–57.

26. Todd Clear, Val Clear, and William Burrell, *Offender Assessment and Evaluation.*

27. Camille Camp and George Camp, *The Corrections Yearbook, 1997,* p. 149.

28. Michael R. Geerken and Hennessey D. Hayes, "Probation and Parole: Public Risk and the Future of Incarceration Alternatives," *Criminology* 31 (1993), pp. 549–564.

29. Petersilia, "Probation in the United States: Practices and Challenges," p. 4.

30. Lauren E. Glaze and Thomas P. Bonczar, *Probation and Parole in the United States, 2005* (Washington, DC: Bureau of Justice Statistics, 2006), p. 1.

31. Vincent O'Leary and Joan Nuffield, *The Organization of Parole Systems in the United States* (Hackensack, NJ: National Council on Crime and Delinquency, 1972).

32. William Parker, *Parole: Origins, Development, Current Practices and Statutes* (College Park, MD: American Correctional Association, 1975).

33. *Morrissey v. Brewer,* 408 U.S. 471 (1972).

34. Michael Gottfredson, S. Mitchell-Herzfield, and T. Flanagan, "Another Look at the Effectiveness of Parole Supervision," *Journal of Research in Crime* 19 (1982), pp. 277–298.

35. See Billie S. Erwin, *Evaluation of Intensive Probation Supervision in Georgia* (Atlanta: Georgia Department of Offender Rehabilitation, February 1985); Todd R. Clear and Edward Latessa, "A Study of Role Perception among

ISP Officers," paper presented to the Academy of Criminal Justice Sciences (Washington, DC, March 1989).

36. Carl B. Klockars, "A Theory of Probation Supervision," *Journal of Criminal Law, Criminology and Police Science* 63 (1972), pp. 550–557.

37. Adult Probation and Parole Services, *Workload Measurement Study* (Richmond, VA: Department of Corrections, Division of Adult Community Corrections, March 1987).

38. Ibid.

39. Don M. Gottfredson, M. G. Neithercutt, Joan Nuffield, and Vincent O'Leary, *Four Thousand Lifetimes: A Study of Time Served and Parole Outcomes* (Davis, CA: National Council on Crime and Delinquency, Research Center, 1973).

40. Glaze and Bonczar, p. 7.

41. M. K. Harris, "Disquisition on the Need for a New Model for Criminal Sanctioning Systems," *West Virginia Law Review* 77 (1974), pp. 263–326.

42. Camille Camp and George Camp, *The Corrections Yearbook, 1997,* p. 50.

43. Norval Morris and Michael H. Tonry, *Between Prison and Probation* (NY: Oxford University Press, 1990).

44. Sandra Evans Skovron, Joseph E. Scott, and Francis T. Cullen, "Prison Crowding: Public Attitudes toward Strategies of Population Control," *Journal of Research in Crime and Delinquency* 25 (1988), pp. 150–169.

45. Joan Petersilia and Elizabeth Piper Deschenes, "What Punishes? Inmates Rank the Severity of Prison versus Intermediate Sanctions," in *Community Corrections: Probation, Parole, and Intermediate Sanctions,* ed. Joan Petersilia (NY: Oxford University Press, 1998), pp. 149–159.

46. *Ex parte Garland,* 71 U.S. 333 (1867).

47. *Burdick v. United States,* 236 U.S. 79 (1915); *People ex rel. Prisament v. Brophy,* 287 N.Y. 132 (1942).

48. Fahy G. Mullaney, *Economic Sanctions in Community Corrections* (Washington, DC: U.S. Department of Justice, National Institute of Corrections, August 1988).

49. Ida Zamist, *Fines in Sentencing: An Empirical Study of Fine Use, Collection and Enforcement in New York City Courts* (NY: Vera Institute of Justice, 1981, revised 1986).

50. Pat Carlen and Dee Cook, eds., *Paying for Crime* (Philadelphia: Open University Press, Milton Keynes, 1989).

51. Barbara Smith, Robert Davis, and Susan Hillenbrand, *Improving Enforcement of Court-Ordered Restitution: A Study of the American Bar Association Criminal Justice Victim Witness Project* (Washington, DC: American Bar Association, August 1989).

52. "Restorative Justice Program Provides Alternatives to Prison, Parole," *Crime Prevention News* 96–17, September 4, 1996, pp. 1–2.

53. James Byrne, A. Lurigio, and S. Baird, "The Effectiveness of the 'New' Intensive Supervision Programs," *Research in Corrections* 5 (1989), p. 2.

54. ISP Fact Sheet, Administration Office of the County, New Jersey, p. 2 (available at www.judiciary.state.nj.us/).

55. Frank S. Pearson, *Research on New Jersey's Intensive Supervision Program: Final Report* (New Brunswick, NJ: Institute for Criminological Research, Rutgers University, 1987).

56. Joan Petersilia, "Georgia's Intensive Probation: Will the Model Work Elsewhere?" in *Intermediate Punishments: Intensive Supervision, Home Confinement and Electronic Surveillance,* ed. Belinda McCarthy (Monsey, NY: Criminal Justice Press, 1987), p. 21.

57. Susan B. Noonan and Edward J. Latessa, "Intensive Probation: An Examination of Recidivism and Social Adjustment for an Intensive Supervision Program," *American Journal of Criminal Justice* 12 (1987), pp. 45–61.

58. Michael Tonry, "Stated and Latent Features of ISP," *Crime and Delinquency* 36 (1990), pp. 174–191; Joan Petersilia and Susan Turner, "Comparing Intensive and Regular Supervision for High Risk Probationers: Early Results from an Experiment in California," *Crime and Delinquency* 36 (1990), pp. 87–111.

59. Dale Parent, *Shock Incarceration: An Overview of Existing Programs* (Washington, DC: National Institute of Justice, 1989), p. 9. See also Jody Klein-Saffran, "Shock Incarceration: Bureau of Prisons Style," *Research Forum* (Federal Bureau of Prisons, Office of Research and Evaluation, July 1992), pp. 1–9.

60. Ibid., p. 7.

61. "New York State Division of Parole, Shock Incarceration: One Year Out of 3" (prepared by the New York Office of Policy Analysis and Information, August 1989), *New Haven Register,* November 10, 1989, p. 15.

62. Doris MacKenzie and Claire Souryal, *Multisite Evaluation of Shock Incarceration* (Washington, DC: National Institute of Justice, 1994).

63. Doris MacKenzie, "Boot Camp Prisons: Components, Evaluations and Empirical Issues," *Federal Probation* 54 (1990), pp. 44–52.

64. Camille Camp and George Camp, *The Corrections Yearbook, 1997,* p. 170.

65. See, e.g., Edward Latessa and Gennaro F. Vito, "The Effects of Intensive Supervision on Shock Probationers," *Journal of Criminal Justice* 16 (1988), pp. 319–330; Faith E. Lutze, "Are Shock Incarceration Programs More Rehabilitative than Traditional Prisons? A Survey of Inmates," *Justice Quarterly* 15 (1998) pp. 547–563.

66. See Gunther Kaiser, *Kriminologie,* 2nd ed. (Heidelberg: C. F. Muller Jur. Verlag, 1988).

67. Edward Latessa and Harry Allen, "Halfway Houses and Parole: A National Assessment," *Journal of Criminal Justice* 10 (1982), p. 156.

chapter 14

68. Joan Petersilia, *Exploring the Option of House Arrest* (Santa Monica, CA: Rand Corporation, 1986).

69. Joan Petersilia, *Expanding Options for Criminal Sentencing* (Santa Monica, CA: Rand Corporation, 1987), p. 32.

70. Paul Hofer and Barbara Meierhoefer, *Home Confinement: An Evolving Sanction in the Federal Criminal Justice System* (Washington, DC: Federal Judicial Center, 1987), pp. 19–20.

71. Christopher Baird and Dennis Wagner, *Evaluation of the Florida Community Control Program* (Madison, WI: National Council on Crime and Delinquency, 1990).

72. Robert Rogers and Annette Jolin, "Electronic Monitoring: A Review of the Empirical Literature," *Journal of Contemporary Criminal Justice* 5 (1989), pp. 133–180; Timothy P. Cadigan, "Electronic Monitoring in Federal Pretrial Release," *Federal Probation* (March 1991), pp. 26–33.

73. Annesley K. Schmidt, "Electronic Monitoring," *Journal of Contemporary Criminal Justice* 5 (1989), pp. 133–180; Annesley K. Schmidt, "Electronic Monitors—Realistically, What Can Be Expected?" *Federal Probation* 55 (1991), pp. 47–53.

74. David C. Anderson, *Sensible Justice: Alternatives to Prison* (NY: New Press, 1998), p. 44.

75. J. Muncie, "A Prisoner in My Home: The Politics and Practice of Electronic Monitoring," *Probation Journal* 37 (1990), pp. 72–77.

76. State of South Carolina State Reorganization Commission, *Evaluation of the Electronic Monitoring Pilot Program, 1988–1989* (March 1990).

77. Petersilia and Turner, "Comparing Intensive and Regular Supervision," pp. 87–111.

78. D. Palumbo, "From Net-widening to Intermediate Sanctions," paper prepared with M. Clifford and Z. Snyder-Joy for the American Correctional Association (Baltimore, 1990).

79. Terry Baumer and Robert Mendelsohn, *The Electronic Monitoring of Non-violent Convicted Felons: An Experiment in Home Detention* (Washington, DC: National Institute of Justice, 1990).

80. Marc Mauer in Dick Whitfield, *Tackling the Tag: The Electronic Monitoring of Offenders* (Winchester, UK: Waterside Press, 1997), p. 37.

81. R. Ball, R. C. Huff, and J. R. Lilly, *House Arrest and Correctional Policy: Doing Time at Home* (Newbury Park, CA: Sage, 1988).

82. Federal Government Information Technology, *Electronic Surveillance and Civil Liberties* (Washington, DC: Congress of the United States, Office of Technology Assessment, 1985).

83. For a detailed discussion of the psycholegal effects of home confinement, see Dorothy K. Kagehiro and Ralph Taylor, "A Social Psychological Analysis of Home Electronic Confinement," in *Handbook of Psychology and Law,* ed. D. K. Kagehiro and W. S. Laufer (NY: Springer-Verlag, 1991).

84. M. Renzema and D. Skelton, *The Use of Electronic Monitoring by Criminal Justice Agencies: 1989* (Kutztown, PA: Criminal Justice Program, 1990).

85. Paulette Hatchett, *The Home Confinement Program: An Appraisal of the Electronic Monitoring of Offenders in Washtenaw County, Michigan* (Lansing: Community Programs Evaluation Unit, Michigan Department of Corrections, 1987).

86. Mark S. Umbreit, "Community Service Sentencing: Last Alternative or Added Sanction?" *Federal Probation* 45 (1981), pp. 3–14.

87. Anderson, *Sensible Justice: Alternatives to Prison,* pp. 24–25, 27.

88. Tonry, *Intermediate Sanctions in Sentencing Guidelines,* p. 11.

89. Barry Krisberg and James Austin, *The Unmet Promise of Alternatives to Incarceration* (San Francisco: National Council on Crime and Delinquency, 1981).

90. James Byrne, "Assessing What Works in the Adult Community Corrections Systems," paper presented to Academy of Criminal Justice Sciences, Denver, March 1990, p. 10. On the experiences with the Kansas Community Corrections Act, see M. Kay Harris, Peter R. Jones, and Gail S. Funke, *The Kansas Community Corrections Act: An Assessment of a Public Policy Initiative* (Philadelphia: Temple University—Edna McConnell Clark Foundation, 1990); Peter R. Jones, "The Risk of Recidivism: Evaluating the Public-Safety Implications of a Community Corrections Program," *Journal of Criminal Justice* 19 (1991), pp. 49–66; and Thomas Ellsworth, *Contemporary Community Corrections* (Prospect Heights, IL: Waveland, 1992).

91. Tonry, *Intermediate Sanctions in Sentencing Guidelines,* p. 13.

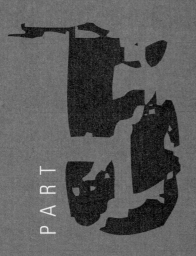

PART

Challenges for the Twenty-First Century

15 Justice for Juveniles and Victims

• Normally, this textbook would have ended with the preceding chapter. Everything you should know about contemporary criminal justice has been fully explored. Yet there are some aspects of criminal justice that are, seemingly, outside the purview of criminal justice texts, perhaps to be covered by other courses in the discipline. But these aspects of criminal justice are, nevertheless, central to the formation of a rational, modern criminal justice policy. These are the topics of juvenile justice and victim-oriented justice.

• It so happens that these topics also pose some of the greatest challenges to our criminal justice system—and to our thinking about criminal justice.

• So, in Chapter 15, we address the challenges to criminal justice that exist with respect to children and victims in the twenty-first century.

CHAPTER

15

JUSTICE FOR JUVENILES AND VICTIMS

In many parts of the world, warlords are pressuring very young children into their militias, teaching and forcing them to commit atrocities. Victimized children become victimizers. In the United States, equally young children are growing up in a gun-and-fatigues culture, and some turn into mass killers of their classmates. In Chicago, not so long ago, two young boys, seven and eight years old, stood charged with having murdered an eleven-year-old girl by striking her with a rock, suffocating her with her underwear, molesting her, and then dragging her body into nearby underbrush. They then made off with her bicycle.[1]

• Caroline Isenberg, a twenty-three-year-old Harvard graduate, died on a cold December night on the roof of her apartment building from twenty-three stab wounds inflicted by her abducter, whose rape and robbery efforts she had resisted. Isenberg is a victim of crime, but not the sole victim. As both the prosecutor and judge at the killer's trial emphasized, there are many victims of this crime: "Miss Isenberg, her family, her friends, the community."[2]

While criminal justice specialists may differ on priorities, most would probably agree to the challenges facing the profession and society at the dawn of the twenty-first century. These challenges, illustrated by the two vignettes at the beginning of this chapter, are described below.

1. Preventing delinquency and administering juvenile justice effectively. The system for controlling juvenile delinquency has become ever more punitive and less and less effective.

2. Alleviating the pain of victimization. A breakthrough is on the horizon, in the form of restorative justice. Taken to its logical conclusion, restorative justice could also do much to return us from an overly retributive criminal justice to one that is more humane, effective, and efficient.

In the two sections of this final chapter, we focus on these specific challenges: juvenile justice and the role of the victim.

The Challenge of Juvenile Justice

Approaches to Juvenile Delinquency

How are we to react to children who commit acts that we call criminal when committed by adults?

The American public and its politicians are confused as to what to do about juvenile delinquency, and especially juvenile violence: Should we get tough, or ever tougher, or should we seek to nurture and guard the nation's youngest, to socialize them to become productive citizens?

There is a historical reason for this confusion. Two thousand years ago, the Romans developed conflicting approaches, and we have used both ever since. One of these approaches is punitive: Children above age seven are potentially subject to criminal liability if their actions show that they were aware of the wrongfulness of their action.

The greatest of English legal scholars, Sir William Blackstone (1723–1780), suggested in his 1758 lectures that if a child of tender years had killed another, evidence that he hid the body might be sufficient to prove he understood the wrongfulness of his action.[3] By age seven, children are socialized enough to attend school. But children below age fourteen may still not be held accountable for their actions if they lack the maturity to realize the wrongfulness of their conduct.

The other ancient root is that of concern for children. It was expressed by the legal concept of *parens patriae* (parent of the country) which to the Romans meant that the emperor, and in medieval times the monarch, could exercise *patria potestas* (parental power) *in loco parentis* (in the place of a parent deemed unable or unworthy) over children in trouble or in danger of becoming wayward. The power of the monarch was eventually transferred to the state, as represented by the juvenile court judge. We find its traces in the concepts used today in juvenile court proceedings.

In re Gault: A Landmark Case

There has been a see-saw battle between these two approaches—the punitive and the caring—ever since. The caring approach gained the upper hand in 1899, when the first American juvenile court was established in Chicago. This approach found adherents all over the world. The switch back to the punitive approach occurred in the 1960s when, faced with rising juvenile crime rates, there was a swing toward a get-tough approach. The spark that fueled the switch was the case of Gerry Gault.

> Gerald Francis Gault, then aged fifteen, was accused of having made obscene phone calls. (He never admitted the charge, nor was it ever proven.) The sheriff—a police officer—arrested Gault. The same officer, now acting as a jailer, kept him in custody. The same officer, now

Video camera records the abduction of a toddler by two 11-year-olds in a Liverpool shopping mall, February 2, 1993. Subsequently, the abductors killed the toddler.

acting as a prosecutor, presented charges against Gault in juvenile court. Gault's family was never properly notified. There was no witness against him, yet the juvenile court ordered him to be confined in a juvenile correctional facility for six years. (An adult could have been punished for this offense, if proven, by a fine of $5 to $50 and a two-month jail term.)

Everything seemed to have gone wrong in the Gault case. A single official had acted as police officer, social worker, prosecutor, and jailer. Having been refused the constitutional right to be confronted by a witness, to receive counsel, to be given notice of the charges, and to be protected against self-incrimination, and having been committed to a multiyear detention sentence (in lieu of perhaps a warning or a fine), the conclusion was inescapable that a young man was being confined for a crime which was never proven, properly or otherwise.

When the case finally reached the U.S. Supreme Court, the Court decided that juveniles in juvenile court must be accorded the same constitutional rights available to adults charged with crime. These rights include:

- The right to receive adequate and timely notice of the charges.
- The right to counsel.
- The right to be confronted by and to examine witnesses.
- The privilege against self-incrimination.[4]

The Supreme Court's decision sent mixed signals. Juvenile court judges were worried that this might mean the end of the benevolent/paternalistic approach to dealing with delinquents. For the politicians, the *Gault* decision raised another issue: If we are to give juvenile offenders the same rights and privileges as adult offenders, why don't we hold them to the same responsibilities and duties? Thus began the effort to adjust juvenile court proceedings to the standards of adult criminal proceedings, and the parallel effort to subject more and more juveniles to adult criminal processes.

Treating Juveniles as Adults

The first step was an initiative by the Institute of Judicial Administration at New York University and the American Bar Association calling for juvenile proceedings to be based on the seriousness of the offense committed.[5]

The states responded with four strategies:

1. Lowering the age at which juveniles are subject to adult criminal liability. Twenty states chose fourteen as the age at which juveniles are liable; two states lowered the age to ten; two allowed no judicial waiver; and fourteen did not specify an age.[6]

2. Reducing the upper age at which juveniles are subject to original juvenile court jurisdiction:

   > In . . . 37 states and the District of Columbia, juvenile courts are initially responsible for all law violations committed by youth under 18. In other words, the juvenile court's "upper age of original jurisdiction" is 17. In 10 states, the upper age of original juvenile court jurisdiction is set at 16 years. . . . In three states . . . the upper age of jurisdiction is 15, which means that all youth age 16 or older face criminal prosecution for any arrest. . . .
   >
   > [In recent years] other states have considered reducing the upper age of juvenile court jurisdiction. . . . If more states follow this trend, large numbers of young offenders will be excluded from juvenile court and automatically handled in adult court.[7]

3. Excluding certain serious offenses from the jurisdiction of juvenile courts altogether (see Table 15.1 and Figure 15.1).

4. Investing prosecutors with the power to **direct file** juveniles for trial in adult criminal courts (mostly for serious offenses).

direct file
Prosecutors' power to try juveniles directly in adult criminal courts.

In many states, prosecutors are empowered to bring charges against juveniles directly in criminal court, bypassing the juvenile justice system altogether. In Florida, where this method is particularly popular, 7,000 juvenile cases were direct filed in criminal court in 1995, nearly equalling the number of juvenile cases waived by judges nationwide.[8]

TABLE 15.1
Offenses Excluded from Juvenile Court Jurisdiction[*]

Offenses	States[†]
Murder[**]	Connecticut, Delaware, District of Columbia, Georgia, Idaho, Illinois, Indiana, Louisiana, Minnesota, Nevada, New Mexico, New York, North Carolina, Ohio, Oklahoma, Pennsylvania, Utah, Vermont.
Rape	Delaware, District of Columbia, Georgia, Idaho, Illinois, Indiana, Louisiana, New York.
Kidnapping	Delaware, Louisiana, Vermont.
Burglary	District of Columbia, Georgia, Louisiana, Vermont.
Armed robbery	District of Columbia, Georgia, Idaho, Illinois, Indiana, Louisiana, Maryland, Vermont.
Other[‡]	Alabama, Connecticut, Florida, Idaho, Illinois, Indiana, Kansas, Kentucky, Nebraska, Rhode Island, Vermont, Washington.
Hawaii:	Class A felonies if one violent prior, or two violent priors in the past two years.
Maryland:	Any crime punishable by the death penalty.
Mississippi:	Any crime punishable by the death penalty.

[*]Criminal courts can try juveniles for such crimes provided they have reached minimum age.
[†]Because of the different offense categories, some states are listed more than once.
[**]This category includes various degrees of criminal homicide, including attempted murder in some states.
[‡]This category includes offense categories such as "any offense."
SOURCE: Barry C. Feld, "The Juvenile Court Meets the Principle of the Offense: Legislative Changes in Juvenile Waiver Statutes," *Journal of Criminal Law & Criminology* 78 (1987), pp. 512–514. Reprinted by special permission of Northwestern University, School of Law.

Of every 100 delinquency cases originally excluded from juvenile court jurisdiction in 3 counties in Pennsylvania in 1996, about one-fourth resulted in criminal court conviction.

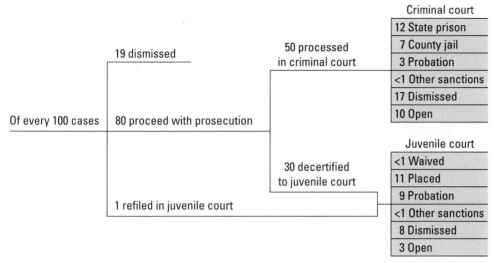

Note: Detail may not add to totals because of rounding. Data based on 473 excluded cases.

FIGURE 15.1   Treating Juveniles as Adults

SOURCE: Howard N. Snyder, Melissa Sickmund, Eileen Poe-Yamagata, *Juvenile Transfers to Criminal Court in the 1990s: Lessons Learned from Four Studies* (Washington, DC: Bureau of Justice Statistics, 2000), p. 3.

The net effect has been an erosion of juvenile court jurisdiction and the transfer of more and more juvenile offenders into the already overburdened adult criminal justice system. How far down on the age ladder should we go? Remember the Chicago kids: At their arraignments they occupied themselves with drawing crayon pictures of houses and hearts, oblivious to their situation, their attorneys and prosecutors, the court, the trial, life and death. As it turned out, the two little boys are probably innocent of the crimes for which they had been arraigned. Their "confessions" had been the result of suggestive police interrogation, and their innocence was corroborated by semen stains on the victim's underwear, which could not possibly have come from a seven- or eight-year-old.[9] Subsequent investigation indicated that the two boys may well have thrown stones at their little victim, but that it was a sex deviant who committed a sexual crime on the body of the little girl.[10]

The magnitude of juvenile delinquency/crime is demonstrated by the following statistics: In 2006, law enforcement agencies made over 1,626,000 arrests of persons under age eighteen, but only 74,000 of these were for violent crimes (see Figure 15.2).[11] (For a discussion of index crimes see Chapter 2.) So the vast majority of those arrested continue to travel the road of juvenile justice, albeit a road paved with due process guarantees.[12]

careers

Changing the Juvenile Justice Process

The steps in the juvenile process are comparable to those of criminal proceedings, though there are some differences in terminology and function:

• While in criminal cases the process normally starts with an arrest, juveniles are actually "taken into custody."
• Booking procedures for juveniles are called "intakes."
• In criminal proceedings, charges are filed to start the process. Juvenile proceedings start with a petition.
• Adults charged with a crime may be bailed or jailed; juveniles are normally released into the custody of their parents before an adjudicatory hearing.

Arrests by Age, 2006 [11, 250 agencies; 2006 estimated population 216,686,722]

Offense Charged	Total All Ages	Ages Under 18	Ages 18 and Over
TOTAL	10,472,432	1,626,523	8,845,909
Total percent distribution[1]	100.0	15.5	84.5
Murder and nonnegligent manslaughter	9,815	956	8,859
Forcible rape	17,112	2,519	14,593
Robbery	93,527	26,092	67,435
Aggravated assault	327,478	44,424	283,054
Burglary	222,192	61,155	161,037
Larceny-theft	801,633	206,187	595,446
Motor vehicle theft	100,775	25,338	75,437
Arson	12,002	5,888	6,114
Violent crime[2]	447,932	73,991	373,941
Violent crime percent distribution[1]	100.0	16.5	83.5
Property crime[2]	1,136,602	298,568	838,034
Property crime percent distribution[1]	100.0	26.3	73.7
Other assaults	952,741	181,965	770,776
Forgery and counterfeiting	79,477	2,583	76,894
Fraud	197,722	5,681	192,041
Embezzlement	14,769	1,037	13,732
Stolen property; buying, receiving, possessing	90,084	15,649	74,435
Vandalism	220,422	86,170	134,252
Weapons; carrying, possessing, etc.	147,623	34,700	112,923
Prostitution and commercialized vice	59,724	1,208	58,516
Sex offense (except forcible rape and prostitution)	63,243	11,516	51,727
Drug abuse violations	1,379,887	143,639	1,236,248
Gambling	9,018	1,620	7,398
Offeneses against the family and children	92,065	3,633	88,432
Driving under the influence	1,038,633	14,292	1,024,341
Liquor laws	469,186	102,755	366,431
Drunkenness	409,490	12,057	397,433
Disorderly conduct	519,046	153,231	365,815
Vagrancy	27,053	3,734	23,319
All other offenses (except traffic)	2,917,803	279,991	2,637,812
Suspicion	1,725	316	1,409
Curfew and loitering law violations	114,313	114,313	–
Runaways	83,874	83,874	–

FIGURE 15.2   Juvenile Arrests for 2006

[1] Because of rounding the percentages may not add to 100.0

[2] Violent crimes are offenses of murder and nonnegligent manslaughter, forcible rape, robbery, and aggravated assault. Property crimes are offenses of burglary, larceny-theft, motor vehicle theft, and arson.

SOURCE: *Crime in the United States, Juvenile Arrests* (Washington, DC: U.S. Government Printing Office, 2007), table 38.

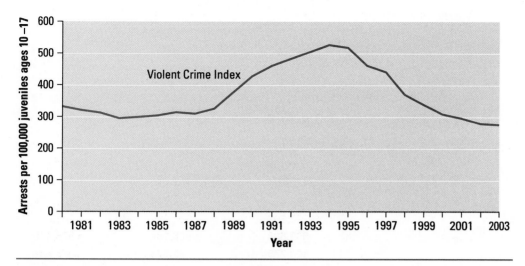

FIGURE 15.3   Juvenile Violent Crime Index, 1981–2003

NOTE: Analysis of arrest data from the FBI and population data from the U.S. Bureau of the Census and the National Center for Health Statistics. The juvenile Violent Crime Index arrest rate in 2003 was lower than in any year since at least 1980 and 48 percent below the peak year of 1994.

SOURCE: Howard Snyder, *Juvenile Arrests 2003* (Washington, DC: National Institute of Justice, 2005), p. 5.

- Adults charged with a crime face a trial; juveniles face an adjudicatory hearing.
- Adults may be found guilty of crimes charged; juveniles may be determined to be delinquent.

There are many divergent calls to change the processes by which juveniles charged with crime are dealt with. Some want the juvenile court to be replaced either by a family court or the placement of all juvenile offenders under adult criminal court jurisdiction. Initiatives to abolish the juvenile court system do not hold much promise. Adult criminal courts are notoriously inept at dealing with juvenile offenders, especially the very young.

The statistical evidence indicates that juvenile violent crime peaked in 1993 and has been declining ever since. While the arrest rates for other offenses with which juveniles are charged have shown divergent patterns, the overall juvenile share of violent crime has been decreasing since 1994 (see Figure 15.3).[13] And there is no evidence that system changes had anything to do with it. But even if they had, many experts believe there is something wrong with the systems we have developed for dealing with juvenile offenders. Children are not simply young adults, and the transformation of an infant into an adult is a complicated process. The challenge for the future, as far as juvenile justice is concerned, is to take this transformational process into account, adjust our procedures accordingly, and develop separate yet integrated approaches for preventing juvenile delinquency on the one hand, and dealing with juvenile offenders on the other.[14] This calls for an open-mind approach that must rely on research in psychology and child development. In all probability, a new approach will emerge, with the following ingredients:

- not to prematurely interrupt childhood;
- not to throw children into the adult world of criminal justice;
- not to subject children to punishment in the adult sense of this term;
  but rather,
- to protect and promote childhood;
- to discourage detrimental (adult) values from intruding on childhood;
- to respond to youthful deviance in a graduated manner which respects crucial developmental differences as a child matures from infancy, to prepubescence, to pubescence, to young adulthood, to maturity.

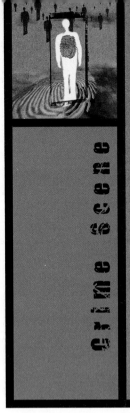

STALKING

Famed TV comedian David Letterman is not easily frightened, even after a recent plot to kidnap his infant son. Yet even he felt threatened when he saw his stalker in the hallway, next to his bedroom door. His stalker—for years—was Margaret Ray (who had also stalked an astronaut), driven to her often-daring stalking escapades by uncontrollable schizophrenic delusions. Her many arrests had no deterrent impact. She ended her life on October 5, 1998, by kneeling in front of a speeding 105-car coal train—following the suicides of two of her schizophrenic siblings.

> Stalk . . . to pursue quarry or prey stealthily . . . to go through (an area) in search of prey or quarry . . .

In times past, "stalking" was a concept used to describe what deer hunters did. Today, stalking is a frightening reality for many human victims. Consider that more than 2 percent of adults have been stalked in their lifetime, and women are nearly four times as likely to be the victim. Stalking victim rates, oddly enough, are highest among Native Americans (nearly five percent of all males and 17 percent of females).[1]

These data are from the National Violence Against Women Survey, a nationally representative telephone survey of 8,000 men and 8,000 women aged eighteen and older. Data were collected from November 1995 to May 1996 using random digit dialing sampling and a computer-assisted interviewing system. The survey defines stalking as a course of conduct directed at a specific person that involves repeated (two or more occasions) visual or physical proximity, nonconsensual communication, or verbal, written, or implied threats (or a combination thereof) that would cause a reasonable person fear. This definition of stalking is similar to the definition of stalking used in the model antistalking code for states developed by the National Institute of Justice.

The Challenge of Victimology: Toward Restorative Justice

The Rediscovery of the Victim

There was a time, and it is only half a century ago, when victims seemed invisible: At most, they appeared as witnesses and were pressured to testify. The criminal justice system, focused on offenders, viewed victims as virtually irrelevant. But it had not always been that way. When humans lived in tribal communities, victims of crime played dominant roles. They determined what should happen to offenders, and they accepted or refused a given amount of compensation. In Western societies all this changed in the Middle Ages when sovereigns considered themselves the principal victims of all crime.

The evidence of vast victimizations during the Nazi era, from 1933 to 1945, inflicted by the German government itself, changed that situation. The renewed focus on victims began with a few scholars, among them Hans von Hentig[15] and Beniamin Mendelsohn,[16] and later Stephen Schafer,[17] all of whom were victims of state-inflicted crimes. **Victimology,** a subdiscipline of criminology, was born. This new science has made many contributions, including the development of victimization surveys to measure the true extent of crime. Victimology's greatest contribution has been the securing of a place for the victim in the criminal justice process and the creation of measures for compensating those harmed by crime. The concern of a handful of scholars has turned into a movement supported by many advocacy groups. These, in turn, have gained the support of research scholars and, ultimately, legislators.

As a result of the victimology movement, important questions have begun to be asked and answered: How many victims fail to report crimes committed against them, why so few, and why do they fail to report crimes? Several Bureau of Justice Statistics surveys have provided interesting findings. Surveys show that presumed reasons for nonreporting—fear of reprisal by the offender or distrust of the police—account for only a small number of nonreports (see Table 15.2). Whatever the reasons for nonreporting, without a report the police are virtually powerless. Victimizations will continue. It is important, then, to deal with the reasons for failure to report.

victimology
Systematic study of the role played by the victim in a criminal incident and in the criminal process.

Stalking is a new crime. State laws define it as the "willful, malicious and repeated following and harassing of another person where there is credible threat of violence against the victim or a member of the victim's family."[2] The laws have grown out of the realization that many women, separated from abusive mates, are insufficiently protected by restraining orders and other court decrees. For years, many people have suffered the traumatic experience of being stalked. Some have been killed by their former mates. The new laws allow the police to arrest stalkers. But, as a new crime, it is not yet properly reflected in statistics. So, thus far, we know very little about the effectiveness of these laws.

Questions for Discussion

1. Some civil rights advocates contend that stalking laws violate the rights of investigative reporters who have to follow people as part of their job. Do you agree? Explain your position.

2. Just as new crimes, like stalking, are being created, acts that once were considered to be crimes may become "noncrimes." Give an example of something that once was criminal but is no longer considered to be so.

SOURCE:

1. U.S. Department of Justice, National Institute of Justice, *Stalking in America: Findings from the National Violence Against Women Survey,* NCJ 169582 (Washington, DC: U.S. Department of Justice, 1998), p. 3.
2. Tamar Lewin, "New Laws Address Old Problem: The Terror of a Stalker's Threat," *The New York Times,* February 8, 1993, p. A1.

Reasons for Reporting to Police	Personal Crimes Total[b]	Property Crimes Total
Number of reasons for reporting victimizations[d]	2,399,330	9,314,820
Total	100%	100%
Stop or prevent this incident	19.7	9.0
Needed help due to injury	2.3	0.3[e]
To recover property	3.5	21.8
To collect insurance	0.0[e]	4.4
To prevent further crimes by offender against victim	19.4	10.6
To prevent crime by offender against anyone	10.5	6.7
To punish offender	7.7	4.5
To catch or find offender	7.1	7.6
To improve police survelliance	3.0	7.2
Duty to notify police	6.2	6.6
Because it was a crime	15.3	17.0
Some other reason	3.7	2.7
Not available	1.7	1.7

TABLE 15.2

Estimated Percent Distribution of Reasons for Reporting Personal and Property Victimizations to Police, by type of Crime, United States, 2005[a]

[a]Detail may not add to total because of rounding.
[b]Includes crimes of violence and purse snatching/pocket picking not listed separately.
[c]Includes rape and sexual assault not listed separately.
[d]Some respondents may have cited more than one reason for reporting victimizations to the police.
[e]Estimate is based on about 10 or fewer sample cases.
SOURCE: U.S. Department of Justice. Bureau of Justice Statistics, *Criminal Victiminzation in the United States, 2005 Statistical Tables,* NCJ 215244. Table 101 [Online]. Available: http://www.ojp.usdoj.gov/bjs/pub/pdf/cvus05.pdf [May 30, 2007]. Table adapted by *Sourcebook* staff.

As important as the first step of the process is, subsequent stages of the criminal justice process also require the participation of victims. The police need *complainants* in their investigation. If victims are not treated with respect, if their reports are not followed up properly, if items reported as stolen are not recovered, then victims will not cooperate as complainants.

During all the steps of prosecution and pretrial proceedings, victims suffer a great deal of inconvenience, such as frequent appearances at hearings, canceled appointments, trouble finding babysitters, lost income on hearing days—all the while feeling relatively unimportant. Instead, victims need supportive responses, such as being duly informed about the status of a case, having a say in bail hearings and plea bargains, and obtaining protection against harassment, intimidation, or even assault.

At trial, in particular, victims—whose testimony is needed—require special consideration. Should they be forced to wait for hours until called? Should they be allowed to testify at sentencing hearings? What is the victim's role at the appellate stage? Should victims be informed of appeals and their outcome? Should they receive notice of a defendant's discharge into the community?

The victims' rights movement has maintained the pressure on legislatures by documenting existing shortcomings and demanding reform. Indeed, this pressure has produced results. As Table 15.3 demonstrates, a massive array of victims, rights measures have already been enacted into law.

Compensation for Victims of Crime

Wealthy or steadily employed citizens who are victimized have traditionally relied on their health or property insurance to compensate them for their losses, though the emotional suffering always remains. The poor, being largely uninsured, have traditionally accepted their losses because of crime and remained uncompensated. Rarely can crime victims receive compensation by suing the perpetrator in a civil damage action, as, unhappily, most perpetrators are poor themselves.

victim compensation
Scheme, usually based on statute, by which victims of violent crime may receive a limited financial award out of public funds for criminal harm suffered.

To remedy this problem, the victims' rights movement zeroed in on legislation under which crime victims may be compensated (**victim compensation**). In a relatively short period (since the 1960s), all fifty states, the District of Columbia, and the Virgin Islands have passed victim compensation legislation. Most of the state compensation schemes are limited to "innocent victims of violent crime" and the amounts awardable are limited. There are other restrictions and limitations that vary by states. Nevertheless, it is astounding that, thanks to the pressure of citizen groups, so many compensation schemes have been created within the span of a generation. Many have even been updated from time to time, by expanding their coverage or the amounts awardable.

Yet, despite all of the progress that has been made, there are still imperfections and inconsistencies. For example, while thirty-nine jurisdictions grant the victim the right to confer with the prosecutor on a plea agreement (the other jurisdictions grant no such right), only six grant such a right with regard to a pretrial release (the others do not). Such inconsistencies pervade the entire victims' rights/victims' compensation program. It has grown up haphazardly and has remained an unfulfilled promise for many victims. What is wrong? Is there something missing?

The Promise of Restorative Justice

If you think of the evolution in philosophies of punishment over the past fifty years, you might imagine a pendulum that swings back and forth between support for retributive and nonretributive theories. So where is the pendulum now? Retributive approaches underlie the sentencing guidelines. Just desserts–based theories also support the massive growth of prison populations. But lurking behind the scenes and ready to emerge is a very different philosophy or theory of justice, one that takes to heart the victim and all of the "stakeholders" to a crime.

The aim of this "restorative" justice is simple: Restore the harm done by crime by elevating the role of the victim in the criminal justice process. When successful, restorative justice allows parties with a stake in a particular offence to reconcile the act done with the aftermath

- Thirty-two states have constitutional rights for crime victims. Eighteen states' victims' rights amendments include the right to restitution.

- In four states, crime victims are given standing to assert their legal rights. Nine states have statutorily designated offices to receive complaints from victims when their rights are violated.

- Forty-one states and the District of Columbia give crime victims the right to attend the trial. In some of these states, a victim is still subject to exclusion if scheduled to testify as a witness.

- At least seven states allow a photograph of a homicide victim taken while the victim was alive to be in the courtroom during the trial of the case.

- In forty-two states, victims are to be notified of canceled or rescheduled hearings. Two additional states require notification of victims when their presence in court is not required.

- Every state and the District of Columbia allow victim impact statements at sentencing. Forty-eight states and the District of Columbia permit victim input concerning parole. In at least ten of those states, victims may submit electronically recorded impact statements for consideration by the paroling authority.

- Victims are provided notice of the escape of a convicted offender in forty-eight states and the District of Columbia, although only twenty-four states require notification of victims when the offender is recaptured.

- In thirty-nine states, separate or secure waiting areas are to be provided where possible to minimize contact between victims' and the offender's family members or friends during court proceedings.

- Forty-six states have enacted legislation providing employment intercession services for victims in an attempt to minimize the risk of employment termination, harassment, and loss of wages or benefits to victims absent from work to attend criminal judicial proceedings or participate in other prosecution-related activities. Thirty-one states provide victims with employment protection by prohibiting employers from discharging an employee who misses work responding to a subpoena to appear at a criminal proceeding.

- Restitution orders in forty-seven states may be enforced in the same manner as civil judgments. Juvenile offenders may be ordered to pay restitution in forty-nine states, and the child's parent or legal guardian may be held responsible for a portion of such restitution in thirty-two states. In addition, civil liability for personal injury, property damage, or both resulting from a child's intentional act may be imposed against the child's parent or guardian in forty-nine states and the District of Columbia.

- Twenty-two states have eliminated the criminal statute of limitations for their most serious sex offense. In eight additional states, a prosecution for the most serious sex offense may be initiated at any time if certain conditions apply, including the availability of DNA evidence. In nine other states, the applicable statute of limitations is extended if DNA evidence is available.

- Forty-nine states and the District of Columbia have adopted laws requiring HIV testing of certain sex offenders.

- Convicted sex offenders are required to register with state or local law enforcement in all fifty states and the District of Columbia. Each state and the District of Columbia also have enacted laws providing for community notification of the release of sex offenders or allow public access to sex offender registration. Thirty-seven states maintain sex offender registry websites, while eight states maintain sex offender websites with limited information.

- Courts in every state and the District of Columbia must consider evidence of domestic violence when determining child custody issues.

- Stalking is a crime in every state and the District of Columbia. Fourteen states classify stalking as a felony upon the first offense, while thirty-four states classify stalking as a felony upon the second offense and/or when the crime involves aggravating factors. Eleven states have created a specific civil cause of action for stalking. At least forty-four states now have laws that explicitly include electronic forms of communication within their stalking or harassment laws. Ten states have video voyeurism laws that specifically address the use of a video camera to secretly tape someone.

- Forty-eight states have enacted legislation related to identity theft. In twenty-five states, identity theft is considered a felony, while four states treat the crime as a misdemeanor. In the remaining nineteen states, varying classifications and penalties are imposed depending on the degree of violation, with the value of the property stolen being the most common determining factor. At least twenty-one states have legislation that specifically requires the offender to make restitution to the victim of the identity theft.

- Fifteen states have laws requiring local school boards to enact antibullying policies.

SOURCE: From the National Center for Victims of Crime, http://www.ncvc.org/ncvc/main.aspx?dbName=DocumentViewer& DocumentID=38725.

TABLE 15.3 National Center for Victims of Crime: Legislative Summary (2003)

of the offence and its implications for the future. Like other approaches, its objectives include the reduction of recidivism by allowing offenders to repair the harm they have caused to victims, to the communities in which the crime took place, and to themselves.

Offenders earn back their place in law-abiding society by repaying their moral debts. In the words of two experts, "when crime is understood as repair and/or healing, and when the importance of active participation by victims and community members in response to crime is emphasized, basic community needs are understood and addressed in different ways."[18]

As discussed in Chapter 11, restorative justice may take many different forms, including victim–offender mediation, restitution to crime victims, victim awareness education programs, victim impact panels, and community reparation boards. The results of experimental research on restorative justice, conducted by Professors Larry Sherman and John Braithwaite, will soon tell us just how effective and practical these different forms are. Until then, anecdotal evidence is very supportive. Consider Jason's experience.

Case Study: A New Approach to Juvenile Offending

An Opportunity to Speak. Thirteen-year-old Jason's face was grim as he looked around at those attending the restorative justice conference and struggled to answer the coordinator's question. "How were you involved in this incident?" Quietly, Jason began his story. He and his friend Michael were on their way to Jason's house that afternoon and cut across the shopping center's parking lot. The car was there. They could see the speakers, and with Michael as lookout, Jason crawled in the car and began pulling out wires. The owner of the car (Rhonda) came out of her office and yelled at them to stop. Jason dropped the speaker, and he and Michael began running. Later that day, Jason heard the sheriff's officer knock on his door and talk to his mother. After the officer questioned Jason and his friend, the boys were handcuffed and taken to the juvenile detention center.

When asked what he was thinking at the time of the incident, Jason replied, "Nothing, just that I saw the speakers and wanted them." Jason struggled when asked who had been affected by his actions, telling the group that *he* had been affected—by being taken to "juvenile." "What about the owner of the car?" asked the coordinator. "Well, I guess because she got her speakers messed up, she was affected." Pausing for a moment, Jason looked at his mother and whispered that she too had been affected by his behavior.

Jason's friend Michael gave his account of what happened, admitting that he wasn't thinking at the time and now knows he made a big mistake. The person most disappointed in Michael, he explained, was his younger brother, and that was the worst part of all this—losing his brother's trust.

Rhonda next described the incident, explaining that she heard the two boys in the parking lot and ran out to see what was happening. "I saw the one boy in my car holding the speaker—I yelled at him to stop and he dropped it and ran." When asked what she wanted to receive from the conference, Rhonda said she wanted to know why the boys had attempted to steal her speakers. She also wanted the boys to understand how she felt and asked them how they would feel if someone took their possessions.

Moving around the circle, the conference coordinator asked the boys' mothers how the incident had affected them. Jason's mother said that at first she was shocked and had a hard time believing her son would be involved in something like this. Jason, she explained, had money from an allowance and didn't need to steal anything. Michael's mother told the group how disappointed she was that her son had participated in the incident. She had always tried to raise her boys to know the difference between right and wrong, and it would take a while to restore her trust in Michael.

Drafting a Contract. After each participant had an opportunity to speak, the contract drafting phase of the conference began. The participants discussed and outlined steps the boys needed to take to make things right. The coordinator asked the boys if they had anything they wanted to say to the victim. Each made a sincere apology for trying to steal Rhonda's speakers. Rhonda said that she believed the boys were remorseful and thought they had learned from their mistake.

When asked if there was anything else she wanted to add to contract, Rhonda explained that because the speakers were replaced and her car had no permanent damage, restitution was not necessary. She suggested, however, that the boys perform community service work. Following Rhonda's suggestion, the conference participants joined in and traded ideas on what type of work would be appropriate and how many hours would be fair. The boys were asked whether they would agree to community service and whether they knew of any work that was needed around their neighborhood. Finally, the participants agreed that Jason and Michael would perform twenty hours of service at a community center to earn money to pay their court fees. The coordinator wrote up the contract, and all of the participants signed it, putting a formal end to the incident.

Benefits of the Process. As the conference participants rose to leave, Jason and Michael shook hands with everyone in the group. Although the boys had been held accountable for their behavior, they knew that people still cared about them and had worked to help them learn from their mistakes. Having received an apology and learned why the boys did what they did, Rhonda felt that she could put the incident behind her. The boys' parents had a chance to express how they felt about their sons' actions, they received support from the group, and they helped point their children back in the right direction.[19]

As Jason's story suggests, testing the efficacy of restorative justice may not resolve, one way or the other, the more significant philosophical questions raised by looking at crime through a restorative lens. After all, what is the nature of the harm? What can and should be done to address a wrong against the community? And, who must ultimately assume responsibility? Of course, these questions could be asked of any sentencing philosophy.

But the momentum is building for restorative justice. In their first pastoral letter to Louisiana's 1.3 million Catholics since 1997, eight bishops recently called for the state's criminal justice system to embrace the values of restorative justice. Is this surprising? "Yes" and "no." After all, Louisiana has the highest per capita rate of incarceration in the United States—93,000 men and women in prison or on probation or parole. "These challenges alone urge us to a new way of thinking and acting," the bishops wrote.[20]

Review

One of the challenges of juvenile justice is our failure to resolve the conflict between a caring and a punitive approach, both of which are deeply rooted in history. Over the last decade, juvenile justice has become more punitive—at least as far as legislation is concerned. The youngest age at which juveniles may be transferred to adult criminal court for trial has been lowered. The upper age limit at which juveniles are subject to being assigned to juvenile court jurisdiction has been reduced. A variety of offenses on the part of juveniles have been excluded from juvenile jurisdiction altogether.

The increased punitiveness of juvenile justice appears to be motivated by political and emotional considerations. Scientific evidence does not support it. The twenty-first century challenges us to resolve the matter on the basis of scientific findings.

Second, while much progress has been made in considering and ameliorating the plight of victims in our criminal justice system, the improvements are spotty and have reached relatively few victims. In search of a more systematic and effective approach to serving victims of crime, the new paradigm of "restorative justice" may offer a solution. Restorative justice involves victims, offenders, and the community in the adjudication process, and it seeks a mutual agreement as to how offenders can pay for the damage they have done to their victims. Such an approach is not necessarily inconsistent with retribution as a limit on what an offender can be expected to do. Offender rehabilitation remains a main goal, and incapacitation must remain available.

The challenges to criminal justice in the new millennium that we have identified are not separate and isolated issues. They are intertwined: All over the world children are being deprived of childhood and driven into an unfortunate adult world of violence and exploitation—whether as child soldiers in the many ethnic conflicts around the globe, or whether as child prostitutes, exported from home to distant places with no chance to return to a life of happiness and harmony. These problems of victimization have long ceased being local. They span the globe.

Thinking Critically about Criminal Justice

1. Should capital punishment be imposed on persons as young as eleven years who are charged with homicide? List the arguments for and against this proposition.

2. Since most criminal cases do not lead to conviction of an offender, how is "restorative justice" applicable in such cases?

Internet Connection

Note: While all of the URLs listed were current as of the printing of this book, these sites often change. Please check our website (http://www. mhhe.com/socscience/crimjustice/adlercj) for updates.

In recent years the tactic of mass rape during war has come to light. Read about victims of rape during war in the context of history and reflect on why this tactic is still used to victimize women and children. See **http://news.bbc.co. uk/2/hi/africa/3549325.stm.**

What kinds of employment opportunities in the field of juvenile justice exist in the private sector versus the state and federal government? See the juvenile justice job bank: **http://www.fsu.edu/~crimdo/jjclearinghouse/jjboard. html.**

Notes

1. Pam Belluck, "Chicago Boys, 7 and 8, Charged in the Brutal Killing of a Girl, 11," *The New York Times,* August 10, 1998, pp. 1, 14.

2. Marcia Chambers, "Life Term Imposed in Rooftop Slaying of Aspiring Actress," *The New York Times,* August 6, 1985, p. A1.

3. Sir William Blackstone, *Commentaries on the Laws of England,* IV (Oxford, England: Clarendon Press, 1765), pp. 22–28.

4. *In re Gault,* 387 U.S. 1 (1967). Subsequent decisions added that juvenile charges must be proven by evidence beyond a reasonable doubt and other rights. See Christopher P. Manfredi, *The Supreme Court and Juvenile Justice* (Lawrence: University of Kansas Press, 1998).

5. Institute of Judicial Administration—American Bar Association, *Juvenile Justice Standards: A Summary and Analysis,* 2nd ed., ed. Barbara Dansiger Flicker (Cambridge, MA: Ballinger, 1982).

6. Eric Fritsch and Craig Hemmens, "Juvenile Waiver in the United States, 1979–1995: A Comparison and Analysis of State Waiver Statutes," *Juvenile and Family Court Journal* 46, no. 3 (1995), pp. 7–35.

7. Jeffrey A. Butts and Adele V. Harrell, *Delinquents or Criminals: Policy Options for Young Offenders* (Washington, DC: The Urban Institute, 1998), pp. 5, 6.

8. Ibid., p. 6.

9. Julie Grace, "The Things Kids Say," *Time,* September 14, 1998, p. 50; "Chicago Police Are Reviewing Juvenile Policy," *The New York Times,* September 9, 1998, p. 26.

10. John McCormick and Peter Annin, "Who Killed Ryan Harris?" *Newsweek,* October 5, 1998, pp. 42–43.

11. Howard H. Snyder, *Juvenile Arrests 2006* (Washington, DC: U.S. Department of Justice, OJJDP, November 1997).

12. Carol J. DeFrances and Kevin J. Strom, *Juveniles Prosecuted in State Criminal Courts* (Washington, DC: U. S. Department of Justice, OJP, BJS, March 1997).

13. Snyder, *Juvenile Arrests 1996.*

14. Coordinating Council on Juvenile Justice and Delinquency Prevention, *Combating Violence and Delinquency: The National Juvenile Justice Action Plan* (Washington, DC: U.S. Government Printing Office, 1996); Kevin Wright and Karen Wright, *Family Life, Delinquency and Crime: A Policymaker's Guide: Research Summary* (Washington, DC: Office of Juvenile Justice and Delinquency Prevention, 1994); Butts and Harrell, *Delinquents or Criminals. United Nations Standard Minimum Rules for the Administration of Juvenile Justice (The Beijing Rules)* (NY: United Nations), in *Compendium of United Nations Standards and Norms in Crime Prevention and Criminal Justice, 1992,* pp. 169–179; *United Nations Guidelines for the Prevention of Juvenile Delinquency (The Riyadh Guidelines)* (NY: United Nations), in *Compendium of United Nations Standards and Norms in Crime Prevention and Criminal Justice, 1992,* pp. 180–191.

15. Hans von Hentig, "Remarks on the Interaction of Perpetrator and Victim," *Journal of Criminal Law and Criminology* 31 (1941), pp. 303–309; Hans von Hentig, *The Criminal and His Victim* (New Haven, CT: Yale University Press, 1948).

16. See Beniamin Mendelsohn, "The Origin of the Doctrine," in *Victimology,* ed. Israel Drapkin and Emilio Viano (Lexington, MA: Lexington Books, 1974), pp. 3–4.

17. Stephen Schafer, *The Victim and His Criminal, A Study in Functional Responsibility* (NY: Random House, 1968).

18. G. Bazemore and M. Umbriet, *Conferences, Circles, Boards and Mediations: Restorative Justice and Citizen Involvement in the Response to Youth Crime* (Washington, DC: OJJDP, 1999).

19. USDOJ, Restorative Justice Conferences as an Early Response to Young Offenders (Washington, DC: BJS, 2000).

20. Bruce Nolan, State Bishops Call for Prison Reform: New Movement for "Restorative" Justice Growing, *The Times-Picayune,* February 2, 2002, p. 14.

The Constitution of the United States of America[1]

We the People of the United States, in Order to form a more perfect Union, establish Justice, insure domestic Tranquility, provide for the common defence, promote the general Welfare, and secure the Blessings of Liberty to ourselves and our Posterity, do ordain and establish this CONSTITUTION for the United States of America.

Article I

Section 1. All legislative Powers herein granted shall be vested in a Congress of the United States, which shall consist of a Senate and House of Representatives.

Section 2. The House of Representatives shall be composed of Members chosen every second Year by the People of the several States, and the Electors in each State shall have the Qualifications requisite for Electors of the most numerous Branch of the State Legislature.

No Person shall be a Representative who shall not have attained to the Age of twenty-five Years, and been seven Years a Citizen of the United States, and who shall not, when elected, be an Inhabitant of that State in which he shall be chosen.

[Representatives and direct Taxes[2] shall be apportioned among the several States which may be included within this Union, according to their respective Numbers, which shall be determined by adding to the whole Number of free Persons, including those bound to Service for a Term of Years, and excluding Indians not taxed, three fifths of all other Persons.][3] The actual Enumeration shall be made within three Years after the first Meeting of the Congress of the United States, and within every subsequent Term of ten Years, in such Manner as they shall by Law direct. The Number of Representatives shall not exceed one for every thirty Thousand, but each State shall have at Least one Representative; and until such enumeration shall be made, the State of New Hampshire shall be entitled to chuse three, Massachusetts eight, Rhode-Island and Providence Plantations one, Connecticut five, New York six, New Jersey four, Pennsylvania eight, Delaware one, Maryland six, Virginia ten, North Carolina five, South Carolina five, and Georgia three.

When vacancies happen in the Representation from any State, the Executive Authority thereof shall issue Writs of Election to fill such Vacancies.

The House of Representatives shall chuse their Speaker and other Officers; and shall have the sole Power of Impeachment.

Section 3. The Senate of the United States shall be composed of two Senators from each State, chosen by the Legislature thereof, for six Years; and each Senator shall have one Vote.

Immediately after they shall be assembled in Consequence of the first Election, they shall be divided as equally as may be into three Classes. The Seats of the Senators of the first Class shall be vacated at the Expiration of the second Year, of the second Class at the Expiration of the fourth Year, and of the third Class at the Expiration of the sixth Year, so that one-third may be chosen every second Year; and if Vacancies happen by Resignation, or otherwise, during the Recess of the Legislature of any State, the Executive thereof may make temporary Appointments until the next Meeting of the Legislature, which shall then fill such Vacancies.

No Person shall be a Senator who shall not have attained to the Age of thirty Years, and been nine Years a Citizen of the United States, and who shall not, when elected, be an Inhabitant of that State for which he shall be chosen.

The Vice President of the United States shall be President of the Senate, but shall have no vote, unless they be equally divided.

The Senate shall chuse their other Officers, and also a President pro tempore, in the absence of the Vice President, or when he shall exercise the Office of President of the United States.

---

[1]This version follows the original Constitution in capitalization and spelling. It is adapted from the text published by the United States Department of the Interior, Office of Education.

[2]Altered by the Sixteenth Amendment.

[3]Negated by the Fourteenth Amendment.

The Senate shall have the sole Power to try all Impeachments. When sitting for that purpose they shall be on Oath or Affirmation. When the President of the United States is tried, the Chief Justice shall preside: And no person shall be convicted without the Concurrence of two thirds of the Members present.

Judgment in Cases of Impeachment shall not extend further than to removal from Office, and disqualification to hold and enjoy any Office of honor, Trust, or Profit under the United States: but the Party convicted shall nevertheless be liable and subject to Indictment, Trial, Judgment, and Punishment, according to Law.

Section 4.   The Times, Places and Manner of holding Elections for Senators and Representatives, shall be prescribed in each State by the Legislature thereof; but the Congress may at any time by Law make or alter such Regulations, except as to the Places of Chusing Senators.

The Congress shall assemble at least once in every Year, and such Meeting shall be on the first Monday in December, unless they shall by Law appoint a different Day.

Section 5.   Each House shall be the Judge of the Elections, Returns and Qualifications of its own Members, and a Majority of each shall constitute a Quorum to do Business; but a smaller number may adjourn from day to day, and may be authorized to compel the Attendance of absent Members, in such Manner, and under such Penalties, as each House may provide.

Each House may determine the Rules of its Proceedings, punish its Members for disorderly Behaviour, and, with the Concurrence of two thirds, expel a Member.

Each House shall keep a Journal of its Proceedings, and from time to time publish the same, excepting such Parts as may in their Judgment require Secrecy; and the Yeas and Nays of the Members of either House on any question shall, at the Desire of one fifth of those Present, be entered on the Journal.

Neither House, during the Session of Congress, shall, without the Consent of the other, adjourn for more than three days, nor to any other Place than that in which the two Houses shall be sitting.

Section 6.   The Senators and Representatives shall receive a Compensation for their Services, to be ascertained by Law, and paid out of the Treasury of the United States. They shall in all Cases, except Treason, Felony, and Breach of the Peace, be privileged from Arrest during their Attendance at the Session of their respective Houses, and in going to and returning from the same; and for any Speech or Debate in either House, they shall not be questioned in any other Place.

No Senator or Representative shall, during the Time for which he was elected, be appointed to any civil Office under the Authority of the United States, which shall have been created, or the Emoluments whereof shall have been increased, during such time; and no Person holding any Office under the United States shall be a Member of either House during his continuance in Office.

Section 7.   All Bills for raising Revenue shall originate in the House of Representatives; but the Senate may propose or concur with Amendments as on other bills.

Every Bill which shall have passed the House of Representatives and the Senate, shall, before it become a Law, be presented to the President of the United States; If he approve he shall sign it, but if not he shall return it, with his Objections, to that House in which it shall have originated, who shall enter the Objections at large on their Journal, and proceed to reconsider it. If after such Reconsideration two thirds of that House shall agree to pass the bill, it shall be sent, together with the objections, to the other House, by which it shall likewise be reconsidered, and if approved by two thirds of that House, it shall become a Law. But in all such Cases the Votes of both Houses shall be determined by Yeas and Nays, and the Names of the Persons voting for and against the Bill shall be entered on the Journal of each House respectively. If any Bill shall not be returned by the President within ten Days (Sundays excepted) after it shall have been presented to him, the Same shall be a Law, in like Manner as if he had signed it, unless the Congress by their Adjournment prevent its Return, in which Case it shall not be a Law.

Every Order, Resolution, or Vote to which the Concurrence of the Senate and House of Representatives may be necessary (except on a question of Adjournment) shall be presented to the President of the United States; and before the Same shall take Effect, shall be approved by him, or being disapproved by him, shall be repassed by two thirds of the Senate and House of Representatives, according to the Rules and Limitations prescribed in the Case of a Bill.

Section 8.   The Congress shall have Power To lay and collect Taxes, Duties, Imposts and Excises, to pay the Debts and provide for the common Defence and general Welfare of the United States; but all Duties, Imposts and Excises shall be uniform throughout the United States;

To borrow money on the credit of the United States;

To regulate Commerce with foreign Nations, and among the several States, and with the Indian Tribes;

To establish an uniform rule of Naturalization, and uniform Laws on the subject of Bankruptcies throughout the United States;

To coin Money, regulate the Value thereof, and of foreign Coin, and fix the Standard of Weights and Measures;

To provide for the Punishment of counterfeiting the Securities and current Coin of the United States;

To establish Post Offices and post Roads;

To promote the Progress of Science and useful Arts, by securing for limited Times to Authors and Inventors the exclusive Right to their respective Writings and Discoveries;

To constitute Tribunals inferior to the Supreme Court;

To define and punish Piracies and Felonies committed on the high Seas, and Offenses against the Law of Nations;

To declare War, grant Letters of Marque and Reprisal, and make Rules concerning Captures on Land and Water;

To raise and support Armies, but no Appropriation of Money to that Use shall be for a Longer Term than two Years;

To provide and maintain a Navy;

To make Rules for the Government and Regulation of the land and naval forces;

To provide for calling forth the Militia to execute the Laws of the Union, suppress Insurrections and repel Invasions;

To provide for organizing, arming, and disciplining the Militia, and for governing such Part of them as may be employed in the Service of the United States, reserving to the States respectively, the Appointment of the Officers, and the Authority of training the Militia according to the discipline prescribed by Congress;

To exercise exclusive Legislation in all Cases whatsoever, over such District (not exceeding ten Miles square) as may, by Cession of particular States, and the acceptance of Congress, become the Seat of the Government of the United States, and to exercise like Authority over all Places purchased by the Consent of the Legislature of the State in which the Same shall be, for the Erection of Forts, Magazines, Arsenals, Dock-yards, and other needful Buildings;—And

To make all Laws which shall be necessary and proper for carrying into Execution the foregoing Powers, and all other Powers vested by this Constitution in the Government of the United States, or in any Department or Officer thereof.

Section 9.　The Migration or Importation of such Persons as any of the States now existing shall think proper to admit, shall not be prohibited by the Congress prior to the Year one thousand eight hundred and eight, but a tax or duty may be imposed on such Importation, not exceeding ten dollars for each Person.

The privilege of the Writ of Habeas Corpus shall not be suspended, unless when in Cases of Rebellion or Invasion the public Safety may require it.

No bill of Attainder or ex post facto Law shall be passed.

No capitation, or other direct, Tax shall be laid unless in Proportion to the Census or Enumeration herein before directed to be taken.

No Tax or Duty shall be laid on Articles exported from any State.

No Preference shall be given by any Regulation of Commerce or Revenue to the Ports of one State over those of another: nor shall Vessels bound to, or from, one State, be obliged to enter, clear, or pay Duties in another.

No Money shall be drawn from the Treasury, but in Consequence of Appropriations made by Law; and a regular Statement and Account of the Receipts and Expenditures of all public Money shall be published from time to time.

No Title of Nobility shall be granted by the United States: And no Person holding any Office of Profit or Trust under them, shall, without the Consent of the Congress, accept of any present, Emolument, Office, or Title, of any kind whatever, from any King, Prince, or foreign State.

Section 10.　No State shall enter into any Treaty, Alliance, or Confederation; grant Letters of Marque and Reprisal; coin Money; emit Bills of Credit; make any Thing but gold and silver Coin a Tender in Payment of Debts; pass any Bill of Attainder, ex post facto Law, or Law impairing the Obligation of Contracts, or grant any Title of Nobility.

No State shall, without the Consent of the Congress, lay any Imposts or Duties on Imports or Exports, except what may be absolutely necessary for executing its inspection Laws; and the net Produce of all Duties and Imposts, laid by any State on Imports or Exports, shall be for the use of the Treasury of the United States; and all such Laws shall be subject to the Revision and Control of the Congress.

No state shall, without the Consent of Congress, lay any duty of Tonnage, keep Troops, or Ships of War in time of Peace, enter into any Agreement or Compact with another State, or with a foreign Power, or engage in War, unless actually invaded, or in such imminent Danger as will not admit of delay.

Article II

Section 1.　The executive Power shall be vested in a President of the United States of America. He shall hold his Office during the Term of four years, and, together with the Vice President, chosen for the same Term, be elected, as follows:

Each State shall appoint, in such Manner as the Legislature thereof may direct, a Number of Electors, equal to the whole Number of Senators and Representatives to which the State may be entitled in the Congress: but no Senator or Representative, or Person holding an Office of Trust or Profit under the United States, shall be appointed an Elector.

[The Electors shall meet in their respective States, and vote by Ballot for two persons, of whom one at least shall not be an Inhabitant of the same State with themselves. And they shall make a List of all the Persons voted for, and of the Number of Votes for each; which List they shall sign and certify, and transmit sealed to the Seat of the Government of the United States, directed to the President of the Senate. The President of the Senate shall, in the Presence of the Senate and House of Representatives, open all the Certificates, and the Votes shall then be counted. The Person having the greatest Number of Votes shall be the President, if such Number be a Majority of the whole Number of Electors appointed; and if there be more than one who have such Majority, and have an equal Number of Votes, then the House of Representatives shall immediately chuse by Ballot one of them for President; and if no Person have a Majority, then from the five highest on the List the said House shall in like Manner chuse the President. But in chusing the President, the Votes shall be taken by States, the Representation from each State having one Vote; a quorum for this Purpose shall consist of a Member or Members from two-thirds of the States, and a Majority of all the States shall be necessary to a Choice. In every Case, after the Choice of the President, the Person having the greatest Number of Votes of the Electors shall be the Vice President. But if there should remain two or more who have equal votes, the Senate shall chuse from them by Ballot the Vice President.][4]

The Congress may determine the Time of chusing the Electors, and the Day on which they shall give their Votes; which Day shall be the same throughout the United States.

No person except a natural-born Citizen, or a Citizen of the United States, at the time of the Adoption of this Constitution, shall be eligible to the Office of President; neither shall any Person be eligible to that Office who shall not have attained to the Age of thirty-five years, and been fourteen Years a Resident within the United States.

In Case of the Removal of the President from Office, or of his Death, Resignation, or Inability to discharge the Powers and Duties of the said Office, the same shall devolve on the Vice President, and the Congress may by Law provide for the Case of Removal, Death, Resignation, or Inability, both of the President and Vice President, declaring what Officer shall then act as President, and such Officer shall act accordingly, until the disability be removed, or a President shall be elected.

The President shall, at stated Times, receive for his Services a Compensation, which shall neither be increased nor diminished during the Period for which he shall have been elected, and he shall not receive within that Period any other Emolument from the United States, or any of them.

Before he enter on the execution of his Office, he shall take the following Oath or Affirmation:—"I do solemnly swear (or affirm) that I will faithfully execute the Office of President of the United States, and will, to the best of my Ability, preserve, protect, and defend the Constitution of the United States."

Section 2.   The President shall be Commander in Chief of the Army and Navy of the United States, and of the Militia of the several States, when called into the actual Service of the United States; he may require the Opinion, in writing, of the principal Officer in each of the executive Departments, upon any subject relating to the Duties of their respective Offices, and he shall have Power to Grant Reprieves and Pardons for Offenses against the United States, except in Cases of Impeachment.

He shall have Power, by and with the Advice and Consent of the Senate, to make Treaties, provided two-thirds of the Senators present concur; and he shall nominate, and by and with the Advice and Consent of the Senate, shall appoint Ambassadors, other public Ministers and Consuls, Judges of the supreme Court, and all other Officers of the United States, whose Appointments are not herein otherwise provided for, and which shall be established by Law: but the Congress may by Law vest the Appointment of such inferior Officers, as they think proper, in the President alone, in the Courts of Law, or in the Heads of Departments.

The President shall have Power to fill up all Vacancies that may happen during the Recess of the Senate, by granting Commissions which shall expire at the End of their next Session.

Section 3.   He shall from time to time give to the Congress Information of the State of the Union, and recommend to their Consideration such Measures as he shall judge necessary and expedient; he may, on extraordinary occasions, convene both Houses, or either of them, and in Case of Disagreement between them, with respect to the Time of Adjournment, he may adjourn them to such Time as he shall think proper; he shall receive Ambassadors and other public Ministers; he shall take care that the Laws be faithfully executed, and shall Commission all the Officers of the United States.

Section 4.   The President, Vice President and all civil Officers of the United States, shall be removed from Office on Impeachment for, and Conviction of, Treason, Bribery, or other high Crimes and Misdemeanors.

Article III

Section 1.   The judicial Power of the United States, shall be vested in one supreme Court, and in such inferior Courts as the Congress may from time to time ordain and establish. The Judges, both of the supreme and inferior Courts, shall hold their Offices during good Behaviour, and shall, at stated Times, receive for their Services, a Compensation, which shall not be diminished during their Continuance in Office.

Section 2.   The judicial Power shall extend to all Cases, in Law and Equity, arising under this Constitution, the Laws of the United States, and Treaties made, or which shall be made, under their Authority;—to all Cases affecting ambassadors, other public ministers and consuls;—to all cases of admiralty and maritime Jurisdiction;—to Controversies to

---

[4]Revised by the Twelfth Amendment.

which the United States shall be a Party;—to Controversies between two or more States;—between a State and Citizens of another State;[5]—between Citizens of different States— between Citizens of the same State claiming Lands under Grants of different States, and between a State, or the Citizens thereof, and foreign States, Citizens, or Subjects.

In all Cases affecting Ambassadors, other public Ministers and Consuls, and those in which a State shall be Party, the supreme Court shall have original Jurisdiction. In all the other Cases before mentioned, the supreme Court shall have appellate Jurisdiction, both as to Law and Fact, with such Exceptions, and under such Regulations as the Congress shall make.

The trial of all Crimes, except in Cases of Impeachment, shall be by Jury; and such Trial shall be held in the State where the said Crimes shall have been committed; but when not committed within any State, the Trial shall be at such Place or Places as the Congress may by Law have directed.

Section 3. Treason against the United States, shall consist only in levying War against them, or in adhering to their Enemies, giving them Aid and Comfort. No Person shall be convicted of Treason unless on the Testimony of two Witnesses to the same overt Act, or on Confession in open Court.

The Congress shall have power to declare the Punishment of Treason, but no Attainder of Treason shall work Corruption of Blood, or Forfeiture except during the Life of the Person attainted.

Article IV

Section 1. Full Faith and Credit shall be given in each State to the public Acts, Records, and judicial Proceedings of every other State. And the Congress may by general Laws prescribe the Manner in which such Acts, Records and Proceedings shall be proved, and the Effect thereof.

Section 2. The Citizens of each State shall be entitled to all Privileges and Immunities of Citizens in the several States.

A Person charged in any State with Treason, Felony, or other Crime, who shall flee from Justice, and be found in another State, shall on demand of the executive Authority of the State from which he fled, be delivered up, to be removed to the State having Jurisdiction of the crime.

No Person held to Service or Labour in one State, under the Laws thereof, escaping into another, shall, in Consequence of any Law or Regulation therein, be discharged from such Service or Labour, but shall be delivered up on Claim of the Party to whom such Service or Labour may be due.

Section 3. New States may be admitted by the Congress into this Union; but no new State shall be formed or erected within the Jurisdiction of any other State; nor any State be formed by the Junction of two or more States, or parts of States, without the Consent of the Legislatures of the States concerned as well as of the Congress.

The Congress shall have Power to dispose of and make all needful Rules and Regulations respecting the Territory or other Property belonging to the United States; and nothing in this Constitution shall be so construed as to Prejudice any Claims of the United States, or of any particular State.

Section 4. The United States shall guarantee to every State in this Union a Republican Form of Government, and shall protect each of them against Invasion; and on Application of the Legislature, or of the Executive (when the Legislature cannot be convened) against domestic Violence.

Article V

The Congress, whenever two-thirds of both Houses shall deem it necessary, shall propose Amendments to this Constitution, or, on the Application of the Legislatures of two-thirds of the several States, shall call a Convention for proposing Amendments, which, in either Case, shall be valid to all Intents and Purposes, as part of this Constitution, when ratified by the Legislatures of three-fourths of the several States, or by Conventions in three-fourths thereof, as the one or the other Mode of Ratification may be proposed by the Congress; Provided that no Amendment which may be made prior to the Year One thousand eight hundred and eight shall in any Manner affect the first and fourth Clauses in the Ninth Section of the first Article; and that no State, without its Consent, shall be deprived of its equal Suffrage in the Senate.

Article VI

All Debts contracted and Engagements entered into, before the Adoption of this Constitution, shall be as valid against the United States under this Constitution, as under the Confederation.

This Constitution, and the Laws of the United States which shall be made in Pursuance thereof; and all Treaties made, or which shall be made, under the Authority of the United States, shall be the supreme Law of the Land; and the Judges in every State shall be bound thereby, any Thing in the Constitution or Laws of any State to the Contrary notwithstanding.

The Senators and Representatives before mentioned, and the Members of the several State Legislatures, and all executive and judicial Officers, both of the United States and of the several States, shall be bound by Oath or

---

[5]Qualified by the Eleventh Amendment.

Affirmation to support this Constitution; but no religious Tests shall ever be required as a qualification to any Office or public Trust under the United States.

Article VII

The Ratification of the Conventions of nine States shall be sufficient for the Establishment of this Constitution between the States so ratifying the same.

Done in Convention by the Unanimous Consent of the States present the Seventeenth Day of September in the Year of our Lord one thousand seven hundred and Eighty seven, and of the Independence of the United States of America the Twelfth. In Witness whereof We have hereunto subscribed our Names.[6]

George Washington

President and Deputy from Virginia

New Hampshire

John Langdon
Nicholas Gilman

Massachusetts

Nathaniel Gorham
Rufus King

Connecticut

William Samuel Johnson
Roger Sherman

New York

Alexander Hamilton

New Jersey

William Livingston
David Brearley
William Paterson
Jonathan Dayton

Pennsylvania

Benjamin Franklin
Thomas Mifflin
Robert Morris
George Clymer
Thomas FitzSimons
Jared Ingersoll
James Wilson
Gouverneur Morris

Delaware

George Read
Gunning Bedford, Jr.
John Dickinson
Richard Bassett
Jacob Broom

Maryland

James McHenry
Daniel of St. Thomas Jenifer
Daniel Carroll

Virginia

John Blair
James Madison, Jr.

North Carolina

William Blount
Richard Dobbs Spaight
Hugh Williamson

South Carolina

John Rutledge
Charles Cotesworth Pinckney
Charley Pinckney
Pierce Butler

Georgia

William Few
Abraham Baldwin

Articles in Addition to, and Amendment of, the Constitution of the United States of America, Proposed by Congress, and Ratified by the Legislatures of the Several States, Pursuant to the Fifth Article of the Original Constitution[7]

[Amendment I]

Congress shall make no law respecting an establishment of religion, or prohibiting the free exercise thereof; or abridging the freedom of speech, or of the press; or the right of the people peaceably to assemble, and to petition the Government for a redress of grievances.

[Amendment II]

A well regulated Militia, being necessary to the security of a free State, the right of the people to keep and bear Arms shall not be infringed.

---

[6]These are the full names of the signers, which in some cases are not the signatures on the document.

[7]This heading appears only in the joint resolution submitting the first ten amendments, known as the Bill of Rights.

[Amendment III]

No Soldier shall, in time of peace, be quartered in any house, without the consent of the Owner, nor in time of war, but in a manner to be prescribed by law.

[Amendment IV]

The right of the people to be secure in their persons, houses, papers, and effects, against unreasonable searches and seizures, shall not be violated, and no Warrants shall issue, but upon probable cause, supported by Oath or affirmation, and particularly describing the place to be searched, and the persons or things to be seized.

[Amendment V]

No person shall be held to answer for a capital or otherwise infamous crime, unless on a presentment or indictment of a Grand Jury, except in cases arising in the land or naval forces, or in the Militia, when in actual service in time of War or public danger; nor shall any person be subject for the same offence to be twice put in jeopardy of life or limb; nor shall be compelled in any criminal case to be a witness against himself, nor be deprived of life, liberty, or property, without due process of law; nor shall private property be taken for public use, without just compensation.

[Amendment VI]

In all criminal prosecutions, the accused shall enjoy the right to a speedy and public trial, by an impartial jury of the State and district wherein the crime shall have been committed, which district shall have been previously ascertained by law, and to be informed of the nature and cause of the accusation; to be confronted with the witnesses against him; to have compulsory process for obtaining witnesses in his favour, and to have the Assistance of Counsel for his defence.

[Amendment VII]

In suits at common law, where the value in controversy shall exceed twenty dollars, the right of trial by jury shall be preserved, and no fact tried by a jury, shall be otherwise reexamined in any Court of the United States, than according to the rules of the common law.

[Amendment VIII]

Excessive bail shall not be required, nor excessive fines imposed, nor cruel and unusual punishments inflicted.

[Amendment IX]

The enumeration in the Constitution, of certain rights, shall not be construed to deny or disparage others retained by the people.

[Amendment X]

The powers not delegated to the United States by the Constitution, nor prohibited by it to the States, are reserved to the States respectively, or to the people.
  [Amendments I–X, in force 1791.]

[Amendment XI][8]

The Judicial power of the United States shall not be construed to extend to any suit in law or equity, commenced or prosecuted against one of the United States by Citizens of another State, or by Citizens or Subjects of any Foreign State.

[Amendment XII][9]

The Electors shall meet in their respective States and vote by ballot for President and Vice-President, one of whom, at least, shall not be an inhabitant of the same State with themselves; they shall name in their ballots the person voted for as President, and in distinct ballots the person voted for as Vice-President, and they shall make distinct lists of all persons voted for as President, and of all persons voted for as Vice-President, and of the number of votes for each, which lists they shall sign and certify, and transmit sealed to the seal of the government of the United States, directed to the President of the Senate;—The President of the Senate shall, in the presence of the Senate and House of Representatives, open all the certificates and the votes shall then be counted;—The person having the greatest number of votes for President, shall be the President, if such number be a majority of the whole number of Electors appointed; and if no person have such majority, then from the persons having the highest numbers not exceeding three on the list of those voted for as President, the House of Representatives shall choose immediately, by ballot, the President. But in choosing the President, the votes shall be taken by states, the representation from each state having one vote; a quorum for this purpose shall consist of a member or members from two-thirds of the states, and a majority of all the states shall be necessary to a choice. And if the House of Representatives shall not choose a President whenever the right of choice shall devolve upon them, before the fourth day of March next following, then the

---

[8]Adopted in 1798.
[9]Adopted in 1804.

Vice-President shall act as President, as in the case of the death or other constitutional disability of the President.— The person having the greatest number of votes as Vice-President, shall be the Vice-President, if such number be a majority of the whole number of Electors appointed, and if no person have a majority, then from the two highest numbers on the list, the Senate shall choose the Vice-President; a quorum for the purpose shall consist of two-thirds of the whole number of Senators, and a majority of the whole number shall be necessary to a choice. But no person constitutionally ineligible to the office of President shall be eligible to that of Vice-President of the United States.

[Amendment XIII][10]

Section 1.   Neither slavery nor involuntary servitude, except as a punishment for crime whereof the party shall have been duly convicted, shall exist within the United States, or any place subject to their jurisdiction.

Section 2.   Congress shall have power to enforce this article by appropriate legislation.

[Amendment XIV][11]

Section 1.   All persons born or naturalized in the United States, and subject to the jurisdiction thereof, are citizens of the United States and of the State wherein they reside. No State shall abridge the privileges or immunities of citizens of the United States; nor shall any State deprive any person of life, liberty, or property, without due process of law; nor deny to any person within its jurisdiction the equal protection of the laws.

Section 2.   Representatives shall be apportioned among the several States according to their respective numbers, counting the whole number of persons in each State, excluding Indians not taxed. But when the right to vote at any election for the choice of electors for President and Vice-President of the United States, Representatives in Congress, the Executive and Judicial officers of a State, or the members of the Legislature thereof, is denied to any of the male inhabitants of such State, being twenty-one years of age, and citizens of the United States, or in any way abridged, except for participation in rebellion, or other crime, the basis of representation therein shall be reduced in the proportion which the number of such male citizens shall bear to the whole number of male citizens twenty-one years of age in such State.

Section 3.   No person shall be a Senator or Representative in Congress, or elector of President and Vice-President, or hold any office, civil or military, under the United States, or under any State, who, having previously taken an oath, as a member of Congress, or as an officer of the United States, or as a member of any State legislature, or as an executive or judicial officer of any State, to support the Constitution of the United States, shall have engaged in insurrection or rebellion against the same, or given aid or comfort to the enemies thereof. But Congress may by a vote of two-thirds of each House, remove such disability.

Section 4.   The validity of the public debt of the United States, authorized by law, including debts incurred for payment of pensions and bounties for services in suppressing insurrection or rebellion, shall not be questioned. But neither the United States nor any State shall assume or pay any debts or obligation incurred in aid of insurrection or rebellion against the United States, or any claim for the loss or emancipation of any slave; but all such debts, obligations, and claims shall be held illegal and void.

Section 5.   The Congress shall have the power to enforce, by appropriate legislation, the provisions of this article.

[Amendment XV][12]

Section 1.   The right of citizens of the United States to vote shall not be denied or abridged by the United States or by any State on account of race, color, or previous condition of servitude—

Section 2.   The Congress shall have power to enforce this article by appropriate legislation.

[Amendment XVI][13]

The Congress shall have power to lay and collect taxes on incomes, from whatever source derived, without apportionment among the several States, and without regard to any census or enumeration.

[Amendment XVII][14]

The Senate of the United States shall be composed of two Senators from each State, elected by the people thereof, for six years; and each Senator shall have one vote. The electors in each State shall have the qualifications requisite for electors of the most numerous branch of the State legislatures.

[10]Adopted in 1865.
[11]Adopted in 1868.

[12]Adopted in 1870.
[13]Adopted in 1913.
[14]Adopted in 1913.

When vacancies happen in the representation of any State in the Senate, the executive authority of such State shall issue writs of election to fill such vacancies: *Provided,* That the legislature of any State may empower the executive thereof to make temporary appointments until the people fill the vacancies by election as the legislature may direct.

This amendment shall not be so construed as to affect the election or term of any Senator chosen before it becomes valid as part of the Constitution.

[Amendment XVIII][15]

Section 1. After one year from the ratification of this article the manufacture, sale, or transportation of intoxicating liquors within, the importation thereof into, or the exportation thereof from the United States and all territory subject to the jurisdiction thereof for beverage purposes is hereby prohibited.

Section 2. The Congress and the several States shall have concurrent power to enforce this article by appropriate legislation.

Section 3. This article shall be inoperative unless it shall have been ratified as an amendment to the Constitution by the legislatures of the several States, as provided in the Constitution, within seven years from the date of the submission hereof to the States by the Congress.

[Amendment XIX][16]

The right of citizens of the United States to vote shall not be denied or abridged by the United States or by any State on account of sex.

Congress shall have power to enforce this article by appropriate legislation.

[Amendment XX][17]

Section 1. The terms of the President and Vice-President shall end at noon on the 20th day of January, and the terms of Senators and Representatives at noon on the 3rd day of January, of the years in which such terms would have ended if this article had not been ratified; and the terms of their successors shall then begin.

Section 2. The Congress shall assemble at least once in every year, and such meeting shall begin at noon on the 3rd day of January, unless they shall by law appoint a different day.

Section 3. If, at the time fixed for the beginning of the term of the President, the President elect shall have died, the Vice-President elect shall become President. If a President shall not have been chosen before the time fixed for the beginning of his term or if the President elect shall have failed to qualify, then the Vice-President elect shall act as President until a President shall have qualified; and the Congress may by law provide for the case wherein neither a President elect nor a Vice-President elect shall have qualified, declaring who shall then act as President, or the manner in which one who is to act shall be selected, and such person shall act accordingly until a President or Vice-President shall have qualified.

Section 4. The Congress may by law provide for the case of the death of any of the persons from whom the House of Representatives may choose a President whenever the right of choice shall have devolved upon them, and for the case of the death of any of the persons from whom the Senate may choose a Vice-President whenever the right of choice shall have devolved upon them.

Section 5. Sections 1 and 2 shall take effect on the 15th day of October following the ratification of this article.

Section 6. This article shall be inoperative unless it shall have been ratified as an amendment to the Constitution by the legislatures of three-fourths of the several States within seven years from the date of its submission.

[Amendment XXI][18]

Section 1. The eighteenth article of amendment to the Constitution of the United States is hereby repealed.

Section 2. The transportation or importation into any State, Territory, or possession of the United States for delivery or use therein of intoxicating liquors, in violation of the laws thereof, is hereby prohibited.

Section 3. This article shall be inoperative unless it shall have been ratified as an amendment to the Constitution by conventions in the several States, as provided in the Constitution, within seven years from the date of the submission hereof to the States by the Congress.

[Amendment XXII][19]

No person shall be elected to the office of the President more than twice, and no person who has held the office of

---

[15]Adopted in 1918.
[16]Adopted in 1920.
[17]Adopted in 1933.

[18]Adopted in 1933.
[19]Adopted in 1961.

President, or acted as President, for more than two years of a term to which some other person was elected President shall be elected to the office of the President more than once.

But this Article shall not apply to any person holding the office of President when this Article was proposed by the Congress, and shall not prevent any person who may be holding the office of President, or acting as President, during the term within which this Article becomes operative from holding the office of President or acting as President during the remainder of such term.

This article shall be inoperative unless it shall have been ratified as an amendment to the Constitution by the legislatures of three-fourths of the several states within seven years from the date of its submission to the states by the Congress.

[Amendment XXIII][20]

Section 1.   The District constituting the seat of Government of the United States shall appoint in such manner as the Congress may direct:

A number of electors of President and Vice-President equal to the whole number of Senators and Representatives in Congress to which the District would be entitled if it were a State, but in no event more than the least populous State; they shall be in addition to those appointed by the States, but they shall be considered, for the purpose of the election of President and Vice-President, to be electors appointed by a State; and they shall meet in the District and perform such duties as provided by the twelfth article of amendment.

Section 2.   The Congress shall have power to enforce this article by appropriate legislation.

[Amendment XXIV][21]

Section 1.   The right of citizens of the United States to vote in any primary or other election for President or Vice-President, for electors for President or Vice-President, or for Senator or Representative in Congress, shall not be denied or abridged by the United States or any state by reason of failure to pay any poll tax or other tax.

Section 2.   The Congress shall have the power to enforce this article by appropriate legislation.

[Amendment XXV][22]

Section 1.   In case of the removal of the President from office or of his death or resignation, the Vice-President shall become President.

Section 2.   Whenever there is a vacancy in the office of the Vice President, the President shall nominate a Vice President who shall take office upon confirmation by a majority vote of both Houses of Congress.

Section 3.   Whenever the President transmits to the President Pro Tempore of the Senate and the Speaker of the House of Representatives his written declaration that he is unable to discharge the powers and duties of his office, and until he transmits to them a written declaration to the contrary, such powers and duties shall be discharged by the Vice-President as Acting President.

Section 4.   Whenever the Vice-President and a majority of either the principal officers of the executive departments or of such other body as Congress may by law provide, transmit to the President Pro Tempore of the Senate and the Speaker of the House of Representatives their written declaration that the President is unable to discharge the powers and duties of his office, the Vice President shall immediately assume the powers and duties of the office as Acting President.

Thereafter, when the President transmits to the President Pro Tempore of the Senate and the Speaker of the House of Representatives his written declaration that no inability exists, he shall resume the powers and duties of his office unless the Vice President and a majority of either the principal officers of the executive departments or of such other body as Congress may by law provide, transmit within four days to the President Pro Tempore of the Senate and the Speaker of the House of Representatives their written declaration that the President is unable to discharge the powers and duties of his office. Thereupon Congress shall decide the issue, assembling within forty-eight hours for that purpose if not in session. If the Congress, within twenty-one days after receipt of the latter written declaration, or, if Congress is not in session, within twenty-one days after Congress is required to assemble, determines by two-thirds vote of both Houses that the President is unable to discharge the powers and duties of his office, the Vice President shall continue to discharge the same as Acting President; otherwise, the President shall resume the powers and duties of his office.

[Amendment XXVI][23]

Section 1.   The right of citizens of the United States, who are eighteen years of age or older, to vote shall not be denied or abridged by the United States or by any State on account of age.

Section 2.   The Congress shall have power to enforce this article by appropriate legislation.

[20]Adopted in 1961.
[21]Adopted in 1964.
[22]Adopted in 1967.

[23]Adopted in 1971.

Glossary

accessoryship Criminal liability of all those who aid the perpetrator of an offense.

accomplice Person who helps another to commit a crime.

acquittal Judicial finding or jury verdict finding the defendant not guilty of the crime charged.

administration bureau Unit of a police department responsible for the management of the department as an organization; includes personnel, finance, and research and development.

aggravated assault Attack on a person in which the assailant inflicts serious harm or uses a deadly weapon.

aggression Use of armed force by a state against the sovereignty or territory of another state, inconsistent with the Charter of the United Nations; an international crime.

alternative sanctions Punishments or other dispositions imposed instead of the principal sanctions currently in use, such as imprisonment or probation.

appellate court Court with the power to review the judgment of a trial court, examining errors of law.

arraignment First stage of the trial process, at which the indictment or information is read in open court and the defendant is requested to respond thereto.

arrest Seizure of the person; the taking of a person into custody.

arrest warrant Written order from a court directing the police to effect an arrest.

arson The malicious burning of the dwelling house of another, or the burning of other structures or even personal property.

assault Unlawful offer or attempt with force or violence to hurt another.

assigned counsel system Judge appoints a private lawyer selected from a list of attorneys to represent indigent defendants in criminal proceedings.

attrition (mortality) rate Rate at which the numbers decrease in the course of the criminal process because persons are diverted out of the system.

bail Security given to ensure the reappearance of a defendant, in order to obtain his or her release from imprisonment.

boil bond agents Private business operators, paid by the defendant, who post the amount required by the court to secure the release of the defendant.

bailiff Officer of the court who administers formal procedures, keeps order, announces a judge's arrival, and administers oaths.

beat Territory covered by a police officer on patrol; derived from hunters' "beating" the bushes for game.

blue curtain Screen that separates police from civilians in society; isolation of police who spend time only with other police officers and their families.

bankruptcy fraud Scam designed to take advantage of loopholes in the bankruptcy laws.

boiler rooms Operations run by stock manipulators who, through deception and misleading sales techniques, seduce unsuspecting and uninformed individuals into buying stocks in obscure and often poorly financed corporations.

bribes Offers of money or goods to police to ensure that they do not enforce the law.

burden of proof In criminal cases, the legal obligation of the prosecution to prove the charges against the defendant beyond a reasonable doubt.

burglary At common law, the nighttime breaking and entering of the dwelling house of another, with the intention to commit a felony or larceny therein; a felony.

challenge for cause Challenge to remove a potential juror because of his or her inability to render a fair and impartial decision in a case. See also *peremptory challenges; voir dire.*

churning Practice of trading a client's shares of stock frequently to generate large commissions.

circuit courts of appeal Federal appellate courts with the power to review judgments of federal district courts. See *appellate court.*

civilian police review boards External control mechanism composed of persons usually from outside the police department.

classification Process that consists of regular procedures through which the custodial, treatment, vocational, and educational needs of each prisoner are determined.

common law Law as developed in England and later in the United States on the basis of court decisions (precedents) and as supplemented by legislation.

community policing Strategy that relies on public confidence and citizen cooperation to help prevent crime and make the residents of a community feel more secure.

community service Sanction that requires an offender to spend a period of time performing public service work.

community service order Sanction in which sentencing judge orders the convict to perform any of a range of services to the community.

conditional pardon Pardon that depends on the fulfillment of specified conditions.

conflict theory Model of crime in which the criminal justice system is seen as being used by the ruling class to control the lower class.

consent search Warrantless search conducted when the party to the search provides "voluntary and intelligent consent" to police.

conspiracy Agreement among two or more persons to commit a crime, making each guilty of conspiracy and all other crimes committed in furtherance of the conspiracy.

consumer fraud The act of causing a consumer to surrender money through deceit or a misrepresentation of a material fact.

contract system Private attorneys from law firms or local bar associations provide defense services to indigent defendants.

conventions International agreements by which several nations commit themselves to common, legally binding obligations.

corporate crime Criminal act committed by one or more employees of a corporation that is subsequently attributed to the organization itself.

correctional facility Facility where convicted offenders serve their sentence; includes county jails and state and federal prisons.

court administrator Chief administrative officer of the court, usually appointed by the state court of last resort, the chief justice of the court of last resort, or a judicial council.

court officers and marshals Persons who provide courtroom security and maintain order. See also *bailiff*.

courts of general jurisdiction Major trial courts that have regular, unlimited jurisdictions over all cases and controversies involving civil and criminal law.

courts of limited jurisdiction Courts (with a justice of the peace, magistrate, or judge presiding) that handle minor criminal cases, less serious civil suits, traffic and parking violations, and health law violations.

courts of special jurisdiction Courts that specialize in certain areas of law: family courts, juvenile courts, and probate courts (transfer of property and money of deceased).

crackdown Intensified effort by the police to deal with a problem in a particular area, or to reduce the incidence of a particular crime.

crimes against humanity Consist of murder, extermination, enslavement, deportation, and other inhumane acts done against any civilian population, or persecution on political, racial, or religious grounds, when such acts are done or such persecutions are carried out in execution of, or in connection with, any act of aggression or any war crime; international crimes.

criminal attempt Act or omission constituting a substantial step in a course of conduct planned to culminate in the commission of a crime.

criminal homicide Unjustified, unexcused killing of another human being.

criminal justice The sum total of society's activities to defend itself against the actions it defines as criminal.

custody Suspect under arrest or deprived of freedom in a significant way.

decoy Police officer disguised as a potential crime victim to attract criminal attacks precipitating an arrest.

defense attorney (in criminal cases) Lawyer retained by an individual accused of committing a crime, or assigned by the court if the individual is unable to pay.

deprivation model Explanation of prison subculture that suggests norms, language, roles, and traditions are developed in the prison to help prisoners adjust to the pains of imprisonment.

detention facility Facility that houses persons arrested and undergoing processing, awaiting trial, or awaiting transfer to a correctional facility.

determinate sentence Sentence to prison that has a fixed term; also called a flat sentence.

deterrence Theory of punishment that holds that potential offenders will refrain from committing crimes for fear of punishment (sometimes called general prevention).

differential response Police response strategy that involves classifying calls for service and using various responses.

directed patrol Patrol officers assigned to specific activities, such as patrolling a high-crime area, chosen after an analysis of crime patterns.

direct file Prosecutors' power to try juveniles directly in adult criminal courts.

district courts Trial courts in the federal and in some state systems.

diversion Removal of the defendant from the normal path of the criminal justice process to an alternative path (for example, a treatment program).

due process of law According to the Fourteenth Amendment, a fundamental mandate that a person should not be deprived of life, liberty, or property without reasonable and lawful procedures.

electronic monitoring Computer-assisted checks on anoffender's movement to ensure that he or she is not going to places in violation of restrictions.

embezzlement The conversion (misappropriation) of property or money with which one is entrusted or for which one has a fiduciary responsibility.

entrapment   Illegal police practice of persuading an initially unwilling party to commit an offense.

exclusionary rule   Rule prohibiting use of illegally obtained evidence in a court of law.

exigent circumstances   Certain emergencies that call for immediate action and therefore do not allow time for a search warrant to be obtained.

extradition   Process of ancient origin by which an alleged offender is transferred from one sovereign country to another for trial.

federal courts   Courts of the federal system, applying federal law, with power to test the constitutionality of state law and adjudicate controversies arising between residents of two or more states.

Federal Witness Protection Program   Program under the Organized Crime Control Act of 1970 to protect witnesses who testify in court, by relocating them and assigning them new identities.

felony   Serious crime, subject to punishment of one year or more in prison, or to capital punishment.

felony murder   Criminal liability for murder for one who participates in a felony that is dangerous to life and causes the death of another.

fine   Sum of money paid as a penalty and/or as an alternative to or in conjunction with incarceration.

fraud   Acquisition of the property of another through deception.

frisk   Patting down a suspect's clothing to search for concealed weapons, under reasonable suspicion.

fruit of the poisonous tree   Evidence obtained through other, illegally obtained evidence, inadmissible because it is tainted by the illegality of the initial search, arrest, or confession.

general deterrence   Threat of punishment intended to induce the general public not to engage in criminal acts.

genetic fingerprinting   Use of DNA as a technique for identifying suspects.

genocide   International crime defined by convention (1948) and consisting of specific acts of violence committed with intent to destroy, in whole or in part, a national, ethnic, racial, cultural, or religious group.

good faith exception   Exception to the exclusionary rule in which evidence obtained by police acting in good faith with a search warrant issued by a neutral and detached magistrate is admissible, even though the warrant is ultimately found to be invalid.

good time system   System under which time is deducted from a prison sentence for good behavior within the institution.

grand jury   Panel of sixteen to twenty-three citizens who screen the prosecution's evidence, in secret hearings, to decide whether someone should be formally charged with a crime.

grass eaters   Officers who accept payoffs for rendering police services or for looking the other way when action is called for.

habeas corpus   Writ requesting that a person or institution detaining a named prisoner bring him or her before a judicial officer and give reasons for the detention.

halfway house   Residential correctional facility in which an offender may have to serve the last portion of his or her sentence outside prison, but not yet in the community.

high-speed chase   The pursuit of a suspect at high speeds.

high-tech crime   The pursuit of illegal activities through the use of advanced electronic media.

homicide   The killing of one person by another.

hot pursuit   Exception to the rule requiring police to have a warrant to conduct a search; applies to cases of pursuit of vehicles and of suspects on foot.

house arrest   Sentence in which convicts are confined to their own residence in lieu of imprisonment in an institution.

hustling   Inmate activity that involves obtaining goods and services that are unavailable through legitimate channels.

importation model   Explanation of prison subculture that suggests norms, language, roles, and traditions are brought into the prison from outside the walls.

incapacitation   Preventing persons from committing crime by physical restraint, for example, incarceration.

incarceration   Sanction that requires a defendant to serve a term in a local jail, state prison, or federal prison.

indeterminate sentence   Sentence for which the legislature allows the judge to impose a minimum and/or a maximum term, the actual length of service depending on the discretion of corrections officials.

index crimes   The eight major crimes included in Part I of the UCR: criminal homicide, forcible rape, robbery, aggravated assault, burglary, larceny-theft, motor vehicle theft, and arson.

indictment   Accusation against a criminal defendant rendered by a grand jury on the basis of evidence constituting a *prima facie* case.

information   Accusation against a criminal defendant prepared by a prosecuting attorney.

inmate code   Informal set of rules that reflect the values of the prison society.

insider trading   Use of material, nonpublic financial information about securities to obtain unfair advantage.

intensive supervision probation (ISP)   Alternative to prison for convicted nonviolent offenders who do not qualify for routine probation; probation subject to stringent supervision.

internal affairs Department responsible for receiving and investigating charges against the police.

International Court of Justice Court of the United Nations with jurisdiction to adjudicate disputes among states. Also known as World Court.

international crimes Crimes, established largely by conventions, violative of international law, including but not limited to crimes against the peace and security of humankind.

international criminal courts Established by the United Nations, ad hoc (temporary) criminal courts created to try defendants accused of crimes under international law. A permanent International Criminal Court was agreed upon in 1998.

international criminal justice Emerging international system for dealing with international and transnational crime.

interrogation Explicit questioning or actions that may elicit an incriminating statement.

involuntary acts Acts that are the product of somnambulism (sleepwalking), unconsciousness, seizures, or involuntary neurological responses.

involuntary manslaughter Unintentionally but recklessly causing the death of another by consciously taking a grave risk.

jail Place of confinement administered by local officials and designed to hold persons for more than 48 hours but usually less than one year.

judge Public officer lawfully instituted (by appointment or election) to decide litigated questions according to law, presiding in a court of law.

jurisdiction Power of a sovereign state to make and enforce its own laws. Also, the power granted to a court to adjudicate matters in dispute within its competence and territory.

just desserts Philosophy of justice that asserts that the punishment should fit the crime and the culpability of the offender.

justice of the peace Originally (est. 1326) an untrained man, normally not learned in the law, usually of the lower nobility, assigned to investigate and try minor cases. Today a judge of a lower court, local or municipal, with limited jurisdiction.

justifications Defenses in which the law authorizes the violation of another law within limits of proportionality.

labeling theory Explanation of deviance in terms of the way a person acquires a negative identity, such as "addict" or "ex-con," and is forced to suffer the consequences of outcast status.

larceny Trespassory taking and carrying away of personal property belonging to another with the intent to deprive the owner of the property permanently.

legalistic style Style characteristic of police departments where work is marked by a professional orientation with an emphasis on law enforcement.

legality Principle that every crime must be clearly defined by common law or legislation prior to its commission.

line functions Law enforcement functions of a police department.

mala in se **(Latin)** Offenses deemed inherently evil.

mala prohibita **(Latin)** Wrongs that are merely prohibited.

mandatory sentence Sentence prescribed by the legislature, which a judge has no choice but to impose.

marshal Federal law enforcement officer of the U.S. Marshal Service. Formerly, federal law enforcement officer in territories.

mass murder The murder of several persons, in one act or transaction, by one perpetrator or a group of perpetrators.

maximum security prison Penal institution designed and operated with the principal goal of preventing escape and avoiding violence on the part of prisoners, virtually to the exclusion of rehabilitation or other programs.

meat eaters Officers who solicit bribes or cooperate with criminals for personal gain.

medium security prison Penal institution with emphasis on control and custody, but not to the exclusion of rehabilitative or other programs.

mens rea **(Latin)** Guilty mind; awareness of wrongdoing. Intention to commit a criminal act, or recklessness.

minimum security prison Penal institution allowing inmates and visitors internal freedom of movement and program participation consistent with incarceration.

Miranda **warning** Warning that explains the rights of an arrestee, and that police recite at the time of the arrest or prior to interrogation.

misdemeanor Crime less serious than a felony and subject to a maximum sentence of one year in jail or a fine.

modus operandi Means and method by which a crime is committed.

motion Oral or written request to a judge, asking the court to make a specified ruling, finding, decision, or order; may be presented at any appropriate moment from arrest until the end of the trial.

murder in the first degree Killing done with premeditation and deliberation or, by statute, in the presence of other aggravating circumstances.

murder in the second degree Killing done with intent to cause death but without premeditation and deliberation.

nolo contendere Defendant pleads no contest (admits criminal liability for purposes of this proceeding only).

operations bureau   Unit of a police department responsible for the functions associated with the primary law enforcement mission.

pardon   Release from the legal penalties of an offense.

parens patriae **(Latin)**   Parent of the country; assumption by the state of the role of guardian over children whose parents are deemed incapable or unworthy.

parole   Release of a prisoner into the community during the last part of a prison term, on promise of good conduct and under supervision.

parole board   Group of citizens, usually appointed by the governor of a state, who determine the eligibility of prisoners for release from prison and the dates for their release from prison and from parole.

parole hearing   Meeting held by members of the parole board to decide whether prisoners will be granted parole.

parole officer   Officer of the executive branch of government responsible for the supervision of convicts released from prison on parole.

penitentiary   Prison or place of confinement and correction for persons convicted of criminal acts; originally a place where convicts did penance.

peremptory challenges   Challenges (limited in number) by which a potential juror may be dismissed by either the prosecution or the defense without assignment of reason. See also *challenge for cause; voir dire.*

plain view   No warrant is needed to conduct a search when the fruits or instrumentalities of a crime are in plain view.

plea   Response to a criminal charge. Traditional pleas are guilty, not guilty, *nolo contendere,* and not guilty by reason of insanity.

plea bargaining   Agreement made between defense and prosecution for certain leniencies in return for a guilty plea.

police brutality   Use of excessive physical force against another person (usually a suspect) by law enforcement officers.

police subculture   Set of norms and values that govern police behavior, brought about by stressful working conditions plus daily interaction with an often hostile public.

police–community relations (PCR) programs   All initiatives, whether from the police or the community, to bridge the gap between law enforcement professionals and the people they serve.

preliminary hearing   Preview of a trial held in court before a judge, in which the prosecution must produce sufficient evidence for the case to proceed to trial.

presentence investigation report   Report prepared by the probation department for a judge; contains information about the offense, the offender, and the history of prior offenses and may include a recommendation of a sentence.

preventive detention   Pretrial incarceration of an accused deemed dangerous.

preventive patrol   Police officers driving or walking through a designated geographic area of responsibility in a varied pattern so that their presence is not predictable.

prima facie **case**   Case in which there is evidence that would warrant the conviction of the defendant unless otherwise contradicted; a case that meets evidentiary requirements for grand jury indictment.

principal   Perpetrator of a criminal act.

prison   Federal or state penal institution in which offenders serve sentences longer than one year.

prison argot   Unique vocabulary used by prisoners.

prison hulks   Decommissioned ships converted into prisons.

prisonization   Socialization process in which new prisoners learn the ways of prison society, including rules, hierarchy, customs, and culture.

probable cause   Set of facts that would induce a reasonable person to believe that the accused committed the offense in question; the minimum evidence requirement for an arrest, according to the Fourth Amendment.

probation   Serving a sentence in the community in lieu of a prison term, on condition of good conduct, compliance with conditions, and under supervision.

probation officer   Officer attached to the trial court who is responsible for administering the court's probation program.

problem-oriented policing   Strategy that seeks to identify the underlying problems within a community so that community and police can work together to solve them.

prosecutor   Attorney and government official who represents the people against persons accused of committing criminal acts.

psychopathy   Condition in which a person has no sense of responsibility; shows disregard for truth; is insincere; and feels no sense of shame, guilt, or humiliation.

public defender system   Public or nonprofit organizations (with staff) that provide defense services to indigent defendants.

radical theory   Theory that crime is the result of a struggle for power and resources between owners of capital and workers.

reasonable suspicion   Warranted suspicion (short of probable cause) that a person has been or may be engaged in the commission of a crime.

recidivism   Repeated or habitual relapses into criminal behavior.

reformation   Voluntary, self-initiated transformation of an individual lacking in social or vocational skills into a productive, normally functioning citizen.

reformatory   Institution designed to reform criminals through individualized treatment, education, and vocational training.

rehabilitation Punishment philosophy that asserts that through proper correctional intervention, such as educational and vocational programs and psychotherapy, a criminal can be reformed into a law-abiding citizen.

release on recognizance (ROR) Release of a defendant on his or her promise to return to court as required.

restitution Compensation (normally court ordered) on the part of an offender to the victim, or a victim substitute, for any losses or harm inflicted, usually in money or services.

restorative justice Model of justice, opposed to retributive justice, aiming at the offender's contribution to offset the harm done, including reconciliation with victims.

retribution "Eye for an eye" philosophy of justice, now known as just desserts.

revocation of parole Return of an offender to prison for the violation of parole conditions.

robbery The taking of the property of another, or out of his or her presence, by means of force and violence or the threat thereof.

search Any governmental intrusion upon a person's reasonable expectation of privacy.

seizure Exercise of control by a government official over a person or thing.

selective incapacitation Targeting of high-risk and recidivistic offenders for rigorous prosecution and incarceration.

selective incorporation Supreme Court practice of incorporating the Bill of Rights selectively, by identifying federal rights that are "implicit in the concept of ordered liberty" and applying them to states through the Fourteenth Amendment's due process clause.

sentencing guidelines System for the judicial determination of a relatively firm sentence based on specific aggravating or mitigating circumstances.

serial murder Killing of several victims over a period of time.

service style Style characteristic of police departments in suburban communities where residents expect and receive a high level of service from local government.

services bureau Unit of a police department that provides technical services to assist in the execution of line functions, such as keeping records.

Sherman Antitrust Act Congress passed this law in 1890 to prohibit any contract, conspiracy, or combination of business interests in restraint of foreign or interstate trade.

shock incarceration Short term of incarceration that subjects offenders to hard work, intense drills, and other character-building exercises.

shock probation Sentence that allows for brief incarceration followed by probation, in an effort to induce law abidance by shocking the offender.

shoplifting Stealing of goods from stores or markets.

simple assault Attack that inflicts little or no physical harm on the victim.

social control The social processes by which the behavior of individuals or groups is regulated. Deviance results when social controls are weakened or break down, so that individuals are not motivated to conform to them.

special deterrence Threat of punishment that deters an offender from engaging in any additional criminal behavior, based on the disagreeable experience with a past punishment.

split sentence Sentence that requires the convicted criminal to serve time in jail followed by probation.

standard operating procedure (SOP) manual Collection of departmental directives governing the performance of duties.

state attorney general Chief legal officer of the state; state counterpart to the U.S. attorney general.

state supreme court State court of last resort (except in those jurisdictions where the supreme court is a trial court of unlimited jurisdiction).

sting operation Deceitful but lawful technique in which police pretend to be involved in illegal activities to trap a suspect.

stock manipulation Brokers who have a stake in a particular security make misleading or false statements to clients to give the impression that the price of the stock is about to rise, creating an artificial demand for it.

stop and frisk Technique used by police to "pat down" a person suspected of being armed or in possession of the instrumentalities of a crime.

strain theory Crime results when the same materialistic goals are held out to all members of society without giving them equal means to achieve them.

subculture A subdivision within the dominant culture that has its own norms, beliefs, and values.

terrorism The use or threat of violence directed at people or governments to punish them for past action or to bring about a change of policy that is to the terrorist's liking.

third degree Torturing a suspect to gain information.

tort Wrong committed by one person against another, other than mere violation of a contract, which entitles the victim to compensation.

transnational crimes Criminal activities extending into, and violating the laws of, several countries.

treaty An agreement, usually among two sovereign states, binding them to abide by common standards and to enforce them.

trial by ordeal In medieval England, subjecting the accused to cruel procedures to reveal God's judgment of the person's guilt or innocence.

trial jury Body of persons legally selected and sworn to inquire into any matter of fact and to give their verdict according to the evidence.

United States attorney   Attorney and government official who prosecutes cases at the federal level.

United States attorney general   Highest ranking official in the United States Department of Justice.

United States Supreme Court   Federal court that has ultimate authority in interpreting the Constitution as it applies to federal and state law; final authority in interpreting federal law.

victim compensation   Scheme, usually based on statute, by which victims of violent crime may receive a limited financial award out of public funds for criminal harm suffered.

victimology   Systematic study of the role played by the victim in a criminal incident and in the criminal process.

vigilante group   Group of private citizens taking the law into their own hands by tracking down criminals and punishing them.

violation   Infraction of the law for which normally only a fine can be imposed.

voir dire   Process in which lawyers and a judge question potential jurors to select those who are acceptable.

voluntary manslaughter   Intentionally but without malice causing the death of another person, as in the heat of passion.

waiver hearing   Hearing in juvenile court to determine whether jurisdiction shall be waived and granted to an adult criminal court.

watchman style   Style characteristic of police departments that concentrate on the order maintenance function.

white-collar crime   A violation of the law committed by a person or group of persons in the course of an otherwise respected and legitimate occupation or business enterprise.

working personality   Effect of police work on an officer's outlook on the world. Danger and authority are important factors.

writ of certiorari   Document issued by a higher court directing a lower court to prepare the record of a case and send it to the higher court for review.

zero tolerance   A new approach to policing that is characterized by a lowering of tolerance to crime and deviance and the use of punitive measures to achieve this goal.

Credits

Photo Credits

Page 2: © EyeWire Images/Getty Images; **12:** © Joel Gordon; **20:** Courtesy Rosanne Russo; **24:** © Reuters/Corbis; **27:** © David Kadlubowski/Sarasota County Sheriff's Office/Corbis; **35:** © Tony Gutierrez/Reuters/Corbis; **40:** Courtesy Cherif Bassiouni; **44-45:** © Brand X Pictures; **46:** © Reuters/ Corbis; **50 top:** © Brand X Pictures/PunchStock; **50 bottom:** © Alfred/ SIPA; **51:** © EFE/SIPA; **54:** © AP Images; **58:** Courtesy Helica Gonzalez; **60:** © Timothy A. Clary/AFP/Getty Images; **62:** © Alex Wong/Getty Images; **92-93:** © Brand X Pictures; **94:** © AP Images; **99:** © Richard Sheinwald/AP Images; **103:** © Bettmann/Corbis; **106:** © AP Images; **112-113:** © BananaStock/ Punchstock; **116:** Frontispiece of The Criminal Prosecution and Capital Punishment of Animals by E.P. Evans (London: Faber, 1987); **117:** © AP Images; **124:** © Bettmann/Corbis; **128:** Courtesy Thomas King; **134-135:** © Bettmann/Corbis; **140:** © Reuters/Corbis; **152:** Courtesy of FBI; **158 top:** Courtesy Tom Harrington; **158 bottom:** © Reuters/Corbis; **162-163:** © Mikael Karlsson/Arresting Images; **164:** © NBC/ Courtesy Everett Collection; **172:** © Brooks Kraft/Corbis; **178:** Courtesy Elliot M Gross; **197 top:** © Robert Spencer/SIPA; **197 bottom:** Federal Bureau of Investigation; **204-205:** Library of Congress; **212:** © Mikael Karlsson/Arresting Images; **214:** © Scott Houston/Sygma/Corbis; **222:** Courtesy of Joe Waters; **224:** US Department of Defense; **225,** © AP Images; **232-33:** © Hisham F. Ibrahim/Getty Images; **236:** © James Duncan Phillips Library/Peabody and Essex Museum; **243:** © AP Images; **245:** © Matthew Cavanaugh/epa/Corbis; **252-253:** © Brand X Pictures; **254:** © Culver Pictures; **257:** © Denny Henry/epa/Corbis; **268:** Courtesy Delores D. Jones-Brown; **278:** © Gary Hershorn/Reuters/Corbis; **284-285:** © AP Images; **290 both:** © Discovery Channel/Vic Blue, Getty Images; **298:** © Michael A. Smith/Time Life Pictures/Getty Images; **302:** Courtesy Terri Kopp; **305:** © Reuters/Corbis; **308-309, 312:** © AP Images; **316:** © James Nubile/The Image Works; **320:** Courtesy Deborah W. Denno; **328:** © Time Pix/Getty Images; **336-337:** © Bill Swersey; **340:** From "The Official Report of the New York State Special Commission on Attica"; **348:** © A. Ramey/Woodfin Camp & Associates; **350:** Courtesy P. F. McManimon Jr.; **360:** © Shannon Sweeney/SIPA; **368-369:** © Damian Doverganes/AP Images; **370:** © Royalty-Free/Corbis; **376:** © Andrew Lichtenstein/Sygma/Corbis; **382:** Courtesy Roberta Richmond; **384:** © A. Ramey/ Stock Boston; **392-393:** © James Nubile/The Image Works; **407:** © Robin Nelson/PhotoEdit; **408:** Courtesy John Lilly; **412:** © Leynse/ Saba/Corbis; **420-421:** © Mikael Karlsson/Arresting Images; **423:** © Matthew Polak/Sygma/Corbis.

Text and Illustration Credits

13: Figure 1.5 Adapted from Samuel Walker, *Sense and Nonsense About Crime.* Reprinted with the permission of Cengage/ Wadsworth. **17:** Figure 1.7 From R.F. Sparks, H.G. Genn, and D.J. Dodd, *Surveying Victims: A Study of the Measurement of Criminal Victimization, Perceptions of Crime, and Attitudes to Criminal Justice.* Reprinted with the permission of John Wiley & Sons, Ltd. **30:** Figure 1.8 From Freda Adler, Gerhard O.W. Mueller, and William S. Laufer, *Criminal Justice: An Introduction.* © 1996. Reprinted by permission of The McGraw-Hill Companies, Inc. **34:** Figure 1.10 From www.privacyinternational.org. Reprinted by permission of Privacy International. **57:** Figure 2.2 From *The Wichita Eagle* (February 29, 2005). Reprinted by permission. **75:** Figure 2.5 From Ko-lin Chin, *Chinese Subculture and Criminality.* © 1990 by Ko-lin Chin. Reprinted by permission of Greenwood Publishing Group, Inc. **86:** Copyright The New Yorker Collection 1990 Arnie Levin from cartoonbank.com. All rights reserved. **98:** Figure 3.1 From Donald J. Shoemaker, *Theories of Delinquency: An Examination of Explanations of Delinquent Behavior, Third Edition.* © 1984, 1990, 1996, 2000 by Oxford University Press, Inc. Reprinted with the permission of Oxford University Press, Ltd. **109:** Figure 3.3 Adapted from Ronald V. Clarke and Derek B. Cornish, "Modeling Offenders' Decisions: A Framework for Research and Policy" from *Crime and Justice, Volume 6,* edited by Michael Tory and Norval Morris. © 1985 by The University of Chicago. All rights reserved. Reprinted with the permission of the University of Chicago Press. **121:** Figure 4.2 © 1962 The Saturday Evening Post, a division of the Benjamin Franklin Library & Medical Society. Reprinted with permission. **222:** Figure 7.2 Adapted from Rolando del Carmen, *Criminal Procedure: Law and Practice.* © 1991. Reprinted by permission of Cengage. **227:** Figure 7.3 From *The New York Times* (February 14, 1999). © 1999 by The New York Times Company. Reprinted with permission. **237:** Figure 8.1 Adapted from Abraham S. Blumberg, *Criminal Justice: Issues and Ironies, Second Edition.* © 1979. Reprinted by permission of Children's Press/Franklin Watts Scholastic Library Publishing. **247:** Figure 8.5 From National Center for State Courts, *Examining the Work of State Courts, 2005.* Reprinted by permission. **280:** Figure 9.6 From *The Justice System Journal* (Fall 1982). Reprinted by permission of the National Center for State Courts. **286:** Figure 10.1 From Kathleen Maguire and Ann L. Pastore (eds.), *Sourcebook of Criminal Justice Statistics, Online,* www.albany.edu/sourcebook/pdf/t592005.pdf. Reprinted by permission. **322:** Figure 11.1 From Andrew von Hirsch, Kay A. Knapp, and Michael Tonry, *The Sentencing Commission and Its Guidelines.* © 1987. Reprinted by permission of Northeastern University Press/University Press of New England. **331:** Figure 11.3 From Death Penalty Information Center. Reprinted by permission. **400:** Figure 14.2 From *Community Corrections: Probation, Parole, and Intermediate Sanctions,* edited by Joan Petersilia. Reprinted with the permission of Oxford University Press, Ltd.